Social Work and the Grand Challenge to Eliminate Racism

Social Work and the Grand Challenge to Eliminate Racism

Concepts, Theory, and Evidence Based Approaches

Edited by
MARTELL L. TEASLEY, MICHAEL S. SPENCER,
AND MELISSA BARTHOLOMEW

OXFORD
UNIVERSITY PRESS

Oxford University Press is a department of the University of Oxford. It furthers the University's objective of excellence in research, scholarship, and education by publishing worldwide. Oxford is a registered trade mark of Oxford University Press in the UK and certain other countries.

Published in the United States of America by Oxford University Press 198 Madison Avenue, New York, NY 10016, United States of America.

© Oxford University Press 2023

All rights reserved. No part of this publication may be reproduced, stored in a retrieval system, or transmitted, in any form or by any means, without the prior permission in writing of Oxford University Press, or as expressly permitted by law, by license, or under terms agreed with the appropriate reproduction rights organization. Inquiries concerning reproduction outside the scope of the above should be sent to the Rights Department, Oxford University Press, at the address above.

You must not circulate this work in any other form and you must impose this same condition on any acquirer.

Library of Congress Cataloging-in-Publication Data
Names: Teasley, Martell L., editor. | Spencer, Michael S., editor. | Bartholomew, Melissa, editor.
Title: Social Work and the Grand Challenge to Eliminate Racism : concepts, theory, and evidence based approaches / Edited by Martell L. Teasley, Michael S. Spencer, Melissa Bartholomew.
Description: New York : Oxford University Press, [2023] | Includes bibliographical references and index.
Identifiers: LCCN 2022053631 (print) | LCCN 2022053632 (ebook) | ISBN 9780197674949 (hardback) | ISBN 9780197674963 (epub) | ISBN 9780197674970
Subjects: LCSH: Racism. | Social service and race relations. | Minorities—Civil rights.
Classification: LCC HT1521 .S543 2023 (print) | LCC HT1521 (ebook) | DDC 305.8—dc23/eng/20221208
LC record available at https://lccn.loc.gov/2022053631
LC ebook record available at https://lccn.loc.gov/2022053632

DOI: 10.1093/oso/9780197674949.001.0001

Printed by Integrated Books International, United States of America

Racism is a grand challenge for the social work profession because the profession has never tackled the centrality of racism as a causal factor, precipitating problem formation in the lives of people.
—Martell L. Teasley

Contents

Contributors	xvii
Introduction	xxi
Racism and Society	xxiv
Race and Social Outcomes	xxv
The Goal of This Book	xxvii
The Challenge of Eliminating Racism	xxx

PART I. HISTORY, RACISM, AND SOCIAL WORK EDUCATION

1. The Meaning and Function of Race and Racism: A Conceptual Understanding	3
Martell L. Teasley	
The Meaning and Function of Race and Racism	9
Racism	12
Institutional Racism	13
Systemic Racism	14
Racial Projects	14
Racializing People	16
Racialized Identity	17
Racial Commonsense Thinking	18
Conclusion	21
2. Anti-Racism Social Work: History and Future Challenges	28
Martell L. Teasley	
Social Work and Racism	31
Racism in Early Social Work	33
Racism and Civil Rights	36
Racism, Diversity, and Social Work Education	39
Racism and Social Work	42
Anti-Racist Social Work	45
ASWB and Racially Biased Licensure Testing	47
Conclusion	51

viii CONTENTS

3. Using Personal-Professional Narratives as a Technique for
Teaching: Social Work Students about the Complexities
of Racism 59
Tracy R. Whitaker, Ruby M. Gourdine, and Robert L. Cosby, Jr.
Racism in the Helping Relationship 61
Challenges in Discussing Racism with Social Work Students 63
Use of Personal-Professional Narratives 66
Personal-Professional Narrative Case Study 67
Juvenile Court Experience 67
Child Welfare Agency 68
Evaluating Outcomes 69
Implications for Practice 71
Summary and Conclusion 71

4. Eradicating Racism: Social Work's Most Pressing Grand
Challenge 76
Abril N. Harris, Smitha Rao, Manuel Cano, Bongki Woo, Ty Tucker,
Dale Dagar Maglalang, and Melissa Wood Bartholomew
Conceptualization of Racism 78
Racism and the History of Social Work 79
Social Work's Efforts to Eradicate Racism 83
Intrapersonal Efforts to Eradicate Racism 83
Interpersonal Efforts to Eradicate Racism 85
Institutional Efforts to Eradicate Racism 86
Conclusion 89

5. Ending Racism: A Critical Perspective 95
Harold E. Briggs and Martell L. Teasley
The Sustainability of Racism in America 99
Racism by Legislative Fiat and De Jure 99
Building a Race Consciousness-Raising and Anti-Racism Practice and
Theory Narrative 101
Structural and Policy Approaches to Anti-Racism Practice 107
Practice Approaches for Addressing Structural
and Interpersonal Racism 109
Behavioral Approach to Understanding Racism and Racial Prejudice 110
Mindfulness and Anti-Racism Practice 110
Combined Practice Approaches for Reducing Racism 111
Addressing Racial Discrimination through Task-Centered Practice 112
Confronting the Denial of Racism 113
Anti-Racism and Anti-Oppression Practice 114
Critique of Anti-Racism and Anti-Oppressive Practice Perspectives 116
Conclusion 116

PART II. RACISM AND INDIVIDUAL AND FAMILY WELL-BEING

6. Ensure Healthy Development for Youth: Expansions and Elaborations for Equity 127
   Valerie B. Shapiro, Amelia Seraphia Derr, Nehal Eldeeb,
   Henrika McCoy, Miguel A. Trujillo, and Cuc T. Vu
   In Matters of Equity, Creating Change Does Not Necessarily
   Create Progress 128
   Re-examining *Unleashing the Power of Prevention*
   for Equity Elaborations 130
   In Matters of Equity, Aspirations and Intentions Are Insufficient 132
   Re-examining the Goal to Establish Equity-Enhancing Interventions 134
   Understanding the Effects of Tested Programs on
   Marginalized Groups 139
   Case Example: An Equity-Enhancing Approach to Program
   Adaptation and Implementation 148
   Equity-Enhancing Interventions Prioritize Participatory Processes 149
   Equity-Enhancing Interventions Are Tailored to Particular Cultures,
   Contexts, and Conditions 150
   Equity-Enhancing Interventions Innovate Delivery Methods to
   Improve Service 152
   Can Unleashing Prevention Be Anti-Racist? 154

7. Ensuring Healthy Development for All Youth: Prevention of
   Psychosis 169
   Melissa E. Smith, Pamela Rakhshan Rouhakhtar,
   and Jason Schiffman
   The Promise of Prevention for All? 169
   Overview of Early Psychosis Prevention 170
   The Grand Challenge of Preventing Serious Mental Illness 170
   The Promise of Prevention: An Update 171
   Setting the Stage: Race and Mental Illness 175
   Brief History of the Social Construction of Mental Illness and Race 175
   Current Racial and Ethnic Disparities in the Identification and
   Treatment of Serious Mental Illness 176
   Role of Structural and Individual Racism in Mental Healthcare 177
   A Mirror Image? Racial and Ethnic Disparities in Psychosis Prevention 178
   Structural Racism, Racial Bias, and Cultural Responsiveness in
   Assessing Youth for Psychosis Risk 178
   Are Promising Evidence-Based Practices for Psychosis Prevention
   Racially and Culturally Responsive? 181

X CONTENTS

Strategies for Reducing Structural Racism and Racial Bias and
Increasing Cultural Responsiveness: Implications for Social
Work Research, Education, and Practice 183
  Development of Racially and Culturally Responsive Evidence-
  Based Practices 186
  Service Provision: Helping Family and Youth Unleash Their Power 186
Summary 187

8. Closing the Health Gap: Addressing Racism,
Settler Colonialism, and White Supremacy 200
Michael S. Spencer, Santino G. Camacho, Bongki Woo,
Roberto E. R. Orellana, and Jessica I. Ramirez
A Holistic View of Health 201
The Association between Racism and Settler Colonialism,
and Physical and Mental Health 203
Eliminating Racism in Health Systems 205
  Health Service Delivery 207
  Workforce Development 210
  Health Information Systems 210
  Equitable Access 212
  Financing Systems 212
  Leadership and Governance 213
  Culturally Relevant Health-Promotion Interventions to
  Reduce Exposure to Racism 213
  Racial Healing 214
  Cultural Coping and Cultural Resilience 215
  Culturally Tailored and Culturally Grounded Interventions 219
  Toward Solutions and Reconciliation 222
Conclusion 224

9. Integrating AASWSW's Grand Challenges of Productive Aging
with Anti-Racism and Health Equity Lenses to
Improve Population Health 235
Ernest Gonzales, Nancy Morrow-Howell, Jacqueline L. Angel, Lisa
Fredman, Lisa A. Marchiondo, Robert Harootyan, Jasmin Choi,
Nandini Choudhury, Kelsi Carolan, Kathy Lee, Erwin Tan,
Patricia Yu, Emily Shea, Cliff Whetung, and Christina Matz
An Integrated Framework of Productive Aging, Anti-Racism, and
Health Equity 236
  Definitions 236
  Public Policy, Culture, and Discrimination 237
  Individual Capacity 241
  Neighborhood Capacity 242
  Institutional Capacity 242

Productive Activities	243
Outcomes among Older Adults	243
Outcomes for Families, Organizations, and Society	244
Contributions of an Integrated Framework	245
Progress to Date and Future Research	246
Implications for Education	248
Conclusion	249

10. **Racism and the Grand Challenge of Ending Family Violence among Black Families** — 258
Alan J. Dettlaff, Reiko Boyd, and Tricia Bent-Goodley

Black Families and Child Maltreatment	259
Black Families and Intimate Partner Violence	261
Historical Overview of Racism and Violence against Black Families	262
Forced Family Separation	262
Laws and Policies to Maintain White Supremacy	264
The Role of Racism in Creating and Perpetuating Risk for Family Violence	267
Racism and Poverty	267
Racism, Health, and Stress	270
Racism, Geographic Contexts, and Structural Inequities	272
Evidence-Based and Evidence-Informed Strategies for Ending Family Violence	277
Applying an Anti-Racist Framework to Violence Prevention	280

11. **Beyond Colorism: The Impact of Racialization in U.S. Latinxs** — 287
Rocío Calvo, Jandel Crutchfield, and Jorge Delva

Healthcare	290
Housing	291
Education	292
Criminal Justice	293
Promising Practices to Counteract the Impact of Racism on Latinxs	294
Conclusion	298

12. **Confronting the History of Racism against Asian Americans in the United States** — 304
Meirong Liu

Introduction	304
Asian Americans and Historical Experiences of Othering	305
Impact of Racism on the Health and Mental Health of Asian Americans	308
Anti-Asian Racism and the Grand Challenges for Social Work	309
Moving Forward: Strategies to Eliminate Anti-Asian Racism	311
Disentangling the Model Minority Myth	311
Fostering Racial Solidarity	313

xii CONTENTS

Reflecting Racism within the Social Work Profession and
Developing an Anti-Asian Racism Workforce 314
    Support Reporting and Bystander Intervention Training 316
    Policy Initiatives on Anti-Asian Racism 317
    The Importance of Community-Based Solutions 318
    Addressing Access to Mental Healthcare 319
    Culturally Sensitive Evidence-Based Intervention 319
    Directions for Future Anti-Asian Racism Research 321
Conclusion 322

PART III. ELIMINATING RACISM THROUGH STRENGTHENING THE SOCIAL FABRIC

13. Strengthening the Social Responses to the Human Impacts of
Environmental Change 335
*Rachel Forbes, Dorlisa J. Minnick, Amy Krings, Felicia M. Mitchell,
Samantha Teixeira, and Shanondora Billiot*
    Chapter Overview 336
    Intersection of Health Equity and Environmental Justice 337
    Pesticide Exposure 338
    Food Systems and Food Security 338
    Water 340
    Extractive Energy and Natural Resource Development 342
    Extreme Weather Events 343
    Urban Heat Islands (UHI) 344
    Tornadoes 345
    Hurricanes and Flooding 345
    Climate Migration 346
    COVID-19 348
    Air Quality 348
    Food Systems 349
    Water 349
    Activism and Advocacy 350
    Conclusion and Moving Forward 355

14. Race and Racism in the Homelessness Crisis in the United
States: Historic Antecedents, Current Best Practices, and
Recommendations to End Racial Disparities in Housing and
Homelessness 365
*Deborah K. Padgett, Benjamin F. Henwood,
and James Petrovich*
    Foreword: A Brief Comment on the Authors' Positionality 365
    Racism in Plain Sight: From Slavery to Jim Crow to

CONTENTS xiii

Post–World War II Housing Exclusion 366
Research on Homelessness: The Missing Significance of Race 369
Current Best Practices in Ending Homelessness: Housing First 371
The HUD-VASH Program for Homeless Veterans: A Rare Success
Story and Lessons Learned 374
  African Americans among Homeless Veterans 374
  The Success of HUD-VASH 375
Structural and Institutional Changes Needed to Address Racial
Inequities in Housing Access and Housing Security 376
Conclusion and Recommendations 377

15. Eradicating Social Isolation: Focus on Social Exclusion and
Racism 383
Sandra Edmonds Crewe, Claudia Thorne, and Natalie Muñoz
Introduction 383
Social Isolation and Social Exclusion 384
  Social Isolation 384
  Social Exclusion 385
Theories: Racism and Social Exclusion 387
  Critical Race Theory 388
  Intersectionality 388
  Racialized Organizations Theory 389
Social Exclusion, Stigma, and Racism 390
  Relationship of Racism to Social Exclusion and Stigma 391
  Income and Wealth 392
  Education 392
  Physical and Mental Health Outcomes 393
Case Vignettes (Racism and Social Exclusion) 394
  Case Vignette # 1: Ms. Jones 395
  Case Vignette #2: Julissa 397
  Case Vignette #3: Michael 399
Conclusion: The Way Forward 401

PART IV. PROGRESSIVE APPROACHES TO ELIMINATING INSTITUTIONAL, SOCIAL POLICY, AND ECONOMIC RACISM

16. Juvenile Justice for Achieving Equal Opportunity and Justice 413
Susan A. McCarter, Bo-Kyung Elizabeth Kim,
Patricia Logan-Greene, and Vanessa Drew
Juvenile Justice and Delinquency Prevention Act 414
Disparate Impacts of Juvenile Justice System Involvement 415
  Micro-Level Impacts 415

xiv CONTENTS

Meso-Level Impacts	416
Macro-Level Impacts	417
Assessing Racial and Ethnic Disparities in Juvenile Justice	418
Reducing Racial and Ethnic Disparities in Juvenile Justice	419
Conclusion and Implications	419

17. From Mass Incarceration to Smart Decarceration 426
Susan A. McCarter, Camille R. Quinn, Charles H. Lea, III, and Laura S. Abrams

Mass Incarceration	427
Racial and Ethnic Disparities in the Criminal Justice System	428
Promote Smart Decarceration Grand Challenge	428
Micro, Meso, and Macro Contributors to RED	429
Micro Factors	430
Meso Factors	432
Macro Factors	433
Strategies to Redress Racial and Ethnic Disparities in the Criminal Justice System	435
Increase the Availability of and Access to Culturally Congruent Reentry Programs	435
Address Collateral Consequences through Racial and Ethnic Equity-Informed Policies and Practices	438
Decriminalize Low-Level Offenses and Invest in Alternatives to Incarceration	439
Repeal Racialized Criminal Justice Legislation and Policies	441
Adopt Racial Impact Statements as a Policy Priority	442
Address Explicit and Implicit Bias along the Carceral Continuum	443
Conclusion/Implications	444

18. Reducing Racialized Barriers to School Success for All Children and Youth 459
Terence Dwight Fitzgerald, Martell L. Teasley, Tasha Seneca Keyes, and Schnavia Hatcher

Race, Gender, and Disproportionality in School Suspension and Expulsion	460
Potential Outcomes of School Suspension and Expulsion	462
Existing Approaches for Tackling Disproportionality	463
Current Approaches	464
Launching the School Success Project (SSP)	466
Collaboration and Capacity-Building	468
Utilizing Evidence-Based and Innovative Methods	468
Completing the Interactive Map	469
Developing a Dissemination Strategy	469
Conclusion	470

CONTENTS XV

19. **Reversing Extreme Inequality: The Legacy and Persistence of Racism Economic Inequality** 476
Trina R. Shanks, Jennifer Romich, Stephanie C. Boddie, Laura Lein, and Dominique S. Crump
The Legacy and Persistence of Racism: Implications and Possibilities for Extreme Economic Inequality 476
  The Significance of the Racial Income and Wealth Gaps 476
  The History of Exclusionary Policies in the United States 479
    Native Americans 482
    Black Americans 483
    Latinx/Hispanic 484
    Asian Americans 485
    White Americans 485
  Labor and Income 486
    Assets and Wealth 489
    Land Loss 491
    Wealth Stripping through Fees and Fines 492
    Policy to Mitigate Economic Inequality by Race 493
    Reparations 494
  What Can Social Workers Do? 495
  Conclusion 496

20. **White Supremacy and American Social Policy: Implications for Racism-Centered Policy Practice** 503
Jerome H. Schiele, Denise McLane-Davison, and Christopher Maith, Sr.
The Reluctance to Address White Supremacy 504
White Supremacy's Foundation 505
Social Policy as Racial Regulation 507
The Denial of Racism 508
Policy Practice to Address White Supremacy 510
  Policy Practitioner Roles 510
Racism-Centeredness in a Social Welfare Policy Course 514
  Womanist Pedagogy and Racism-Centeredness 514
  Course Assignments 515
  Congressional Black Caucus Foundation (CBCF) Annual Conference 518
Conclusion 519

21. **Policy, Practice, and Institutional Barriers to Financial Capability and Asset Building Related to Race (Racism) in the United States** 524
Jenny L. Jones, Julie Birkenmaier, Lissa Johnson, Gena G. McClendon, Yunju Nam, Jin Huang, and Eyitayo Onifade
The Economics of Racism 525

xvi CONTENTS

The Challenges of Economics and Race/Racism	525
Race and Financial Education	526
Financial Socialization	527
Financial Education	528
For example, some schools	529
Financial Guidance	530
Impacts of Financial Education on Financial Behaviors and Well-Being	531
Race and Household Financial Access	534
Basic Financial Access: Banked Status	534
Alternative Financial Service (AFS) Use	535
Policy and Practice Suggestions to Increase Rate of Banked Products and Services Use	536
Credit Reports, Credit Scores, and Credit Use	536
Policy and Practice Suggestions Regarding Consumer Credit	537
Retirement Savings	538
Policy and Practice Suggestions Regarding Retirement Accounts	539
Racism as a Barrier to Achieving Financial Capability and Asset Building for All	539
Racial Wealth and Disparity	540
Race and FCAB and Social Work Education	543
Conclusion	545
Index	555

Contributors

Laura S. Abrams, PhD, MSW, University of California, Los Angeles

Jacqueline L. Angel, PhD, MA, University of Texas, Austin

Melissa Wood Bartholomew, PhD, JD, MDiv, MSW, Center for Diversity, Inclusion, & Belonging, Harvard Divinity School

Tricia Bent-Goodley, PhD, MSW, Professor Emeritus, Howard University

Shanondora Billiot, PhD, MSW, University of Illinois

Julie Birkenmaier, PhD, MSW, LCSW, St. Louis University

Stephanie C. Boddie, PhD, MSW, Baylor University

Reiko Boyd, PhD, MSW, University of Houston

Harold E. Briggs, PhD, AM, University of Georgia

Rocio Calvo, PhD, MA, Boston College

Santino G. Camacho, MPH, University of Washington

Manuel Cano, PhD, MSW, Arizona State University

Kelsi Carolan, PhD, MSW, University of Connecticut

Jasmin N. Choi, BSW, Boston University

Nandini Choudhury, MSW, LCSW, MPH, Center for Innovation in Social Work and Health, Boston University

Robert L. Cosby, PhD, MSW, Jr, Howard University

Sandra Edmonds Crewe, PhD, MSW, Howard University

Dominique S. Crump, LLMSW, University of Michigan

Jandel Crutchfield, PhD, MSW, University ot Texas at Arlington

Jorge Delva, PhD, MSW, Boston University

Amelia Seraphia Derr, PhD, MSW, Seattle University

Alan J. Dettlaff, PhD, MSW, University of Houston

Vanessa Drew, EdD, LSW, Elon University

Nehal Eldeeb, University of California, Berkeley

xviii CONTRIBUTORS

Terence Dwight Fitzgerald, PhD, EdM, MSW, Council for Mental Wellbeing

Rachel Forbes, MSW, University of Denver

Lisa Fredman, PhD, MSPH, Boston University

Ernest Gonzales, PhD, MSSW, New York University

Ruby M. Gourdine, DSW, MSW, Howard University

Robert (Bob) Harootyan, MA, MS, University of North Carolina, Wilmington

Abril N. Harris, PhD, MSW, University of Washington

Schnavia Hatcher, PhD, MSW, University of Alabama

Anna Hayward, PhD, MSW, State University of New York, Stonybrook

Benjamin F. Henwood, PhD, MSW, LCSW, University of Southern California

Jin Huang, PhD, MSW, St. Louis University

Lissa Johnson, MBA, MSW, LCSW, Washington University, St. Louis

Jenny L. Jones, PhD, MSW, Clark Atlanta University

Tasha Seneca Keyes, PhD, MSW, California State University San Marcos

Bo-Kyung Elizabeth Kim, University of Southern California

Amy Krings, PhD, MSW, Loyola University Chicago

Charles H. Lea, III, PhD, MSW, University of Houston

Kathy Lee, PhD, MSW, University of Texas at Arlington

Laura Lein, PhD, MA, University of Michigan

Meirong Liu, PhD, MS, LLM, Howard University

Patricia Logan-Greene, University of Buffalo

Dale Dagar Maglalang, PhD, MA, MSW, Brown University

Christopher Maith, Sr, PhD, MBA, Morgan State University

Lisa A. Marchiondo, PhD, University of New Mexico

Christina Matz, PhD, MSW, Boston College

Susan A. McCarter, PhD, MSW, MS, University of North Carolina, Charlotte

Gena G. McClendon, PhD, ML, Washington University, St. Louis

Denise McLane-Davison, PhD, MA, Toronto Metropolitan University

Dorlisa J. Minnick, PhD, MSW, Shippensburg University

Felicia M. Mitchell, PhD, MSW, Arizona State University

Nancy Morrow-Howell, PhD, Washington University, St. Louis

CONTRIBUTORS xix

Natalie Muñoz, PhD, MSW, Howard University

Yunju Nam, Ph.D., MSW, University of Buffalo

Eyitayo Onifade, PhD, MSW, Clark Atlanta University

Roberto E. R. Orellana, PhD, MPH, MSW, University of Washington

Deborah K. Padgett, PhD, MPH, MA, New York University

James Petrovich, PhD, LCSW, Texas Christian University

Meredith Powers, PhD, MSW, University of North Carolina, Greensboro

Camille R. Quinn, PhD, LCSW, LISW-S, University of Michigan

Jessica I. Ramirez, PhD, MSW, MPH, University of Washington

Smitha Rao, PhD, MA, The Ohio State University

Jennifer Romich, PhD, MA, University of Washington

Pamela Rakhshan Rouhakhtar, PhD, University of Maryland, Baltimore County

Jerome H. Schiele, DSW, MSW, Morgan State University

Jason Schiffman, PhD, MA, University of California Irvine

Trina R. Shanks, PhD, MSW, University of Michigan

Valerie Shapiro, PhD, University of California Berkeley

Emily Shea, MSW, MPH, City of Boston

Melissa E. Smith, PhD, MSSW, University of Maryland

Michael S. Spencer, PhD, MSSW, University of Washington

Erwin Tan, MD, Research & International Affairs Director, AARP Thought Leadership

Martell L. Teasley, PhD, MSW, University of Utah

Samantha Teixeira, PhD, MSW, Boston College

Claudia Thorne, PhD, LISW, LCSW, Coppin State University

Miguel A. Trujillo, PhD, LCSW, University of Denver

Ty Tucker, PhD Candidate, MSW, Boston College

Cuc T. Vu, City of Seattle

Cliff Whetung, PhD Candidate, MSW, NYU Silver School of Social Work

Tracy R. Whitaker, PhD, MSW, Howard University

Bongki Woo, PhD, MSW, University of South Carolina

Patricia Yu, Ph.D., LCSW, Executive Office of Health and Human Services at the Commonwealth of Massachusetts

Introduction

The Grand Challenges for Social Work (GCSW) have galvanized the profession, serving as a catalyst for change in bridging collaborative, scholarly, and public initiatives with innovative approaches, backed by science, to tackle long-standing and seemingly intractable social welfare problems. Launched in 2015 as a 10-year project, the American Academy of Social Welfare GCSW selected 12 initial concept papers under three domains. A plethora of consortiums, forums, conferences, workshops, webinars, advocacy efforts, and policy initiatives continue to take place, along with special journal editions, books, and research articles, all dedicated to the GCSW. Additionally, social work education programs have integrated the GCSW into curricula and instruction, university programs, and faculty-led initiatives.

While acknowledging the growing success of the GCSW, voices from within the social work profession questioned the glaring absence of racism as a central focus for the initiative. Although many of the scholarly papers that make up the Grand Challenges underscore the need to include race and discrimination as variables, the distinctiveness of racism as an overarching and casual factor is not captured within the initial set of concept papers. Native American scholars were particularly concerned about a lack of acknowledgment of their plight as First Nation, Indigenous people, and the recognition of their continuous struggle for human rights, anti-oppressive practices, and sovereignty. As voices grew, the topic gained the attention of the Grand Challenges Executive Committee, who then facilitated a discussion to consider the possible integration of racism as a new Grand Challenge. For some, the pervasiveness of racism is viewed as a nearly impossible task for the social work profession to tackle. For others, the idea of generating a set of Grand Challenges for the profession is incomplete without specific attention to racism as a root cause of oppression and inequality. From another perspective, the social work profession's signature value of social justice is obviously linked to the need for racial justice, and thus, there were calls for the integration of racism within all of the

Social Work and the Grand Challenge to Eliminate Racism. Edited by: Martell L. Teasley, Michael S. Spencer, and Melissa Bartholomew, Oxford University Press. © Oxford University Press 2023. DOI: 10.1093/oso/9780197674949.001.0001

xxii INTRODUCTION

Grand Challenges, from a sort of metatheoretical perspective; that is, as a formal system that describes the many structural problems and outcomes related to race and racism in society. In some ways, this would mean sprinkling race and racism among the Grand Challenges, which could be meaningful, but would not be enough. Such an approach is good as a method of understanding the veracity of racism and its manifestations across social problems. Yet, it neglects the centrality of racism as a causal factor impacting the lives of people.

To think critically, based on what we know about the malleability of race and racism, all of these perspectives have merit and become points of departure in attempts to comprehend the veracity of racism. However, there are also those who contend that "[b]ecause race is socially constructed, all cultural and experiential products from a racial perspective remain suspect" (Curry, 2017, p. 5). From this position, any search for racial narratives and meaning to explain social experiences and outcomes is a search for racial reification. Thus, race consciousness is problematized and rejected as unproven prima facie and narrow thought (Curry, 2017). However, this position neglects to honestly examine the centrality of racism and denies the real and meaningful experience of racialized people as personified throughout history and contemporary times, along with its omnipresent collate, racism (see Chapter 1). Nor will such an approach garner meaningful changes in the lives of people who intentionally and unintentionally are victims of racialized thoughts and practices. It is important to understand how the malleability of White supremacy and racism took hold in different forms and systems of materializing racial practices in North America, South America, Europe, and the Netherlands (Reid-Merritt, 2017). For this reason, "definitions and perceptions of race are complex, confusing, contradictory, controversial and imprecise"; but they continue to be used as a classification system of groups around the world (Reid-Merritt, 2017, p. 5). Race and racism are the only way in which people can situate certain lived experiences and their outcomes. The deleterious effects of racism are not on the margins of the lived experience of people and groups, and therefore, approaches to eliminating racism cannot be on the margins or serve as a secondary social problem.

In the United States, although the Black and White binary of racism continues, the growing significance of race and racism within and between all racial and ethnic groups demands greater attention by the social work profession. Laws and customs that disavow overt racism have given way to more complex and covert forms of racism, including the complexities of structural inequalities. Thus, any study of racism at one point in time must take into consideration the fluidity and flexibility of racism to morph into varied institutional and structural forces within society (Omi & Winant, 2015). And we cannot forget the benefactor of racism: whiteness. While there is nothing wrong with being a White person, benefiting from whiteness is a form of silent complicity seldom discussed. The historical problem is that whiteness has been based on skin color, certain physical characteristics, intelligence quota, and even the superiority of spiritual systems, all contrasting with blackness, Black people, and has been pitted relative to skin tone against people of other hues. Thus, part of undoing racism means undoing whiteness (Asante, 2017; Reid-Merritt, 2017).

There is also the continuing growth and belief in White supremacy, which exacerbates racism and contributes to growing inequality within the United States. Many people in the United States were astonished and stricken when they tuned into their televisions and other media forms on August 11 and 12, 2017, as they witnessed the Unite the Right and neo-Nazi rally on the campus of the University of Virginia in Charlottesville. These protestors included self-admitted members of the alt-right, White nationalist, right-wing militias, neo-Confederates, and neo-fascists groups. Columns of White males marched in unison shouting racist and anti-Semitic remarks. Undoubtedly, White supremacy is on the rise in the United States and throughout Europe, and unless stopped, its malignance will only exacerbate into either outright discriminatory and racist practices or growing covert forms of racism, all of which are unfolding (Mishra, 2017). According to the Southern Poverty Law Center, the number of White nationalist groups within the United States increased by 55% from 2017 to 2019 to a total of 940. Their visibility is becoming greater through their appearances at Black Lives Matter protests and COVID-19 protests, wearing insignia and brandishing weapons. Whether in the closet or upfront and vocal, White supremacy of any kind, even in its silence, is pernicious, volatile, and ultimately violent.

White people are essential to any possibility that the nation will change course and head down a pathway to eliminating racism. Understandably, this is a tough haul because of the polarizing nature and the painful reality of discussing race, racism, whiteness, and White supremacy in this country. White denial, as well as ignorance of the contours of whiteness, foreshadow sincerity, clarity of thought, and intellectual rigor, leading to substantive outcome models for change, both inside and outside the social work profession. At the crux of indifference to change is economic and institutional vested

xxiv INTRODUCTION

interest in maintaining the structure and functioning of the status quo. In the words of W. E. B. Du Bois, "Everyone is in favor of justice so long as it costs them no effort" (1929, p. 45). Thus, people cannot be outraged about injustice if they take no action.

As the U.S. population continues to diversify to a non-White majority, a number of important transformations are taking place in terms of the intellectual justifications for racism, from the voting booth, fears of non-White immigration, to the prison-industrial complex. Professional leadership in this area means having a frank and honest discussion about the complexities and the clear and present danger of institutional and structural racism in the twenty-first century. Such a conversation must lead to planned and substantiated advocacy and action aimed at results. Although racism permeates nearly every aspect of U.S. society, including social interactions, there has been significant and continuous social progress in reducing its vestiges. Thus, ending racism is not an insurmountable project; it is one that requires commitment and persistence from every member of society.

Racism is a Grand Challenge for the social work profession because the profession has never tackled the centrality of racism as a causal factor precipitating problem formation in the lives of people. At the root of many clinically diagnosed problems that call for social work intervention are a host of structural and systemic issues that culminate and place disenfranchised communities, families, and people at risk for unhealthy outcomes. Institutional, structural, cultural, economic, and political racism is at the forefront of these issues. In this respect, the Grand Challenge to Eliminate Racism represents an excellent vehicle to ameliorate, lessen, and even eradicate racism within targeted domains of the social work profession and its fields of practice. The GCSW are a call to action, seeking innovative ways to tackle long-standing social problems using evidence-based methods an innovative approach to problem-solving. Scientific approaches to undermining the many facets of racism within society will require innovation and new ways to approach old racialized problems, disciplinary and interdisciplinary collaboration, as well as longitudinal commitment. And we cannot forget the internal challenges of racism within the social work profession, a problem briefly discussed later in this chapter.

Racism and Society

Racism has played itself out in many forms in the United States, including slavery, indentured servitude, segregation, Jim Crow laws, genocide, and settler colonialism. Today, structural racism, bias, and discriminatory practices continue to promote racial inequality in a myriad of ways (Lipstiz, 2011). "The dominant white frame still views whites as a group to be generally superior and virtuous and people of color as groups to be generally of less social, economic and political consequence" (Feagin, 2020, p. 168). Institutional racism within the criminal justice and child welfare systems and public education continues long-standing practices resulting in inequitable treatment and racialized outcomes. While the progress of the Civil Rights movement is notable and far-reaching, the apparent need to continuously address race relations is evidenced by the ongoing violence against Black and Brown people by police, the desecration of Indigenous lands and lives, anti-immigration policies, constraints on voting privileges, high rates of incarceration of Black and Brown people, and disproportionate rates of chronic illnesses that impact people of color—all buttressed by society's general lack of understanding of the pernicious effects of White privilege and gross income and wealth gaps between racial and ethnic groups. Moreover, a national lack of awareness and status quo thinking such as "this is the way things have always been" allow racist systems to continue unchecked and to further generate methods to reify the maintenance of the social order. Thus, racism is a unique Grand Challenge, as it is inextricably linked to all of the existing 12 Grand Challenges, while having its own distinctive qualities. Racism infiltrates nearly all social welfare problems, including health, the quality of life for the elderly, child welfare, mental health, substance use, wealth distribution, poverty, homelessness, environmental injustice and climate change, incarceration rates, and perhaps, the biggest challenge of all, race and ethnic relations.

Race and Social Outcomes

While racial inequalities are associated with a wide range of negative economic, social, and health outcomes, these inequalities become exacerbated when there is a crisis. The COVID-19 pandemic is a perfect example of this. Since the first outbreaks, COVID-19 attacked our most vulnerable communities. Besides the elderly, age-adjusted rates of COVID-19 morbidity and mortality were significantly higher for African Americans, Latinx Americans, and Native Hawaiian/Pacific Islanders, American Indians, and Alaska Native racial and ethnic groups (Artiga & Orgera, 2020). The Brookings Institute reported in June 2020 that national death rates from COVID-19 were higher for African Americans and Latinx within all age

xxvi INTRODUCTION

categories. For example, African Americans ages 55–64 have a higher death rate from COVID-19 that Whites ages 65–74. Among those aged 45–54, African Americans and Latinx death rates are at least six times higher than for Whites (Ford, Reber, & Reeves, 2020). Why does this happen?

First, many of these groups have a history of economic disadvantage, whether it is inequality in education, income, technological deficits, networking opportunities, working a low-wage essential job, or unemployment as a result of racist policies that differentially fund school districts, the legacy of segregation and redlining, discriminatory and predatory practices in lending and financing, and the inability to accumulate assets (American Sociological Association, 2003; Schiele, 2020). Economic disadvantage lends itself to deficiencies in access to healthy food, healthcare, digital access, housing, and other basic necessities to survive (Ford, Reber, & Reeves, 2020). More than two-thirds of the country's Black (67%) and Hispanic (70%) populations live in zip codes with higher than average unemployment rates. Second, as Lipsitz (2011) explains in *How Racism Takes Place*, relations between races are relations between places. In other words, physical space undergirds how racism takes place. Lipsitz contends that geographic racism in America is part of the "White spatial imaginary" shaping where people live. One only needs to read the history of many geographic dwellings, and how they become the domicile of minoritized populations, to find how communities and neighborhoods were racialized. Environmental and geographic racism normally relegates poor minoritized populations to geographic areas where there are income, wealth, education, employment and health disparities. For example, at the time of this writing, Blacks are 18% of the population in New York but made up a whopping 33% of those contacting COVID-19. In Illinois, 43% of those who died from COVID-19 were Black, but they are only 15% of the population. Similarly, Michigan's Black population accounted for 40% of the state's COVID-19 deaths, while Blacks are only 4% of the population (Gordon, 2020).

Third, there is evidence that existing chronic illnesses put individuals with COVID-19 at a greater risk of mortality. There is clear evidence of disparities in the distribution of chronic illness in the United States. These disparities are rooted in both interpersonal and institutional experiences with health systems that are rooted in White supremacy and privilege, including unethical medical experimentation, greater likelihood of receiving a more invasive treatment (e.g., amputations), provider bias, lack of culturally appropriate providers, as well as the health risks compounded by economic disadvantage.

INTRODUCTION   xxvii

Fourth, there is a cultural and deeper "soul wound" among people that exists through intergenerational trauma that is passed down, both as a means of protecting communities from White supremacy, and as a reminder that the country still has a long way to go to in order to live up to its promise of life, liberty, and the pursuit of for happiness for all its citizens. We also cannot forget the plight of today's immigrant populations, who so often represent the poor huddled masses seeking liberty, similar to the forerunners of the Pax Americana. Beyond economic and social cost, racism wounds people. This soul wound is exacerbated under the COVID-19 crisis when people are isolated, anxious, depressed, and angry. Incidence of overt racism, such as the murder of George Floyd and other Black and Brown individuals, the 45th president of the United States calling COVID-19 the "Chinese virus" and subsequent acts of racism against Asian Americans, as well as stricter immigration policies for non-White individuals, are now resonating with people as a call to action. Continued racialized practices means that many racialized groups continue to deal with covert or ordinary, everyday racism (e.g., microaggressions), which deepen the wounds and heed intergenerational and collective healing (Kendi, 2019). Unfortunately, the buildup of frustration and anger resulting in protests and riots further put minoritized communities at risk for greater harm, both in contracting the virus or in encountering further violence from police. Thus, racism attacks those most vulnerable at more than one level; it attacks holistically, systemically, and unapologetically.

The Goal of This Book

This book examines the centrality of racism in tackling a number of long-standing social welfare problems. Focusing on the effects of systemic racism and its impact on well-being during the life cycle, authors take on many of the topical areas covered under the initial 12 GCSW, as well as exploring new subject areas. The text also examines internal problems with race and racism within the social work profession. In many ways, this text represents an opening salvo for the June 2020 announcement of the Social Work Grand Challenge to Eliminate Racism. Its content is symbolic of the considerable amount of work to be done to include the identification of problem formation, planning strategies, contemplation of methods, attempts at changes, and ongoing assessment. Taking a solution-focused stance to understanding

xxviii INTRODUCTION

problem formation, the authors of the text place an emphasis on evidence-based and innovative approaches to solving social welfare problems impacted by racism.

Ironically, the planning of the announcement for the Social Work Grand Challenge to Eliminate Racism came one month after the murder of George Floyd by Minneapolis police officer Derek Chauvin on May 25, 2020, which triggered first national, then worldwide protests against racism and police violence. Leaders within the social work profession agree that there are internal challenges that need to be addressed. At a June 26, 2020, virtual meeting held by the Council on Social Work Education, the general sentiment among professional social work organization leaders was, "we need to clear up our own house first," as stated by NASW CEO Angelo McClain. The social work profession has attempted a variety of approaches to deal with the challenge of racism, both internal to the profession and within the wider society.

As demonstrated within this book, a considerable amount of internal work in this area needs to be conducted. A range of power dynamics within institutions, organizations, agencies, and workplace settings should be part of such a process, along with adhering to the reality of organizational diversity. At the personnel level, there is a need to have micro-level discussions of White privilege, as well as analysis of social systems that sustain social relations and stratification based on whiteness. Again, this is necessary for the social work profession as well as within the larger society. This book fills a void within the social work profession in its dedication to examining social justice and welfare topics related to the Grand Challenge to Eliminate Racism.

The purpose of this book is to address the long-overdue challenge within the social work profession to provide a road map for deepening our understanding of how racism infiltrates our society and what social work, in collaboration with allied sciences and professionals, can do to eliminate it. We take special measures in this book to not only look at racism as a root cause of oppression, but also find solutions, grounded in evidence and practice-based knowledge. Macro-, meso-, and micro-level implications are examined and social work values are addressed throughout the chapters. The authors address a wide range of social work and long-standing societal grand challenges, and address not only the far-reaching implications of racism, but also the challenge of White supremacy.

Focusing on the effects of systemic racism and its impact on well-being during the life cycle, 79 authors within 21 chapters of this book take on a plethora of social welfare problems and their connection to institutional, structural, organizational, and interpersonal racism. Major objectives for this book are designed to assist the reader in:

- Examining various forms of racism and their distinctions and impact on racial groups;
- Promoting evidence- and practice-based research that cultivates improvements in the daily lives of people affected by racism, facilitating systemic change on the individual, organizational, community, and societal levels;
- Advancing community empowerment and advocacy to address and eliminate racism and White supremacy;
- Identifying the link between racism and the social determinants of health and social well-being;
- Moving towards "upstream" preventive practices as opposed to more costly "downstream" inteventions;
- Fostering the development of an anti-racist social work workforce that promotes access to resources and opportunities and encompasses transdisciplinary collaboration;
- Examining the link between historical racial oppression and contemporary racialized economic injustice;
- Promoting teaching and learning within social work education programs that examine structural inequalities and White privilege, and their impact on individual and group outcomes; and
- Developing a policy agenda for eliminating racism and white supremacy from institutions and organizations, where structural racism is evident and causes the most damage.

Many of the authors are writers of the initial 12 GCSW, and there are a host of new authors who add fresh perspectives to the discourse on race and racism with innovative approaches to eliminate racism. Although this book is not intended to deeply explore whiteness, it invokes a necessary conversation on whiteness that cannot be avoided if there is sincerity in the elimination of racism. Anti-racism practices include the study of whiteness, which contains implications for how we can eliminate White supremacy, and how White privilege can be used to combat racism (Bonilla-Silva, 2010). We also highlight the ways in which social work interventions can be damaging if White privilege and racism are not revealed and harnessed. The editors of this book

The Challenge of Eliminating Racism

Today, more than 60 years past the famed Civil Rights movement, the country is in the midst of a resurgence of a human rights struggle where cities are again experiencing major protests, rioting, and the inevitable characteristics of American violence. Over time, the nation has divided itself along political ideologies, and race serves a central role in that division. The growing resurgence of White supremacy groups; a growing wealth gap; police extrajudicial killings; environmental racism; and serious health, educational, and employment disparities among racial and ethnic groups drive the clarion call for human rights and change in our social contract with Black, Indigenous, and People of Color (BIPOC). In what may be viewed as a new civil rights movement, the primary target is systemic racism.

Unlike the Progressive era, there is no planned advocacy and policymaking force among social work organizations that can stand up to prevailing societal forces that dictate our current national and declining state of social welfare—the fragmentation among social work organizations does not help this cause. The *fire this time* is among us and Black Lives Matter, Moral Mondays, Repairers of the Breach, Color of Change, and many others that have emerged as grassroots organizations born out of necessity, now galvanizing the nation and the world. They have become the face and leaders in the call for social change. What visual and notable roles will the social work professional play in this twenty-first-century call for racial justice? The social work profession must identify its collective niche in this new era, and its organizations, coalitions, leaders, and professional members must ask themselves, what will be the resolve and response of the profession to the heightened demand for racial and economic justice in the era of hypercapitalism? History will record its efforts during this critical time. The Grand Challenge to Eliminate Racism is late to the party, particularly for a profession predicated on social justice. However, if the social work profession wants to be part of the last dance, standing tall, and recognizable for social justice in this new era, it will have to "step up" its game and demonstrate leadership in the movement for change.

Authors' note: We have no known conflicts of interest to disclose.

References

Artiga, S., & Orgera, K. (2020, May 14). COVID-19 presents significant risks for American Indian and Alaska Native People. Coronavirus Statistics. Centers for Disease Control. Retrieved from https://www.kff.org/coronavirus-covid-19/issue-brief/covid-19-presents-significant-risks-for-american-indian-and-alaska-native-people/.

Asante, M. K. (2017). Race and racism in American Society: Evolution towards new thoughts. In P. Reid-Merritt (Ed.), Race in America (pp. 23–42). Santa Barbara, CA: Praeger

American Sociological Association (2003). *The importance of collecting data and doing social scientific research on race*. Washington, DC: American Sociological Association.

Curry, T. (2017). *The man-not: Race, class, genre, and the dilemmas of Black manhood*. Philadelphia: Temple University Press.

Du Bois, W. E. B. (1929). The denial of economic justice to Negros. In Foner, P. S. (1970) (Ed.), *W. E. B. Du Bois speaks: Speeches and addresses 1920–1963* (pp. 43–46).

Ford, T., Reber, S., & Reeves, R. V. (2020). Race gaps in COVID-19 deaths are even bigger than they appear. Up Front Brookings. Retrieved from https://www.brookings.edu/blog/up-front/2020/06/16/race-gaps-in-covid-19-deaths-are-even-bigger-than-they-appear/.

Gordon, S. (2020, May 7). Black, minority populations hit harder by COVID-19. *UPI Health Day News*. United Press International, Inc. Retrieved from https://www.upi.com/Health_News/2020/05/07/Black-minority-populations-hit-harder-by-COVID-19/8801588860415/

Kendi, I. X. (2019). *How to become an antiracist*. New York: Random House

Lipsitz, G. (2011). *How racism takes place*. Philadelphia: Temple University Press.

Mishra, P. (2017). *Age of anger: A history of the present*. New York: Penguin Books.

Omi, M., & Winant, H. (2015). *Racial formation in the United States* (3rd ed.). New York: Routledge.

Reid-Merritt, P. (2017). Race in America: Social constructs and social realities: An introduction In P. Reid-Merritt (Ed.), *How a pseudoscientific concept shaped human interaction* (Vol. 2, pp. 3–22). Santa Barbara, CA: Praeger.

Schiele, J. H. (2020). *Social welfare policy: Regulation & resistance among people of color* (2nd ed). San Diego, CA: Cognella.

PART I

HISTORY, RACISM, AND SOCIAL WORK EDUCATION

Racism is imbued within the structures of our society and has been nesting comfortably within the social work profession since its inception (see Chapter 1). The 13th Grand Challenge is boldly calling social workers to extract this systemic stronghold from its profession and breathe new life into a field that has the capacity to transform society. To facilitate this necessary disruption, social workers must be willing to critically engage in an exploration of the meaning of racism and its impact on social work in order to work toward its elimination from society and the profession. The chapters in Part I provide a robust examination of race and racism, its role in social work, and the profession's movement toward a posture of anti-racism. In Chapter 1, "The Meaning and Function of Race and Racism," Martell Teasley lays important groundwork required for this deep exploration of race, racism, and the social work profession. The author examines ways in which institutional norms produce racial commonsense thinking as part of normative consciousness, discourse, and social practice. Beginning with the fundamentals, he then provides the scaffolding necessary for understanding the function of race and racism at the micro, meso, and macro levels.

Teasley carries this discussion forward in Chapter 2, "Anti-racism Social Work: History and the Challenge Ahead," where he sheds light on the persistent efforts of many within the profession throughout the years to advance this conversation and to focus on race and racism in a way that would take root. He illuminates the challenges along the journey toward the goal of centering race and racism in the curriculum and programming of social work education. The author demonstrates how and why that the social work profession continues to struggle with its approach to race and racism in its efforts to promote social justice. This chapter provides a review of efforts by the Council on Social Work Education (CSWE), the National Association

2 HISTORY, RACISM, AND SOCIAL WORK EDUCATION

of Social Workers (NASW), and other organizations in order to demonstrate the ebb and flow of the struggle to grapple with race and racism while continuing to promote social justice within the social work profession. In Chapter 3, "Using Personal-Professional Narratives as a Technique for Teaching Social Work Students about the Complexities of Racism," Tracy R. Whitaker, Ruby M. Gourdine, and Robert L. Cosby, Jr., offer a way to further this goal. Their chapter explores the benefits and challenges of utilizing narratives as a method for exposing social work students to a realm beyond the classroom and the textbooks. The authors will examine the incongruency between articulated and practiced behaviors in social work, including how racism persists, even within the context of helping relationships. They highlight how educators can offer narratives as a vehicle for helping students understand the function of race and racism in the lives of clients and the systems and structures in which they live.

In Chapter 4, "Eradicating Racism: Social Work's Most Pressing Grand Challenge," Abril Harris, Smitha Rao, Manual Cano, Bongki Woo, Ty Tucker, Dale Arvy Maglalang, and Melissa Bartholomew provide further grounding in racism and the history of social work. They highlight the critical need for social workers to address the way racism functions personally within White and BIPOC (Black, Indigenous, and People of Color) social workers. They underscore the need for ongoing self-examination to be part of the work of eradicating racism within the profession. The chapter wbegins with a critical conceptualization of racism and its extensive effect on institutions and the well-being of populations. In Chapter 5, the final chapter of this section, "Ending Racism: A Critical Perspective," Harold Briggs and Martell Teasley continue the theme of Chapter 4, helping readers to envision the end of racism through an examination of the clinical and organizational research supporting frameworks for approaches that help address the function of racism at the interpersonal and systemic levels. This chapter reviews the available clinical and organizational research to present conceptual frameworks to use in designing practice approaches for the elimination of racism at the interpersonal and the systemic levels of attention.

1

The Meaning and Function of Race and Racism

A Conceptual Understanding

Martell L. Teasley

I knew I was not a racist, so I thought.

—James Baldwin

It is important to understand that in a country predicated on race and racism from its origins, through colonial denomination and genocide, slavery, exclusion, internment, Jim Crow, and the growing backlash to a non-European, multiethnic majority, there remain elements within American society serving from one era to another in the maintenance of racism (Lipsitz, 2011; Mills, 1997; Reid-Merritt, 2017). For this reason, race and racism have many characteristics and meanings that have development over time (Feagin, 2020; Omi & Winant, 2015). Understanding the complexities of race and racism and the assignment of their meaning and social value is important for the social work profession in its service to diverse populations and quest for social justice.

In this chapter, I set the stage for a conversation on race, racism, and the social work profession as part of critical discourse. I discuss a series of definitions as part of a conceptual understanding of how to think about race and racism. This chapter is an attempt to provide the reader with an understanding of the endemic ways in which race and racism are embedded within the structure of American society, often in everyday and ordinary ways. Understanding the centrality of racism within the American context may seem to be a nebulous task; mainly, because race and racism are part of the everyday and ordinary social milieu and are fully integrated within

Martell L. Teasley, *The Meaning and Function of Race and Racism* In: *Social Work and the Grand Challenge to Eliminate Racism.* Edited by: Martell L. Teasley, Michael S. Spencer, and Melissa Bartholomew, Oxford University Press. © Oxford University Press 2023. DOI: 10.1093/oso/9780197674949.003.0001

American society. I attempt to promote an understanding of how to conceptualize race and racism based on micro, meso, and macro levels within the social work profession.

Critical thought about race and racism means a continued study of the fluid and flexible meanings of these concepts within a given social era and/or context, and how they are addressed within institutional norms and practices, and everyday interpersonal and situational narratives. For example, it was unfashionable and politically incorrect to say "Black Lives Matter" in many mainstream settings prior to the murders of George Floyd, Breonna Taylor, and Ahmed Aubrey in the spring of 2020. However, these triggers became a global tipping point for demands to stop out-of-control policing of black bodies, which resulted in widespread protest, civil unrest, rioting in some states, and international condemnation and protest. After the May 2020 murder of George Floyd by Minneapolis police officer Derek Chauvin, and his fellow officers as accomplices, the social acceptance of Black Lives Matter (BLM) became a way for people to distance themselves from the public, overt, and calculated execution of Floyd, with the police officers knowingly being video recorded. Seemingly overnight, BLM became a battle cry for racial justice as citizens of all hues, major leagues sports, many Fortune 500 companies, major media outlets, and prominent White political figures endorsed BLM, as well as some local and state governments.

The momentum from this period resulted in other symbolic gestures taking place throughout society—bringing down Civil War era statues; removing the names of known racists from buildings; and acknowledging the legitimacy of BLM. While meaningful, these acts represent a sort of camouflage that does little to change power dynamics between police and minority communities—the source of much discontent among African Americans and Latinos. Parenthetically, none of these activities tackles systemic racism found in a lack of corporate organizational diversity, draconian minority-community lending practices by banks, discriminatory employment and housing practices, urban community divestment, gentrification projects, and zip code disparities in public school funding. Calls to defund or reduce funding to police departments resulted in some attempts to reduce funding, and some attempts to increase funding. Congressional legislation on police reform based on measures to enhance training and place greater oversight on local policing ended without accomplishments. Conversely, one year after the May 2020 police killing of George Floyd, 21 U.S. states passed legislation focused on police oversight (Buchholz, 2021). State driven legislation to reduced the dispropionality of legthal death by police of unarmed minoritized groups did help to calm the public and served as a meaningful victory to the psyche of African Americans, particularly those from the Civil Rights generation, and those from other ethnic groups, who have for generations decried and pushed for the need to remove nationalized symbols of white supremacy. However, according to the research group, Mapping Police Violence, there is little in the abatement of police killings of unarmed African Americans and other minoritiezed groups since the enactment of legislation to end racial disparities in deaths by police. One year after to the Floyd murder, . . . "25 states saw a decrease, 19 states an increase and seven states had the same number of police killings compared with the same period" a year earlier (Haddad, 2021, online).

The activities of BLM and other social activist groups have resulted in a heighted racial consciousness among many social work professionals, particularly among students within social work education programs. In fact, "[t]he 2020 Black Lives Matter's call to defund the police has at times carried a call for refunding social services" (Burghardt, 2021, p. xxiv). In a backlash against many mainstream institutions during this period, groups of young professional and student social workers went as far as questioning the worth of the National Association of Social Workers (NASW), and have even called for its defunding.

For all of the social work profession's efforts to develop knowledge, critical thinking, values, and skills in the promotion of diversity and inclusion, the profession finds itself in the twenty-first century asking many questions in this area, and needing greater understanding of the complexities of race and racism (Maylea, 2020). Many point to the lack of attention to macro practice by frontline social workers as a salient factor in why the profession lacks meaningful efforts and a creditable voice at the table of political advocacy for racial reconciliation. There are also concerns about the curriculum in many social work education programs. Part of this is the seemingly "implicit imperative that focuses on preparing [social work education] students and frontline professional for private practice" (Burghardt, 2021, p. xxv). The divided house among micro, meso, and macro practice cannot stand if the social work profession is to make meaningful gains on the grand challenge to eliminate racism and other traditional forms of practice. Consequently, the current era represents a critical period for the social work profession as it attempts to navigate the backlash against the nearly singular professional focus on clinical entrepreneurship over the values of social justice and the need to remedy racialized inequalities.

The social work profession in not alone in its need to thoroughly address racism throughout its scope of education and practice. Other social and behavioral sciences have similar struggles; most have emerged from the era of pseudo-science and blatant scientific racism and intelligence testing. Yet, reform is still needed, as many reinforce vestiges of the past and practices based on racial commonsense thinking. Standardized testing, such as the American College Testing (ACT) exam and the Scholastic Aptitude Test (SAT), are being abandoned as necessary assessments for college readiness. In January 2021, the oldest national physicians' association in the country, the American Psychiatric Association, issued an apology from its Board of Trustees "to its members, patients, their families, and the public for enabling discriminatory and prejudicial actions within the APA and racist practices in psychiatric treatment for Black, Indigenous and People of Color" . . . (online). Following suit, in October 2021, the American Psychological Association declared that the organization "failed in its role leading the discipline of psychology, was complicit in contributing to systemic inequities, and hurt many through racism, racial discrimination, and denigration of communities of color, thereby falling short on its mission to benefit society and improve lives" (online).

Chapter 2 discusses approaches since the 1960s in which the social work profession attempted to address race and racism within the profession and within practice. The spring of 2020 witnessed the development of the Grand Challenge to Eliminate Racism, which is quite an undertaking, even just to deal with racialized challenges within the profession. Nevertheless, if the social work profession is sincere about the call to eliminate racism, then it must deal with the centrality of race and racism as causal factors influencing the lived experiences of people. In referring to the centrality of racism, I define it as a primary and casual factor shaping the lived experiences and circumstances of people (Mills, 1997). This includes generalized presuppositions about race and ethnicity; the complexities of structural inequalities; socialized racial identities, attitudes, and behaviors; the pervasive power of whiteness; and the power and structure of institutions and organizations in which racialized people interact within the social milieu. The centrality of race and racism means having hard discussions, deliberation, and decision-making surrounding racial understanding, equity, and inclusion (King, 2018). Approaches to understanding race and racism from a diversity and inclusion perspective are often void of an examination of the centrality of race and racism, and therefore contribute to a lack of understanding of the fluid and dynamic aspects of race and racism within American society (DiAngelo, 2021). As I have written elsewhere:

> Part of understanding the centrality of race and racism consists of how one views, investigates, and examines the structural system, its operations and actions including the cultural context, and the ability to pinpoint the ripple effects of problems grounded in racialized policies and practices. It is important to understand that although race and racism were central factors throughout the development and maintenance of the America experience, they have been relegated to the margins or peripheral of our discourse on causal factors to explain racial group socioeconomic disparities and outcomes, and racialized behaviors. In the proposed colorblind society, race is not a factor and at worse is conceived as a marginal factor in society—racism as a form of happenstance. Although there are times when race is a marginal factor, the fact that many in society are uninformed and often unaware of how race and racism worked as central factors in the functionality of a historical caste system hinders our ability to create an antiracist society. This is because there is an absence of forethought on the reality of race and racism in American, which has resulted in the development of a form of social cognitive dissonance, manifested from the canons of Western knowledge serving as the foundation of the American schooling process. Overtime, standards of whiteness as the optimal state of being and as a form of achievement for citizenship status, in the creation of the American dream, fomented racialized thought and practice as the norm. (Teasley, n.p.)

Finally, in examining the centrality of race and racism, one is compelled to examine the conceptualization of Whites versus non-Whites, and the reality of White racial entitlement versus non-White subordination, including the many internal distinctions between these categories (Jeyasingham, 2012; Jones, 2020; Mill, 1997). As Mills pragmatically states in *The Racial Contract*, many non-Whites see race as, paradoxically, "everywhere" and "nowhere" in structuring their lives, which is a process that is formally missed or not recorded morally or politically, mainly, because such existence seems quite normal in a racialized society. Consequently, Mills proclaims, "But in a racially structure polity the only people who can find it psychologically possible to deny the centrality of race are those who are racially privileged, for whom race is invisible precisely because the world is structured around them . . ." (1997, p. 76). Those who deny the centrality of race do so because it is invisible to them as a non-factor in their privilege. As a metaphor, Mills contends, "The fish do not see the water, and whites do not see the racial nature of a white polity because it is natural to them, the element in which they move" (p. 76). Therefore, the investigation of racism requires careful study, critical thought, and engagement in order to decipher the ways in which race is applied and given meaning in the social milieu.

Non-White populations are not the only groups affected by the realities of race. As Baldwin notes, White supremacy forces Whites to engage in fantastic rationalization to support their belief system, which borders on the pathological given its insistence of superiority. According to Baldwin in his 1963 bestseller, *The Fire Next Time*, this pathological approach to understanding race generated a torched existence for Whites, accompanied by a "sort of structured ignorance" of the reality of non-Whites, such that one cannot raise certain issues with Whites. Simply put, as long as whiteness exists, racism will exist. From this line of thought, one wonders what subjects are taboo about whiteness within the social work profession (Jeyasingham, 2012). To investigate such thinking means that a bold search for truth must take place in the midst of White self-deception, and the accompanying denial and disagreement.

What is clear from this position is that if the social work profession is going to tackle eliminating racism as a grand challenge, it must extend the professional knowledge base though a historical lens, conceptual and theoretical approaches, research methods, and practical approaches to inform macro, meso, and micro perspectives in order to better understand the centrality of race and racism. The review of race and racism within this chapter attempts to promote greater understanding of the breadth and depth of race and racism in our lived experiences. It is not intended to be a comprehensive overview, but more a narrative illustration of the fluid and flexible meanings of these concepts and how they transition from time and place while maintaining meaning.

One of the positions discussed in the *Eliminate Racism* working paper is the *development of an anti-racism social workforce that promotes access to resources, opportunities, and transdisciplinary collaboration and advances community empowerment to build racial equity* (Teasley et al., 2021). Of necessity in this process is the development of a workforce that understands the centrality of race and racism. This chapter hopes to contribute to that understanding. Igniting a sense of critical consciousness in the development of an anti-racism workforce is a major challenge for social work education and practice, involving the inclusion of supporting organizations. If individuals, agencies, and organizations commit to transition this murky road of anti-racist thought and practice, it must begin with self-reflection based on understanding the manifestation and development of race and racism within our own lives, including the presuppositions normed in our individual and group socialization process, much of which continues.

In many ways, it is our lack of individual self-reflection that impedes our understanding of the centrality of race and racism. Those who claim to "not see race" and to be "color-blind" in thought and attitude about race and/or who have limited knowledge of the history of race and racism in America will have the hardest time in the self-reflection process. For many entering social work education, without curriculum and instruction that concretely promote self-reflection and critical consciousness about race and racism in a knowledge- and skills-building capacity, they cannot arrive at, say, where author James Baldwin found himself after deep introspection, "I knew I was not a racist, so I thought."

The Meaning and Function of Race and Racism

Shaping the concept of race has a long and varied history. Although there is a litany of documentation on race and racism from ancient times to the present, according to author Ibram Kendi, the first acknowledgment of the concept of race comes from the French author Jacques de Breze in his 1481 poem, "The Hunt." It is in the year 1606 that race first appears in the dictionary, where French diplomat Jean Nicot stated that "race" means descent: ". . . It is said that a man, a horse, a dog or another animal is from good or bad race." It is racism that led to the concept of race as a method of identifying and determining the worth and status of people from differing groups with the human family. The ideological formation of race in America starts with the European movement and rapid expansion into the so-called new world as a developed psychological justification for hierarchically classifying human beings for the purpose of legal and institutional control, and the assignment of value. In forming a global social contract, race became a way of ranking people by class. Thus, the concept of race gained its social legitimacy as a useful and organized system of power and control (Omi & Winant, 2015).

As a young country, the United States gave racial classifications realness with the one-drop rule and the classification of people based on skin color and ancestral descent (Wilkenson, 2020). Even Nazi Germany, which studied the US system of racial apartheid, would not go as far as the one-drop rule in classifying a person who had majority German ancestry as totally Jewish (Wilkenson, 2020). Early American law and jurisprudence supported *total* legal inequality based on race until the passage of the Fourteenth Amendment in 1868, which granted citizenship to African Americans. After the passage of the Fifteenth Amendment in 1870, which granted voting rights to black men, the country then stripped African Americans of these rights through Jim Crow laws, which lasted until the 1960s.

Today, race continues to serves as a basis for the distribution of social privileges and resources. As a concept created to support and privilege whiteness, the concept of race has both biological and social dimensions. As Karenga (2017) explains, from a biological perspective, in reference to physical features, race is used to distinguish different kinds of human beings. Thus, given the history of classifying human beings based on phenotypic similarities and differences, *race is ocular*, as explained by Omi and Winant (2015). Human bodies are visually read and assessed for symbolic meaning and association with time, place, and setting.

Key to understanding race as a concept is the assignment of social values within a cultural content and the symbolic meaning of physical features (Burton et al., 2010; Karenga, 2017). Yet, race is more than what meets the eye, not just about skin color, physical features such as the size of nose and lips, and hair texture. In its social dimensions, we live race through class, gender, status, sexual identity, nationality, religion, and in many other ways (Lopez, 2006). Because of its long history and the elongated movement to give it meaning, race carries presuppositions acquired during the socialization process. Humans are saturated with a variety of ways in which race is used and assigned meaning in society though cultural messaging. The assignment of race is a central principle for social organization, particularly surrounding ethnic identify, and serves as an ingrained feature of our social system (Burton et al., 2010). Over time, based on the reification of the concept and its social meaning, race has become key to our cultural orientation, and therefore takes on substantive meaning in the lives of people. Thus, it is

THE MEANING AND FUNCTION OF RACE AND RACISM   11

important that race be viewed as more than a pseudoscientific concept or a social construct that has no substantive meaning. As Karenga points out:

> ... to say that race is specious is to deny the reality of it in its social embrace and social consequences. Indeed, it is important to remember that concepts are not simply real and imaginary descriptions of reality, for they actually become forms of reality itself when people embrace these ideas and use them to inform, explain, and direct their lives, and such is the history of race and the system for which it is the foundation stone—that is, racism. (2017, pp. 27–28)

It is important to understand that race is particularly malleable when it comes to identity formation. According to Feagin (2020), the European Enlightenment and colonization helped to forge White racial identity as a form of racial capital to include significant socioeconomic benefits, privileges, and the institutionalization of White social status. Mills (1997) contends that the making of a global social contract based on a racial hierarchy created social ladder-like levels, with Whites at the top of the hierarchy and the lowest levels reserved for African Americans and Native Americans. Subsequently, the importance of racial identify and pride is among the myriad of reasons why racial and ethnic groups often jockey for power, status, and recognition as forms of national pride and positionality in the world. Because of this, race has a swath of meanings within historical, social, religious, scientific, cultural, and political contexts, and there are always a number of racial projects within the social order (Omi & Winant, 2015). Subsequently, groups and individuals form identities based on racial classifications as a sense of who they are within a worldview, and as forms of status in society.

Given this backdrop, designating groups as "people of color" or as "non-White," as well as who has whiteness as an identity, and the privileges that accompany it, is central to racial formation in the United States. Take for example the nearly forgotten early prerequisite cases from 1868 until 1952—those based on racial restrictions for naturalization—which determined which immigrants and populations within new U.S. territory would be naturalized with whiteness (Lopez, 2006). Using the pseudoscientific research of the time to achieve political and legal victories, the prerequisite courts tied temperament, linked cultural and cognition, examined physical features, intellect, political acuity, and treated the question of behavior as innate elements of human biology instead of aspects of acquired identity

(Lopez, 2006). For fifty years following the Civil War, naturalization laws were central in determining the status of immigrant newcomers. In the early 1900s, the persistence of anti-Asian agitation groups kept prerequisite laws at the forefront of national popular politics. For example, the Asiatic Exclusion League constructed arguments for restrictive interpretations of the "White person" prerequisite. In 1910 they [White America] claimed that Asian Indians were not "White," but an "effeminate, caste-ridden, and degraded" race who did not deserve citizenship (Lopez, 2006, p. 3). For nearly one hundred years, federal law restricted immigration to the United States on the basis of race through the Chinese exclusion laws of the 1880s until the dismantling of racial quota restrictions by Congress in 1965.

From a Marxist perspective, race is a tool in the determination of "productive humanity" and "disposable humanity," which is based on the shifting production of race as a logic of depreciation in the market value of surplus labor (Singh, 2019). Shifting ideas about race and the racialization of people became a necessary component in the maintenance of social relations and social worth in the capitalist order of America (Mill, 1997). State management of property, jurisprudence, labor, and the regulation of violence enforce this scheme. From the start of the 1619 Project, race and anti-Black racism were intrinsically linked to capitalisms' mode of production, with its system of chattel slavery (Stevenson, 2019). Out of slavery came fear and the need to control Black people; and paradoxically, everything to do with American exceptionalism: its constitutional system of governance, industrial power, economic might, popular music, slang, folklore, legal and electoral systems, educational system, forms of inequities, approaches to public health, proclivity for violence, and "the example it sets for the world as a land of freedom and equality," including "the endemic racial fears and hatreds that continue to plague it to this day" (Stevenson, 2019, p. 1).

Racism

Racism resulted from the strict rules governing race and the political, sociocultural, economic, and psychological consequences of such an arrangement (Mann, 2017). Racism is the exercising of power and dominance by one racial group over another racial group, frequently and consistently resulting in the disadvantage of the dominated group at the expense of the dominating group (Asante, 2017; Feagin, 2020; Karenga, 2017; Omi & Winant, 2015).

THE MEANING AND FUNCTION OF RACE AND RACISM   13

Racism is transmitted across generations by cultural values, institutional policies and practices, individual behaviors, and cultural norms and mores. Over time, such practices became systematic and codified into institutional and legal practices throughout the American cultural landscape. The trauma experienced by racism, from a psychological perspective, that is, racialized trauma, is associated with a host of consequences, including anxiety, depression, and other serious, sometimes debilitating conditions such as substance use disorder, and post-traumatic stress disorder. Stress caused by racism can also contribute to physical problems such as cardiovascular and other physical diseases (American Psychological Association, 2020).

Institutional Racism

"Institutional racism refers to the kinds of practices and actions that exist within and operate through the existing institutional arrangements of social life" (Bell, 2014, p. 27). Karenga (2017) argues that institutional racism in our society is one of three basic ways in which racism takes place. Second is to create an *ideology* of domination and social worth based on skin color and anatomic features—thus, the use of race as a construct to assign meaning and value to people based on specific characteristics related to their class and status in society. This was buttressed by religious doctrine intertwined with the concept of a hierarchy of the human race, and the ideas behind scientific racism. Racist ideology provides the justification for inequality and for engaging in oppressive practices that place people in an imposition. Third, racism as *imposition* is in essence a method of imposing power and oppression on people, based on aggression, intimidation, sanction, and violence against targeted individuals and groups (Karenga, 2017; Mills, 1997). It often begins as an interruption in and destruction and appropriation of people's history and the appropriation of their "productive capacity in racial terms through assault, conquest, occupation, annexation, dispossession, segregation, apartheid, deculturalization, exploitation, genocide, enslavement, holocausts, and other forms of massive violence and oppression" (Karenga, 2017, p. 29). Today, the imposition of people based on race and racism can be found in community redlining and predatory lending practices, gentrification projects, school zoning, zero-tolerance policies, stop-and-frisk, a racialized criminal justice system, and a host of structural inequalities that imposition people: first as human being in the social environment, and

14 MARTELL L. TEASLEY

second in their quest for well-being, advancement, and self-actualization. Thus, by examining residential and school segregation, mortgage and insurance redlining, taxation and transportation policies, the location of environmental and toxic hazards, policing strategies, and the design of highways and byways, we can gain an understanding of all spatial ways in which racism takes place (Bobo, 2015; Lipsitz, 2011).

Systemic Racism

Systemic racism is found within the structures of institutions in our society to include the courts, legal systems, schools, universities, religious organizations, corporations, and many processes and practices that ensure continued dominance and power in the advancement of White privilege (Karenga, 2017). The general assumption behind systemic racism was the contention that major parts of life for a White person would be directly different from those of the racialized person of color (Bobo, 2015; Omi & Winant, 2015). Rooted in its past foundation, "systemic racism today is composed of intersecting, overlapping, and codependent racist institutions, policies, practices, ideas, and behaviors that give an unjust amount of resources, rights, and power to white people while denying them to people of color" (Cole, 2019, p. 1). Many long-standing public policy initiatives and activities started as racial projects. including residential housing, homesteading, farming policy, public school zoning and taxation, and eminent domain highway development (Bell, 2004; Lipsitz, 2011).

To wit, institutional and ideological elements and the imposition of racism are components of systemic racism, and all three operate in a similar fashion to what the eighteenth-century economist Adam Smith referred to as the "invisible hand" of capitalism—the process whereby individuals guide capitalism and the free market, knowingly or unknowingly, through promoting the public interest in the production of capital. Here, the invisible hand of racism operates intentionally and unintentionally through the waning and waxing of racial projections that create a sort of ebb-and-flow to the production and maintenance of systemic racism in society.

Racial Projects

As the building blocks of racial formation, racial projects are the linkage between structure and representation. Racial projects help to shape social structures through ideology and practice, and they help to connect and assign meaning in shaping racial formation (Bobo, 2015; Feagin & Bennefield, 2014). "Racial projects connect what race means in a particular discursive or ideological practice and the way in which both social structures and everyday experiences are racially organized, based on that meaning" (Omi & Winant, 2015, p. 125). Stop-and-frisk, mass incarceration, zero tolerance policies within the criminal justice system and in schools, state restrictions on voting access, the banning of teaching Critical Race Theory, and immigrant detention camps are all examples of racial projects. Each of these areas are backed politically by acceptable social narratives stated to legitimate their practices, such as views that espouse solely the promotion of law and order, services for students' mental well-being in schools, enforcing safe schools, prevention of voter fraud, and protecting the border. Furthermore, there are long-standing ideologies that support the implementation and imposition of racial projects (e.g., the yellow peril, the model minority, job-stealing immigrants, Black laziness and criminality, angry Black man, crackhead, self-made man) and contemporarily (the Chinese virus, No Child Left Behind, tough on crime, detention camps for unwanted immigrants, birtherism, concealed carry and stand-your-ground gun laws).

Racial projects are important to understand because, in many ways, they represent the DNA of structural inequalities. "A racial project can be defined as racist if it *creates or reproduces structures of domination based on racial significant and identifies*" (Omi & Winant, 2015, p. 128). Because of its origins in xenophobic slants against Latino migrant populations, particularly in categorizing them as gang members, thugs, and narco-drug runners, and as "freeloaders" on the U.S. social welfare systems, the call for building and completing the Mexico–U.S. border wall is a racial project. It has resulted in thousands of Latino immigrants placed for prolonged periods in inhumane and overcrowded detention camps. The bombastic and consistent rhetorical message from the Trump administration helped to dehumanize Latino immigrants from Central America, allowing for family and child separation, a lack of legal due process, overcrowded and unhealthy living conditions, and the continued detention of over 11,000 children (Serwer, 2019). Already perceived as "people of color," casting Latino immigrants as an existential threat to the American way of life, the need for a wall was publicly dramatized as a national crisis and a clear-and-present state of emergency (Bischoff, 2019). Emboldened by a stable political following, the Trump administration consciously used immigration enforcement as the rationale to incarcerate and dehumanize undocumented immigrants and their American relatives (Serwer, 2019). Serving as red meat for "what is wrong with America," Latino

16 MARTELL L. TEASLEY

immigrants served to delight part of Trump's constituency that revels in the use of draconic policy and state violence "against those they see as trying to take their country from them . . ." (Serwer, 2019, p. 3).

Racializing People

Part of the imposition in the maintenance of racism is the problem of racialized people of color having to define their existence as a racial being in a racially stratified society (Wilkerson, 2020). This practice, within itself, further speaks to a level of privilege because it subliminally leaves Whites outside of the identify politics of race. The health, welfare, and security of people around the world are affected by the ordering of people into racial categories. Similar to a caste system, racial categories help to determine one's social status, group affiliations, interactions, and people's sense of belonging to one another (Wilkerson, 2020). As a method in the maintenance of the status quo, "white racial framing" includes not only racial bias and discrimination, but racial ideologies based on narratives, images, and inclinations (Feagin & Bennefield, 2014). Research demonstrates that the United States has profound stratification and presuppositions of people based on skin tone (Monk, 2018). For example, racial stereotypes of those deemed as part of the "yellow race" are often cognitively perceived as those of Asian descent, with no distinction between ethnic groups. As Kawai points out, we often "do not distinguish yellows here from yellows there—Asian Americans from Asians, Chinese from Japanese, or Koreans from Vietnamese; that is, stereotyping Asian Americans is both Asian and American" (Kawai, 2005, p. 111). Skin color is a central feature in the racialization of African Americans. In the United States and internationally, the darkest people are the poorest and most racialized. Research findings demonstrate that African Americans with darker skin tone reported significantly lower or less educational attainment, employment opportunities, income status, marital status, home ownership, and political representation, as well as longer prison sentences (Culbreth, 2006; Monk, 2018; Ladson-Billings, 2000).

Presuppositions that underscore the identity politics of race often make people socially uncomfortable in direct discussions about who they are as racialized beings, particular in the White and Black binary of race relations. For example, racialized identity politics compelled Britain's Prince Harry and Meghan Markle to declare abdication as senior royals, as the Duke and Duchess of Sussex. This took place in spite of claims of their accepted marriage representing a symbol of Britain's post-racial and postcolonial positionality. Talent, good looks, and her growing reputation as a humanitarian were not enough to overcome Meghan Markle's mixed-race heritage. Members of the British press continuously racialized her experience and questioned her fit as a member of British royalty. In one blatant example, after Harry and Meghan's son was born, a BBC radio host, who was eventually fired, tweeted, "Royal baby leaves hospital," which was a statement above a black-and-white 1920s photo of a baby chimp holding hands with a humble white couple in the doorway of a building.

Racialized Identity

Another problem with racializing people is referring to a person or group as "people of color." The invention of "people of color" as a category is part of the discourse of the dominant group, who by the power of the nation-state attempts to controls the system of racial classification (Mann, 2017). This common statement implies the presupposition that we are not speaking of White people as part of this umbrella term. The term *person or people of color* is a metonym for race, whereas whiteness stands outside of such characterization. Such a practice restricts Whites from racial regulation as people of color (Schiele, 2020). Based on this condition, people of color must continuously negotiate the trappings of race and identity politics (Metzl & Hansen, 2014). The powerful in-group is void of the negative stigma associated with racialized identity politics, unless it chooses to do so, which is essentially on its own terms. From an anti-racist approach, "it is important not to replicate racism in discussions about ending racism by falling into the people-of-color trap (Mann, 2017, p. 68).

Asante (2017, p. 50) points out that whether intentional or unintentional, "those who claim to be 'white' maintain racism in all of its institutional forms because they dominate those sectors that have the capacity to change the life" of racialized people. To some degree, the sheer power of whiteness as a standalone category compiles many non-White people of lighter hue to, by some means, free themselves from the albatross of racialized identity politics by gravitating toward whiteness as a preferred state of mind and consciousness. The impact of unchecked whiteness has can have many pernicious outcomes. For example, in the area of healthcare, Feagin and Bennefield's

(2014, p. 7) review of research literature concluded, ". . . institutionalized white socioeconomic resources, discrimination, and racialized framing from centuries of slavery, segregation, and contemporary white oppression severely limit and restrict access to many Americans of color to adequate socioeconomic resources. . . ."

Focusing on the obvious hypocrisy of racialized thinking, author James Baldwin writes in the *Fire Next Time*, "as long as you are white, I am black." Here, Baldwin flips the responsibility of human categorization by race to highlight and examine the normality of unquestionable whiteness. He noted that there will be no real examination of race unless and until whites examine themselves and their pretense of innate superiority. Baldwin's work is instructive because it realizes that when it comes to questions of race, there seems to be an autonomic need to examine the victims of racism, instead of the problematic notion of whiteness and its pernicious effects (Asante, 2017).

Racial Commonsense Thinking

In general, commonsense thinking helps people organize the world based on what is known—though sensory perception and what we learn from society—and provides rules for people to operate in a given setting. It gives people guidelines to operate in the world and helps them understand how things should work (Chomsky & Waterstone, 2021). Common sense is based on experiences that are reinforced over time though socialization and behavior modification. It is an extra sense that allows people to make meaningful and organize what their senses tell them about the world. People are acculturated on views, values, and practices, and operate in the world based on a set of normative rules from those experiences. Similarly, the normalization of racialized thinking has become so commonplace in America that it serves as a central organizing theme in public life, and provides presupposition to human relations and interactions, and has been codified though acculturation and socialization. In conjunction with racial projects, racial commonsense thinking often determines where people live; who and what are considered beautiful, good, or bad; skin color and power relations; our sense of law and order; where to build schools; who deserves to go to jail; where to place employment opportunities and toxic waste; housing patterns; forms of recreation; hospital location; restaurant identification, auto sales, and much more.

As a way of thinking, racial commonsense thinking benefits the status quo in terms of social relations and discounts the lived experiences of non-Whites (Omi & Winant, 2015). It takes for granted a system of practices within social institutions, organizations, and government that often discriminates against minoritized populations. To think critically, based on our socialization process, as a society and as individuals, we often engage in racial commonsense thinking as a sort of autonomic process. In some instances, it triggers the fight-or-flight principle in people, such as a woman clutching her purse tighter when a Black man enters an elevator that she occupies, or the policeman who stops a Black make driving in a predominately White neighborhood. The systemic and economic benefits of institutionalized racism have led to a country steeped in racial commonsense thinking as a normalized part of thought, discourse, and practice. The practice of White privilege has become a way of organizing our thinking about places and people in the world and has been reinforced though practice and socialization. Over time, the relation among government, law enforcement, and the legal system has normalized racial commonsense thinking, particularly though the persistent historical classification of individuals as racial group members of society based on skin color.

As an artifact of the racial state, racial commonsense thinking cuts across race and ethnic lines, class, and status. Internalized oppression provides a conduit for so-called people of color to think along the lines of common narratives that support the dominant narrative and status quo. Consequently, let there be no mistake that racial commonsense thinking is not an attribute only cognitively processed and acted upon by White people. Take, for example, the early myth during the Coronavirus pandemic in March 2020, in which some African American social media outlets engaged in public discourse and discussion contending that African Americans could not catch COVID-19. Such a focus harkens back to a time when African Americans were thought to have less sensitivity to pain, and at times were considered painless and therefore thought to suffer less from disease affliction, or not at all. Thus, racial commonsense thinking has *ahistorical* vestiges where "not knowing" and even "knowing better" are supplanted for the dominant and normalized realities of institutionalized racial thought and practice.

Finally, racial commonsense thinking is void in the consideration of race and racism as real and meaningful expressions of the American cultural experience for all people, including Whites. *Racial amnesia*, the process whereby individuals and groups forget the connection between historical racist events and their influence on the present, is a product of racial commonsense thinking, as people and society, in general, have suppressed racialized problems from the past and their effects on the present. It is the essence of post-racial thinking, which surmises that America is free of preferences, prejudice, and discrimination, and has become color-blind or, at least, non-racist in legal jurisprudence, thought, and social practice.

There are countless historical examples of racial commonsense thinking. To illustrate, Frederick Douglass complained in a meeting with Abraham Lincoln about the treatment of Black soldiers during the Civil War. Douglass lamented that Black Union Army soldiers were paid less money, were undersupplied in comparison to White soldiers, and were treated unequally as fellow soldiers. Lincoln simply replied that such treatment was the price that Black troops paid for being allowed to fight in the Civil War. Frederick Douglass's complaint was a matter of pragmatic circumstances for Lincoln, who expressed that his real goal was to "save the Union" during the Civil War, and that the lives of Black Americans were an instrument to be used toward that end, nothing more (Blight, 2018).

As a present-day example, we can find racial commonsense thinking in the long-running narrative referred to as the American "war on drugs." During the crack-cocaine epidemic of the 1980s, which predominately affected urban Black communities, crack-cocaine users and addicts were stereotyped as hypersexual predators who were overly violent. Among other hyped-up claims, the federal government ushered in judicial disparity between offenses for crack and powder cocaine, with a sentencing ration of 100:1. The 1986 Federal Anti-Drug Abuse Act led to mandatory minimum prison sentencing, which punished crack-cocaine offenses more harshly than powder-cocaine offenses. The law "unjustly and disproportionately penalize[d] African American defendants for drug trafficking comparable to that of white defendants" (Vagin & McCurdy, 2006, p. 6). Just four years after the enactment of mandatory minimum sentencing, the average federal drug sentence for African Americans was 49% higher than that of Whites (Vagin & McCurdy, 2006). As a racial project, it led to droves of Black men being incarcerated, helping to form today's prison industrial complex. Beyond the hype, there never was scientific or penological justification for the 100:1 sentencing (Vagin & McCurdy, 2006).

Conversely, contemporarily we are witness to an opioid epidemic, which has captured the attention of the entire nation and has killed many more people than crack cocaine did. Yet, because it is associated with people from all backgrounds, and mainly because of its dramatic effect on affluent white

THE MEANING AND FUNCTION OF RACE AND RACISM   21

families, it is socially viewed as a medical emergency. Now, as it should have been in the past, treatment is the order of the day. States and localities now supply opioid addicts with free naloxone kits, which block or reverse the effects of opioid medications. During the 1980s, states supplied hand-cuffs to Blacks, based on the rationale from politicians—and their corporate sponsors—who demonized them as predators, worthy of harsh prison sentencing guidelines for using and selling crack cocaine (Vagin & McCurdy, 2006).

Most within the United States do not understanding how the present-day battle with deaths of despair among White America, as outlined in Metzl's (2019) *Dying of Whiteness: How the Politics of Racial Resentment Is Killing America's Heartland*, is related to the normalization of racialized practices, including the reality of whiteness. It is based on generations of the purposeful socialization of racial commonsense thinking, and attempts to make synonymous a person's race as a priori to individual and group social worth and well-being. The impact of racial commonsense thinking has classically conditioned the American psyche, creating the conditions and the context in which the populace believe that the despair and death of non-Whites, based on the social determinants of health, result from the bane of their existence as non-Whites. To the contrary, the reality is that deaths of despair from suicide, drug overdoses and alcoholic liver disease threaten the public health and wellbeing of the entire country. As the fastest-growing cause of death, the evidence demonstrates that many are concentrated among whites without higher education degrees (Case & Deaton, 2020). Beyond the politics of race and racism, inequality and deaths of despair jointly result from social change driven by politic, power, and technology, which has helped to decimate good paying jobs for America's working class leading to it desolution (Case & Deaton, 2020). Moreover, Whites without university degrees report less health, more daily pain, and feeling less happy. Marriage as an institution is failing, and trends in governmental and public policy do not support family formation. Corporations, once in sync with the needs of the American worker though unionization, are now only beholden to their shareholders, with worker rights sidelined.

Conclusion

This opening chapter is an attempt to promote an understanding of how to conceptualize the meaning and function of race and racism in thought and practice. Table 1.1 provides a list of micro, meso, and macro factors that

Table 1.1 Items to Consider in Conceptualizing the Centrality of Racism across Practice Domains

Micro	Meso	Macro
Individual Racialized Practices	*Broader Community Racialized Practices*	*Institutional Practices*
Anti-blackness	Banking locations and lending practices	Affirmative action
Avoidant Racism	Book banning	Anti-racism
Bigotry	Child welfare practices	Criminal justice
Colorblindness	Community policing	Cultural narratives
Colorism	Community and public relations	Employment opportunity
Gender bias	Community history and iconographic images	Environmental policy
Implicit bias	Educational access and outcomes	Federal and state laws
Internalized oppression	Food insecurity	Governmental resource allocations
People of color	Gerrymandered voting districts	Governmental policies
Prejudice	Hate crimes	Higher education
Racial bias	Health care access and inequality	Healthcare access
Racial equity	Juvenile justice systems	Immigration policies
Racialization	Local employment opportunities	Institutional racism
Racial identify	Media coverage	Legal surveillance
Racial profiling	Mortgage and home financing	Institutional programming
Racial socialization	Noise pollution	National political representation
Racial discrimination	Policing and surveillance	Social justice
Racial micro-aggressions	Political representation	Societal norms
Stigma	Racial hierarchy in community governance	Structural inequalities
Racial trauma/stress	Racial and ethnic community formation	Systemic racism
Racism and race	Racial relations	Racial commonsense thinking
Racial oppression	Regulatory oversight	Racial projects
Unconscious bias	Residential redlining	Racial regulation
White supremacy	School zoning	Racialized policies and procedures
Whiteness	School-to-prison-pipeline	Racial justice
White privilege	Social welfare benefits	Racial wealth gaps
Xenophobia	Zoning practices	Wealth disparities

social work professionals should thoroughly understand as researchers and practitioners. In doing so, a focus on the centrality of race must become a lens of discernment, examining how variables fit together when racialized practices are involved. It is important to determine the volume of racialized practices across domains on individual or group experiences as a way of determining the impact of racism on outcomes. Greater information on items identified within Table 1.1 can be found within the reference literature cited for this chapter. Items within columns are not an exhaustive list, and they are not mutually exclusive, as many apply across domains. Micro factors are those that may be experienced by individuals though social interaction, while meso factors are part of a broader community experience. Macro factors are the product of larger social institutions, systems, and structural forces that drive meso- and macro-based factors.

Why is challenging and changing racial common sense so important to the elimination of racism in our society and beyond? Because "[i]f we want to change people's minds and think about the world operating differently, we have to contend with those deeply embedded and virtually held conceptions of how the world operates" (Chomsky & Waterstone, 2021, p. 7). The United States can eliminate racism the same way the country established it as a conceptual reality within institutional and systemic supports and structures—this took some doing over time. The challenge is to educate the public on the problems that racialized thinking and practices have cost individuals, groups, and the social fabric from past to present, and the future cost of continued approaches to the social milieu steeped in racial commonsense thinking and practice. Acknowledging that this is no easy feat, it can be accomplished; however, the country's political climate does not favor such an approach. Unfortunately, in America and throughout most of the Westernized world, racial commonsense thinking is more pervasive than not.

While we must continue to rely on the scientific process and evidence-based approaches to social welfare problem formation, many of which are discussed in this book, it is likewise necessary to change the presuppositions and fermented notions that uphold racialized thinking based on Westernized canons (Lopez, 2006). Thus, the minds and hearts of America matter in the struggle to eliminate racism. It will take nothing less than a long-term change in commonsense thinking to eliminate racism. "In order to change people's minds and operate differently, it is vitally important that we connect with our deeply embedded notions and conception of how the world works" (Chomsky & Waterstone, 2021, p. 7). In order to move down this pathway, all racial and ethnic groups within the country must work together to change their conceptual understanding of humanity based on skin tone, hair texture, other physical features, and other racialized attributes. However, such change "will not be achieved without the broad and relentless struggle required for the racial reconstruction of societies whose history and current practice of racism are evident and undeniable" (Karenga, 2017, p. 26).

As for the Grand Challenge to Eliminate Racism, the social work profession must contend with its own presuppositions and embedded concepts about race and racism, prior to any attempt to serve as stewards of eliminating racism in society. This is to say, the profession must struggle with its own racial commonsense thinking among its higher education programs, approaches to public policy, research, and the professional practice domain. Historically and contemporarily, there have been attempts to move in this direction, and while progress has taken place, there is much to be done.

Study Questions

1. How has your understanding of racism and how it works evolved during your lifetime?
2. Describe the effects of the death of George Floyd on our national understanding of racism.
3. Define and discuss systemic racism and how it affects individuals and communities.
4. Discuss the experiences that minoritized populations encountered in taking standardized tests.
5. Discuss your personal (past or present) presuppositions about three racial/ethnic groups other than your own.
6. What are your thoughts about social presuppositions related to your racial/ethnic group?
7. If you had to use an alternative term to the concept "people of color," what would that term be? Give an example of how you would use it.
8. Identify and discuss a contemporary "racial project" linked to micro, meso, and macro practice, as well as implications for social work practice in each area.
9. Define "whiteness" and its association with deaths of despair as discussed in this chapter.

10. Define racial commonsense thinking and provide an example of how it affects a social welfare program.

References

APA apologizes for its support of racism in psychiatry (2021). Message from the President. Retrieved from https://www.psychiatry.org/newsroom/news-releases/apa-apologizes-for-its-support-of-racism-in-psychiatry.

Asante, M. K. (2017). Race and racism in American Society: Evolution towards new thoughts. In P. Reid-Merritt (Ed.), *Race in America* (pp. 23–42). Santa Barbara, CA: Praeger.

Baldwin, J. (Writer) (2017). I am not your negro [Film] Bagnolia Pictures.

Baldwin, J. (1963). *The fire next time*. New York: Random House.

Bell, D. (2004). *Silent covenants: Brown v. Board of Education and the unfulfilled hopes for racial reform*. New York: Oxford University Press.

Bell, J. M. (2014). *The Black Power movement and American social work*. New York: Columbia University Press.

Bischoff, B. (2019). Immigrant detention conditions were atrocious under Obama. Here's why they're so much worse under Trump. *SLATE News & Politics*. Retrieved from https://slate.com/news-and-politics/2019/06/trump-child-immigrant-detention-no-toothpaste-obama.html.

Blight, D. W. (2018). *Frederick Douglass: Prophet of freedom*. New York: Simon & Schuster.

Bobo, Lawrence D. (2015). A troublesome recurrence: Racialized realities and racist reasoning today. *Du Bois Review: Social Science Research on Race, 12*(1), 1–4. doi: 10.1017/s1742058x15000077.

Buchholz, K. (2021, May). Statista. *Which states have acted on police reform*: https://www.statista.com/chart/22172/legislation-on-police-reform-by-state/

Burghardt, S. (2021). *The end of social work: A defense of the social worker in times of transformation*. San Diego, CA: Cognella.

Burton, L. M., Bonilla-Silva, E., Ray, V., Buckelew, R., & Freeman, E. H. (2010). Critical race theories, colorism, and the decade's research on families of color. *Journal of Marriage and Family, 72*(3), 440–459. https://doi.org/10.1111/j.1741-3737.2010.00712.x.

Case, A., & Deaton, A. (2020). *Deaths of despair and the future of capitalism*. Princeton, NJ: Princeton University Press.

Chomsky, N., & Waterstone, M. (2021). *Consequences of capitalism: Manufacturing discontent and resistance*. La Vergne, IL: Haymarket Books.

Cloyd, K. (2020, June 5). Nice does not equal not racist. Scary Mommy. Retrieved from: https://www.scarymommy.com/never-considered-myself-racist-done-racist-things

Cole, N. L (2020). *Definition of systemic racism in sociology: Beyond prejudice and micro-aggressions*. Retrieved from https://www.thoughtco.com/systemic-racism-3026565.

Culbreth, D. (2006). Employment discrimination in the 21st century: An empirical investigation of the presence of intraracial colorism among Black Americans in the workplace. *Dissertation Abstracts International, 67*(07), 164A (UMI No.3226798).

DiAngelo, R. (2021). *Nice racism: How progressive white people perpetuate racial harm*. Boston: Beacon Press.

Feagin, J. R. (2020). *The white racial frame: Centuries of racial framing and counter-framing*. New York: Taylor & Francis.

Feagin, J., & Bennefield, Z. (2014). Systemic racism and US healthcare. *Social Science & Medicine, 103*, 7–14. http://dx.doi.org/10.1016/j.socscimed.2013.09.006.

Haddad, M. (2021, May). Aljazzeera News. *How many people have been killed by US police since George Floyd?* https://www.aljazeera.com/news/2021/5/25/how-many-people-have-police-killed-since-george-floyd

Harvard Library (n.d.). Confronting anti-black racism. Scientific racism. Retrieved from https://library.harvard.edu/confronting-anti-black-racism/scientific-racism.

Jeyasingham, D. (2012). White noise: A critical evaluation of social work education's engagement with whiteness studies. *The British Journal of Social Work, 42*(4), 660–686.

Karenga, M. (2017). Race and racism: A critical examination of a pathology of oppression. In P. Reid-Merritt (Ed.), *Race in America: How a pseudoscientific concept shaped human interaction* (Vol. 1) (pp. 43–58). Santa Barbara, CA: Praeger.

Kawai, K. (2005). Stereotyping Asian Americans: The dialectic of the model minority and the yellow peril. *The Howard Journal of Communications, 16*, 109–130.

King, R. (2018). *Mindful of race: Transforming racism from the inside out*. Boulder, CO: Sounds True.

Ladson-Billings, G. (2000). *Brazil, South Africa, the United States: Beyond racism*. Atlanta, GA: Comparative Human Relations Initiative, the Southern Education Foundation.

Lipsitz, G. (2011). *How racism takes place*. Philadelphia: Temple University Press.

Lopez, I. H. (2006). *White by law: The legal construction of race*. New York: New York University Press.

Mann, A. B. (2017). Socially misconstrued usage of the racial concept in contemporary America. In P. Reid-Merritt (Ed.), *Race in America* (pp. 59–76). Santa Barbara, CA: Praeger.

Mapping Police Violence (2022, November). https://mappingpoliceviolence.org/

Maylea, C. (2020). The end of social work. *British Journal of Social Work, 51*, 772–789.

Melamed, J. (2015). Racial capitalism. *Critical Ethnic Studies, 1*, 76–85.

Metzl, J. (2019). *Dying of Whiteness: How the politics of racial resentment is killing America's heartland*. New York: Basic Books.

Metzl, J. M., & Hansen, H. (2014). Structural competency: Theorizing a new medical engagement with stigma and inequality. *Social Science & Medicine, 102*, 126–133.

Mills, C. W. (1997). *The racial contract*. Ithaca, NY: Cornell University Press.

Monk, E. P. (2018). The color of punishment: African Americans, skin tone, and the criminal justice system. *Ethnic and Racial Studies, 42*(10), 1593–1612. https://doi.org/10.1080/01419870.2018.1508736.

Omi, M., & Winant, H. (2015). *Racial formation in the United States* (3rd ed.). New York: Routledge.

Reid, P. (2017). Race in America: Social constructs and social realities—An introduction. In P. Reid-Merritt (Ed.), *Race in America: How a pseudoscientific concept shaped human interaction* (Vol. 1) (pp. 3–22). Santa Barbara, CA: Praeger.

Schiele, J. H. (2020). *Social welfare policy: Regulation and resistance among people of color* (2nd ed.). San Diego, CA: Cognella.

Serwer, A. (2019). A crime by any name: The Trump administration's commitment to deterring immigration through cruelty has made horrifying conditions in detention

THE MEANING AND FUNCTION OF RACE AND RACISM   27

facilities inevitable. *The Atlantic*. Retrieved from https://www.theatlantic.com/ideas/archive/2019/07/border-facilities/593239/.

Singh, A. A. (2019). *The racial healing handbook: Practical activities to help you challenge privilege, confront systemic racism and engage in collective healing.* Oakland, CA: New Harbinger Publications.

Stevenson, B. (2019). Mass incarceration. *New York Times Magazine.* The 1619 Project. Retrieved from https://www.nytimes.com/interactive/2019/08/14/magazine/prison-industrial-complex-slavery-racism.html?mtrref=www.nytimes.com&gwh=F3B70 E91189FC89534E85370C9ECEFC7&gwt=pay&assetType=PAYWALL.

Teasley, M. L., McCarter, S., Woo, B., Conner, L. R., Spencer, M. S., & Green, T. (2021). *Eliminate racism* (Grand Challenges for Social Work Initiative Working Paper No. 26). Cleveland, OH: American Academy of Social Work & Social Welfare.

Vagins, D. J., McCurdy, J. (2006, October). *Cracks in the system: Twenty years of the unjust federal crack cocaine, policy counsel for civil rights and civil liberties.* American Civil Liberties Union, Washington, DC. Retrieved from https://www.aclu.org/other/cracks-system-twenty-years-unjust-federal-crack-cocaine-law?redirect=criminal-law-ref orm/cracks-system-twenty-years-unjust-federal-crack-cocaine-law.

Wilkerson, I. (2020). *Caste: The origin of our discontents.* New York: Random House.

2

Anti-Racism Social Work

History and Future Challenges

Martell L. Teasley

> *We condemn racism, yet many of us do not fully understand what it is and how it operates within our society and especially within our own social work educational settings.*
>
> —John Longres (1973)

Speaking at the Annual Program Meeting of the Council on Social Work Education in January 1971, John Longres outlined his assessment of why racism was pervasive within the social work profession. Longres makes the case that although the social work profession condemns racism, many within the profession do not know what racism is, or how it operates in society and within social work educational settings. In many ways, his speech that day, published in the journal *Education for Social Work* (1972), laid out the perimeters of racism as a grand challenge for social work education. Speaking in a candidate tone at the 2016 Society for Social Work Research national conference, Davis (2016) voiced that the country and the social work profession have far too long ignored conversations about race, racism, and injustice. Davis went further to say that undoing the deleterious effects of race and racism for historically oppressed groups is a grand challenge for America and the social work profession (Briggs, Briggs, & Briggs, 2019).

For sure, the social work profession's long-term engagement with diversity and inclusion has not resolved the challenge of racism within the profession and the larger society. On this topic, Davis (2016, p. 397) spoke plainly at the conference:

Martell L. Teasley, *Anti-Racism Social Work* In: *Social Work and the Grand Challenge to Eliminate Racism*. Edited by: Martell L. Teasley, Michael S. Spencer, and Melissa Bartholomew, Oxford University Press.
© Oxford University Press 2023. DOI: 10.1093/oso/9780197674949.003.0002

I believe that in our efforts to be inclusive, social work professionals have lost our way with regards to the issue of race and racism. For some time now, individuals of all racial and ethnic groups have too often been engaged in discussions focusing on celebrating differences and diversity. I believe these discussions have served to avert our attention from the more difficult—and more challenging—conversations on race and racism, diverting efforts from the action needed to move us toward a more racially just society. Indeed, discussions focusing on diversity might actually be serving to diffuse truly useful discussion on any of the groups that the term diversity is meant to encompass.

To his point, from a racial justice perspective, many social work professionals continue to encounter situational narratives within the practice setting that contribute to disparities in outcomes along racial lines (Briggs et al., 2019). Children welfare practice in the form of schools (Schiele, 2020), juvenile justice, mental health diagnosis, and the foster care system all have histories of problematic racialized outcomes (Lowery, 2019). What is it within foster care and school-based settings, as interdisciplinary practices settings, where health and healthcare professionals are involved, that so profoundly leads to the development of disparities based on race? Although there are social work education programs with courses and a curriculum focused on understanding and challenging racism, the profession's intersectional approach to curriculum development, as stated in the 2015 Education Policy Accreditation Standards (EPAS), suggests that the centrality of racism and its complexities are not likely to be unfolded in many programs.

To be fair and balanced, it is not totally the responsibility of social work education programs to cover the multiplicity of ideas and thoughts about race and racism. It is also well-known that some instructors are better than others in the teaching and learning process on the topic of racism. However, the idea of *doing no harm* applies as a minimal professional standard for the profession. For this reason, at the minimal, the social work profession must obligate itself to address the contours of race and racism within its programming and practices, and to better understand why there are disparities in outcomes in settings in which social workers practice. It is also important that social work education programs provide students with road maps to bodies of knowledge relevant to professional practice, advocacy, and policy formations aimed at the well-being of diverse racial and ethnic groups

(Bryant & Kolivoski, 2021). Then, too, any educated person understands the need to be a lifelong learner.

The research is scant to nonexistent on the knowledge base that students acquire in social work education programs for dealing with racism within the practice settings and in policy analysis (Schiele, 2020). At times, social work faculty and students cringe, suffer through, and detest classroom discussion and assignments on race and racism; there is often a sort of avoidance in going down this road as a part of diversity and inclusion discussions (Bryant & Kolivoski, 2021). What is more, carrying the diversity burden, minority faculty members too often endure the backlash of teaching diversity and inclusion courses in predominantly white institutions. On the flipside, there are students who gain significant information, knowledge, and skill development from diversity and inclusion courses within social work education programs (O'Neill & Miller, 2015). Nevertheless, I suspect, but do not have the research backing, that the most profound critiques of our racialized climate are found in Black Feminist Theory, Critical Race Theory, Afrocentric Theory, and the growing presence of anti-racism practices, which are not part of the narratives found within core curriculum for the majority of white faculty within social work education programs.

It is ironic that the mainstream of the social work profession has for the most part purposefully resisted the scholarly revolution over the past two decades coming from Africana and Black Studies. Scholars from these disciplines recognized racism in America and its origins in slavery as a foundational American institution in organizing the development of the nation's political and legal systems, economy base, institutional structures, and even cultural practices in the determination of life's chances in moving through society (Mills, 1997). Under the cloak of "lacking evidence," and the use of intellectual name calling such as "Black essentialism," "neo-Marxism," and "identity politics," Afrocentric scholars received a de facto boycott from the most prestigious social work faculty positions, and were ignored within prestigious practice and clinical settings, even those serving African Americans. Even today, Afrocentric, Latinx, Native American, Intersectional, and perspectives on the Asian American experience are lacking across the curricula of many social work education programs and social work licensing examinations.

Whether leaders within the social work profession realize it or not, the absence of the Black Studies paradigm continues to be a major blow to any attempt at engaging in discourse, teaching and learning, practice, research, and policy analysis that examines the centrality of race as the primary factor in the drive and causal push for specific outcomes. As with any theoretical body of knowledge and derived practices, there are complications within Black Studies and other diverse theoretical orientations. Nevertheless, that does not dismiss the need for critical examination of alternative approaches to social work and social welfare from the underlying assumptions and basic tenets derived from the experiences of minoritized people. Consequently, understanding social welfare problem formation from the perspectives of minoritized groups has to this day not make appropriate inroads within social work scholarship, policy formation, and practice.

The reader will glea from this chapter that there is a pattern within social work history where minoritized groups, particularly African Americans, have attempted to provide a pathway for the profession to deal with the centrality of race and racism and forge new pathways toward anti-racist practices, only to see their ideas and efforts fizzle out. Parenthetically, quite often in America, the seemingly sincere promise brought on by minority group protest becomes less than the pledge and promise of change within the social work profession and the larger society.

Social Work and Racism

In addressing racism as a grand challenge, it is important to discuss the contours of race and racism. In this chapter, I engage in a conversation on the social work profession's attempt to address the challenge of race and racism as a profession, particularly in light of its professional pledge and body of ethical values dedicated to anti-racist practices and social justice. I explore conceptual understandings of race and racism as examples of the utility and elasticity of these concepts, and their use and effects within society. I identify and discuss central challenges for the social work profession in its attempt to make progress on the Grand Challenge to Eliminate Racism.

With more than 50 years gone by, I harken back to the work of Longres, who unbeknownst at the time, identified and built a case for racism as a grand challenge for the social work profession. He expanded on two provocative points during his presentation. First, ". . . how social work education has contributed to and been affected by racism in the past and what it must do to rid itself of racism in the future." Second, ". . . why social work education has contributed to racism and why it may be difficulty for social work education to commit itself to a course of action which will eradicate racism" (p. 295). I end the chapter on what I refer to as the "new frontier" of advocacy in the need to protest for reform of the social work liscensing examination as developed by the Association of Social Work Boards (ASWB).

In reflecting on how the social work profession has dealt with the conundrum of race and racism over time, I hope to explore the meaning of Longres's two points of interest expressed in his 1971 speech. In many ways, I operate from the same position as Longres when he further stated, "we will assume that social work educators are collectively desirous of putting an end to racial strife in the United States by putting an end to racism" (p. 295). I assume that the social work profession, as represented by the American Academy of Social Welfare, the Society for Social Work Research, the Council on Social Work Education (CSWE), the Association of Baccalaureate Social Work programs, the National Association of Deans and Directors of Social Work, and the Association of Social Work Boards, is sincere and serious in its attempts to galvanize the profession to eradicate racism as a Grand Challenge for the profession. Of necessity in this quest, it is important to provide a sense of how the profession has approached the study of race and racism in educating students to be knowledge and understand the machinations and deleterious effects of race and racism. In moving down this pathway, I take a brief dive into early history of the profession and the internal challenges with racism within the profession. I further examine measures taken by the profession to meet the challenge of race and racism since the Civil Rights movement. In the end, I hope to demonstrate why eliminating racism as a Grand Challenge for the social work profession serves as, perhaps, its biggest challenge.

The social work profession continues its commitment to a diverse profession with representation from racial and ethnic groups, gender identity groups, those from varied religious backgrounds, and those with disabilities woven into its professional ranks, standards of practice, educational programming, and governance as a profession. Movement to diversify the profession started in the 1960s with legal mandates based on civil rights legislation and tension from inside and outside of the social work profession to recruit minority practitioners, faculty, and students to the profession. African Americans were the early pioneers of calling for racial inclusion inside the social work profession (Bell, 2014; Calton-LaNey, 1994). Reminded of past struggles for racial justice and equality, Briggs, Briggs, and Briggs (2017, p. 16) explain that "[t]he dearth of emphasis on race and the issues

ANTI-RACISM SOCIAL WORK   33

impacting African American well-being is ironic given the contributions of early African American scholars in historically black universities and colleges (HBCUs) to social work education."

Racism in Early Social Work

In placing White structural racist practices over its cordial relationships with African Americans, from its conception, the social work profession failed in its approach to practice with Black Americans. The origins of African Americans' need for education in the post–Civil War era began as a means of self-help and improvement of community life. In the examination of community life, early Black educators could not find themselves in the curriculum they were studying (Carlton-LaNey, 1999). Black educators were vulnerable to the whims and wishes of White authority in Jim Crow school systems. For the most part, early African American social workers accepted White domination and approaches to practice, which were inconsistent with the needs of the Black community. Commenting on the determination of African American social work pioneers, social work historian Iris Carlton LaNey (1999) writes, "The strength of these pioneers' convictions, gave them the tenacity to continued their work in spite of the institutionalized forces militated against their success" (p. 6).

Part of settlement house developments in the 1920s for African Americans started with the great migration from the South to the North. "Typically, neither black women nor men were chronicled in the list of prominent social-welfare pioneers in the period from 1890–1930" (Armfield, 2012, p. 41). Records of the contributions of African American work in Black hospitals and other organizations were not preserved, making their contributes nearly invisible. When White social workers served the Black migrant population, they implemented Jim Crow guidelines. Some White settlement houses created separate agendas for Black and White newcomers; however, the general rule was that White settlement houses were not open to African Americans (Armfield, 2012). Even the beloved icon of the social work profession, Jane Adams, who cut her teeth in African American settlement homes, started Hull House as a segregated settlement house. As Carle (2013, p. 86) explains:

African American charitable work had been occurring for decades—indeed, it was Jane Addams's participation in African American mission house work that lifted her from a depression she fell into during her early adult years and provided her with a vision for how she could pursue a meaningful life of service to others. But Adams had decided to focus our efforts on acculturating the many (white) immigrant "races" arriving in the United States, and Hull House sat in the mist of white immigrant neighborhoods. Hull House quite explicitly did not serve African Americans.

Addams, who helped start the National Association for the Advancement of Colored People (NAACP), was elected the first woman president of the National Conference of Charities and Corrections (later the National Conference of Social Work, NCSW). "Though the NCSW did not officially discriminate [Black] social workers encountered racist attitudes and Jim Crow policies" in people, agencies, and organizations (Armfield, 2012, p. 45). For example, appointed in 1916 as executive secretary of the National Urban League, Eugene Knuckles Jones, a prominent African American intellectual and social work pioneer, was the first African American elected to the NCSW as a board member (1926–1933) and he was the first Black president of the organization. Jones was a staunch advocate for African American social and economic viability, health, and housing, community-based practice, and self-help. He was instrumental in professionalizing Black social work in America and helping the larger profession form a national identity, particularly in vocational education and community-based practice. Yet, for the most part—other than among African Americans—Jones is not recognized in the annals of the profession for his accomplishments (Armfield, 2012). Nor were the lessons learned from his activism for African American communities institutionalized as part of the social work profession.

Starting in the 1940s and picking up steam during the 1960s, separation developed within the profession between micro-, meso-, and macro-based practice. In retrospect, this proved to be poor timing, as divisions among clinical, community-based, and policy advocacy emerged within the profession. However, as the American politicians started to move families from the benefits of the so-called welfare state to a marketplace reality, with a focus on two-parent-working families as necessary for participation in the middle class, racism became pervasive in different ways and impinged on micro-level and macro-level systems and organizational structures (Rodgers, 2015, p. 1). To date, there is no definitive history on race or racism within the social work profession. If one engages in a scholarly internet search on social work and racism, few studies, articles, or textbooks will emerge. Yet, contributions are coming forward. In *Facilitating Injustice*, Park (2020) documents the social work profession's complicity in the forced removal and incarceration of Japanese Americans during the World War II internment of approximately 120,000 Asian Americans. Similarly, Bell (2014) documents the experiences of African Americans and the social work profession during the Black Power movement.

In the general scope and field of social work research and practice, there are no profession-wide major projects aimed at reducing racial disparities in the social determinants of health. A 2006 National Association of Social Workers (NASW) workforce study determined that:

> In terms of racial and ethnic diversity, overall, the profession has not kept pace with population trends in terms of its ability to attract social workers of color. . . . As frontline providers, social work needs to expand the racial and ethnic diversity within its ranks, particularly because children and adolescents are the most racially and ethnically diverse age group in the U.S. population. (Whitaker et al., 2006, p. 16)

Understanding the changing demographic of America, in 1973 the CSWE established a diversity standard requiring accredited social work programs to make continuous efforts to diversify their student body at all levels of instruction as well as their research personal. During the same period, the NASW launched research to understand the revolutionary needs of the labor force for the profession. In spite of these efforts, "[f]rom 1974 through about 1990, enrollment for White students held steady at about 80% of the graduate student total" (Bowie et al., 2018, p. 271). However, the percentage of White MSW (master of social work) graduates dropped to 64%. Latino enrollment in MSW programs was less than 2% from 1974 to 1990.

Longres opined that given the profession's movement toward mental health treatment and clinical entrepreneurship in the 1960s and 1970s, the social work profession was steered away from examining deficiencies in social structure—focusing more on the need for individual change rather than social change. He further asserted that the profession was more committed to helping White middle-class America rather than the non-White and poor. "Moreover, social work appears more committed to following the footsteps of psychiatry than in carving out a unique professional identity committed to the poor and to social reform," stated Longres (1973).

Racism and Civil Rights

In the promotion of professional equity and social change during the 1960s and 1970s, anti-racism movements led to the development of platforms against racism and low minority representation within professional organizations and institutions of higher education. This period witnessed the development of the Black Power movement and the formation of independent professional organizations in succession from White-dominated professional organizations in law, business, anthropology, sociology, psychology, counseling, etc. (Bell, 2014). The National Association of Black Social Workers (NABSW) resulted from the leadership of African American social work scholars as a call for the profession to concentrate on the specific needs of African American communities and in protest of the pervasive institutional racism within the social work profession. Similar to other Black Power independent organizational movements, NABSW was the creation of anti-racism and culturally responsive practices, with Black leadership and commitment to Black communities (Bell, 2014). During this period, the widespread racist ideology of the Moynihan analysis, which pathologized the structure and functioning of Black families, and particularly demeaned Black males as aloof and absent fathers, captured the mainstream of American. As a racial project designed to reduce White culpability for the problematic socioeconomic condition of African Americans, the Moynihan Report heavily influenced the social work profession, other than the resistance found within historically Black colleges and universities. It resulted in a call-to-action for Black social workers. It was unfortunate that the broader society and the social work profession did not accentuate the problem of gross underemployment and unemployment, the criminal justice fixation—with federal assistance— on Black male incarceration, and the negative impact that the U.S. social welfare system had on Black families. "It was unfortunate that the economic issue, employment for African American males noted by Moynihan, never received sufficient focus in the national debate" (Bowle et al., 2016, p. 124).

Seeking community uplift as a professional occupation along with greater educational access, the late 1960s and early 1970s witnessed an influx of African Americans into the ranks of social workers. By 1965, the CSWE education was first among national accreditation bodies to develop a nondiscrimination standard (Bell, 2014). CSWE moved from its 1952 suggestions of social work education programs considering cultural, social, and spiritual experiences in practice, to a 1972 mandate within curriculum guidelines for programs to "recognize, understand, and appraise, human behavior in the light of personal and cultural norms and values . . ." (Bell, 2014, p. 132). CSWE further formed a task force to develop methods to increase diversity within the numbers of faculty teaching in social work education programs. "These task forces were convened for American Indians, Puerto Ricans, and Chicanos in 1970, and later for African Americans and Asian Americans in 1971" (Bell, 2014, p. 129).

Yet, full inclusion in the development of curriculum, programming, and practice methods with minority communities lagged, and in many areas, still needs development within the profession. Hinting at the use of racial commonsense thinking and racial projects with the intention of maintaining power relationships within the social work profession, Longres writes in 1971 that mainstream social work minority recruitment programs were "frequently a search for the good 'nigger,' the non-White who will be grateful for the hand-out and who will not make waves. There was a cautious analysis, he further articulates, "of numbers so that too many will not come about too soon" (p. 297).

During the Civil Rights era, with greater numbers of African Americans entering the social work profession, tenure in promotion standards in university and college settings with social work education programs did not acknowledge the needs of Black communities, and therefore placed many African American social work scholars in a compromising situation. This situation continues today. Many students from minoritized groups entered the profession to do something about the conditions and circumstances within their communities, only to find out that such projects are not part of the academic scholarship landscape. Although this situation is gaining attention and even some change within the mainstream of social work, efforts lags in terms of commitment and the design of appropriate standards within mainstream academia.

There were equal if not greater challenges from African American social work practitioners. Accusations of workplace, client-centered, and institutional racism were rampant among African American social workers. African Americans further lacked opportunity within the profession, and faced biased treatment and marginalization within organizations from White coworkers (Bell, 2014). Tensions culminated in 1968 with the walkout of 400 Black social workers at the April 1968 National Conference of Social Welfare.

Consequently, in the spring of 1968, the CSWE conducted a survey of nondiscriminatory practices among accredited graduate social work programs. Findings showed no evidence of program violations; however, the criteria for nondiscriminatory practices "had signified the omission of any consideration of race, color, creed, or ethnic origin in the determination of student admission and faculty selection" (Mirelowitz, 1979, p. 302). In response to internal pressure and activism from African Americans and the NABSW, the CSWE developed Standard 1234A in 1973, which specified that schools must make special and continued efforts to enrich programming "by providing racial, ethnic, and cultural diversity in its student body and at all levels of instructional and research personnel and by providing corresponding educational support"; Bell, 2014, p. 129). The development of the NASW Standards and Indicators for Cultural Competence in Social Practice date back to a start on the 1969 Delegate Assembly for the Task Force on Minority Concerns. In addition, there was the development of the CSWE Black Task Force in 1973, designed to address the curricular and instructional needs of African Americans within social work education programs.

Arguably, the lack of follow-through on recommended educational objectives by the Black Task Force underscores why the social work profession did not take the elimination of racism seriously, even within its professional ranks. In many ways, the social work profession has yet to make good on the goals set forth by the Task Force: (1) An understanding of how the economic, social, political, and class forces that determine social policies are implicitly influenced by racism; (2) an ability to analyze how social policy is formulated by legislation, by the courts, and by government bureaucracies, and how this formulation is influence by racism; (3) an awareness of the impact of institutional racism on Black Americans and other ethnic minorities with a particular reference to the distribution of societal resources and the patterns of delivery of educational, health, and social services (Bell, 2014, p. 131).

Bell (2014) pragmatically states that Black Task Force findings were "a harsh critique of social work education, but the force also offered a way forward" for the profession (p. 132). However, to achieve these objects would have meant a profound shift in social work education, practice and policy formation—none of which took place. Instead, the road to cultural competence was paved as the profession's method to affront racism and other forms of injustices. In this way, the hardnose politics and tough conversations on racism were diluted and reduced to a menu of "isms," which educators and professional practitioners could claim as their individualized flavor of social justice advocacy (Davis, 2016). The recommendations of the Black Task

Force findings were ultimately consumed within continuing iterations of CSWE diversity curriculum standards, which have been the gold standard for articulating guidelines for diversity and inclusion within the social work profession. In terms of the centrality of race and racism, there was always a problem with "the broad-based emphasis on diversity in social work, [because] there is a lesser emphasis placed on race and the injustices encountered by historically marginalized and oppressed groups such as African Americans" (Brigg et al., 2019, p. 20). Multicultural social work only dibbled and dabbled in racial parlance; it did not exemplify the type of critical thought about race and racism. Finally, the separation of micro, meso, and macro resulted in today's high focus on clinical entrepreneurship and movement toward lower contact with indigent clients. As Specht and Courtney assert in *Unfaithful Angels* (1994), the social work profession sacrificed a great deal of its commitment to social development during stretches of its history to focus on professionalism and psychotherapy. A stalwart commitment to racial justice was among the losers of professional attention.

Racism, Diversity, and Social Work Education

Much of the research on race and racism within the context of the social work profession is in the area of diversity and cultural competence. Cultural competence refers to the set of attitudes, practices, values, skills, and policies that enables a person or agency to work well with people from different cultural groups (Abrams & Moio, 2009). Efficacy studies on diversity and cultural competence in social work education are limited, and needs greater attention by the profession (Briggs et al., 2019; Larson & Bradshaw, 2017). In general, existing studies provide little information on evidence-based approaches to intervention with culturally specific groups. (Copeland, 2006; Briggs et al., 2019; Larson & Bradshaw, 2017; Sue & Zane, 2006). Briggs et al.'s review of literature on cultural competence in social work found that systematic reviews of research on outcomes studies on culturally competent interventions with African Americans are absent from the research literature.

A comprehensive review of outcomes studies in social work using culturally competent interventions with Latinos found that "there remains a paucity of intervention outcome research regarding the Latino population" (Jani et al., 2009, p. 192). Larson and Bradshaw's review of literature found that teachers who engage in cultural competence are those who demonstrate cultural sensitivity, use culturally relevant teaching methods, incorporate historical views of marginalized populations, and address and discuss discrimination in practices. Their systematic review of literature found that many normative scales used to examine practitioners' levels of cultural competence are (a) self-report measures and (b) prone to social desirability bias. Abrams and Moio (2009) argue that the use of cultural competence models has been "largely ineffective and that its tendency to equalize oppressions under a 'multicultural umbrella' unintentionally promotes a color-blind mentality that eclipses the significance of institutionalized racism" (p. 245).

Given social work's broad-based interest in diversity as the target for understanding and reflecting social justice, and the fluidity of racism, the contextual development of racial projects lacks proper attention by the profession (Abrams & Moio, 2009). In order to strengthen approaches to cultural competence training in social work education programs and in consideration of the centrality of race and racism, Briggs et al. (2019) suggest that students must examine the structural determinants of culture as a way of understanding and combating racial injustice: (1) making use of socio-emotional intelligence in addressing racial consciousness and racial diversity in the pursuit of well-being; (2) understanding and appraising the structural determinants of White privilege and power; (3) developing, documenting, and putting forth best practices that promote social responsibility and culturally competent social justice models of practice; and (4) learning evaluation skills, including the documentation of lessons learned from culturally specific practices.

Students must understand structural inequalities and racial regulation in order to understand what and how change needs to occur. Structural inequalities are often deeply woven rules, regulations, norms, and process, within our society, within institutions and organizations, businesses, educational systems, healthcare systems, and government. Miller and Garran (2007, p. 33) couch institutional racism as "a web of oppression which obstructs economic, social, and political mobility for people of color while white people are issued passports of privilege." In order for the social work profession to consider an internal approach to eliminating racism, a concerted change is needed within social work education in order to teach students about structural change and its link to institutional racism. The education of social work students, particularly at the graduate level, must of necessity provide an understanding and create student self-awareness of how institutional practices support and result in inequalities for individual clients and communities. It is hard for individuals to tackle a structural system riddled with inequalities. The first order for change in this situation is to understand exactly what you want changed and the dynamics of the system involved. Efforts in this area will require leadership, advocacy, organization, coalition and capacity building, political engagement, sustained effort, and the drive to build off small victories as well as rebound from setbacks. The function of social work education from an anti-racist perspective is to ensure that students are equipped with such knowledge and relevant skills when they exit social work education programs. All social work students should be given the challenge of grappling with how to engage in anti-racist practices and commit to livelong advocacy for one or perhaps several anti-racist projects as a signature professional goal. Students should be provided with examples of social work activists who have demonstrated such tenacity.

It follows that students will need to gain comprehensive understanding of macro, meso, and micro factors within a social work education program in order to realize the elimination of racism as a Grand Challenge for the profession. The is necessary in order for students to gain a sense of the centrality of race and racism, and so that they will grasp the full spectrum and meaning of racialization over the life cycle, while developing the cognitive dispensation to engage in anti-racist practices. In order to combat structural racism, macro practice cannot be specialized learning, or be viewed as distinct from a generalist approach to social work education or licensing. Of necessity, social work education programs must, en masse, end their consistent marriage to clinical practice as the mainstay of the social work profession. The politics, policies, structural contours, and realities of race and racism warrant knowledge of institutional functioning by social workers who take on an anti-racist persona. Preparation for anti-racist social work education means that social work education programs will need to end the structural distinctions in MSW program offerings among micro, meso, and macro practice. Students must understand the link between client needs in the environment, the socioeconomic context within the community setting, and the larger structural system in order to tackle structural racism. There can be no cursory review of these systems, but more so, an in-depth study as part of program competencies. Moreover, as a means of cultivating racial justices, it is paramount that students learn the institutional contours of modern-day forms of oppression, racial regulation, power, and White privilege.

Racism and Social Work

In June 2021 the NASW issued an apology for racist practices in American social work. Reflecting on the profession's efforts to engage in anti-racist practice through the continued promotion of social justice, the article cites the following racialized practices undertaken by the profession:

- Progressive era social workers built and ran segregated settlement houses.
- Social worker suffragists blocked African Americans from gaining the right to vote.
- Prominent social workers supported eugenics theories and programs.
- Social workers helped recruit Black men into the infamous Tuskegee Experiment.
- Social workers participated in the removal of Native American children from their families and placement in boarding schools.
- Social workers also took part in intake teams at Japanese internment camps during World War II.
- And since the founding of the profession, bias among some social workers has limited delivery of healthcare, mental health treatment, and social services to people of color. (NASW, 2021)

While these uncomfortable truths and sober assessment are admirable, contemporary challenges of racism for the social work profession are many. For example, it is widely known throughout the social work profession that historically oppressed groups are overrepresented in the nations' child welfare systems, and research demonstrates that they receive unequal treatment compared to their Caucasian counterparts (Fong, McRoy, & Dettlaff, et al., 2014; Briggs et al., 2019). Child welfare represents a major area of needed revolutionary change for the social work professional. In fact, long-term problems with child welfare and the foster care system are one reason for a call to end the child welfare system and start anew (Burghardt, 2019; Dettlaff & Boyd, 2020). Not to exclude the racial disparities as a problem with the juvenile justice system, there is now the school (or foster care) to prison pipeline populated mainly by African Americans. Unfortunately, for a myriad or reasons beyond the scope of this text, there are glaring and long-standing overrepresentation and outcome disparities for many minoritized children and youth within U.S. child welfare systems.

The foster care system is replete with racialized problems and represents a major field of social work practice that can be the target of the Grand Challenge to Eliminate Racism for the profession. For more than 40 years, African American, Native American, and Alaska Native children have been overrepresented in the U.S. foster care system when compared to Caucasian children and youth (Howze & McKeig, 2019). Data from 2017 collected by the U.S. Department of Health and Human Services identify African Americans as at nearly 15% of the child welfare population but 23% of all youth in the foster care system. Whereas Latinx children represent 25% of the US child population, they are 21 percent of children in foster care. "And Asian and Native Hawaiian kids make up 5% of the U.S. child population but only 1% of its foster care population" (The Annie Casey Foundation, 2020, online). Black children enter earlier, remain in foster care longer, experience the most restrictive treatment, and are more likely to have parental rights removed, as well as interact with the juvenile justice system, when compared to other racial and ethnic groups (Myers, 2011). While race and poverty are significant factors in the overrepresentation of minoritized populations in the foster care system, scholars have identified stress, bias, family composition, cultural misunderstandings, differential treatment, and distrust between child welfare decision-makers and the families they serve as contributing to disparate outcomes (Dettlaff, & Boyd, 2020; Fong, McRoy, & Dettlaff, 2014; Howze & McKeig, 2019).

School social work practice represents the largest field of child welfare practice for the profession. According to 2019 data from the U.S. Bureau of Labor Statistics, child, family, and school social workers numbered 342,500 of the 713,200 overall employed workforce during that period. School social workers are often part of interdisciplinary teams within school settings; they have the task of promoting child and youth school success and healthy developmental outcomes. Although the root causes of educational inequality are complex, institutionalized racism and socioeconomic disparities continue to advantage White children and youth (U.S. Government Accountability Office, 2020, online). African American and Latinx children and youth are overrepresented within pre-K–12 public school systems among those identified with an emotional disturbance or a learning disability, and they are disproportionately diagnosed with behavioral problems (U.S. Government Accountability Office, 2020, online). The advent of zero-tolerance policies, leading to overuse of exclusionary discipline practices in the form of suspension and expulsion from schools, has become a major problem, with nationwide disproportionate representation among African American, Native American, and Latinx children and youth (Lowery, 2019; Teasley, et al, 2017). Most notable, problems start early in the schooling experience for Black children. According to a report by Scientific American (Novak, 2023, online), although 18 stated have banned preschool expulsions, nationwide, "half of the 250 kids expelled from preschool each day are Black boys." African American preschool-aged children make up just 19% of preschool-aged children but comprise 47% of preschoolers suspended more than once (Gilliam, Maupin, Reyes, Accavitti, & Shic, 2016). Within every state in the nation, African Americans are disproportionality suspended and expulsed from public schools. Cultural insensitivity, bias, discrimination, over-referral, discrepancies in consequences for behavioral factors, and referrals and exclusionary practices have all be identified within research literature (Gilliam et al., 2016; Teasley et al., 2017).

There are also gross racial disparities within the juvenile justice system with the overrepresentation of minoritized youth (Fong et al., 2014; Marshall & Haight, 2014). With 1.5 million youth seen in juvenile courts in 2009, 34% were African American, although they represented only 15% of youth ages 10–17 who were incarcerated. Latino youth represented 19% of youth ages 10–17, but 25% of youth who were incarcerated (Fong et al., 2014). The structural problem referred to as the "push out" phenomenon in public schools—the disproportionate suspensions and expulsions of African America, Latinx, and Native American children—comes full circle, for children with an association with entry into the juvenile justice system and its role in the now infamous school-to-prison pipeline (Lowery, 2019). Characteristic of mainly urban areas, this problem exists in nearly all 50 states and impacts an entire generation of youth. This is an important social justice issue and must be considered as central to anti-racist practices in schools.

All of these areas of child welfare experience are the domains of social work professionals. While not the primary professional service within many child welfare settings, it is important to underscore the critical roles and ethical responsibility engendered by social work professionals practicing within child welfare settings. It is well known that social work professionals are bound to seek out and repair indifference and inequities, take measures to reduce and remove oppression and marginalization, and *do no harm* as an ethical responsibility. At present, social workers within child welfare settings, schools, and juvenile justice settings have not developed models of practices that ameliorate or eliminate disproportionality and disparities in outcomes for racialized children and youth.

Anti-Racist Social Work

Intuitively, anti-racist projects are those that undo or resist structures of domination based on racial significance and identities. Anti-racist projects are responsible for diminishing overt forms of racism, which often results in subtle and more implicit forms of racism, as witnessed in the current area. As the public and particularly minoritized populations start to dismantle racial projects, new vestiges of structural impediments become the building blocks of racial formation. Anti-racism projects were responsible for the Black radical tradition in the early 1900s, which preceded and, in many ways, gave birth to the Civil Rights movement in America. Black Lives Matter is an anti-racist project, which gained its agency out of a wave of police killings of unarmed African Americans, including children.

Regarding social control measures, Williams and Parrott (2014) explain that it is often hard to find spatial arrangements within social work education programs to engage in anti-racist discourse. What they refer to as "predominately White areas" often marginalizes discourse about anti-racist practices and whiteness based on misplaced assumptions about the intent of such perspectives. As a partial remedy to this drawback, Schiele (2020) argues that a racism-centered perspective is needed throughout the social work profession. A basic assumption from a racism-centered perspective is that a key function of American social policy development and implementation is social control through racial formation and subsequent racial projects (Schiele, 2020). The policies and practices that emerge from the underlying assumption of social control are understood as having regulatory intentions and results that aim to monitor and change the behavior of those deemed socially deviant or politically threating. From this viewpoint, social policies are instruments that enforce the cultural norms and mores of dominant groups among those who demonstrate nonconformity.

Placing race at the center of our analysis means moving from a non-racist perspective to anti-racist practices (DiAngelo, 2021). There is a distinct difference between not being racist and being an anti-racist. Just because people do not believe that they are racist says nothing of their ability to identify and locate the roots of racism within power and policies, which lead to programs,

46 MARTELL L. TEASLEY

practices, and personal interactions that help reduce racism—the task of the anti-racist. To *not* be a racist is a position of neutrality. To the contrary, Kendi (2019, pp. 9–10) states, there is no neutrality in the racism struggle. The opposite of being a racist isn't "not being a racist"—it is being an *anti-racist*:

> One endorses either the idea of a racial hierarchy as a racist, or racial equality as an antiracist. One either believes problems are rooted in groups of people, as racist, or locates the root of problems in power and policies, as an antiracist. One either allows racial inequities to persevere, as a racist, or confronts racial injustice, as an antiracist. The is no in-between safe space of not racist.

Finally, the problem with just being not racist is that we live in a world where people are okay with the existence of racism, they just do not want to be known as an individual racist. This gives the common person "a way out" or maybe a "colorblind pass" and therefore serves as a form of racial common sense thinking, maintaining the status quo. Plainly stated and as the old saying goes, if the shoe fits, wear it! The claim of non-racism neutrality is a mask for racism (Kendi, 2019).

Although the use of the anti-racist perspective has history within the social work profession, there is a need for greater focus on anti-racism within the profession (Abrams & Gibson, 2007). As long as social work practice is synonymous with diversity management as a form of competence development, the profession will remain unable to reconcile being a "good" social worker with being an anti-racist practitioner. However, one of the more general barriers to such discussions within social work education programs is students' feelings of discomfort and resistance "including guilt, shame, and anxiety when discussing anti-racism in the classroom. Along with student resistance and discomfort comes faculty unease, such as the concern that teaching anti-racism can lead to negative course evaluations" (Hamilton-Mason & Schneider, 2018, p. 338). The 2022 Education Policy Accreditation Standards (EPAS) are dedicated to anti-racist competencies for social work education. Although EPAS is revised every seven years, the murder of George Floyd in May 2020 and the international protect that followed sparked a call for change, which reverberated throughout the social work profession. For example, the new EPAS was constructed with input from an assembled CSWE Task Force to Advance Anti-Racism in Social Work Education, which designed an action plan to strengthen the profession's approach to anti-racist education, practice, research, and policy advocacy. As with past iterations of EPAS, designed to change social work practices to improve diversity, equity, and inclusion, this version resulted from a call-to-action by many young professionals, including students who called out the gap between the profession's values and the reality of content within education programming and practice. Areas to be impacted include curriculum and instruction; student, faculty, and program equity; decolonizing the research enterprise; the amplification of Critical Race Theory; the development of a clearinghouse for anti-racist resources; assurance that field placement is committed to anti-racist practices; program diversity; and providing support for HBCUs and tribal colleges. This set of activities is much more comprehensive than past efforts at diversity, inclusion, and culturally competency practice. However, it will take some time to assess the outcome of these efforts and their ability to promote change within the profession in the facilitation of anti-racist practices (CSWE, 2021).

ASWB and Racially Biased Licensure Testing

In 1969 the NASW approved regulation to develop the Association of Social Work Boards (ASWB) to coordinate state regulator practices (Kim, 2022). This led to all states requiring licensing for clinical practice for several categories of the master of social work (MSW) and bachelor of social work (BSW) degrees. Surprisingly, "[d]espite the prevalence and significance of social work licensure, the conceptual and empirical literature is surprisingly rare" (Kim, 2002, p. 2). There is no body of literature outlining and detailing the psychometric properties within various iterations and levels of the social work licensure examinations (Albright & Thyer, 2010).

Though there are a plethora of issues within the social work profession that can be informed by an anti-racist lens, the long-awaited August 2022 release of basic demographic data on licenture test-takers and the revealed, significant racial disparities in passage rates has become a tipping point, placing the social work profession in an internal crisis, with larger public implications. At the BSW level, data revealed that from 2011 to 2021, there was an 82% passage rate for Whites, 38% for Blacks, 64% for Asians, and 71% for Native Americans as first-time test-takers; 81% of all test-takers eventually passed the licensure at the BSW level. At the MSW level, 91% of Whites, 52% of Blacks, 72% of Asians, and 72% of Native Americans passed as first-time

48   MARTELL L. TEASLEY

test-takers; 86% of all test-takers eventually passed the master's licensure exam. As for the clinical MSW licensure exam, 91% of Whites, 57% of Blacks, 80% of Asians, and 74% of Native Americans passed as first-time test-takers, with 88% of all test-takers eventually passing the licensure exam. Prior to the release there were nationwide assumptions of racial disparities among the passage rate of test-takers. Although there is limited research (Senreich and Dale, 2021), the evidence was glaring, as state after state and social work education programs noticed gaps between Whites and other racialized groups.

Ignoring requests by state licensing organizations, schools of social work education programs, researchers, and practitioners, the ASWB openly refused to release any statistical analysis of the exam, as well as any basic demographic data on test-takers, until August 2022. As recently as 2021, the claim from ASWB leadership was that the organization did not have comprehensive demographic data, and that existing data were inadequate or too incomplete to release (DeCarlo, 2021). Perhaps, part of their resistance belongs to the lack of a public call to release licensing exam data from the CSWE and the NASW—arguably the two major organizations within the profession. That such a posture persisted within the profession for over 50 years is a testament to the pervasiveness of racial commonsense thinking within a profession that touts social justice and equality above all. As Senreich and Dale (2021, p. 20) astutely point out:

> by not insisting that ASWB report licensing exam passing rates by demographic groups, the major social work profession organization the U.S. licensure boards have allowed a testing system to continue that does not ensure that there is a lack of discrimination against nonwhite racial groups as well as gender and age groups.

With the data release of demographic data on test-takers from ASWB, an outcry mounted among practitioners, researchers, and a host of state social work organizations, including the National Association of Deans and Directors (NADD) of Social Work and the Association of Baccalaureate Social Work Program Directors. Along with other demands, both organizations wrote letters to the CEO and president of ASWB calling for reform in the licensing examinations. Even leadership from ASWB states the obvious in its published letter titled "Beyond Data: A Call to Action," dated August 30, 2022, acknowledging systemic and institutional racism as being "core to the racial disparities evidenced by the recently released licensing exam pass rate data." The NADD Task Force on Licensing letter to ASWB CEO Stacey Hardy-Chandler and President Roxroy Reid states:

> This call to action indicates a commitment to reform from racially-biased testing. However, there is also a need to repair the harm that past racially-biased testing has caused. Part of NADD's request is for even greater transparency on factors related to the social work licensing examination. This includes releasing the psychometric properties of the exam (or working with impartial psychometricians to conduct necessary analyses), providing detailed information on the constellation of theoretical approaches used in constructing the exam, and placing the exam in Spanish, similar to placing the exam in French as a provision of entering the Canadian market for social work licensing examinations.

Having released the July 2022 Education Policy and Accreditation Standards with a focus on anti-racist practices, the Commission on Accreditation noted that ASWB's "descriptive statistics suggest significant race and age disparities in exam pass rates" and thus "voted to remove licensing exam pass rates for social work education from its program accreditation standards." Backed by CSWE in September 2022, the Commission on Accreditation leadership informed the profession that after the release of test-taker demographics by ASWB, swift action was taken to ensure the EPAS "supports social work education programs in developing a workforce of social workers who are knowledgeable about the ways positionality, power, privilege, and diversity affect all levels of practice" (CSWE 2022, online).

ASWB's safeguards against racial bias in testing are inadequate. ASWB's approach to diversity, equity, and inclusion in the design of its licensing exams has been to diversify the examination of test-item analysis through the use of minoritized racial group members as part of examination question development (Marson et al., 2010). As former ASWB CEO Dwight Hymans expressed, "We do not track the outcome, in other words, the pass rate for different groups. But what we do know about standardized testing is that generally speaking across any exam . . . it's fairly common knowledge that there are disparities in outcomes" (DeCarlo, 2021, online). Conversely, with Whites comprising nearly 80% of social workers, this approach has limitations. It is not the same as engaging in the examination of concurrent validity with the use of diverse populations in the construction and testing of items. It is not same as making use of diverse theoretical perspectives, used within social practice based on research findings, in item construction within the ASWB content areas of communication, therapeutic relations, issues of diversity, clinical practice, clinical supervision, service delivery, and human development and behavior in the environment.

In ASWB's pledge to protect the public, test-takers are viewed as a "competent social worker" based on those who pass the exam; and those who fail are considered an "incompetent social worker," at the particular level of licensure practice (Mason & DeAngelis, 2018). According to Owens (2021, n.p.), licensing "[i]tems are continually monitored for reliability, validity, potential bias, and Differential Item Functioning." Emphasis has been placed on test item construction as the primary method for proving test validity for the licensure exam (Marson, DeAngelis, & Mittal, 2010). To the contrary, Albright and Thyer (2010) explain that the exam does not determine competence for the profession given that it is not tested for concurrent and predictive validity. Social work involves the ability to empathizes and engage in many interpersonal skills not captured by multiple choice tests (Senreich & Dale, 2021). Such skills are often nuanced to particular cultural and community context.

If ASWB is serious about diversity, equity and inclusion and anti-racist practices in its testing, then racial and ethnic subgroups would be independently tested for exam scoring competency, using normative statistical tools for reality and validity testing outcomes. To underscore, the organization would further examine content and constructs from Afrocentric, Latinx, Native American, Critical Race Theory, Intersectional, and perspectives on the Asian American experience as part of item construct and subscale development. Diverse perspectives for social work practice and subsequent research findings should be use in item construction within ASWB's content areas of communication, therapeutic relations, issues of diversity, clinical practice, clinical supervision, service delivery, and human development and behavior in the environment. In addition to these measures, Morrow (2022, p. 8), chair of the Commission on Accreditation, states plainly that much needed change should include narrowing

> the gap between Council on Social Work Education standards and Association of Social Work Boards exam content, improving licensure preparation in educational settings, resolving macro practice concerns about social work licensure, developing consistency across license titles, providing transparency in exam pass rate demographics, achieving

practice mobility, and advancing empirical research on testing and practice competence.

In spite of popular knowledge, and with a profit over $6 million annually, ASWB is not a social work organization; it is a regulatory organization that claims accountability only to its membership (DeCarlo, 2021). The organization has a nationwide monopoly on social work licensing and has operated without sufficient linkage to CSWE EPAS, and without competition since its inception. It is doubtful that ASWB will outright reform its practices without advocacy and competition. The organization appears satisfied with a profitable and racially biased exam that has not been independently assessed for reliability and validity among racial and ethnic subgroups (DeCarlo, 2021). Consequently, mobilization against the continuation of current ASWB practices needs to be a priority for the social work profession—this is a "call to action" for social work advocacy, as racialized disparities in licensure have forged a dividing line between the haves and the have-nots. As Nienow, Sogabe and Husain (2023, p. 81) underscore, the social work profession "faces a moment of reckoning regarding systemic racism, specifically within its regulatory system." A minimum cumulative grade point average of 3.0 is required for all graduate social work programs, "based upon observation and application of practice behavior." However, "the licensure exam process relies upon assessment of knowledge of cognitive systems only." In many way, this reckoning represents a new frontier from the profession in the needs to tackle a major organization related to its missions and legitimacy as a profession. This will not be easy but represents a major thrust towards antiracist social work practice and is instrumental to the elimination of racism within the profession. What many within the profession need to realize is that "it is our collective responsibility as social workers to create new institutions that assess practitioner competency in a way that is community-owned, open source, inclusive, and congruent with our professional values" (DeCarlo, 2021, online).

Conclusion

Returning to the prophetic words of James Baldwin (1962, pp. 50–51), who stated, "People are not, for example, too terribly anxious to be equal (equal, after all, to what, and to whom?) but they love the idea of being superior." And this translates to conceived superior forms of freedom based on "the shifting sands of status" within society (p. 51) that individuals and groups attempt to obtain and maintain. According to Baldwin, most of us do not really have the desire to push for freedom other than for ourselves, and those we hold dear. Indeed, promoting, pushing, and struggling for freedom for others is hard to bear. It is a selfless exercise and can becomes the ultimate form of service to others. The lesson here is that freedom based on the "individual currency of self," as an ultimate goal, is less than optimal freedom. Eschewing both Nazi Germany and Russian Communist rule, Polish poet Czeslaw Milosz (1955, 23:01) explains, "freedom from something is a great deal, yet, not enough. It is much less than freedom for something."

In the profession's commitment to a fuller freedom for those less fortunate, social work professionals must strive to repair problems within the profession that represent long-standing racial bias as a constraint on freedom. Although the social work profession has attempted to deal with the conundrums of racism, the profession has not dealt with White privilege and its contours within the profession, to include the practice setting and social work licensure (Jeffery, 2006; Jeyasingham, 2013). Anti-racism social work practice means of necessity struggling for freedom from oppressive practices that undergird the dynamics of racism within the profession, which made it necessary to push for the 13th Grand Challenge to Eliminate Racism. Anti-racism means the social work profession must end racialized disproportionality in social welfare practice; confront and resolve the myriad of racialized social welfare problems outlined within this text; rid the profession of gender bias; and transform its "people of color" theories and the racialization of people into expressions of freedom. Just as importantly, it must end the standalone category of whiteness within its professional practice, based on the superiority and domination of those deemed White (Odera et al., 2021).

The imposition of White supremacy and its consecration in whiteness took place not only at the expense of Blacks and other minoritized groups, but also on Whites. Creating social work practitioners who are educated to solve the social welfare problems and challenges of Whites was at the heart of Longres's lament against the profession in the 1970s. Today, as a country, the United States is now in an era where the burden of whiteness, once viewed as the need to save non-White people in the world from backwardness, is now a struggle, in many spaces, to maintain homeostasis among many Whites, let alone achieve the so-called American dream.

The investment of many Whites in maintaining an imaginary racial hierarchy atop other racialized groups is failing, and ironically, harms the well-being of White Americans as a demographic group (Metzl, 2019). Thus, freedom from racism means freedom from White supremacy and the imposition of whiteness, for all. For sure, such an approach will engender major personal discomfort, but the profession must undergo this conversion if it wants to demonstrate a commitment to change and advocate for anti-racist policies and practices throughout society.

Should the social work profession make strides to "clean its own house" of racism, the realities of the United States and its lingering caste system (Wilkerson, 2020) is that collective revolutionary action is required to eliminate racism (Rodgers, 2015). Surely, the pervasive problem of racism will not be resolved solely by the efforts of social workers; even if the profession solves its internal racialized practices, it will have to form a collective effort and build coalition.

Truth be told, over time, and on the backs of many people and interest groups who struggled for social and racial justice, the United States has made major strides in harnessing and curtailing overt racism; but vestiges of the past are clear and present dangers for the future. A multi-racial and ethnic coalition can be led by dedicated social workers to lead the Grand Challenge to Eliminate Racism. Such a coalition should include individuals, groups, organizations, and corporations who engage in intellectual pursuits, research, the development of program and practice, protests, community organization, education and teaching, policy formation, and grassroots social activism, until racism is condemned socially, and its true effects becomes untenable to the future of humanity (Rodgers, 2015).

Study Questions

1. How can the social work profession avoid past misdeeds within practice and policy domains such as those that led the National Association of Social Workers (NASW) to apologize in 2021 for racist practices in American social work?
2. Identify and discuss your views on achievements and shortcomings in the development and implementation of past and present diversity standards for social work education by the Council on Social Work Education (CSWE).

3. What is the meaning of the term "anti-racist," and how does it differ from the term "non-racist?"
4. What can social work education programs do to ensure that students become knowledgeable and effective anti-racist professionals?
5. Discuss ways in which the NASW can promote anti-racist practices.
6. Why are classroom discussions on racism challenging for students and instructors?
7. What indicators would demonstrate evidence that the social work profession has made important strides to eliminate racism within the profession?
8. Identify and discuss your personal approach to advocacy in an attempt to have the Association of Social Work Boards (ASWB) reform racialized disparities in licensure testing practices.
9. What is your opinion of EPAS 2022 and its focus on creating anti-racist social work professionals?
10. What are ways you can personally promote anti-racist practices in your personal life and in the workplace setting?

References

Abrams, L. S., & Gibson, P. (2007). Teaching Notes: Reframing multicultural education: Teaching White privilege in the Social Work Curriculum. *Journal of Social Work Education, 43*, 147–160. https://doi.org/10.5175/JSWE.2007.200500529

Abrams, L. S., & Moio, J. A. (2009). Critical race theory and the cultural competence dilemma in social work education. *Journal of Social Work Education, 45*(2), 245–261. https://doi.org/10.5175/JSWE.2009.200700109.

Albright, D. L., & Thyer, B. A. (2010). A test of the validity of the LCSW examination: Quis custodiet ipsos custodes? *Social Work Research, 34*, 229–234. doi:10.1093/swr/34.4.229

Armfield, F. L. (2012). *Eugene Kinckle Jones: The National Urban League and black social work, 1910–1940*. Urbana: University of Illinois Press.

Baldwin, J. (1962). *The fire next time*. New York: Random House, Inc.

Bell, J. M. (2014). *The Black Power movement and American social work*. New York: Columbia University Press.

Bowie, S. L., Nashwan, A. J. J., Thomas, V., Davis-Buckley, R. J., & Johnson, R. L. (2018). An assessment of social work education efforts to recruit and retain MSW students of color. *Journal of Social Work Education, 54*, 270–286.

Bowles, D. D., Hopps, J. G., & Clayton, O. (2016). The impact and influence of HBCUs on the social work profession. *Journal of Social Work Education, 52*(1), 118–132. doi: https://doi.org/10.1080/10437797.2016.1112650.

Briggs, H. E., Briggs, V. G., & Briggs, A. C. (2019). *Integrative practice in and for larger systems*. New York: Oxford University Press.

ANTI-RACISM SOCIAL WORK 55

Bryant, D., & Kolivoki, K. M. (2021). The stories we tell: Examining the persistence and impacts of normative whiteness and white supremacy within social work education. *Advances in Social Work, 21*(2), 481–489.

Bureau of Labor Statistics, U.S. Department of Labor. (2021, March). *Occupational outlook handbook: Social workers.* Retrieved from https://www.bls.gov/ooh/community-and-social-service/social-workers.htm.

Carle, S. D. (2013). *Defining the struggle: National organizing for racial justice, 1880–1915.* New York: Oxford University Press.

Carlton-LaNey, I. (1994). Introduction: The legacy of African American leadership in social welfare. *Journal of Sociology and Social Welfare, 21*, 5–12.

Carlton-LaNey, I. (1999). African American social work pioneer's response to need. *Social Work, 44*(4), 311–321. https://doi.org/10.1093/sw/44.4.311.

Copeland, V. C. (2006). Disparities in mental health service utilization among low-income African American adolescents: Closing the gap by enhancing practitioner's competence. *Child and Adolescent Social Work Journal, 23*(4), 407–431. doi: 10.1007/s10560-006-0061-x.

Council on Social Work Education (2021). An update from the Anti-Racism Task Force. Retrieved from https://www.cswe.org/news/news/an-update-from-the-anti-racism-task-force/.

Council on Social Work Education. (2022). 2002 EPAS and licensing exam pass rates. Retrieved from: https://www.cswe.org/news/news/coa-removes-licensing-exam-pass-rates-from-the-2022-epas/

Davis, L. (2016). Race: America's Grand Challenge. *Journal of the Society for Social Work and Research, 7*(2), 395–403. Retrieved from https://www.journals.uchicago.edu/doi/full/10.1086/686296.

DeCarlo, M. P. (2021). Racial bias and ASWB exams: A failure of data equity. Editorial. *Social Work and Social Policy, 32*(3), 255–258. Retrieved from https://journals.sagepub.com/doi/epub/10.1177/10497315211055986.

Dettlaff, A. J., & Boyd, R. (2020). Racial disproportionality and disparities in the child welfare system: Why do they exist, and what can be done to address them? *The Annals of the American Academy, 692*, 253–274.

DiAngelo, R. (2021). *Nice racism: How progressive white people perpetuate racial harm.* Boston: Beacon Press.

Fong, R., McRoy, R., & Dettlaff, A. (2014). Disproportionality and disparities. In *Encyclopedia of Social Work.* National Association of Social Workers Press and Oxford University Press. Retrieved from https://oxfordre.com/socialwork/view/10.1093/acrefore/9780199975839.001.0001/acrefore-9780199975839-e-899.

Gilliam, W. S., Maupin, A. N., Reys, C. R., Accavitti, M., & Shic, F (2016, September 28). *Do early educators' implicit biases regarding sex and race relate to behavior expectations and recommendations of preschool expulsions and suspensions?* (Research Study Brief). Yale Child Student Center. Retrieved from https://medicine.yale.edu/childstudy/policy-and-social-innovation/zigler/publications/preschool%20implicit%20bias%20policy%20brief_final_9_26_276766_54643_v1.pdf

Hamilton-Mason, J. & Schneider, S. (2018). Antiracism expanding social work education: a qualitative analysis of the undoing racism workshop experience. *Journal of Social Work Education, 43*(2), 337–348.

Howze, K., & McKeig, A. K. (2019). The greenbook and the overrepresentation of African American, Hispanic, and Native American Families in the Child Welfare System. *Juvenile and Family Court Journal, 70*, 103–118. https://doi.org/10.1111/jfcj.12154

Jani, J. S., Ortiz, L., & Aranda, M. P. (2009). Latino outcome studies in social work: A review of the literature. *Research on Social Work Practice, 19*(2), 179–194.

Jeyasingham, D. (2013). White noise: A critical evaluation of social work education's engagement with whiteness studies. *The British Journal of Social Work, 42*(4), 660–686.

Jeffery, D. (2006). 'What good is anti-racist social work if you can't master it?': Exploring a paradox in anti-racist social work education. *Race Ethnicity and Education, 8*(4), 409–425. doi: 10.1080/13613320500324011.

Kendi, I. X. (2019). *How to be an antiracist*. New York: One World.

Kim, J. J. (2022). Racial disparities in social workers' licensing rates. *Research on Social Work Practice, 32*(4), 374–387. doi: 10.1177/10497315211066907.

Larson, K. E., & Bradshaw, C. P. (2017). Cultural competence and social desirability among practitioners: A systemic review of the literature. *Children and Youth Services Review, 76*, 100–111.

Lawler, M. J., LaPlante, K. D., Giger, J. T., & Norris, D. S. (2012). Overrepresentation of Native American children in foster care: An independent construct? *Journal of Ethnic and Cultural Diversity in Social Work, 21*(2), 95–110. doi:10.1080/15313204.2012.647344.

Longres, J. (1973). The impact of racism on social work education. In J. A. Goodman (Ed.), *Dynamics of racism in social work practice* (pp. 291–305). Washington, DC: NASW Press.

Lowery, P. G., & Burrow, J. D. (2019). Concentrated disadvantage, racial disparities, and juvenile institutionalization within the context of attribution theory. *Criminal Justice Studies, 32*, 330–355.

Marshall, J. M., & Haight, W. (2014). Understanding racial disproportionality affecting African American Youth who cross over from the child welfare to the juvenile justice system: Communication, power, race and social class. *Children and Youth Services Review, 9*(42), 82–90.

Marson S. M., DeAngelis D., & Mittal N. (2010). The association of social work boards' licensure examinations: A review of reliability and validity processes. *Research on Social Work Practice, 20*, 87–99. https://doi.org/10.1177/1049731509347858

Metzl, J. M. (2019). *Dying of whiteness: How the politics of racial resentment is killing America's heartland*. New York: Basic Books.

Mills, C. W. (1997). *The racial contract*. Ithaca, NY: Cornell University Press.

Miller, J., & Garran, A. M. (2007). The web of institutional racism. *Smith College Studies in Social Work, 77*, 33–67.

Miller, J. L., & Garran, A. M. (2017). *Racism in the United States: Implications for the helping professions* (2nd ed.). New York: Springer.

Miłosz, C. (1955). *The Captive Mind* (J. Zielonko, Trans.). New York: Vintage Books.

Mirelowitz, S. (1979). Implications of racism for social work practice. *The Journal of Sociology & Social Welfare, 6*(3), 297–312.

Morrow, D. F. (2022). Social work licensure and regulation in the United States: Current trends and recommendations for the future. *Research on Social Practice, 33*, 8–14. https://doi.org/10.1177/10497315221114175

Myers, Jr., S. L. (2011). *Response to a research synthesis on child welfare disproportionality and disparities*. In J. Fluke, B. J. Harden, M. Jenkins, & A Reuhrdanz (Eds.), Disparities and disproportionality in child welfare: Analysis of the research. Papers from a Research Symposium Convened by the Center for the Study of Social Policy and The

Annie E. Casey Foundation on behalf of the Alliance for Racial Equity Child Welfare (pp. 107–112).

NASW (2021). NASW apologizes for racist practices in American social work. New Releases. Retrieved from: https://www.socialworkers.org/News/News-Releases/ID/2331/NASW-apologizes-for-racist-practices-in-American-social-work.

Nienow, M., Sogabe, E., & Husain, A. (2023). Racial disparity is social work licensure exam pass rates. *Research on Social Work Practice, 33*, 76–83.

Novak, S. (2023, January 12). Half of the 250 Kids expelled from preschool each day are Black boys. *Scientific American.* https://www.scientificamerican.com/article/half-of-the-250-kids-expelled-from-preschool-each-day-are-black-boys/

Odera, S., Wagaman, M. A., Staton, A., & Kemmerer, A. (2021). Decentering Whiteness in Social Work Curriculum: An Autoethnographic Reflection on a Racial Justice Practice Course. *Advance in Social Work, 21,* 2/3, 801–820.

O'Neill, P. & Miller, J. (2015). Hand and glove: How the curriculum promotes an anti-racism commitment in a school for social work. *Smith College Studies in Social Work, 85*(2), 159–175. doi:10.1080/00377317.2015.1021222

Owen, S. (2021, September). How does ASWB guard against bias on the social work licensing exams. *The New Social Worker.* Retrieved from: https://www.socialworker.com/feature-articles/education--credentials/aswb-guard-against-bias-social-work-licensing-exams/

Park, Y. (2020). *Facilitating injustice: The complicity of social workers in the forced removal of and incarceration of Japanese Americans 1941–1946.* New York: Oxford University Press.

Rodgers, S. T. (2015, August). *Racism.* In C. Franklin (Ed.), Encyclopedia of social work online (ESWO) (21st ed.). New York, NY: Oxford University Press. https://doi.org/10.1093/acrefore/9780199975839.013.1009.

Schiele, J. H. (2020). *Social welfare policy: Regulation and resistance among people of color* (2nd ed.). San Diego, CA: Cognella.

Senreich, E., & Dale, T. (2021). Racial and age disparities in licensing rates among a sample of urban MSW graduates. *Social Work, 66,* 1, 19–28.

Specht, H., & Courtney, M. E. (1993). *Unfaithful angels: How social work has abandoned its mission.* New York: Free Press.

Sue, S., & Zane, N. (2006). Ethnic minority populations have been neglected by evidence-based practices. In J. C. Norecross, L. E. Beutler, & R. F. Levant (Eds.), *Evidence based practices in mental health* (pp. 329–337) Washington, DC: American Psychology Association.

Teasley, M. L., McRoy, R. G., Joyner, M., Armour, M., Gourdine, R. M., Crewe, S. E., Kelly, M., Franklin, C. G. S., Payne, M., Jackson, J., & Fong, R. (2017). Increasing success for African American children and youth (Grand Challenges for Social Work initiative Working Paper No. 21). Cleveland, OH: American Academy of Social Work and Social Welfare.

The Annie Casey Foundation. (2020, April 13). *Black children continue to be disproportionately represented in foster care.* Kids Count Data Center. https://datacenter.kidscount.org/updates/show/264-us-foster-care-population-by-race-and-ethnicity#:~:text=By%20comparison%3A%20White%20kids%20represent%2050%25%20of%20the,but%20only%201%25%20of%20its%20foster%20care%20population

Whitaker, T., Weismiller, T., & Clark, E. (2006). *Assuring the sufficiency of a frontline workforce: A national study of licensed social workers. Special report: Social work services for children and families.* Washington, DC: National Association of Social Workers.

Wilkerson, I. (2020). *Caste: The origin of our discontents.* New York: Random House.

William, C., & Parrott, L. (2014). Anti-racism and predominantly 'white areas': Local and national referents in the search for race equality in social work education. *British Journal of Social Work, 44*(2), 290–309.

3

Using Personal-Professional Narratives as a Technique for Teaching

Social Work Students about the Complexities of Racism

Tracy R. Whitaker, Ruby M. Gourdine, and Robert L. Cosby, Jr.

When we share our stories, we are reminded of the humanity in each other. When we take the time to understand each other's stories, we become more forgiving, more empathetic and more inclusive.
— Michelle Obama

One of the most pervasive and laudable goals of the social work profession is the creation of a society that is just and equitable for all its citizens. This goal was recently underscored in The Grand Challenges for Social Work, in which four of the 12 challenges focus primarily on the promotion of a just society (Grand Challenges, n.d.). The social work profession relies heavily on its educational apparatus to ensure that aspiring social workers not only are familiar with the goals of the profession, but also that they are provided the skills with which to achieve them. Social work education uses a competency-based framework that promotes the integration and application of knowledge, values, and skills. This framework also requires the demonstration and assessment of student competence. Social workers are trained to push toward the realization of an equitable society through their ability to engage persons of diverse and different backgrounds, and their ability to actively work toward social justice aims.

Two of the eight core competencies of social work education address diversity and difference and the advancement of social justice (CSWE, 2015). Competency Two specifically requires that social work programs

Tracy R. Whitaker, Ruby M. Gourdine, and Robert L. Cosby, Jr., *Using Personal-Professional Narratives as a Technique for Teaching* In: *Social Work and the Grand Challenge to Eliminate Racism*. Edited by: Martell L. Teasley, Michael S. Spencer, and Melissa Bartholomew, Oxford University Press. © Oxford University Press 2023. DOI: 10.1093/oso/9780197674949.003.0003

educate their students to "engage diversity and difference in practice," while Competency Three addresses the requirement that social work practitioners are able to "advance human rights and social, economic, and environmental justice" (CSWE, 2015, p. 7). Competency Two is explicit in its wording about understanding dimensions of diversity, power, oppression, and privilege; and Competency Three describes fundamental human rights and the role of social work in eliminating oppressive structural barriers. However, understanding and combating racism are not explicitly defined as core knowledge and skills that social work students should attain. These gaps notwithstanding, social work educators have a responsibility to address barriers to social justice in a way that facilitates the preparation of the next generation of social work practitioners (Edmonds-Cody & Wingfield, 2017). This preparation is particularly important as racism retains its place as one of the most intractable problems of the past four centuries (Crewe & Gourdine, 2019).

The overwhelming election and acceptance of Barack Obama as the 44th president of the United States led many to believe that the nation had overcome racism and had entered a "post-racial" period for the first time in the country's history. However, a flurry of disdain and hatred, fueled by some congressional leaders, ushered in a new era of increased racism and dampened the country's optimism. The nation saw relentless attacks, both political and personal, and President Obama's policy initiatives were opposed at every juncture (Enck-Wanzer, 2011). Understanding that all these issues were tied to race and racism provides teachable moments where history can offer and become the best way to enter into dialogue.

Racism persists as a major social justice barrier in part due to the inability of different groups of people to fully appreciate the complexities of racism (Miller & Garran, 2017). Racism is part of the social fabric of the United States and can be experienced on both individual and group levels. Racism can be codified into policies that deny access or benefits, constrict movement within and across sectors of the society, or thwart the economic and social progress of a particular group (Blank et al., 2004). Racism can be experienced broadly by several members of a group simultaneously, for example, Jim Crow Laws. However, racism can also be one of the most profoundly personal experiences a person can have. The experience of being discriminated against, targeted, attacked, or denied fundamental access to basic rights can engender feelings of anger, hostility, shame, depression, and hopelessness (Carter & Forsyth, 2010). Racism can also result in outcomes that extend beyond feelings and exhibit as undue stress, health disparities, food insecurity, poverty, and worse life chances (Crewe & Gourdine, 2019; Wan, 2019). The experience of racism is as complex and multilayered as the phenomenon itself.

Racism in the Helping Relationship

The current political climate bombards the society with the vestiges of White supremacy, intolerance, discrimination, and racism (Southern Poverty Law Center, 2020). Social workers, despite their fidelity to the principles of human rights and social justice, are not immune from the effects of racism. Some helping professionals are "targeted by it, others benefit from it, and still others have experiences of both privilege and oppression" (Miller & Garran, 2017, p. 105). Neither are they necessarily exempt from engaging in professional practice behaviors that are racist or oppressive.

Social workers ascribe to a professional code of ethics that encourages empowerment, respect, and partnership with client populations (NASW, 2017), but social work practice, both historically and currently, has been strongly linked to social control (Burman, 2004; Harp & Bunting, 2019; Wahab, 2002). The social work profession has often been criticized for not "practicing what it preaches" regarding racism (Clark et al., 2006; McMahon & Allen-Meares, 1992; Jeffery, 2006; NASW, 2007). James Dumpson, a social work educator, decried the hypocrisy of the social work profession, as he noted that there is a discrepancy between what we say we do and what we actually do (as cited in Gourdine & Brown, 2016).

In 2005, the National Association of Social Workers convened a "Social Work Congress" to identify social work imperatives for the next decade. Two of the twelve imperatives specifically addressed racism in social work education and practice (Clark et al., 2006). In the current climate, social work educators are challenged to help students understand racism as a complex phenomenon and its accompanying dynamics of exclusion and exploitation.

Indeed, even social workers' interventions with clients and communities can unwittingly be marred by racism, micro-aggressions, and the perpetuation of stereotypes (Constantine, 2007; Weng & Gray, 2020; Williams, 2013). Social workers and other clinicians can dismiss or minimize race-based trauma in the lives of their clients or ascribe to "colorblind" ideologies (Williams, 2013). Social work practice can also involve the support of agency and national policies that discriminate against people of color.

From field education to professional practice, social workers work with people who, by virtue of their proximity to social workers, need assistance with some aspect of their social functioning (Karls & Wandrei, 1994). In addition, the professionalization process itself can create or reinforce a false dichotomy, in which emerging professionals learn to present themselves as immune from the personal or social justice challenges that affect their clients. These challenges can include addiction, mental illness, poverty, and racism. Sometimes, social work educators use the "voice of clients" to help students better understand client motivations and to promote empathy. These narratives also provide models of discrimination, injustice, and inequality (Burack-Weis et al., 2017). "Stories" about clients can be interesting, but also seductive and voyeuristic. Although these narratives provide insight into lives that social work students would not ordinarily access, they may also reinforce the idea of the client as "the other," or someone with whom the student has limited opportunities for interaction or engagement. Social work educators must be careful that the use of narratives about client populations does not further stigmatize the people whom social work seeks to serve. Members of client populations can be exoticized to the point of non-recognition as members of the human family. Unlike client narratives, personal-professional narratives from faculty can model how to appropriately engage in self-disclosure and how to use authenticity in communication.

When working with client populations, social workers strive to be genuine, while maintaining appropriate professional boundaries. Navigating personal boundaries is important in learning to be skillful in delivering social services. Social work had historically advised emerging professionals to disclose truths about themselves to clients, carefully, guardedly, and rarely (Petersen, 2002; Raines, 1996) However, as the use of self-disclosure gained acceptance as an appropriate clinical tool (Anderson & Mandell, 1989), it has become more important that social workers know how to appropriately use this tool. Self-disclosure is an issue that social workers identify as a weakness in their social work education (Knight, 2012). Many social work students struggle to be authentic, while simultaneously not disclosing personal information about themselves to clients. The use of authenticity with clients can be controversial, as the art of self-disclosure should benefit the client, not the worker's need to share (Hepworth et al., 2016). Hepworth et al. (2016) define authenticity as "the sharing of self by relating in a natural, sincere, spontaneous, open, and genuine matter" (p. 117). Social work students may simultaneously want to be authentic, but also to be guaranteed a safe space for their authenticity.

When discussing sensitive topics such as racism and social justice issues, the classroom must become a safe space and provide an opportunity for students to practice using their authentic voices. Having discussions about social and racial justice issues, particularly as they relate to social policies, might be a way of enlightening students to the possible contradictions they may face as they work with and advocate for their clients. For example, they might begin to notice that some policies have dire consequences for the people they serve. These conversations must be broad and capable of having divergent opinions and can cause all involved to engage in self-reflection.

Challenges in Discussing Racism with Social Work Students

More than 60 years following the civil rights movement, conversations about race are still fraught with landmines. DiAngelo (2018) describes racism as the most complex dilemma since the founding of this country, and its associated challenges are equally complex. They include challenges of perspective; challenges of upbringing, of personal experience, of position, and of privilege, and some say a genealogy of racism (Su Rasmussen, 2011) with a pedigree of oppression and exploitation. Teaching the subject of racism can be daunting, as perspectives of otherness appear to separate the known White supremacists from the seemingly indifferent and benign observer who takes no stand against those "far right" folks (Goodman & Johnson, 2013; Saull, 2018).

In fact, to avoid discussing racism, some people ascribe to "colorblind" ideologies, or the idea that racism no longer exists. Bonilla-Silva (2014) posits that White people do not see themselves as evil or immoral, so the idea of being racist is diminished for them. DiAngelo (2018) asserts that racism speaks to moral character. In classrooms across the country, professors and students are reluctant to teach about it or to create opportunities to discuss firsthand experiences of racism, as dialogues about racism can elicit unpleasant emotions from all participants (Decuir-Gunby & Williams, 2007; Miller et al., 2004). If the student body is diverse with a majority of White students, the issue of privilege can be controversial. Racism is often denied, as most people do not acknowledge personal racism and bias. If African

Americans discuss racism, the victims of racism are often viewed as people who are angry, out of control, or doing something that justifies the racism. An example is the emergence of the Black Lives Matter movement that was born out of efforts to stop race-based policing. Until very recently, this movement had been widely viewed as a radical group and garnered negative reactions by many in society who countered this movement with "all lives matter" and "blue lives matter" mantras (Smith, 2017). Other people of color, who are not born in the United States, often have different experiences with racism and may not feel the "sting" of racism that African Americans often express. Given these dynamics, how can the university classroom become a safe and supportive place to discuss racism?

Racism is not experienced in a monolithic or homogeneous way. Racism affects social work students differently depending a variety of factors, including their experiences, their level of racial identity, and their cultural backgrounds (Miller & Garran, 2017). Students of color may have had direct experiences with racism, and those experiences are likely to exist on a continuum in terms of intensity and frequency. Similarly, White students' experiences with racism may also exist on a continuum that ranges from active participant to anti-racist ally. These differences aside, social work education strives to develop common ground from which social workers can effectively combat racism and engage in anti-racist practices. This common ground requires that social work students understand the ways that racism can manifest, as well as the consequences of its manifestation. One way to expose social work students to the complexities of racism is through the shared experiences of trusted mentors. Faculty members have a unique opportunity to influence the next generation of social workers through personal-professional narratives that explore the events and consequences of racism.

Teaching about the complexities of racism requires careful and thoughtful development of curricula, building from a perspective of strength with an eye toward inclusivity. Social work educators are called to speak truth to power, but presenting the information and giving social work students the opportunity to gain from that knowledge must be considered and shared in different ways.

The challenges of how faculty and students teach and learn about race and racism are not seen simply from a participant or observer standpoint. Discussing racism is one of the more difficult subjects to broach. Those who have not experienced racism often believe that is akin to other forms of discrimination, and there are obvious truths in those assumptions.

A particular barrier to understanding the complexities of racism is the difference in the perception of locus of control among different racial groups. White people in the United States tend to have a strong internalized sense of locus of control, and for many, their consequences are the direct result of their action or lack of action. African Americans and other people of color, however, experience consequences that do not always result from their actions, but from their occupation of black and brown bodies. For them, an externalized sense of locus of control is ordinary and they realize that many things are simply out of their control. Thus, when an African American is killed by the police, it makes sense for White people to immediately question, "what did he/she *do*?" They simply lack the context and experience of having or witnessing negative consequences without provocation. To many, it is inconceivable that a person would be harassed simply for existing. An extreme depiction of this dissonance is the alt-right term "dindu nuffin." This pejorative term is used to mock African Americans who are victims of police shootings. The term originated after the shooting of Michael Brown in Ferguson, Missouri. One "dindu nuffin" meme depicts a movie promo featuring a shirtless, young African American male, pointing a gun with a menacing expression. Across his chest is a blood-splatter, with the title, "Dindu Nuffins. He was a good boy," while the names of Trayvon Martin, Michael Brown, Darrien Hunt, and Jordan Davis appear behind his head as though they are the stars of the movie. Although this meme and term represent an extreme and horrific point of view, aspects of this view are clearly shared as victims of police shootings are criminalized in the media, although they are killed during the non-commission of crimes.

For social work educators of color, racial identity is not an abstract concept, but a very real and complex entity that contextualizes their personal and professional lives every day (Winston et al., 2004). They understand the duality of living with an internal locus of control, while accepting the inevitability of the external locus of control. Racialized experiences are a part of their life experiences, from the family member who picked cotton or tobacco, or the parent who was denied a mortgage loan, or the sale of their home because of imminent domain, to the parents who have had "the talk" with their children. When faculty share these experiences, they can breathe life into the classroom curriculum and teaching experience.

Use of Personal-Professional Narratives

Narratives can be used to allow social work students to reflect on their experiences as helping professionals (Riessman & Quinney, 2005) as well as to educate social work students about social justice issues (Bell, 2010). Personal-professional narratives can promote equity by elevating voices that reveal the extent of racism in the current society and by providing a lens through which others can gain insight into their own biases (Miller et al., 2020). Miller et al. (2020) use the term "counter-narrative" to include critical storytelling, counter-stories, and counter-narratives that are directly framed by Critical Race Theory and that promote equity by providing an alternative perspective to that of the mainstream. The use of personal-professional narratives by social work faculty of color provides rare glimpses into the lived experiences of social workers confronting social injustice in their own lives (Cosby & Grant, 2018; Crewe, 2004; Gourdine, 2004; Whitaker, 2018). For students from oppressed groups, these narratives can be empowering and affirming examples of using both their personal and professional "voices." For students from groups of privilege, these narratives can provide context for understanding the complexity of social justice. These personal-professional narratives allow educators to communicate with students in powerful, authentic ways that can lead to "courageous conversations" in and outside the classroom.

Faculty at an HBCU (historically Black college or university) in the Mid-Atlantic region of the country have used narratives in a variety of ways in the classroom. Through its history and legacy, the faculty have adopted a philosophy of the "Black Perspective," which has six guiding principles. These principles are incorporated throughout the curriculum, giving relevancy to the experiences of African Americans and other oppressed peoples.

In the first semester social work methods class, students are assigned the works of full-time faculty, which include some narratives. Among other issues, these narratives detail the faculty members' experiences with integration and with early career racism (Crewe, 2004; Gourdine, 2004). Other experiences included the use of a video narrative that expressed the pain associated with being a Black mother in the ongoing era of state violence against Black people (Whitaker, 2018). The school also produced a monograph on racism which collected first-person narratives that spoke to the experiences of African Americans who have confronted the painful experiences of racism. The use of the monograph in a class focused on the intersection of race, class, and gender proved to be helpful in exploring race and racism from different perspectives of social workers (Cosby & Grant, 2018).

USING PERSONAL-PROFESSIONAL NARRATIVES   67

These experiences are poignant, as students can see themselves through faculty experiences and determine that they too can address racism. Students with different life experiences can also began to learn about social justice issues that they might have not faced themselves, but now have a better understanding of how these issues might affect others. For example, an immigrant student may encounter and understand racism differently than an African American or White student. Giving space for that acknowledgment and discussion hopefully makes a more enlightened social worker.

Personal-Professional Narrative Case Study

Our social work program focuses on social justice and the civil rights of all. The faculty adopts as its philosophy the Black Perspective mentioned above, which is a set of six principles that focuses the students on social justice, affirmation, strengths, vivification, diversity, and internationalization. In an effort to practice authenticity, personal stories of challenges and successes of issues surrounding social justice are often shared. These stories and experiences, for faculty who are primarily African American and other people of color, often resonate with a population of students who fit the same description. This case will describe the experiences of one faculty member that is published in the journal *Reflections: Narratives of Professional Helping* (Gourdine, 2004). This account is assigned reading for foundation-level students.

The article begins with a brief description of a faculty member's upbringing during the civil rights era and her coming of age as civil rights were beginning to be implemented for many African Americans. However, the ascent into roles and positions that were primarily and previously assigned to White people was not easy and caused some consternation among her colleagues. This faculty member describes two job experiences as a new and young professional.

Juvenile Court Experience

I joined the juvenile court employee as a temporary worker. As a new college graduate, I was pleased to accept the position. The court system was segregated by race, so in essence there were two parallel systems. As an African American, I worked with African American women as the probation officer. I worked with four men and one other woman. A woman was a supervisor of the unit. I had the most affirming experience among these wonderful people. They were protective, as I was the youngest person there and new to the job. They were willing to help me learn the job and provided good life lessons as I worked to prove myself in this important position. They gave me confidence in my growing independence. However, in a conversation with the youngest male probation officer, we recognized that we were carrying very large caseloads which at times topped 100 cases, while the White probation caseloads were typically around 20 cases. We were not pleased about the disparity.

One day we saw an opportunity to address this disparity. The chief judge, who was a White man, appeared on a radio call-in show to describe the services of the court. The young man and I called in the show and queried him why the court was still segregated. He was not pleased, and I believed he was embarrassed to have to address this sensitive issue so publicly. I tell this story because it demonstrates advocacy, but also demonstrates that my colleague and I had no planned strategy beyond publicly announcing the problem. We were reprimanded for our actions. Advocacy may involve facing consequences. In retrospect, we could have done a better job of planning. However, we did see the court change its policies and began to integrate as expected, by law. There are a lot of lessons in this narrative. The questions that this process raised for me were:

1. Did desegregation change job opportunities for Blacks and Whites?
2. Did the courts believe any training was necessary for this transformation?
3. Did clients receive better services?

Child Welfare Agency

The next job I worked with was child welfare intake. I was recruited to apply for this position as the child welfare department had few Black workers. I was the youngest and only Black person in the unit. This job did not have the nurturing aspect of my first job; there, I had support from several Black administrators who checked in on me regularly to offer advice and support. My supervisor was supportive even though she did not always understand my perspective on issues as it related to race. Discussions during meetings with my coworkers were disturbing to me. There were incidences of macro- and microaggressions in that there was the use of a version of the "n" word regarding African American/Black clients. There were also comments about my reactions to these aggressions. I did not react initially but found that eventually I would speak out. Each coworker impacted me differently, as they saw race from their own vantage points. With the exception of one person who I felt was particularly insensitive, the others thought their ways of dealing with Blacks were the accepted norms. The major workplace challenge from my perspective was their need to develop the sensitivity required to address racism. I was able to learn from coworkers but also was awakened by their lack of sensitivity in some cases. Even my supervisor, who was the most open to racial issues, could make comments that made one gasp in disbelief.

It is not just the telling of these types of stories but analyzing them that is most helpful for students. How could one have responded? Were the strategies appropriate? Was there support for your approach? How did you handle these situations? How did they affect your self-esteem? These conversations allow for students to share their experiences when facing social justice issues, and to think about how they might respond to them and how they will use their change agency to address the inequalities in society.

In the example presented, the author had pioneering experiences with racism. However, other racialized experiences that are common today can also be explored, such as racism in the workplace, microaggressions, experiences while shopping, the misuse of summoning police, responses to complaints about racism, and strategies that parents employ to protect their children in racially hostile environments.

Evaluating Outcomes

At this crucial juncture in both American and social work history, it is imperative that students can demonstrate shifts in their understanding and behaviors regarding racism as a result of their social work education. Personal-professional narratives can be powerful sources of pain, authenticity, and marginalization, but sharing stories is not enough. Miller, Liu, and Ball (2020) have examined the use of narratives and their use in advancing the goals of educational equity for people of color for students in elementary education. Findings from the study show that these narratives are invaluable in revealing aspects of racialized reality, but there is less clarity regarding whether these narratives move into transformative action (Miller et al., 2020). The authors encourage the use of narratives to help students "develop their agency as well as their voices" (Miller et al., 2020, p. 293).

Evaluating students' understanding of the impact of racism on the lives of individuals, groups and communities from the use of narratives can happen in a number of ways. One way is to measures shifts in students' understanding of the complexities of racism. The students are given a "pretest" measuring their familiarity with and understanding of racialized experiences. The pretest consists of a set of statements provided to students at the beginning of the course, prior to the introduction of the narratives. These statements are broad, commonly held beliefs about behaviors attributed to people based on race, such as:

- Police officers' instructions are more likely to be ignored by African Americans.
- Affirmative action ensures that only the most qualified person is hired or promoted.
- People of color see discrimination when it does not exist.
- All parents have "the talk" with their children to keep them safe.
- Most of the time, police do not stop people unless they have a good reason to do so.
- "Black Lives Matter" excludes other people whose lives also matter.
- The judicial system is fair to all people, regardless of race.
- More Black people are in jail because Black people commit more crimes than White people.
- Grocery stores are evenly distributed throughout the city.
- People receive predictable consequences and rewards for their actions.

Students anonymously rate their agreement with the statements on a five-point scale ranging from strongly disagree to strongly agree. The instructor aggregates the scores for each item and presents them to the students as a starting point. After the narratives have been introduced and discussed, the same statements are presented to the students and scored as a post-test. The post-test results are reviewed for areas of shifting opinions. After the second set of scores is presented to students, the instructor engages in a discussion with students about what changed for them and why.

Implications for Practice

Sharing personal-professional narratives can move the social work profession toward more authentic conversations about understanding and eradicating racism (Miller et al., 2020). They can also mitigate the discomfort of discussing racism in the classroom and strengthen students as anti-racist practitioners.

Unlike policy discussions, narratives are from a single viewpoint and are not debatable regarding their veracity. Although they are personal, narratives do not end, but rather, can start conversations that promote growth and understanding. When students can understand the pain of racism from a person for whom there is already affinity and positive regard, the experience can be transformative. These narratives allow the student to "walk in the shoes" of someone familiar and safe, but with different life experiences. Students can also bear witness to the fear and courage that racism elicits. They can also begin to see their faculty as multidimensional people, with their own histories. Most importantly, they can understand how their social work voices can be powerful, even when they are vulnerable.

Summary and Conclusion

Using narratives as a part of social work education is a well-established practice. This approach is articulated in various social work texts and journal articles. What has been explicated here is a way to use narratives in an authentic way to have the difficult discussion about race. This chapter demonstrates the ways an HBCU has approached race discussions in the classroom. While acknowledging the difficulty of these conversation is important, it is also important to acknowledge that the education of social workers requires these conversations. Choosing silence over discomfort is not an acceptable option for social workers and constitutes too high a price for social work clients. Combating racism calls for a ready intervention in the social work profession. Regarding racism, there is a gap between the mission of social work and its actual practice. The profession should be a catalyst of change and demonstrate a real commitment to racial equity.

This chapter provides an opportunity for those who educate social workers to use personal-professional narratives as a technique to provide opportunities for real discussions on race. It is undeniable that racism has impacted the social work profession, and we now are seeing in real time, through videos, the ways in which racism can hurt people of color. Encouraging faculty to be open about their own experiences can be a solid first step in helping social work students understand the complexities of racism. Assessing students' understanding and their emotional affect from being exposed to such experiences can enhance knowledge and strengthen skill development in the creation of anti-racism practices. The time has come for the social work profession to confront this grand challenge and actively participate in the eradication of racism.

Study Questions

1. How is racism imbedded into social policies?
2. What are some of the ways that racism is perpetuated in communities?
3. Is there a role for social work education in eradicating racism?
4. How can narratives help students gain a greater sensitivity toward another person's experience with racism?
5. Should students use their authentic voices when working with clients, especially if there are racial/class differences? Identify potential pitfalls.
6. How do personal/professional narratives differ from client narratives?
7. Are there potential risks for faculty of color in sharing narratives with their students? What are some examples?
8. How can someone examine whether their own biases promote racist ideology?
9. What does it mean to be anti-racist?
10. Should social work students be expected to be anti-racist? Why or why not?

References

Anderson, S. C., & Mandell, D. L. (1989). The use of self-disclosure by professional social workers. *Families in Society, 70*(5), 259–267. https://doi.org/10.1177/10443894890 7000501.

Bell, L. A. (2010). *Storytelling for social justice: Connecting narrative and the arts in anti-racist teaching*. New York: Routledge.

USING PERSONAL-PROFESSIONAL NARRATIVES   73

Blank, R. M., Dabady, M., & Citro, C. F. (Eds.). (2004). *Measuring racial discrimination: Panel on methods for assessing discrimination.* National Research Council. Washington, DC: The National Academies Press.

Bonilla-Silva, E. (2014). *Racism without racists: Color-blind racism and the persistence of racial inequality in the United States* (4th ed.). Lanham, MD: Rowman & Littlefield.

Burack-Weis, A., Lawrence, L. S., & Mijangos, L. B. (2017). *Narrative in social work practice: The power and possibility of story.* New York: Columbia University Press.

Burman, S. (2004). Revisiting the agent of social control role: Implications for substance abuse treatment. *Journal of Social Work Practice, 18*(2), 197–209. doi:10.1080/0265053042000231016.

Carter, R. T., & Forsyth, J. (2010). Reactions to racial discrimination: Emotional stress and help-seeking behaviors. *Psychological Trauma: Theory, Research, Practice, and Policy, 2*(3), 183–191. https://doi.org/10.1037/a0020102.

Clark, E., Weismiller, T., Whitaker, T., Waller, G., Zlotnik, J., & Corbett, B. (2006). *2005 Social Work Congress: Final report.* Washington, DC: NASW Press.

Constantine, M.G. (2007). Racial microaggressions against African American clients in cross-racial counseling relationships. *Journal of Counseling Psychology, 54*(1), 1–16.

Cosby, R., & Grant, R. (Eds.). (2018). *Race and the intersection of abuse, power and control: Research & reflections from the Black perspective.* Washington, DC: Howard University School of Social Work and the Multidisiciplinary Gerontology Center.

Council on Social Work Education. (2015). *2105 Educational policy and accreditation standards for baccalaureate and master's social work programs.* Alexandria, VA: CSWE.

Crewe, S. E. (2004). A time to be silent and a time to speak up. *Reflections: Narratives of Professional Helping, 10*(1), 16–25.

Crewe, S. E., & Gourdine, R. M. (2019). Race and social policy: Confronting our discomfort. *Social Work in Public Health, 34*(1), 1–11.

Decuir-Gunby, J. T., & Williams, M. R. (2007). The impact of race and racism on students' emotions: A critical race analysis. In Paul A. Schutz & Reinhard Pekrun (Eds.), *Emotion in Education* (pp. 205–219). Cambridge, MA: Elsevier, Academic Press. https://doi.org/10.1016/B978-012372545-5/50013-7.

DiAngelo, R. (2019). *White fragility: Why it's so hard for white people to talk about racism.* Boston: Beacon Press.

Edmonds-Cody, C., & Wingfield, T. (2017). Social workers: Agents of change or agents of oppression? *Social Work Education, 36*(4), 430–442.

Enck-Wanzer, D. (2011). Barack Obama, the Tea Party, and the threat of race: On racial neoliberalism and born-again racism. *Communication, Culture & Critique, 4*(1), 23–30.

Goodman, S., & Johnson, A. J. (2013). Strategies used by the far right to counter accusations of racism. *Critical Approaches to Discourse Analysis across Disciplines, 6*(2), 97–113.

Gourdine, R. M., & Brown, A. W. (b2016). *Social action, advocacy and agents of change: Howard University School of Social Work in the 1970s.* Baltimore, MD: Black Classic.

Gourdine, R. M. (2004). A beginning professional's journey toward understanding equality and social justice in the field of social work. *Reflections: Narratives of Professional Helping, 10*(1), 73–81.

Grand Challenges. (n.d.). Grand challenges for social work. Retrieved from https://grand challengesforsocialwork.org/#the-12-challenges.

Harp, K. L., & Bunting, A. M. (2019). The racialized nature of child welfare policies and the social control of black bodies. *Social Politics: International Studies in Gender, State & Society*, 27(2), 258–281. https://doi.org/10.1093/sp/jxz039.

Hepworth, D. H., Rooney, R. H., Rooney, G. D., & Strom- Gottfried, K. (2016). *Direct social work practice: Theory and skills*. Boston, MA: Cengage Learning.

Jeffery D. (2006) What good is anti-racist social work if you can't master it? Exploring a paradox in anti-racist social work education. *Race, Ethnicity and Education*, 8(4), 409–425. doi:10.1080/13613320500324011.

Karls, J. M., & Wandrei, K. E. (1994). *Person-in-Environment system: The PIE classification system for social functioning problems*. Washington, DC: NASW Press.

Knight, C. (2012). Social workers' attitudes towards and engagement in self-disclosure. *Clinical Social Work Journal*, 40(3), 297–306.

McMahon, A., & Allen-Meares, P. (1992). Is social work racist? A content analysis of recent literature. *Social Work*, 37, 533–539. https://doi.org/10.1093/sw/37.6.533.

Miller, J., Hyde, C. & Ruth, B. (2004). Teaching about race and racism in social work: Challenges for white educators. *Smith College Studies in Social Work*, 74(1), 409–426.

Miller, J. L., & Garran, A. (2017). *Racism in the United States: Implications for the helping professions* (2nd ed.). New York: Springer.

Miller, R., Liu, K., & Ball, A. (2020). Critical counter-narrative as transformative methodology for educational equity. *Review of Research in Education*, 44, 269–300.

National Association of Social Workers. (2007). *Institutional racism and the social work profession: A call to action*. Washington, DC: NASW Press.

National Association of Social Workers. (2017). *Code of ethics of the National Association of Social Workers*. Washington, DC: NASW Press.

Peterson, Z. D. (2002). More than a mirror: The ethics of therapist self-disclosure. *Psychotherapy: Theory, Research, Practice, Training*, 39(1), 21–31. https://doi-org.proxyhu.wrlc.org/10.1037/0033-3204.39.1.21.

Raines, J. (1996). Self-disclosure in clinical social work. *Clinical Social Work Journal*, 24(4), 357–375.

Reissman, C. K., & Quinney, L. (2005). Narrative in social work: A critical review. *Qualitative Social Work*, 44(4), 391–412.

Saull, R. (2018). Racism and far right imaginaries within neo-liberal political economy. *New Political Economy*, 23(5), 588–608.

Smith, D. (October 31, 2017). The backlash against Black Lives Matter is just more evidence of injustice. *The Conversation.com*. Retrieved from https://theconversation.com/the-backlash-against-black-lives-matter-is-just-more-evidence-of-injustice-85587.

Southern Poverty Law Center. (2020). Hate and extremism. Retrieved from https://www.splcenter.org/issues/hate-and-extremism.

Su Rasmussen, K. (2011). Foucault's genealogy of racism. *Theory, Culture & Society*, 28(5), 34–51.

Wahab, S. (2002) "For their own good?": Sex work, social control and social workers, a historical perspective. *The Journal of Sociology & Social Welfare*, 29(4), 39–57.

Wan, W. (August 2, 2019). Racism has devastating effects on children's health, pediatricians warn. *Washington Post*. Retrieved from https://www.washingtonpost.com/health/racism-has-devastating-effects-on-childrens-health-pediatricians-warn/2019/08/02/ce5fc96a-b313-11e9-8f6c-7828e68cb15f_story.html.

Weng, S. S., & Gray, L. (2020) Racial microaggressions within social work: Perceptions of providers. *Journal of Social Work Practice, 34*(1), 67–80. doi:10.1080/02650533.2018.1553871.

Whitaker, T. (2018). The fatigue of racism. In R. Cosby & R. Grant (Eds.), *Race and the intersection of abuse, power and control: Research and reflections from the Black perspective* (pp. 60–63). Washington, DC: Howard University School of Social Work and the Multidisciplinary Gerontology Center.

Williams, M. (June 30, 2013). How therapists drive away minority clients. *Psychology Today*. Retrieved from https://www.psychologytoday.com/us/blog/culturally-speaking/201306/how-therapists-drive-away-minority-clients.

Winston, C. E., Rice, D. W., Bradshaw, B. J., Lloyd, D., Harris, L. T., Burford, T. I., et al. (2004). Science success, narrative theories of personality and race self-complexity: Is race represented in the identify construction of African American adolescents? *New Directions for Child and Adolescent Development, 106*, 55–77.

4

Eradicating Racism

Social Work's Most Pressing Grand Challenge

Abril N. Harris, Smitha Rao, Manuel Cano, Bongki Woo, Ty Tucker,
Dale Dagar Maglalang, and Melissa Wood Bartholomew

> *I have almost reached the regrettable conclusion that the Negro's great stumbling block in the stride toward freedom is not the white Citizens Councilor or the Ku Klux Klanner, but the white moderate who is more devoted to order than to justice.*
>
> —Martin Luther King Jr. (1963)

In 2019, over half (58%) of U.S. adults reported poor race relations in the country (Horowitz et al., 2019). Scholars argue that the widening discord among racial groups is associated with the "Trump effect"—the upsurge of hate crimes related to former president Donald J. Trump's discriminatory rhetoric targeting Black, Indigenous, and People of Color (BIPOC) and other oppressed groups (Edwards & Rushin, 2018). The global uprising in the demand for racial justice in response to the deaths of George Floyd, Breonna Taylor, Ahmaud Arbery, and many other Black individuals, including Black trans man Tony McDade, at the hands of the police in the United States, and white people, as in the case of Arbery, is a harrowing reminder that systemic racism and white supremacy remain rampant. These murders, along with countless other racially motivated murders, such as the murders of 23 Latinx individuals of Mexican heritage who died as a result of the mass shooting in El Paso, Texas, in August 2019, are contemporary examples of racial violence. Furthermore, the racist rhetoric of associating the COVID-19 virus with Asian Americans incited over 2,500 hate crimes targeting Asian Americans

Abril N. Harris, Smitha Rao, Manuel Cano, Bongki Woo, Ty Tucker, Dale Dagar Maglalang, and Melissa Wood Bartholomew, *Eradicating Racism* In: *Social Work and the Grand Challenge to Eliminate Racism*. Edited by: Martell L. Teasley, Michael S. Spencer, and Melissa Bartholomew, Oxford University Press. © Oxford University Press 2023. DOI: 10.1093/oso/9780197674949.003.0004

during March–August 2020 alone (Darling-Hammond et al., 2020; Jeung & Nham, 2020).

Nevertheless, it is imperative to acknowledge that racism has been ever-present, even before the colonization of the United States, fueled by capitalist endeavors, and actualized through the murder of Native Americans and the enslavement of Africans (Sweet, 1997). Racism was built and embedded over time in ideologies, policies, institutions, and systems that situated white people at an advantage (Kendi, 2016). Whereas it is one of the numerous forms and systems of oppression in this country and globally, we explicitly name racism as an antecedent that dictates and influences how groups are able to access institutions and power (Bassett, 2017). Evidently, in analyzing racism, intersectionality (Crenshaw, 1989, 1991) must also be considered to understand how socially constructed categories that touch upon power and oppression (Nash, 2008) are distributed, maintained, and transformed (Cho et al., 2013).

The Grand Challenges of Social Work (GCSW) initiative by the American Academy of Social Work & Social Welfare (AASWSW), anchored by leading members of the social work profession, articulate the foremost societal challenges that social workers need to tackle. Until AASWSW announced eliminating racism as the new 13th Grand Challenge in 2020, race and racism were not as explicitly interwoven into the initial 12 grand challenges, even though they remain central to the issues social workers grapple with. A content analysis of the 21 concept papers making up the initial 12 Grand Challenges showed gaps in how race/ethnicity and racism are present within the explications of the challenges before the profession (Rao et al., 2021). While mentions of race/ethnicity were fairly high, racism was not a common consideration in the extant concept papers. Challenges specifically examining outcomes for racial minorities were explicit about racism and the pernicious impacts thereof, but most challenges either steered clear or alluded to some form of discrimination without naming racism. Hence, the newly created Grand Challenge to Eliminate Racism is a much-needed stepping stone to make our commitment to racial justice and anti-racism more explicit and intentional across all ecological dimensions of social work. This chapter provides a lens and context for social workers to introspect and understand our profession's history and current stature, to be able to imagine how we can be agents of change in order to help create a more just and equal society.

78 ABRIL N. HARRIS ET AL.

In this chapter, we examine the history of racism and the use of race as a differentiating factor in the United States as well as in the social work profession. We begin with a conceptualization of race and racism and the conditions that led to racism being embedded into institutions and systems as we know them today. It is critical to understand this history, not just in the case of the country, but also what it means for the profession of social work to continue disrupting systems that perpetuate this form of oppression. We then take a look at how social work institutions such as the Council for Social Work Education (CSWE) engage with race and racism, with examples from the profession of committees working to address and dismantle racism. This background helps to situate the urgency of why eradicating racism needs to be front and center for a profession that aims to tackle intersecting systems of oppression. Racism is the foremost challenge of America (Davis, 2016) and social work needs to reckon with our own positionality and responsibilities in inheriting, furthering, not questioning (enough), and not challenging the status quo of racism in the United States.

Conceptualization of Racism

The formation of race as a category to differentiate between colonized and enslaved groups of people by Western Europeans, through false biological beliefs of the superiority of white people and whiteness over other groups (Cooper & David, 1986), has bestowed and operationalized racism as we know it. Racism as a concept has been operating for several centuries (Fredrickson, 2015). However, its first recorded use was in 1902 when Richard Henry Pratt, advocate of the establishment of boarding houses for Native Americans, articulated it in a speech criticizing racial segregation (Demby, 2014). Over time, the definition of racism has been contested by scholars to comprehend what it truly comprises. David Wellman's definition of racism states that racism is a system of advantage based on race (Wellman, 1993). Wellman argues that white supremacy culture afforded white people an unjust advantage in all institutions, creating a system that benefits them disproportionately compared to others. Bonilla-Silva (2006) extended our understanding of racism and proposed "color-blind racism" to encompass the subtle forms of discrimination based on race that those in power use through the employment of race-neutral words and terms that otherwise gesture the racialization of groups, thus maintaining white supremacy.

Others characterize racism as a combination of power and prejudice which, as Hoyt Jr. (2012) contends, relieves people of color from being held accountable to performing what would be considered racist behaviors and attitudes. Instead, Hoyt (2012) offers the use of race-based oppression to delineate the use of power and authority over a group of people based on their race to discriminate against them at micro (interpersonal) and macro (institutional) levels. Alternatively, Kendi's (2019) definition suggests that racism is a collection of racist policies, supported by racist ideas, that forge racial inequity. In this chapter, we conceptualize racism as an inequitable system and power based on race.

Racism and the History of Social Work

Since its inception, social work has consistently demonstrated its reluctance to take an anti-racist approach to the social problems plaguing society (Berman-Rossi & Miller, 1994; Stubbs, 1984). By acknowledging and confronting the racist history of social work, we can rectify our wrongs and move toward a practice of liberation (Freire & Moch, 1990; Reisch, 2002). Often, the history of social work is presented in ways that highlight the charitable nature and commitment to social justice among early social workers. The early social workers showed dedication to uplifting communities and demanding policy measures that provided resources and welfare to communities that needed them (Reisch, 2002). However, service provision in the late nineteenth and early twentieth centuries by social workers reveals a more sinister legacy that has implications for the current state of the profession in the United States (Garcia, 1971; Park, 2008; Reisch, 2008).

Social work ideas and practice germinated from charitable work practiced by white women, predominantly belonging to the middle to upper echelons of society. Designated as "friendly visitors," they anchored their charitable welfare in morality, based on Protestant religiosity, and the recipients of their good deeds were assessed for moral fiber and "deservingness" (Reisch & Andrews, 2002). The influx of immigrants during the early 1900s encouraged others to begin thinking about addressing the needs of these new members of American society (Carlton-LaNey, 1999; Reisch & Andrews, 2002). Wealthy, educated white women who were unable to participate in legitimate professions of the time were able to find their niche and dedicate their lives to improving the lives of the poor and downtrodden (Reisch & Andrews, 2002).

While this women-led field generated key policy changes and provision of goods and services to those who needed it, there was a systematic exclusion of Black, Indigenous, Latinx, and Asian people from the beneficence of these early social workers (Carlton-LaNey, 1999; Garcia, 1971; Park; 2008; Reisch, 2008, Weaver, 2000).

Radicalism is evidentiary throughout social work history, as many of the revered social work pioneers were involved in creating social change and were active in policymaking. Despite this history, there are lesser-known truths about how white social workers limited their radical tactics to certain groups. During the Progressive era, social work responses were often rooted in the dominant white culture that focused on ideas of assimilation, separatism, and "color blindness" (Reisch, 2008). These approaches to social welfare continued to beset the social work profession and greatly impacted how they interacted with and provided services to racial minorities (Weaver, 2000). The history of social work often focuses on the accomplishments of social work pioneers like Jane Addams and Mary Richmond and shows social work as a "benevolent institution requiring only superficial fine tuning" to meet the needs of racial minorities (Stubbs, 1984, p. 7). Further investigation demonstrates that the clear individualistic nature of early social work did little to address the structural issues faced by racial minorities.

Settlement houses, the crown jewels in social work history, were segregated and were largely reserved for poor European immigrants (Berman-Rossi & Miller, 1994; Stubbs, 1984). Due to the essentialism of the European immigrant experience, racial minorities were often excluded from the social welfare opportunities provided to whites (Carlton-LaNey, 1999). A majority of settlement houses refrained from providing services to Black people; in 1911, 10 of the 413 settlement houses were exclusively serving Black people (Berman-Rossi & Miller, 1994). While acknowledging the contributions of social workers in creating a more just society in critical periods of U.S. history that shaped policies and institutions (Reisch & Andrews, 2002), our purpose here is to expound on the ways in which the social work profession supported institutionalized racism through racial segregation.

Consistent with the ideology of the 1920s and beyond, early social workers were convinced that the etiology of social problems was due to cultural and genetic deficiencies (Berman-Rossi & Miller, 1994; Gibson, 2015; Park, 2008). Social workers actively incorporated eugenics into social responses to the impoverished and/or racial groups not classified as white (LaPan & Platt, 2005). Francis Galton, an English scientist and statistician, theorized the inherently racist "science" of eugenics that attributed deviant behavior and low intelligence to genetic deficiencies and encouraged societies to promote the breeding of those with superior "human fitness," as to prevent the degeneration of the human race (Gibson, 2015). Social workers during the Progressive era, at the height of the eugenics movement, engaged in classifying young women as degenerates. Young women who had the misfortune of receiving such a classification were policed and often were recommended for institutionalization, and in extreme cases, sterilization (Kennedy, 2008). Consistent with cultural and genetic deficiency theories of the day, young African American women were more likely to be designated as degenerates by social workers of the time (Kennedy, 2008). Eugenic ideals did not remain prominent in social work practice, but the implicit understanding of whites as the model of "human fitness" persisted (Loya, 2011). Thus, the exclusion of racial minorities from social welfare benefits was pervasive and long-lasting. Due to the neglect experienced by racial minorities during the development of the welfare state, many communities of color were forced to rely on fostering their own groups' success in the midst of a racially hostile environment (Reisch, 2008).

As part of the Great Migration from the South to the North, Black Americans created their own settlement housing and social service programming that focused on cultural ideals like mutual aid, racial pride, and self-help (Carlton-LaNey, 1999). Black reformers formed their own social work schools to train Black social workers who were equipped to deal with the needs in their community. Like the Black community, Latinx and Asian communities were virtually ignored by white social workers for decades (Reisch, 2008). Due to the lack of attention and scarcity of resources provided by "legitimized" social welfare organizations, many of these communities asserted their own autonomy. Chicano communities modeled their efforts based on their informal kinship systems (Reisch, 2008). Their social welfare community responders, known as *mutualistas*, created mutual aid responses that aligned with the cultural heritage and identity of Chicanos (Garcia, 1971; Reisch, 2008). Chicanos rejected notions of assimilation and instead developed housing resources, legal services, emergency loans, and resistance to racial discrimination, using their own practices (Reisch, 2008). The diverse composition of the Asian American diaspora during the early twentieth century caused fragmentation in service provision, with cultural enclaves using different methods to address the needs in Japanese, Chinese, Korean, and Filipino communities (Park, 2008). However, Asian immigrant enclaves were able to create agricultural associations, provide care for the sick, and establish other internal organizations that provided a wide range of social welfare resources (Reisch, 2008; Park, 2008).

While social welfare providers of color were advocating and working to uplift their communities, the social work field participated in the domination and hindrance of any progress that communities of color attempted to make (Berman-Rossi & Miller, 1994). Social workers have been described as an "extension of colonization" because they often work in bureaucratic systems on behalf of the state. Social workers working in partnership with the U.S. government have helped facilitate racist and traumatic policies that continue to impact people today. The California State Department of Social Welfare and its social workers actively participated in evacuating, relocating, and ultimately interning people of Japanese ancestry in concentration camps during World War II (Park, 2008). While German and Italian immigrants were groups of interest due to the role of their countries of origin in the war, they were not identified as candidates for exclusion (Park 2008). Social workers referred to Japanese residents and citizens as "alien enemies" and assisted in their transfer (Park, 2008). Years prior, social workers were agents in the removal of Native American children from their homes to be relocated to boarding schools to morph young Native Americans to fit within the dominant culture (Park, 2008; Weaver, 2000). Social work's role in creating environments of trauma for Native American youth has had a lasting impact on the community, with Native communities still distressed at the recall of being removed from their families (Weaver, 2008). These historical elisions highlight the disciplinary dilemmas that the field of social work continues to wrestle with today.

American social work was conceptualized in the minds of middle- and upper-class white women, and in pursuit of legitimacy and professionalization, the field then continuously measured its worth by the standards set by white middle- and upper-class men (Berman-Rossi & Miller, 1994). This origin story set the tone for how social work continued to develop since the early nineteenth century (Carlton-LaNey, 1999; Reisch, 2008). Social workers continue to struggle with activism around issues pertaining to racism and other forms of oppression (Carlton-LaNey, 1999; Reisch, 2002). The needs of Black, Indigenous, Latinx, and Asian communities still warrant attention within social work practice, research, and policy. Incremental diversion to more individualized practice and social service institutionalization have also impacted the ability of the field to address the egregious harms created by systemic oppression, namely racism (Reisch, 2002; Stubbs,

1984). The residues of such ideologies echo in the present, as scholars continue to interrogate whether or not social work is racist through the paucity and invisibilization of BIPOC literature in the social work canon (Corley & Young, 2018; McMahon & Allen-Meares, 1992). Freire shares that history "is made by us, and as we make it, we are made and remade by it" (Freire & Moch, 1990, p. 6). Upon reflection, it is clear that it will take immense mobilization and accountability to confront the racist and obstructionist history of the social work profession.

Social Work's Efforts to Eradicate Racism

The history of the discipline offers an important contextual foundation for the necessary work of self-examination that social workers must continually engage in. This section explores how racism manifests at different levels, including at the intrapersonal, interpersonal, and institutional levels, and offers some ways forward.

Intrapersonal Efforts to Eradicate Racism

The first step toward liberation begins with transforming the mind (Freire, 1970). Beginning at the intrapersonal level, eradicating racism requires a continual exploration of personal biases, privileges, and positions that each individual carries. The social work profession has permeated the intimate environment of people's homes, as well as government institutions in the United States. The National Association of Social Workers (NASW) Code of Ethics dedicates a section on ethical standards related to cultural awareness and diversity in social work practice with others, and yet, there is no ethical standard that requires an individual social worker to engage in self-reflective work that would equip them to intensely comprehend how their own biases and perceptions might impact their work in diverse communities. Internalized oppression and domination are terms rarely used in social work; a review of the social work code of ethics and competencies reveals no evidence of a consideration of the impact of internalized oppressive ideologies on the profession (Green et al., 2005).

Social work education focuses on teaching diversity, or courses focused on equity and inclusion of racial minorities, to prepare students for practice in multicultural communities. In doing so, the underlying assumption is that white is normal and the experiences of BIPOC are, by contrast, a departure from this norm (Loya, 2011). Orientation in the dominant culture among social workers, in particular white social workers, can be detrimental to communities that encounter racially uncritical practitioners (Garcia, 1971; Nicotera, 2010). Internalized racism among people of color is defined as the "inculcation of racist stereotypes, values, and images perpetuated by the white dominant society about one's racial group" (Pyke, 2010, p. 553). However, among white people this phenomenon is referred to as internalized domination, and those same racist ideals and values are internalized, fostering beliefs that they are superior and that their privileged status is the societal norm (Bell et al., 2016). This makes it more likely that one will encounter racial minorities and attribute their experiences to individualized factors as opposed to the structural racism that maintains inequities in society. A study by Green et al. (2005) found that white social workers, in general, have overwhelmingly positive views of racial minorities, but when topics of affirmative action and desire to have close relationships with people of color were posed, they were more inclined to show some reluctance. Loya's (2011) study on "color-blind" racial attitudes among white social workers found that white social workers did not deny the validity of institutional racism, but demonstrated decreased ability to acknowledge racial privilege and critical racial issues. Interestingly, in a sample (n = 995) of white social workers, nearly 95% saw themselves as culturally competent. Culturally responsive social work becomes impossible if a social worker has little to no knowledge of the ways that they may be perpetuating Eurocentric ideals and values onto communities of color (Nicotera, 2010).

Engaging in critical self-investigation is important for both minoritized social workers and those social workers who benefit from white privilege. Yet, white social workers may struggle with internalized domination, while working within systems and institutions created for their benefit (De Silva et al., 2007). Nearly 85% of licensed social workers self-identify as white, and thus the likelihood that a white social worker will be working in a BIPOC community is high (Loya, 2011). People of color have been known to experience culturally irresponsible interactions with white social workers (Garcia, 1971; LaNey, 1999; Weaver, 2000), but these harmful interactions can be minimized or eradicated with critical self-work. Lack of self-awareness of privileges and unwillingness to take responsibility for one's own learning and unlearning processes precludes allyship in the fight for racial justice

(Spencer, 2008). Progressive social work can only be achieved through the union of "what is said" and "what is done"; one cannot cling to ideals of anti-racism and yet continue to perpetuate racist ideals in practice (Freire & Moch, 1990, p. 9).

In order to confront biases and privilege, it is necessary to consider one's social position/perspective and to challenge inherent assumptions. Many institutions in which social workers are immersed are steeped in "Western," "Eurocentric," "white," cis-gendered, heteronormative, and neoliberal structures, perspectives, values, and practices, as highlighted by theories of whiteness:

> Our educational and clinical institutions are not culturally empty spaces within which people from different cultural contexts engage. Rather, they are firmly penetrated by the values and commitments of authoritarian, white perspectives. (Allen, 2006, p. 72)

Eradicating racism requires acknowledging and challenging the often-overlooked implicit frames of reference that social workers may hold, wherein white is the standard and the norm, and all else is deemed "the other" (Davis, 2018; Nylund, 2006).

Interpersonal Efforts to Eradicate Racism

Social workers have an ethical call to understand the importance of diversity in shaping the human experience while managing personal biases and presenting as learners (as opposed to experts) of others' experiences (Council on Social Work Education, 2015). Social workers are also responsible for learning about, recognizing, and acknowledging historical as well as current oppression, inequity, and exclusion. Efforts to eradicate racism are often conceptualized around actions at a societal, policy, or institutional level, and understandably so. Nevertheless, eradicating racism is a commitment (albeit implicit) that must pervade both intrapersonal and interpersonal levels. This commitment manifests across multiple personal and professional roles, including, for example, the social worker as a lifelong learner (e.g., by choosing to study race and racism), the social worker as a practitioner (e.g., by validating others' accounts of racial/ethnic discrimination), or the social worker as an academic (e.g., by investigating and uncovering racial/ethnic disparities).

At the interpersonal level, social workers can work toward eradicating racism both in how they intentionally and unintentionally relate to others. Although cultural competence has traditionally been viewed as the standard for interacting with individuals associated with racial/ethnic minority groups, cultural competence proposes to attain the unattainable—becoming competent in understanding other cultures (Fisher-Borne et al., 2015). Cultural humility, on the other hand, recognizes the ongoing and never-ending process of "self-reflection and self-critique" that demands perhaps not so much knowledge of the "other" as a change in one's attitudes and approach toward others (Fisher-Borne et al., 2015). Social workers who advocate for anti-racist practices must engage in and be exposed to ongoing opportunities to explore implicit biases in order to better understand the journeys, struggles, and barriers that BIPOC have endured.

Unbeknownst to many social workers, merely understanding human diversity and social differences does little to eradicate racism. An anti-racist agenda acknowledges that actions centered on dismantling racism do not begin with conversations centered on celebrating racial/ethnic differences (Davis, 2016), but rather with conversations centered on the biases and inequities that such racial/ethnic constructions cause and perpetuate. While systemic changes are key to eradicating racism, it is at the intra- and interpersonal levels that such changes might originate, by adopting and fostering anti-racist attitudes and interactions that are needed to spark higher-order change. Furthermore, ongoing efforts directed at eradicating racism will demand actions that extend beyond the professional realm. As individuals embedded into multiple and overlapping domains, social workers are responsible for applying an anti-racist agenda in every part of their lives and interactions.

Institutional Efforts to Eradicate Racism

Social workers are responsible for recognizing the institutional racism surrounding them and using their professional knowledge to ameliorate it through practices at every level (De Silva et al., 2007). Social work organizations, including the National Association of Social Workers (NASW), the Council on Social Work Education (CSWE), and the National Association of Deans and Directors of Schools of Social Work (NADD), have identified that racism needs to be addressed through social work education and practice

(Clark et al., 2006; De Silva et al., 2007). Since institutional racism manifests at the socioeconomic, educational, and political levels within which social workers operate, a thoughtful self-assessment of the profession can help to gain a better understanding of racism and to make institutional-level efforts to eradicate racism.

Social work educational institutions strive to meet the educational guidelines of the CSWE's (2015) accreditation standard that requires programs to "provide a learning environment that models affirmation and respect for diversity and differences" (p. 14). However, there have been concerns that the emphasis on cultural diversity and multicultural practice can detract from the deep-rooted institutionalized racism and racial stratification (Abrams & Gibson, 2007; Davis, 2016). Relatedly, a content analysis of social work explicit curricula revealed that, although social work courses have largely promoted diversity and differences, there are opportunities to allocate greater attention to disparities and inclusion to promote active engagement in essential conversations around injustice and oppression (Woo et al., 2022). It would behoove CSWE to make anti-racism an explicit requirement in social work education curricula in order for social work programs to maintain or obtain accreditation.

One important curricular effort to challenge racism and a Eurocentric approach to social work is to integrate content such as Critical Race Theory, white privilege, and internalized racism into social work curricula and all aspects of education (Abrams & Gibson, 2007; National Association of Social Work [NASW], 2007; Miller et al., 2004). Educating students regarding this content can foster students' critical racial consciousness and help them learn how to more effectively intervene in institutional racism that permeates social work concerns (Abrams & Gibson, 2007). In addition, an emphasis on BIPOC scholars' voices and work in the curriculum can help racial/ethnic minority students and faculty find representation in the school and curriculum and can equip students with capacities to promote inclusion in working with their clients and agencies (Woo et al., 2022). To effectively teach this content in the classroom, instructors need support from their peers (e.g., co-teaching courses on racism and other systems of oppression with professors from various racial backgrounds) and institutions (e.g., program's commitment to the content; Abrams & Gibson, 2007; Comerfold, 2003). Additionally, department search committees should intentionally search and hire BIPOC faculty and administrators and be critical of hiring white faculty researching BIPOC communities, in order to decolonize research spaces (Fine et al., 2000). In doing so, social work education institutions can periodically assess the extent to which their implicit and explicit curricula have given attention to the content around disparities, inclusion, and anti-racism.

Social work organizations possess the potential to become anti-racist entities (NASW, 2007). Individual members of the organization can constantly engage in professional development to better recognize racism surrounding their clients and their communities and to acquire necessary knowledge and skills (NASW, 2007). In addition to individual social workers' efforts, the organizational decision-makers' role is crucial in taking deliberate steps to fight racism. Leadership can explicitly address the organization's intention to avoid institutional racism at all levels and to develop clearly defined goals, benchmarks, and measurable plans to prioritize culturally inclusive practices (Walter et al., 2017). In doing so, organizations can create senior management positions, such as a racial justice ambassador who creates continued institutional processes (e.g., staff training programs, supervision, and/or evaluation protocols), promotes abilities (e.g., searches, recruits, interviews, hires, and mentors a diverse workforce), and creates a culture of dialogue (e.g., to constructively facilitate and manage essential conversations on race and anti-racist practices) (Cano, 2020), to promote inclusion, equity, and justice within organizations. Further, active partnerships with other organizations and groups in racial/ethnic minority communities can help the organization understand concerns and their perceptions in the community and help to build community-focused solutions to address racism (Walter et al., 2017; McLeod et al., 2017).

In addition, social work associations, such as the NASW, CSWE, and NADD, must continue to play key leadership roles in promoting the profession's commitment to eradicating racism on a larger scale (NASW, 2007). For example, though CSWE does not provide a discussion on race/racism within the code of ethics, the organization does have the Council on Racial, Ethnic, and Cultural Diversity (CRECD). The CRECD is a council of the Commission for Diversity and Social and Economic Justice that promotes expanding the knowledge base for educators, students, and alumni through education and by disseminating and encouraging research about members of historically and emerging underrepresented groups (Council of Social Work Education, 2015). The NASW and CSWE have a unique leadership role in addressing and eradicating racism. NADD, in its role to engage in developing leaders for the social work profession, created and implemented an Anti-racism Action Plan in 2021. There are several academic institutions that have utilized their leadership and position to address racism within the profession, but these examples remain few and far between.

Institutions devoted to social work education, policy, or practice must continually consider whether their institutional policies are perpetuating a status quo that is dominated by white perspectives to the exclusion of all others. Such policies may relate to staff recruitment, hiring, workforce management, and service provision, among others. Institutions must also endeavor to foster an organizational climate that makes their commitment toward anti-racism explicit, and may begin by defining, operationalizing, and monitoring initiatives for the dismantling of racism. Institutions must recognize that they cannot bring BIPOC individuals into a space that is racist and rely on optics to absolve themselves from committing to anti-racism. Often, inclusionary tactics entail that white people are "including" BIPOC people into their space by enacting policies and practices that are palatable to their comfortability. Rather, it should involve the dismantling of this white space itself.

Conclusion

The social work profession is rooted in service, social justice, dignity and worth of the person, importance of human relationships, integrity, and competence (NASW, 2008). These core beliefs are the foundation to our profession and have informed ethics, curriculum, scholarship, and practice. Although these beliefs were designed to be flexible within the context and complexity of the human experience, we have allowed the inimical realities of racism to be easily erased by more agreeable terms like "diversity" and "inclusion.: Rev. Dr. Martin Luther King, Jr.'s words at the beginning of this chapter caution us that a moderate approach to change will not lead to the structural and social transformation that is required to eradicate racism. When social workers do not challenge existing white supremacist systems, and therefore maintain the status quo, they become a greater stumbling block to freedom, liberation, and self-determination for all. Nearly 60 years hence, the moderate approach to incremental change and reform have done more to stall racial justice efforts than the now normalized white supremacist structures. This chapter has provided a brief grounding of social work's history that we need to remain cognizant of, and offers possible avenues to upend white supremacy culture at multiple levels: the personal, interpersonal, and institutional. This collective redress can go a long way in addressing systemic racism in social work and the society that our profession is embedded in. We must make social work's commitment to eradicating systemic racism explicit and institutionalized through the 13th Grand Challenge if we are resolute in our desire to attain racial justice for us all and for future generations.

Study Questions

1. What are some of the ways in which social work has been complicit in maintaining white supremacy and racist practices?
2. We assert that social workers have been described as an "extension of colonization" because of their entanglements with bureaucratic state systems that have helped to facilitate racist and traumatic policies. What are some contemporary examples of social work policies and/or practices that are extensions of colonization?
3. How does an uncritical view of the history of social work affect present-day practice and research, and how can we confront it?
4. Has reading about the racist history of social work impacted your understanding of how racism functions and what is required to eradicate it within U.S. society and culture? If so, how?
5. Examine social work's settlement house movement through an anti-racist lens. What key elements should be added to social work syllabi to present a complete historical account of the settlement house movement?
6. What are some examples of social reform, service provision, and mutual aid championed by and for communities of color in the United States? What sets them apart from the established models of service provision?
7. What will you do as a social worker to advance anti-racist praxis across intrapersonal, interpersonal, and institutional levels?
8. If you are a social worker who identifies as white, what specific steps can you take in your institution to illuminate the existence of racism and white supremacy culture, particularly for other white social workers, and to advance the work of eradication?
9. Can you identify efforts your organization is making to ensure that it is not perpetuating "a status quo that is dominated by white perspectives to the exclusion of all others"?

ERADICATING RACISM   91

References

Abrams, L. S., & Gibson, P. (2007). Teaching notes: Reframing multicultural education: Teaching white privilege in the social work curriculum. *Journal of Social Work Education, 43*(1), 147–160.

Allen, D. G. (2006). Whiteness and difference in nursing. *Nursing Philosophy, 7*(2), 65–78.

Bassett, M. T. (2017). Public health meets the problem of the color line. *American Journal of Public Health, 107*(5), 666–667. https://doi.org/10.2105/AJPH.2017.303714.

Bell, L. A., Funk, M. S., Joshi, K.Y., & Valdivia, M. (2016). Racism and White privilege. In M. Adams, L. A. Bell, D. J. Goodman, & K. Y. Joshi (Eds.), *Teaching for Diversity and Social Justice* (3rd ed., pp. 133–182). New York, NY: Routledge.

Berman-Rossi, T., & Miller, I. (1994). African-Americans and the settlements during the late nineteenth and early twentieth centuries. *Social Work with Groups, 17*(3), 77–95. https://doi.org/10.1300/J009v17n03_06.

Bonilla-Silva, E. (2006). *Racism without racists: Color-blind racism and the persistence of racial inequality in the United States* (2nd ed.). Lanham, MD: Rowman & Littlefield Publishers.

Cano, M. (2020). Diversity and inclusion in social service organizations: Implications for community partnerships and social work education. *Journal of Social Work Education, 56*(1), 105–114.

Carlton-LaNey, I. (1999). African American social work pioneers' response to need. *Social Work, 44*(4), 311–321. https://doi.org/10.1093/sw/44.4.311.

Cho, S., Crenshaw, K. W., & McCall, L. (2013). Toward a field of intersectionality studies: theory, applications, and praxis. *Signs: Journal of Women in Culture and Society, 38*(4), 785–810. https://doi.org/10.1086/669608.

Clark, E. J., Weismiller, T., Whitaker, T., Waller, G. W., Zlotnik, J. L., & Corbett, B. (Eds.). (2006). *2005 Social Work Congress: Final report.* Washington, DC: NASW Press.

Comerfold, S. A. (2003). Enriching classroom learning about diversity: Support and strategies from a qualitative study. *Journal of Social Work Education, 23*, 159–183.

Cooper, R., & David, R. (1986). The biological concept of race and its application to public health and epidemiology. *Journal of Health Politics, Policy and Law, 11*(1), 97–116. https://doi.org/10.1215/03616878-11-1-97.

Corley, N. A., & Young, S. M. (2018). Is social work still racist? A content analysis of recent literature. *Social Work, 63*(4), 317–326. https://doi.org/10.1093/sw/swy042.

Council on Social Work Education (CSWE). (2015). Educational policy and accreditation standards for baccalaureate and master's social work programs. Retrieved from https://www.cswe.org/getattachment/Accreditation/Standards-and-Policies/2015-EPAS/2015EPASandGlossary.pdf.

Crenshaw, K. (1989). Demarginalizing the intersection of race and sex: A Black feminist critique of antidiscrimination doctrine, feminist theory and antiracist politics. *University of Chicago Legal Forum, 1989*(1), 139–168. https://chicagounbound.uchicago.edu/uclf/vol1989/iss1/8.

Crenshaw, K. (1991). Mapping the margins: Intersectionality, identity politics, and violence against women of color. *Stanford Law Review, 6*, 1241–1300. https://heinonline.org/HOL/P?h=hein.journals/stflr43&i=1257

Darling-Hammond, S., Michaels, E. K., Allen, A. M., Chae, D. H., Thomas, M. D., Nguyen, T. T., Mujahid, M. M., & Johnson, R. C. (2020). After "the China virus" went viral: Racially charged coronavirus coverage and trends in bias against Asian

Americans. *Health Education & Behavior, 47*(6), 870–879. https://doi.org/10.1177/1090198120957949

Davis, C. U. (2018). Laying new ground: Uprooting white privilege and planting seeds of equity and inclusivity. *Journal of Dance Education, 18*(3), 120–125.

Davis, L. E. (2016). Race: America's grand challenge. *Journal of the Society for Social Work and Research, 7*(2), 395–403.

De Silva, E. C., Jackson, V., Oldman, V., Schachter, R., Wong, J., Lopez, L., & Richards, D. (2007). *Institutional racism and the social work profession: A call to action.* Washington, DC: National Association of Social Workers.

Demby, G. (2014). The ugly, fascinating history of the word "racism." *NPR.* https://www.npr.org/sections/codeswitch/2014/01/05/260006815/the-ugly-fascinating-history-of-the-word-racism.

Fine, M., Weis, L., Weseen, S., & Wong, L. (2000). For whom? Qualitative research, representations, and social responsibilities. In N. Denzin and Y. Lincoln (Eds.), *Handbook of Qualitative Research* (pp. 167–207). Thousand Oaks, CA: Sage.

Fisher-Borne, M., Cain, J. M., & Martin, S. L. (2015). From mastery to accountability: Cultural humility as an alternative to cultural competence. *Social Work Education, 34*(2), 165–181.

Fredrickson, G. M. (2015). *Racism: A short history.* Princeton, NJ: Princeton University Press. http://www.jstor.org/stable/j.ctvc779fw.

Freire, P. (1970). *Pedagogy of the oppressed* (M. B. Ramos, Trans.). New York: Continuum.

Freire, P., & Moch, M. (1990). A critical understanding of social work. *Journal of Progressive Human Services, 1*(1), 3–9.

Garcia, A. (1971). The Chicano and social work. *Social Casework, 52*(5), 274–278.

Gibson, M. F. (2015). Intersecting deviance: Social work, difference and the legacy of eugenics. *The British Journal of Social Work, 45*(1), 313–330.

Green, R. G., Kiernan-Stern, M., & Baskind, F. R. (2005). White social worker's attitudes about people of color. *Journal of Ethnic and Cultural Diversity in Social Work, 14*, 47–68. doi: 10.1300/J051v14n01_03.

Horowitz, J. M., Brown, A., & Cox, K. (2019). Race in America 2019. Pew Research Center. Retrieved from https://www.pewsocialtrends.org/2019/04/09/race-in-america-2019/.

Hoyt, C., Jr. (2012). The pedagogy of the meaning of racism: Reconciling a discordant discourse. *Social Work, 57*(3), 225–234. https://doi.org/10.1093/sw/sws009.

Jeung, R., & Nham, K. (2020). *Incidents of coronavirus-related discrimination: A report for A3PCON and CAA.* Retrieved from http://www.asianpacificpolicyandplanningcouncil.org/wp-content/uploads/Stop_AAPI_Hate_Weekly_Report_4_3_20.pdf.

Kendi, I. X. (2016). *Stamped from the beginning: The definitive history of racist ideas in America.* New York, NY: Nation Books.

Kendi, I. X. (2019). *How to be an antiracist.* New York, NY: One World.

Kennedy, A. C. (2008). Eugenics, "degenerate girls," and social workers during the Progressive Era. *Affilia: Journal of Women and Social Work, 23*(1), 22–37. doi: 0.1177/0886109907310473.

King, M. L. (1963, April 16). Letter from the Birmingham jail. Retrieved from https://kinginstitute.stanford.edu/king-papers/documents/letter-birmingham-jail.

LaPan, A., & Platt, T. (2005). 'To stem the tide of degeneracy': The eugenic impulse in social work. In S.A. Kirk (Ed.), *Mental disorders in the social environment: Critical perspectives* (pp. 139–164). New York: Columbia University Press.

Loya, M. (2011). Color-blind racial attitudes in White social workers: A cross-sectional study. *Smith College Studies in Social Work, 81*, 201–217. doi: 10.1080/00377317.2011.589341

McLeod, B. A., Gilmore, J., & Jones, J. T. (2017). Solutions to structural racism: One organization's community-engaged approach in the aftermath of civil unrest. *Social Work, 62*(1), 77–79.

McMahon, A., & Allen-Meares, P. (1992). Is social work racist? a content analysis of recent literature. *Social Work, 37*(6), 533–539. https://doi.org/10.1093/sw/37.6.533.

Miller, J., Hyde, C. A., & Ruth, B. J. (2004). Teaching about race and racism in social work: Challenges for White educators. *Smith College Studies in Social Work, 74*, 409–426.

Nash, J. C. (2008). Re-thinking intersectionality. *Feminist Review, 89*(1), 1–15. https://doi.org/10.1057/fr.2008.4

National Association of Social Workers. (2007). *Institutional racism and the social work profession: A call to action*. Washington, DC: NASW.

National Association of Social Workers. (2008). *Code of ethics of the National Association of Social Workers*. Washington, DC: NASW.

Nicotera, N., Walls, N. E., & Lucero, N. M. (2010). Understanding practices issues with American Indians: Listening to practitioner voices. *Journal of Ethnic & Cultural Diversity in Social Work, 19*, 195–216. doi: 10.1080/15313204.2010.499321.

Nylund, D. (2006). Critical multiculturalism, whiteness, and social work: Towards a more radical view of cultural competence. *Journal of Progressive Human Services, 17*(2), 27–42.

Park, Y. (2008). Facilitating injustice: Tracing the role of social workers in the World War II internment of Japanese Americans. *Social Service Review, 82*(3), 447–483. doi: 0037-7961/2008/8203-0004

Pyke, K. D. (2010). What is internalized racial oppression and why don't we study it? Acknowledging racism's hidden injuries. *Sociological Perspectives, 53*(4), 551–572.

Rao, S., Woo, B., Maglalang, D. D., Bartholomew, M., Cano, M., Harris, A., & Tucker, T.B. (2021). Race and ethnicity in social work grand challenges. *Social Work, 66*(1), 9–17. https://doi.org/10.1093/sw/swaa053

Reisch, M. (2002). Defining social justice in a socially unjust world. *Families in Society, 83*(4), 343–354.

Reisch, M. (2008). From melting pot to multiculturalism: The impact of racial and ethnic diversity on social work and social justice in the USA. *British Journal of Social Work, 38*, 788–804. doi: 10.1093/bjsw/bcn001.

Reisch, M., & Andrews, J. (2002). *The road not taken: A history of radical social work in the United States*. New York, NY: Brunner-Routledge.

Edwards, G. S., & Rushin, S. (2018, January 18). The effect of President Trump's election on hate crimes. *SSRN Electronic Journal*, 1–24. https://doi.org/10.2139/ssrn.3102652.

Spencer, M. S. (2008). A social worker's reflections on power, privilege, and oppression. *Social Work, 53*(2), 99–101.

Stubbs, P. (1984). The employment of Black social workers: From ethnic sensitivity to anti-racism. *Critical Social Policy, 4*(12), 6–27.

Sweet, J. H. (1997). The Iberian roots of American racist thought. *The William and Mary Quarterly, 54*(1), 143–166. https://doi.org/10.2307/2953315.

Walter, A. W., Ruiz, Y., Tourse, R. W. C., Kress, H., Morningstar, B., MacArthur, B., & Daniels, A. (2017). Leadership matters: How hidden biases perpetuate institutional racism in organizations. *Human Service Organizations: Management, Leadership & Governance, 41*(3), 213–221.

Weaver, H. N. (2000). Activism and American Indian issues. *Journal of Progressive Human Services, 11*(1), 3–22. doi: 10.1300/J059v11n01_02.

Wellman, D. T. (1993). *Portraits of white racism.* Cambridge: Cambridge University Press.

Woo, B., Cano, M., & Pitt-Catsouphes, M. (2022). Equity and justice in social work explicit curriculum. *Journal of Social Work Education, 58*(3), 611–618.

5

Ending Racism

A Critical Perspective

Harold E. Briggs and Martell L. Teasley

> *If we are to seek new goals for our struggles, we must first reassess the worth of the racial assumptions on which, without careful thought, we have presumed too much and relied on too long.*
>
> —Bell (2018, p. 14)

The fulfillment of a democracy that exacts equal justice to all requires reflection. Given the present climate, it is critical to review our storied past to retrace how we have arrived at our current state of racial strife. Consequently, examining the origins of whiteness surfaces as the best segue to commence our critical discourse. The genesis of structural inequalities and the receipt of all resources as well as the quality-of-life benefits to be reaped in America has historical roots that can be traced back to laws and policies (Themba-Nixon, 2001). These laws and policies preserved such entitlements of White privilege to Caucasian Americans (Irons, 2022; Rothstein, 2017). Such privilege exists for Caucasian Americans, while exact justice for people of color remains unobtainable (Themba-Nixon, 2001). The metastasized effects of structural racism are best highlighted in the 1967 Kerner Commission Report, its 2017 follow-up study (Christopher, 2021), and in research by Du Bois and Eaton (1899).

Reputed as landmark research of the effects of racism on African Americans, the Du Bois and Eaton study is informative and instructive. It is the earliest record of the study of the effects of systemic racism on African Americans. The study data showed how racism is a socially constructed infection when inextricably linked to poverty, disease, and poor health and leads to chronic illness and early death (Jones-Eversley & Dean, 2018). The study memorializes the period of time following legalized slavery, the Jim Crow era, in which America continued to lack moral clarity to mitigate the

Harold E. Briggs and Martell L. Teasley, *Ending Racism* In: *Social Work and the Grand Challenge to Eliminate Racism*. Edited by: Martell L. Teasley, Michael S. Spencer, and Melissa Bartholomew, Oxford University Press.
© Oxford University Press 2023. DOI: 10.1093/oso/9780197674949.003.0005

furtherance of legalized structural racism. No longer lawful, reputed as excessive by Adolph Hitler, and marveled by the Dutch, who used it to establish the South African system of apartheid, the impact of Jim Crow laws on its victims is expected to be far reaching yet remains unknown.

Despite its morally clear mission to pursue equal justice socially responsibly for the vulnerable, the profession of social work failed to act to mitigate the sustained unjust treatment of African Americans post-slavery. What would life have been like if the original Civil Rights Act of 1866 legislation would have been inspired by the profession and was fully ratified? Let's do not forget, as we envision a post-apartheid America, that our justice mandate includes social policies that reduce the racial wealth gap and reverse the nonexistent wealth-generation status of non-White citizens. If the early framers of this country can charitably pay former Caucasian slaveowners reparations for losing their slave investments, we can task our current leadership with authorizing payment of compensatory damages to the Black and Brown survivors of structural racism and inequalities. Visualize if the Supreme Court of 1883 had decided not to authorize housing segregation which would have violated the 1866 Civil Rights Act legislation (Rothstein, 2017). The absence of the 1883 Supreme Court decision to allow housing segregation would have upheld the intent of the 1866 Civil Rights Act. Further imagine that the Homestead Act allowed African Americans and First Nation people to own land and sell land to Caucasian because the Homestead Act paid for the land owned by the First Nations. To preserve collaboration between nations, the United States in partnership with the First Nations enacted an equal opportunity lottery for claiming land. To complete this dream, imagine the 40 acres and a mule reparation policy was fully ratified. What a dream! Does it remind you of Martin Luther King's dream? Exact justice or nothing. Redressing its civil rights missteps requires social work to own and advance such a post-apartheid vision in twenty-first-century America. It also requires social work to mitigate its perpetuation of white supremacy (Hafen, 2022), cease and avoid advancing use of the "anything but race" perspective and to call out racism in all forms (Thomas, n.d; https://citeseerx.ist.psu.edu).

To date and of note is the dearth of research that examines the empirical foundations of anti-racism approaches in mitigating structural racism. As far back as post-slavery, social assistance to African Americans was defined as race work (Banks et al., 2018). Race work was not condoned as social work, which was named "good works" (Banks et al., 2018). Aiding African Americans was an unpopular act of social responsibility, tantamount to a social taboo. There was a considerable degree of risk of attacks from White supremacy sympathizers that accompanied giving aid to African Americans prior to the 1960s. Race work was taken up by a few activists and civic-minded foot soldiers who wanted to help African Americans (Bowles et al., 2016).

Race work was excluded from the profession's originating agenda of gender preferences, enhancing its methodological capacity (Claghorn, 1927), and preserving its envisioned inter-professional status as a science (Reid, 2001; Thyer, 2004). These aims took priority over its ethical commitment to confront oppression and obtain equal justice (Briggs et al., 2019). Relegation of its obligations to redress anti-Black racism was an act of racism. The profession betrayed its mission and ethical foundations. For social work to establish its credibility as a social justice profession, it must avoid aiding in the direct and indirect proliferation of structural racism. For example, social workers need to recognize the upstream and downstream role that racial bias and anti-racism inaction has in preserving the racial disproportionate and disparate experiences. African American families are tethered to government surveillance, child welfare, and temporary need assistance through family service systems. Freeing families from such bondage requires a responsive anti-racism paradigm (Briggs et al., 2021).

To prioritize anti-racism as a key performance indicator of the profession of social work's mission and social justice aims, we suggest the following: (1) the profession of social work attenuate practices of *seeing no evil* (denying racism), *saying no evil* (censoring speech on racism), *doing no evil* (voter suppression legislation and lack of civil rights enforcement protections); (2) the profession of social work partner with specific organizations to aid in achieving the closing in of the racial wealth gap and the acquisition of the social determinants of health for African American, First Nation, and other people of color (Yearby, 2018); (3) abolish the use of structural racism and gender privileging pathways embedded within the institutional and inter-institutional cultures of academic and professional social work (Jones, 2018); and (4) endorse equal justice for African Americans and other indigenous groups as a profession-wide anti-racism, achievable aim within this generation. Beyond committing to these aims, the profession of social work owes African Americans and other people of color an overdue apology for its participation in racism (Christopher, 2021). Committing to these aims alone will not pardon the profession from its abdication of its equal justice ethical foundations. Social work's racial indifference and conspiracy of silence amid well-documented accounts of its social justice omissions are evidence of its glaring inaction (Banks et al., 2018; Briggs, Holosko, et al., 2018; Hopps, 1982; Poole, 2006; Bowles et al., 2016).

The profession-wide pursuit of anti-racism aims is both emblematic and a time-sensitive social welfare imperative. Transparently launching a full-scale anti-racism paradigm in real time will challenge us to learn publicly from our micro- and macro-aggressions, blatant errors, and omissions due to race. Pursuing an anti-racism paradigm will need to be guided by a process of privileging anti-racism, which brings with it the shift in equitable access to power and equal justice as a human right. Unlike a diversity framework. an anti-racism paradigm involves the deliberate naming and adoption of the profession's post-apartheid vision and strategic anti-racism paradigm through which it will hold itself and society accountable. The profession-wide adoption of a post-apartheid vision and an anti-racism paradigm would undeniably demonstrate the profession's intent to abolish racism, and obtain exact justice and racial equity. In furtherance of these formidable aims and despite its recent currency, whiteness, racial inequality, and White privilege, which are woven into U.S. culture, institutions, and individual behaviors of many Whites, can be traced back historically to the country's founding (Chrobot-Mason et al., 2020, p. 4). In contemporary America, their sustainability is due in part to the aftereffects of the early misinterpretation of the U.S. Constitution, along with systemic forces with embedded racial distinctions across and within institutions (Baron, 1969; Bowser, 2017; Harp & Bunting, 2020; Irons, 2022; Rothstein, 2017). In fact, many present-day structural inequalities and lack of access to resources that enhance well-being have been accompanied by the criminalization of social problems (Davis, 2000). Such structural inequalities result from attempts to solve overt and legal forms of inequality that were simultaneously crafted to maintain the interests of Whites (Rothstein, 2017). Thus, structural racism is a legal invention shielded by U.S. law (Irons, 2022). Ironically, attenuating structural racism will depend on legal redress and new legislation.

With this backdrop in mind, this chapter reviews the available clinical and organizational literature to present conceptual frameworks to use in designing practice approaches to eliminate racism at the interpersonal and systemic levels of attention. In this chapter, we discuss: (1) the sustainability of racism in America; (2) the origins of racism by legislative fiat and policy de jure in America; (3) building a race consciousness-raising and anti-racism practice and theory development narrative; (4) realizing structural and policy approaches to use in achieving the aims of anti-racism; and

(5) examining anti-racism practice perspectives and methods for addressing structural and interpersonal racism.

The Sustainability of Racism in America

A major reason racism is sustained in America is due to the sanction of structural racism through institutional policies, inter-institutional arrangements, and laws (Briggs & Paulson, 1996; Irons, 2022). It is also sanctioned by the conspiracy of silence reflected in the sustained trauma and life-threatening deprivation experienced by non-White, minoritized populations (Danielle, 1998). By definition, a conspiracy of silence involves the reframing of typical noxious reactions; the numbing of adverse reactions to trauma exposure by both the victims and the perpetrators (Heldke & O'Connor, 2004). Briggs, Briggs, and Briggs (2019) lament the consequences of the conspiracy of silence involving African Americans as the normative and predictable silence within society that is often upheld by the people who benefit and know better (p. 22).

Consequently, insulated structural and interpersonal racism systems, White supremacy, and White privilege are inextricably linked as functions of social control. First, they inconspicuously preserve Whites' self-interest, while assuring their dominance in the United States (Briggs et al., 2019; Themba-Nixon, 2001). Second, they are the intractable conduits, which preserve the racial disparities and racial disproportionate burdens encountered by racial and ethnic people and communities (Roberts, 2008; Themba-Nixon, 2001).

Racism by Legislative Fiat and De Jure

The privileging of laws and policies with embedded distinctions that assign both benefits and penalties on the basis of race guarantees the proliferation of structural racism in America (Briggs & Paulson, 1996; Irons, 2022; Rothstein, 2017). Privileging racism occurs when acts of racial injustice such as voting rights restriction are deemed lawful, despite their racist intent and effects. Voting rights suppression laws are not uniform nationwide. Voting rights suppression laws differ across jurisdictions from one form of exclusionary race-based policy and/or system of voter suppression regulation to another. What they share in common is the disproportionate fate of voter suppression on Black and Brown voting people. For example, the Thirteenth and Fourteenth Amendments to the U.S. Constitution, which were established to help solidify the legal freedom of Black Americans, played a dual function. With the initial intent to strengthen the rights of citizenship, they helped to preserve the integrity of dominance, power, privilege, and practices that disallow access to civil and human rights for Black and Brown people. Ratified into law in 1865, the Thirteenth Amendment was stated to abolish slavery; yet it codifies peonage as the continuation of slavery beyond the Emancipation Proclamation. Stated in the following clause of the Thirteenth Amendment: "Neither slavery nor involuntary servitude, except as a punishment for crime whereof the party shall have been duly convicted, shall exist within the United States, or any place subject to their jurisdiction" (p. xx). The exceptions clause within the Thirteenth Amendment, referring to those "duly convicted," led to convict leasing laws and statutes after the Civil War lasting into the 1940s. Black codes were simultaneously enacted throughout Southern states, creating the legal context for the convict leasing system. To put it plainly, even though the Thirteenth Amendment abolished slavery and involuntary servitude, it left room for using punishment of a crime as a surrogate.

In contemporary times, the spirit and intent of the Thirteenth Amendment provides the legal grounds assisting in the creation of a nationwide for-profit prison-industrial complex that predominately and disproportionately incarcerates Black and Latinx populations. Although the rate has declined significantly since 2007, African Americans are 13% of the U.S. population, but constitute 33% of the prison sentence population, which is six times that of Whites (Epperson et al., 2018; Gramlich, 2019). Conversely, Caucasians represent "64% of adults but 30% of prisoners. And while Hispanics represented 16% of the adult population, they accounted for 23% of inmates" (Gramlich, 2019, p. 1).

Furtherance of the denial of remedies for racial injustices against Black and Brown people is articulated in the Fourteenth Amendment of the U.S. Constitution. Passed in 1868, the Fourteenth Amendment safeguards against reparations for the loss of slaves due to emancipation and legal remedies for the institutionalized mistreatment of enslaved people in this country. In particular, sections one and two of the Fourteenth Amendment provide protections for all people born within the United States as citizens with the right to vote, and just as important, provided due process and equal protection under the law. However, "[d]espite legislation intended to provided enforcement of these rights, the laws were poorly enforced, and most were subsequently declared unconstitutional" (Bell, 2004, p. 11).

Despite legal declaration of equal treatment under the law, systemic racism then shifted to legal segregation as the method to maintain White dominance and power. The standard-bearer for legal segregation was codified with the case of *Plessy v. Ferguson*. In 1896, a Black man, Homer Plessy, attempted to ride in a Whites-only railroad car on a train in New Orleans, Louisiana. Arrested and convicted under Louisiana's 1890 segregation law, Plessy petitioned the U.S. Supreme Court for redress. In acknowledging absolute equality under the law as found in the Fourteenth Amendment, the U.S. Supreme Court contended that the Amendment did not intend "to abolish distinction based on color. . . ." This decision gave the green light to continue and enhance legal segregation throughout the country, which it did. For public schools, hotels, stores, entertainment, water fountains, and even cemeteries, legal segregation was the order of the day until the *Brown* decision in 1954.

Building a Race Consciousness-Raising and Anti-Racism Practice and Theory Narrative

From a critical race perspective, this is all an illustration of the interest-convergence covenants, as defined by Bell (2004). He observed, "Black rights are recognized and protected when and only so long as policymakers perceived that such advances will further interests that are their primary concern" (p. 49). The *Brown* decision was timely, in that it coincidently came about as the United States battled communist threats to American democracy; thus it had international symbolism of America's movement toward racial equality. Conversely, the "all deliberate speed" clause in *Brown II* (1957) set up a legal loophole for states and localities. Its vagueness allowed states to disregard any pressing mandate to integrate public schools. Over time, coupled with major legal battles over school zoning laws and suburban municipalities' ability to restrict tax revenues, today's public-school systems are, in general, a microcosm of racial disparities in wealth, housing, and other asset holdings. Hence, school access is a race latent factor in America that reflects racialized disparities in outcomes.

Any serious effort in ending racism in twenty-first-century America will need to align its nonviolent anti-racism and equal justice efforts to achieve racial equity in the treatment of Black and Indigenous people in America. The first step in addressing the elimination of racism within organizations is to create a culture of critical race conscience, which involves calling out racism and injustice. Assessing the means and conditions that create advantages for Caucasians while disadvantaging persons of color is essential to naming, shaming, taming, and calling out racism. Simply put, racism is also a mental process and learned behavior to which people are exposed in the socialization process. If the country wants to eliminate racism, it must likewise educate people to be anti-racist in the socialization process.

Calling out injustice by authentically exposing racism and its intractable effects is extremely valuable, even if it causes pain to recount the experience. Expelling the silence breaks the denial of its existence. Calling out racism breaks up the relationship between inaction and indifference, which are the dependable accomplices in sustaining social injustice. In social work, Larry Davis (2016) urged social work researchers to focus more on studying issues of race and racism, which he believes are both America's original sin and forgotten grand challenge. Increasing the number and scope of research on race and racism is expected in the profession of social work, given the recent calls to actions by Corley and Young (2018) and others such as Banks, Hopps, and Briggs (2018) and Briggs, Holosko, Banks, Parker, and Huggins-Hoyt (2018). The increased focus on the study of racism is expected given the recent decision to identify ending racism as the 13th Grand Challenge for social work by the American Academy of Social Work and Social Welfare in 2020. Along with increased research, the profession will experience an intense focus on theory development in the future study of racism in social work.

As a context for ending racism, some scholars have called for theory development to facilitate understanding of the perpetual nature of racism. In this vein, Bowser (2017) calls to action the further development of a testable theory of racism that integrates cultural, institutional, and individual explanations of racism into a single theory of racism capable of policy and practice applications.

Beginning with the advent of American slavery up to the present, the character of structural racism has been established and sustained by a legal and policy infrastructure. African Americans' social oppression began with slavery, which was abolished (Bowser, 2017). Yet, racial exclusionary practices evolved from slavery to the Black Codes, which were formalized into Jim Crow laws and legislation that sanctioned the second system of structural racism, which has now been replaced by a third system of structural racism. This third system is highlighted in Michelle Alexander's treatise *The New Jim Crow* (2011). Alexander (2011) asserts that the prison system has advanced the broad social, economic, and political interests of Whites in this country for centuries. As with the first system, the third system of structural racism shields the proliferation of whiteness while drawing on the anything other than race perspectives to disguise it.

There are those who believes racism's sustainability is due to its elusive and enigmatic character, which he believes is misunderstood (Bowser, 2017). There are some who argue that cultural racism is not a separate theory. In his analysis, racism's cultural domain is a separate level contained within a more comprehensive broad-base single theory of racism (Bowser, 2017). In this vein, structural racism is enabled through interlocking reinforcing levels by which racial exclusions operate to subordinate African Americans, with each level of racism performing a perpetuating function, enabling the inextricably linked levels of racism. In this context the cultural level enshrines the value base and ideological assumptions of White supremacy and racial inferiority of non-White racial and ethnic groups. The history of housing segregation laws and statutes in America and its impact on the limitation of twenty-first-century wealth generation by African Americans provides a perfect lesson of the interface of individual, institutional, and cultural forms of racism sanctioned by government-sponsored laws and policies. Rothstein's (2017) account of government-sponsored legislation and policies and the judiciary-sanctioned housing segregation of Black and White residents in the United States is informative and instructive for future study of the application of a broad-base three-pronged theory of the strands and tapestry of racism.

Applying an operant theory framework allows for a functional analysis of Bowser's (2017) three-pronged interdependent levels of racism (Briggs & Paulson, 1996). In this vein, the cultural level of racism embodies a White supremacy value base and belief system, which functions as an important antecedent to the institutional level of racism (Bowser, 2017). According to Bowser (2017), "without racist cultural scripts, institutional expressions of racism would not occur" (p. 581). The relationship between each level can be explained through a behavioral contingency theory of racism. As Caucasian manifest destiny is the antecedent condition, White supremacy is the behavioral condition illustrated through inter-institutional expressions of structural racism (Yearby, 2018). White privilege functions as the reinforcing consequence of structural racism. Structural racism further embolden and justify individual expressions of racism (Briggs et al., 2019; Bowser, 2017; Briggs & Paulson, 1996).

The system of racial exclusions is sustained at the institutional level as long as each participating organization upholds advantages for Whites relative to racial and ethnic counterparts (Bowser, 2017). Bowser (2017) asserts that removing resources that maintain racial distinctions will result in that institution experiencing abandonment and loss of value and existence. The defunding of public education and the marginal support of charter schools are examples of institutions that were abandoned when White students were no longer in the majority (Bowser, 2017). With the increase in schools' attendance by non-White students, there has been a decline in the quality and resource base, which threatens public schools' overall survival. Bowser (2017) points to the consequences and impact of White flight on the decline in public education quality, abandoning marginalized low-income communities occupied by racial minorities.

In sum, through Bowser's (2017) multidimensional theoretical view, cultural, institutional, and individual expressions of racism are mutually reinforcing conditions. The cultural level serves as the White supremacy value base facilitating the structure of a racial hierarchy where Caucasians are viewed as superior to African Americans (Bowser, 2017). The institutional level of racism is manifested indirectly. Racial distinctions are embedded in laws in housing and public schools, unfair real estate and mortgage banking practices, and rampant inequalities in employment and municipal services (Bowser, 2017). The individual level of racism is expressed sometimes through hate crimes by individuals, which are perceived as justified by the existence of institutional racism and belief in the inferiority of minority groups and people (Bowser, 2017).

To advance the future study of the theoretical characteristics that make up and sustain racism as viewed by activists, it has been recommended that such investigations at a minimum require monitoring for new forms of cultural racism and the development of new institutional practices. From the three-pronged theory of racism, cultural shifts lead to institutional practices, and individual racial behaviors are integrated and preconditioned to one another and are mutually reinforcing. The use of Bowser's (2017) three-pronged single theory of racism is needed now, given the rise in focus on racism and its obvious impact during the pandemic of COVID-19, accompanied by police murder of Black Americans, polarizing anti-immigration policies, and growing, violent White nationalism. One must also take a hard look at the events surrounding the insurrection on the U.S. Capitol on January 6, 2021. Not since the 1812 attack by the British has the U.S. Capitol building been under siege. Outnumbered, the Capitol Police and U.S. House and Senate Sergeant at Arms learned that the mob was given carte blanch by the remaining officers, who surrendered control to insurrectionist members of the mob.

The aftermath of this event exposed a sense of White racial solidarity among many right-wing Whites, small elements of the Capital Police force, members of the Republican Party, and President Trump. Alter the violent attack on the capital, including unlawful entry, insurrectionists captured by law enforcement were gently escorted off Capitol grounds, released, and told to go home. Subsequent investigations determined that a few Capitol Police assisted insurrectionists before and after January 6, 2021. Compared to the Black Lives Matter protest during the summer of 2020 at the nation's capital, which resulted in an attack on the protesters by the Capitol Police and National Guard, the insurrection, incited by then President Trump, was allowed to linger for hours despite the curfew imposed by the African American female mayor of the District of Columbia. Both events were preplanned but were handled completely differently and along racial lines.

The redress of structural racism became a major political platform issue in the 2020 presidential election. Ironically, the Republican president's right-wing response to the possibility of losing the 2020 presidential election was to invent and spread a lie that the election was stolen. The approach was to seek judicial intervention to allow voter suppression, by fiat, in the elections in the states of Georgia, Pennsylvania, and Michigan. Unsuccessful in swaying election outcome through legal channels, after the 2020 presidential election, lawmakers from several states, most notably in the South, legislated racialized practices that restrict voting opportunities and the impartial oversight of ballots cast and counted. Such denial of voter participation would disqualify residents from several densely populated urban centers with high numbers of African Americans.

Thus, schools of social work education launching efforts of decolonization of their organizational cultures, beginning with their curricula, must model their commitment to equal justice. Faculty and leaders of schools of social work ought to join at least one organization standing for anti-racism campaign issues, such as ratification of the John Lewis Voters Rights Act to defeat the contagious spread of voter rights restriction laws proliferating across the country since the 2020 presidential election. While authentically joining a campaign, schools of social work should commit to a truth and conciliation process, instigated by conducting an institutional self-study and acknowledgment of their own identified racists policies and practices that privilege Whites and that require modification to permit opportunities for equity and inclusion. In this way, curriculum decolonization is not the primary anti-racism outcome of the school. Abolishing un-access to exact justice throughout becomes the profession's anti-racism goal (Hafen, 2022).

The profession of social work has work to do to realign its commitment to the redress of racism and protracted oppression of African Americans. It might benefit from beginning with the aforementioned apology, followed by a truth and reconciliation process, which would include subsequent reforms and social action (Christopher, 2021). Why is an apology required? Social work is a social justice profession. Ironically, knowledge development and professional training of social workers in the United States evolved during the Jim Crow era. To reiterate what has been said earlier, to ignore the knowledge of the harsh treatment of Black people and other people of color during the period of legalized segregation was a breach of professional ethics. The profession's diversity agenda at the time excluded race (Banks et al., 2018). It is unconscionable that there was no anti-racism campaign organized and launched by social work (Briggs, Holosko, et al., 2018).

Stridently, moving toward the endorsement of race consciousness involves a commitment to anti-racism, structurally, interpersonally, and culturally. Race consciousness and feminist perspectives share the same anti-empirical philosophy of science knowledge development paradigm. At a minimum, a social worker must adopt a critical race consciousness perspective, reflected in the Council on Social Work Education (CSWE) standards that govern schools of social work, and through questions posed on the national social work licensure examination. CSWE 2022 Educational Policy and Accreditation Standards makes inroads into this area with requirements for anti-racism practices; however, it will be up to individual programs to take on the organization analysis, long-term planning, and commitment to providing curriculum and instruction to undo the predictable and modifiable downward spiral experience of African Americans reported by Du Bois and Eaton (1899). Moving forward, social work inaction toward racism is now antithetical.

Structural and Policy Approaches to Anti-Racism Practice

In this section, we emphasize useful approaches to anti-racism practices. To start, we highlight the American Public Health Association's campaign against racism (Jones, 2018). The campaign's priorities involved three objectives: (1) naming racism, (2) assessing how racism is manifested within institutional systems, and (3) defining and creating next steps to achieve anti-racism. In naming racism, Jones (2018) depicts structural racism as a rigged opportunity structure embedded within a racial hierarchy that ensures advantages for some, while concurrently ensuring inaccessibility to some deemed as unprivileged and whose unjust plight is relegated to a lesser priority in the domestic policy arena. In this vein, the deliberate use of race and the lack of race as a consideration can produce structural racism.

Yet, racism costs us all. For example, based on a Citigroup study (2020), the country lost $16 trillion over a 20-year period due to discrimination against African Americans (Peterson & Mann, 2020). Jones (2018) believes racism is manifested along three levels that include institutional, personally mediated, and internalized expressions. She asserts that to remedy the broader society of racism by focusing on the institutional expression of racism is fundamental to anti-racism practice. She believes the understanding achieved by dismantling the process of structuring racial exclusions and White preference opportunities is an important aim of anti-racism practice. Jones (2018) asserts that the character of racism is embedded within "our structures, policies, practices, norms, and values, which are different elements of decision-making" (p. 232).

Jones (2018) elaborates on the application of the 5 Ws (who, what, why, when, where) and the 1 H (how) to decision-making questions to assess how racism is operating within a system. Jones (2018, p. 232) asserts that the assessment of the structures, policies, practices, norms, and values of the system should include a database review that inventories how racism is privileged and the challenges to anti-racism practice. In Jones's (2018) view: "we need to become vigilant in identifying and addressing inaction in the face of need" (p. 232). She extolls the benefits of organizations authentically pursuing anti-racism practice through explicitly investigating the seminal question: "How is racism operating here?" (Jones, 2018, p. 232).

To fulfill the third aim of the campaign against racism, Jones (2018) proposed an anti-racism collaborative as an organizational entity for organizing the future efforts of the anti-racism campaign. To support the massive undertaking of the anti-racism campaign, she designed an eight-team collective infrastructure to channel "the wisdom and energy of anti-racism activity across the country and world" (p. 232). The proposed collaborative was jointly adopted by UCLA's Center for the Study of Racism, Social Justice, and Health and the Social Medicine Consortium.

Griffith and Semlow (2020) articulate strategies such as the fine arts as a mechanism for educating and mobilizing Whites to adopt anti-racism and health equity practice standards. They argue that efforts to redress social oppression, racism, and White domination have persisted for centuries. The authors indicate that ever since the writings and efforts of W. E. B Du Bois, there has been attention given to the promotion of health equity and the elimination of racism. Griffith and Semlow (2020) indicate that the random clinical trial research data that endorses anti-racism practice within and across institutions has not been established.

Hardeman, Medina, and Kozhimannll (2016) recommend a five-fold critical self-consciousness-building strategy for dismantling structural racism and achieving health equity. The strategy they highlight includes (1) recognizing the origins of racism and the devaluing of African Americans in the United States; (2) acknowledging that racism has shaped falsehoods justifying health disparities as consequences of genetic predisposition and cultural makeup of African Americans; (3) explicitly recognizing, identifying, and classifying the existence of racism; (4) acknowledging the opportunities that accompany race and racism; and (5) engaging in a process of critical self-consciousness of one's status as you privilege the voices and perspectives of the disempowered and marginalized segments of society. For example, on behalf of the editorial board of *Advances in Radiation Oncology*, Jackson et al. (2020) commits to broad-scale change as a context for the ending of racism system-wide in radiation oncology.

To rid their field of racism, the editorial board established an initial action plan, which includes a focus on accountability to an anti-racism agenda involving diversifying journal authors, article reviewers, and editorial board members. They are committed to using their power and influence with other journals to broaden their focus on health disparities, health equity, inclusion, and diversity. They seek to mount an education campaign that sponsors and directs research on diversity, inclusion, equity, and disparities in health. They also seek to sustain a focus and ongoing discussion on systemic barriers and biases within their field. To ensure buy-in, the editorial board sought to retain engagement of its Black authors and to investigate any and all instances of bias and barriers to publishing in their journal.

Along similar lines, Brown, Kijakazi, Runes, and Turner (2019) assert that too little attention is paid to the factors and conditions that give rise to racial and ethnic disparities reported in policy research. To reverse these shortcomings, the authors seek to address the existence of structural racism in organizations that conduct research and policy analysis. Brown, Kijakazi, Runes, and Turner (2019) believe that the strategies research and policy organizations use to address issues of structural racism are influenced and shaped by the organization's mission, funding base, size, and internal structure of operations. To avoid the lack of attention to structural racism in research and policy analysis, the authors recommend (1) increasing staff learning about structural racism and novel ways to investigate it; (2) rethink using race primarily as a dummy variable while expanding types of research that privilege voices of the community survivors of racism as paid survey respondents; and (3) enhancing communication.

Practice Approaches for Addressing Structural and Interpersonal Racism

There is minimal focus on racism in the behavioral analysis research literature (Matsuda et al., 2020). Of the limited behavioral literature that exists, much of it was published during the 1970s, but subsequently was followed by a reduction in emphasis (Matsuda et al., 2020). The sparse emphasis on racism in the behavioral literature has concentrated on the interpersonal aspects of racism. Racism results in a number of effects that include its adverse influence on economic development, physical and mental health, and academic achievement (Matsuda, Garcia, Catagnus, & Brandt, 2020, p. 336). In their review, racism is defined as "a belief that one's own racial or ethnic group is superior, or that other such groups represent a threat to one's cultural identity, racial integrity, or economic well-being" (merriam-webster. com/dictionary/racism; Matsuda et al., 2020, p. 337). Citing Briggs and Paulson (1996) and Lai et al. (2016), Matsuda, Garcia, Catagnus, and Brandt (2020) in their behavior analytic review of literature indicate that racial prejudice is a type of racism "involving socially inappropriate and discriminatory behaviors, including verbal behavior, directed at members of an ethnic group" (Matsuda et al., 2020, p. 337).

Racism from this vantage point is primarily limited given its concentration on the individual expression of racism, which we discussed earlier (Bowser, 2017). Thus, the review of behavioral literature on racism that follows does not include a focus on the cultural and institutional levels of racism (Bowser, 2017). Despite this gap in knowledge, others such as Briggs and Paulson (1996) and Matsuda, Garcia, Catagnus, and Brandt (2020) believe that behavior analysis is useful in facilitating understanding and reduction in racism, broadly defined. Matsuda, Garcia, Catagnus, and Brandt (2020) support their assertion by distilling a behavioral analytic definition of racial prejudice and reviewing research about racial prejudice. They also summarize the research on the existence and persistence of bias, examining the research to reduce bias, and highlighting interventions to reduce racial prejudice. In the following sections, we highlight a number of approaches to understand and deal with racism and anti-racism.

Behavioral Approach to Understanding Racism and Racial Prejudice

Matsuda, Garcia, Catagnus, and Brandt (2020) discuss the role of reinforcement and punishment contingencies involved in learning bias. They highlight the behavioral analytic formulations of racism and prejudice through responding, operant, and social learning processes. In this way, racism and prejudice are understood as a learned behavior that is cued by precipitating conditions or actions and is sustained by reinforcement or punishment consequences. Racial prejudice and other racist actions can also be a result of learning. Learning by witnessing the commission of a racist act may increase the perpetuation of racist behaviors (Briggs & Paulson, 1996; Matsuda et al., 2020).

Mindfulness and Anti-Racism Practice

The authors report the usefulness of acceptance and commitment treatment for reducing racial prejudice. The authors explain that acceptance and commitment therapy prepares its learners to reduce racial bias behaviors. In this vein, mindfulness focuses on being present in the moment, which the authors link to reduction in implicit racial bias. Acceptance involves learning to confront and face adversity with less distress; diffusion enables us to stay the course and avoid being derailed. It also involves decreasing rigid preoccupation with self and verbal behaviors. Mindfulness aids in minimizing performance anxiety actions, such as over-attending to self-talk and other attention-deflecting cues, by realigning attention to the present moment.

The authors report that acceptance and commitment therapy also involves three other processes: self-as-context, values, and committed action (Matsuda et al., 2020). Self-as-context involves forming a perspective about ourselves through self-examination. As for values, the authors define values as regulations that modify the consequences of other behavior. Matsuda, Garcia, Catagnus, and Brandt (2020) illustrate the role of values in reducing racial prejudice in the following example, "a student may say, 'I want to help decrease racism in my school.' The deliberate commitment to anti-racism becomes a powerful antecedent that alters the reinforcing value of engaging in behaviors such as connecting with local organizations to combat racism or informing others about ways to support ethnic minorities" achieve equal justice (Matsuda et al., 2020, p. 341). Committed actions, unlike values, which represents rules or standards of conduct, are the tasks that are consistent with obeying and adhering to said rules.

Combined Practice Approaches for Reducing Racism

Matsuda, Garcia, Catagnus, and Brandt (2020) highlight the mindfulness and acceptance, training perspective taking, and behavior analytic and combined approaches as specific interventions for reducing racial prejudice. Mindfulness and acceptance interventions are promising practices for reducing racial prejudice (Matsuda et al., 2020). It is an evidence-based intervention with broad application in areas involving eating disorders and weight management, mental health disorders, aggression, and behavioral disruptive behaviors (Matsuda et al., 2020).

A second intervention involves teaching people to adopt the perspectives of the oppressed as their mindset and mitigates racial bias (Matsuda et al., 2020). Research studies reviewed by Matsuda, Garcia, Catagnus, and Brandt (2020) provide evidence that training people to adopt marginalized and oppressed views has positive behavioral effects on reducing racial prejudice in college students. It helps the person to authentically identify with what unprivileged minoritized people are thinking and feeling through visualization

112 HAROLD E. BRIGGS AND MARTELL L. TEASLEY

or personal self-imaging of what the experience of being racially excluded actually manifest. Such training is also reported to mitigate stereotyping and attenuating in-group favoritism (Matsuda et al., 2020). As for the use of behavioral analytic intervention, self-monitoring and performance feedback have been used to praise equity behaviors among school-age children. As a call to action for applied behavioral research on reducing institutional prejudice and racism, the authors recommended a number of profession-wide investigations.

Addressing Racial Discrimination through Task-Centered Practice

Reid (2000) provides a practice intervention to use with individual victims and anti-racist allies and accomplices in organizations addressing racial discrimination in the workplace. For people who have experienced racial discrimination, the author recommends the following: (1) document each occurrence, along with demographic information that identifies the witnesses and alleged perpetrators of the alleged instances; (2) use informal means to address allegations rather than engaging in inaction or using formal venues to file incident reports; (3) if the alleged act violates the law or the victim believes they experienced a law violation, the equity and inclusion or human resource department would be able to assist the victim in filing the necessary paperwork, which will include an interview, followed by a compliant investigation. Consider whether or not an employment discrimination attorney is warranted.

For small groups of allies or accomplices to anti-racism/social justice practice, Reid (2000) recommends that they (1) review the organization's policies on violations of racial discrimination, (2) host organization-wide meetings about racial discrimination in the workplace, to allow for a collectivity of support and dialogue leading to the design of an anti-racist/anti-discrimination plan of change; (3) establish a formal change action plan that addresses goals for organization climate, "recruitment, hiring, promotion, and retention" activities that mitigate racial discrimination in hiring and any other area of the organization "that might be affected by racial discrimination" (p. 200); (4) implement a diversity and inclusion "exposure strategy" (p. 200). Such a strategy involves creating "situations" that involve a diverse

ENDING RACISM 113

group of people engaging in a work process that requires diversity contact, thereby reducing racial homogeneity (p. 200).

Confronting the Denial of Racism

A major reason structural racism has survived is the denial of its existence by government and leaders representing the vested interests of political and power elite groups (Babacan, 2008). Investigating the root causes of racism and financing its elimination is political suicide for either major party platform. Ending racism has not been a winnable political campaign aim. Denying the existence of racism fuels the popularity and use of any other perspectives than race, best articulated by Thomas (n.d.; https://citeseerx.ist. psu.edu). Thus, the debunking of the denial of racism is a critical milestone amid the bevy of essential tasks to the distillation of anti-racism culture and practice.

The denial of the existence of racism is manifested in a number of ways. Changing the focus to adopting cultural diversity frameworks shields Caucasians from addressing racism and the power imbalances maintained through "color-blind "policies (Babacan, 2008; Briggs & Leary, 2001). Racism denial is a deliberate action and a real adverse phenomenon (Babacan, 2008). There is an array of consequences that follow racism denial. First, as racism's existence is minimized, there is the unlikely acknowledgement of whiteness and White privilege. Second, as an alternative to recognizing whiteness and White privilege, there is a rejection of the label of whiteness and an adoption of the view that White people are survivors of oppression (Babacan, 2008). The denial of racism reinforces the permanence of racism. It also disqualifies the victims' account of mistreatment and invalidates the lived experiences of non-White people aggrieved by social injustices (Babacan, 2008).

The denial of racism is accompanied by a lack of any strategic intention to conduct "research into the area of racism and ensures there is very little evidence as how racism is constructed, where and how it is manifested, and what works in terms of anti-racism strategies" (Babacan, 2008, p. 6). Another consequence of denial is the lack of any policy prescriptions to redress racism and its protracted effects (Babacan, 2008). It is further reinforced by the underreporting of racist experiences by people of color or others who witness its occurrence (Babacan, n.d). Persons of color are labeled as being

114 HAROLD E. BRIGGS AND MARTELL L. TEASLEY

alarmist and overreacting to events defined as racist (Babacan, 2008). The denial of racism nurtures and reinforces its proliferation (Babacan, 2008).

Anti-Racism and Anti-Oppression Practice

Corneau and Stergiopoulos (2012) present the usefulness of anti-racism and anti-oppression practices for diverse mental health services consumers. Seven strategies emerge when combining these compatible approaches for practicing with racially diverse groups and people. These include empowerment, education, alliance building, language, alternative healing methods advocacy, social justice/activism, and foster reflexivity.

Empowerment is achieved when service users who are persons of color are involved in decision-making across the full spectrum of care. It also involves providers affirming the customs, "life experience, pride, belief systems, and strengths" of its racially diverse service user clientele (Corneau & Stergiopoulos, 2012, p. 269). Education focusing on anti-racism practice encompasses learning activities to facilitate broad institutional and system changes to achieve equity by mitigating racism and oppression (Corneau & Stergiopoulos, 2012). Education on anti-racism practice includes comprehending "the historical roots of racism, its definitions, its manifestations within institutions, its impact on poverty, the job market and on the treatment of visible minorities in the media" (2012, p. 270).

Building alliances with other activist-centered and social justice action groups and allies is a fundamental component of anti-racism and anti-oppression practices. Developing allyships with like-minded social justice advocates allows for the mobilization of collective power and influence. Building this network enables the mounting of a campaign of change through protests and massive resistance as a show of strength. Such a sign of strength allows activists to "challenge power" (2012, p. 271).

Advancing a culture of anti-racism involves the use of language that dignifies, honors, and respects individuals and groups and avoids stigmatizing and reproducing oppressive forces, which is an essential part of anti-racism and anti-oppressive practices. Language that achieves an egalitarian structure and avoids a division and power hierarchy is embedded in anti-racism and anti-oppression practices. Language that avoids judgment and deficit thinking is welcomed and used throughout anti-racism and anti-oppressive practices. This language sanctions the views and perspectives of all (Corneau & Stergiopoulos, 2012).

Alternative healing strategies that differ from Western medicine's approach such as yoga, Chinese medicine, and other culturally diverse practices of healing are an important component of anti-racism and anti-oppressive practices. Such alternative methods promote harmony and interdependence, while Western approaches promote personal autonomy and individualism (Corneau & Stergiopoulos 2012, p. 271). Alternative healing strategies promote holistic healing as opposed to the use of medication and biomedical forms of treatment. Alternative healing approaches incorporate diverse knowledge bases and worldviews on healing and recovery.

Advocacy and social justice activism involve aiding people of color in achieving anti-racism aims, rather than directing their desired change efforts. By empowering decision-making by persons of color, the advocate avoids the onerous possibility of disempowering the client by deciding for them what their endpoints and course of action should be to fulfill their social justice aims. Yet, championing the choices and "rights" of persons of color is a fundamental function to anti-racism and anti-oppressive practices.

Fostering reflexivity is the final and equally important strategy used in anti-racism and anti-oppressive practices. Reflexivity involves self-learning and self-modification, which begins with self-examination, according to Corneau and Stergiopoulos (2012). In this way, people learn their identity, location, perspective, and activism aims with respect to the nature and extent of racism and its broad-base manifestations. Through anti-racism/anti-oppressive practice, the approach involves the trainee identifying as either oppressed or oppressor (Corneau & Stergiopoulos, 2012, p. 273).

Through anti-racism and anti-oppressive practices, people of color privilege racial pride, racial history, and racial identity. People of color are also expected to self-examine to assess for "internalized racism" (Corneau & Stergiopoulos, 2012, p. 273). Alternatively, anti-racism practice involves Caucasian advocates to self-examine by undergoing a racial humility self-assessment. Self-racial appraisal helps Caucasian people recognize the impact of the persistence of whiteness, White privilege, and White supremacy. The self-racial appraisal aids privileged people to recognize the transactional nature of institutional and cultural expressions of racism.

Critique of Anti-Racism and Anti-Oppressive Practice Perspectives

There are a few drawbacks to the anti-racism paradigms that are noteworthy. Anti-racism theory lacks an acknowledgment of the interface of racial oppression with additional expressions of oppression involving gender, class, and sexuality (Corneau & Stergiopoulos, 2012, p. 274). In fact, the authors believe that the examination of racism strictly within the "Black/White dichotomy" disenfranchises and disempowers persons who are also marginalized and fit outside the Black/White schism (Corneau & Stergiopoulo, 2012, p. 274). Thus, anti-racism does not acknowledge the intersectional expressions of racism. Jeffrey (2005), cited in Corneau and Stergiopoulos (2012), put it best: "anti-racism by its theoretical nature is removed from practice, especially in the field of social work where anti-racism is part of the training curriculum, yet hard to apply in practice within a profession that tends to reproduce whiteness" (p. 274).

Compared to anti-racism, the major criticism of the anti-oppressive practice (AOP) framework is its homogeneous view of oppression (Corneau & Stergiopoulos, 2012). Equalizing the oppressive experiences across groups claiming minority status in this country has reignited an earlier question posed by Hopps (1982). She asks whether social work is approaching the issue of social oppression as a common experience or as unique to each culturally diverse group. Schiele (2007) poses a similar question. To date, the literature does not provide much guidance to clarify what is meant as oppression for each group.

AOP has been criticized as being a tool that legitimizes the best interests of people whose qualifications to judge oppression are questionable (Corneau & Stergiopoulos, 2012). A major drawback to the authentic use of AOP is the absence of the leadership voices that have evolved from the vulnerable groups with lived experiences "impacted by oppression" (p. 274). Also, AOP does not include lifelong ethical self-review and behavior-modification practice tools needed by professionals advancing the aims of AOP through the "privilege positions" they occupy (Corneau & Stergiopoulos, 2012, p. 274).

Conclusion

Actualizing a national post-apartheid America requires leadership by social justice experts as accomplices in advancing anti-racism policy and practice to rid the country of the permanence of racism. Achieving anti-racism will require legislative, policy, institutional, cultural, interpersonal, and individual change. Change can be done. First, we must understand that structural racism is a legal invention that is shielded by the law, whose modification is determined by the law. The permanence of structural racism reinforces White privilege, White supremacy, and whiteness as learned cognitive processes with behavioral norms that perpetuate each other. It will take a massive, focused effort as a society, yet people can learn to eliminate structural racism, and only when they achieve the moral clarity about how obtaining equal justice benefits rather than furthers inequality.

Ending racism will advance racial equity. A truth and reconciliation approach similar to the process used in South Africa may further mitigate injustice and serve as an equal justice paradigm shift in America. Neither, however, will resolve the issue of whiteness and White supremacy. For whiteness and White supremacy are mindsets of Europeans with historical roots to ideologies such as manifest destiny. Research shows that attitudes are longer to change than actions. Future research will bear witness to whether addressing the companion issues of whiteness and White supremacy following intervening on structural racism was the correct course of action to follow.

To attenuate whiteness and White supremacy may require rethinking the possible link between racism and psychiatric functioning. E. Franklin Fraser first hypothesized the relationship and was forced to leave Georgia to avoid capture by White supremacy sympathizers (Barrow, 2007). Years later, Briggs (2001) hypothesized the relationship between racism and psychiatric disorder. Also, through electronic literature search he uncovered the conceptual interface between the concept of cultural diversity and furtherance of structural racism through meritocracy-driven systems.

To undue the legal infrastructure of structural racism, the Civil Rights Division of the Department of Justice (DOJ) needs to be reimagined as a check-and-balance system to protect the country from returning to pre–civil rights existence. Enforcement protections are an important response against racial discrimination. It means that the Civil Rights Division has the power of prosecution and legal remedies for victims of racial discrimination. The COVID-19 pandemic hit Black and Brown communities at a greater rate, which further reflected the racial health disparities that prevent access to the social determinants of health. As the COVID pandemic grew in stature, so did the rise in frequent televised killings of unarmed African Americans by police. These killings served as the catalyst for protests against racism and demands for racial equity and social justice across the nation.

Ending racism must not be an exercise in behavior modification of individual Caucasian citizens. Such an aim is tantamount to a fool's errand. As we see it, the end of structural racism involves reforming its legally constructed infrastructure, White privilege, and the barriers to the upward mobility and access to opportunities for minoritized populations relative to advantages reserved for White communities (Irons, 2022).

Ending racism will enable the preservation of democracy. Democracy, an experimental form of government that exacts equal justice in America, is based on ordered liberty, which makes it an imperfect union, subject to contradiction. Since time immemorial, America has passed laws, told untruths, preserved whiteness, denied manifest destiny to people of color through structural inequalities while advancing its economic and political vested interest (Claghorn, 1927; Alexander, 2011). Oppression of Black and Indigenous people is America's founding sin.

The U.S. legacy of institutionalized inhumane and uncivilized traditions is undeniable. Examples of its legacy of inhumanity and human torture, including the American slavery era, the Reconstruction era, the Black Codes, Jim Crow era, the domestic terrorism of First Nations, the U.S. Department of Justice Family and Child Separation Policy, and the police killing of unarmed African Americans, exemplify the zoomorphism of people of color as an American tradition. By definition, zoomorphism is the assignment of animal qualities and characteristics to human beings and inanimate objects. The zoomorphism of people of color is reinforced by an infrastructure of laws and policies that furthers whiteness, ethnocentrism, and White supremacy.

Ending racism is needed now; its furtherance with Black and Brown people is predictable yet structurally intractable. For example, in twenty-first-century America, immigration policy and practice have resulted in thousands of Haitian, Latin, and Hispanic immigrants, who are seeking political asylum, experiencing zoomorphism and structural racism that resemble the Jim Crow experience of African Americans. Protracted zoomorphism leads to exposure to the social determinants of health disparities and early death, which was first reported by Du Bois and Eaton (1899). They concluded that structural racism is a social infection that leads to morbid disease and early death in their study of the effects of structural racism on Blacks in the seventh ward in Philadelphia during the Jim Crow era.

In closing, Paul Robeson consistently reminded us that the battlefront is everywhere in terms of striving for racial equality. Black and indigenous people of color (BIPOC) bear the unearned responsibility of addressing

ENDING RACISM 119

racism across a myriad of fronts. In this way, we all are duty bound to pursue the aims of anti-racists or to inherit the conspiracy of silence of racism and the inevitable legacy of racial conflict. As forecasted by Chinua Achebe (1998), "as long as one people sit on another and are deaf to their cry, so long will understanding and peace elude all of us" (p. 49).

Study Questions

1. Which scholarly work best highlighted structural racism and is reputed as landmark research of the effects of racism on African Americans?
2. How have American laws and social policies created structural inequality for BIPOC?
3. Why was "race work" considered different and independent from social work?
4. What are the three steps that the author recommends to ensure the key performance indicator (KPI) of social work's aim, especially for overcoming racism?
5. What is one major reason that racism is sustained in America?
6. What is a "conspiracy of silence" and what impacts does it have on social equity and equality?
7. How does the Thirteenth Amendment continue to protect "legal" forms of slavery in modern times?
8. What, according to Alexander (2011), is modern slavery?
9. What is the Hardeman, Medina, and Kozhimannll (2016) fivefold critical self-consciousness-building strategy, and how can it be used to dismantle structural racism?
10. Explain Bowser's (2017) three-pronged theory of racism and apply it to current racial tension in the United States.

References

Achebe, C., & Lyons, R. (1998). *Another Africa*. New York: Anchor Books.

Alexander, M. (2010). *The New Jim Crow: Mass incarceration in the age of colorblindness.* New York: New York Press.

Babacan, H. (2008). *Addressing denial: The first step in responding to racism.* Melbourne: Institute for Community, Ethnicity and Policy Alternatives.

Banks, L., Hopps, J. G., & Briggs, H. E. (2018). Cracks in the ceiling? Historical and contemporary trends of African American deans of schools of social work. *Research on Social Work Practice, 28*(3), 288–299.

Baron, H. (1969). The web of urban racism. In I. Knowles & K. Prewitt (Eds.), *Institutional racism in America* (pp. 134–176). Englewood Cliffs, NJ. Prentice Hall.

Barrow, F. H. (2007). Forrester Blanchard Washington and his advocacy for African Americans in the New Deal. *Social Work, 52*(3), 201–208. https://doi.org/10.1093/sw/52.3.201.

Bell, D. (2004). The interest-convergence covenants. In D. Bell, *Silent Covenants* (pp. 49–58). Oxford: Oxford University Press.

Bell, D. (2018). *Faces at the bottom of the well: The permanence of racism.* New York: Basic Books.

Bowles, D. D., Hopps, J. G., & Clayton, O. (2016). The impact and influence of HBCUs on the social work profession. *Journal of Social Work Education, 52*(1), 118–132.

Bowser, B. P. (2017). Racism: Origin and theory. *Journal of Black Studies, 48*(6), 572–590.

Briggs, H. E. (2001). Cultural diversity: A latter day Trojan horse. *Psychology and Education: An Interdisciplinary Journal, 38*(1), 3–11.

Briggs, H. E., Briggs, V. G., & Briggs, A. C. (2019). *Integrative practice in and for larger systems.* New York: Oxford University Press

Briggs, H. E., & Leary, J. D. (2001). Shields and Walls: The Structure and Process of Racism in America. *Psychology and Education-Orangeburg-, 38*(2), 2–14.

Briggs, H. E., Hardeman, C. P., Banks, L., Briggs, A. C., Allen, J. L., Hopps, J. G., & McCrary, D. (2021). Do race, racial disproportionality, and disparities remain foci of child welfare? *Child Welfare, 98*(5), 93–117.

Briggs, H. E., Holosko, M. J., Banks, L., Huggins-Hoyt, K. Y., & Parker, J. (2018). How are African Americans currently represented in various social work venues? *Research on Social Work Practice, 28*(3), 275–287.

Briggs, H. E., & Paulson, R. I. (1996). Racism. In M.A. Mattaini & B.A. Thyer (Eds.), *Finding solutions to social problems: Behavioral strategies for change* (pp. 147–177). Washington, DC: American Psychological Association.

Brown, K. S., Kijakazi, K., Runes, C., & Turner, M. A. (2019). *Confronting structural racism in research and policy analysis.* Washington, DC: Urban Institute.

Christopher, G. C. (2021). Truth, racial healing, and transformation: Creating public sentiment. *Health Equity, 5*(1), 668–675.

Chrobot-Mason, D., Campbell, K., & Vason, T. (2020). Whiteness in organizations: From white supremacy to allyship. New York: Oxford Research Encyclopedia, Business and Management. doi: 10.1093/acrefore/9780190224851.013.195.

Claghorn, K. H. (1927). The problem of measuring social treatment. *Social Service Review, 1*(2), 181–193.

Corley, N. A., & Young, S. M. (2018). Is social work still racist? A content analysis of recent literature. *Social work, 63*(4), 317–326.

Corneau, S., & Stergiopoulos, V. (2012). More than being against it: Anti-racism and anti-oppression in mental health services. *Transcultural Psychiatry, 49*(2), 261–282.

Danieli, Y (Ed.). (1998). *International handbook of multigenerational legacies of trauma.* New York: Plenum Press.

Davis, A. (2000). Masked racism: reflections on the prison industrial complex. [Article reprinted from *Colorlines*]. *Indigenous Law Bulletin, 4*(27), 4–7.

Davis, L. E. (2016). Race: America's grand challenge. *Journal of the Society for Social Work and Research, 7*(2), 395–403.

Du Bois, W. E. B., & Eaton, I. (1899). *The Philadelphia Negro: A social study.* Philadelphia: University of Pennsylvania Press.

Epperson, M. W., Pettus-Davis, C., Grier, A., & Sawh, L. (2018). Promote smart decarceration. In R. Fong, J. E. Lubben, & R. Barth (Eds.), *Grand Challenges for Social Work and Society* (Volume 1, pp. 181–203). New York: Oxford University Press.

Gramlich, J. (2019). The gap between the number of blacks and whites in prison is shrinking. Pew Research Center, *FACTANK News in the Numbers.* Retrieved from https://www.pewresearch.org/fact-tank/2019/04/30/shrinking-gap-between-number-of-blacks-and-whites-in-prison/

Griffith, D. M., & Semlow, A. R. (2020). Art, anti-racism and health equity: Don't ask me why, ask me how! *Ethnicity & Disease, 30*(3), 373–380.

Hafen, Q. (2022). Critical whiteness theory and social work education: Turning the lens inward. *Social Work Education*, 1–18.

Hardeman, R. R., Medina, E. M., & Kozhimannil, K. B. (2016). Dismantling structural racism, supporting black lives and achieving health equity: Our role. *The New England Journal of Medicine, 375*(22), 2113.

Harp, K. L. H., & Bunting, A. M. (2020). The radicalized nature of child welfare policies and the social control of Black bodies. *Social Politics, 27*(20), 258–281.

Heldke, L. M., & O'Connor, P. (2004). *Oppression, privilege, and resistance: Theoretical perspectives on racism, sexism, and heterosexism.* New York: McGraw-Hill Humanities, Social Sciences & World Languages.

Hopps, J. G. (1982). Editorial page: Oppression based on color. *Social Work*, 3–5.

Irons, P. (2022). *The roots of systemic racism: White men's law.* New York: Oxford University Press.

Jackson, I., Deville, C., Jr., Tsai, J., Goyal, S., Hintenlang, K. M., Videtic, G. M., & Miller, R. C. (2020). Addressing the impact of systemic racism in radiation oncology: *Advances in Radiation Oncology* commits to addressing systemic, institutionalized racism in academic medicine. *Advances in Radiation Oncology, 5*(5), 791.

Jeffery, D. (2005). "What good is anti-racist social worker, if you can't master it?": Exploring the paradox in anti-racist social work education. *Race, Ethnicity, and Education, 8*(4), 409–425.

Jones, C. P. (2018). Toward the science and practice of anti-racism: Launching a national campaign against racism. *Ethnic Discrimination, 28*(Suppl 1), 231–234. doi: 10.18865/ed.28.S1.231. PMID: 30116091; PMCID: PMC6092166.

Jones-Eversley, S. D., & Dean, L. T. (2018). After 121 years, it's time to recognize W. E. B. Du Bois as a founding father of social epidemiology. *The Journal of Negro Education, 87*(3), 234–245.

Lai, C. K., Skinner, A. L., Cooley, E., Murrar, S., Brauer, M., Devos, T., . . . Nosek, B. A. (2016). Reducing implicit racial preferences: II. Intervention effectiveness across time. *Journal of Experimental Psychology: General, 145*(8), 1001.

Matsuda, K., Garcia, Y., Catagnus, R., & Brandt, J. A. (2020). Can behavior analysis help us understand and reduce racism? A review of the current literature. *Behavior Analysis in Practice, 13*(2), 336–347.

Peterson, D. M., & Mann, C. L. (2020). *Closing the racial inequality gaps: The economic cost of Black inequality in the US.* Citi GPS: Global Perspectives & Solutions. https://ir.citi.

com//PRxPvgNWu319AU1ajGf+sKbjJjBJSaTOSdw2DF4xynPwFB8a2jV1FaA3Idy7vY59bOtN2lxVQM=

Poole, M. (2006). *The segregated origins of social security: African Americans and the welfare state.* Chapel Hill: University of North Carolina Press.

Reid, W. J. (2000). *The task planner: An intervention resource for human service professionals.* New York: Columbia University Press.

Reid, W. J. (2001). The scientific and empirical foundations of clinical practice. In H. E. Briggsand & K. Corcoran (Eds)., *Social work practice: Treating client common problems,* (pp. 36–65). Chicago: Lyceum Books.

Roberts, D. E. (2008). The racial geography of child welfare: Toward a new research paradigm. *Child Welfare, 87*(2), 125.

Rothstein, R. (2017). *The color of law.* New York: Liveright; W. W. Norton.

Schiele, J. (2007). Minority fellowship program: Implications of the equality-of-oppression paradigm for curriculum content on people of color. *Journal of Social Work Education, 43*(1), 88–100.

Themba-Nixon, M. (2001). *The persistence of white privilege and institutional racism in US policy: A report on US government compliance with the International Convention on the Elimination of All Forms of Racial Discrimination.* Oakland, CA: Transnational Racial Initiative.

Thyer, B. A. (2004). Science and evidence-based social work practice. In H. E. Briggs and T. L. Rzepnicki (Eds.), *Using evidence in social work practice: Behavioral perspectives* (pp.74–90). Chicago: Lyceum Books.

Yearby, R. (2018). Racial disparities in health status and access to healthcare: The continuation of inequality in the United States due to structural racism. *American Journal of Economics and Sociology, 27*(3–4), 1113–1152.

PART II
RACISM AND INDIVIDUAL AND FAMILY WELL-BEING

Of major concern to the social work profession is the impact of racism on the health and well-being of racial/ethnic communities. In Part II, we move from defining and understanding racism toward the insidiousness of racism within the context of the Grand Challenges for Social Work (GCSW). Authors of chapters emphasize the role of racism within the context of the Grand Challenge by interrogating existing evidence and the inclusion of racism as a factor for examining outcomes. This includes representation of diverse populations in research, biases within assessment and treatment protocols, as well as the inclusion and/or exclusion of protective factors that are rooted in culture and context. Chapters also provide evidence for successful interventions that address the impact of racism on health and well-being, as well as future recommendations for how these challenges can more explicitly include racism and White supremacy across multiple levels, including individuals, communities, organizations, and institutions.

Under "Enabling Healthy Development for Youth," we provide two chapters that highlight the power of prevention for young people to prevent behavioral health problems through the life course by means of empirical scientific evidence. Chapter 6 by Shapiro and colleagues considers the goal of reducing racial disparities in behavioral health problems through science-based and equity-enhancing prevention. They also examine the extent to which the concept of racism among diverse young people has been represented among contributing studies. Chapter 7 by Smith and colleagues focuses on issues of racism and bias in the assessment, prevention, and treatment of early psychosis among racial/ethnic minority youth and presents several conceptual frameworks for reducing racial and socioeconomic disparities through prevention intervention.

124 RACISM AND INDIVIDUAL AND FAMILY WELL-BEING

Chapter 8 highlights disparities in health outcomes that racial/ethnic communities experience, but also provides a holistic and multidimensional viewpoint that targets racism within individuals, organizations, and systems as the source of these inequities. Authors begin with a review of the problem, interventions, and solutions that have been used to address racism in health at individual, organizational, and systemic levels. Next, authors discuss potential moderators of this association, specifically those that promote positive coping and health. We discuss interventions for communities of color that address racism and health through culturally grounded, community-driven solutions that promote health and provide opportunities for positive active coping. Spencer and colleagues also provide examples of health interventions that demonstrate promise which are grounded in communities and their culture. In Chapter 9, Gonzales and colleagues tackle the Grand Challenge on productive aging though a health equity and anti-racist lens. The goal is to help identify solutions for inequities in health, and to enhance opportunities for engagement in employment, volunteering, and caregiving. The general premise is that health inequities across the life course are associated with differential opportunities for productivity, purposeful living, and quality ties to others. The objectives of this chapter are to integrate productive aging and health equity, two concepts and grand challenges advanced by the American Academy of Social Work & Social Welfare, to help identify solutions for inequities in health, and to enhance opportunities for engagement in employment, volunteering, and caregiving. The general premise is that health inequities across the life course are associated with differential opportunities for productivity, purposeful living, and quality ties to others.

Dettlaff and colleagues in Chapter 10 examine how racism is a particularly insidious impetus for family violence among Black Americans and how protective factors within these families have been largely neglected within the context of prevention and intervention strategies. This chapter examines how violence imparted since this country's inception through systemic racism against Black families contributes to current racial disparities in interpersonal family violence. This chapter discusses strengths and resilience of Black families and explores how such largely neglected protective factors might be harnessed in the context of prevention and intervention strategies to promote conditions of equity and racial justice that will truly bring an end to family violence. Strategies are provided within the context of recognizing that ending family violence in this country can only occur when we end White supremacy.

Finally, Part II contains two chapters that demonstrate how racism in the form of colorism plays out among two U.S. racial/ethnic groups, Latinxs and Asian Americans. Specifically, Calvo and colleagues (Chapter 11) argue that Latinx populations in the United States have been constructed as non-White and therefore appropriate for exploitation. This chapter analyzes the racialization process of Latinxs associated with symbolic indicators of colorism, origin, language, or cultural traits. After discussing how this process has normalized Latinxs as appropriate for exploitation, authors review the consequences of this process on Latinxs' socioeconomic well-being. The authors conclude by providing an account of evidence-based interventions that have shown promise in counteracting the negative impact of racialization on different Latinx communities. The authors also discuss the consequences of this on the well-being of the Latinx community and put forward evidence-based interventions that have been found to be useful in counteracting the impact of racialization on these communities. Similarly, Liu (Chapter 12) examines the experience of discrimination among Asian Americans and the interaction between race and gender. The author then investigates the impact of such racial discrimination on the Asian American community, including mental health and help-seeking behavior. The last section of the chapter investigates the literature on the recent anti–Asian American sentiment and the significant rise of attacks on the Asian American community, including older adults and women, during the COVID-19 pandemic. Implications for Asian American help-seeking and well-being are also discussed.

6

Ensure Healthy Development for Youth

Expansions and Elaborations for Equity

Valerie B. Shapiro, Amelia Seraphia Derr, Nehal Eldeeb, Henrika McCoy, Miguel A. Trujillo, and Cuc T. Vu

Taking action does not necessarily lead to change, and change does not necessarily indicate progress.
                    —Aché Lytle, *Our Resilience Is Our Revolution*

The Grand Challenge to Ensure Healthy Development for Youth calls upon social work scholars, educators, and practitioners to "imagine a world where only a modest number of behavioral health problems in young people are treated, controlled, or remediated—because most are prevented from occurring in the first place" (Shapiro & Bender, 2018, p. 499). Problems that threaten the healthy development of youth include anxiety; depression; alcohol, tobacco, and drug abuse; violence; absenteeism and disengagement from school; risky sexual activity; among other undesirable outcomes. Practice innovations and scientific validation suggest that the prevention of these behavioral health problems in youth is possible. Many policies and programs have been developed, tested, and demonstrated to effectively reduce the incidence of these behavioral health problems in study samples (Jenson & Bender, 2014). Yet, the Centers for Disease Control and Prevention (CDC) estimates that Americans only receive preventive healthcare at about half the recommended rate (CDC, 2009). For many young people, and the adults who scaffold their development, effective prevention is not available, affordable, accessible, accommodable, or acceptable (Penchansky & Thomas, 1981), and the prevalence of behavioral health problems in young people remains high.

Valerie B. Shapiro, Amelia Seraphia Derr, Nehal Eldeeb, Henrika McCoy, Miguel A. Trujillo, and Cuc T. Vu, *Ensure Healthy Development for Youth* In: *Social Work and the Grand Challenge to Eliminate Racism*. Edited by: Martell L. Teasley, Michael S. Spencer, and Melissa Bartholomew, Oxford University Press. © Oxford University Press 2023. DOI: 10.1093/oso/9780197674949.003.0006

128 VALERIE B. SHAPIRO ET AL.

As part of the Grand Challenge Initiative, the Coalition for the Promotion of Behavioral Health (CBPH; www.coalitionforbehavioralhea lth.org) advocated for *Unleashing the Power of Prevention*, with the ultimate goal of reducing behavioral health problems in young people—and reducing embedded racial and socioeconomic disparities—by 20% within a decade (Hawkins et al., 2015). The 2015 white paper envisions social policies and programs in every community that reduce the adversities experienced by young people and disrupt, with various protective mechanisms, the causal chain between adversity and behavioral health problems. Seven broad strategies have been envisioned for achieving these goals (e.g., raising public awareness of the power of prevention, increasing the infrastructure available to support the high-quality implementation of preventive initiatives). The original white paper articulates steps to guide the coalition's actions within these seven strategic areas in order to reduce the *overall rates* of behavioral health problems in young people. The plan to address the *embedded racial and socioeconomic disparities*, however, is less explicitly articulated. Here, we take the standpoint that such omissions are one way in which racism manifests and hierarchies of dominance are maintained (Jones, 2000).

In Matters of Equity, Creating Change Does Not Necessarily Create Progress

Many behavioral health problems in young people, featured in this Grand Challenge, share a common set of risk and protective factors: the preceding characteristics and conditions which shape the likelihood that the problem manifests. Yet, the distribution of the risk and protective factors among youth are not random; they reflect and perpetuate social inequities. Therefore, different social groups—characterized by gender, race, ethnicity, citizenship, (dis)ability, sexual orientation, gender identity, and class—experience dramatically different levels of behavioral health. As reiterated by the CBPH original chairpersons, evidence suggests that public policies *responding* to behavioral health problems have increased social inequality, contributing to well-known ethnic and racial disparities (Jenson & Hawkins, 2017; Gilman, 2014; Western & Pettit, 2010). For example, a recent study of young adults revealed that White survey respondents were more likely than Black respondents to self-report perpetrating illegal behaviors (53% and 32%, respectively), White and Black respondents were equally likely to report perpetrating violent or property crimes, and yet, Black respondents were more likely than White respondents to experience arrest (15% and 6%, respectively; McGlynn-Wright et al., 2020). Furthermore, Black people living in the United States are more likely to be diagnosed with schizophrenia, and less likely to be diagnosed with mood disorders, compared to White people living in the United States with the same symptoms (American Psychiatric Association, 2017). A societal reckoning with the reality of inequality, caused by racist social forces and actors, has resulted in renewed calls for broad societal change. Yet, our classic calls to redistribute social control measures to those who actually pose the greatest threat, and to redistribute intervention services to those with the greatest need, however necessary, are insufficient to address this problem (Morsy & Rothstein, 2019; The National Academy of Sciences, 2019; Shapiro, 2015). We must also advocate for a societal investment in structural arrangements that *prevent* the need for behavioral health interventions in the first place.

Although *Unleashing the Power of Prevention* will not, in isolation, dismantle the racist systems that organize our world, the initiative has promise to contribute to equity transformations by shifting attention and investment to upstream (i.e., social-structural) determinants of well-being, alleviating the disparate burden of illness and disease, and reducing harmful (e.g., biased, stigmatizing) encounters with problematic service systems. This requires proceeding thoughtfully and deliberately, however, to avoid embedding the same structures of oppression in a prevention-oriented society that are entrenched in the society we seek to change. The 1985 federal Heckler Report recognized "the 'national paradox of phenomenal scientific advancement and steady improvement in overall health status' accompanied by 'persistent, significant health inequities [that] exist for minority Americans'" (Koh et al., 2011, p. 1822); a paradox which remains entrenched in our society 35 years later. Similarly, the grand challenge to Ensure Healthy Youth Development runs the risk of using available science to improve the health of some young people, shifting population level averages, without catalyzing change in the larger, social contexts in which young people develop disparately (Biglan et al., 2012; Ginwright et al., 2005). In matters of equity, making a change does not necessarily mean making progress (Lytle, 2020; Swoboda et al., 2018). Therefore, this chapter seeks to reexamine the Power of Prevention, with explicit attention to the intersecting Grand Challenge to *Eliminate Racism.*

130 VALERIE B. SHAPIRO ET AL.

Re-examining *Unleashing the Power of Prevention* for Equity Elaborations

Calls for *health equity* insist that obstacles be removed and resources be provided so that all people have a fair and just opportunity for health (Braveman et al., 2017, 2018). The principle of health equity requires the elimination of *health disparities*, or differences in healthcare, status, or outcomes between groups (Carter-Porkas & Baquet, 2002), adversely impacting *marginalized* (i.e., treated as insignificant or peripheral) or *minoritized* (i.e., given less power or representation in society) groups.[1] For example, 48% of Latinx and 47% of Black adolescents between the ages of 13–17, compared to 42% of their White counterparts, reported ever experiencing a mental health disorder (Alegria et al., 2015), and Black teenagers were more likely to attempt suicide than White teenagers (Centers for Disease Control, 2019). When the 2010 Affordable Care Act promised "a revitalized era for prevention" (Koh & Sebelius, 2010, p. 1296), it was well articulated that "without an explicit focus on equity, reform will leave millions of Americans behind" (Siegel & Nolan, 2009, p. 2401). CBPH's original white paper (Hawkins et al., 2015) did describe some of the behavioral health disparities experienced by Black and Indigenous youth relative to non-Hispanic White youth, but did not elaborate on their mechanisms or meanings. The white paper was also implicitly guided by the U.S. Department of Health and Human Services' (US DHHS) *Action Plan to Reduce Racial and Ethnic Health Disparities* (2011) and the National Partnership for Action (NPA) to End Health Disparities' *National Stakeholder Strategy for Achieving Health Equity* (NPA, 2011), but this was not made explicit. These well-aligned health equity initiatives sought to (1) raise awareness of disparities; (2) build capacity for leadership, planning, implementation, and accountability through local multi-sector partnerships; (3) improve access to preventive services by improving coverage and reducing costs; (4) strengthen workforce competence; and (5) mobilize communities to collect and monitor data over time and adopt the most effective strategies to reduce disease and eliminate disparities. The federal agenda and strategies to reduce racial and ethnic disparities in behavioral health are embedded in CPBH's work, yet their influence and alignment were omitted.

Unleashing the Power of Prevention envisions state-supported, local coalitions of community residents, young people, and cross-sector collaborations between professionals acting together to transform existing

ENSURE HEALTHY DEVELOPMENT FOR YOUTH   131

youth services to reduce behavioral health problems and enhance equity. The ways in which the CPBH advocates for transformed services to reflect the three main activities of *science-based prevention* have been articulated elsewhere (e.g., Hawkins et al., 2002; Shapiro et al., 2013; Shapiro et al., 2015), but here we make more explicit the ways in which the CPBH advocates for *equity-enhancing prevention*. First, science-based prevention requires *collecting* local epidemiological data to look at nuanced profiles of risk and protection. Equity-enhancing prevention additionally requires *disaggregating* these population-level profiles by meaningful subgroups of the community. Second, science-based prevention requires using epidemiological data to *prioritize* risk and protective factors to target for change, and *creating* action plans composed of programs and practices, from among those tested and demonstrated to be effective in changing the targeted risk/ protective factors and problem behaviors. Equity-enhancing prevention requires using *participatory* processes to collect and interpret the data, and to select programs and policies that are (a) consistent with local values, (b) desirable to intended beneficiaries, and (c) have been tested and demonstrated to be effective for diverse and minoritized socio-demographic groups. Finally, science-based prevention requires regularly collecting data to *monitor* programs and policies and ensure they are well implemented and effective in the local context. Equity-enhancing prevention requires monitoring levels and quality of participant engagement to overcome programmatic and structural barriers to inclusion, and completing subgroup analyses to *ensure* that population-level disparities in access and outcomes are narrowing. A community-randomized trial of this approach to prevention planning, called Communities That Care (Hawkins et al., 1992), has demonstrated efficacy for reducing the prevalence of adolescent substance use and violence in small towns (Hawkins et al., 2009; Hawkins et al., 2014), with pilot and evaluation projects exploring the approach to prevention in urban neighborhoods, Indian Country, and in a variety of high- and low-resource countries throughout the world (Brown et al., 2014; Fagan, Hawkins et al., 2019; Guttmannova et al., 2017). Community systems for science-based and equity-enhancing prevention require very robust systems of supports for research and innovation, data monitoring, training, and service delivery (Beadle & Graham, 2011; O'Connell et al., 2009; Spoth et al., 2013). These supports are exceedingly important for prevention research and practice to be successful in large, transient, underserved, diverse, and marginalized communities (Cheadle et al., 2001; Eisenberg et al., 2020; Fagan, Hawkins, et al., 2019). The action steps in the CPBH's Strategic Plan (2019) seek to invigorate this system of supports, without which disparate outcomes in behavioral health are likely to persist (Fagan, Bumbarger, et al., 2019).

In Matters of Equity, Aspirations and Intentions Are Insufficient

Despite intentions to include all young people in all communities in our vision for science-based and equity-enhancing prevention, our[2] original white paper (Hawkins et al., 2015) did not sufficiently elaborate on matters of race and ethnicity. Race and ethnicity are socially constructed ideas used to group people based on observed or attributed shared attributes, cultures, traditions, or national origins; the concepts have been leveraged to hierarchically determine human worth and entitlement (Chisom & Washington, 1997; Rao et al., 2021). In our original white paper, we omitted an oft-referenced literature which has shown that many common risk and protective factors can be assessed reliably across adolescents of diverse race and ethnicities (Choi et al., 2005; Deng & Roosa, 2007; Roosa et al., 2011; Sullivan & Hirschfield, 2011; Williams et al., 1999). We did not explicitly name experiences with micro-aggressions, discrimination, and racial trauma (Comas-Diaz et al., 2019; Trent et al., 2019) as risk factors for poor behavioral health outcomes, nor positive cultural identity and related constructs as potential protective factors (Spencer et al., 1991). We also failed to articulate the ways in which bias is likely to enter the process of prioritizing the risk and protective factors that communities target. Research has shown that within-child characteristics are often used to explain the behavioral health problems of Black youth, whereas external factors are often used to explain the behavioral health problems of White youth, and judgments as to whether risk and protective factors are malleable with a given context are subject to similar racialized expectations and interpretations (McCoy & Pearson, 2019). In our original white paper, we only briefly mentioned a federal effort (i.e., CDC's Racial and Ethnic Approaches to Community Health [REACH] initiative) shown to have some success in reducing disparities in health behaviors (e.g., early childhood immunization rates, cholesterol and cancer screening, cigarette smoking, exercise; Cohen et al., 2010), described a small number of universal interventions (e.g., Raising Healthy Children; Staying Connected with Your Teen) that have shown promise for narrowing disparities over time

(Haggerty et al., 2007; Hawkins et al., 2008; Hill et al., 2014), and described some culturally specific interventions (e.g., Familias Unidas) that have shown improvements in the mental and behavioral health of marginalized young people (Perrino et al., 2014; Prado et al., 2007; Prado et al., 2012). We failed to acknowledge that many marginalized youth are likely to receive universal interventions that fail to recognize trauma, terror, and other important correlates of their behavioral health (Marsigili & Booth, 2015; Scott & McCoy, 2018; McCoy et al., 2016), and inversely, that many system-involved youth who could benefit from universal prevention practices do not have access to such programs (McCoy & McKay, 2006). Although our original white paper has been independently assessed as among the 57% of Grand Challenge Initiative papers in which race and ethnicity were an explicit and integrated theme, *Unleashing the Power of Prevention* was not among the 43% that even mentioned racism as a construct (Rao et al., 2021). Accordingly, we believe that our original white paper failed to be sufficiently explicit about the challenges of fully enacting our goals for equity-enhancing prevention. For example, if attitudes toward prevention are favorable, funding is available, and a racially diverse community is ready to adopt an effective prevention practice, can coalition members identify a program that has been studied and demonstrated to prevent behavioral health problems in young people who identify as Black, Indigenous, or other People of Color? If a program has not yet been studied and demonstrated to be effective for marginalized youth, have protocols been developed for intervention modification and use? These are important pragmatic questions; we are not the first to raise them (e.g., Alvidrez et al., 2019; Barrera et al., 2017; Ford & Airhihenbuwa, 2010; Marsiglia & Booth, 2015; Jaggers et al., 2020; Stanley et al., 2020) but we reiterate that they remain unresolved.

The definitional emphasis of the Grand Challenge Initiative on "discrete interventions and measurable progress" predicated on "[existing] scientific evidence . . . that the challenge can be completely or largely solved" (Fong et al., 2017, p. 8) within a decade, likely inspired certain social problems to be prioritized and certain strategies for improvement to be emphasized (Howard & Garland, 2015). Similar to the interdisciplinary literatures upon which we draw, it has been observed in our social work literature that only 7% of articles published in four major social work journals between 2005 and 2015 included content related to "racial and ethnic minorities" (Corley & Young, 2018), and that race and ethnicity were more often statistically partialed out of analyses than treated as worthy of substantive inquiry (Woo

134 VALERIE B. SHAPIRO ET AL.

et al., 2018). These circumstances, among others, converged and lured us into centering White youth and treating their experiences as a normal from which all others may deviate. Years of scientific funding to predominantly White researchers (Ginther et al., 2011), testing interventions on predominantly White samples (e.g., LaRoche & Christopher, 2008; Pacific Northwest Evidence-based Practice Center, 2019; Rowe & Trickett, 2018), led the Grand Challenge to Ensure Healthy Development for Youth to rely on a remarkably robust, but admittedly narrow, scientific knowledge base, and to focus on "scaling up" (i.e., promote broad access to) existing preventive interventions, with the authentic and heartfelt aspiration to benefit *all* youth, while overlooking gaps in theory, research, policy, and practice that specifically pertain to marginalized youth.

Re-examining the Goal to Establish Equity-Enhancing Interventions

In an effort to bring some focused attention and effort to CBPH's third goal (i.e., to establish and implement criteria for preventive interventions that are effective, sustainable, *equity-enhancing*, and cost-beneficial), the CPBH (2019) strategic plan suggests the following activities: (a) examine existing definitions for equity, endorse criteria for equity-enhancing interventions, and promote the use of these criteria; (b) develop and promote research guidelines for examining equity-enhancing preventive interventions; (c) develop an initiative encouraging prevention researchers to "look back" at their data to find and report information characterizing equity-enhancing effects; and (d) establish a taskforce to identify and disseminate preventive strategies to reduce disparities and guidance for tailoring and testing such strategies. Our 2020 reflections upon our 2019 plans recognize that our goals may take for granted that the scholarship and science, as applied to prevention, are sufficiently developed and ready to be subjected to synthesis, evaluation, and dissemination. There is an important line of scholarly critique suggesting that if the CPBH does not clarify, in ways that might make power unambiguous, the actors (who) and actions (how) that sustain siloed scholarship and incomplete science as related to our ambitious equity goals, we inherit and perpetuate the existing structural arrangements that have enabled disparities to persist (Leonardo, 2004). Even if well coordinated, as suggested in our Strategic Plan, with selected state representatives, the Society for Prevention

Research taskforce on disparities, or the National Institute of Minority Health and Disparities (NIMHD), our coalition cannot proceed with these advocacy objectives without first recognizing and remediating underlying oversights.

Two exemplar oversights come to mind. First, we need to explicitly attend to more sophisticated conceptualizations of race and racialization in order to facilitate the equity-enhancing acts of disaggregating epidemiological data and analyzing intervention effects by subgroups. The risk of using race atheoretically is twofold; it reifies a construction of race that obscures within-group heterogeneity and the actual roots and impacts of structural disadvantage on disease status and response-to-intervention (Saperstein & Penner, 2012). Second, we need to appreciate the complexity of endorsing criteria for equity-enhancing interventions, and the requisite conceptual work necessary to unearth the implicit assumptions embedded within various possibilities for how this is accomplished. In our 2020 grappling with our 2019 plan to "develop an initiative encouraging prevention researchers to 'look back' at their data to find and report information characterizing equity-enhancing effects," we recognize both the tremendous need for this information and the tremendous limitations of any conclusions that can be drawn by investigations of this nature. Yet, by ignoring race in our analyses, we abdicate our responsibility as researchers to provide evidence central to local prevention planning, implicitly devolve the responsibility of determining what works for whom to local communities, and then bemoan the failures of communities to use science to inform their practice. Instead, we now view a focus on diversity, equity, and inclusion as a primary pathway to achieving the goal of unleashing the power of prevention.

To this end, we attempt here to progress a discussion of what it means to be an equity-enhancing intervention. We posit four conceptualizations upon which criteria for equity-enhancing interventions may be based, which we respectively term: centering, reducing, protecting, and promoting. We do not endorse any particular approach, but believe that a discussion of the complexities of these definitions, their relative advantages and disadvantages, and their implications, should be an important next step toward the work of Ensuring Healthy Development for Youth. First, a *centering* approach to determining whether an intervention is equity-enhancing would foreground questions of relevance to the well-being of marginalized youth, rendering comparisons to other groups a distraction from that purpose. Under these terms, an intervention may be deemed equity-enhancing if it is demonstrated as effective for a marginalized group. This approach is consistent with the National Institute of Minority Health and Health Disparities' recent consensus report that describes the need to study marginalized populations, regardless of the presence of disparities (Duran & Perez-Stable, 2019). It does, however, leave open the possibility that, in the absence of a comparison, marginalized groups could be receiving an inferior service or attaining a worse behavioral health status relative to other groups.

A second approach to determining whether an intervention is equity-enhancing is one we have termed *reducing*. This approach would prioritize a reduction of disparate care and outcomes between structurally advantaged and disadvantaged groups. Under these terms, an intervention may be deemed equity-enhancing if moderation of the intervention effect is observed, such that the care or status of the disadvantaged group improves more than the care or status of the advantaged group. This approach is born from a disparity reduction framework, and reflects its ideals. It does, however, leave open the possibility that an equity-enhancing intervention could benefit the disadvantaged group while the advantaged group does not benefit at all, or even deteriorates.

A third conceptualization of equity-enhancing interventions, *protecting*, would be predicated on the ideal that all youth should benefit the same amount from an intervention. Benefiting *the same amount* may be important, as interventions that benefit advantaged groups more than they benefit disadvantaged groups, even when everyone benefits, actually exacerbate inequities (Lorenc & Oliver, 2014). Using the protecting approach, an intervention may be deemed equity-enhancing (or perhaps, technically, equality-enhancing) if main effects of the intervention are detected for all groups, but there are no significant interactive effects detected by racial groups. We have termed this approach *protecting*, as it seeks to protect all youth from behavioral health problems, but also largely maintains the disproportionate disease burden by race, thereby protecting the status quo.

Last but not least, a *promoting* approach to determining whether an intervention is equity-enhancing would assess the extent to which obstacles could be removed, and resources be provided, so all youth can benefit in ways that maximize their behavioral health. This follows the framework of *targeted universalism* (powell et al., 2019), whereas the goals are the same for all groups, but the strategies to achieve the goals are targeted (i.e., differentiated in accordance to diverse cultures, contexts, and conditions). A targeted strategy may be required under conditions when there are different presentations of the problem, different etiological factors that contribute to the emergence of the problem, differential access to or engagement in available interventions, or differential effectiveness between groups (Castro et al., 2010; Lindsey et al., 2019). Using a promoting approach, the equity-enhancing effect of an intervention may be explored through diverse research methods; it may be deemed equity-enhancing if it includes sufficient guidance for the circumstances in which to tailor an intervention, a well-articulated process for providing resources and removing barriers (i.e., adapting an intervention to various individual cultures, contexts, and conditions), the adaptation process is tested with marginalized youth, and satisfaction, engagement, and intervention effects of the adapted intervention are demonstrated for the targeted group. Although it may seem like promotion approaches to equity-enhancement will require infinite resources to adapt and test interventions for endless subdivisions of young people into smaller and more homogeneous groups, it may be helpful to think less about narrow categories of people with shared appearances or lineages, and to instead think more about individuals with shared sociocultural or lived experiences in the United States that render effective interventions differentially available, affordable, accessible, accommodable, and acceptable to diverse populations. In other words, rather than think about race as a fixed exogenous variable with an inherent biological basis (Morning, 2008), researchers could think about a shared lived experience of racism and resistance as a variable in their research (Kauffman & Cooper, 2001).

Classic methodological debates are evoked when considering the disaggregation and analysis of preventive intervention effects by race (Kauffman & Cooper, 2001). How should race be determined? How should race be bounded such that it represents something meaningful, given within-group variance in broad categories that are neither rank ordered nor mutually exclusive? How should race variables be coded in quantitative research? How should small samples be analyzed and interpreted, and how should studies be adequately powered to determine efficacy by subgroup and detect subgroup differences? Should researchers only test for moderation by race (i.e., when intervention effects *differ* by race) when a main effect for race (i.e., when intervention effects are *associated* with race) is detected? The ways in which comparisons are drawn and these questions are answered have implications for the size, significance, and interpretation of the intervention effects, and readily, if not transparently, embed the researcher's worldview in their research.

We hope that this initial presentation of criteria and methods for demonstrating equity enhancement will continue to benefit from expansion and elaboration. We recognize that interventions with evidence of equity enhancement are not necessarily universally equity-enhancing; interventions may promote equity for some population segments on some indicators of behavioral health, and not on or with others. We are hopeful that as our technological capacity grows for efficiently aggregating, analyzing, and visualizing high-quality data, so does our capacity for identifying specific risk and protective factors for behavioral health among groups experiencing the adverse effects of racism, studying the effectiveness of equity-enhancing strategies, and ultimately delivering highly contextualized and adaptive precision-based strategies for health promotion (Dolley, 2018; Supplee et al., 2018). We wrestled with the inherent contradictions in the two examples we have provided: calling for more sophisticated conceptualizations of race and racialization, while also suggesting using simplistic racial characterizations to segment the population and observe intervention effects. We believe that documenting disparities in behavioral health status and intervention outcomes by broad racial categories should continue for the sake of calling attention to the downstream consequences of racism. And yet, we understand this to be a beginning and not an endpoint. Observing racial disparities does not, in and of itself, motivate a community coalition to prioritize the needs of a marginalized group (McCoy, 2020a), illuminate the socio-structural mechanisms through which disparities persist, or identify possible strategies to promote health equity. We need to go beyond calls to scale up *programs*, but must also call to scale up *the conditions* in which programs can benefit marginalized youth. This involves advocating for poverty remediation and anti-discrimination policies, as well as the elimination of other conditions that constrain the authentic choice-making upon which the success of many psychoeducational programs are predicated (Trent et al., 2019). We posit that health equity depends upon centering questions of relevance to the well-being of marginalized youth (Wallerstein & Duran, 2010), understanding the effects of new and previously tested programs on diverse and marginalized socio-demographic groups (Gottfredson et al., 2015), and demonstrating how a community may overcome programmatic and structural barriers to inclusive adaptation and implementation (Barerra et al., 2011).

Like our colleagues attempting to scale up evidence-based interventions more broadly, we assume that our persistent legacies of White supremacy and minoritization have shaped our current lists (i.e., curated repositories) of effective prevention programs. Many of the prevention programs on such lists were designed with the underlying intention to be culture-blind; however, they have embedded an assumption of White hegemonic neutrality. They then evolved to be rhetorically inclusive (i.e., illustratively including names and images from people presumed not to be White so as to encourage adoption in diverse communities), but largely have not been structurally situated within or adapted to norms or beliefs beyond White cultural contexts (Castro et al., 2004). As written by Kumpfer et al. (2002):

> Most universal prevention programs are generic programs developed for popular American culture or youth culture, which is heavily influenced by White, middle class values. Professional training has stressed "the melting pot" model of American culture, resulting in few culturally-specific models (McGoldrick & Giordano, 1996). The theoretical constructs, definitions of protective or risk factors, appropriate intervention strategies, and research evaluation strategies have all been influenced by mainstream American values (Turner, 2000). Commercial developers seek to develop generic programs culturally acceptable by diverse families; thus, making their products widely marketable. (p. 242)

In the remainder of this chapter, we consider how racism intersects with the sixth CPBH goal: increase the number of young people receiving effective preventive interventions. We intend to do so without disparaging the ideals and contributions of science-based prevention, the promise of curated lists of rigorously tested programs, or the programs currently on those lists which have demonstrated effects on the behavioral health of young people. Fundamentally, we believe that science-based prevention can and should be a pathway to equity. Yet, we also believe that without explicit scrutiny and action to advance equity, scientific processes alone will not be able to overcome the racist societal systems in which they function.

Understanding the Effects of Tested Programs on Marginalized Groups

The Blueprints for Healthy Youth Development is a registry of "experimentally proven programs" intended to guide decision-makers toward effective prevention practice (Mihalic & Elliott, 2015). We examine the Blueprints

140 VALERIE B. SHAPIRO ET AL.

list because we think it is the best available menu of evidence-based prevention programs. Distinction as a "model" program typically requires two randomized controlled trials (RCTs), with sustained positive (at least 12 months after the program ends), and no iatrogenic, effects. Given the rigor of the registry, it is the virtual place where communities conducting science-based prevention are advised to visit to select an effective prevention program for use. It is unclear, however, who is included in the studies buttressing the evidence base of model programs and whether some subgroups benefit from promoted interventions more than others (Shapiro et al., 2022). Further synthesis is required to understand the extent to which studies supporting these tested-effective prevention programs are inclusive and have assessed differential effects by racial subgroups.

We conducted a scoping review of the studies buttressing Blueprints "model" programs (i.e., "Blueprints Certified Studies") to examine the extent to which these studies (Q1) describe their samples, (Q2) include marginalized youth, (Q3) include race and/or ethnicity in their analytic models, and (Q4) analyze intervention effects by racial and/or ethnic subgroups of youth. To be clear, this initial review is not intended to be a systematic review of the prevention literature, but rather an attempt to identify knowledge gaps and to clarify information needs within a set of papers underlying a set of rigorously tested programs (Munn et al., 2018). For the sake of this review, we report the ways in which samples are described in the original language of these studies. We acknowledge the limitations of broad racial categories that are largely silent on what these socio-demographic categories represent, who is represented, or the realities of experiencing intersecting systems of oppression. Our intention is to understand this literature from the perspective of a research-user, in all of its utility and its shortcomings. If a community coalition member visits the Blueprints website (https://www.blueprintsprograms.org/) today, as envisioned by the CPBH, with the hopes of increasing the number of young people in their community receiving effective preventive interventions, what information could they glean from Certified Studies about effective prevention for racially and ethnically marginalized youth?

As depicted in Figure 6.1, The Blueprints registry listed 17 "model" programs in April 2020, based on evidence from 44 Blueprints Certified studies ($M = 2.6$ per program), described in 62 peer-reviewed papers published during 1973–2018 (median year = 2006). The programs embedded in these studies were universal ($n = 5$), selective ($n = 3$), indicated ($n = 4$), or multi-tiered ($n = 5$). Studies explored diverse outcomes

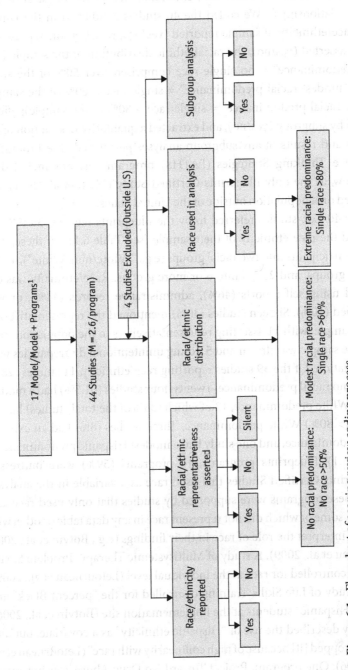

Figure 6.1. Flow chart of scoping review coding process.
17 Model and Model Plus programs as of April 2020.

142 VALERIE B. SHAPIRO ET AL.

(e.g., problem behavior, education, emotional well-being, physical health, positive relationships). We coded the 40 studies conducted in the United States: race/ethnicity of sample reported (yes/no), racial/ethnic representativeness asserted (yes/no), the racial/ethnic distribution of the sample ("no racial predominance" = no single race comprised over 50% of the study sample, "modest racial predominance" = single race > 60% of the sample, "extreme racial predominance" = single race > 80% of the sample); effects analyzed by subgroup (yes/no), and extracted a qualitative description of the methods and results of any subgroup analyses performed. The Promoting Alternative Thinking Strategies (PATHS) program was not included in this review, as the only Blueprints Certified Study (Malti et al., 2011) was conducted on a population outside of the United States.

Of the 40 U.S. studies referred to by the Blueprints registry, 39 (97.5%) described the race/ethnicity of their sample (see Table 6.1). Of these, 31% divided participants into two racial groups (e.g., "White/non-White"), 43.5% into 3–5 groups, and 25.5% into 6 or more groups. Race/ethnicity was determined using self-reports (46%), administrative records (44%), or was unspecified (10%). Sixteen studies (40%) mentioned the representativeness of their sample, with 11 asserting representativeness to the population from which the sample was drawn and 5 noting unintentional discrepancies with the population. Of the 39 studies reporting race/ethnicity, 11 studies (28%) reported no racial predominance. Twenty-four studies (61.5%) had a modest (> 60%) White predominance, 13 of which (33% of the total studies) had an extreme (> 80%) White predominance. Three studies (8%) had an extreme Black predominance, and one study had a modest Hispanic predominance.

Of the 17 Blueprints programs, 10 programs (59%) were buttressed by Blueprints Certified Studies that used race as a variable in the analysis. Five of these programs were supported by studies that only used race as a covariate, some of which did not represent race in any data table or otherwise report or interpret the role of race in their findings (e.g., Botvin et al., 2006; Letourneau et al., 2009). A study of Multisystemic Therapy–Problem Sexual Behavior controlled for race at the individual level (Letourneau et al., 2009), while a study of Life Skills Training controlled for the "percent Black" and "percent Hispanic" students at the implementation site (Botvin et al., 2006). One study described the use of "Hispanic ethnicity" as a covariate, but ultimately "dropped [it] because of high collinearity with race" (Letourneau et al., 2009, p. 96). One program, Project Toward No Drug Abuse, was buttressed by three studies that used race as a covariate, although each in somewhat

ENSURE HEALTHY DEVELOPMENT FOR YOUTH 143

Table 6.1 U.S. Studies Buttressing Blueprints "Model" Distinction: Sample Diversity and Intention to Analyze Subgroup Effects by Race

Prevention Program	Study[1]	Authors and Year	Racial/Ethnic Distribution of Sample[2]	Intention to Analyze Subgroup Effect by Race
Early College High School (ECHS)	1	Haxton et al., 2016	No	Yes
	2	Edmunds et al., 2017	Predominance Modest: White	Yes
Functional Family Therapy (FFT)	13	Gottfredson et al., 2018	Extreme: Black	No
LifeSkills Training (LST)	1	Botvin et al., 1995	Extreme: White	No
	7	Botvin et al., 2006	No	No
	9	Spoth et al., 2002	Predominance Extreme: White	No
Multisystemic Therapy (MST)	3	Borduin et al., 1995	Modest: White	No
Blues Program	1	Rohde et al., 2014	Modest: White	No
	2	Sticeet al., 2008; Stice et al., 2010	No Predominance	No
Body Project	1	Stice et al., 2006	Modest: White	Yes
	2	Stice et al., 2003	Modest: White	No
	3	Stice et al., 2001	Modest: White	No
	4	Stice et al., 2009; Stice et al., 2011	Extreme: White	No
	5	Stice et al., 2013; Stice et al., 2015	Modest: White	No
Brief Alcohol Screening and Intervention for College Students (BASICS)	1	Baer et al., 2001;	Extreme: White	No
	2	Marlatt et al., 1998	Extreme: White	No
	5	Borsari & Carey, 2000 Turrisi et al., 2009	Extreme: White	No
GenerationPMTO	1	DeGramo et al., 2004; Forgatch et al., 2009; Forgatch et al., 1999; Patterson et al., 2010	Extreme: White	No
Maryland Ignition Interlock License Restriction	1	Beck et al., 1999	Extreme: White	No
	2	Rauch et al., 2011	Extreme: White	No
Multisystemic Therapy – Problem Sexual Behavior (MST-PSB)	1	Borduin et al., 1990	Modest: White	No
	2	Borduin et al., 2009	Modest: White	No
	3	Letourneau et al., 2009	No Predominance	No
New Beginnings	1	Wolchik et al., 2002	Extreme: White	No
	2	Wolchik et al., 1993	Extreme: White	

(continued)

144 VALERIE B. SHAPIRO ET AL.

Table 6.1 Continued

Prevention Program	Study[1]	Authors and Year	Racial/Ethnic Distribution of Sample[2]	Intention to Analyze Subgroup Effect by Race
Nurse-Family Partnership (NFP)	1	Olds et al., 1997; Olds et al., 1986; Olds et al., 1998; Olds et al., 2002 Kitzman et al., 1997; olds et al., 2004	Extreme: White No Predominance Extreme: White	No No No
	2			
	3			
ParentCorps	1	Brotman et al., 2011 Brotman et al., 2013; Brotman et al., 2016	No Predominance Extreme: Balck	Yes No
	2			
Positive Action	1	Beets et al., 2009; Snyder et al., 2010 Lewis et al., 2014; li et al., 2009	No Predominance No Predominance	No No
	2			
Project Towards No Drug Abuse (TNDA)	1	Simon et al., 2002; Sussman et al., 1998 Dent et al., 2001 Sussman et al., 2002; Sussman et al., 2003 Sun et al., 2008	No Predominance No Predominance No Predominance Modest: Hispanic	No No No No
	2			
	3			
	4			
Treatment Foster Care Oregon	1	Chamberlain et al., 1996; Eddy et al., 2004 Chamberlain et al., 2007; Leve et al., 2005 Kerr et al., 2009	Extreme: White Modest: White Modest: White	No No No
	6			
	7			

[1] Study number according to Blueprints registry retrieval and review. This does not necessarily reflect chronological order.

[2] No predominance = no single race >50% of sample; modest predominance = single race >60% of sample; extreme predominance = single race>80% of sample.

different ways. Sussman and colleagues (2003) used an "ethnicity" variable (among other variables) to predict two-year retention in their study, and then used "propensity for retention" as an ultimately nonsignificant covariate when examining treatment effects. Sun and colleagues (2008) observed an attrition bias in their study, such that the retained sample (compared to the loss-to-follow up sample) was less likely to be "African American" than "White" and more likely to be "Latino" than "White." Ethnicity was therefore used as a covariate, but like the aforementioned studies, the study authors did not report the parameters or interpret them in their analysis of program effects. Simon and colleagues (2002) adjusted for race in their logistic regression models and observed (as conveyed in a data table, with no mention in text) that "Hispanic" and "Non-Hispanic black" youth across conditions had greater odds of violent victimization than "Non-Hispanic whites," among male youth one-year post-intervention. A fourth program, Positive Action, was buttressed by a study that included "ethnicity" (among other demographic characteristics and measures of baseline problem behaviors) as an individual-level control variable "to reduce potential confounding effects and increase statistical precision." (Li et al., 2011, p. 193). Parameters (as conveyed in a data table, with no mention in text) conveyed that "Hispanic" and "White" students, across conditions, were less likely than "Black" students to self-report bullying behavior. A Maryland Ignition Interlock study included race as a potential "risk-factor" for alcohol-related traffic violations, including it as a covariate in their survival analysis (Rauch et al., 2011). This study found "African-Americans," across conditions, had a significantly higher hazard rate of alcohol-related traffic violations during the two-year post-intervention period. The group to whom "African-Americans" were compared in this analysis is not immediately apparent (Rauch et al., 2011). None of the aforementioned analyses that controlled for race examined program efficacy by race, which would require a subgroup analysis.

Of the 17 Blueprints programs, only 5 (29%) were buttressed by Blueprints Certified Studies that expressed intentions to examine treatment effects by race. Because race did not directly predict outcomes independent of other covariates, one study did not pursue an interaction (Olds et al., 1998). Two papers assessing the Body Project stated that there was "no evidence that participant ethnicity moderated the intervention" without any specification of method or display of data further explicating this claim (Stice et al., 2011, p. 504; 2006, p. 268). It is unclear whether such analyses, when completed, were sufficiently powered to detect interaction effects; one aforementioned study suggesting that there "was no evidence that participant age or ethnicity moderated the intervention effects" also wrote that "the sample was relatively homogeneous with regard to ethnicity and socioeconomic status, suggesting that care should be taken in generalizing the results to move diverse populations" (Stice et al., 2011, p. 504). A study examining Multisystemic Treatment (MST) evaluated the effects of several potential moderators, including race, on post-treatment arrests by examining the cross-product term of the treatment group and the moderating variable, entered last in a sequential regression model (Borduin et al., 1995). A nonsignificant change in R^2

for the cross-product term was interpreted to mean that MST was "equally effective with youths of different . . . ethnic backgrounds" (Borduin et al., 1995, p. 576). ParentCorps and Early College High School Initiative (ECHS) reported significant intervention effects by racial group. The ParentCorps study (Brotman et al., 2011) observed no primary outcomes (neither effective parenting practices nor child behavior problems) moderated by race (families characterized as "Black" or "Latino"), but did observe moderation of a secondary outcome (parental involvement), such that there was only an effect for "Black" families. In one ECHS study (Haxton et al., 2016), findings are interpreted by the authors as reducing a disparity (i.e., there was a stronger effect for "minority youth" than for "nonminority youth" on "post-secondary degree attainment") on one of the five outcomes examined. In a second ECHS study (Edmunds et al., 2017), however, the intervention exacerbated a disparity (i.e., there was a stronger effect for "not underrepresented" than for "underrepresented youth" on "college credits accrued" and "percentage of students who received any postsecondary credential"). Reviewing this selection of intervention studies begins to illustrate some of the complexities of analyzing subgroup effects in ways that advance equity in research and inform practice and policy decisions.

In summary, it appears that when evidence-users try to ascertain whether a model Blueprints study sample includes young people like those in the community in which they live or work, they may not be able to make this determination. Although U.S.-based studies buttressing the Blueprints model prevention programs do describe the race and/or ethnic composition of their study sample, the ways in which race is conceptualized, measured, and used could be improved. The studies buttressing Blueprints model program distinctions have been conducted on predominantly White samples, although four studies centered marginalized youth. Two of the four studies that centered marginalized youth benchmarked their findings (Hill et al., 2008) against policy-relevant performance gaps (Brotman et al., 2013, 2016) or effect sizes observed when studying the same program within a different sample (Kitzman et al., 1997). Although seven studies used race as a control variable in their analysis, very few studies reported on subgroup effects by race. This provides little information as to whether rigorously tested prevention programs perpetuate, sustain, or remediate racial and ethnic disparities in behavioral healthcare and outcomes.

Our findings generally comport with results website visitors would encounter when using target group filters embedded in the Blueprints website.

ENSURE HEALTHY DEVELOPMENT FOR YOUTH 147

There is currently only one model program (GenerationPMTO) listed as efficacious with Hispanic/Latino youth, no model programs listed as efficacious with African American youth, and no programs listed as efficacious with American Indian/Alaskan youth.[3] We also observed instances of model programs that are first described on their Blueprints Fact Sheet as applicable to "Race/Ethnicity: All" but subsequently nuanced with important additional information on an expandable menu containing "Race/Ethnicity/ Gender Details." For example, New Beginnings is listed as a program applicable to all races and ethnicities, but then nuanced to say that "significant moderated effects showed that the intervention had greater benefits for non-Hispanic White families than Hispanic families" (Blueprints, 2022).[4] Our follow-up review of the primary source revealed a study asking important questions, using appropriate methods, and finding that "many of these moderated effects showed positive benefits for non-Hispanic White families but not for Hispanic families. The findings indicate . . . the need for further adaptations to make the program effective for Hispanic parents" (Sandler et al., 2020, p. 60).

Without explicit evidence of efficacy for marginalized youth, the justification for "scaling up" programs requires maintaining an assumption of White universalism. Recognizing that withholding effective prevention programs from understudied populations could also adversely impact the behavioral health of marginalized youth, we join the call of Aarons and colleagues (2017) for researchers to work as urgently on scaling *out* effective prevention programs (i.e., adapting to novel populations or delivery systems) as on scaling them up, and in the meantime, "borrow strength" from previous studies to propel forward a prevention agenda and guide program adaptations. Our research funders, journal editors, and repository curators need to support, circulate, and track scale-out efforts (Alvidrez et al., 2019) such that they do not encounter the same challenges encountered by replication studies (Aos et al., 2011; Valentine et al., 2011).

A fully executed systematic review may be able to determine if there is additional knowledge available which can help answer these important user-oriented questions that is simply not part of the evidence Blueprints used to make an efficacy determination. Assuming momentarily that Blueprints does make good use of and promote available evidence, future randomized controlled trials (RCTs) of prevention programs should increase sample diversity and describe their samples more comprehensively. Primary and secondary analyses should assess subgroup effects in order to understand

148 VALERIE B. SHAPIRO ET AL.

whether prevention programs have sustained positive, and no iatrogenic, effects for marginalized youth, close health disparity gaps, and assess the extent to which they promote health equity. Importantly, observing the current state of transparency, inclusion, and subgroup analyses among Blueprints Certified Studies should not limit future work to filling these gaps. In the next section, we provide an illustration that describes the way one community circumvented these gaps, and adapted a program to expand access to an effective prevention program by immigrant and refugee families of color.

Case Example: An Equity-Enhancing Approach to Program Adaptation and Implementation

The Seattle Office of Immigrant and Refugee Affairs (OIRA), a Seattle government office, was established by city ordinance in 2012 to "improve the lives of Seattle's immigrant and refugee communities by engaging them in decisions about the City of Seattle's future and improving the City's programs and services to meet the needs of all constituents" (https://www.seattle.gov/iandraffairs/about-us). This office was therefore well positioned to coordinate a process of transforming services through the activities of science-based and equity-enhancing prevention to promote the healthy development of young people.

As consistent with OIRA's mission, ensuring the healthy development of all youth required centering the experiences of immigrant and refugee families. These families often share structurally situated etiological characteristics, unique from the experiences of dominant groups, that shape their risk for behavioral health problems. These include experiences of acculturative stress, bi/multi-cultural parenting expectations, language barriers, anti-immigrant racism, navigating new systems of care (e.g., schools, healthcare, social services, law enforcement), disruptions to social support, and uncertainty caused by shifting immigration policies. Evidence-based programs (EBPs) could help support immigrant and refugee families facing these challenges, but these same challenges may result in differential access to, engagement with, or effectiveness of available prevention programs. The work of Seattle OIRA provides an example of how a community might address these barriers to pursue healthy development for all youth.

This case illustrates an innovative approach to adapting the Strengthening Families 10–14 Program (SFP), a Blueprints for Healthy Youth Development

Certified Promising Program. The adapted SFP was delivered over the course of seven weeks per program cycle at a local community center. Sessions were held on Saturday mornings for 3.5 hours and were conducted in English with live interpretation. Participating families originated from Vietnam, Somalia, Eritrea, Ethiopia, Mexico, and Paraguay, and spoke six preferred languages (English, Somali, Vietnamese, Amharic, Tigrinya, and Spanish). In order for OIRA to utilize the EBP successfully across a wide variety of cultural contexts, the EBP required adaptations for fit and relevance in those contexts, but also required fidelity to the core elements of the program that have been shown to create successful outcomes (Hasson et al., 2020). Guided by the aforementioned idea of scaling out an intervention, we "borrowed strength" from existing evidence, and then used a *promoting* approach to explore SFP's potential as an equity-enhancing intervention. This case highlights three key practices: (1) utilizing a participatory approach in all phases of prevention planning and implementation; (2) tailoring an intervention to the unique cultures, contexts, and conditions of targeted beneficiaries; and (3) developing innovative service-delivery models that yield engagement, satisfaction, and intervention effects for program participants. We elaborate on each of these practices as we discuss our processes of program selection, adaptation, delivery, and evaluation.

Equity-Enhancing Interventions Prioritize Participatory Processes

Equity-enhancing prevention should use participatory processes to select and implement programs that are desirable to, engaging with, and effective for intended beneficiaries (Frerichs et al., 2016; Marsiglia & Booth, 2015). This can require an assessment of the extent to which intervention tailoring is needed in order for the program to be accessible, contextually relevant, culturally aligned, and meet the self-expressed needs of intended participants (Barrera et al., 2011; Colby et al., 2013). The use of participatory processes in program selection, adaptation, delivery, and evaluation can increase the likelihood that an intervention will include these essential elements because potential participants are involved in decision-making and can advise directly on program relevance as well as barriers to access and inclusion (Barrera et al., 2017). By participatory processes we mean the explicit and consistent prioritization of the intended program beneficiaries as equal planning partners with service providers throughout all phases. We acknowledge this may represent a paradigm shift from more traditional approaches to service delivery and may require additional resource and time allocation up front. Taking the long view, utilizing such approaches may actually conserve resources by increasing the likelihood that resulting programs will more authentically meet the needs of the participants, remove barriers to access and inclusion, and ultimately expand the benefits of such programs to more community members, which will have a greater impact on public health (Aarons et al., 2017; Jagers et al., 2019).

In our case example, this city-supported, local coalition of community residents, young people, and cross-sector professionals used a participatory approach beginning in the needs assessment phase. OIRA staff—including service providers, administration, and interpreters—worked in tandem with potential program beneficiaries to identify community needs that could be met through implementation of an EBP. Community partners in this process were solicited through previously developed relationships, either because they were prior participants in other OIRA programs or through community-outreach efforts with local immigrant and refugee organizations. What emerged from this process was a prioritized need for support in strengthening parenting skills, family cohesion, and preventing youth from becoming involved in crime, drug/alcohol use, and disengaging from school. After a search for effective EBPs to support this purpose, we were unable to find strong evidence for a program demonstrated to work for the population we intended to serve—new immigrant and refugee families of color from a variety of cultural and geographic backgrounds, speaking multiple preferred languages. We decided to choose the Strengthening Families 10–14 Program (SFP) because it was one of the few with a curriculum that included both parents and youth working together, a priority for community members. The participatory processes we cultivated during the initial phases of prevention planning were then catalyzed into collaborative partnerships that became essential for an effective SFP adaptation process.

Equity-Enhancing Interventions Are Tailored to Particular Cultures, Contexts, and Conditions

Equity-enhancing interventions require an adaptation process that ensures relevance to the cultural context of the participants while also delivering the

ENSURE HEALTHY DEVELOPMENT FOR YOUTH   151

curriculum components that have demonstrated effectiveness (Chambers & Norton, 2016). Collaborative partnerships between program developers, service users, and service providers increase the likelihood that this process will result in adaptation decisions that balance fidelity and fit because multiple relevant points of view are considered at crucial decision points (Baum et al., 2006). The kind of collaborative adaptation teams we are suggesting here are ideal for identifying and targeting curriculum fit efforts that take into consideration what Resnicow et al. (2000) refer to as *surface structure* and *deep structure* modifications. Surface structure fit efforts are concerned with matching intervention materials and content to the specific cultural contexts of the intended participants. Deep structure fit efforts incorporate historical, environmental, social, and cultural issues that shape participant behavioral health experiences. Both surface and deep structure concerns should be incorporated into intervention adaptation efforts and are best identified by a collaborative team that represents multiple lived experiences in relation to the curriculum material.

In our case, once SFP was identified as the best option, we invited the SFP developers from the University of Iowa to meet with our implementation team in Seattle for three days. Our implementation team included OIRA staff, intended program facilitators, a cadre of interpreters who had been working with OIRA in other community-based programs, and potential program participants. The purpose of the meeting was to train the team in the SFP curriculum and to collaboratively address adapting it for intended participants while maintaining fidelity with critical curricular components. A detailed review of every phase of the SFP curriculum was conducted for cultural relevance and potential access and inclusion barriers. When areas of discrepancy were identified, the collaborative team worked through the following process: (1) define the discrepancy in detail and the reason that particular curriculum element did not "fit"; (2) understand from the SFP developers if the identified part of the curriculum is necessary for fidelity; and (3) with those questions answered, create an adaptation that fits the cultural contexts of the participants and also maintains program fidelity. Using this process, we were able to make adaptations that did not change essential curriculum components as identified by the SFP developers.

Because we were not adapting SFP for one monocultural/monolinguistic group, but working with multiple culture and language contexts, this was a complicated and time-intensive process, at times requiring a variety of different adaptations for each identified discrepancy. However,

152 VALERIE B. SHAPIRO ET AL.

equity-enhancing interventions depend upon identifying programmatic and structural barriers to access and inclusion, such as cultural relevance, language barriers, and pragmatic issues of transportation, childcare, and cost. Having a collaborative adaptation and implementation team that represented program developers, providers, and users allowed us to more accurately identify potential barriers and plan our approach to overcoming them.

Equity-Enhancing Interventions Innovate Delivery Methods to Improve Service

A collaborative and successful adaptation process does not ensure that all barriers to access and inclusion are resolved; new programmatic and structural barriers to inclusion and retention will arise throughout service delivery. Equity-enhancing interventions require flexible and creative service-delivery methods to monitor for and address barriers, both in the adaptation phase of program adoption and during program implementation (August & Gewirtz, 2019; Barrera et al., 2017; Gottfredson et al., 2015)— an approach we refer to as responsive service delivery. Utilizing responsive service delivery promotes practices that increase participant engagement, satisfaction, and retention.

In our case, the collaborative partnerships nurtured during the adaptation process yielded a commitment to three central strategies for responsive service delivery. First, we *provided for the material needs* of program participants that, if not met, would have prohibited participation. We offered transportation to and from program sessions, a meal before and after each session, childcare during the session for children too young to participate in the SFP, and a small stipend for each family. Second, we *prioritized language accessibility* through translating all curriculum materials into relevant languages and providing live interpretation during each session. Because our program participants spoke six different preferred languages, we had to address the unique needs of multilingual program delivery. In order to do so, we provided one interpreter per family unit who sat with each family and provided live interpretation, allowing the participants to take part in all of the interactive elements of the curriculum. Our third and most important strategy for ensuring responsive service delivery was *expanding the role of interpreters* beyond providing language access. In our model, the interpreters were essential partners in program delivery who functioned as a bridge, connecting each family with the program material and also connecting the service-provision team to each family's unique needs. It was only through utilizing interpreters in this way that we were able to monitor for and address adaptation concerns, barriers to participation, and particular family circumstances that required additional resources. The program-delivery team, including interpreters, met each week in between sessions to debrief the prior session and plan for the upcoming session. During these team meetings, interpreters were able to share their observations regarding participant engagement, satisfaction, and need for further adaptation or adjustments to the curriculum. They also alerted the team to resource needs beyond the scope of the program (e.g., social, legal, and educational services), which allowed us to connect the family to the appropriate support. During the course of working on this project, some interpreters became interested in becoming SFP facilitators themselves and were provided support in getting trained to do so, which expanded the reach of the SFP program.

This case example of a practitioner-led adaptation (Alvidrez et al., 2019) of an EBP was characterized by participatory and collaborative processes that guided all phases of prevention planning and implementation and a responsive service-delivery approach. Evaluation of the program was guided by the question of whether the adapted version of SFP was successful in achieving the original curriculum learning outcomes. Participants were given the retrospective pre-post test included in the SFP curriculum (Molgaard et al., 1997), a single-administration self-report survey. It measures curriculum learning outcomes through participant-reported use of tools and skills covered in the curriculum, which are central to SFP's positive impact on risk and protective factors (Molgaard & Spoth, 2001). The survey was translated from English into five additional languages, youth and parents were surveyed separately, and interpretation was provided. Results indicate that the adapted SFP curriculum achieved the original SFP learning outcomes. Parents retrospectively reported increased use of all 20 parenting effectiveness tools, and youth retrospectively reported increased use of 13 of the 15 social/emotional skills taught in the curriculum. Despite adaptations done to tailor SFP for immigrant/refugee families, our outcomes show that the program had similar results to non-adapted implementations (C. Hockaday, personal communication, November 4, 2018). We share this experience in hopes that it will further our consideration for how youth services, using repositories of effective programs, may be transformed toward science-based and equity-enhancing prevention.

Can Unleashing Prevention Be Anti-Racist?

We write and conclude this chapter during a moment of broad recognition that *structural racism* (i.e., "laws, rules, and practices, sanctioned and even implemented by various levels of government, and embedded in the economic system as well as in cultural and societal norms" (Bailey et al., 2020, p. 768) create health disparities. To counteract structural racism, the role of racism in prevention research and practice must be made explicit. Like the vaccines developed to *prevent* severe COVID-19 disease, which were initially scarce in the United States, we recognize that the stated and unstated assumptions built into the prevention delivery system had powerful impacts on the potential of scientific advancement to translate into individual and societal well-being. It was true that different people, by nature of their individual characteristics (e.g., age, preexisting health condition) and contextual circumstances (e.g., residential density; nature of employment) had different profiles of risk for COVID-19 disease. We recognize that these profiles of risk were not random; many reflected the injustices of the society in which we all live. We also recognized that severe COVID cases, at the time of initial vaccine distribution, had been disproportionately experienced by Black, Indigenous, and Hispanics, who respectively, compared to Whites, had 2.47, 3.11, and 5.82 times the odds of COVID mortality among Medicare fee-for-service beneficiaries (Izurieta et al., 2020). Yet, the *absolute majority* of COVID mortalities among these Medicare beneficiaries did not come from Black (16%), Indigenous (1%), or Hispanic (5%) individuals, but rather from White (72%) individuals. Despite disparate risk, attending to those in the racially defined high-risk groups will not be the most *efficient* path to lowering the *overall* incidence of disease. We see here a prevention paradox (Rose, 1981), which also applies to behavioral health. Focusing on the overall prevalence and incidence of behavioral health disorders may obscure, if not disrupt, progress toward the reduction of behavioral health disparities between dominant and marginalized racial groups (Frohlich & Potvin, 2008).

We also write this chapter while calls for anti-racist scholarship appear from our professional societies (SSWR Social Policy Committee, 2020) and in our leading professional journals (Herrenkohl et al., 2020), asking social work scholars to lead an anti-racist agenda. We humbly submit that before the CBPH scholars are positioned to lead, we need to listen to and catch up with the leadership coming from our student, practitioner, and community activist coalition members and non-members, as well as scholars whose voices have not yet been amplified in the Grand Challenge to Ensure Healthy Youth Development. It is important to recognize that those who are assaulted by racism are the experts; experts must be given the room to speak hard truths (McCoy, 2021). We reiterate here Dr. McCoy's (2020b) warning that contemporary forces could inspire enthusiasm for hasty actions that may be ill-informed and misguided. As an antidote to counterproductive anti-racist intentions, she reminds us of our responsibility to include informed and engaged Black researchers on our teams and to ensure our research processes, from conceptualization to interpretation, are "filtered through eyes that do not benefit from white privilege" (p. 472). She further suggests that we treat race as a control (i.e., treat as a constant in statistical analysis) variable only in cases where we theorize experiences associated with race to be equal across race, and that we attribute racial differences to the historic and contemporary consequences of racism rather than to race itself. Finally, we should not question the legitimacy of research centered on the well-being of marginalized youth or require a comparison to youth from dominant groups in order to have the research contribute to our understanding of the world in which we live.

To ensure the healthy development of youth, we continue to envision state-supported, local coalitions of community residents, young people, and cross-sector collaborations acting together to transform existing youth services to prevent behavioral health problems and enhance equity. A robust body of evidence suggests that unleashing the power of prevention can improve the well-being of young people, on average, but we recognize that the path to reducing population rates of behavioral health problems, while also reducing disparities in behavioral health, is a true Grand Challenge at the intersection of *Ensuring Healthy Youth Development* and *Eliminating Racism*. Without explicit scrutiny and action to advance equity, scientific processes alone will not be able to overcome the racist societal systems in which they function. We can only achieve our goals by catalyzing a change in the larger, undesirable social contexts in which (a) young people develop disparately, (b) prevention research is conducted without careful consideration of the pervasive effects of racism, and (c) prevention services are scaled up to more youth without being scaled out to include more diverse youth. We have come to view a focus on diversity, equity, and inclusion as a primary pathway to achieve the goal of unleashing the power of prevention. We hope that you will join us.

Dedication

This chapter is dedicated to Elizabeth Angela Circo (1978–2020).

Acknowledgments

We write this chapter in appreciation to the Academy of Social Work and Social Welfare whose leadership team gave us the Grand Challenge framework through which to think deeply about the potential impacts of our science on society. We are indebted to all of the authors of the "original white paper" which articulates the Grand Challenge to Unleash the Power of Prevention, and the founding co-leads of the grand challenge, J. David Hawkins and Jeffrey M. Jenson, who have given the vision vibrant life over the past five years. We appreciate members of the Coalition for the Promotion of Behavioral Health (CPBH), and the CPBH Steering Committee. Further, we are grateful to the scholars (Martell Tesley, Michael Spencer, and others) who advanced a 13th Grand Challenge to Eliminate Racism. We have had tremendous thought-partners, including incoming Grand Challenge Initiative co-chairs joining Shapiro (Kimberly Bender and Melissa Lippold), members of the Center Prevention Research and Social Welfare (B. K. Elizabeth Kim, Kelly Ziemer, and Juyeon Lee), CPBH equity consultants (James Herbert Williams and Jacqueline Lloyd), SPR Advocacy Committee Chair (Lauren Supplee), and research assistant (Erica Gleason). Shapiro's work is funded by the William T. Grant Scholars Program and nurtured by their network of scholars striving to reduce inequality. We are honored to have worked with the Seattle Office of Immigrant and Refugee Affairs Strengthening Families 10–14 Program participants, interpreters, facilitators, and support staff. Statements in this chapter do not necessarily represent claims of these individuals or organizations.

Study Questions

1. When Aché Lytle says that in matters of equity, taking action does not necessarily lead to change, and change does not necessarily lead to progress, what do you think she means? What does it mean for the Grand Challenge of Ensuring Healthy Development for Youth and Unleashing the Power of Prevention? What does it mean for you?

ENSURE HEALTHY DEVELOPMENT FOR YOUTH 157

2. This chapter is predicated on the notion that seemingly innocuous omissions can reflect and perpetuate racism. Do you agree? Where do you observe these types of omissions in your contributions to social work research and practice?

3. This chapter suggests we must advocate for a societal investment in structural arrangements that prevent health problems in youth. What are some of the structural arrangements for which you advocate?

4. How does the Coalition for the Promotion of Behavioral Health (CBPH) describe equity-enhancing prevention throughout this chapter?

5. What are possible conceptualizations of race, racialization, and racism that could be used in intervention research to better convey the lived experiences of young people?

6. What do you think are the relative advantages and disadvantages of the four approaches conceptualized (centering, reducing, protecting, promoting) for determining whether an intervention is equity-enhancing? What are the implications of using each of the approaches and any potential for unintended consequences?

7. How do you think racial subgroup analyses should be conducted? Is it important to make comparisons, and if so, of what nature?

8. In what ways does the Seattle Office of Immigrant and Refugee Affairs (OIRA) delivery of Strengthening Families 10–14 Program use an equity-enhancing prevention framework to unleash the power of prevention?

9. What challenges emerge when we attempt to reduce the overall incidence of behavioral health problems in a population while we simultaneously attempt to reduce the racial and ethnic disparities in these problems? What will it take to achieve both of these goals within a decade? What are some examples of progress that are explored in this chapter?

Notes

1. People with experiences of anti-Black racism have different preferred terms for the language used to characterize people sharing this experience. In our use of these terms, we intend to emphasize the politically constructed and structurally embedded nature of oppression, but not so entrenched as to be irremediable. We proceed in this chapter using the term *marginalized*, as the term *minoritized* may be less familiar to our readers, and we do not wish to inadvertently introduce yet another negative term to describe the circumstances of Black people.

2. As current members of the CPBH, some of whom contributed to the original white paper and others who did not, we now write in the first-person plural to take

158 VALERIE B. SHAPIRO ET AL.

collective ownership of the powerful contributions and omissions of the CPBH framing documents in order to assess the work for the perpetuation of racism and make recommendations for future directions.

3. The justification for listing GenerationPMTO as efficacious for Hispanic/Latino youth is a study (Martinez & Eddy, 2005) that is not among the *Blueprints Certified Studies* that officially buttress the model program designation, although it is a good example of using a promoting approach to explore the equity-enhancing effects of an intervention.

4. Although referenced on the Blueprints web pages associated with this program, this study was not listed as among the *Blueprints Certified Studies* (and therefore not included in our prior review).

References

Aarons, G. A., Sklar, M., Mustanski, B., Benbow, N., & Hendricks Brown, C. (2017). "Scaling-out" evidence-based interventions to new populations or new health care delivery systems. *Implementation Science, 12,* 111. https://doi.org/10.1186/s13 012-017-0640-6

Alegria, M., Green, J. G., McLaughlin, K. A., & Loder, S. (2015). Disparities in child and adolescent mental health and mental health services in the U.S. New York, NY: William T. Grant Foundation.

Alvidrez, J., Nápoles, A. M., Bernal, G., Lloyd, J., Cargill, V., Godette, D., Cooper, L., Horse Brave Heart, M. Y., Das, R., & Farhat, T. (2019). Building the evidence base to inform planned intervention adaptations by practitioners serving health disparity populations. *American Journal of Public Health, 109*(S1), S94–S101. https://doi.org/10.2105/AJPH.2018.304915.

American Psychiatric Association (2017). Mental health disparities: African Americans. Retrieved from https://www.psychiatry.org/File%20Library/Psychiatrists/Cultural-Competency/Mental-Health-Disparities/Mental-Health-Facts-for-African-Americ ans.pdf.

Aos, S., Cook, T. D., Elliott, D. S., Gottfredson, D. C., Hawkins, J. D., Lipsey, M. W., & Tolan, P. (2011). Commentary on Valentine, Jeffrey, et al. Replication in prevention science. *Prevention Science, 12*(2), 121.

August, G. J., & Gewirtz, A. (2019). Moving toward a precision-based, personalized framework for prevention science: Introduction to the special issue. *Prevention Science, 20,* 1–9.

Baer, J. S., Kivlahan, D. R., Blume, A. W., McKnight, P., & Marlatt, G. A. (2001). Brief intervention for heavy-drinking college students: 4-year follow-up and natural history. *American Journal of Public Health, 91,* 1310–1316.

Bailey, Z. D., Feldman, J. M., & Bassett, M. T. (2020). How structural racism works: Racist policies as a root cause of U.S. racial health inequities. *New England Journal of Medicine, 384*(8), 768–773.

Barrera, M., Berkel, C., & Castro, F. G. (2017). Directions for the advancement of culturally adapted preventive interventions: Local adaptations, engagement, and sustainability. *Prevention Science, 18*(6), 640–648.

Barrera, M., Castro, F. G., & Holleran-Steiker, L. K. (2011). A critical analysis of approaches to the development of preventive interventions for subcultural groups. *American Journal of Community Psychology, 48,* 439–454.

Baum, F., MacDougall, C., & Smith, D. (2006). Participatory action research. *Journal of Epidemiology & Community Health, 60*(10), 854–857.

Beadle, M. R., & Graham, G. N. (2011). Collective action to end health disparities. *American Journal of Public Health, 101*(S1), S16–S18.

Beck, K. H., Rauch, W. J., Baker, E. A., & Williams, A. F. (1999). Effects of ignition interlock license restrictions on drivers with multiple alcohol offenses: A randomized trial in Maryland. *American Journal of Public Health, 89,* 1696–1700.

Biglan, A., Flay, B. R., Embry, D. D., & Sandler, I. N. (2012). The critical role of nurturing environments for promoting human well-being. *American Psychologist, 67*(4), 257.

Blueprints. (2022). New Beginnings Fact Sheet. https://www.blueprintsprograms.org/programs/613999999/new-beginnings-for-children-of-divorce/

Borduin, C. M., Henggeler, S. W., Blaske, D. M., & Stein, R. J. (1990). Multisystemic treatment of adolescent sexual offenders. *International Journal of Offender Therapy and Comparative Criminology, 35,* 105–114.

Borduin, C. M., Mann, B. J., Cone, L. T., Henggeler, S. W., Fucci, B. R., Blaske, D. M. & Williams, R. A. (1995). Multisystemic treatment of serious juvenile offenders: Long-term prevention of criminality and violence. *Journal of Consulting and Clinical Psychology, 63,* 569–578.

Borduin, C. M., Schaeffer, C. M., & Heiblum, N. (2009). A randomized clinical trial of Multisystemic Therapy with juvenile sexual offenders: Effects on youth social ecology and criminal activity. *Journal of Consulting and Clinical Psychology, 77,* 26–37.

Borsari, B., & Carey, K. B. (2000). Effects of a brief motivational intervention with college student drinkers. *Journal of Consulting and Clinical Psychology, 68,* 728–733

Botvin, G. J., Baker, E., Dusenbury, L., Botvin, E. M., & Diaz, T. (1995). Long-term follow-up results of a randomized drug abuse prevention trial in a white middle-class population. *Journal of the American Medical Association, 273,* 1106–1112.

Botvin, G. J., Griffin, K. W., & Nichols, T. R. (2006). Preventing youth violence and delinquency through a universal school-based prevention approach. *Prevention Science, 7,* 403–408.

Braveman, P., Arkin, E., Orleans, T., Proctor, D., Acker, J., & Plough, A. (2017). *What is health equity? And what difference does a definition make?* Princeton, NJ: Robert Wood Johnson Foundation.

Braveman, P., Arkin, E., Orleans, T., Proctor, D., Acker, J., & Plough, A. (2018). What is health equity? *Behavioral Science & Policy, 4*(1), 1–14.

Brown, E. C., Hawkins, J. D., Rhew, I. C., Shapiro, V. B., Abbott, R. D., Oesterle, S., ... Catalano, R. F. (2014). Prevention system mediation of Communities That Care effects on youth outcomes. *Prevention Science, 15*(5), 623–632.

Brotman, L. M., Calzada, E., Huang, K., Kingston, S., Dawson-McClure, S., Kamboukos, D., Rosenfelt, A., Schwab, A., & Petkova, E. (2011). Promoting effective parenting practices and preventing child behavior problems in school among ethnically diverse families from underserved, urban communities. *Child Development, 82*(1), 258–276.

Brotman, L. M., Dawson-McClure, S., Calzada, E. J., Huang, K., Kamboukos, D., Palamar, J. J., & Petkova, E. (2013). Cluster (school) RCT of ParentCorps: Impact on kindergarten academic achievement. *Pediatrics, 131*(5), 1521–1529.

Brotman, L. M., Dawson-McClure, S., Kamboukos, D., Huang, K., Calzada, E., Goldfeld, K., & Petkova, E. (2016). Effects of ParentCorps in prekindergarten on child mental health and academic performance: Follow-up of a randomized clinical trial through 8 years of age. *Journal of the American Medical Association Pediatrics, 170*(12), 1149–1155.

Carter-Pokras, O., & Baquet, C. (2002). What is a "health disparity"? *Public Health Reports, 117*(5), 426–434. doi: 10.1093/phr/117.5.426.

Castro, F. G., Barrera, M., Jr., & Holleran Steiker, L. K. (2010). Issues and challenges in the design of culturally adapted evidence-based interventions. *Annual Review of Clinical Psychology, 6,* 213–239.

160 VALERIE B. SHAPIRO ET AL.

Castro, F. G., Barrera, M., & Martinez, C. R. (2004). The cultural adaptation of prevention interventions: Resolving tensions between fidelity and fit. *Prevention Science*, 5(1), 41–45.

Centers for Disease Control and Prevention (2009). Preventive health care. Retrieved June 28, 2020, from http://web.archive.org/web/20190525141113/https://www.cdc.gov/healthcommunication/toolstemplates/entertainmented/tips/preventivehealth.html.

Centers for Disease Control and Prevention (2019). High school youth risk behavior survey data. Retrieved from https://nccd.cdc.gov/Youthonline/App/Default.aspx.

Chambers, D. A., & Norton, W. E. (2016). The adaptome: Advancing the science of intervention adaptation. *American Journal of Preventative Medicine*, 51(4S2), S124–S131.

Cheadle, A., Wagner, E. H., Walls, M., Diehr, P., Bell, M. A., Anderman, C., McBride, C. M., Catalano, R. F., Pettigrew, E., Simmons, R., & Neckerman, H. J. (2001). The effect of neighborhood-based community organizing: Results from the Seattle Minority Youth Health Project. *Health Services Research*, 36(4), 671–689.

Choi, Y., Harachi, T. W., Gillmore, M. R., & Catalano, R. F. (2005). Applicability of the social development model to urban ethnic minority youth: Examining the relationship between external constraints, family socialization, and problem behaviors. *Journal of Research on Adolescence*, 15(4), 505–534.

Coalition for the Promotion of Behavioral Health (2019). Ensuring the healthy development for all youth: Unleashing the power of prevention strategic plan. Retrieved from https://www.coalitionforbehavioralhealth.org/strategic-plan.

Cohen, L., Chavez, V., & Chehimi, S. (2010). *Prevention is primary: Strategies for community well being* (2nd edition). San Francisco: Josey-Bass.

Colby, M., Hecht, M. L., Miller-Day, M., Krieger, J. L., Syvertsen, A. K., Graham, J. W., & Pettigrew, J. (2013). Adapting school-based substance use prevention curriculum through cultural grounding: A review and exemplar of adaptation processes for rural schools. *American Journal of Community Psychology*, 51(1), 190–205.

Comas-Diaz, L., Hall, G. N., & Neville, H. A. (2019). Racial trauma: Theory, research and healing: Introduction to special issue. *American Psychologist*, 74(1), 1–5.

Corley, N. A., & Young, S. M. (2018). Is social work still racist? A content analysis of recent literature. *Social Work*, 63(4), 317–326.

DeGarmo, D. S., Patterson, G. R., & Forgatch, M. S. (2004). How do outcomes in a specified parent training intervention maintain or wane over time? *Prevention Science*, 5, 73–89.

Deng, S., & Roosa, M. W. (2007). Family influences on adolescent delinquent behaviors: Applying the social development model to a Chinese sample. *American Journal of Community Psychology*, 40(3–4), 333–44.

Dent, C., Sussman, S., & Stacy, A. (2001). Project Towards No Drug Abuse: Generalizability to a general high school sample. *Preventive Medicine*, 32, 514–520.

Dolley, S. (2018). Big data's role in precision public health. *Frontiers in Public Health*, 6, 68.

Duran, D. G., & Pérez-Stable, E. J. (2019). Novel approaches to advance minority health and health disparities research. *American Journal of Public Health*, 109(S1), S8–S10. https://doi.org/10.2105/AJPH.2018.304931.

Eddy, J., Whaley, R., & Chamberlain, P. (2004). The prevention of violent behavior by chronic and serious male juvenile offenders: A 2-year follow-up of a randomized clinical trial. *Journal of Emotional and Behavioral Disorders*, 12(1), 2–8.

Edmunds, J. A., Unlu, F., Glennie, E., Bernstein, L., Fesler, L., Furey, J., & Arshavsky, N. (2017). Smoothing the transition to postsecondary education: The impact of the early college model. *Journal of Research on Educational Effectiveness*, 10(2), 297–325.

Eisenberg, N., Brown, E. C., Pérez-Gómez, A., Mejía-Trujillo, J., Paredes-Aguilar, M., Cardozo-Macias, F., . . . Guttmannova, K. (2020). Community utilization of risk

ENSURE HEALTHY DEVELOPMENT FOR YOUTH   161

and protective factor data for prevention planning in Chile and Colombia. *Health Promotion International, 36*(2), 417–429.

Fagan, A. A., Bumbarger, B. K., Barth, R. P., Bradshaw, C. P., Cooper, B. R., Supplee, L. H., & Walker, D. K. (2019). Scaling up evidence-based interventions in US public systems to prevent behavioral health problems: Challenges and opportunities. *Prevention Science, 20*, 1147–1168. https://doi.org/10.1007/s11121-019-01048-8

Fagan, A. A., Hawkins, J. D., Catalano, R. F., & Farrington, D. P. (2019). *Communities that care: Building community engagement and capacity to prevent youth behavior problems.* New York: Oxford University Press.

Ford, C. L., & Airhihenbuwa, C. O. (2010). The public health critical race methodology: Praxis for antiracism research. *Social Science & Medicine, 71*(8), 1390–1398.

Forgatch, M., & DeGarmo, D. (1999). Parenting through change: An effective prevention program for single mothers. *Journal of Consulting and Clinical Psychology, 67*(5), 711–724.

Forgatch, M. S., Patterson, G. R., DeGarmo, D. S., & Beldavs, Z. (2009). Testing the Oregon delinquency model with 9-year follow-up of the Oregon Divorce Study. *Development and Psychopathology, 21*(5), 637–660.

Fong, R., Lubben, J., & Barth, R. P. (Eds.). (2017). *Grand challenges for social work and society.* Oxford: Oxford University Press.

Frerichs, L., Hassmiller-Lich, K., Dave, G., & Corbie-Smith, G. (2016). Integrating systems science and community-based participatory research to achieve health equity. *American Journal of Public Health, 106*(2), 215–222.

Frohlich, K. L., & Potvin, L. (2008). The inequality paradox: The population approach and vulnerable populations. *American Journal of Public Health, 98*(2), 216–221.

Gilman, A. B. (2014). *Incarceration and the life course: Predictors, correlates, and consequences of juvenile incarceration* (Doctoral dissertation). University of Washington.

Ginther, D. K., Schaffer, W. T., Schnell, J., Masimore, B., Liu, F., Haak, L. L., & Kington, R. (2011). Race, ethnicity, and NIH research awards. *Science, 333*(6045), 1015–1019.

Ginwright, S., Cammarota, J., & Noguera, P. (2005). Youth, social justice, and communities: Toward a theory of urban youth policy. *Social Justice, 32*, 24–40.

Gottfredson, D. C., Cook, T. D., Gardner, F. E., Gorman-Smith, D., Howe, G. W., Sandler, I. N. & Zafft, K. M. (2015). Standards of evidence for efficacy, effectiveness, and scale-up research in prevention science: Next generation. *Prevention Science, 16*, 893–926.

Gottfredson, D. C., Kearley, B., Thornberry, T. P., Slothower, M., Devlin, D., & Fader, J. J. (2018). Scaling-up evidence-based programs using a public funding stream: A randomized trial of Functional Family Therapy for court-involved youth. *Prevention Science, 19*(7), 939–953. doi 10.1007/s11121-018-0936-z.

Guttmannova, K., Wheeler, A. C., Hill, K. G., Evans-Campbell, T. A., Hartigan, L. A., Jones, T. M., Hawkins, J. D., Catalano, R. F. (2017). Assessment of risk and protection in Native American youth: Steps toward conducting culturally relevant, sustainable prevention in Indian Country. *Journal of Community Psychology, 45*(3), 346–362.

Haggerty, K. P., Skinner, M. L., MacKenzie, E. P., & Catalano, R. F. (2007). A randomized trial of Parents Who Care: Effects on key outcomes at 24-month follow-up. *Prevention Science, 8*, 249–260. http://dx.doi.org/10.1007/s11121-007-0077-2.

Hasson, H., Grondal, H., Hedberg Rundgren, A., Avby, G., Uvhagen, H., & vonThiele Schwarz, U. (2020). How can evidence-based interventions give the best value for users in social services? Balance between adherence and adaptations: A study protocol. *Implementation Science Communications, 1*(15), 1–9.

162 VALERIE B. SHAPIRO ET AL.

Hawkins, J. D., Catalano, R. F., Jr., & Associates. (1992). *Communities that care: Action for drug abuse prevention*. San Francisco, CA: Jossey-Bass.

Hawkins, J. D., Catalano, R. F., & Arthur, M. W. (2002). Promoting science-based prevention in communities. *Addictive Behaviors, 27*(6), 951–976.

Hawkins, J. D., Jenson, J. M., Catalano, R., Fraser, M. W., Botvin, G. J., Shapiro, V., . . . Stone, S. (2015). Unleashing the power of prevention. *American Journal of Medical Research, 3*(1), 39.

Hawkins, J. D., Kosterman, R., Catalano, R. F., Hill, K. G., & Abbott, R. D. (2008). Effects of social development intervention in childhood 15 years later. *Archives of Pediatrics and Adolescent Medicine, 162*, 1133–1141. http://dx.doi.org/10.1001/archpedi.162.12.1133.

Hawkins, J. D., Oesterle, S., Brown, E. C., Arthur, M. W., Abbott, R. D., Fagan, A. A., & Catalano, R. F. (2009). Results of a type 2 translational research trial to prevent adolescent drug use and delinquency: A test of Communities That Care. *Archives of Pediatrics & Adolescent Medicine, 163*(9):789–798.

Hawkins, J. D., Oesterle, S., Brown, E. C., Abbott, R. D., & Catalano, R. F. (2014). Youth problem behaviors 8 years after implementing the Communities That Care prevention system: A community randomized trial. *JAMA Pediatrics, 168*(2), 122–129.

Haxton, C., Song, M., Zeiser, K., Berger, A., Turk-Bicakci, L., Garet, M. S. Knudson, J., & Hoshen, G. (2016). Longitudinal findings from the Early College High School Initiative Impact Study. *Educational Evaluation and Policy Analysis, 38*(2), 410–430.

Herrenkohl, T. I., Wooten, N. R., Fedina, L., Bellamy, J. L., Bunger, A. C., Chen, D. G., ... Solomon, P. (2020). Advancing our commitment to antiracist scholarship. *Journal of the Society for Social Work and Research, 11*(3), 365–368.

Hill, C. J., Bloom, H. S., Black, A. R., & Lipsey, M. W. (2008). Empirical benchmarks for interpreting effect sizes in research. *Child Development Perspectives, 2*(3), 172–177.

Hill, K. G., Bailey, J. A., Hawkins J. D., Catalano, R. F., Kosterman, R., Oesterle, S., & Abbott, R. D. (2014). The onset of STI diagnosis through Age 30: Results from the Seattle Social Development Project intervention. *Prevention Science, 15*(Suppl 1), S19–S32.

Howard, M. O., & Garland, E. L. (2015). Social work research: 2044. *Journal of the Society for Social Work and Research, 6*(2), 173–200.

Izurieta, H. S., Graham, D. J., Jiao, Y., Hu, M., Lu, Y., Wu, Y., Chillarige, Y., Wernecke, M., Pratt, D., . . . Kelman, J. (2021). Natural history of COVID-19: Risk factors for hospitalizations and deaths among > 26 million US Medicare beneficiaries. *The Journal of Infectious Diseases, 223*(6), 945–956.

Jagers, R. J., Rivas-Drake, D., & Williams, B. (2019). Transformative social and emotional learning (SEL): Toward SEL in service of educational equity and excellence. *Educational Psychologist, 54*(3), 162–184.

Jenson, J. M., & Bender, K. A. *Preventing child and adolescent problem behavior: Evidence-based strategies in schools, families, and communities*. Oxford: Oxford University Press, 2014.

Jenson, J. M., & Hawkins, J. D. (2017). Ensure healthy development for all youth: Unleashing the power of prevention. In R. Fong, J. Lubben, & R.P. Barth (Eds.), *Grand challenges for social work and society: Social progress engineered by science* (pp. 18–35). New York: Oxford University Press.

Kerr, D. C. R., Leve, L. D., & Chamberlain, P. (2009). Pregnancy rates among juvenile justice girls in two randomized controlled trials of Multidimensional Treatment Foster Care. *Journal of Counseling and Clinical Psychology, 77*(3), 588–593.

Kitzman, H., Olds, D. L., Henderson, C. R., Hanks, C., Cole, R., Tatelbaum, R., McConnochie, K.M., Sidora, K., Luckey, D. W., Shaver, D., Engelhardt, K., James, D., & Barnard, K. (1997). Effect of prenatal and infancy home visitation by nurses on pregnancy outcomes, childhood injuries, and repeated childbearing. *Journal of the American Medical Association, 278*(8), 644–652.

Koh, H. K., Graham, G., & Glied, S. A. (2011). Reducing racial and ethnic disparities: the action plan from the department of health and human services. *Health Affairs, 30*(10), 1822–1829.

Koh, H. K., & Sebelius, K. G. (2010). Promoting prevention through the affordable care act. *New England Journal of Medicine, 363*(14), 1296–1299.

Kumpfer, K. L., Alvarado, R., Smith, P., & Bellamy, N. (2002). Cultural sensitivity and adaptation in family-based prevention interventions. *Prevention Science, 3*(3), 241–246.

Leonardo, Z. (2004). The color of supremacy: Beyond the discourse of "white privilege." *Educational Philosophy and Theory, 36*(2), 137–152.

Letourneau, E. J., Henggeler, S. W., Borduin, C. M., Schewe, P. A., McCart, M. R., Chapman, J. E., & Saldana, L. (2009). Multisystemic Therapy for juvenile sexual offenders: 1-year results from a randomized effectiveness trial. *Journal of Family Psychology, 23*, 89–102.

Leve, L. D., Chamberlain, P., & Reid, J. B. (2005). Intervention outcomes for girls referred from juvenile justice: Effects on delinquency. *Journal of Consulting and Clinical Psychology, 73*(6), 1181–1185.

Lewis, K. M., Bavarian, N., Snyder, F. J., Acock, A., Day, J., DuBois, D. L., Ji, P., Schure, M. B., Silverthorn, N., Vuchinich, S., & Flay, B. R. (2012). Direct and mediated effects of a social-emotional and character development program on adolescent substance use. *The International Journal of Emotional Education, 4*(1), 56–78.

Li, K. K., Washburn, I., DuBois, D. L., Vuchinich, S., Ji, P., Brechling, V., Day, J., Beets, M. W., Acock, A. C., Berbaum, M., Snyder, F., & Flay, B. R. (2011). Effects of the Positive Action program on problem behaviors in elementary school students: A matched-pair randomized control trial in Chicago. *Psychology & Health, 26*, 187–204.

Lindsey, M. A., Sheftall, A. H., Xiao, Y., & Joe, S. (2019). Trends of suicidal behaviors among high school students in the United States: 1991–2017. *Pediatrics, 144*(5), 1–11.

Lorenc, T., & Oliver, K. (2014). Adverse effects of public health interventions: a conceptual framework. *Journal of Epidemiology & Community Health, 68*(3), 288–290.

Lytle, A. (2020). Our resilience is our revolution. Scholars Retreat Keynote Presentation. William T. Grant Foundation.

Malti, T., Ribeaud, D., & Eisner, M. P. (2011). The effectiveness of two universal preventive interventions in reducing children's externalizing behavior: A cluster randomized controlled trial. *Journal of Clinical Child & Adolescent Psychology, 40*(5), 677–692.

Marlatt, G. A., Baer, J. S., Kivlahan, D. R., Dimeff, L. A., Larimer, M. E., Quigley, L. A., Somers, J. M., & Williams, E. (1998). Screening and brief intervention for high-risk college student drinkers: Results from a 2-year follow-up assessment. *Journal of Consulting and Clinical Psychology, 66*, 604–615.

Marsiglia, F. F., & Booth, J. M. (2015). Cultural adaptation of interventions in real practice settings. *Research on Social Work Practice, 25*(4), 423–432.

Martinez, C. R., & Eddy, J. M. (2005). Effects of culturally adapted parent management training on Latino youth behavioral health outcomes. *Journal of Consulting and Clinical Psychology, 73*(4), 841–851.

McCoy, H. (2020a). Gun violence in urban communities must get the same attention as suburban school shootings [OpEd]. *The Hill.* https://thehill.com/opinion/civil-rights/490669-gun-violence-in-urban-communities-must-get-the-same-attention-as-white.

McCoy, H. (2020b). Black lives matter, and yes, you are racist: The parallelism of the twentieth and twenty-first centuries. *Child and Adolescent Social Work Journal, 37*(5), 463–475.

McCoy, H. (2021). What do you call a Black woman with a PhD? A N*****: How race trumps education no matter what. *Race and Justice, 11*(3), 318–327.

164   VALERIE B. SHAPIRO ET AL.

McCoy, H., Leverso, J., & Bowen, E. A. (2016). What the MAYSI-2 can tell us about anger/ irritability and trauma. *International Journal of Offender Therapy and Comparative Criminology, 60*(5), 555–574. doi: 10.1177/0306624X14555855.

McCoy, H., & McKay, C. (2006). Preparing social workers to identify and integrate culturally affirming bibliotherapy into treatment. *Social Work Education, 25*(7), 680–693.

McCoy, H., & Pearson, E. (2019). Racial disparities in the juvenile justice system. In *Encyclopedia of Social Work*. Oxford: Oxford University Press. https://doi.org/10.1093/acrefore/9780199975839.013.1288

McGlynn-Wright, A., Crutchfield, R. D., Skinner, M. L., & Haggerty, K. P. (2020). The usual, racialized, suspects: The consequence of police contacts with Black and White youth on adult arrest. *Social Problems, 69*(2), 299–315.

McGoldrick, M., Giordano, J., & Garcia-Preto, N. (1996). Overview: Ethnicity and family therapy. *Ethnicity and Family Therapy, 2*, 1–27.

Mihalic, S. F., & Elliott, D. S. (2015). Evidence-based programs registry: Blueprints for healthy youth development. *Evaluation and Program Planning, 48*, 124–131.

Molgaard, V. K., Kumpfer, K. L., & Fleming, E. 1997. *The Strengthening Families program: For parents and Iowa youth 10–14 leader guide*. Ames, IA: Iowa State University Extension.

Molgaard, V., & Spoth, R. (2001) The Strengthening Families program for young adolescents: Overview and outcomes. *Residential Treatment for Children & Youth, 18*(3), 15–29. doi: 10.1300/J007v18n03_03.

Morning, A. (2008). Reconstructing race in science and society: Biology textbooks, 1952– 2002. *American Journal of Sociology, 114*(S1), S106–S137.

Munn, Z., Peters, M. D., Stern, C., Tufanaru, C., McArthur, A., & Aromataris, E. (2018). Systematic review or scoping review? Guidance for authors when choosing between a systematic or scoping review approach. *BMC Medical Research Methodology, 18*(1), 143.

The National Academy of Sciences (2019). *The promise of adolescence: Realizing opportunity for all youth*. Washington, DC: National Academies Press. https://www.nap.edu/resource/25388/Adolescent%20Development.pdf.

National Partnership for Action to End Health Disparities. (April 2011). National Stakeholder Strategy for Achieving Health Equity. Rockville, MD: U.S. Department of Health & Human Services, Office of Minority Health. Retrieved from: https://web.archive.org/web/20150906111658/http://www.minorityhealth.hhs.gov/npa/files/Plans/NSS/NSS_07_Section3.pdf.

O'Connell, M. E., Boat, T., & Warner, K. E. (2009). *Preventing mental, emotional, and behavioral disorders among young people: Progress and possibilities*. Washington, DC: National Academies Press.

Olds, D. L., Eckenrode, J., Henderson, C. R., Kitzman, H., Powers, J., Cole, R., Sidora, K., Morris, P., Pettitt, L. M., & Luckey, D. (1997). Long-term effects of home visitation on maternal life course and child abuse and neglect: 15-year follow-up of a randomized trial. *Journal of the American Medical Association, 278*(8), 637–643.

Olds, D. L., Henderson, C. R., Chamberlin, R., & Tatelbaum, R. (1986). Preventing child abuse and neglect: A randomized trial of nurse home visitation. *Pediatrics, 78*, 65–78.

Olds, D. L., Henderson, C. R., Cole, R., Eckenrode, J., Kitzman, H., Luckey, D., Pettitt, L., Sidora, K., Morris, P., & Powers, J. (1998). Long-term effects of nurse home visitation on children's criminal and antisocial behavior: 15-year follow-up of a randomized controlled trial. *Journal of the American Medical Association, 280*(14), 1238–1244.

ENSURE HEALTHY DEVELOPMENT FOR YOUTH   165

Olds, D. L., Kitzman, H., Cole, R., Robinson, J., Sidora, K., Luckey, D. W., Henderson, C. R., Hanks, C., Bondy, J., & Holmberg, J. (2004). Effects of nurse home visiting on maternal life course and child development: Age 6 follow-up results of a randomized trial. *Pediatrics, 114,* 1550–1559.

Olds, D. L., Robinson, J., O'Brien, R., Luckey, D. W., Pettitt, L. M., Henderson, C. R., Ng, R. K., Sheff, K. L., Korfmacher, J., Hiatt, S., & Talmi, A. (2002). Home visiting by paraprofessionals and by nurses: A randomized, controlled trial. *Pediatrics, 110,* 486–496.

Pacific Northwest Evidence-Based Practice Center. (2019). *Achieving health equity in preventative services.* Rockville, MD: U.S. Department of Health and Human Services. https://web.archive.org/web/20201021054501/https://effectivehealthcare.ahrq.gov/sites/default/files/pdf/cer-222-report-health-equity-preventive-services.pdf.

Patterson, G. R., Forgatch, M. S., & DeGarmo, D. S. (2010). Cascading effects following intervention. *Development and Psychopathology, 22,* 949–970.

Penchansky, R., & Thomas, J. W. (1981). The concept of access: Definition and relationship to consumer satisfaction. *Medical Care, 19*(2), 127–140.

Perrino, T., Pantin, H., Prado, G., Huang, S., Brincks, A., Howe, G., Beardslee, W., Sandler, I., & Brown, C. H. 2014. Preventing internalizing symptoms among Hispanic adolescents: A synthesis across Familias Unidas trials. *Prevention Science, 15*(6), 917–928.

Powell, J. A., Menendian, S., & Ake, W. (2019). *Targeted universalism: Policy & practice.* Haas Institute for a Fair and Inclusive Society. Berkeley: University of California.

Prado, G., Pantin, H., Briones, E., Schwartz, S. J., Feaster, D., Huang, S., Sullivan, S., Tapia, M. I., Sabillon, E., Lopez, B., & Szapocznik, J. (2007). A randomized controlled trial of a parent-centered intervention in preventing substance use and HIV risk behaviors in Hispanic adolescents. *Journal of Consulting and Clinical Psychology, 75*(6), 914–926.

Prado, G., Cordova, D., Huang, S., Estrada, Y., Rosen, A., Bacio, G. A., Leon Jimenez, G., Pantin, H., Brown, C. H., Velazquez, M. R., Villamar, J., Freitas, D., Tapia, M. I., & McCollister, K. 2012. The efficacy of Familias Unidas on drug and alcohol outcomes for Hispanic delinquent youth: Main effects and interaction effects by parental stress and social support. *Drug and Alcohol Dependence, 125*(Suppl 1), S18–S25.

Rauch, W. J., Ahlin, E. M., Zador, P. L., Howard, J. M., & Duncan, G. D. (2011). Effects of administrative ignition interlock license restrictions on drivers with multiple alcohol offenses. *Journal of Experimental Criminology, 7,* 127–148.

Resnicow, K., Soler, R., Braithwaite, R. L., Ahluwalia, J. S., & Butler, J. (2000). Cultural sensitivity in substance use prevention. *Journal of Community Psychology, 28*(3), 271–290.

Rohde, P., Stice, E., Shaw, H., & Briere, F. N. (2014). Indicated cognitive behavioral group depression prevention compared to bibliotherapy and brochure control: Acute effects of an effectiveness trial with adolescents. *Journal of Consulting and Clinical Psychology, 82*(1), 65–74.

Roosa, M. W., Zeiders, K. H., Knight, G. P., Gonzales, N. A., Tein, J.-Y., Saenz, D., O'Donnell, M., & Berkel, C. (2011). A test of the social development model during the transition to junior high with Mexican American adolescents. *Developmental Psychology, 47*(2), 527–37.

Rose, G. (1981). Strategy of prevention: lessons from cardiovascular disease. *British Medical Journal, 282,* 1847–1851.

Rowe, H. L., & Trickett, E. J. (2018). Student diversity representation and reporting in universal school-based social and emotional learning programs: Implications for generalizability. *Educational Psychology Review, 30*(2), 559–583.

166 VALERIE B. SHAPIRO ET AL.

Sandler, I., Wolchik, S., Mazza, G., Gunn, H., Tein, J. Y., Berkel, C., Jones, S., & Porter, M. (2020). Randomized effectiveness trial of the New Beginnings Program for divorced families with children and adolescents. *Journal of Clinical Child and Adolescent Psychology, 49*(1), 60–78.

Saperstein, A., & Penner, A. M. (2012). Racial fluidity and inequality in the United States. *American Journal of Sociology, 118*(3), 676–727.

Scott, L. D., Jr., & McCoy, H. (2018). Correlates of somatic symptoms among African American males transitioning from a public system of care. *American Journal of Men's Health, 12*(2), 274–282. doi: 10.1177/1557988316630304.

Shapiro, V. B. (2015). Resilience: Have we not gone far enough? A response to Larry E. Davis. *Social Work Research, 39*(1), 7–10.

Shapiro, V. B., & Bender, K. (2018). Seven action steps to unleash the power of prevention. *Journal of the Society for Social Work and Research, 9*(4), 499–509.

Shapiro, V. B., Lippold, M., & Bender, K. (2022). Ensuring healthy development for youth by unleashing the power of prevention: An update on progress and priorities. In R. P. Barth, J. T. Messing, T. R. Shanks, & J. H. Williams (Eds.), *Grand Challenges for Social Work and Society: Milestones Achieved and Opportunities Ahead, 2nd edition*. Oxford University Press.

Shapiro, V. B., Hawkins, J. D., & Oesterle, S. (2015). Building local infrastructure for community adoption of science-based prevention: The role of coalition functioning. *Prevention Science, 16*(8), 1136–1146.

Shapiro, V. B., Hawkins, J. D., Oesterle, S., Monahan, K. C., Brown, E. C., & Arthur, M. W. (2013). Variation in the effect of Communities That Care on community adoption of a scientific approach to prevention. *Journal of the Society for Social Work and Research, 4*(3), 154–164.

Siegel, B., & Nolan, L. (2009). Leveling the field: Ensuring equity through National Health Care Reform. *New England Journal of Medicine, 361,* 2401–2403.

Simon, T. R., Sussman, S., Dahlberg, L. L., & Dent C. W. (2002). Influence of a substance-abuse-prevention curriculum on violence-related behavior. *American Journal of Health Behavior, 25,* 103–110.

Snyder, F., Vuchinich, S., Acock, A., Washburn, I., Beets, M., & Kin-Kit, L. (2010). Impact of the Positive Action program on school-level indicators of academic achievement, absenteeism, and disciplinary outcomes: A matched-pair, cluster randomized, controlled trial. *Journal of Research on Educational Effectiveness, 3*(1), 26–55.

Society for Social Work & Research Social Policy Committee. (2020). SSWR call and commitment to ending police brutality, racial injustice, and white supremacy. Retrieved from: https://secure.sswr.org/sswr-call-and-commitment-to-ending-police-brutality-racial-injustice-and-white-supremacy/.

Spencer, M. B., Swanson, D. P., & Cunningham, M. (1991). Ethnicity, ethnic identity, and competence formation: Adolescent transition and cultural transformation. *The Journal of Negro Education, 60*(3), 366–387.

Spoth, R. L., Redmond, C., Trudeau, L., & Shin, C. (2002). Longitudinal substance initiation outcomes for a universal preventive intervention combining family and school programs. *Psychology of Addictive Behaviors, 16,* 129–134.

Spoth, R., Rohrbach, L. A., Greenberg, M., Leaf, P., Brown, C. H., Fagan, A., Catalano, R. F., Pentz, M. A., Sloboda, Z., Hawkins, J. D., & Society for Prevention Research Type 2 Translational Task Force Members and Contributing Authors. (2013). Addressing core challenges for the next generation of type 2 translation research and systems: The translation science to population impact (TSci impact) framework. *Prevention Science, 14*, 319–351.

Stanley, L. R., Swaim, R. C., Kaholokula, J. K. A., Kelly, K. J., Belcourt, A., & Allen, J. (2020). The imperative for research to promote health equity in indigenous communities. *Prevention Science, 21*(1), 13–21.

Stice, E., Butryn, M., Rohde, P., Shaw, H., & Marti, C. (2013). An effectiveness trial of a new enhanced dissonance eating disorder prevention program among female college students. *Behaviour Research and Therapy, 51*(12), 862–871.

Stice, E., Chase, A., Stormer, S., & Appel, A. (2001). A randomized trial of a dissonance-based eating disorder prevention program. *International Journal of Eating Disorders, 29*, 247–262.

Stice, E., Rohde, P., Butryn, M., Shaw, H., & Marti, C. N. (2015). Effectiveness trial of a selective dissonance-based eating disorder prevention program with female college students: Effects at 2- and 3-year follow-up. *Behaviour Research and Therapy, 71*, 20–26.

Stice, E., Rohde, P., Gau, J., & Shaw, H. (2009). An effectiveness trial of a dissonance-based eating disorder prevention program for high-risk adolescent girls. *Journal of Consulting and Clinical Psychology, 77*(5), 825–834.

Stice, E., Rohde, P., Gau, J. M., & Wade, E. (2010). Efficacy trial of a brief cognitive-behavioral depression prevention program for high-risk adolescents: Effects at 1- and 2-year follow-up. *Journal of Consulting and Clinical Psychology, 78*(6), 856–867.

Stice, E., Rohde, P., Seeley, J. R., & Gau, J. M. (2008). Brief cognitive-behavioral depression prevention program for high-risk adolescents outperforms two alternative interventions: A randomized efficacy trial. *Journal of Consulting and Clinical Psychology, 76*(4), 595–606.

Stice, E., Rohde, P., Shaw, H., & Gau, J. (2011). An effectiveness trial of a selected dissonance-based eating disorder prevention program for female high school students: Long-term effects. *Journal of Consulting and Clinical Psychology, 79*(4), 500–508.

Stice, E., Shaw, H., Burton, E., & Wade, E. (2006). Dissonance and healthy weight eating disorder prevention programs: A randomized efficacy trial. *Journal of Consulting and Clinical Psychology, 74*(2), 263–275.

Stice, E., Trost, A., & Chase, A. (2003). Healthy weight control and dissonance-based eating disorder prevention programs: Results from a controlled trial. *International Journal of Eating Disorders, 33*, 10–21.

Sullivan, C. J., & Hirschfield, P. 2011. Problem behavior in the middle school years: An assessment of the social development model. *Journal of Research in Crime and Delinquency, 48*(4), 566–593.

Sun, P., Sussman, S., Dent, C. W., & Rohrbach, L. A. (2008). One-year follow-up evaluation of Project Towards No Drug Abuse (TND-4). *Preventive Medicine, 47*, 438–442.

Supplee, L. H., Parekh, J., & Johnson, M. (2018). Principles of precision prevention science for improving recruitment and retention of participants. *Prevention Science, 19*(5), 689–694.

Sussman, S., Dent, C. W., Craig, S., Ritt-Olsen, A., & McCuller, W. J. (2002). Development and immediate impact of a self-instruction curriculum for an adolescent indicated drug abuse prevention trial. *Journal of Drug Education, 32*(2), 121–137.

Sussman, S., Dent, C., Stacy, A., & Craig, S. (1998). One-year outcomes of Project Towards No Drug Abuse. *Preventive Medicine, 27*, 632–642.

Sussman, S., Sun, P., McCuller, W. J., & Dent, C. W. (2003). Project Towards No Drug Abuse: Two-year outcomes of a trial that compares health educator delivery to self instruction. *Preventive Medicine, 37*, 155–162.

168 VALERIE B. SHAPIRO ET AL.

Swoboda, C. M., Benedict, J. A., Hade, E., McAlearney, A. S., & Huerta, T. R. (2018). Effectiveness of an infant mortality prevention home-visiting program on high-risk births in Ohio, *Public Health Nursing, 35*, 551–557.

Trent, M., Dooley, D. G., & Dougé, J. (2019). The impact of racism on child and adolescent health. *Pediatrics, 144*(2), 1–14.

Turner, W. (2000). Cultural considerations in family-based primary prevention programs in drug abuse. *Journal of Primary Prevention, 21*(3), 285–303.

Turrisi, R., Larimer, M. E., Mallett, K. A., Kilmer, J. R., Ray, A. E., Mastroleo, N. R., Geisner, I. M., Grossbard, J., Tollison, S., Lostutter, T. W., & Montoya, H. (2009). A randomized clinical trial evaluating a combined alcohol intervention for high-risk college students. *Journal of Studies on Alcohol and Drugs, 70*, 555–567.

U.S. Department of Health and Human Services. (April 2011). *HHS Action Plan to Reduce Racial and Ethnic Disparities: A Nation Free of Disparities in Health and Health Care*. Washington, D.C.: U.S. Department of Health and Human Services. Retreived from: https://web.archive.org/web/20150813150051/http://minorityhealth.hhs.gov/npa/files/Plans/HHS/HHS_Plan_complete.pdf

Valentine, J. C., Biglan, A., Boruch, R. F., Castro, F. G., Collins, L. M., Flay, B. R., . . . Schinke, S. P. (2011). Replication in prevention science. *Prevention Science, 12*(2), 103.

Wallerstein, N. & Duran, B. (2010). Community-based participatory research contributions to intervention research: The intersection of science and practice to improve health equity. *American Journal of Public Health*, 100, S40–S46.

Western, B., & Pettit, B. (2010). Incarceration & social inequality. *Daedalus, 139*(3), 8–19.

Williams, J. H., Ayers, C. D., Abbott, R. D., Hawkins, J. D., & Catalano, R. F. (1999). Racial differences in risk factors for delinquency and substance use among adolescents. *Social Work Research, 23*(4), 241–256.

Wolchik, S., Sandler, I., Millsap, R. E., Plummer, B. A., Greene, S. M., Anderson, E. R., Dawson-McClure, S. R., Hipke, K., Haine, R. A. (2002). Six-year follow-up of preventive interventions for children of divorce: A randomized controlled trial. *JAMA, 288*(15), 1874–1881.

Wolchik, S., West, S., Westover, S., Sandler, I., Martin, A., Lustig, J., Tein, J. Y., Fisher, J. (1993). The children of divorce parenting intervention: Outcome evaluation of an empirically based program. *American Journal of Community Psychology, 21*(3), 293–331.

Woo, B., Figuereo, V., Rosales, R., Wang, K., & Sabur, K. (2018). Where is race and ethnicity in social work? A content analysis. *Social Work Research, 42*(3), 180–186.

7

Ensuring Healthy Development for All Youth

Prevention of Psychosis

Melissa E. Smith, Pamela Rakhshan Rouhakhtar, and Jason Schiffman

> *Only during the civil-rights era did emerging scientific understandings of schizophrenia become enmeshed in a set of historical currents that marked particular bodies, and particular psyches, as crazy in particular ways. The tensions of that era then changed the associations that many Americans made about persons with schizophrenia. Ultimately, recent American racial history altered more than the meaning of mental illness: it changed the meaning of mental health as well.*
>
> —Jonathan M. Metzel, *The Protest Psychosis: How Schizophrenia Became a Black Disease*

The Promise of Prevention for All?

Youth and young adults at risk for, or on a trajectory toward, serious mental illness related to psychosis (e.g., schizophrenia, schizoaffective disorder) often experience subclinical levels of psychosis (i.e., attenuated psychosis) prior to full illness development, or a manifestation of other severe psychopathology (Kelleher et al., 2014), without ever transitioning to a psychotic disorder. Given the potential for improved outcomes in psychotic disorders with early intervention, as well as the negative psychosocial outcomes associated with attenuated symptoms regardless of eventual transition to full threshold disorders (Salokangas et al., 2013), the field has increasingly focused attention on developing an understanding of and treatment for subthreshold psychosis symptoms.

Melissa E. Smith, Pamela Rakhshan Rouhakhtar, and Jason Schiffman, *Ensuring Healthy Development for All Youth* In: *Social Work and the Grand Challenge to Eliminate Racism.* Edited by: Martell L. Teasley, Michael S. Spencer, and Melissa Bartholomew, Oxford University Press. © Oxford University Press 2023.
DOI: 10.1093/oso/9780197674949.003.0007

170 SMITH, RAKHSHAN ROUHAKHTAR, AND SCHIFFMAN

The preponderance of work in this emerging field, however, has been conducted with individuals from majority racial/ethnic groups, with little attention on how issues of racism and sociocultural context may impact early identification and treatment for minoritized racial/ethnic groups at risk for psychosis. The 13th Grand Challenge of social work will call for the "[preparation] of the profession to address structural racism and its impact on ourselves and our clients" (American Academy of Social Work & Social Welfare, 2014, np). It thus follows that the Grand Challenge to ensure healthy development for all youth by preventing psychosis and serious mental illnesses such as schizophrenia should be examined through a lens of racial equity and justice in research and clinical practice. In this chapter, we will first review early psychosis prevention in the context of the Grand Challenge proposal to prevent psychosis, after which we will turn our attention to racial and cultural issues impacting psychosis prevention.

Overview of Early Psychosis Prevention

Consistent with the conceptualization of mental health concerns existing on a spectrum of severity, identifying risk for psychosis is rooted in recognizing symptoms similar in nature but lesser in severity and/or conviction relative to fully formed hallucinations, delusions, and disorganized thinking as experienced by those with serious mental illness. Moving into the realm of diagnosable disorders or syndromes, psychosis-risk symptoms associated with distress and/or impairment have been codified with the creation of standardized self-report and semi-structured interview tools (McGlashan et al., 2010; Yung et al., 2005). For the purposes of this chapter, we will refer to people experiencing psychosis-risk symptoms defined by attenuated or subclinical levels of psychosis as at risk for psychosis or at clinical high-risk (CHR) for psychosis, while those diagnosed with a fully diagnosable psychotic disorder such as schizophrenia will be referred to as having a serious mental illness (SMI).

The Grand Challenge of Preventing Serious Mental Illness

As a part of the Grand Challenges for Social Work initiative spearheaded by the American Academy of Social Work and Social Welfare, DeVylder (2016) described the state of the field and the goals and measurable outcomes for preventing serious mental illness, linking to the broader mission of ensuring healthy development for all youth. These goals (pp. 452–453) included:

Aim 1: Development of brief non-stigmatizing screening by existing human service organizations;
Aim 2: Development of rigorous testing of novel treatment approaches;
Aim 3: Testing the bonus benefits for early intervention (person-centered approach, addressing all needs);
Aim 4: Creating regional centers of excellence on prevention and early intervention for psychosis;
Aim 5: Educating social work students, with emphasis on early detection and intervention.

In addition, the proposal included three innovative strategies to promote interdisciplinary collaboration and cross-sector approaches to prevent psychosis that give social workers a prominent seat at the table in multiple settings (e.g., mental health, school). These strategies (pp. 454–455) were:

Innovation 1: "Focused prevention in mental health" that uses a "middle-ground approach" between the clinical staging model (which targets general mental health symptoms with broad interventions) and targeted psychosis prevention;
Innovation 2: "Psychosocial treatment as a primary intervention for psychotic disorders" without pharmacological intervention;
Innovation 3: "Community agencies as points of early detection for [serious] mental illness."

The Promise of Prevention: An Update

In the relatively short time since the inaugural Grand Challenges proposal for the prevention of serious mental illness (DeVylder, 2016), early psychosis scholars and practitioners have made meaningful strides in the development and implementation of assessments and interventions for youth at risk for psychosis.

Screening and detection. A wide variety of self-report and interview-based tools have been validated for use to screen and assess for psychosis-risk symptoms. These include gold standard self-report measures like the PRIME screen (Miller et al., 2004) or the Prodromal Questionnaire-Brief (PQ-B; Loewy et al., 2011), among others (Daneault & Stip, 2013). Recent adaptations building upon this foundation offer promise for wider implementation or more accurate use of screening tools for psychosis-risk, including a brief, two-item measure for use in nonspecialized clinical settings (Phalen et al., 2018), online tools (McDonald et al., 2018), and sophisticated analytic techniques to develop more accurate screening (Brodey et al., 2018; Brodey et al., 2019). To date, there is preliminary evidence for the validity of these screening tools (Addington et al., 2015; Kline & Schiffman, 2014), although more work is needed to determine appropriate adaptations across diverse settings and populations (Savill et al., 2018; Schiffman, 2018).

The Structured Interview for Psychosis Risk Syndromes (SIPS; McGlashan et al., 2010) and the Comprehensive Assessment of At-Risk Mental States (CAARMS; Yung et al., 2005) are the two gold standard semi-structured interviews currently used to diagnose psychosis risk syndromes and evaluate psychosis-risk symptom severity in youth and young adults. In terms of prediction to psychosis, semi-structured interviews assessing psychosis risk perform well with clinical populations with high sensitivity, albeit low specificity (Fusar-Poli et al., 2020). Approximately 25% of people who meet criteria for a risk syndrome based on one of these interviews will develop a diagnosable illness with psychosis.

Despite the gains made in the development, evaluation, and implementation of screening tools and semi-structured interviews, assessing for risk in the context of stigma associated with psychosis (Aim 1) remains a challenge. Reports from a recent review (Colizzi et al., 2020) indicate higher levels of internalized stigma in youth at risk for psychosis as compared to peers without mental health concerns or diagnoses other than those on the psychosis spectrum, with stigma associated with poorer outcomes across functional and psychosocial domains. Although there are positive aspects to psychosis-risk labels reported by some individuals, negative consequences were also endorsed, seeming to indicate the need for more work targeted toward reduction of stigma associated with psychosis-risk diagnoses. These findings have important implications for assessment tools. Shan and colleagues (2020) found that levels of internalized stigma moderated the relation between screening measures and diagnostic outcome on clinical interviews, with individuals reporting low internalized stigma showing good concordance between self-report and interview diagnoses, whereas those

ENSURING HEALTHY DEVELOPMENT FOR ALL YOUTH   173

with high internalized stigma did not have a statistically significant relation between self-report scores and interview derived diagnoses. Future work is needed to identify aspects of screening tools, or the screening process, that may contribute to levels of internalized stigma, leading to the development and implementation of adaptations to address these issues.

Prevention intervention services, psychosocial treatment, and holistic outcomes. Growing evidence supports the efficacy of prevention intervention with youth at risk for psychosis to reduce symptoms, increase functioning, and in some cases prevent transition to a fully diagnosable psychotic disorder (Aim 2) (Glenthøj et al., 2017; Stafford et al., 2013; van der Gaag et al., 2013). A recent study examining international implementation of prevention services reported that specialty care for those at risk for psychosis frequently included psychosocial interventions such as those recommended in the Grand Challenges proposal (e.g., clinical monitoring, crisis management, supportive therapy, family psychoeducation, and psychotherapy such as Cognitive Behavioral Therapy [CBT]; Kotlicka-Antczak et al., 2020). Of note, it is important to highlight that these interventions were typically implemented *alongside* psychopharmacological interventions, rather than as standalone or first-line treatments as proposed in the original Grand Challenge (Innovation 2).

To date, CBT has been recommended widely as a primary prevention intervention, due to its effectiveness as well as economic benefits, alongside other psychosocial interventions that attend to other areas of concern, such as functioning, quality of life, and other comorbid disorders (Campion et al., 2019; Okuzawa et al., 2014; van der Gaag et al., 2019). Other promising interventions addressing functioning in domains beyond psychosis/psychosis-risk, include cognitive remediation (which has shown some effectiveness in improving cognitive and social functioning), and family-focused therapy (Glenthøj et al., 2017; Stafford et al., 2013; Thompson et al., 2015). It is important to note that despite a range of interventions available, no specific strategy has demonstrated clear superiority over others (Fusar-Poli et al., 2020).

In addition to the shift from a symptom-focused approach to a more expansive, holistic conceptualization of treatment outcomes, gold standard treatments for youth at risk for psychosis and adults in the early stages of psychosis are increasingly embracing a transdiagnostic approach to conceptualization and treatment. Shah and colleagues (2020) released an international consensus statement on early intervention treatment, promoting an approach

174 SMITH, RAKHSHAN ROUHAKHTAR, AND SCHIFFMAN

to care that flexibly applies to both typical and atypical presentations and progressions of illness and that leads to individualized treatment and a more nuanced understanding of client mental health (Aim 3).

Centers of excellence and focused prevention. There are now a number of regional centers of excellence in the majority of U.S. states (e.g., EASA Center for Excellence, 2016) that identify and treat youth at risk for or in the early stages of psychosis (Aim 4). In addition, an increasing number of programs provide outreach/education, assessment, and intervention services for those in the at-risk phase of illness (e.g., Friedman-Yakoobian et al., 2018). There are also federal policy and funding efforts currently underway, with awards granted to 21 clinics across the United States for the purpose of creating new treatment programs within community provider agencies to provide intervention for youth and young adults at CHR for psychosis (SAMHSA, 2018). These intervention programs, in addition to larger funding initiatives at the state (Johnson et al., 2021; ; Neindam et al., 2019) and federal levels (NIH, 2018a, 2018b) to develop regional hubs for the purpose of standardization, evaluation, and harmonization of early intervention programs, signify substantial accomplishment in the development of centers of excellence for at-risk and early psychosis treatment. It is important to note that all the initiatives and programs described above are in keeping with proposed innovation strategies (Innovation 3; DeVylder, 2016) regarding focused prevention and incorporating interventions of varying types and intensity across a broad range of systems, from generalized to specialized (Sale et al., 2018).

Education of social workers. DeVylder's final goal (Aim 5) for prevention of schizophrenia and SMI aimed to incorporate information about psychosis-risk assessment and screening among social workers in particular (2016). A number of promising studies and program protocols targeting general community and mental healthcare provider education have demonstrated initial effectiveness in providing training to a wide range of practitioners, increasing knowledge of early warning signs of psychosis and generating appropriate referrals (Sutton et al., 2018; McFarlane & Jaynes, 2017; Lynch et al., 2016). For example, the Portland Identification and Early Referral (PIER) program consists of a broad range of techniques to promote education regarding psychosis-risk/early psychosis, including strong outreach and education efforts among school social work practitioners, as well as offering continuing education credits (CEUs) for trainings (McFarlane & Jaynes, 2017). A recent pilot program that shows promise in integrating early identification and intervention education for all social workers as a part of the standard curriculum is a National Institute of Mental Health (NIMH)–funded study, *Social Work Training to Reduce Duration of Untreated Psychosis* (Andorko et al., 2021). This ongoing protocol is currently evaluating a novel online risk-assessment training curriculum for social work practitioners across Maryland. Features of the training include availability to all social workers in Maryland for continuing education credits regardless of interaction with early intervention services, and linkage to early intervention consultation and referral resources.

Setting the Stage: Race and Mental Illness

Despite the potential benefits of prevention services and the demonstrable steps taken toward the goals put forth by DeVylder in 2016, structural racism and other disparities in the mental healthcare system may put minoritized racial and ethnic youth and young adults at a disadvantage with respect to early detection and intervention. With minoritized racial and ethnic status being identified as a reliable risk factor for early psychosis (Fusar-Poli et al., 2019), questions abound regarding the mechanisms behind this risk. The perpetuation of generational structural racism, disparities in the mental health system, and biases that lead to misdiagnosis of racial and ethnic populations resulting in inappropriate and/or ineffective treatment and poor outcomes all serve as candidate drivers of the link between minority status and early psychosis.

Brief History of the Social Construction of Mental Illness and Race

To contextualize current racial and ethnic disparities in access, diagnosis, quality of care, and outcome related to SMI, a brief history of the social construction of mental illness and race is warranted. In 1851, Samuel Cartwright coined the term *Drapetomania* (i.e., runaway slave syndrome) pathologizing Africans who ran away from slavery (Cartwright, 1851). The "treatment" for Drapetomania was removal of the big toes of enslaved people (White, 2002), with brutal whipping serving as "prevention" (Cartwright, 2004). The systematic means of categorizing a normal response to collective trauma serves as an example of how structural racism was infused into the early conceptualization of psychopathology in the United States. Patterns of structural racism continued to arise as the mental health field grew and manifested itself with widespread racial disparities. This included racial bias in how we historically and currently misattribute thoughts and behaviors in Black populations as pathological or in some cases psychotic.

At the advent of institutionalized mental health treatment in the nineteenth and early twentieth centuries, separate but unequal racial segregation resulted in disparities in mental health asylum conditions for Black patients. Patients in Black asylums experienced disproportionate levels of improper nutrition and medical treatment; infectious diseases; sexual violence (specifically against Black women); and labor exploitation (Kannani, 2011). In *The Protest Psychosis: How Schizophrenia Became a Black Disease*, Metzl (2010) documents the political racialization of the diagnosis of schizophrenia in the 1960s and 1970s. The "schizophrenic" label was systematically applied to people of color (Black people in particular) in psychiatric discourse, research, and popular media to explicitly and implicitly marginalize and minimize the credibility and voice of civil rights protestors, the Black Power movement, and the Nation of Islam, among others. Although many would argue that the structure and associated parity of the mental health system has improved over the past 50 to 60 years, challenges codified in the past have not all been overcome, and this history provides some context to the current and contemporary disparities that continue to plague mental health services for minoritized racial and ethnic groups with SMIs in the United States.

Current Racial and Ethnic Disparities in the Identification and Treatment of Serious Mental Illness

Since the 1980s, research has consistently documented the over- and misdiagnosis of Black individuals with schizophrenia (Barnes, 2008; Baskin et al., 1981; Blow et al., 2004; Pavkov et al., 1989; Strakowski et al., 1996). Over- and misdiagnosis has been attributed to racial biases and related social constructions of Black populations as violent, aggressive, and paranoid (Kannani, 2011). Disparities also exist along the continuum from pathways to care to mental health and recovery outcomes. Racial and ethnic disparities have been documented in quality of care related to psychiatric hospital admission rates, receipt of mental health services, and prescription of antipsychotic medication (Bessaha et al., 2017; Horvitz-Lennon et al., 2014;

Yamada et al., 2009). A recent literature review has documented that for Black adults with schizophrenia spectrum disorders there is a dearth of research examining the effectiveness of widely accepted evidence-based treatment practices established in primarily White samples (Smith et al., 2019), with the existing literature suggesting differential impacts of evidence-based practices for White versus Black adults (Eack & Newhill, 2012).

Role of Structural and Individual Racism in Mental Healthcare

Inherent in the history of mental health treatment of Black populations (in particular African Americans) with SMIs is a strong element of structural racism. Only recently has there been a call to examine how the intersection of mental illness and other socially disadvantaged identities (e.g., being Black) has adversely impacted those situated within these intersecting identities (Alang, 2019; Oexle & Corrigan, 2018). The issues surrounding Black populations seeking or receiving treatment in the mental healthcare system are illustrated in the lived experiences of Black individuals who have identified how race impacted their unmet mental health needs. Experiences of other oppressive systems; the intersection of racial discrimination and mentalism (discrimination based on mental health status); mistrust due to historical treatment of Black populations in the mental health system; and racial micro-aggressions from providers all negatively contribute to a pattern of experiences of structural and individual racism (Alang, 2019).

Inherent in this history are two overlapping phenomena that have an interactive and multiplicative impact on Black people. Black people are overdiagnosed *as well as* discriminated against. Overdiagnosis leads to mismatches in treatment as well as a sense of helplessness, disempowerment, worthlessness, and stigmatization—all outcomes that can paradoxically create a contextual-fulfilling prophecy toward the original misdiagnosis of psychosis. Additionally, facing undue stress and trauma associated with discrimination (which can take many forms, including overdiagnosis) can also exacerbate vulnerability toward psychosis. In the context of systemic stress and trauma, resilience in a given moment has the potential to mask possible long-term impacts that might contribute to psychosis. These factors interact to convey risk while at the same time possibly obscure that risk, impacting the ability to receive the right types of interventions at the right time.

A Mirror Image? Racial and Ethnic Disparities in Psychosis Prevention

Given the relative infancy of early psychosis prevention research and practice, there are many questions about the danger of practice and research perpetuating the racial and ethnic disparities prevalent in mental health treatments for adults with serious mental illness. International studies have reported no differences in quality of care (Byrne et al., 2019), but poorer recovery in psychosocial functioning following treatment (Salokangas et al., 2013) for minoritized racial/ethnic youth and youth adults compared to their White counterparts. With respect to access to care, limited research suggests a trend toward racial and ethnic disparities in service access for youth and young adults with early psychosis (He et al., 2019).

Young people from racial and ethnic minority groups experiencing early psychosis often enter mental health treatment via toxic treatment pathways that include traumatizing interactions with the police and disempowering emergency hospitalizations (Myers et al., 2018, p. 184).

Structural Racism, Racial Bias, and Cultural Responsiveness in Assessing Youth for Psychosis Risk

Despite the promising progress made in the development of assessment for youth at risk for psychosis, significant concerns remain regarding generalizability of these tools in all race and culture groups. Specifically, early evidence suggests that some self-report and clinical-assessment tools for psychosis risk may lead to over-pathologizing or mislabeling minoritized racial/ethnic youth and young adults (Millman et al., 2019). Although it may be the case that elevated levels of psychosis-spectrum symptoms seen in minoritized racial/ethnic youth as compared to their majority group peers are a function of elevated levels of stressors (e.g., discrimination, trauma [both related to race/minoritized group status as well as other trauma]) reflective of a diathesis-stress model, it is also likely that current measurement tools lack validity in certain minoritized racial/ethnic groups, whether due to a misinterpretation of contextual and/or societal factors resulting in distress (e.g., racism) or benign/positive cultural beliefs/experiences (e.g., religion; Schiffman et al., 2019).

Cross-cultural issues of validity may manifest in both the psychometric properties of measures, as well as the ways in which concepts are understood and function across groups (Leong et al., 2010). Preliminary evidence of psychosis-risk self-report measures suggests issues across both these domains for minoritized racial/ethnic group members in the United States. Cicero and colleagues (2016, 2019) evaluated the measurement invariance (i.e., indication that a construct is being measured equivalently and may be meaningfully compared across groups) of two self-report measures of psychosis risk (the Prodromal Questionnaire-Brief and Schizotypal Personality Questionnaire) in a population of individuals identifying as Asian, Multiethnic, Pacific Islander, or White. Results from both studies indicated that although the measures achieved basic levels (configural and metric) of measurement invariance, both measures were partially variant at the scalar level based on self-reported race, indicating that mean comparisons of these commonly used screening tools are not appropriate for all race groups without further evaluation and modification.

In a study evaluating the factor structure of the Prime Screen self-report tool in two racially diverse, help-seeking samples, Rakhshan Rouhakhtar and colleagues (2018) found evidence for a two-factor structure of the Prime Screen in both samples, with one factor showing strong associations with early psychosis/psychosis-risk diagnoses, social functioning deficits, and self-reported mental health scores, with the other four-item factor showing no significant relations with diagnoses or functional impairment. The nature of the items comprising the latter factor (e.g., belief in ability to predict future, belief in mind reading, acting differently because of superstitions, and having supernatural gifts/talents) seems to suggest that some Prime Screen items may lack validity as a measure of psychosis risk, particularly for minoritized racial/ethnic group members with beliefs/experiences outside the dominant culture. Expanding on these findings, Rakhshan Rouhakhtar, Pitts, and Schiffman (2019) evaluated differences in the Prime Screen in a general sample of Black and White college students, with results indicating problematic validity of some Prime items, particularly for Black participants. Importantly, although scores on Prime items were significantly correlated with self-reported well-being among White participants for 7 of the 12 items on the measure, only one Prime item was significantly associated with well-being scores for Black participants. Similarly, Millman and colleagues (2019) found that the concordance between Prime Screen scores and clinical interview diagnosis of psychosis risk varied by race in a help-seeking sample of Black and White youth, with a high level of agreement between self-report and interview among White participants, while no relation was found for their Black peers. Evaluating the nature of this phenomenon at an item level, it appeared that differences in scores among at-risk and low-risk participants varied as a function of race, with White participants in the at-risk group typically showing higher mean scores as compared to their low-risk peers, as expected. In contrast, however, Black at-risk participants showed similar or even lower mean item scores on some Prime Screen items. Considered in aggregate, these findings seem to suggest that self-report measures of psychosis-risk may lack validity—and possibly lead to problematic outcomes—when administered to individuals of minoritized racial/ethnic groups.

Although the research is sparse, in addition to screening tools, there are indications of potential for racial biases impacting the validity and generalizability of psychosis-risk clinical interviews to racially/ethnically diverse individuals. In a sample of mostly Black help-seeking youth at CHR for psychosis, Wilson and colleagues (2016) reported that neighborhood crime was associated with levels of suspiciousness, even when controlling for severity of psychosis-risk symptoms, suggesting that contextual factors like crime levels may influence symptom ratings in clinical assessments of psychosis risk. These findings were in large part independently replicated in a different city (Vargas et al., 2020). Although not conducted among people in the at risk phase of illness, in a study of people with psychosis using the *Diagnostic and Statistical Manual of Mental Disorders* (5th edition; DSM-5) cultural formulation interview (CFI) to re-evaluate historical diagnoses in an ethnically diverse sample initially diagnosed by community providers, Adeponle and colleagues (2012) found that a meaningful number of initial psychosis diagnoses were updated to non-psychotic disorders, while only a nominal number of initial non-psychotic disorders were altered to a psychotic disorder. Qualitative analyses of providers using the CFI to assist when making psychosis diagnoses indicated that this tool facilitated a systematic process for resolving normative or diagnostic uncertainty with regard to psychosis (Adeponle et al., 2015).

Despite the well-documented role of racial biases in the diagnostic process for racial/ethnic minority individuals, as well as the significant role of clinical judgment in resolving normative uncertainty in psychosis-risk diagnostic interviews, no work has yet evaluated the presence, extent, or impact of racial bias held by interviewers/practitioners in psychosis-risk clinical assessment.

This is particularly problematic given the recent efforts to shorten/modify psychosis-risk clinical interviews to facilitate quick administration in busy clinical settings (e.g., mini-SIPS; Woods et al., 2020) that could potentially lead to practices more susceptible to provider biases.

Irrespective of the means of assessment, endorsement of what may be interpreted by practitioners as suspicious or paranoid thinking needs to be situated in an individual's given sociopolitical climate. For example, structural racism and systemic inequality have condoned community violence and perpetuated police brutality on Black populations. Exposure to discrimination and racially targeted violence (e.g., police violence), whether experienced personally (oneself or one's family), witnessed through media, or in the community (both acute instances of violence as well as cumulative exposure), may be a root cause of a "healthy mistrust," as opposed to a pathological suspiciousness, as some Black people try to navigate their safety in a world that often devalues and physically threatens their lives (Terrel et al., 2009). At the same time, it is important to recognize that such experiences can engender experiences related to psychosis in and of themselves. DeVylder and colleagues noted that people who self-reported police victimization (disproportionately Black males) were at increased risk for psychosis-like experiences (DeVylder et al., 2017). Similarly, Smith and colleagues (2020) found that Black individuals were disproportionately exposed to gun violence and that individuals exposed to gun violence, regardless of race had higher levels of mental health symptoms including psychosis-like experiences compared to individuals who did not report such exposure.

Are Promising Evidence-Based Practices for Psychosis Prevention Racially and Culturally Responsive?

Cognitive Behavioral Therapy (CBT). Effectiveness studies with racial/ethnic youth and young adults experiencing psychosis-risk symptoms is limited (Kim et al., 2011; Rathod et al., 2013). Within the psychosis intervention literature, international research has begun to examine the impact of treatment on minoritized racial/ethnic youth and young adults with psychosis risk as well as with diagnosable psychotic disorders. CBT with youth and young adults experiencing psychosis-risk symptoms has shown preliminary effectiveness with youth in Korea (Kim et al., 2011). CBT for schizophrenia among Black and minoritized ethnic adults with schizophrenia has also been evaluated in the United Kingdom (Rathod et al., 2010; Rathod et al., 2013). With input from Black and ethnic clients and lay community members as well as providers, Rathod and colleagues culturally adapted CBT for psychosis (Rathod et al., 2010; Rathod et al 2013). Important areas for adaptation included understanding cultural explanations for mental illness, talking about impacts of racism, talking about religion and spirituality, and attending to cultural-bound beliefs and meaning of voices.

Family Focused Therapy. As a promising practice for youth at risk for psychosis, family-focused therapy should take into account the importance of family and culture for minoritized racial/ethnic families. On the whole, family psychoeducational interventions and Family Focused Therapy (FFT; McFarlane et al., 2012; Miklowitz et al., 2014; Miklowitz et al., 2018; O'Brien et al., 2006) have demonstrated modest efficacy in improving family functioning and reducing the severity of psychosis-risk symptoms and improving psychosocial functioning. Despite the promise of this intervention, to the authors' knowledge no work to date has evaluated whether interventions like FFT show equivalent effects across all race groups, or whether adaptations for treatment are needed for optimal use with minoritized racial/ethnic group families. Additionally, minoritized racial/ethnic group individuals have been less included in research on family interventions for early psychosis than White individuals, indicating that efficacy of these interventions for individuals not belonging to White racial groups is as of yet unestablished (Claxton et al., 2017).

Given that an underlying treatment target of FFT is high levels of parental criticism, hostility, or overprotectiveness, there is reason to believe additional research on early psychosis/psychosis-risk family interventions and race may be vital to the success of family interventions in minoritized populations (Miklowitz et al., 2014). Research seems to indicate that while high levels of critical comments and overinvolvement may be predictive of negative outcomes for White youth at risk for psychosis, this finding may not be true across all cultural/racial/ethnic groups (O'Driscoll et al., 2019; Sing et al., 2013), with some research indicating that critical comments and overinvolvement may be related to *better* illness outcomes for minoritized racial/ethnic individuals with psychosis (Gurak & Weisman de Mamani, 2017; Rosenfarb et al., 2006). Thus, family-based interventions for psychosis-risk/early psychosis may benefit from adaptation based on cultural norms related to expressed emotion in the family.

ENSURING HEALTHY DEVELOPMENT FOR ALL YOUTH   183

Culturally Informed Treatment for Schizophrenia (CIT-S; Weisman et al., 2006; Weisman de Mamani et al., 2014) and Culturally-adapted Family Intervention (CaFI; Edge et al., 2016; Edge et al., 2018) have been implemented with promising early results for people with SMI, indicating feasibility and acceptability of culturally adapted treatments that could be applicable for those at risk. Adaptations of these interventions include incorporation of spirituality and collectivist family culture or culturally different aspects of family structure, ensuring concepts in treatment are culturally consistent, using communication with families that is culturally appropriate, as well as understanding and centering treatment around relevant adaptive and maladaptive practices and beliefs specific to each family, among other changes (Edge et al., 2018; Weisman de Mamani et al., 2014). Culturally informed adaptations for preventive treatments for minoritized racial/ethnic groups at risk for psychosis similar to those pioneered by Weisman de Mamani and colleagues may offer advantages to standard care created for majority cultures.

Strategies for Reducing Structural Racism and Racial Bias and Increasing Cultural Responsiveness: Implications for Social Work Research, Education, and Practice

Across research, education, and practice for minoritized racial and ethnic youth and young adults at risk for psychosis, effective, racially unbiased, and culturally responsive mental health services must be achieved through interdisciplinary collaboration advocating for anti-racist policies and practices. At the level of early identification, as described above, assessment and diagnostic tools used in research and practice are not empirically validated across racial groups. Conceptual and metric equivalency (Leong et al., 2010) should be established for all existing psychosis-risk measures, both self-report and clinical interviews. Analyses should include evaluation of measurement invariance (Fischer & Karl, 2019) and development, testing, and implementation of any adaptations to measures resulting from these studies should be embarked upon with sensitivity to diverse stakeholders. Additionally, mixed-method analyses, in addition to longitudinal studies, should be undertaken to reach these goals (e.g., Earl et al., 2015; Peltier et al., 2017). Given the improvements in prediction of CHR status seen in measures when using distress ratings (Kline et al., 2014), it is likely that integration of distress scales in those measures that do not yet include them, or reliance on scoring methods and norms based on distress scales for those measures that already use them, will result in more culturally competent assessment. In addition to revamping existing measures, should findings suggest that no amount of adaptation helps in creating a reliable and valid screening measure for minoritized groups, participatory action research engaging a range of stakeholders could facilitate new measurement tools from the ground up.

Semi-structured interviews are by their nature reliant upon clinical judgment, and hence subject to influence of an interviewer's racial/ethnic biases. It is therefore important that research evaluate the ways in which practitioners and interviewers resolve normative uncertainty when diagnosing psychosis-risk syndromes in racially/ethnically diverse populations, highlighting aspects of, or items in, gold-standard clinical interviews that are particularly sensitive to biases, and creating and testing mechanisms that promote culturally sensitive assessment (Adeponle et al., 2015). Complementing these efforts, research (both qualitative and quantitative) should identify what culturally sensitive assessment of psychosis risk looks like from a client perspective. Longitudinal work determining changes in predictive validity for future transition to psychosis or other outcomes associated with true psychosis-risk syndromes in typical vs. adapted clinical-interview measures will assist in understanding the impact of culturally sensitive measurement on psychometrics in psychosis-risk. Following standards and guidelines vis-à-vis the DSM-5 cultural formulation interview can help to minimize bias and yield more accurate assessment results.

Beyond the scope of most diagnostic interviews, understanding the environmental context that surrounds youth and young adults will help contextualize any potential symptoms or experiences reported during clinical evaluations. For instance, high levels of policing and community violence can alert practitioners to consider issues of trauma that could either resemble or potentially trigger psychosis. Regardless, practitioners would be well advised to probe for and monitor potential signs of risk for psychosis over time in these situations. The task of practitioners is to glean when suspiciousness (a subclinical level of paranoia) is warranted and when it is in excess of the environmental dangers. For example, a Black youth who has directly or vicariously experienced police brutality may exhibit levels of suspiciousness paired with other functional impairments and distress. If this is interpreted as a symptom of psychosis risk, the practitioner may lead the youth down a trajectory of early psychosis intervention, prescription of antipsychotic medication with long-term side effects, and a possible misdiagnosis of schizophrenia as "symptoms" progress. At the same time, sensitive intervention would not totally dismiss the possibility that police brutality and consequent associated stress could lead to psychosis risk in the future. Thus addressing the issues at hand, while also monitoring the possible development of additional symptoms, offers an inclusive path to care.

Understanding of larger systemic issues impacting Black communities locally, nationally, and internationally (especially if working with immigrant populations) gives practitioners a more inclusive and informative sociocultural context in which to assess, engage, and treat (see Shai, 2019, for a framework that assists practitioners in addressing sociocultural context, structural racism and oppression in service provision). Once the provider has a clearer understanding of the impact of oppression and racism on their client's presentation, they will be better able to assess if this presentation represents risk of psychosis; responses to environmental stressors causing other forms of pathology (e.g., trauma-related stress, depression, anxiety); or no/little risk of pathology.

Training in psychosis risk assessment can also provide inroads in addressing disparities, with specific attention being paid toward sensitizing providers to cultural and contextual factors that may otherwise account for what appears to be risk for psychosis. In an example of this approach, Andorko and colleagues (2021) attempted to ensure integration of cultural and contextual factors into the assessment of psychosis-risk through a large-scale training of social workers. The training infused attention to race and sociocultural context in teaching trainees to use screening tools for psychosis risk in community settings (e.g., schools, child welfare). For example, the trainers (authors Melissa Smith and Jason Schiffman) addressed issues of appropriate mistrust among Black youth that may result from systemic racism (e.g., police harassment and violence) or neighborhood context (e.g., community violence) that could be misinterpreted as paranoia. Continuing education training such as these, coupled with attention to structural racism and systemic oppression, can shape practitioners toward assessing risk for psychosis within an anti-racist and culturally responsive context.

Regardless of the assessment tools or practices in place, the "process" of implementation will dictate their ultimate utility. Schiffman and colleagues (2019) suggest that providers administering psychosis risk assessments should be encouraged to "allow time for clients to share their individual and cultural views around what are intended as [psychosis risk] probes, such as their possible experiences of discrimination, social deprivation, and/or trauma related to their surrounding neighborhood context" (p. 2).

Development of Racially and Culturally Responsive Evidence-Based Practices

At this point we must acknowledge that promising psychosis prevention evidence-based practices will only be racially unbiased and culturally responsive with the dismantling of structural racism in healthcare, housing, education, employment, and poverty, given the intersection of these socioeconomic indicators with mental health. We can, however, start by developing and testing prevention services, (1) in and with communities of color that show preliminary effectiveness in youth at risk for psychosis among majority groups (CBT, Cognitive Remediation, Family Focused therapy), (2) that incorporate cultural beliefs of minoritized racial/ethnic groups, and (3) that address mistrust issues in the community that stem from historical and structural racism in medical and research settings. The limited psychosis-prevention literature, coupled with behavioral health research with youth and young adults, can provide a blueprint for the psychosis prevention field, including development, engagement, dissemination, delivery, and sustainability (Barrera et al., 2017; Ngo et al., 2008; Novins et al., 2012). For instance, focus on education about race, privilege, and oppression for behavioral health practitioners (Alang, 2019), and anti-racist education to provide just and equitable services to minoritized racial/ethnic groups (Ford & Airhihenbuwa, 2010; Hardeman et al., 2016) are all strategies that would likely be applicable for providers working with people with early psychosis. Similarly, social workers have proposed using frameworks for incorporating larger systemic issues of structural inequality, social oppression, and racism into everyday practice and education that would translate well to support those at risk for psychosis (Cultural Humility: Fisher-Borne et al., 2015; SHARP: Shaia, 2019).

Service Provision: Helping Family and Youth Unleash Their Power

If a youth or young adult presents as at risk for psychosis or exhibits other underlying psychopathology, it is the practitioner's role to provide services or refer them to services that can meet their immediate needs. For families and youth alike, their immediate focus may be on symptom amelioration, and decreasing individual and family distress. We recommend providing youth and families with treatment options consistent with their needs and goals that includes any necessary cultural adaptations, as mentioned earlier. Additionally, the Council on Social Work Education (CSWE) provides a comprehensive list of readings on cultural adaptations for different racial/ethnic groups across a range of interventions which we encourage readers to consult.

As youth and family become more engaged and are better able to manage their at-risk symptoms and functioning, the service provider should think through organizational, community, and/or political advocacy with their clients, that tap into the family and youths' strengths and how they can affect change to impact policies and structures. Similar to psychoeducation, practitioners can provide clients with socioeducation, that is, "the act of assisting clients to reinterpret their experiences through the lens of SET [socially-engineered trauma: traumatic events rooted in social forces of oppression and inequality]" (Shaia et al., 2019, p. 238). In the case of a Black youth experiencing symptoms consistent with psychosis risk (or other non-psychosis symptoms such as trauma), the social worker may explore with the youth and the family how symptoms and associated distress may be related to or understood in the context of structural racism or other forms of oppression, co-developing a plan for individual and/or collective advocacy (W. Shaia, personal communication, June 24, 2020). This may result in an outcome such as the youth and family deciding to join a local National Alliance for Mental Illness (NAMI) chapter or other national or local group focusing on topics such as community organizing and policies for minoritized racial/ethnic groups with mental illness. Effective pursuit of these strategies requires practitioners to increase their knowledge of resources to include local and national advocacy and political organizations focused on mental health issues.

Summary

Considerable progress has been made since DeVylder (2016) outlined a vision for the prevention of SMI. Aligned with the articulated aims, early identification and person-centered treatment strategies have been implemented in an ever-growing network of early psychosis centers of excellence, with social workers providing leadership and training to the emerging workforce. Despite this progress, attention to the issues of race, ethnicity, and health disparities has lagged behind. In order for all people in the at-risk phase of psychosis to be afforded opportunities toward prevention, the historical and contextual realities of institutionalized racism and internal biases need to be examined so that we can create a mental healthcare system that is culturally responsiveness for minoritized racial/ethnic youth and young adults at clinical high risk for psychosis. There is tremendous need for ongoing research and attention in this area and we offer the following recommendations for the field to critically adopt as part of the next grand challenge.

1. Increased education of the social work workforce regarding the impact of historical racism and oppression on communities of color, with the goal of using this knowledge in collaboration with clients for community involvement and advocacy;
2. Additional research on the creation of racially unbiased and culturally sensitive psychosis risk-assessment tools (self-report and practitioner administered);
3. Incorporation of culturally responsive explanatory models of psychosis risk and mental illness that are driven by clients and families, and that do not pathologize culturally normative behavior;
4. Adaptation of existing, or creation of new, intervention strategies that incorporate cultural values and are responsive to race, ethnicity, and identity.

Across areas of practice research, an underlying discussion ensues regarding how to ensure that the core elements of an "evidence-based" practice are provided, while at the same time attuning to cultural nuances of youth being treated so that these practices are equally effective for minoritized racial/ethnic youth. As Ngo et al. (2008) stated, "What seems to be important is to strike a balance between fidelity to evidence-based treatment and culturally informed care" (p. 858). There is an urgency to understand issues of structural racism that may impact service delivery or experiences of treatment in psychosis-prevention research and practice. Our recommendations include the call for social workers to be a guide in the field of psychosis risk in promoting contextually informed practice, racial equity, and justice

ENSURING HEALTHY DEVELOPMENT FOR ALL YOUTH 189

consistent with the NASW Code of Ethics and now attended to as the 13th Grand Challenge of social work.

Study Questions

1. What is attenuated psychosis, or psychosis-risk symptoms? How do they differ from full-threshold symptoms of psychosis?

2. What is the aim of prevention and treatment services for youth that may be at risk for psychosis? What are the current recommendations for prevention and treatment, and how effective are they?

3. How did structural racism influence the conceptualization of mental illness? How has structural racism impacted current mental health diagnosis and treatment?

4. What are the major concerns in using current assessment tools with minoritized racial and ethnic youth?

5. What are the promising evidence-based practices for psychosis prevention? Are they racially and culturally responsive? If so, discuss key elements or adaptations that contribute to racial and cultural responsiveness. If not, what is lacking?

6. Discuss three strategies for reducing structural racism and racial bias and increasing cultural responsiveness in the assessment and diagnosis of psychosis risk.

7. Discuss three strategies for reducing racial bias and increasing cultural responsiveness in evidence-based treatment practices for youth at risk for psychosis.

8. Case Study: Devon is a 16-year-old cisgender African American male who attends a public high school in an urban, low-income, predominantly Black neighborhood. Devon was referred to you, the school social worker, by his teacher. Devon's grades have been lower than normal in the past year, and his teacher noted that he has become more withdrawn in class. When you meet with Devon, he shares that he has been feeling isolated from other classmates recently, wondering if they are talking about him behind his back, or are out to get him somehow. You suspect that he may be showing early signs of psychosis and administer a psychosis risk assessment. When prompted about the level of distress and interference related to his feelings about his classmates,

Devon shared that it makes it hard to talk in class, participate in group projects, and he skips classes on occasion. He also shared that he thinks he has been hearing the voice of his grandmother the past few months after her passing, but he's not sure that's even possible. He stated that he was initially scared but has found it comforting given that he was very close to her.

a. What are some initial biases you should attend to before assessing Devon?

b. What more would you want to learn about Devon's experiences?

c. What contextual and/or cultural factors would you need to consider before providing your assessment?

d. If Devon attended a high school in a predominantly White neighborhood, would that change your assessment of his behaviors and experiences? Why or why not?

e. What historical factors might be at play with respect to Devon's interfacing with the mental health system?

f. Knowing that a partnership with Devon would require input from him and his family, brainstorm ways to connect with them and generate some initial ideas for treatment planning.

Suggested Readings

* Fisher-Borne, M., Cain, J. M., & Martin, S. L. (2015). From mastery to accountability: Cultural humility as an alternative to cultural competence. *Social Work Education, 34*(2), 165–181. doi: 10.1080/02615479.2014.977244.

* Gehlert, S., & Mozersky, J. (2018). Seeing beyond the margins: Challenges to informed inclusion of vulnerable populations in research. *Journal of Law, Medicine & Ethics, 46*(1), 30–43. https://doi-org.proxy-hs.researchport.umd.edu/10.1177/107311051 8766006.

Hardeman, R. R., Medina, E. M., & Kozhimannil, K. B. (2016). Structural racism and supporting black lives: The role of health professionals. *The New England Journal of Medicine, 375*(22), 2113–2115. doi: 10.1056/NEJMp1609535.

* Ngo, V., Langley, A., Kataoka, S. H., Nadeem, E., Escudero, P., & Stein, B. D. (2008). Providing evidence-based practice to ethnically diverse youths: Examples from the Cognitive Behavioral Intervention for Trauma in Schools (CBITS) program. *Journal of the American Academy of Child and Adolescent Psychiatry, 47*(8), 858–862. doi: 10.1097/CHI.0b013e3181799f19.

Novins, D. K., Boyd, M. L., Brotherton, D. T., Fickenscher, A., Moore, L., & Spicer, P. (2012). Walking on: Celebrating the journeys of Native American adolescents with substance use problems on the winding road to healing. *Journal of Psychoactive Drugs, 44*(2), 153–159. doi: 10.1080/02791072.2012.684628.

ENSURING HEALTHY DEVELOPMENT FOR ALL YOUTH   191

* Rivas-Drake, D., Camacho, T. C., & Guillaume, C. (2016). Just good developmental science: Trust, identity, and responsibility in ethnic minority recruitment and retention. In S. S. Horn, M. D. Ruck, & L. S. Liben (Eds.), *Advances in child development and behavior* (Vol. 50, pp. 161–188). Ann Arbor, MI: Elsevier Academic Press.

* Shaia, W. (2019). SHARP: A framework for addressing the contexts of poverty and oppression during service provision in the United States. *Journal of Social Work Values and Ethics, 16*(1), 16–26.

Wagner, E. F., Hospital, M. M., Graziano, J. N., Morris, S. L., & Gil, A. G. (2014). A randomized controlled trial of guided self-change with minority adolescents. *Journal of Consulting and Clinical Psychology, 82*(6), 1128–1139. doi: 10.1037/a0036939.

* Washington, H. A. (2006). *Medical apartheid: The dark history of medical experimentation on Black Americans from colonial times to the present.* New York: Random House.

* = Written all or in part by social work researchers, educators, or practitioners.

References

Addington, J., Stowkowy, J., & Weiser, M. (2015). Screening tools for clinical high risk for psychosis. *Early Intervention in Psychiatry, 9*(5), 345–356. doi: 10.1111/eip.12193.

Adeponle, A. B., Groleau, D., & Kirmayer, L. J. (2015). Clinician reasoning in the use of cultural formulation to resolve uncertainty in the diagnosis of psychosis. *Culture, Medicine and Psychiatry, 39*(1), 16–42. https://doi.org/10.1007/s11013-014-9408-5.

Adeponle, A. B., Thombs, B. D., Groleau, D., Jarvis, E., & Kirmayer, L. J. (2012). Using the cultural formulation to resolve uncertainty in diagnoses of psychosis among ethnoculturally diverse patients. *Psychiatric Services, 63*(2), 147–153. https://doi.org/10.1176/appi.ps.201100280.

Alang, S. M. (2019). Mental health care among Blacks in America: Confronting racism and constructing solutions. *Health Services Research, 54*(2), 346–355. doi: 10.1111/1475-6773.13115.

American Academy of Social Work & Social Welfare (2014). Prepare the profession to address structural racism and its impact on ourselves and our clients [Press release]. Retrieved from https://grandchallengesforsocialwork.org/grand-challenges-for-soc ial-work/prepare-the-profession-to-address-structural-racism-and-its-impact-on-ourselves-and-our-clients/.

Andorko, N. D., Fitzgerald, F., Roemer, C., Solender, E., Petti, E., Rakhshan Rouhakhtar, P., McNamara, K. E., Smith, M. E., Buchanan, R. W., Schiffman, J., & DeVylder, J. (2021). Social work training to reduce duration of untreated psychosis: Methodology and considerations of a web-based training for community providers. *Early Intervention in Psychiatry, 16*(4), 3939–3401. doi: 10.1111/eip.13178.

Barnes, A. (2008). Race and hospital diagnoses of schizophrenia and mood disorders. *Social Work, 53*(1), 77–83. doi: 10.1093/sw/53.1.77.

Barrera, M., Jr., Berkel, C., & Castro, F. G. (2017). Directions for the advancement of culturally adapted preventive interventions: Local adaptations, engagement, and sustainability. *Prevention Science, 18*(6), 640–648. doi: 10.1007/s11121-016-0705-9.

Baskin, D., Bluestone, H., & Nelson, M. (1981). Ethnicity and psychiatric diagnosis. *Journal of Clinical Psychology, 37*(3), 529–537. doi: 10.1002/1097-4679(198107)37:3<529::aid-jclp2270370315>3.0.co;2-3.

192 SMITH, RAKHSHAN ROUHAKHTAR, AND SCHIFFMAN

Bessaha, M. L., Shumway, M., Smith, M. E., Bright, C. L., & Unick, G. J. (2017). Predictors of hospital length and cost of stay in a national sample of adult patients with psychotic disorders. *Psychiatric Services, 68*(6), 559–565. doi: 10.1176/appi.ps.201600312.

Blow, F. C., Zeber, J. E., McCarthy, J. F., Valenstein, M., Gillon, L., & Bingham, C. R. (2004). Ethnicity and diagnostic patterns in veterans with psychoses. *Social Psychiatry and Psychiatric Epidemiology, 39*(10), 841–851. doi: 10.1007/s00127-004-0824-7.

Brodey, B. B., Girgis, R. R., Favorov, O. V., Addington, J., Perkins, D. O., Bearden, C. E., . . . Brodey, I. S. (2018). The early psychosis screener (EPS): Quantitative validation against the SIPS using machine learning. *Schizophrenia Research, 197*, 516–521. doi: 10.1016/j.schres.2017.11.030.

Brodey, B. B., Girgis, R. R., Favorov, O. V., Bearden, C. E., Woods, S. W., Addington, J., . . . Cadenhead, K. S. (2019). The early psychosis screener for internet (EPSI)-SR: Predicting 12 month psychotic conversion using machine learning. *Schizophrenia Research, 208*, 390–396. doi: 10.1016/j.schres.2019.01.015.

Byrne, M., Codjoe, L., Morgan, C., Stahl, D., Day, F., Fearon, P., . . . Valmaggia, L. (2019). The relationship between ethnicity and service access, treatment uptake and the incidence of psychosis among people at ultra high risk for psychosis. *Psychiatry Research, 272*, 618–627. doi: 10.1016/j.psychres.2018.12.111.

Campion, J., Taylor, M. J., McDaid, D., Park, A. L., & Shiers, D. (2019). Applying economic models to estimate local economic benefits of improved coverage of early intervention for psychosis. *Early Interventions in Psychiatry, 13*(6), 1424–1430. doi: 10.1111/eip.12787.

Cartwright, S. (1851). Diseases and peculiarities of the Negro race. *De Bow's Review: Southern and Western States, XI*, 5 v. Retrieved from http://hdl.handle.net/2027/njp.32101065216424.

Cartwright, S. (2004). Report on the diseases and physical peculiarities of the Negro race. In Arthur Caplan, James J. McCartney & Dominic A. Sisti (Eds.), *Health, Disease, and Illness: Concepts in Medicine* (pp. 28–39). Washington, DC: Georgetown University Press.

Cicero D. C. (2016). Measurement invariance of the Schizotypal Personality Questionnaire in Asian, Pacific Islander, White, and Multiethnic populations. *Psychological Assessment, 28*(4), 351–361. https://doi.org/10.1037/pas0000180

Cicero, D. C., Krieg, A., & Martin, E. A. (2019). Measurement invariance of the Prodromal Questionnaire-Brief Among White, Asian, Hispanic, and Multiracial Ppopulations. *Assessment, 26*(2), 294–304. https://doi.org/10.1177/1073191116687391.

Claxton, M., Onwumere, J., & Fornells-Ambrojo, M. (2017). Do family interventions improve outcomes in early psychosis? A systematic review and meta-analysis. *Frontiers in Psychology, 8*, 371. https://doi.org/10.3389/fpsyg.2017.00371.

Colizzi, M., Ruggeri, M., & Lasalvia, A. (2020). Should we be concerned about stigma and discrimination in people at risk for psychosis? A systematic review. *Psychological Medicine, 50*(5), 705–726. doi: 10.1017/S0033291720000148.

Daneault, J. G., & Stip, E. (2013). Genealogy of instruments for prodrome evaluation of psychosis. *Frontiers in Psychiatry, 4*(25), 1–9. doi: 10.3389/fpsyt.2013.00025.

DeVylder, J. E. (2016). Preventing schizophrenia and severe mental illness: A grand challenge for social work. *Research on Social Work Practice, 26*(4), 449–459. doi: 10.1177/1049731515622687.

DeVylder, J. E., Oh, H. Y., Nam, B., Sharpe, T. L., Lehmann, M., & Link, B. G. (2017). Prevalence, demographic variation and psychological correlates of exposure to police

ENSURING HEALTHY DEVELOPMENT FOR ALL YOUTH 193

victimisation in four US cities. *Epidemiology and Psychiatric Sciences, 26*(5), 466–477. https://doi.org/10.1017/S2045796016000810.

Eack, S. M., & Newhill, C. E. (2012). Racial disparities in mental health outcomes after psychiatric hospital discharge among individuals with severe mental illness. *Social Work Research, 36*(1), 41–52. doi: 10.1093/swr/svs014.

Earl, T. R., Fortuna, L. R., Gao, S., Williams, D. R., Neighbors, H., Takeuchi, D., & Alegría, M. (2015). An exploration of how psychotic-like symptoms are experienced, endorsed, and understood from the National Latino and Asian American Study and National Survey of American Life. *Ethnicity & Health, 20*(3), 273–292. https://doi.org/10.1080/13557858.2014.921888.

EASA Center for Excellence (2016). *Program directory of early psychosis intervention programs.* Portland, OR: EASA Center for Excellence.

Edge, D., Degnan, A., Cotterill, S., Berry, K., Drake, R., Baker, J., . . . Abel, K. (2016). Culturally-adapted family intervention (CaFI) for African-Caribbeans diagnosed with schizophrenia and their families: A feasibility study protocol of implementation and acceptability. *Pilot and Feasibility Studies, 2*(1), 39. doi: 10.1186/s40814-016-0070-2.

Edge, D., Degnan, A., Cotterill, S., Berry, K., Baker, J., Drake, R., & Abel, K. (2018). Culturally adapted Family Intervention (CaFI) for African-Caribbean people diagnosed with schizophrenia and their families: A mixed-methods feasibility study of development, implementation and acceptability. *NIHR Journals Library.* https://pubmed.ncbi.nlm.nih.gov/30222284/

Fischer, R., & Karl, J. A. (2019). A primer to (cross-cultural) multi-group invariance testing possibilities in R. *Frontiers in Psychology, 10*(1507), 1–18. doi: 10.3389/fpsyg.2019.01507.

Fisher-Borne, M., Cain, J. M., & Martin, S. L. (2015). From mastery to accountability: Cultural humility as an alternative to cultural competence. *Social Work Education, 34*(2), 165–181. doi: 10.1080/02615479.2014.977244.

Ford, C. L., & Airhihenbuwa, C. O. (2010). Critical race theory, race equity, and public health: Toward antiracism praxis. *American Journal of Public Health, 100 Suppl 1*(Suppl 1), S30–S35. doi: 10.2105/AJPH.2009.171058.

Friedman-Yakoobian, M. S., West, M. L., Woodbery, K. A., O'Donovan, K. E., Zimmet, S. V., Gnong-Granato, A., . . . Seidman, L. J. (2018). Development of a Boston treatment program for youth at clinical high risk for psychosis: Center for early detection, assessment, and response to risk (CEDAR). *Harvard Review of Psychiatry, 26*(5), 274–286. doi: 10.1097/HRP.0000000000000181.

Fusar-Poli, P., Salazar de Pablo, G., Correll, C. U., Meyer-Lindenberg, A., Millan, M. J., Borgwardt, S., . . . Arango, C. (2020). Prevention of psychosis: Advances in detection, prognosis, and intervention. *JAMA Psychiatry, 77*(7), 755–765. doi: 10.1001/jamapsychiatry.2019.4779.

Fusar-Poli, P., Sullivan, S. A., Shah, J. L., & Uhlhaas, P. J. (2019). Improving the detection of individuals at clinical risk for psychosis in the community, primary and secondary care: An integrated evidence-based approach. *Frontiers in Psychiatry, 10*, 774. doi: 10.3389/fpsyt.2019.00774.

Glenthøj, L. B., Hjorthøj, C., Kristensen, T. D., Davidson, C. A., & Nordentoft, M. (2017). The effect of cognitive remediation in individuals at ultra-high risk for psychosis: A systematic review. *NPJ Schizophrenia, 3*, 20–20. doi: 10.1038/s41537-017-0021-9.

Gurak, K., & Weisman de Mamani, A. (2017). Caregiver expressed emotion and psychiatric symptoms in African-Americans with schizophrenia: An attempt to understand the paradoxical relationship. *Family Process, 56*(2), 476–486. https://onlinelibrary. wiley.com/doi/abs/10.1111/famp.12188.

Hardeman, R. R., Medina, E. M., & Kozhimannil, K. B. (2016). Structural racism and supporting Black lives: The role of health professionals. *The New England Journal of Medicine, 375*(22), 2113–2115. doi: 10.1056/NEJMp1609535.

He, E., Brooks, C., Gardner, N., & Li, H. (2019). F116. Help-seeking barriers for youth at clinical high risk of developing psychosis: by demographic information. *Schizophrenia Bulletin, 45*(Suppl 2), S298–S298. doi: 10.1093/schbul/sbz018.528.

Horvitz-Lennon, M., Volya, R., Donohue, J. M., Lave, J. R., Stein, B. D., & Normand, S.-L. T. (2014). Disparities in quality of care among publicly insured adults with schizophrenia in four large U.S. states, 2002–2008. *Health Services Research, 49,* 1121–1144. doi:10.1111/1475-6773.12162.

Johnson, K. A., Guyer, M., Öngür, D., Friedman-Yakoobian, M., Kline, E., Carol, E., Davis, B., & Keshavan, M. (2021). Early intervention in psychosis: Building a strategic roadmap for Massachusetts. *Schizophrenia Research, 229*(2021), 43–45. doi: 10.1016/ j.schres.2021.01.026

Kannani, N. (2011). Race and madness: Locating the experiences of racialized people with psychiatric histories in Canada and the United States. *Critical Disability Discourses/ Discours critiques dans le champ du handicap, 3,* 1–14. Retrieved from https://cdd.journ als.yorku.ca/index.php/cdd/article/view/31564/31232.

Kelleher, I., Devlin, N., Wigman, J. T., Kehoe, A., Murtagh, A., Fitzpatrick, C., & Cannon, M. (2014). Psychotic experiences in a mental health clinic sample: Implications for suicidality, multimorbidity and functioning. *Psychological Medicine, 44*(8), 1615–1624. doi: 10.1017/s0033291713002122.

Kim, K. R., Lee, S. Y., Kang, J. I., Kim, B. R., Choi, S. H., Park, J. Y., . . . Kwon, J. S. (2011). Clinical efficacy of individual cognitive therapy in reducing psychiatric symptoms in people at ultra-high risk for psychosis. *Early Intervention in Psychiatry, 5*(2), 174–178. doi: 10.1111/j.1751-7893.2011.00267.x.

Kline, E., & Schiffman, J. (2014). Psychosis risk screening: A systematic review. *Schizophrenia Research, 158*(1-3), 11–18. https://doi.org/10.1016/j.schres.2014.06.036

Kline, E., Thompson, E., Bussell, K., Pitts, S. C., Reeves, G., & Schiffman, J. (2014). Psychosis-like experiences and distress among adolescents using mental health services. *Schizophrenia Research, 152*(2), 498–502. doi: https://doi.org/10.1016/j.schres.2013. 12.012.

Kotlicka-Antczak, M., Podgórski, M., Oliver, D., Maric, N. P., Valmaggia, L., & Fusar-Poli, P. (2020). Worldwide implementation of clinical services for the prevention of psychosis: The IEPA early intervention in mental health survey. *Early Intervention in Psychiatry, 14*(6), 741–750. doi: 10.1111/eip.12950.

Leong, F. T., Leung, K., & Cheung, F. M. (2010). Integrating cross-cultural psychology research methods into ethnic minority psychology. *Cultural Diversity & Ethnic Minority Psychology, 16*(4), 590–597. https://doi.org/10.1037/a0020127.

Loewy, R. L., Pearson, R., Vinogradov, S., Bearden, C. E., & Cannon, T. D. (2011). Psychosis risk screening with the Prodromal Questionnaire–brief version (PQ-B). *Schizophrenia Research, 129*(1), 42–46. doi: 10.1016/j.schres.2011.03.029.

Lynch, S., McFarlane, W. R., Joly, B., Adelsheim, S., Auther, A., Cornblatt, B. A., Migliorati, M., Ragland, J. D., Sale, T., Spring, E., Calkins, R., Carter, C. S., Jaynes, R., Taylor, S. F., & Downing, D. (2016). Early detection, intervention and prevention of psychosis

ENSURING HEALTHY DEVELOPMENT FOR ALL YOUTH 195

program: Community outreach and early identification at six U.S. sites. *Psychiatric Services*, *67*(5), 510–516. https://doi.org/10.1176/appi.ps.201300236

McDonald, M., Christoforidou, E., Van Rijsbergen, N., Gajwani, R., Gross, J., Gumley, A. I., . . . Uhlhaas, P. J. (2018). Using online screening in the general population to detect participants at clinical high-risk for psychosis. *Schizophrenia Bulletin*, *45*(3), 600–609. doi: 10.1093/schbul/sby069.

McFarlane, W. R., & Jaynes, R. (2017). Educating communities to identify and engage youth in the early phases of an initial psychosis: A manual for specialty programs. Retrieved from http://nri-inc.org/media/1560/nri_educating_communities_identify _engage.pdf.

McFarlane, W. R., Lynch, S., & Melton, R. (2012). Family psychoeducation in clinical high risk and first-episode psychosis. *Adolescent Psychiatry*, *2*(2), 182–194. doi: 10.2174/ 2210676611202020182.

McGlashan, T. H., Walsh, B. W., & Woods, S. W. (2010). *The psychosis-risk syndrome: Handbook for diagnosis and follow-up*. Oxford: Oxford University Press.

Metzl, J. M. (2010). *The protest psychosis: How schizophrenia became a black disease*. Boston: Beacon Press.

Miklowitz, D. J., O'Brien, M. P., Schlosser, D. A., Addington, J., Candan, K. A., Marshall, C., . . . Cannon, T. D. (2014). Family-focused treatment for adolescents and young adults at high risk for psychosis: Results of a randomized trial. *Journal of the American Academy of Child and Adolescent Psychiatry*, *53*(8), 848–858. doi: 10.1016/j.jaac.2014.04.020.

Miklowitz, D. J., O'Brien, M. P., Schlosser, D. A., Sullivan, A. E., George, E. L., Taylor, D. O., . . . Cannon, T. D. (2018). Clinicians' treatment manual for family-focused therapy fo early-onset youth and young adults (FFT-EOY). Retrieved from https://www.semel. ucla.edu/champ/downloads-clinicians.

Miller, T. J., Cicchetti, D., Markovich, P. J., & Woods, S. (2004). The SIPS Screen: A brief self-report screen to detect the schizophrenia prodrome. *Schizophrenia Research*, *70*(1 supplement), 78. doi: https://doi.org/10.1016/j.schres.2004.06.006.

Millman, Z. B., Rakhshan Rouhakhtar, P. J., DeVylder, J. E., Smith, M. E., Phalen, P. L., Woods, S. W., . . . Schiffman, J. (2019). Evidence for differential predictive performance of the prime screen between Black and White help-seeking youths. *Psychiatric Services*, *70*(10), 907–914. doi: 10.1176/appi.ps.201800536.

Myers, N., Sood, A., Fox, K. E., Wright, G., & Compton, M. T. (2018). Decision making about pathways through care for racially and ethnically diverse young adults with early psychosis. *Psychiatric Services*, *70*(3), 184–190. doi: 10.1176/appi.ps.201700459.

National Institutes of Health [NIH]. (2018a). Early Psychosis Intervention Network (EPINET): Practice-based research to improve treatment outcomes. (RFA-MH-19-150). Retrieved from https://grants.nih.gov/grants/guide/rfa-files/RFA-MH-19-150.html.

National Institutes of Health [NIH]. (2018b). Early Psychosis Intervention Network (EPINET): Data coordinating center. (RFA-MH-19-151). Retrieved from https://gra nts.nih.gov/grants/guide/rfa-files/RFA-MH-19-151.html.

Ngo, V., Langley, A., Kataoka, S. H., Nadeem, E., Escudero, P., & Stein, B. D. (2008). Providing evidence-based practice to ethnically diverse youths: Examples from the Cognitive Behavioral Intervention for Trauma in Schools (CBITS) program. *Journal of the American Academy of Child and Adolescent Psychiatry*, *47*(8), 858–862. doi: 10.1097/CHI.0b013e3181799f19.

Niendam, T. A., Sardo, A., Savill, M., Patel, P., Xing, G., Loewy, R. L., Dewa, C. S., & Melnikow, J. (2019). The rise of early psychosis care in California: An overview of community and university-based services. *Psychiatric Services, 70*(6), 480–487. https://doi. org/10.1176/appi.ps.201800394

Novins, D. K., Boyd, M. L., Brotherton, D. T., Fickenscher, A., Moore, L., & Spicer, P. (2012). Walking on: Celebrating the journeys of Native American adolescents with substance use problems on the winding road to healing. *Journal of Psychoactive Drugs, 44*(2), 153–159. doi: 10.1080/02791072.2012.684628.

O'Brien, M. P., Gordon, J. L., Bearden, C. E., Lopez, S. R., Kopelowicz, A., & Cannon, T. D. (2006). Positive family environment predicts improvement in symptoms and social functioning among adolescents at imminent risk for onset of psychosis. *Schizophrenia Research, 81*(2–3), 269–275. doi: 10.1016/j.schres.2005.10.005.

O'Driscoll, C., Sener, S. B., Angmark, A., & Shaikh, M. (2019). Caregiving processes and expressed emotion in psychosis, a cross-cultural, meta-analytic review. *Schizophrenia Research, 208*, 8–15. doi: https://doi.org/10.1016/j.schres.2019.03.020.

Oexle, N., & Corrigan, P. W. (2018). Understanding mental illness stigma toward persons with multiple stigmatized conditions: Implications of intersectionality theory. *Psychiatric Services, 69*(5), 587–589. doi: 10.1176/appi.ps.201700312.

Okuzawa, N., Kline, E., Fuertes, J., Negi, S., Reeves, G., Himelhoch, S., & Schiffman, J. (2014). Psychotherapy for adolescents and young adults at high risk for psychosis: A systematic review. *Early Intervention in Psychiatry, 8*(4), 307–322. https://doi. org/10.1111/eip.12129

Pavkov, T., Lewis, D., & Lyons, J. (1989). Psychiatric diagnoses and racial bias: An empirical investigation. *Professional Psychology: Research and Practice, 20*, 364–368. doi: 10.1037/0735-7028.20.6.364.

Peltier, M. R., Cosgrove, S. J., Ohayagha, K., Crapanzano, K. A., & Jones, G. N. (2017). Do they see dead people? Cultural factors and sensitivity in screening for schizophrenia spectrum disorders. *Ethnicity & Health, 22*(2), 119–129. https://doi.org/10.1080/13557 858.2016.1196650

Phalen, P. L., Rouhakhtar, P. R., Millman, Z. B., Thompson, E., DeVylder, J., Mittal, V., . . . Schiffman, J. (2018). Validity of a two-item screen for early psychosis. *Psychiatry Research, 270*, 861–868. doi: https://doi.org/10.1016/j.psychres.2018.11.002.

Rakhshan Rouhakhtar, P. J., Phalen, P. L., Thompson, E., Andorko, N., Millman, Z. B., Sun, S., & Schiffman, J. (2018). Factor analysis of the Prime Screen: Introducing the Prime-8. Paper presented at the 5th Biennial American Psychological Association Division 45 Society for the Psychological Study of Culture, Ethnicity, and Race Conference, Austin, Texas.

Rakhshan Rouhakhtar, P., Pitts, C. S., & Schiffman, J. (2019). Associations between race, discrimination, community violence, traumatic life events, and psychosis-like experiences in a sample of college students. *Journal of Clinical Medicine, 8*(10). 1573. doi :10.3390/jcm8101573.

Rathod, S., Kingdon, D., Phiri, P., & Gobbi, M. (2010). Developing culturally sensitive cognitive behaviour therapy for psychosis for ethnic minority patients by exploration and incorporation of service users' and health professionals' views and opinions. *Behavioral Cognitive Psychotherapy, 38*(5), 511–533. doi: 10.1017/ s1352465810000378.

Rathod, S., Phiri, P., Harris, S., Underwood, C., Thagadur, M., Padmanabi, U., & Kingdon, D. (2013). Cognitive behaviour therapy for psychosis can be adapted for minority ethnic groups: A randomised controlled trial. *Schizophrenia Research, 143*(2–3), 319–326. doi: 10.1016/j.schres.2012.11.007.

Rosenfarb, I. S., Bellack, A. S., & Aziz, N. (2006). Family interactions and the course of schizophrenia in African American and White patients. *Journal of Abnormal Psychology, 115*(1), 112–120. https://doi.org/10.1037/0021-843X.115.1.112.

Sale, T., Humensky, J., Baker, M., Hardy, K., Noordsy, C. D., & Adelsheim, S. (2018). The integration of early psychosis services in a system of care framework: Opportunities, issues. Retrieved from http://www.easacommunity.org/PDF/integration-ep-svcs-soc.pdf.

Salokangas, R. K. R., Nieman, D. H., Heinimaa, M., Svirskis, T., Luutonen, S., From, T., . . . The EPOS Group. (2013). Psychosocial outcome in patients at clinical high risk of psychosis: A prospective follow-up. *Social Psychiatry and Psychiatric Epidemiology, 48*(2), 303–311. doi: 10.1007/s00127-012-0545-2.

SAMHSA (2018). *Community programs for outreach and intervention with youth and young adults at clinical high risk for psychosis.* (Funding Opportunity Announcement No. SM-18-012). Retrieved from https://www.samhsa.gov/grants/grant-announcements/sm-18-012.

Savill, M., D'Ambrosio, J., Cannon, T. D., & Loewy, R. L. (2018). Psychosis risk screening in different populations using the Prodromal Questionnaire: A systematic review. *Early Intervention in Psychiatry, 12*(1), 3–14. doi: 10.1111/eip.12446.

Schiffman, J. (2018). Considerations for the development and implementation of brief screening tools in the identification of early psychosis. *Schizophrenia Research, 199,* 41–43. doi: 10.1016/j.schres.2018.03.002.

Schiffman, J., Ellman, L. M., & Mittal, V. A. (2019). Individual differences and psychosis-risk screening: Practical suggestions to improve the scope and quality of early identification. *Frontiers in Psychiatry, 10,* 6–6. doi: 10.3389/fpsyt.2019.00006.

Shah, J. L., Scott, J., McGorry, P. D., Cross, S. P. M., Keshavan, M. S., Nelson, B., . . . for the International Working Group on Transdiagnostic Clinical Staging in Youth Mental Health. (2020). Transdiagnostic clinical staging in youth mental health: A first international consensus statement. *World Psychiatry: Official Journal of the World Psychiatric Association (WPA), 19*(2), 233–242. doi: 10.1002/wps.20745.

Shaia, W. (2019). SHARP: A framework for addressing the contexts of poverty and oppression during service provision in the United States. *Journal of Social Work Values and Ethics 16*(1), 16–26.

Shaia, W. E., Avruch, D. O., Green, K., & Godsey, G. M. (2019). Socially-engineered trauma and a new social work pedagogy: Socioeducation as a critical foundation of social work Practice. *Smith College Studies in Social Work, 89*(3–4), 238–263.

Shan, L., Millman, Z. B., DeLuca, J., Klaunig, M. J., Rouhakhtar, P. R., Lucksted, A., & Medoff, D. R. (2020). S27. Examining discrepancies between self-report and clinician-rated assessments of psychosis risk: Does internalized stigma matter? *Schizophrenia Bulletin, 46*(Suppl 1), S41–S41. doi: 10.1093/schbul/sbaa031.093.

Singh, S. P., Harley, K., & Suhail, K. (2013). Cultural specificity of emotional overinvolvement: a systematic review. *Schizophrenia Bulletin, 39*(2), 449–463. doi: 10.1093/schbul/sbr17.0

Smith, M. E., Sharpe, T. L., Richardson, J., Pahwa, R., Smith, D., & DeVylder, J. (2020). The impact of exposure to gun violence fatality on mental health outcomes in four U.S. urban settings. *Social Science & Medicine. 246,* 112587. doi: https://doi.org/10.1016/j.socscimed.2019.112587

Smith, M. E., Yamada, A.-M., Barrio, C., Pahwa, R., Hurlburt, K., & Brekke, J. S. (2019). A quick scoping review of psychosocial treatment recommendations for African Americans with schizophrenia spectrum disorders. *Journal of Ethnic & Cultural Diversity in Social Work, 28*(3), 263–281. doi: 10.1080/15313204.2019.1640823.

Stafford, M. R., Jackson, H., Mayo-Wilson, E., Morrison, A. P., & Kendall, T. (2013). Early interventions to prevent psychosis: Systematic review and meta-analysis. *BMJ: British Medical Journal, 346*, f185. doi: 10.1136/bmj.f185.

Strakowski, S. M., Flaum, M., Amador, X., Bracha, H. S., Pandurangi, A. K., Robinson, D., & Tohen, M. (1996). Racial differences in the diagnosis of psychosis. *Schizophrenia Research, 21*(2), 117–124. doi: 10.1016/0920-9964(96)00041-2.

Sutton, M., O'Keeffe, D., Frawley, T., Madigan, K., Fanning, F., Lawlor, E., . . . Clarke, M. (2018). Feasibility of a psychosis information intervention to improve mental health literacy for professional groups in contact with young people. *Early Intervention Psychiatry, 12*(2), 234–239. doi: 10.1111/eip.12410.

Terrell, F., Taylor, J., Menzise, J., & Barrett, R. K. (2009). Cultural mistrust: A core component of African American consciousness. In H. Neville, B. Tynes, & S. O. Utsey (Eds.), *The handbook of African American psychology* (pp. 299–310). Thousand Oaks, CA: Sage Publications.

Thompson, E., Millman, Z. B., Okuzawa, N., Mittal, V., DeVylder, J. E., Skadberg, T., . . . Schiffman, J. (2015). Evidence-based early interventions for individuals at clinical high risk for psychosis: A review of treatment components. *The Journal of Nervous and Mental Disease, 203*(5), 342–351. doi: 10.1097/nmd.0000000000000287.

van der Gaag, M., Smit, F., Bechdolf, A., French, P., Linszen, D. H., Yung, A. R., . . . Cuijpers, P. (2013). Preventing a first episode of psychosis: Meta-analysis of randomized controlled prevention trials of 12 month and longer-term follow-ups. *Schizophrenia Research, 149*(1–3), 56–62. doi: 10.1016/j.schres.2013.07.004.

van der Gaag, M., van den Berg, D., & Ising, H. (2019). CBT in the prevention of psychosis and other severe mental disorders in patients with an at risk mental state: A review and proposed next steps. *Schizophrenia Research, 203*, 88–93. doi: 10.1016/j.schres.2017.08.018.

Vargas, T., Rakhshan, P., Schiffman, J., Zou, D., Rydland, K., & Mittal, V. (2020). Neighborhood crime, socioeconomic status, and suspiciousness in adolescents and young adults at Clinical High Risk (CHR) for psychosis. *Schizophrenia Research, 215*, 74–80.

Weisman, A., Duarte, E., Koneru, V., & Wasserman, S. (2006). The development of a culturally informed, family-focused treatment for schizophrenia. *Family Process, 45*(2), 171–186. doi: 10.1111/j.1545-5300.2006.00089.x.

Weisman de Mamani, A., Weintraub, M. J., Gurak, K., & Maura, J. (2014). A randomized clinical trial to test the efficacy of a family-focused, culturally informed therapy for schizophrenia. *Journal of family psychology: JFP: Journal of the Division of Family Psychology of the American Psychological Association (Division 43), 28*(6), 800–810. https://doi.org/10.1037/fam0000021.

White, K. (2002). *An introduction to the sociology of health and illness.* London: Sage Publications.

Wilson, C., Smith, M. E., Thompson, E., Demro, C., Kline, E., Bussell, K., . . . Schiffman, J. (2016). Context matters: The impact of neighborhood crime and paranoid symptoms on psychosis risk assessment. *Schizophrenia Research, 171*(1–3), 56–61. doi: https://doi.org/10.1016/j.schres.2016.01.007.

Woods, S., Walsh, B., & Cannon, T. D. (2020). Mini-SIPS: Abbreviated clinical structured interview for DSM-5 attenuated psychosis syndrome. Retrieved from https://cpb-us-w2.wpmucdn.com/campuspress.yale.edu/dist/d/120/files/2020/05/Mini-SIPS-version-1-0-041920.pdf.

Yamada, A. M., Barrio, C., Atuel, H., Harding, C. M., Webster, D., & Hough, R. L. (2009). A retrospective study of delayed receipt of initial psychiatric services in a tri-ethnic community sample of adults with schizophrenia. *Schizophrenia Research, 108*(1–3), 305–306. doi: 10.1016/j.schres.2008.11.001.

Yung, A. R., Yuen, H. P., McGorry, P. D., Phillips, L. J., Kelly, D., Dell'Olio, M., . . . Buckby, J. (2005). Mapping the onset of psychosis: The comprehensive assessment of at-risk mental states. *Australia and New Zealand Journal of Psychiatry, 39*(11–12), 964–971. doi: 10.1080/j.1440-1614.2005.01714.x.

8

Closing the Health Gap

Addressing Racism, Settler Colonialism, and White Supremacy

Michael S. Spencer, Santino G. Camacho, Bongki Woo,
Roberto E. R. Orellana, and Jessica I. Ramirez

In *Kānaka Maoli* (Native Hawaiian) culture, illness is considered to be derived from *ma'i* or imbalance. Thus, it is the healer's role to find the source of the *ma'i* in order to correct it. To *Kānaka Maoli, ola,* or health, is holistic; it factors in the harmonious relationship between one's mind, body, and spirit and how these components interact with the world (OHA, 2019). The Ulukau Hawaiian Electronic Library translates *ola* as: life, health, well-being, living, livelihood, means of support, salvation; alive, living; curable, spared, recovered, healed, to live, to spare, save, heal, grant life, survive, thrive (Mau et al., 2010). Our definition of health in this chapter is based on the concepts of *ma'i* and *ola.*

Health is more than just living; it is surviving, thriving, recovering, and healing; it is nurtured by the connection one has to one's culture, community, and ancestors. If 2020 has taught us anything, specifically the disproportionate impact of the Coronavirus pandemic and the racial justice movement that accorded following the witnessing of George Floyd's murder by police, it is that we still have a major source of *ma'i* in our society. Today, we must reckon with this toxic ailment that we have yet to cure in society—*racism*—as experienced through White supremacy and settler colonialism. Racism strikes at the very source of our wellbeing or *ola.* Therefore, we must understand how racism impacts Black, Indigenous, and other People of Color (BIPOC) communities holistically so that we can identify and address all sources of systematic racism and eliminate them. We, as healers, must continue to identify and address the sources of *ma'i* in order to eliminate

Michael S. Spencer, Santino G. Camacho, Bongki Woo, Roberto E. R. Orellana, and Jessica I. Ramirez, *Closing the Health Gap* In: *Social Work and the Grand Challenge to Eliminate Racism.* Edited by: Martell L. Teasley, Michael S. Spencer, and Melissa Bartholomew, Oxford University Press. © Oxford University Press 2023. DOI: 10.1093/oso/9780197674949.003.0008

them, in every sphere of influence we belong to. Bigotry has no place in our communities, organizations, and institutions, particularly those that are responsible for our health. We are at a watershed moment in time. If we are to thrive holistically, we cannot have racism in society. BIPOC communities have known about this *ma'i* for centuries and have been fighting it without rest. But, 2020 has exposed the horrors of racism to the world in a different light, and it calls on all of us, BIPOC communities and allies to respond forcefully and decidedly to eliminate racial injustice from our society.

A Holistic View of Health

We choose to go beyond defining health as just physical in this chapter for a number of reasons. First, we understand that racism can physically attack the body, both directly and indirectly. We need to look no further than the ample evidence of police violence and police brutality in our society against BIPOC communities (Alexander, 2010; Kendi, 2019; Oluo, 2018). However, racism does more than injure us physically. It is chronic, cumulative, evolving, dynamic, and in the air that we breathe and the water we drink, both literally and figuratively. Racism not only impacts our bodies, but deeply cuts into the health of our minds and spirits.

Led by the work of David R. Williams, health research has long established the association between racial discrimination and both physical and emotional well-being for African Americans (Williams & Mohammed, 2009; Williams & Williams-Morris, 2000). Racism's impact on the physical, psychological and emotional wellbeing of BIPOC communities includes outcomes such as chronic illness, poorer health status, depression, anxiety, and other mental health outcomes and is robust across different racial/ethnic groups (Berger & Sarnyai, 2015; Elkins et al., 2019; English et al. 2014; Gee et al., 2007a; Kwate & Goodman, 2015).

In addition to mind and body, racism can also take a toll on one's spirit. BIPOC communities express spirituality in endless ways. Indigenous communities' spiritual health is often connected to our relationship with our ancestors and our land, expressed through our cultural values and practices. Historically *Makana*, or ancient CHamoru healers, held special connections to the spiritual world and often advised people on ways to improve their health through traditional medicines and through the connections to spirits and their ancestors (Cunningham, 1992; Hattori, 2004; Salas, 2019). These practices are carried on today by modern day CHamoru healers known as *yo'åmte siha (also known as suruhånu/a)* as well as the use of *åmot* (traditional herbal medicines) (Lizama, 2014, Bevacqua, 2019). *Kåna*, similar to the Hawaiian term *mana*, is loosely the spiritual energy that exists within and around us that we draw power from; that connects us to our lands, waters, and ancestors; and that influences our health. Thus, engaging with one's cultural practices is a direct form of connecting with one's ancestors. Colonial practices of epistemicide and cultural suppression were tools used by settler colonialists to eliminate cultural practices and to take power from Indigenous people (Hall & Tandon, 2017). From an Indigenous worldview, spiritual health, and a connection to one's ancestors are crucial to understanding the health and wellness of all people (Walters et al., 2011). Within African American communities, spirituality may be tied to one's faith and faith communities. There is an established literature that has demonstrated that religiosity is not only important to African American communities, but that it can act as a buffer for the impact of racism on mental health, as well as among other cultural groups (Ellison et al., 2017).

The health of the land is also integral to and in relationship with our health and well-being. We continue to see indigenous land and BIPOC communities fall victim to pollution, exploitation, desecration, and destruction. The BIPOC diaspora, as a result of capitalism, slavery, genocide, settler colonialism, and imperialism, has separated us from our relationship with our land (Spencer et al., 2020). As our lands die, so will all that live upon it. Any assault on this Earth is a physical wound to us as people. Whether it is pollutants and toxins dumped on Native and Indigenous lands (e.g., Barker, 2012; Mackenzie et al., 2007; Whyte, 2017) or the abandonment and destruction of inner-city neighborhoods through redlining and White flight to the suburbs (Hicken et al., 1982), physical environments affect our health. BIPOC communities experience disproportionate exposure to toxics and hazards in our environments due to environmental racism, and Indigenous communities experience ongoing desecration and exploitation of their lands, and thus bear the burden of poor health as a result (Bryant, 1995; Bullard, 2001; Whyte, 2017; Spencer et al., 2020; Slimming et al., 2014).

In Detroit Head Start neighborhoods, African American mothers were provided with Environmental Justice 101 training and were presented with maps that identified the neighborhoods in the city with the highest levels of toxins. The mothers were infuriated. Many knew that asthma was common in their community, but did not really understand the connection between their experiences and environmental racism. Armed with this new information, the mothers organized a community town hall to share the results of their Photovoice exhibition on environmental justice and to engage community and policy-makers in dialogue. The mothers also developed an environmental justice curriculum for their own Head Start sites and eventually offered them to the entire Detroit Head Start community (Spencer et al., 2012). This case example provides evidence of both the power of lifting the shroud of structural and environmental racism, as well as the power of the community to enact social change through community organizing and engagement.

The Association between Racism and Settler Colonialism, and Physical and Mental Health

Understanding the types of imbalances that racism produces is critical to understanding the associations between racism and health holistically. As noted, the connection between racism and health has long been established. Racism is systemic, structural, and institutional, and is enacted through racist policies and racist ideas that perpetuate racial inequity (Kendi, 2019). It exists globally and locally. Several theories and bodies of research have established that racism, on interpersonal, cultural, institutional, and structural levels, drives negative health outcomes experienced by BIPOC people (e.g., Dressler et al., 2005; Gee & Ford, 2011; Williams & Mohammed, 2013; Krieger, 2014; Hicken et al., 2018; Spencer et al., 2010; Woo et al., 2019). Experiences of racism, intended or not by the perpetrator, can create racism-related stress for BIPOC individuals (Harrell, 2000). This stress can take a toll on BIPOC bodies, resulting in trauma, potentially both chronic and acute, which in turn impacts their physical and emotional well-being (e.g., Walters et al., 2011; Meyer, 2015; Bryant-Davis & Ocampo, 2005; Helms et al., 2010; Elkins et al., 2019). The chronic fatigue from everyday racism (Essed, 1991) can be overwhelming for BIPOC individuals, and this chronic fatigue can also lead to stress and negative health outcomes.

At an interpersonal level, stress and coping models suggest that instances of interpersonal racism such as racial discrimination and microaggressions act as psychological stressors that have a negative impact on BIPOC's health and well-being (e.g., Dressler et al., 2005; Kaholokula et al., 2012; Krieger, 2014; Spencer, 2019). Various studies have demonstrated that experiences of racial discrimination are associated with higher levels of psychological and physiological stress (e.g., Lebrón et al., 2017; Williams & Mohamed, 2013; Town et al., 2018). Evidence applying stress and coping models to examine the association of racism with physical and mental health have also found that various forms of racism, such as acute and chronic instances of racial discrimination and microaggressions, impact the health of BIPOC communities (e.g., Kaholokula, 2016; Brondolo et al., 2019; Din-Dzietham et al., 2004; Kaholokula et al., 2012; Gee et al., 2007b; Schulz et al., 2006; Spencer, 2019; Williams et al., 2003).

At a societal/cultural level, racism, White supremacy, and settler colonialism have been sources of both historical trauma and contemporary trauma experienced by BIPOC communities (Fieland et al., 2007; Comas-Diaz, 2016). For most BIPOC communities, U.S. imperialism and settler colonialism continue to mean loss of lives, family, identity, land/nation, language, spirituality, livelihood, values, practices, and norms. Settler colonialism uniquely drives health inequities for Indigenous people through colonial-related trauma and epistemicide, which ultimately impacts their health and wellbeing (Walters & Simoni, 2002; Walters et al., 2009). Killing a community's culture is taking their spirit, ancestors, and ultimately their health. Blaisdell (1996) identified "cultural historical trauma" as the psychological, physical, social and cultural aftermath of colonialism that many Indigenous people have experienced, including loss of social structures, land, and ways of life. Collectively, this is experienced as "cultural wounding" or disruptions that impact one's sense of self and health-seeking behaviors. Historical trauma and the negative impacts it has on Indigenous communities have been consistently identified as an important cause of health and mental health inequities (Braveheart et al., 2011; Campbell & Evans-Campbell, 2011; Smallwood et al., 2020; Walters et al., 2011).

At an institutional and structural level, racist policies and systems like housing segregation, other forms of social segregation, immigration policies, and the criminal justice system interact with one another to perpetuate poor health outcomes for BIPOC communities (Gee & Ford, 2011; Williams & Mohammed, 2013; Krieger, 2014). Cultural racism, experienced through White supremacy and settler colonialism, places less value on the lives and strengths of BIPOC communities, including cultural values and practices, and more value on policies and practices that perpetuate systemic and institutional racial inequities in health (Williams & Mohamed, 2013; Hicken

CLOSING THE HEALTH GAP 205

et al., 2018; Kendi, 2019). Cultural and institutional levels of racism compound and lead to injustices experienced by BIPOC communities, such as the desecration and annexation of Indigenous lands in the continental United States and the Pacific, the mass incarceration of Black Americans, and the unjust detention of undocumented immigrants. Interactions of racism on all levels have perpetuated racial inequities for BIPOC health.

Race and socioeconomic status are closely linked to numerous poor health outcomes and conditions (Gee & Ford, 2011; Phelan & Link, 2015). Racial capitalism, which theorizes that racialized exploitation and capital accumulation are mutually constitutive, examines the numerous ways that racism and capitalism explain how the United States has become a global capitalist power on the backs and lands of BIPOC communities, and how it still occurs today, as evidenced by such events as the Flint water crisis and the Coronavirus pandemic (Robinson, 1983). Multiple historical and present-day factors have created the syndemic conditions within which BIPOC communities experience disparate outcomes (Laster Pirtle, 2020; Poteat, 2020). An examination of racial capitalism and its many manifestations might offer important opportunities to develop a more expansive understanding of racialized oppression within the context of health and health services.

Eliminating Racism in Health Systems

A model for strengthening health systems to improve health outcomes globally is the World Health Organization (WHO) framework which organizes health systems in six building blocks (Box 8.1): service delivery, health workforce, information, medical products and technologies, financing, and governance and leadership (WHO, 2007). Each building block is accompanied by aims and desirable attributes of the health system. While not directly addressing racism, if implemented with a critical racial lens, we can potentially extrapolate the necessary practices and policies that might be viewed as oppressive by BIPOC communities. We use these building blocks and intended outcomes to understand how health care systems have attempted to eliminate racism in health care. We define health systems as including all actors, institutions, and resources whose primary intentions are to promote, maintain, or restore health.

Similarly, the National Academies' recent consensus study on integrating social needs care into the delivery of healthcare (NASEM, 2019) identifies the

206 MICHAEL S. SPENCER ET AL.

Box 8.1 The Six Building Blocks of a Health System

- Good **health services** are those which deliver effective, safe, quality personal and non-personal health interventions to those that need them, when and where needed, with minimum waste of resources.
- A well-performing **health workforce** is one that works in ways that are responsive, fair, and efficient to achieve the best health outcomes possible, given available resources and circumstances (i.e., there are sufficient staff, fairly distributed; they are competent, responsive, and productive).
- A well-functioning **health information system** is one that ensures the production, analysis, dissemination, and use of reliable and timely information on health determinants, health system performance, and health status.
- A well-functioning health system ensures **equitable access** to essential medical products, vaccines, and technologies of assured quality, safety, efficacy, and cost-effectiveness, and their scientifically sound and cost-effective use.
- A good health **financing system** raises adequate funds for health, in ways that ensure people can use needed services, and are protected from financial catastrophe or impoverishment associated with having to pay for them. It provides incentives for providers and users to be efficient.
- **Leadership and governance** involve ensuring strategic policy frameworks exist and are combined with effective oversight, coalition-building, regulation, attention to system-design, and accountability.

Source: WHO (2007).

---

growing need for understanding upstream factors that impact the delivery and outcomes of healthcare, including stable housing and nutritious food. Racism must be included as a critical upstream factor that impacts delivery and outcomes. The NASEM report makes several recommendations for integrating social care. We use these recommendations, as well as the WHO framework, to extend our analysis on incorporating the impact of racism as a critical and causal social determinant of health.

Health Service Delivery

Racial inequities within health systems also have been well documented. The 2003 Institute of Medicine report *Unequal Treatment: Confronting Racial and Ethnic Disparities in Health Care* documented race and ethnicity as persistent and significant predictors for quality of care, even accounting for socioeconomic status (Smedley et al., 2003). The report found numerous sources contributing to disparities, both at the institutional level—e.g., medical care financing—and at the level of the clinical encounter—e.g., provider bias. Specifically, it discusses how providers' cognitive load during encounters with patients/clients, such as assessment, diagnosis, and treatment, within the constraints of time, resources, and personal attention to existing racial biases, could lead to lower levels of quality care and invasive treatments, such as amputations. Thus, we see how racial biases, professional practice, and policies all intersect to produce negative outcomes for BIPOC communities.

Furthermore, research has demonstrated that most health care providers appear to have implicit bias in terms of positive attitudes toward Whites and negative attitudes toward BIPOC individuals. In a systematic review of racial/ethnic implicit bias and its influence on health-related outcomes, it was found that implicit bias was significantly related to patient–provider interactions, treatment decisions, treatment adherence, and patient health outcomes. Additionally, the review found that implicit attitudes were more often significantly related to patient–provider interactions and health outcomes than treatment processes (Hall et al., 2015). A greater understanding is needed on awareness of implicit biases and how they are rooted in a system of White supremacy through our socialization in a racist, settler colonial society (Kendi, 2019).

Most health services research on racial inequities is focused on the differential health outcomes for BIPOC communities compared to Whites, or disparities. However, approaches to reducing disparities are often not centered on the root causes of racism and White supremacy, but rather behavioral change on the part of the BIPOC individual based historically on theories and worldviews of dominant White America. If we are to eliminate racism in the delivery of health services, we must move away from addressing only risk factors and behavioral change and focus on evidence- and practice-based models that cultivate innovations to improve the daily life conditions of BIPOC communities by eliminating racism.

Organizations should make and communicate a commitment to addressing racism and settler colonialism and its impact on the delivery of health services, as well as how it impacts patients/clients ability to meet their social needs. Policies and practices need to facilitate systemic change on the individual, organizational, community, and societal levels and integrate this into the design of healthcare delivery. The five healthcare activities for designing an integrative system are: awareness, adjustment, assistance, alignment, and advocacy (NASEM, 2019). Similarly, we must begin with an awareness of racism as a societal problem that impacts the well-being of all people. Next, we must look for what adjustments we can make to the system that might address racial inequities and provide assistance to those systems requiring support. Alignment with anti-racist aims of the organization and advocacy for ongoing change within the system would assure that changes are adapted, implemented, and sustained.

Cultural competence interventions. Within health systems, interventions generally focus on improving cultural competency among staff, such as diversity training. Interventions for cultural competency vary greatly, but have been defined in a systematic review as interventions that aim at improving the accessibility and effectiveness of healthcare for people from racial/ethnic minorities by increasing the awareness, knowledge, and skills of healthcare providers or patients, as well as modifying policies and practices of organizations (Truong et al., 2014). Cultural competency may be aimed at the healthcare provider—patient/client level (e.g. interpersonal interactions) or more broadly at the organizational level (e.g. integration of cultural competency into policies, plans and processes). Truong and colleagues also noted that cultural competency training in healthcare demonstrated moderate improvement in provider outcomes and healthcare access and utilization outcomes and weaker improvements in patient/client outcomes.

Methodological rigor often was lacking in these studies, which often lacked objective evidence of intervention effectiveness, consideration of organizational factors, or did not include patient/client outcomes (Truong et al., 2014). The types of interventions reviewed by Truong and colleagues included training/workshops/programs for health practitioners (e.g. doctors, nurses and community health workers), culturally specific/tailored education or programs for patient/clients, interpreter services, peer education, patient navigators, and exchange programs. Finally, moving toward understanding cultures and communities as dynamic is often forgotten in cultural competence models. Culturally humility (Tervalon &

Murray-Garcia, 1998) accomplishes this by fostering an attitude of life-long learning that challenges healthcare providers to be open to diversity in people's worldviews (Tervalon & Murray-Garcia, 1998). This process can be described as having greater openness, self-awareness and self-reflection, and self-critique (Foronda et al., 2016).

Intergroup dialogue. Although training and interventions for cultural competence have evolved over time, giving rise to new terms such as "cultural humility," which emphasizes one's lack of achieving full cultural competence and openness to new learning. Trainings and interventions are sometimes strengthened by applying the principles of intergroup dialogue with an anti-racist/social justice versus multicultural lens (Dessel et al., 2008; Gurin et al., 2013; Spencer, 1999). Intergroup dialogue is often focused on attitudinal and behavioral changes toward co-learning, openness and intercultural under-standing. Rooted in nonviolence, racial dialogues are often centered on both BIPOC and White experiences within the context of White supremacy. Aims often involve raising awareness of ways that racism plays a significant role in our daily lives/workplace and how we perpetuate it. Recognition and acknowledgment of unearned privilege due to one's social position and a commitment to change and action are emphasized. Facilitation skills for intergroup conflict and dialogue are central to this process and can impact effectiveness of interventions or training (Spencer et al., 2011). Intergroup dialogues should be ongoing, and when successful, can lead to changes in individuals' or group attitudes and behaviors. Intergroup dialogue and facili-tation courses in higher education have been implemented, but often are not offered or required in the health sciences. Social work has had success with the integration of intergroup dialogue principles and often brings these skills into the practice environment.

While awareness-to-action is the ultimate goal, most cultural compe-tence or cultural humility interventions are not ongoing but are offered in-frequently, making sustainability difficult. Similarly, intergroup dialogues can dissipate over time or never quite reach the action stage. Also, BIPOC communities often bear the burden of developing and implementing these cultural competency interventions, or at least organizing the logistics of the speaker. Many times, they are not mandatory. This can result in primarily BIPOC and a few White allies in attendance, while those who are in power or members of the dominant group, opt out or do not prioritize this in their schedules. Feelings of hopelessness and discouragement are felt, as well as disrespect for the emotional and time-consuming work that goes into

210 MICHAEL S. SPENCER ET AL.

planning, when it is evident that change from the status quo of White supremacy was never the institution's intention. BIPOC communities can also experience triggers and further traumatization as a part of educating White colleagues who are disinterested in change. Making these interventions or training mandatory is unlikely to create necessary change without a commitment to eliminating racism and White supremacy from every fiber of the organization, and a deep and ongoing commitment to anti-racist work, social justice and health equity. Emerging models of White ally dialogues or caucus groups have become more visible and represent a model of agents of oppression "doing their own work" and not at the expense of BIPOC communities. Research on the effectiveness of ally caucus groups is needed.

Workforce Development

Developing a deep sense of commitment to social justice among health professionals can be achieved through continuous and ongoing opportunities for addressing racism in ourselves, our environments, and our health systems through *interprofessional education*. These opportunities could be offered across health science disciplines or transdisciplinary units. Anti-racism and anti-bigotry should be core content, integrated into every course, and should acknowledge how our socialization into White supremacy permeates our understanding of the world, and therefore our practices and policies. Racism and bigotry cannot be tolerated in our educational programs. Content should also include a process of unlearning and developing new and innovative ways that our former practices and policies can be reconceptualized to promote a better society for all. Skills for identifying White supremacy and settler colonialism in our practices and policies, dismantling them, and putting just practices and policies in their place are critical to all aspects of our professional education. Education must innovate and go beyond cultural competence and attitudinal change if we are to eliminate racism. This is especially true post-2020 as we are observing a greater call for action.

Health Information Systems

One area that the health-serving organization can prioritize is monitoring health inequities within their institutions. The advent of electronic

CLOSING THE HEALTH GAP 211

medical records now makes monitoring patients' outcomes relatively simple. Analyzing these data by social identifiers could not only allow institutions to better understand the reasons for these disparities, but also assist in the development of programs and policies seeking to address and continue to monitor the issue. The inclusion of individuals who have a critical racial understanding of the problem, such as BIPOC providers and patients, should be included in these conversations. If medical records are incomplete or difficult to access, healthcare systems can partner with social epidemiologists from local universities or public health departments. For example, healthcare organizations can create a team of anti-racism consultants, evaluators, community leaders, and other pertinent organizational staff that collect data (e.g., perceived racial climate, perceived cultural competence of staff, etc.), conduct the critical assessment of policies and procedures, and disseminate the findings (Griffith et al., 2007).

For example, King County Public Health in Washington State often hosts collaborative projects with University researchers and community members to monitor and narrow health inequities in communities of color. Their Vulnerable Populations Strategic Initiative engages public health researchers at University of Washington, emergency services, and community leaders to implement 9-1-1 language access interventions to communities with limited English proficiency. These teams could have success in using epidemiological data and methods to inform healthcare systems. Interprofessional collaboration among community-engaged researchers and community organizations could lead to innovative solutions as team members vary in what they consider evidence, in their training and backgrounds, and in their approach to translating evidence into policy and practice (Wallerstein et al., 2011). Finally, holding individuals and entities responsible and accountable to a historical legacy of White supremacy is also necessary. Our organizations and institutions must take the lead here, as individual efforts can only go so far. Organizations and institutions can also take accountability by uncovering their own history with racism and White supremacy and developing potent strategies to reconcile and atone for their actions.

Public/private partnership should establish a large-scale social determinant digital infrastructure and provide resources so that health servicing organizations and consumers can interact with each other and with the healthcare system. This digital infrastructure should regularly report disparities in outcomes among organizations and develop action plans for eliminating these disparities in partnership with the communities most

212 MICHAEL S. SPENCER ET AL.

impacted by those disparities. Action plans should recognize that racism and a history of White supremacy are responsible for these disparities and solutions should be targeted at racism and the structures it creates as a central problem.

Equitable Access

We have previously discussed the issue of access without equity, and the importance of assuring that those entering health systems are not only well-functioning but also free of racism and settler colonialism. The WHO model focuses on quality and also cost-effectiveness. While wasteful and irresponsible spending is not condoned, there must be further evaluation of what factors are communicated when considering costs. As discussed in Smedley's Institute of Medicine report, clinical decisions have a great deal of subjectivity and bias affiliated with them. Therefore, cost alone cannot be a determining factor without careful consideration of social determinants, including racism.

Financing Systems

The Centers for Medicare & Medicaid Services should clearly define which aspects of social care Medicaid can pay for as covered services to dismantle structural racism. These should include services that not only provide culturally appropriate and relevant services, but also support and finance innovative efforts to promote culturally grounded approaches to health and wellbeing occurring within the community. Any efforts toward restructuring institutions to becoming anti-racist should also be funded as part of a large-scale effort to reconcile the human violations that have occurred and to regain the public trust of BIPOC communities. We have seen that a growing number of health systems promote physical activity through gym memberships and other incentives as long-term cost reduction efforts. Similarly, culturally relevant physical activities could also be promoted. Federal and state agencies, payers, providers, delivery systems, and foundations should contribute to advancing research on and evaluating the effectiveness and implementation of social care practices, including practices that go beyond providing basic needs, but that address the reasons why people are without basic needs and why there is a significantly greater need among BIPOC communities.

Leadership and Governance

Institutionally, organizations are increasingly seeking to promote *diversity, equity, and inclusion (DEI)* as a mechanism to acknowledge the value of DEI institutionally to develop concrete plans for undoing past wrongs, (e.g., lack of access, racial climate). DEI policies and practices often offer or require diversity training to staff, examine recruitment and retention of BIPOC, and seek activities and events that promote diversity and inclusion. These interventions are necessary, particularly in combination with attitudinal change, because they promote equity as a value and uncover how racism and White supremacy permeate our lived experiences. However, most would agree that these interventions only go so far. Putting emphasis solely on diversity or differences may dilute the critical discussion of disparities, injustice, and oppression (Davis, 2016). Moreover, DEI programs are unfunded or underfunded, and when implemented poorly, can place BIPOC individuals with the responsibility of educating White people who do not see the problem to be as urgent as those most impacted. If the appropriate time and resources are not provided to support DEI initiatives, accompanied by greater attitudinal change, racism will continue to fester and evolve.

The recruitment of BIPOC individuals into health-serving professions is also an ongoing challenge. Not only must we continue these efforts at recruitment and retention, we must train diverse student populations for positions of leadership and governance. Voice must be given to those underrepresented, both among professional staff and leadership. Emphasizing our commitment to anti-racist policies and practices will likely assist us in our recruitment.

Culturally Relevant Health-Promotion Interventions to Reduce Exposure to Racism

Chin and colleagues (2007) developed a conceptual model for interventions to reduce racial and ethnic disparities that articulates multiple points of action, including interventions that strengthen access, or the linkage between communities and healthcare systems. National policies, such as universal health care, and local interventions, such as community health workers who serve in the role of health navigators, are examples of interventions that strengthen access to healthcare (Spencer et al., 2019). Chin and colleagues also note that while communities and healthcare systems exist within different and often conflicting environments, interventions that integrate the two worlds more seamlessly are needed. Social norms such as individual, internalized, and institutional racism and the distrust between communities and healthcare systems fuel these conflicts and therefore must be addressed and confronted.

As we begin a new decade of research, there is a great need for interventions that go beyond increasing access, but promote healing among and within the patient/client and the healthcare environment. Innovations are necessary that bring these two environments together to identify how White supremacy is defined in our policies and practices and to design ways to correct them. We must go beyond improving access, because if these systems remain unjust at their core, access will only be increasing the number of people entering an unjust system. The Affordable Care Act is critical to promoting access to healthcare, when individuals are able to do so, but it is not the only answer to addressing racism in health.

Racial Healing

With a continuously growing number of health disparities among marginalized populations, the health science world turned to trauma informed care (TIC) in an attempt to effectively address some of the disparities, specifically ones that stemmed from trauma (Harris & Fallot, 2001) experienced by BIPOC youth (Levenson, 2017). Although TIC has been widely used in health sciences, especially in social work, the framework is incomplete when addressing racial healing among BIPOC communities. TIC is limiting in that it cannot fully address the long history of racism, White supremacy and colonization. Interventions that aim to foster racial healing need to first address the root causes of trauma while exposing systemic racism, white supremacy and colonization that greatly impact BIPOC communities (Ginwright, 2018). With these needs in mind, a healing-centered engagement is a more appropriate and needed framework to promote racial healing for BIPOC communities.

The healing-centered engagement framework offers a more holistic approach that fosters well-being among BIPOC communities by highlighting how trauma and healing can be experienced collectively rather than solely individually (Ginwright, 2018). Healing-centered engagement also shifts from what Tuck (2009) calls "damage-centered narratives" to more strength and asset-based approaches to healing and well-being (Ginwright, 2018). This type of approach to racial healing ultimately moves away from solely focusing on the health disparities BIPOC communities face, by centering the cultural strengths and assets that BIPOC communities have been utilizing for decades to survive and thrive. Such examples of these racial healing practices include but are not limited to cultural coping and cultural resilience, ethnic/racial identity, ethnic/racial socialization, cultural values and practices, and culturally-tailored and culturally-grounded interventions. It is important for scholars to deeply consider a healing-centered engagement framework for future interventions that aim to foster racial healing among BIPOC communities.

Cultural Coping and Cultural Resilience

While BIPOC communities await change from interventions at the individual, organizational, and societal levels to eliminate racism, BIPOC communities have taken their health into their own hands. Many grassroots organizations led by BIPOC people create community-based health interventions that work to address health disparities in their communities (Wallerstein & Duran, 2006), while synchronously healing the "soul wounds" that racism causes (Duran et al., 1998). Interventions to improve risk factors for poor health outcomes and behavioral change in lifestyles are numerous; however, reducing risk factors and creating behavioral change do not eliminate racism. Among BIPOC communities, there is a need to further develop and sustain models that prevent the negative impact of racism and White supremacy on our well-being and that promote holistic health, including our communities' strengths and resources.

In most models of prevention and health promotion for BIPOC communities, cultural moderators that reduce the impact of racism are critical to overall health and well-being. These moderators serve as cultural coping resources and sources of cultural resilience and include factors such as racial/ethnic identity, racial socialization, cultural values, and cultural practices. These factors often address our core being or our spiritual/cultural self. There are many examples from research that demonstrate BIPOC communities' resilience and coping despite higher levels of racism-related stress exposure. For example, Keyes (2009) found that African Americans are shown to be more mentally resilient to the influences of social inequity and discrimination than Whites. Similarly, Latinxs tend to display better health status than Whites, though Latinxs frequently experience psychosocial risk factors due to racial discrimination (Gallo et al., 2009; Stone et al., 2016).

To understand these patterns, a cumulative body of research has situated racism as measured by racial discrimination (both acute and chronic) within the specific sociocultural contexts where it plays out, and has identified potential cultural resources that could attenuate the harmful effects of racism. We discuss three major forms of cultural coping resources—ethnic/racial identity, ethnic-racial socialization, and cultural values and practices—that can mitigate the health burden of interpersonal and structural racism.

Ethnic/racial identity. Ethnic/racial identity is an integral part of self-identity because it instills a sense of identification with a given group's cultural values, kinship, and beliefs (Phinney, 1996). Because of this, ethnic/racial identity may influence individuals' perception of race-related stressors, as well as the extent to which they find those stressors psychologically damaging (Carter, 2007; Stevenson & Arrington, 2009). Ethnic/racial identity can serve as a coping resource to buffer the health burden of racism in several ways. First, according to social identity theory, racism functions as a rejection from the mainstream society and may make individuals seek a sense of belonging to and acceptance in their in-group communities (Tajfel & Turner, 2004). Hence, by protecting self-concept and adjustment, strong ethnic/racial identity can equip the individuals to cope with the threats posed by racism (Yip et al., 2019).

Given the potential buffering effect of ethnic/racial identity, a growing body of research has investigated how ethnic/racial identity moderates the health impact of racism. For example, a meta-analysis of 51 studies found that ethnic/racial identity commitment (i.e., an affirmation of an ethnic/racial identity) conferred protection (Yip et al., 2019). Conversely, ethnic/racial identity exploration (i.e., exploring the meaning of one's ethnicity/race) was found to increase vulnerability associated with racial discrimination, calling for a more nuanced understanding of the moderating role of ethnic/racial identity (Yip et al., 2019). Additionally, this study also found that the moderating role of ethnic/racial identity is not necessarily uniform across ethnic/racial groups (Yip et al., 2019). Other studies also documented that the moderating effect of ethnic/racial identity is often more pronounced among the U.S.-born, compared to their foreign-born counterparts (Woo et al., 2019; Yip et al., 2008). Future research should take account of the complex and dynamic nature of ethnic/racial identity and how it can be used as a way to buffer adverse effects of racism for different BIPOC and nativity groups.

Ethnic-racial socialization. The ethnic-racial socialization literature focuses on family as one of the primary contexts that shape the identity and development of youth (Erikson, 1968; Garcia Coll et al., 1996). Many BIPOC families utilize ethnic-racial socialization as a way to communicate, make sense of, and ultimately prepare BIPOC youth for the racialized experiences they encounter (Anderson & Stevenson, 2019). The ways BIPOC families socialize their children are known to be important contributors that influence how race and racial discrimination lead to the variations in BIPOC youth developmental competencies (Garcia Coll et al., 1996). Through ethnic-racial socialization, parents educate and share their own racialized experiences with their children about the significance of their race, ethnicity, and culture, and prepare them to cope with racism and discrimination (Hughes et al., 2006; Anderson & Stevenson, 2019). Ethnic-racial socialization can affect how BIPOC youth cope with racism (Hughes et al., 2006). For example, in one study, authors created a culturally responsive intervention using ethnic-racial socialization and found that Black youth who participated in the intervention were able to express themselves more freely and release feelings of anger that stemmed from racism and/or discrimination (Anderson et al., 2018). In another study working with African American families, authors found that children were less likely to use passive coping strategies if their parents believed that children should respond proactively to discriminatory situations (Johnson, 1994). However, it should be noted that not every ethnic-racial socialization promotes adaptive coping strategies (Brega & Coleman, 1999), and more research is needed to illuminate these differences.

Researchers have documented that various ethnic-racial socialization processes may have distinct effects on psychological and behavioral outcomes (e.g., Caughy et al., 2002; Liu & Lau, 2013; Rumbaut, 1994). Studies examining ethnic-racial socialization suggest relations with positive youth outcomes (Caughy et al., 2002; Johnston et al., 2007; Reynolds & Gonzales-Backen, 2017) and internalizing symptoms and depression (Liu & Lau, 2013; McHale et al., 2006). However, when it comes to preparation for bias and promotion of mistrust, some studies suggest associations with positive outcomes (Bowman & Howard, 1985; Scott, 2003), and others indicate negative outcomes, such as depression and deviant behaviors (Banergee et al., 2015; Biafora et al., 1993; Liu & Lau, 2013). These mixed findings suggest that more evidence is needed to understand the intended and unintended outcomes of cultural socialization as a protective mechanism (Hughes et al., 2006). Overall, ethnic-racial socialization is a crucial cultural process for BIPOC youth and young adults that can equip them with strategies to cope with racism (Neblett et al., 2012).

Cultural values and practices. Adherence to cultural values and practices can influence how BIPOC communities manifest psychological and health problems and how they handle various issues and stressors. Existing literature has tested the effect of adhering to cultural values and practices on health and well-being. For example, some existing literature has identified cultural values and practices as important cultural resources that promote resilience and social development (e.g., Gonzales et al., 2008; Knight & Carolo, 2012) among Mexican American youth, and self-esteem and life satisfaction among African American adolescents (e.g., Constantine et al., 2006), and lower depressive symptoms among American Indian adults (Whitebeck et al., 2002). In contrast, other studies found that adherence to cultural values inversely predicted willingness to seek professional psychological help among Asian college students, reflecting that admitting psychological problems can result in shame to the family (e.g., Kim & Omizo, 2003). These findings indicate that cultural values may not always provide unconditional buffering effects.

Based on the stress-buffering effect of ethnic identity and ethnic-racial socialization, a handful of studies also tested whether being grounded in one's culture may help attenuate the stress associated with racial discrimination. For example, Whitebeck et al. (2002) found that regular participation in traditional practices (e.g., traditional powwow activities, knowledge, and use of the tribal language) buffers the association between discrimination and higher depressive symptoms among American Indians living in the Midwest. A study among South Asians found that the association between discrimination and anger was mitigated by stronger traditional cultural beliefs (e.g., religious ceremonies or rituals, the spiritual practice of fasting, consuming traditional ethnic foods and spices, a joint family living structure) (Nadimpalli et al., 2016). While these two studies found the moderating effect of cultural values and practices, other studies have found them as

CLOSING THE HEALTH GAP   219

mediators that function as risk reducers. Studies of Mexican American adolescents found that racial discrimination is associated with a stronger endorsement of Mexican American values (e.g., familism, religiosity), which in turn is related to higher prosocial tendencies (Brittian et al., 2013) and lower externalizing and internalizing symptoms (Berkel et al., 2010). The results of these studies support the notion of the protective effects of cultural values and practices on mitigating the health burden of discrimination.

Culturally Tailored and Culturally Grounded Interventions

Most evidence-based interventions (EBI) are developed using Western-centric theories of behavior change and behavioral strategies tested in samples of predominantly non-Hispanic Whites. This is often reflected in differential outcomes between ethnic groups and non-Hispanic Whites, with Whites often doing better (Kaholokula et al., 2018; Kumanyika et al., 2002; West et al., 2008). To address this, recent efforts have been made toward culturally tailored interventions that are responsive to and are situated within the context of an individual's cultural group. Tailoring can include anything from linguistic preferences to symbols and other representations of their culture added to the intervention.

While there is evidence that culturally tailored interventions have promise and can be effective, particularly within the context of community-engaged research (Chin, 2007; Spencer et al., 2018), researchers have more recently called for interventions to move beyond culturally tailored and toward culturally centered and culturally grounded interventions (Walters et al., 2018). This goes beyond situating research and interventions within communities, but rather grounding interventions in the core values, norms, and practices of the community. There is recognition that adaptive social structures and systems exist within and emerge from the local economy, and cultural beliefs and practices support and promote well-being in communities (McGregor et al., 2003). These interventions, whether they be ethnocentric (e.g., Afrocentric) or Indigenous in nature, honor the wisdom of communities and their ancestors, as well as their contributions to developing interventions that counteract and/or moderate the negative impact of racism. Interventions that emerge from the local community and promote community empowerment, cultural values and practices, capacity building, and indigenous and ancestral wisdom are holistic and accessible.

One example of culturally grounded interventions that has demonstrated promising evidence to address substance abuse and improve mental health among Indigenous populations in the United States is the Talking Circle. Among Indigenous cultures, a Talking Circle provides social support through the process of gathering in a place where stories are shared in a genuine, warm, and respectful manner and in a context of complete acceptance by members of the group (Lowe et al., 2012). Indigenous populations have long used the Talking Circle to celebrate the sacred interrelationship that is shared with one another and with their world (Simpson, 2000). The idea of the Talking Circle permeates the traditions of Indigenous people to this day. It symbolizes an entire approach to life and to the universe in which each being participates in the Circle and each one serves an important and necessary function that is valued no more or no less than that of any other being (Lowe et al., 2012). By honoring the Circle, human beings honor the process of life and the process of growth that is an ever-flowing stream in the movement of life energy (Garrett & Carroll, 2000). A recent Talking Circle intervention, guided by the Native-Reliance theoretical framework, which is based on Indigenous ways of knowing, cultural identity, and indigenous health perspectives (Lowe, 2019; Lowe et al., 2009), delivered to Native American youth in Florida, provided evidence that the culturally grounded intervention was significantly more effective in enhancing well-being and reducing substance use interest among participants, when compared an standard (i.e., not culturally based) youth-focused EBI (Wimbish-Cirillo et al., 2020). Several Talking Circle interventions designed by Lowe and colleagues have also shown effectiveness in substance abuse prevention and other health-promoting areas such as cardiovascular disease (Kelley & Lowe, 2018) and HIV prevention (Lowe, 2008).

Several other culturally grounded interventions have demonstrated success in improving health in Indigenous communities. One intervention that has shown success in improving health beliefs and attitudes of Choctaw women is the Yappalli: Choctaw Road to Health. The Yappalli intervention utilizes Indigenous ceremony, practices, language, and original instructions and indigenous knowledge of Choctaw health in tandem with Western practices of information-motivational-behavior to promote health among Choctaw women (Walters et al., 2018). This intervention has shown efficacy in improving the health beliefs, attitudes, and behaviors of Choctaw women (Schultz et al., 2016; Fernandez et al., 2020).

In Hawai'i, the Kā-HOLO project utilizes hula (traditional Kānaka Maoli dance) in the management of hypertension and prevention of cardiovascular disease among Kānaka Maoli (Walters et al., 2018). The practice of hula engages in traditional forms of Kānaka Maoli storytelling and transference of ancestral knowledge and values while promoting one's spiritual and physical well-being (Walters et al., 2018). This intervention has been shown in an early pilot study to improve hypertension among Native Hawaiians (Kaholokula et al., 2017). Finally, Tālanoas, a pan-Polynesian form of conversation grounded in balance, sacredness, and mana (potency) (Tecun et al., 2018), has been shown to improve health literacy among Sāmoan and Tongan youth. Although commonly utilized as a research methodology among Tongan scholars, Tālanoas involve having organic dialogue and sharing stories while practicing Pasifika values of respect and relationality. McGrath and Ka'ili (2010) demonstrated that utilizing Tālanoas to educate Washington Sāmoan and Tongan youth on sexual and reproductive health improved their health literacy about HIV. All of these projects utilized community-based participatory research (CBPR) methods and engaged community members in research protocols to ensure the interventions were grounded in Indegenous epistemologies.

Often using CBPR and other community-engaged approaches, culturally grounded interventions are driven by community-identified needs and community participation at all levels of the research process. Culturally grounded interventions also do not rely on White communities to end racism, but rather promote culturally adaptive resources within a White supremacist, settler-colonial society. The Coronavirus pandemic of 2020, along with the global movement for racial justice following the killings of Breonna Taylor, George Floyd, Ahmaud Arbery, Tony McDade, and many other Black lives, demonstrate how in a perfect storm, BIPOC communities have successfully mobilized and engaged their communities locally and nationally—mobilizing their resilience and resources in creating mutual aid to promote community well-being, and protesting in solidarity against the long-standing history of racial injustices and systemic racism experienced by their communities to this day. Despite how the United States chooses to deal with structures and institutions built on White supremacy and settler colonialism, BIPOC communities are adaptive and resilient, as evidenced by their survival in the face of constant genocide, ethnocide, and epistemicide.

Toward Solutions and Reconciliation

Many of the recommendations that were derived from the 2015 Close the Health Gap Grand Challenge in Social Work report (Walters et al., 2016) still apply as we examine racism as a causal factor for health inequities, but as most recommendations go, improvements can always be made. Understanding how to close the health gap depends on the positionality of the speaker and how they understand the problem. How one goes about reducing individuals' health risks and promoting a healthy lifestyle is relative to one's social position and worldview. While culturally competent Western medicine may promote health and well-being, it does not address the most potent causes of the health equity gap: racism, settler colonialism, and White supremacy. The newest Grand Challenge for Social Work, Eliminating Racism, directly addresses this root cause of health inequities at a time when the world has a heightened awareness of the problem. How can we take advantage of this moment in history to create structural change for health equity?

Health as a human right. We can begin with the notion that health and healthcare are a human right and a social justice issue. Second, we must acknowledge that the health outcomes for BIPOC populations are the result of an extensive history of racist policies and practices upon which current policies and practices have been built. Under a nation enacting imperialistic and White supremist policies and practices, BIPOC histories include invasion, colonization, genocide, ethnocide, slavery, Jim Crow, and numerous other human rights violations. Today, racist policies and practices rooted in our history continue to enact injury and harm to our mind, body, and spirit through means such as surveillance and policing, environmental racism, desecration of lands and sacred place, suppression of voting rights, and housing and food insecurity. When traditional lands and people's livelihoods are taken and replaced with polluted neighborhoods, low wages, inadequate, culturally detached healthcare, and culturally insensitive education, processed foods, and suppression of history and voice, our health, our *ola*, is seriously compromised. The harm that White supremacy and contemporary racism has done to BIPOC populations is inexcusable and should be viewed as no less than human rights violations.

Reconciliation. The Close the Health Gap Grand Challenge promotes access to healthcare for all, which brings aid to those without financial resources. But again, this will not eliminate racism, just greater access to a system with its own racist history and practices. Rather, there is a need for healthcare organizations to examine the disparities that exist within their own systems, through data of patient outcomes, partnerships with communities and community-based organizations, and dialogues with not only patients but individuals who have been hurt by or are distrustful of healthcare systems. The process of reconciliation may be a useful model.

Reconciliation is a complex set of processes that involve building or rebuilding relationships, often in the aftermath of widespread human rights violations, which could be applied to healthcare systems as well as other institutions that impact health and well-being of BIPOC communities. Reconciliation can occur at the individual, interpersonal, sociopolitical, and institutional levels. The International Center for Transitional Justice (ITCJ, 2017, p. 2) describes the process of transitional justice as "context specific and to understand the issues that are likely to be most significant in determining appropriate and effective approaches in the aftermath of massive human rights violations." Four aims of the process include: (1) confronting impunity for violations; (2) recognition of the dignity of victims of human rights violations as citizens and human rights bearers; (3) restoration of citizens' trust in state institutions, especially ones charged with guaranteeing fundamental human rights; and (4) prevention of future serious human rights violations.

Any discussion of reconciliation as to its meanings and aims will vary from place to place and the level of reconciliation being sought. These processes should include stakeholders within the patient/client environment and should be open and honest. Such processes will also require courageous leadership and support from multiple sectors, e.g., pharmaceutical, third-party payers, and state and federal health departments, as well as cross-racial coalitions and alliances that include White allies and allied organizations. While far more complex and difficult than cultural competency professional development, it is necessary that BIPOC communities restore their trust in the systems that support our health and well-being through reconciliatory processes.

Community empowerment and population health. The Close the Health Gap Grand Challenge also recommends community empowerment and research on population health through innovative setting- and place-based interventions. Community-academic partnerships that promote community empowerment through participatory principles (e.g., CBPR, Participatory Action Research) are examples of this work. Community-engaged research that de-centers systems rooted in White supremacy and re-centers interventions around the cultural strengths and resources grounded in community can promote health and well-being. Theoretically applying a critical race lens in the conceptualization, implementation, dissemination, and uptake of our interventions in partnership with community is a decolonizing and liberating approach to research and implementation science. Culturally grounded approaches, in combination with anti-racist, participatory principles, can moderate the impact of racism.

Conclusion

Within institutions of higher learning, there is a need to train professionals to systematically examine our institutions and organizations for structural inequalities and White supremacy and their impact on individual and group outcomes. Arguably, this should be done at home from birth and throughout our education. Experiential learning that includes an understanding of how oppression impacts our patients and clients and how to effectively advocate for change is a practical place to start. Experiential learning develops a culture of co-learning versus the expert model that can carry over into professional settings with colleagues and patients/clients. When this co-learning is done in an interprofessional or transdisciplinary environment, a common set of values for a socially just institution may emerge. When backed by accreditation standards that also reflect the urgency of anti-racist and anti-oppressive practices and policies, and implemented by competent instructors, we may finally become free to innovate, explore, and expand the ways that we can enhance health and well-being at individual, organizational, and societal levels.

Educational and professional institutions responsible for the health of BIPOC populations must address the horrific acts of racial violence perpetrated physically, emotionally, and spiritually/culturally in a holistic and comprehensive way. If done in a piecemeal fashion, we will require another half century before progress toward eliminating racism as a determinant of health is to be seen. While we wait, communities must be allowed to pursue their health without further external harm or violence. Minimally, the basic rights to clean air, water, food, housing, land, and access to culturally relevant healthcare must be provided. Currently, White supremacy and settler colonialism affect BIPOC communities across all of these basic needs. Lack of action by those in power within these institutions will mean that BIPOC communities will end up faring for themselves once again, but

CLOSING THE HEALTH GAP 225

we will rise. We have survived great atrocities and stand tall in the face of inequality. Continued leadership, innovation, and healing will come from BIPOC communities, and new leadership will rise with greater voice and more power. We must continue to bend the arrow of justice toward health and well-being: mind, body, and spirit.

Study Questions

1. In addition to physical violence, how else has racism impacted health?
2. What colonial practices were used by settler colonists to eliminate culture practices and take power from Indigenous people?
3. Explain the ways in which American settlers/colonists affected Indigenous peoples' spiritual and mental health.
4. Explain how environmental destruction and Indigenous land impact the mental and spiritual health of BIPOC.
5. What was the environmental discrimination among multiple Head Start neighborhoods in Detroit?
6. Explain how even "unintentional" racism impacts the health of BIPOC.
7. Which theory states that racialized exploitation and capital accumulation are mutually constitutive and examines ways in which racism and capitalism explain how the United States has become a global capitalist "super power," built upon the backs and lands of BIPOC?
8. Explain your thoughts in regard to the implicit bias that exists among healthcare providers who have positive attitudes toward Whites and negative attitudes toward BIPOC folks.
9. Why is cultural competency an effective intervention for clinicians working with BIPOC in healthcare?
10. If the World Health Organization focuses on quality and cost-effectiveness, explain the non-equitable access to healthcare for BIPOC Americans. Why do you think this disparagement exists?
11. Which mechanism is currently very popular (and very effective) among organizations for diversity training? Do you believe it promotes racial healing? Why or why not?
12. Are culturally grounded interventions useful to improve BIPOC health? Why or why not?
13. How can using a "Critical Race Theory lens" impact the healthcare gap?

References

Alexander, M. (2010). *The new Jim Crow: Mass incarceration in the age of colorblindness*. New York: The New Press.

Anderson, R. E., & Stevenson, H. C. (2019). RECASTing racial stress and trauma: Theorizing the healing potential of racial socialization in families. *American Psychologist, 74*(1), 63.

Anderson, R. E., McKenny, M., Mitchell, A., Koku, L., & Stevenson, H. C. (2018). EMBRacing racial stress and trauma: Preliminary feasibility and coping responses of a racial socialization intervention. *Journal of Black Psychology, 44*(1), 25–46.

Banerjee, M., Rowley, S. J., & Johnson, D. J. (2015). Community violence and racial socialization: Their influence on the psychosocial well-being of African American college students. *Journal of Black Psychology, 41*(4), 358–383.

Barker, H. M. (2012). *Bravo for the Marshallese: Regaining control in a post-nuclear, post-colonial world*. Nelson Education. Belmont, CA.

Berger, M., & Sarnyai, Z. (2015). "More than skin deep": stress neurobiology and mental health consequences of racial discrimination. *Stress (Amsterdam, Netherlands), 18*(1), 1–10. https://doi.org/10.3109/10253890.2014.989204.

Berkel, C., Knight, G. P., Zeiders, K. H., Tein, J. Y., Roosa, M. W., Gonzales, N. A., & Saenz, D. (2010). Discrimination and adjustment for Mexican American adolescents: A prospective examination of the benefits of culturally related values. *Journal of Research on Adolescence, 20*(4), 893–915.

Bevacqua, M. L. (2019). *Låncho: Ranch*. Retrieved from: https://www.guampedia.com/lancho-ranch/

Biafora, F. A., Jr., Warheit, G. J., Zimmerman, R. S., Gil, A. G., Apospori, E., Taylor, D., & Vega, W. A. (1993). Racial mistrust and deviant behaviors among ethnically diverse Black adolescent boys 1. *Journal of Applied Social Psychology, 23*(11), 891–910.

Blaisdell, R. K. (1996, Winter). The meaning of health. *Asian American and Pacific Islander journal of health, 4*(1–3), 232.

Bowman, P. J., & Howard, C. (1985). Race-related socialization, motivation, and academic achievement: A study of Black youths in three-generation families. *Journal of the American Academy of Child Psychiatry, 24*(2), 134–141.

Braveheart, M. Y. H., Chase, J., Elkins, J., & Altschul, D. B. (2011). Historical trauma among indigenous peoples of the Americas: Concepts, research, and clinical considerations. *Journal of Psychoactive Drugs, 43*(4), 282–290.

Brega, A. G., & Coleman, L. M. (1999). Effects of religiosity and racial socialization on subjective stigmatization in African-American adolescents. *Journal of Adolescence, 22*(2), 223–242.

Brittian, A. S., O'Donnell, M., Knight, G. P., Carlo, G., Umana-Taylor, A. J., & Roosa, M. W. (2013). Associations between adolescents' perceived discrimination and prosocial tendencies: The mediating role of Mexican American values. *Journal of Youth and Adolescence, 42*(3), 328–341.

Brondolo, E., Ver Halen, N. B., Pencille, M., Beatty, D., & Contrada, R. J. (2009). Coping with racism: A selective review of the literature and a theoretical and methodological critique. *Journal of Behavioral Medicine, 32*(1), 64–88.

Bryant, B. (1995). *Environmental justice: Issues, policies*. Washington, DC: Solutions, Island Press.

Bryant-Davis, T., & Ocampo, C. (2005). The trauma of racism: Implications for counseling, research, and education. *The Counseling Psychologist, 33*(4), 574–578.

CLOSING THE HEALTH GAP 227

Bullard, R. D. (2001). Environmental justice in the 21st century: Race still matters. *Phylon (1960-)*, *49*(3-4), 151–171.

Campbell, C. D., & Evans-Campbell, T. (2011). Historical trauma and Native American child development and mental health: An overview. *American Indian and Alaska Native children and mental health: Development, context, prevention, and treatment*, 1–26.

Carter, R. T. (2007). Racism and psychological and emotional injury: Recognizing and assessing race-based traumatic stress. *The Counseling Psychologist*, *35*(1), 13–105.

Caughy, M. O. B., O'Campo, P. J., Randolph, S. M., & Nickerson, K. (2002). The influence of racial socialization practices on the cognitive and behavioral competence of African American preschoolers. *Child Development*, *73*(5), 1611–1625.

Chin, M. H., Walters, A. E., Cook, S. C., & Huang, E. S. (2007). Interventions to reduce racial and ethnic disparities in health care. *Medical Care Research and Review*, *64*(5_suppl), 7S–28S.

Comas-Díaz, L. (2016). Racial trauma recovery: A race-informed therapeutic approach to racial wounds.

Constantine, M. G., Alleyne, V. L., Wallace, B. C., & Franklin-Jackson, D. C. (2006). Africentric cultural values: Their relation to positive mental health in African American adolescent girls. *Journal of Black Psychology*, *32*(2), 141–154.

Cunningham, L. J. (1992). *Ancient Chamorro Society*. Honolulu, Hawai'i: Bess Press.

Davis, L. E. (2016). Race: America's grand challenge. *Journal of the Society for Social Work and Research*, *7*(2), 395–403.

Dessel, A., & Rogge, M. E. (2008). Evaluation of intergroup dialogue: A review of the empirical literature. *Conflict Resolution Quarterly*, *26*(2), 199–238.

Dessel, A., Rogge, M. E., & Garlington, S. B. (2006). Using intergroup dialogue to promote social justice and change. *Social Work*, *51*(4), 303–315.

Din-Dzietham, R., Nembhard, W. N., Collins, R., & Davis, S. K. (2004). Perceived stress following race-based discrimination at work is associated with hypertension in African–Americans: The metro Atlanta heart disease study, 1999–2001. *Social Science & Medicine*, *58*(3), 449–461. https://doi.org/https://doi.org/10.1016/S0277-9536(03)00211-9.

Dressler, W. W., Oths, K. S., & Gravlee, C. C. (2005). Race and ethnicity in public health research: models to explain health disparities. *Annual Review of Anthropology*, *34*, 231–252. http://doi.org/10.1146/annurev.anthro.34.081804.120505

Duran, E., Duran, B., Heart, M. Y. H. B., & Horse-Davis S. Y. (1998). Healing the American Indian Soul Wound. In: Y. Danieli (Ed.), *International Handbook of Multigenerational Legacies of Trauma*. The Plenum Series on Stress and Coping. Springer, Boston, MA. https://doi.org/10.1007/978-1-4757-5567-1_22

Elkins, J., Briggs, H. E., Miller, K. M., Kim, I., Orellana, R., & Mowbray, O. (2019). Racial/ethnic differences in the impact of adverse childhood experiences on posttraumatic stress disorder in a nationally representative sample of adolescents. *Child and Adolescent Social Work Journal*, *36*(5), 449–457.

Ellison, C. G., DeAngelis, R. T., & Güven, M. (2017). Does religious involvement mitigate the effects of major discrimination on the mental health of African Americans? Findings from the Nashville Stress and Health Study. *Religions*, *8*(9), 195.

English, D., Lambert, S. F., & Ialongo, N. S. (2014). Longitudinal associations between experienced racial discrimination and depressive symptoms in African American adolescents. *Developmental psychology*, *50*(4), 1190–1196. https://doi.org/10.1037/a0034703.

228 MICHAEL S. SPENCER ET AL.

Erikson, E. H. (1968). *Identity: Youth and crisis.* New York: W. W. Norton.

Essed, P. (1991). *Understanding everyday racism: An interdisciplinary theory* (Vol. 2). Sage. Newbury Park, CA.

Fernandez, A. R., Evans-Campbell, T., Johnson-Jennings, M., Beltran, R. E., Schultz, K., Stroud, S., & Walters, K. L. (2020). "Being on the walk put it somewhere in my body": The meaning of place in health for Indigenous women. *Journal of Ethnic & Cultural Diversity in Social Work,* 1–16. https://doi.org/10.1080/15313204.2020.1770652.

Fieland, K. C., Walters, K. L., & Simoni, J. M. (2007). Determinants of health among two-spirit American Indians and Alaska Natives. In *The health of sexual minorities* (pp. 268–300).

Foronda, C., Baptiste, D.-L., Reinholdt, M. M., & Ousman, K. (2016). Cultural humility: A concept analysis. *Journal of Transcultural Nursing, 27*(3), 210–217.

Gallo, L. C., Penedo, F. J., Espinosa de los Monteros, K., & Arguelles, W. (2009). Resiliency in the face of disadvantage: Do Hispanic cultural characteristics protect health outcomes? *Journal of Personality, 77*(6), 1707–1746.

Garcia Coll, C., Crnic, K., Lamberty, G., Wasik, B. H., Jenkins, R., Garcia, H. V., & McAdoo, H. P. (1996). An integrative model for the study of developmental competencies in minority children. *Child Development, 67*(5), 1891–1914.

Garrett, M. T., & Carroll, J. J. (2000). Mending the broken circle: Treatment of substance dependence among Native Americans. *Journal of Counseling & Development, 78*(4), 379–388.

Gee, G. C., & Ford, C. L. (2011). Structural racism and health inequities: Old issues, new directions 1. *Du Bois Review: Social Science Research on Race, 8*(1), 115.

Gee, G. C., Spencer, M., Chen, J., Yip, T., & Takeuchi, D. T. (2007a). The association between self-reported racial discrimination and 12-month DSM-IV mental disorders among Asian Americans nationwide. *Social Science & Medicine, 64*(10), 1984–1996.

Gee, G. C., Spencer, M. S., Chen, J., & Takeuchi, D. (2007b). A nationwide study of discrimination and chronic health conditions among Asian Americans. *American Journal of Public Health, 97*(7), 1275–1282.

Ginwright, S. (2018). The Future of Healing: Shifting From Trauma Informed Care to Healing Centered Engagement. Retrieved from https://medium.com/@ginwright/the-future-of-healing-shifting-from-trauma-informed-care-to-healing-centered-eng agement-634f557ce69c

Gonzales, N. A., Germán, M., Kim, S. Y., George, P., Fabrett, F. C., Millsap, R., & Dumka, L. E. (2008). Mexican American adolescents' cultural orientation, externalizing behavior and academic engagement: The role of traditional cultural values. *American Journal of Community Psychology, 41*(1–2), 151–164.

Griffith, D. M., Mason, M., Yonas, M., Eng, E., Jeffries, V., Plihcik, S., & Parks, B. (2007). Dismantling institutional racism: theory and action. *American Journal of Community Psychology, 39*(3–4), 381–392.

Gurin, P., Nagda, B. R. A., & Zuniga, X. (2013). *Dialogue across difference: Practice, theory, and research on intergroup dialogue.* New York: Russell Sage Foundation.

Hall, B. L., & Tandon, R. (2017). Decolonization of knowledge, epistemicide, participatory research and higher education. *Research for All, 1*(1), 6–19. https://doi.org/10.18546/RFA.01.1.02.

Hall, W. J., Chapman, M. V., Lee, K. M., Merino, Y. M., Thomas, T. W., Payne, B. K., Eng, E., Day, S. H., & Coyne-Beasley, T. (2015). Implicit racial/ethnic bias among health care

CLOSING THE HEALTH GAP 229

professionals and its influence on health care outcomes: A systematic review. *American Journal of Public Health, 105*(12), e60–e76.

Harrell, S. P. (2000). A multidimensional conceptualization of racism-related stress: Implications for the well-being of people of color. *American Journal of Orthopsychiatry, 70*(1), 42–57.

Harris, M., & Fallot, R. D. (2001). Envisioning a trauma-informed service system: A vital paradigm shift. *New Directions for Mental Health Services, 2001*(89), 3–22. doi:10.1002/yd.23320018903

Hattori, A. P. (2004). *Colonial dis-ease: US Navy health policies and the Chamorros of Guam, 1898–1941* (Vol. 19). Honolulu: University of Hawaii Press.

Helms, J. E., Nicolas, G., & Green, C. E. (2010). Racism and ethnoviolence as trauma: Enhancing professional training. *Traumatology, 16*(4), 53–62.

Hicken, M. T., Kravitz-Wirtz, N., Durkee, M., & Jackson, J. S. (2018). Racial inequalities in health: Framing future research. *Social Science & Medicine (1982), 199*, 11–18. https://doi.org/10.1016/j.socscimed.2017.12.027

Hughes, D., Rodriguez, J., Smith, E. P., Johnson, D. J., Stevenson, H. C., & Spicer, P. (2006). Parents' ethnic-racial socialization practices: A review of research and directions for future study. *Developmental Psychology, 42*(5), 747.

International Center for Transitional Justice. (2017). *ICTJ briefing - international center for transitional justice.* ICTJ.org. Retrieved January 25, 2023, from https://www.ictj.org/sites/default/files/ICTJ-Briefing-Paper-Reconciliation-TJ-2017.pdf

Johnson, D. J. (1994). Parental racial socialization and racial coping among middle class Black children. In XIII empirical conference in black psychology (pp. 17–38).

Johnston, K. E., Swim, J. K., Saltsman, B. M., Deater-Deckard, K., & Petrill, S. A. (2007). Mothers' racial, ethnic, and cultural socialization of transracially adopted Asian children. *Family Relations, 56*(4), 390–402.

Kaholokula, J. K. (2016). Racism and physical health disparities. In A. N. Alvarez, C. T. H. Liang, & H. A. Neville (Eds.), *The cost of racism for people of color: Contextualizing experiences of discrimination* (pp. 163–188). American Psychological Association. https://doi.org/10.1037/14852-008

Kaholokula, J. K. A., Grandinetti, A., Keller, S., Nacapoy, A. H., & Mau, M. K. (2012). Association between perceived racism and physiological stress indices in Native Hawaiians. *Journal of Behavioral Medicine, 35*(1), 27–37.

Kaholokula, J. K. A., Ing, C. T., Look, M. A., Delafield, R., & Sinclair, K. i. (2018). Culturally responsive approaches to health promotion for Native Hawaiians and Pacific Islanders. *Annals of Human Biology, 45*(3), 249–263. https://doi.org/10.1080/03014460.2018.1465593.

Kaholokula, J. K. A., Look, M. A., Wills, T. A., de Silva, M., Mabellos, T., Seto, T. B., & Buchwald, D. (2017). Kā-HOLO Project: A protocol for a randomized controlled trial of a native cultural dance program for cardiovascular disease prevention in Native Hawaiians. *BMC Public Health, 17*(1), 321. https://doi.org/10.1186/s12889-017-4246-3.

Kelley, M. N., & Lowe, J. R. (2018). A culture-based Talking Circle intervention for Native American youth at risk for obesity. *Journal of Community Health Nursing, 35*(3), 102–117. https://doi.org/10.1080/07370016.2018.1475796.

Kendi, I. X. (2019). *How to be an antiracist.* One World, New York.

Keyes, C. L. (2009). The Black–White paradox in health: Flourishing in the face of social inequality and discrimination. *Journal of Personality, 77*(6), 1677–1706.

Kim, B. S., & Omizo, M. M. (2003). Asian cultural values, attitudes toward seeking professional psychological help, and willingness to see a counselor. *The Counseling Psychologist, 31*(3), 343–361.

Knight, G. P., & Carlo, G. (2012). Prosocial development among Mexican American youth. *Child Development Perspectives, 6*(3), 258–263.

Krieger, N. (2014). Discrimination and health inequities. *International Journal of Health Services, 44*(4), 643–710.

Kumanyika, S. K., Espeland, M. A., Bahnson, J. L., Bottom, J. B., Charleston, J. B., Folmar, S., Wilson, A. C., Whelton, P. K., & Group, T. C. R. (2002). Ethnic comparison of weight loss in the Trial of Nonpharmacologic Interventions in the Elderly. *Obesity Research, 10*(2), 96–106.

Kwate, N. O. A., & Goodman, M. S. (2015). Cross-sectional and longitudinal effects of racism on mental health among residents of Black neighborhoods in New York City. *American Journal of Public Health, 105*(4), 711–718.

Laster Pirtle, W. N. (2020). Racial capitalism: A fundamental cause of novel coronavirus (COVID-19) pandemic inequities in the United States. *Health Education & Behavior, 47*(4), 504–508.

LeBrón, A. M., Spencer, M., Kieffer, E., Sinco, B., Piatt, G., & Palmisano, G. (2017). Correlates of interpersonal ethnoracial discrimination among Latino adults with diabetes: findings from the REACH Detroit Study. *Journal of Ethnic & Cultural Diversity in Social Work, 26*(1–2), 48–67.

Levenson, J. (2017). Trauma-informed social work practice. *Social Work (New York), 62*(2), 105–113. doi:10.1093/sw/swx001

Liu, L. L., & Lau, A. S. (2013). Teaching about race/ethnicity and racism matters: An examination of how perceived ethnic racial socialization processes are associated with depression symptoms. *Cultural Diversity and Ethnic Minority Psychology, 19*(4), 383.

Lizama, T. A. (2014). Yo'åmte: A deeper type of healing exploring the state of Indigenous Chamorro healing practices. *Pacific Asia Inquiry, 5*(1), 97–106.

Lowe, J. (2008). A cultural approach to conducting HIV/AIDS and hepatitis C virus education among Native American Adolescents. *The Journal of School Nursing, 24*(4), 229–238. https://doi.org/10.1177/1059840508319866

Lowe, J., Liang, H., Riggs, C., Henson, J., & Elder, T. (2012). Community partnership to affect substance abuse among Native American adolescents. *The American Journal of Drug and Alcohol Abuse, 38*(5), 450–455.

Lowe, J., Riggs, C., Henson, J., Elder, T., & Liehr, P. (2009, Spring). Cherokee self-reliance and word-use in stories of stress. *Journal of Cultural Diversity, 16*(1), 5–9. https://pub med.ncbi.nlm.nih.gov/20669397   https://www.ncbi.nlm.nih.gov/pmc/articles/PMC 2914319/.

Lowe, J., Wagner, E., Hospital, M. M., Morris, S. L., Thompson, M., Sawant, M., Kelley, M., & Millender, E. (2019). Utility of the Native-reliance theoretical framework, model, and questionnaire. *Journal of Cultural Diversity, 26*(2), 61–68.

MacKenzie, M. K., Serrano, S. K., & Kaulukukui, K. L. (2007). Environmental Justice for Indigenous Hawaiians: Reclaiming Land and Resources. *Natural Resources & Environment, 21*(3), 37–79. http://www.jstor.org/stable/40924828

Mau, M., Blanchette, P., Carpenter D., Kamaka, M., & Saito, E. (2010). *Health and health care of Native Hawaiian and other Pacific Islander Older Adults.* https://www.oha.org/health.

McGrath, B. B., & Ka'ili, T. O. (2010). Creating Project Talanoa: A culturally based community health program for U.S. Pacific Islander adolescents. *Public Health Nursing*, 27(1), 17–24. https://doi.org/10.1111/j.1525-1446.2009.00822.x

McGregor, D. P., Morelli, P. T., Matsuoka, J. K., Rodenhurst, R., Kong, N., & Spencer, M. S. (2003). An ecological model of Native Hawaiian well-being. *Pacific Health Dialog*, 10(2), 106–128.

McHale, S. M., Crouter, A. C., Kim, J. Y., Burton, L. M., Davis, K. D., Dotterer, A. M., & Swanson, D. P. (2006). Mothers' and fathers' racial socialization in African American families: Implications for youth. *Child Development*, 77(5), 1387–1402.

Meyer, I. H. (2015). Resilience in the study of minority stress and health of sexual and gender minorities. *Psychology of Sexual Orientation and Gender Diversity*, 2(3), 209–213. https://doi.org/10.1037/sgd0000132

Nadimpalli, S. B., Kanaya, A. M., McDade, T. W., & Kandula, N. R. (2016). Self-reported discrimination and mental health among Asian Indians: Cultural beliefs and coping style as moderators. *Asian American Journal of Psychology*, 7(3), 185.

National Academies of Sciences, Engineering, and Medicine. (2019). Integrating social care into the delivery of health care: Moving upstream to improve the nation's health. National Academy of Sciences. Washington, DC.

Neblett, E. W., Jr., Rivas-Drake, D., & Umaña-Taylor, A. J. (2012). The promise of racial and ethnic protective factors in promoting ethnic minority youth development. *Child Development Perspectives*, 6(3), 295–303.

Office of Hawaiian Affairs. (2019). *Mauli ola: The determinants of health*. Office of Hawaiian Affairs (OHA). Retrieved November 5, 2022 from https://www.oha.org/health#:~:text=The%20Hawaiian%20framework%20of%20Mauli,spiritual%20health%20of%20our%20people.&text=These%20factors%20are%20also%20known,are%20all%20determinants%20of%20health.

Oluo, I. (2018). *So You Want to Talk About Race*. Seal Press. Hachette United Kingdom.

Phelan, J. C., & Link, B. G. (2015). Is racism a fundamental cause of inequalities in health? *Annual Review of Sociology*, 41, 311–330.

Phinney, J. S. (1996). Understanding ethnic diversity: The role of ethnic identity. *American Behavioral Scientist*, 40(2), 143–152.

Poteat, T., Millett, G. A., Nelson, L. E., & Beyrer, C. (2020). Understanding COVID-19 risks and vulnerabilities among Black communities in America: The lethal force of syndemics. *Annals of Epidemiology*, 47, 1–3.

Reynolds, J. E., & Gonzales-Backen, M. A. (2017). Ethnic-racial socialization and the mental health of African Americans: A critical review. *Journal of Family Theory & Review*, 9(2), 182–200.

Robinson, C. J. (2000). *Black Marxism: The making of the Black radical tradition*. Chapel Hill: University of North Carolina Press.

Rumbaut, R. G. (1994). The crucible within: Ethnic identity, self-esteem, and segmented assimilation among children of immigrants. *International Migration Review*, 28(4), 748–794.

Salas, M. C., Chamness, T., Tayama, M., Uy, N., Cruz, G., San Nicolas, F., Olaguera, R. F., & Argenal, M. (2019). Ancient CHamoru Medicine Making. Guampedia. Retrieved from https://www.guampedia.com/ancient-chamorro-medicine-making/

Schultz, K., Walters, K. L., Beltran, R., Stroud, S., & Johnson-Jennings, M. (2016, 2016/07/01/). "I'm stronger than I thought": Native women reconnecting to body, health, and place. *Health & Place, 40,* 21–28. https://doi.org/https://doi.org/10.1016/j.healthplace.2016.05.001.

Schulz, A. J., Gravlee, C. C., Williams, D. R., Israel, B. A., Mentz, G., & Rowe, Z. (2006). Discrimination, symptoms of depression, and self-rated health among African American women in Detroit: Results from a longitudinal analysis. *American Journal of Public Health, 96*(7), 1265–1270.

Scott, L. D., Jr. (2003). The relation of racial identity and racial socialization to coping with discrimination among African American adolescents. *Journal of Black Studies, 33*(4), 520–538.

Simpson, L. (2000). Stories, dreams, and ceremonies: Anishinaabe ways of learning. *Tribal College, 11*(4), 26–29.

Slimming, P. A. T., Orellana, E. R., & Maynas, J. S. (2014). Structural determinants of indigenous health: A photovoice study in the Peruvian Amazon. *AlterNative: An International Journal of Indigenous Peoples, 10*(2), 123–133.

Smallwood, R., Woods, C., Power, T., & Usher, K. (2021). Understanding the impact of historical trauma due to colonization on the health and well-being of Indigenous young peoples: A systematic scoping review. *Journal of Transcultural Nursing, 32*(1), 59–68. doi:10.1177/1043659620935955

Smedley, B. D., Stith, A. Y., & Nelson, A. R. (2003). Racial and ethnic disparities in diagnosis and treatment: A review of the evidence and a consideration of causes. In *Unequal Treatment: Confronting Racial and Ethnic Disparities in Health Care, 417,* 1–38.

Spencer, M., Kohn-Wood, L., Dombrowski, R. D., Keeles, O., & Birichi, D. (2012). Environmental justice and the well-being of poor children of color: Building capacity in Head Start parents through Photovoice. In D. K. Nagata, L. Kohn-Wood, & L. A. Suzuki (Eds.), *Qualitative strategies for ethnocultural research* (pp. 143–160). Washington, DC: American Psychological Association. https://doi.org/10.1037/13742-008.

Spencer, M., Martineau, D., & Warren, N. (2011). Extending intergroup dialogue facilitation to multicultural social work practice. In *Facilitating intergroup dialogues: Bridging differences, catalyzing change* (pp. 147–160).

Spencer, M. S. (2019). *Microaggressions and social work research, practice and education.* Routledge. New York, NY.

Spencer, M. S., Chen, J., Gee, G. C., Fabian, C. G., & Takeuchi, D. T. (2010). Discrimination and mental health–related service use in a national study of Asian Americans. *American Journal of Public Health, 100*(12), 2410–2417.

Spencer, M. S., Fentress, T., Touch, A., & Hernandez, J. (2020). Environmental justice, Indigenous knowledge systems, and Native Hawaiians and other Pacific Islanders. *Human Biology, 92*(1), 45–57.

Spencer, M. S., Walters, K. L., Allen, H. L., Andrews, C., Begun, A., Browne, T., & Uehara, E. (2018). Close the health gap. *Grand Challenges for Social Work and Society,* 36–55.

Stevenson, H. C., & Arrington, E. G. (2009). Racial/ethnic socialization mediates perceived racism and the racial identity of African American adolescents. *Cultural Diversity and Ethnic Minority Psychology, 15*(2), 125.

Tecun, A., Hafoka, I., ʻUluʻave, L., & ʻUluʻave-Hafoka, M. (2018). Talanoa: Tongan epistemology and Indigenous research method. *AlterNative: An International Journal of Indigenous Peoples, 14*(2), 156–163. https://doi.org/10.1177/1177180118767436

Stone, J., Kwan, V. S. Y., Ruiz, J. M., Hamann, H. A., Mehl, M. R., & O'Connor, M.-F. (2016). The Hispanic health paradox: From epidemiological phenomenon to contribution opportunities for psychological science. *Group Processes & Intergroup Relations, 19*(4), 462–476.

Tajfel, H., & Turner, J. C. (2004). The Social Identity Theory of Intergroup Behavior. In J. T. Jost & J. Sidanius (Eds.), *Political psychology: Key readings* (pp. 276–293). Psychology Press. https://doi.org/10.4324/9780203505984-16.

Tecun, A., Hafoka, I., 'Ulu'ave, L., & 'Ulu'ave-Hafoka, M. (2018). Talanoa: Tongan epistemology and Indigenous research method. *AlterNative: An International Journal of Indigenous Peoples, 14*(2), 156–163. https://doi.org/10.1177/1177180118767436.

Tervalon, M., & Murray-Garcia, J. (1998). Cultural humility versus cultural competence: A critical distinction in defining physician training outcomes in multicultural education. *Journal of Health Care for the Poor and Underserved, 9*(2), 117–125.

Town, M. A., Walters, K. L., & Orellana, E. R. (2021). Discriminatory distress, HIV risk behavior, and community participation among American Indian/Alaska Native men who have sex with men. *Ethnicity & Health, 26*(5), 646–658. https://doi.org/10.1080/13557858.2018.1557115

Truong, M., Paradies, Y., & Priest, N. (2014). Interventions to improve cultural competency in healthcare: a systematic review of reviews. *BMC Health Services Research, 14*(1), 1–17.

Tuck, E. (2009). Suspending Damage: A Letter to Communities. *Harvard Educational Review, 79*(3), 409–428.

Wallerstein, N. B., & Duran, B. (2006). Using Community-Based Participatory Research to Address Health Disparities. *Health Promotion Practice. Society for Public Health Education, 7*(3), 312–323.

Wallerstein, N. B., Yen, I. H., & Syme, S. L. (2011). Integration of social epidemiology and community-engaged interventions to improve health equity. *American Journal of Public Health, 101*(5), 822–830.

Walters, K. L., Johnson-Jennings, M., Stroud, S., Rasmus, S., Charles, B., John, S., Allen, J., Kaholokula, J. K. A., Look, M. A., de Silva, M., Lowe, J., Baldwin, J. A., Lawrence, G., Brooks, J., Noonan, C. W., Belcourt, A., Quintana, E., Semmens, E. O., & Boulafentis, J. (2020, 2020/01/01). Growing from our roots: Strategies for developing culturally grounded health promotion interventions in American Indian, Alaska Native, and Native Hawaiian communities. *Prevention Science, 21*(1), 54–64. https://doi.org/10.1007/s11121-018-0952-z.

Walters, K. L., Mohammed, S. A., Evans-Campbell, T., Beltrán, R. E., Chae, D. H., & Duran, B. (2011). Bodies don't just tell stories, they tell histories: Embodiment of historical trauma among American Indians and Alaska Natives. *Du Bois Review: Social Science Research on Race, 8*(1), 179–189.

Walters, K. L., & Simoni, J. M. (2002). Reconceptualizing native women's health: an "indigenist" stress-coping model. *American Journal of Public Health, 92*(4), 520–524. https://doi.org/10.2105/ajph.92.4.520.

Walters, K. L., Spencer, M. S., Smukler, M., Allen, H. L., Andrews, C., Browne, T., Maramaldi, P., Wheeler, D. P., Zebrack, B., & Uehara, E. (2016). Eradicating health inequalities for future generations. AASWSW. Retrieved from http://aaswsw. org.

Walters, K. L., Stately, A., Evans-Campbell, T., . . . Guerrero, D. (2009). "Indigenist" Collaborative Research Efforts in Native American Communities. In A. Stiffman (Ed.), *The Field Research Survival Guide* (pp.146–173). Oxford University Press.

West, D. S., Prewitt, T. E., Bursac, Z., & Felix, H. C. (2008). Weight loss of black, white, and Hispanic men and women in the Diabetes Prevention Program. *Obesity, 16*(6), 1413–1420.

Whitbeck, L. B., McMorris, B. J., Hoyt, D. R., Stubben, J. D., & LaFromboise, T. (2002). Perceived Discrimination, Traditional Practices, and Depressive Symptoms among American Indians in the Upper Midwest. *Journal of Health and Social Behavior, 43*(4), 400–418. https://doi.org/10.2307/3090234

Whyte, K. (2017). The Dakota access pipeline, environmental injustice, and US colonialism. *Red Ink: An International Journal of Indigenous Literature, Arts, & Humanities, 19*(1).

Williams, D. R., & Mohammed, S. A. (2009). Discrimination and racial disparities in health: evidence and needed research. *Journal of Behavioral Medicine, 32*(1), 20–47.

Williams, D. R., & Mohammed, S. A. (2013). Racism and health I: Pathways and scientific evidence. *American Behavioral Scientist, 57*(8), 1152–1173.

Williams, D. R., Neighbors, H. W., & Jackson, J. S. (2003). Racial/ethnic discrimination and health: Findings from community studies. *American Journal of Public Health, 93*(2), 200–208.

Williams, D. R., & Williams-Morris, R. (2000). Racism and mental health: The African American experience. *Ethnicity & Health, 5*(3–4), 243–268.

Wimbish-Cirilo, R., Lowe, J., Millender, E., & Orellana, E. R. (2020). Addressing substance use utilizing a community-based program among urban Native American youth living in Florida. *Genealogy (Basel), 4*(3), 79. https://doi.org/10.3390/genealogy4030079.

Woo, B., Fan, W., Tran, T. V., & Takeuchi, D. T. (2019). The role of racial/ethnic identity in the association between racial discrimination and psychiatric disorders: A buffer or exacerbator? *SSM-Population Health, 7.* https://doi.org/10.1016/j.ssmph.2019.100378

Woo, B., Kravitz-Wirtz, N., Sass, V., Crowder, K., Teixeira, S., & Takeuchi, D. T. (2019). Residential segregation and racial/ethnic disparities in ambient air pollution. *Race and Social Problems, 11*(1), 60–67.

World Health Organization. (2007). Everybody's business: Strengthening health systems to improve health outcomes: WHO's framework for action, 1–56. https://apps.who.int/iris/bitstream/handle/10665/43918/9789241596077_eng.pdf

Yip, T., Gee, G. C., & Takeuchi, D. T. (2008). Racial discrimination and psychological distress: the impact of ethnic identity and age among immigrant and United States-born Asian adults. *Developmental Psychology, 44*(3), 787.

Yip, T., Wang, Y., Mootoo, C., & Mirpuri, S. (2019). Moderating the association between discrimination and adjustment: A meta-analysis of ethnic/racial identity. *Developmental Psychology, 55*(6), 1274.

9

Integrating AASWSW's Grand Challenges of Productive Aging with Anti-Racism and Health Equity Lenses to Improve Population Health

Ernest Gonzales, Nancy Morrow-Howell, Jacqueline L. Angel,
Lisa Fredman, Lisa A. Marchiondo, Robert Harootyan, Jasmin Choi,
Nandini Choudhury, Kelsi Carolan, Kathy Lee, Erwin Tan, Patricia Yu,
Emily Shea, Cliff Whetung, and Christina Matz

This chapter brings together perspectives from anti-racism, health equity, and productive aging to advance an equitable, healthy, and productive society.

The shift of the age distribution from younger to older people within nations and across the world is one of the most profound transformations in human history and presents many challenges and opportunities. National discourse has focused primarily on the deficits of aging by emphasizing disabilities, declines, disease, national deficits, and death and dying. Much less attention has been given to the growing diversity and capacity of the older population and adjacent growing proportion who need and/or want to work, volunteer, and provide care at older and older ages. In this chapter, we argue that anti-racism and health equity perspectives allow for a more thorough understanding of current challenges and opportunities for productive aging.

Ernest Gonzales, Nancy Morrow-Howell, Jacqueline L. Angel, Lisa Fredman, Lisa A. Marchiondo, Robert Harootyan, Jasmin Choi, Nandini Choudhury, Kelsi Carolan, Kathy Lee, Erwin Tan, Patricia Yu, Emily Shea, Cliff Whetung, and Christina Matz, *Integrating AASWSW's Grand Challenges of Productive Aging with Anti-Racism and Health Equity Lenses to Improve Population Health* In: *Social Work and the Grand Challenge to Eliminate Racism*. Edited by: Martell L. Teasley, Michael S. Spencer, and Melissa Bartholomew, Oxford University Press. © Oxford University Press 2023. DOI: 10.1093/oso/9780197674949.003.0009

An Integrated Framework of Productive Aging, Anti-Racism, and Health Equity

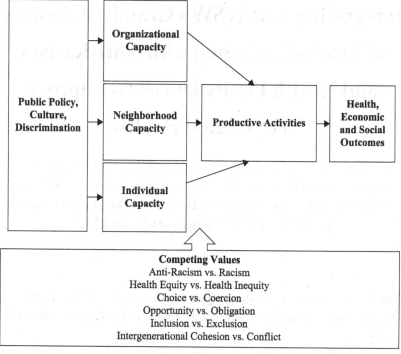

Figure 9.1 Integrated Framework of Productive Aging

Definitions

Productive aging is defined as any activity that produce goods and services by older adults, whether paid or not (Bass et al., 1993). Paid employment, formal volunteering, and informal caregiving represent the three most common productive activities in gerontological social work literature (Gonzales et al., 2015). These activities are shaped by institutional and social structures (Burr et al., 2005; Morrow-Howell et al., 2001) and are associated with health, economic, and social outcomes to individuals, families, communities, and the greater society. Proponents of the productive aging perspective emphasize a core set of values to guide knowledge development: inclusion, opportunity, intergenerational harmony, and choice, as opposed to elitism, obligation, intergenerational conflict, and coercion (Estes & Mahakian, 2001; Morrow-Howell et al., 2001). In this chapter, we introduce two additional core values: anti-racism and health equity.

Anti-racism requires scholars and practitioners in the field of aging to identify and dismantle systemic racist policies and practices that undermine health, economic, and social opportunities for Black, Indigenous, and People of Color (BIPOC). Table 9.1 reviews a wide range of economic, social, and environmental inequities by race and ethnicity. Gerontologists must be committed to implementing and advocating for policies and practices that eliminate these inequities, systems of oppression and power imbalance (Gonzales et al., 2020). Anti-racism points our attention to public policy and culture that shape individual, neighborhood, and institutional capacities for meaningful engagement in work, volunteering, and family caregiving. Similarly, health equity is defined as "the absence of systematic disparities in health between groups with different levels of underlying social advantage/disadvantage— that is, wealth, power, or prestige" (Bravemen & Gruskin, 2003, p. 254). Anti-racism and health equity perspectives bring our focus to exposure to risks across the life-course that are unjust, avoidable, and closely tied to economic, social, or environmental (dis)advantages based on race and ethnicity as well as gender, age, disability, sexual orientation, religion, socioeconomic status, geographic location, and immigration status.

Public Policy, Culture, and Discrimination

Public policy, culture, and discrimination interact in complex ways to create inequities at the individual, neighborhood, and organizational levels. The War on Drugs, mandatory sentences, and incarceration policies have led to unjust imprisonment, fractured families, and stymied opportunities for higher education for BIPOC (Alexander, 2010; Britton, 2019; Epperson & Pettus-Davis, 2016). Some argue the old age insurance provisions of the 1935 Social Security Act—which are often lauded as anti-poverty policies for adults in later life—systematically excluded African Americans and women when the Act was first developed and implemented. African Americans and women were primarily employed in agriculture and domestic work, two sectors not covered by Social Security. The rationale for excluding this type of work was because of administrative burdens involving tax-collection procedures (DeWitt, 2010, p. 1).

Table 9.1 Inequities by Race and Ethnicity among Older Adults in the Health and Retirement Study in 2016

	Total Sample	White	Black/AA	Latinx	Significant Group Differences
	18,298 (100%)	11,087 (78.3%)	4,104 (11.7%)	3,007 (10.5%)	
Variable					
Age (50–107)	66.0 (10.9)	68.5 (11.2)	63.1 (9.5)	53.7 (9.5)	L<B<W
Gender (% women)	54.0%	53.7%	56.5%	61.2%	W<B<L
Married	64.4%	67.3%	44.3%	64.0%	B<L<W
Education					
Less than HS	14.0%	9.6%	21.7%	45.7%	W<B<L
HS	28.6%	29.4%	29.3%	22.2%	L<B<W
Some College	25.8%	26.3%	29.3%	19.0%	L<B<W
College +	31.5%	35.7%	19.8%	13.2%	L<B<W
Income	$95,734 ($185,002)	$106,276 ($156,643)	$53,180 ($73,979)	$51,814 ($104,950)	L<B<W
Assets	$599,783 ($1,519,003)	$714,028 ($1,657,845)	$155,030 ($441,392)	$214,052 ($626,445)	B<L<W
Chronic Health Index	2.1 (1.4)	2.1 (1.5)	2.3 (1.4)	1.9 (1.4)	L<W<B
Total cognition	15.8 (4.3)	15.8 (4.3)	13.5 (4.6)	13.5 (4.4)	B=L<W
Depressed (CESD <= 8)	14.0%	12.9%	18.5%	21.0%	W<B<L
Employment and Volunteering					
Current work status					
Works full-time	34.3%	34.5%	31.9%	35.3%	B<W=L
Works part-time	4.7%	4.5%	4.6%	6.9%	B=W<L
Unemployed	1.9%	1.5%	3.4%	3.5%	W<B=L
Partly retired	7.5%	8.2%	5.1%	4.6%	B=L<W
Retired	45.5%	46.7%	45.9%	36.0%	L<B<W

Disabled	2.6%	1.7%	6.3%	5.5%	W<L<B
Not in labor force	3.5%	3.0%	2.9%	8.3%	B=W<L
Physical job strain (most/all of the time)	($n = 7,484$)	($n = 4,341$)	($n = 1,733$)	($n = 1,410$)	
Requires lots of physical effort	32.5%	29.5%	46.8%	41.9%	W<L<B
Requires heavy lifting	13.7%	12.1%	17.9%	22.1%	W<B<L
Requires stooping/kneeling/crouching	26.1%	24.6%	28.0%	35.9%	W<B<L
Requires good eyesight	87.7%	88.2%	87.8%	84.0%	L<B=W
Job involves lots of stress (agree/strongly agree)	61.6%	63.3%	56.1%	54.2%	L<B<W
Volunteer activity (last 12 months)					
Did not volunteer	63.7%	61.7%	64.7%	77.3%	W<B<L
Volunteered < 100 hours	22.3%	23.2%	21.6%	16.6%	L<B<W
Volunteered >= 100 hours	14.0%	15.1%	13.8%	6.2%	L<B<W
Discrimination Experiences	$n = 5,576$	$n = 3,915$	$n = 975$	$n = 689$	
Major discrimination experiences					
Unfairly dismissed from a job	19.9%	18.6%	20.1%	15.1%	L<W<B
Unfairly not hired for a job	8.4%	7.0%	12.6%	5.1%	L<W<B
Unfairly denied a promotion	10.0%	8.5%	15.3%	8.9%	W<L<B
Unfairly denied a bank loan	5.2%	3.9%	11.1%	5.1%	W<L<B
Unfairly stopped by police	6.5%	4.6%	13.9%	6.9%	W<L<B
Unfairly denied health care	2.8%	2.4%	3.6%	3.9%	W<L=B
Major discrimination experiences					
0	67.5%	68.4%	58.3%	68.2%	B<L=B
1	19.7%	19.6%	20.4%	19.3%	L=W<B

(*continued*)

Table 9.1 Continued

	Total Sample	White	Black/AA	Latinx	Significant Group Differences
2+	12.8%	12.0%	21.3%	12.6%	W<L<B
Everyday discrimination events					
0	37.8%	37.8%	32.3%	45.5%	B<W<L
1	43.7%	45.2%	39.5%	31.9%	L=B<W
2+	18.6%	17.2%	29.3%	22.5%	W<L<B
Everyday discrimination attributions					
Ancestry	4.3%	1.8%	18.6%	15.9%	W<L<B
Gender	9.6%	10.6%	7.1%	1.8%	B<L<W
Race	3.1%	1.2%	20.1%	5.6%	W<L<B
Age	17.6%	19.4%	5.4%	11.1%	B<L<W
Religion	0.1%	0.8%	1.3%	0.7%	B<W<L
Weight	3.1%	3.4%	1.7%	1.5%	B=L<W
Disability	1.2%	1.2%	1.1%	1.0%	L<W<B
Physical appearance	2.6%	2.8%	0.7%	2.6%	B<L=W
Sexual orientation	0.2%	0.3%	0.0%	0.0%	B=L=W
Socioeconomic position	2.4%	2.3%	1.5%	3.8%	B<W<L
Other	9.2%	9.8%	4.4%	7.6%	B<L<W
No attribution/Other	46.1%	46.7%	38.1%	48.4%	B<L<W
Social Cohesion Index (1–7)	5.5 (1.3)	5.6 (1.3)	4.8 (1.5)	4.9 (1.6)	L=B<W
Physical Order Index (1–7)	5.5 (1.4)	5.6 (1.3)	4.7 (1.6)	5.0 (1.6)	B<L<W

Racial segregation continues today. The U.S. workforce is more racially segregated now than a generation ago (Ferguson & Koning, 2018). BIPOC are in employment contexts that pay less, have fewer health and retirement benefits, and involve more physically challenging work conditions. Women of color are particularly susceptible to lower paying jobs, physically demanding jobs, and have less workplace flexibility when compared to non-Hispanic White women and men. And without a national paid family and medical leave policy, women—and especially women of color—are less likely to be in the paid-labor force with social policy protections such as Social Security and employer-based pensions. These social policies elevate the risk of poverty for BIPOCs and women of color.

Individual Capacity

Adverse socio-ecological conditions interact with genetic factors early in life and produce inequities in health that are unjust and avoidable (Angel et al., 2015; Sadana et al., 2016). BIPOC report a high probability of having a low socioeconomic position over their lifetimes, as compared to non-Hispanic Whites (Lui et al., 2006). BIPOC also experience higher levels of incivility and unfair mistreatment across their lifetimes (Gonzales et al., 2021). Carter and colleagues found that early life stress led to sustained negative affective states in emerging adulthood among African Americans and may lead to heightened risk for accelerated biological aging, disease, and mortality (Carter et al., 2019). From a life-course perspective, poverty in childhood is associated with premature mortality, respiratory illness, and cardiovascular disease in later life (Miller & Chen, 2013; Shonkoff, 2010) and BIPOC carry a heavier burden of these early adverse life experiences (Geronimus et al., 2006; Goldbach et al., 2015).

Education is strongly associated with higher-paying jobs, occupational attainment, increased job security, and better mental and physical health across all racial and ethnic groups (Braveman & Gruskin, 2003; House, 2002). Educational systems and labor markets are linked to early stratification processes that magnify across the lifespan (Schafer et al., 2013). Racial minority groups, on average, are less educated than their non-Hispanic White counterparts and represent a disproportionate share of the health and economically disadvantaged in the United States. They are more likely to be employed in low-wage industries and jobs and are therefore less likely to build wealth than their non-minority counterparts (Lui et al., 2006). Moreover, minorities, especially immigrants, often take lower-paying jobs, many of which provide limited access to health insurance. Such patterns of socioeconomic stratification stem from the systematic racism and unequal allocation of power, prestige, and material aid (Williams et al., 2019; House, 2002; Ruger & Kim, 2006).

Neighborhood Capacity

The proposed integrated framework emphasizes the importance of neighborhood and community-level factors as determinants to health and productivity more so than previous conceptual frameworks (Fried et al., 2004; Morrow-Howell et al., 2001; Matz-Costa et al., 2016). Given present and historical neighborhood racial segregation tied to redlining and gentrification (Williams et al., 2019), it is essential to consider how race and ethnicity intersect with the quality of neighborhoods, health, and productive activities (Gonzales et al., 2016). Racially segregated neighborhoods undermine economic well-being in adulthood due to reduced access to quality schools. Racial and ethnic minorities, as compared to non-Hispanic Whites, are exposed to higher levels of social disorganization, violence, limited transportation, and environmental hazards in segregated neighborhoods (McBride et al., 2004; Musick et al., 2000). A study by Gonzales, Lee, and Marchiondo (2019) revealed that low social cohesion and high physical disorder undermined mental health and led to earlier retirement. Johnson, Latham-Minuts, and Poey (2018) found that a one-unit increase in neighborhood social cohesion increased the odds of moderate- and high-intensity volunteering.

Institutional Capacity

Social scientists have emphasized modifying organizational conditions to facilitate and expand access to formal and informal labor market activities (Morrow-Howell et al., 2001; McBride, 2006). Specification of role(s), dissemination of information, role availability, compensation for expenses, in-kind incentives, skill development, role flexibility and recognition, accommodation, complexity of tasks, and social integration, can facilitate the recruitment and retention of older adults into productive activities (Andel et al., 2015; Lee et al., 2022; McBride, 2006; McBride et al., 2011). Yet, BIPOC are often employed in low-paying jobs with few benefits, such as employer-sponsored pensions, and with little flexibility on when, where, and how to do the work (Brown, 2012; Brown, 2016; Brown & Warner, 2008; Glynn et al., 2016).

Productive Activities

Productive activities necessitate physical and cognitive stimulation, social interaction, and emotional exchange. And as a result, these activities activate biopsychosocial mechanisms including biomarkers (e.g., allostatic load, insulin resistance, blood pressure, cortisol levels), functional health (e.g., strength, gait, balance, falls), mental health (e.g., cortical plasticity, executive functioning, memory, processing speed), social engagement (e.g., social support and reciprocity), psychological appraisals (e.g., life satisfaction, purpose in life, self-efficacy), and health behaviors (e.g., exercise, medication adherence, diet, and substance use). Job demands also vary by race and ethnicity. There is a consistent pattern of job insecurity and strain among racial and ethnic minorities when compared to Whites (Landsbergis et al., 2012). Further research is needed to examine how the demands of jobs, volunteer roles, and informal caregiving vary by race and ethnicity, which may help explain enduring health inequities (Gonzales, et al., 2022; Lee et al., 2022).

Outcomes among Older Adults

Findings from population aging and health studies suggest that working longer is associated with a relatively smaller decline in instrumental and basic activities of daily living (ADLs and IADLs) and psychological functioning, and a reduced risk of mortality (Bowen et al., 2010; Calvo, 2006; Jang et al., 2018; Staudinger et al., 2016). Although more rigorous research is needed, there is some evidence that delaying retirement can reduce the risk of dementia and Alzheimer's disease (Dufouil et al., 2014), pointing to the importance of workplace complexity, intellectual stimulation, and social engagement (Fisher et al., 2017). Similarly, volunteering is associated

244 ERNEST GONZALES ET AL.

with improved physical health (Lum & Lightfoot, 2005), mental health (Greenfield & Marks, 2004; Musick & Wilson, 2003), life satisfaction (Van Willigen, 2000), self-rated health (Luoh & Herzog, 2002; Morrow-Howell et al., 2003), and reduced mortality (Lum & Lightfoot, 2005; Musick et al., 1999). Increasing evidence suggests that informal caregivers live longer than their non-caregiving counterparts, supporting the notion that the activity itself bolsters health, despite caregivers reporting more psychological distress, social isolation, and caregiving strain (Pinquart & Sörensen, 2003; Roth et al., 2015; Roth et al., 2009). Research has not yet identified how working longer, volunteering, or informal caregiving affects various dimensions of health across race and ethnicity. An anti-racism lens can be applied to empirically test heterogeneity across and within racial and ethnic groups. This is an important area for future research (National Academies of Sciences, Engineering, and Medicine, 2022).

Outcomes for Families, Organizations, and Society

The benefits of productive aging can extend to younger generations, families, communities, and society. Organizations that employ older workers benefit from their labor in several ways (Inkson & Richardson, 2013), including a positive return-on-investment by hiring and training older employees (Towers Perrin, 2005). When a broad array of job functions were assessed in a meta-analysis, Ng and Feldman (2008) concluded that "older workers demonstrate . . . greater safety-related behavior . . . [and they] appear to engage in fewer counterproductive work behaviors in general and exhibit less workplace aggression, on-the-job substance use, tardiness and voluntary absence in particular" (p. 403). Borsch-Supan and Weiss (2013) found increases in the average age-productivity profile of employees up to age 65.

Programs in which older adult volunteers tutor children who are at risk of not completing high school or college, such as AARP's Experience Corps, have the potential to alter the economic and health trajectories of children, the majority of whom are racial and ethnic minorities living in under-resourced neighborhoods. Caregiving to grandchildren (i.e., grandparenting) may not only improve the health of grandparents, but is also beneficial to young children's learning and development (Hughes et al., 2007; Kenner et al., 2007) and can alleviate financial strain for families by lowering parents' out-of-pocket childcare costs (Mutchler & Baker, 2009). Spousal caregiving may be associated with improved outcomes among the spouses receiving care (Lawrence et al., 1998).

Although organizations may also benefit from the volunteer labor of older adults, especially charitable or mission-driven nonprofit organizations, concrete performance-based outcomes have been more difficult to quantify (Salamon et al., 2011). Organization-level value can be assessed through estimates of the worth of the added activities that organizations are able to undertake as a result of volunteer contributions (i.e., "outputs," such as increased number of services delivered or community members reached, higher staff morale, improved community engagement, access to new streams of funding, etc.) or the value of the work that the volunteer puts into the community/organization (i.e., "inputs," such as time, skills, knowledge, experience) (Salamon et al., 2011).

Volunteer work by adults age 65 or older was valued at nearly $100 billion in 2012 (Corporation for National and Community Service, 2012); and informal caregiving by older adults has been estimated at between $100 and $500 billion annually (Corporation for National and Community Service, 2012; Johnson & Schaner, 2005; Reinhard et al., 2015). Further, because productive engagement is associated with better individual health, such improved health may then translate to lower healthcare costs (Everard et al. 2000; Umberson & Montez, 2010). Given that most of older adults' healthcare in the United States is covered by public funding (Medicare) and Medicaid for low-income older adults, such improvements could carry substantial economic benefit.

Contributions of an Integrated Framework

An anti-racism, health equity, and productive aging framework makes several contributions to the field. First, more than other productive aging models, this framework highlights modifiable life-course factors as precursors for productive engagement and health in later life and underscores systemic racism as a cultural context that limits capacity and choices for racial and ethnic minorities in mid- and later-life. This perspective can be used to address a common concern that adults who enter later life with certain disadvantages will be further marginalized if productive involvement is an expectation. All older adults cannot be expected to engage in certain work, volunteer, and caregiving roles (or will experience negative

246 ERNEST GONZALES ET AL.

outcomes if they do) unless they enter this stage of life with requisite health, social, and economic resources. Productive activities must be in alignment with older adults' capacity, motivations, and preferences. Implications are not only to eliminate health inequities across the life course, but to support people through public policies and programs to be as engaged as they can be, and want to be, when they enter later life.

This integrated framework underscores the importance of working across the American Academy of Social Work & Social Welfare (AASWSW) Grand Challenges. Gerontologists with expertise in productive aging should work with colleagues to eliminate racism (Teasley et al., 2021) and promote health equity (Walters et al., 2016) to promote population health across the life span for all. Interventions, including services, programs, and policy, cannot be isolated to any part of the life course. We must intervene across macro, meso, and micro levels and at all life stages of life to promote health and productivity.

Progress to Date and Future Research

Members of the Grand Challenge Initiative have been conducting research to help inform policies, programs, and advocacy efforts to reduce health disparities through employment, volunteering, and caregiving. Below are a few examples of how this research has already expanded the focus to race and ethnicity, and consequently, research findings are helping to inform efforts to reduce health inequities. More research is necessary to examine heterogeneity among an aging population that is becoming more racially and ethnically diverse.

Employment

A longitudinal population-based aging and health study revealed perceived discrimination and neighborhood conditions undermined mental health and hastened earlier retirement from age 65 to 62 among older Whites, Blacks, and Latinx populations (Gonzales et al., 2021; Gonzales et al., 2018). Older workers who perceived age-based discrimination had higher levels of depression, worse self-rated health, job dissatisfaction, and higher levels of retirement intentions (Marchiondo et al., 2017; Marchiondo et al., 2015). These studies support aspects of the strength and vulnerability integration model (SAVI model; Charles, 2010), which suggests that older adults exhibit and benefit from greater emotion-regulation skills, yet when a stressor becomes chronic, such as discrimination at work, it overwhelms older adults' regulatory skills and triggers harmful physiological responses.

The Senior Community Service and Employment Program (SCSEP) is the only federally funded program to help low-income older adults, with larger percentages of racial and ethnic minorities, obtain employment. While there are ongoing debates about its effectiveness, emerging evidence revealed how this training program improved cognitive, mental, emotional, and physical health, as well as reduced the risk of homelessness, especially for low-income women with chronic health conditions (Carolan et al., 2020; Gonzales et al., 2020; Halvorsen & Yulikova, 2020; Halvorsen et al., 2020). These studies are important because they emphasized the importance of SCSEP authorized by Title V of the Older Americans Act and administered by the Department of Labor as federal policy, and that the program improves health among unemployed and low-income older adults (U.S. Department of Labor, 2015). Future research is required to fully assess causal factors associated with long-term health and employability.

Older workers, and especially older racial and ethnic minorities, have been acutely impacted by COVID-19 (Barnes, 2020; Bui et al., 2020; Gonzales et al. 2021). Long-standing discriminatory practices based on age, race, and Hispanic ethnicity exacerbated underlying attitudes toward older workers as weak and vulnerable (Morrow-Howell & Gonzales, 2020). Labor force participation rate for older workers dropped significantly in the first quarter of 2020 due to COVID (Ghilarducci, 2020). For workers remaining in the labor force, racial and ethnic minority workers often do not have access to flexible work or paid sick leave, and many are employed in low-paying essential jobs in grocery and retail stores. For these reasons, older racial and ethnic minorities were at greater risk of contagion and death from the virus (Gonzales et al., 2021; Halvorsen & Yulikova, 2020).

Volunteering

AARP's Experience Corps is an intergenerational tutoring program of older adults (aged 50+), aimed to help improve the health of older adults as well as the reading and math skills of racial and ethnic minority children in kindergarten to third grade in under-resourced communities. Experimental and quasi-experimental research found that older volunteers, the majority of whom were African American, experienced decreased frailty and falls; fewer depressive symptoms; enhanced memory, strength, balance, walking speed,

248 ERNEST GONZALES ET AL.

cortical plasticity, and executive functioning; increased social and psychological engagement; and improved mobility and IADLs (Carlson et al., 2015; Fried et al., 2013; Hong & Morrow-Howell, 2010; Morrow-Howell et al., 2008). A randomized field trial of elementary school children offers evidence that the intervention showed improvement in students' passage comprehension and reading skills, both of which are key factors to attending and completing college (Gattis et al., 2010; Lee et al., 2012). Older volunteers reported that their families and friends also benefited from the program: older volunteers tutored grandchildren at home; volunteers brought additional resources, information, and new skills back to the family; older volunteers had better relationships and communication with family; and friends and family also got involved with volunteering (McBride et al., 2011).

Caregiving

The United States is the only developed country without paid sick and family leave for all workers. Although family caregiving is the backbone of this country's long-term care system and saves the nation billions of dollars annually, it imposes health and economic costs on informal caregivers and families. Older caregivers, especially women, jeopardize their own economic security by missing employment opportunities and incurring out-of-pocket expenses (Gonzales et al., 2015; Greenfield, 2013; Lee et al., 2015; Wabayashi & Donato, 2006), which has led to a strong and concerted effort to pass legislation on paid family and medical leave at the state and federal levels (Morrow-Howell et al., 2017). In 2017, over 100 experts in aging and work signed a Call to Congress to address the nation's caregiving crisis and support paid family and medical leave (National Partnership for Women & Families, 2017) and there appears to be bipartisan support for passing federal legislation.

Implications for Education

Curricular innovations are attainable and realistic, given that social workers and public health practitioners apply a strengths-based approach, an ecological perspective to health promotion and healthcare practices and programs. Existing social work and public health educational programs need to extend and highlight knowledge and skills related to racism, health equity, and productive roles that matter for older adults. Social work education tends to reinforce aging from a deficits perspective, with a focus on decline, disability, dependency, and dementia rather than a strengths-based and assets perspective to aging. Further, students need exposure to empirically supported programs and policies that are informed from an anti-racist lens, such as Experience Corps. Social service providers and policymakers can stay abreast with emerging health and productive aging issues through on-going training and certificate programs.

Conclusion

Integrating critical lenses of anti-racism and health equity within productive aging scholarship will likely promote a sharper focus for eliminating systemic racism and structural barriers that impede equal access across employment, volunteering, and caregiving contexts. Researchers, policymakers, practitioners, and advocates in social work and allied professions can assist with evaluating and expanding evidence-based programs and policies to reduce racial and ethnic inequities in health that are avoidable and unjust. Social workers are well positioned to work with diverse populations across the life course to advance long and productive lives for everyone. In addition, we need to change the national narrative and cultural images of older adults as assets to society, rather than a burden. Ensuring that all older adults have access to equal opportunities for engagement in productive activities can yield health and economic benefits to them, to younger generations, to families, to communities, and to society.

Acknowledgments

This work was supported by the James Weldon Johnson Professorship (PI: Gonzales), Peter T. Paul Career Development Award (PI: Gonzales); The Center for Innovation in Social Work and Health at Boston University; the National Institute on Minority Health and Health Disparities' Loan Repayment Program (Gonzales, PI), and New York University's Silver School of Social Work. We thank Donna Butts, Executive Director to Generations United, Dean Sandro Galea at Boston University, School of Public Health, Dr. Bronwyn Keefe and Nina Levine at Boston University, School of Social Work for contributions to earlier versions.

Study Questions

1. Please identify 5 research gaps in the areas of anti-racism, health equity, and productive aging. Rank them from "high importance" to "lower importance" and explain your ranking.
2. What federal policies exist to help low-income older adults, many of whom are racial and ethnic minorities, gain employment in later life? What advocacy efforts should social workers engage in to ensure continued federal support for employment?
3. What federal and not-for-profit organizations exist that aim to eliminate the academic achievement gap across racial and ethnic groups? What role can older volunteers play in reshaping academic trajectories for racial and ethnic minority children?
4. Please describe current policy and advocacy efforts to support informal caregivers. How might employment policies support informal caregivers? And how might informal caregivers of color benefit from expanding flexible work options?
5. What evidence exists that perceived discrimination undermines mental health and hastens retirement?
6. How do you define a "good job"? Why might racial and ethnic minorities have less access to good jobs?
7. How might work be beneficial to health? And why might some racial and ethnic minorities' health be compromised by working longer?
8. How might volunteer organizations recruit more older racial and ethnic minorities? And why?
9. Think critically on the value society places on being productive. Why might being "productive" in later life actually be harmful for some older adults? How might it be beneficial for others?

References

Alexander, M. (2010). *The new Jim Crow: Mass incarceration in the age of colorblindness*. New Press.

Andel, R., Crowe, M., Pedersen, N. L., Mortimer, J., Crimmins, E., Johansson, B., & Gatz, M. (2015). Complexity of work and risk of Alzheimer's disease: A population-based study of Swedish twins. *The Journals of Gerontology: Psychological Sciences*, *60B*(5), 251–258. doi: 10.1093/geronb/60.5.P251.

Angel, J. L., Mudrazija, S., & Benson, R. 2015. Racial and ethnic inequalities in health. In L. K. George & K. F. Ferraro (Eds.), *Handbook of aging and the social sciences* (pp. 123–141). San Diego, CA: Elsevier.

Barnes, P. (2020, March 13). Did U.S. response to COVID-19 lag due to age discrimination? *Forbes.* https://www.forbes.com/sites/patriciagbarnes/2020/03/13/did-us-respo nse-to-covid-19-lag-due-to-age-discrimination/#3d79c1491784.

Bass, S. A., & Caro, F. G. (1993). *Achieving a productive aging society.* Westport, CT: Auburn House.

Börsch-Supan, A., & Weiss, M. (2013). *Productivity and age: Evidence from work teams at the assembly line.* (Research Memorandum No. 29). Maastricht, Netherlands: Masstricht University School of Business and Economics.

Bowen, C. E., Noack, C. M. G., & Staudinger, U. M. (2010). Aging in the work context. In K. W. Schaie (Ed.), *Handbook of the psychology of aging.* (pp. 263–278). San Diego, CA: Elsevier Academic Press.

Braveman, P., & Gruskin, S. (2003). Defining equity in health. *Journal of Epidemiology & Community Health, 57*(4), 254–258. doi: 10.1136/jech.57.4.254.

Britton, T. (2019). Does locked up mean locked out? The effects of the anti-drug act of 1986 on black male students' college enrollment (IRLE Working Paper No. 101-19).

Brown, T. (2012). The intersection and accumulation of racial and gender inequality: Black women's wealth trajectories. *The Review of Black Political Economy, 39*(2), 239–258. https://doi.org/10.1007/s12114-011-9100-8

Brown, T. H. (2014). Diverging fortunes: Racial/ethnic inequality in wealth trajectories in middle and late life. *Race Social Problems, 8,* 29–41. https://doi.org/10.1007/s12 552-016-9160-2.

Brown, T. H., & Warner, D. F. (2008). Divergent pathways? Racial/ethnic differences in older women's labor force withdrawal. *The Journals of Gerontology Series B: Psychological Sciences and Social Sciences, 63*(3), S122–S134.

Bui, T., Button, P., & Picciotti, E. (2020). Early evidence on the impact of coronavirus disease 2019 (COVID-19) and the recession on older workers. *Public Policy & Aging Report, 30*(4), 154–159. https://doi.org/10.1093/ppar/praa029.

Burr, J. A, Choi, N. G., Mutchler, J. E., & Caro, F. G., (2005). Caregiving and volunteering: Are private and public helping behaviors linked? *The Journals of Gerontology. Series B, Psychological Sciences and Social Sciences, 60*(5), S247–S256. https://doi-org.ezproxy.bu.edu/10.1093/geronb/60.5.S247.

Calvo, E. (2006, February). Does working longer make people healthier and happier? *SSRN Electronic Journal,* (Issue Brief No. 2). doi: 10.2139/ssrn.2302705.

Carlson, M. C., Kuo, J. H., Chuang, Y. F., et al. (2015). Impact of the Baltimore Experience Corps Trial on cortical and hippocampal volumes. *Alzheimers Dement, 11*(11):1340–1348. doi: 10.1016/j.jalz.2014.12.005

Carolan, K., Gonzales, E., Lee, K., & Harootyan, B. (2020). Institutional and individual factors affecting health and employment among low-income women with chronic health conditions. *Journals of Gerontology: Social Sciences, 75*(5),1062–1071. doi: 10.1093/geronb/gby149.

Carter, S. E., Ong, M. L., Simons, R. L., Gibbons, F. X., Lei, M. K., & Beach, S. R. H. (2019). The effect of early discrimination on accelerated aging among African Americans. *Health Psychology, 38*(11), 1010–1013. https://doi.org/10.1037/hea0000788

Charles, S. T. (2010). Strength and vulnerability integration: A model of emotional well-being across adulthood. *Psychology Bulletin, 136*(6), 1068–1091. https://doi.org/10.1037/a0021232

Corporation for National and Community Service (2012). *Volunteering and civic life in America 2012: Key findings on the volunteer participation and civic health of the nation.* Annual Report. Washington, DC. Retrieved from http://www.volunteeringinamerica.gov/assets/resources/FactSheetFinal.pdf.

DeWitt, L. (2010). The decision to exclude agricultural and domestic workers from the 1935 Social Security Act. *Social Security Bulletin, 70*(4), 49–68.

Dufouil, C., Pereira, E., Chêne, G., Glymour, M. M., Alpérovitch, A., Saubusse, E., Risse-Fleury, M., Heuls, B., Salord, J. C., Brieu, M. A., & Forette, F. (2014). Older age at retirement is associated with decreased risk of dementia. *European Journal of Epidemiology, 29*(5), 353–361. https://doi.org/10.1007/s10654-014-9906-3

Epperson, M., & Pettus-Davis, C. (2016, September). *Policy recommendations for meeting the grand challenge to promote smart decarceration* (Grand Challenges for Social Work Initiative Policy Brief No. 9). American Academy of Social Work & Social Welfare.

Estes, C. L., & Mahakian, J. (2001). The political economy of productive aging. In N. Morrow-Howell, J. E. Hinterlong, & M. N. Sherraden (Eds.), *Productive aging: Concepts and challenges* (pp. 197–213). Johns Hopkins University Press.

Everard, K. M., Lach, H. W., Fisher, E. B., & Baum, M. C. (2000). Relationship of activity and social support to the functional health of older adults. *The Journals of Gerontology Series B: Psychological Sciences and Social Sciences, 55*(4), S208–S212.

Ferguson, J.-P., & Koning, R. (2018). Firm turnover and the return of racial establishment segregation. *American Sociological Review, 83*(3), 445–474. https://doi.org/10.1177/0003122418767438

Fisher, G. G., Chaffee, D. S., Tetrick, L. E., Davalos, D. B., & Potter, G. G. (2017). Cognitive functioning, aging, and work: A review and recommendations for research and practice. *Journal of Occupational Health Psychology, 22*, 314–336. https://doi.org/10.1037/ocp0000086

Fried, L. P., Carlson, M. C., Freedman, M., Frick, K. D., Glass, T. A., Hill, J., McGill, S., Rebok, G. W., Seeman, T., Tielsch, J., Wasik, B. A., & Zeger, S. (2004). A social model for health promotion for an aging population: initial evidence on the Experience Corps model. *Journal of Urban Health: Bulletin of the New York Academy of Medicine, 81*(1), 64–78. https://doi.org/10.1093/jurban/jth094

Fried, L. P., Carlson, M. C., McGill, S., Seeman, T., Xue, Q. L., Frick, K., . . . Piferi, R. (2013). Experience Corps: A dual trial to promote the health of older adults and children's academic success. *Contemporary Clinical Trials, 36*(1), 1–13. doi: 10.1016/j.cct.2013.05.003.

Gattis, M. N., Morrow-Howell, N., McCrary, S., Lee, M., Jonson-Reid, M., McCoy, H., Tamar, K., Molina, A., & Invernizzi, M. (2010). Examining the effects of new york experience corps® program on young readers. *Literacy Research and Instruction, 49*(4), 299–314. https://doi.org/10.1080/19388070903117948

Geronimus, A. T., Hicken, M., Keene, D., & Bound, J. (2006). "Weathering" and age patterns of allostatic load scores among blacks and whites in the United States. *American Journal of Public Health, 96*(5), 826–833.

Ghilarducci, T., & Farmand, A. (2020). Older Workers on the COVID-19-Frontlines without Paid Sick Leave. *Journal of aging & social policy, 32*(4-5), 471–476. https://doi.org/10.1080/08959420.2020.1765685

INTEGRATING AASWSW'S GRAND CHALLENGES   253

Goldbach, J. T., Amaro, H., Vega, W., & Walter, M. D. (2015). The grand challenge of promoting equality by addressing social stigma. The American Academy of Social Work & Social Welfare, Working Paper No. 18. Retrieved on September 25, 2017, from http://aaswsw.org/wp-content/uploads/2016/01/W16-The-Grand-Challenge-of-Promoting-Equality-by-Addressing-Social-Stigma1-1-2.pdf.

Gonzales, E., Gordon, S., Whetung, C., Connaught, G., Collazo, J., & Hilton, J. (2021). Acknowledging systemic discrimination in the context of a pandemic: Advancing an anti-racist and anti-ageist movement. *Journal of Gerontological Social Work, 64*(3), 223–237. doi: 10.1080/01634372.2020.1870604.

Gonzales, E., Lee, K., & Harootyan, B. (2020). Voices from the field: Ecological factors that promote employment and health among low-income older adults with implications for direct social work practice. *Clinical Social Work Journal, 48*(2), 211–222. doi: 10.1007/s10615-019-00719-x.

Gonzales, E., Lee, Y., & Brown, C. (2015). Back to work? Not Everyone. Examining the longitudinal relationships between informal caregiving and paid work after formal retirement. *The Journals of Gerontology: Series B, 72*(3), 532–539. https://doi.org/10.1093/geronb/gbv095

Gonzales, E., Lee, J. Y., Padula, W. V., & Jung, L. S. (2018). *Exploring the consequences of discrimination and health for retirement by race and ethnicity: Results from the health and retirement study.* Chestnut Hill, MA: Center for Retirement Research at Boston College.

Gonzales, E., Matz-Costa, C., & Morrow-Howell, N. (2015). Increasing opportunities for the productive engagement of older adults: A response to population aging. *The Gerontologist, 55*(2), 252–261. https://doi.org/10.1093/geront/gnu176.

Gonzales, E., & Nowell, N. (2017). Social capital and unretirement: Exploring the bonding, bridging, and linking aspects of social relationships. *Research on Aging, 39*(10), 1100–1117. https://doi.org/10.1177/0164027516664569

Gonzales, E., Perry, T., Shen, H., & Wang, Y. (2018). Intersections of home, health and social engagement in old age: Formal volunteering as a protective factor to health after relocation. *Research on Aging, 41*(1), 31–53. https://doi.org/10.1177/0164027518773125

Gonzales, E., Shen, H., Wang, Y., Sprague Martinez, L., & Norstrand, J. (2016). Race and place: Exploring the intersection of inequity and volunteerism among older black and white adults. *Special Issue on Community and Neighborhoods: Journal of Gerontological Social Work, 59*(5), 381–400. https://doi.org/10.1080/01634372.2016.1224787.

Gonzales, E., Whetung, C., Lee, Y. J., & Kruchten, R. (2022). Work demands and cognitive health inequities by race and ethnicity: A Scoping Review. *The Gerontologist.* https://doi.org/10.1093/geront/gnac025.

Greenfield, E. A., & Marks, N. F. (2004). Formal volunteering as a protective factor for older adults' psychological well-being. *The Journals of Gerontology Series B: Psychological Sciences and Social Sciences59*(5), S258–S264. doi: 10.1093/geronb/59.5.s258.

Greenfield, J. C. (2013). The long-term costs of caring: How caring for an aging parent impacts wealth trajectories of caregivers. *All Theses and Dissertations (ETDs).* Paper 1108.

Halvorsen, C. J., & Yulikova, O. (2020). Older workers in the time of COVID-19: The Senior Community Service Employment Program and implications for social work. *Journal of Gerontological Social Work, 63*(6–7), 530–541. doi: 10.1080/01634372.2020.1774832.

Halvorsen, C. J., & Yulikova, O. (2020). Job training and so much more for low-income older adults: The Senior Community Service Employment Program. *Clinical Social Work Journal, 48*(2), 223–229. https://doi.org/10.1007/s10615-019-00734-y.

Halvorsen, C. J., Werner, K., McColloch, E., & Yulikova, O. (2023). How the senior community service employment program influences participant well-being: A participatory research approach with program recommendations. *Research on Aging, 45*(1), 77–91. https://doi.org/10.1177/01640275221098613

House, J. S. (2002). Understanding social factors and inequalities in health: 20th century progress and 21st century prospects. *Journal of Health and Social Behavior, 43*(2), 125–142.

Hughes, M. E., Waite, L. J., LaPierre, T. A., & Luo, Y. (2007). All in the family: The impact of caring for grandchildren on grandparents' health. *The Journals of Gerontology Series B: Psychological Sciences and Social Sciences, 62*(2), S108–S119.

Hughes, M. E., Waite, L. J., LaPierre, T. A., & Luo, Y. (2007). All in the family: The impact of caring for grandchildren on grandparents' health. *The Journals of Gerontology Series B: Psychological Sciences and Social Sciences, 62*(2), S108–S19.

Inkson, K., Richardson, M., & Houkamau, C. (2013). New patterns of late-career employment. In J. Field, R. J. Burke, & C. L. Cooper (Eds.), *The SAGE Handbook of Aging, Work and Society* (pp. 141–156). SAGE Publications Ltd. https://dx.doi.org/10.4135/978144 6269916.

Jang, H., Fengyan, T., Gonzales, E., Lee, Y. S., & Morrow-Howell, N. (2018). Formal volunteering as a protector of health in the context of social losses. *Journal of Gerontological Social Work, 61*(8), 834–848. doi: 1080/01634372.2018/1476945.

Johnson, K. J., Latham-Mintus, K., & Poey, J. L. (2018). Productive aging via volunteering: Does social cohesion influence level of engagement? *Journal of Gerontological Social Work, 61*(8), 817–833. https://doi.org/10.1080/01634 372.2018.1467523

Johnson, R. W., & Schaner, S. G. (2005). *Value of unpaid activities by older Americans tops $160 billion per year.* Washington, DC: The Urban Institute.

Kenner, C., Ruby, M., Jessel, J., Gregory, E., & Arju, T. (2007). Intergenerational learning between children and grandparents in east London. *Journal of Early Childhood Research, 5*(3), 219–243. doi: 10.1177/1476718x07080471.

Landsbergis, P. A., Grzywacz, J. G., & LaMontagne, A. D. (2014). Work organization, job insecurity, and occupational health disparities. *American Journal of Industrial Medicine, 57*, 495–515. https://doi.org/10.1002/ajim.22126

Lawrence, R. H., Tennstedt, S. L., & Assmann, S. F. (1998). Quality of the caregiver–care recipient relationship: Does it offset negative consequences of caregiving for family caregivers? *Psychology and Aging, 13*(1), 150.

Lee, Y. J., Gonzales, E., & Andel, R. (2022). Multifaceted demands of work and their associations with cognitive functioning: Findings from the Health and Retirement Study. *The Journals of Gerontology. Series B, Psychological Sciences and Social Sciences, 77*(2), 351–361. https://doi.org/10.1093/geronb/gbab087

Lee, Y. S., Morrow-Howell, N., Jonson-Reid, M., & McCrary, S. (2012). The effect of the Experience Corps® Program on student reading outcomes. *Education and Urban Society, 44*(1), 97–118. https://doi.org/10.1177/0013124510381262

Lee, Y., Tang, F., Kim, K. H., & Albert, S. M. (2015). The vicious cycle of parental caregiving and financial well-being: A longitudinal study of women. *The Journals of Gerontology, Series B: Psychological Sciences and Social Sciences, 70*, 425–431. doi: 10.1093/geronb/gbu001.

INTEGRATING AASWSW'S GRAND CHALLENGES 255

Lui, M., Robles, B., Leondar-Wright, B., Brewer, R., & Adamson, R. (2006). *The color of wealth: The story behind the US racial wealth divide*. New York: The New Press.

Lum, T. Y., & Lightfoot, E. (2005). The effects of volunteering on the physical and mental health of older people. *Research on Aging, 27*(1), 31–55. doi: 10.1177/0164027504271349.

Luoh, M. C., & Herzog, A. R. (2002). Individual consequences of volunteer and paid work in old age: Health and mortality. *Journal of Health and Social Behavior, 43*(4), 490–509. doi:c10.2307/3090239.

Marchiondo, L., Gonzales, E., & Ran, S. (2015). Development and validation of the workplace age discrimination scale (WADS). *Journal of Business and Psychology, 31*, 493–513. doi: 10.1007/s10869-015-9425-6

Marchiondo, L. A., Gonzales, E., & Williams, L. J. (2017). Trajectories of perceived workplace age discrimination and long-term associations with mental, self-rated, and occupational health. *The Journals of Gerontology, Series B: Psychological Sciences and Social Sciences*, 1–9. doi: 10.1093/geronb/gbx095

Matz-Costa, C., Carr, D., McNamara, T., & James, J. (2016). Physical, cognitive, social, and emotional mediators of activity involvement and health in later life. *Research on Aging, 38*(7), 791–815. https://doi.org/10.1177/0164027515606182

McBride, A. M. (2006). Civic Engagement, Older Adults, and Inclusion. *Generations: Journal of the American Society on Aging, 30*(4), 66–71. https://www.jstor.org/stable/26555488

McBride, A. M., Gonzales, E., Morrow-Howell, N., & McCrary, S. (2011). Stipends in Volunteer Civic Service: Inclusion, Retention, and Volunteer Benefits. *Public Administration Review, 71*(6), 850–858. https://doi.org/10.1111/j.1540-6210.2011.02419.x

McBride, A. M., Sherraden, M. S., & Pritzker, S. (2004). *Civic engagement among low-income and low-wealth families: In their words (CSD Working Paper No. 04-14)*. St. Louis, MO: Washington University, Center for Social Development.

Miller, G. E., & Chen, E. (2013). The biological residue of childhood poverty. *Child Development Perspectives, 7*(2), 67–73. doi: 10.1111/cdep.12021.

Morrow-Howell, N. (2010). Volunteering in later life: Research frontiers. *The Journals of Gerontology: Series B, 65*(4), 461–469. https://doi.org/10.1093/geronb/gbq024.

Morrow-Howell, N. & Gonzales, E. (2020). *Recovering from Covid-19: Resisting ageism and recommitting to a productive aging perspective*. Public Policy and Aging Report. Washington, DC: Gerontological Society of America.

Morrow-Howell, N., Gonzales, E., Harootyan, B., Lee, Y., & Lindberg, B. (2017). Approaches, policies, and practices to support the productive engagement of older adults. *Journal of Gerontological Social Work, 60*, 193–200. https://doi.org/10.1080/01634372.2016.1275912.

Morrow-Howell, N., Gonzales, E., Matz-Costa, C., & Greenfield, E. (2015). Increasing productive aging in later life (Grand Challenges for Social Work Initiative Working Paper No. 8). Cleveland, OH: American Academy of Social Work and Social Welfare.

Morrow-Howell, N., Hinterlong, J., Rozario, P., & Tang, F. (2003). Effects of volunteering on the well-being of older adults. *The Journals of Gerontology Series B: Psychological Sciences and Social Sciences, 58*(3), S137–S145. https://doi.org/10.1093/geronb/58.3.S137.

Morrow-Howell, N., Hinterlong, J., Sherraden, M., & Rozario, P. (2001). Advancing research on productivity in later life. In N. Morrow-Howell, J. Hinterlong, & M. Sherraden (Eds.), *Productive aging: Concepts and challenges* (pp. 285–313). Baltimore: Johns Hopkins University Press.

Morrow-Howell, N., Proctor, E., Choi, S., Lawrence, L., Brooks, A., Hasche, L., Dore, P., & Blinne, W. (2008). Depression in public community long-term care: implications for intervention development. *Journal of Behavioral Health Services and Research, 35*(1), 37–51. https://doi.org/10.1007/s11414-007-9098-7

Musick, M. A., Herzog, A. R., & House, J. S. (1999). Volunteering and mortality among older adults: Findings from a national sample. *The Journals of Gerontology Series B: Psychological Sciences and Social Sciences, 54*(3), S173–S180. doi: 10.1093/geronb/54b.3.s173.

Musick, M. A., & Wilson, J. (2003). Volunteering and depression: The role of psychological and social resources in different age groups. *Social Science & Medicine, 56*(2), 259–269. doi: 10.1016/s0277-9536(02)00025-4.

Musick, M. A., Wilson, J., & Bynum, W. B., Jr. (2000). Race and formal volunteering: The differential effects of class and religion. *Social Forces, 78*(4), 1539–1570. doi: 10.1093/sf/78.4.1539.

Mutchler, J. E., & Baker, L. A. (2009). The implications of grandparent coresidence for economic hardship among children in mother-only families. *Journal of Family Issues, 30*(11), 1576–1597. doi: 10.1177/0192513x09340527.

National Academies of Sciences, Engineering, and Medicine. (2022). *Understanding the Aging Workforce: Defining a Research Agenda.* Washington, DC: The National Academies Press. https://doi.org/10.17226/26173.

National Partnership for Women & Families. (2017). *More than 100 Aging and Work Experts Call on Congress to Address the Nation's Caregiving Crisis with a Strong Paid Leave Plan.* Retrieved from https://www.nationalpartnership.org/our-impact/newsroom/press-statements/more-than-100-aging-and-work-experts-call-on-congress-to-address-the-nations-caregiving-crisis-with-a-strong-paid-leave-plan.html

Ng, T. W. H., & Feldman, D. C. (2008). The relationship of age to ten dimensions of job performance. *Journal of Applied Psychology, 93*(2), 392–423. doi: 10.1037/0021-9010.93.2.392.

Pinquart, M., & Sörensen, S. (2003). Differences between caregivers and noncaregivers in psychological health and physical health: A meta-analysis. *Psychology and Aging, 18*(2), 250–267. doi: 10.1037/0882-7974.18.2.250.

Reinhard, S. C., Feinberg, L. F., Choula, R. & Houser, A. (2015). Valuing the invaluable: 2015 update. Undeniable progress, but big gaps remain. *AARP.* Retrieved January 4, 2018, from https://www.aarp.org/content/dam/aarp/ppi/2015/valuing-the-invaluable-2015-update-new.pdf.

Roth, D. L., Fredman, L., & Haley, W. E. (2015). Informal caregiving and its impact on health: a reappraisal from population-based studies. *Gerontologist, 55*(2), 309–319. https://doi.org/10.1093/geront/gnu177

Roth, D. L., Haley, W. E., Hovater, M., Perkins, M., Wadley, V. G., & Judd, S. (2013). Family caregiving and all-cause mortality: Findings from a population-based propensity-matched analysis. *American Journal of Epidemiology, 178*(10), 1571–1578. doi: 10.1093/aje/kwt225.

Roth, D. L., Perkins, M., Wadley, V. G., Temple, E. M., & Haley, W. E. (2009). Family caregiving and emotional strain: Associations with quality of life in a large national sample of middle-aged and older adults. *Quality of Life Research, 18*(6), 679–688. doi: 10.1007/s11136-009-9482-2.

Ruger, J. P., & Kim, H. J. (2006). Global health inequalities: An international comparison. *Journal of Epidemiology & Community Health, 60*(11), 928–936.

Sadana, R., Blas, E., Budhwani, S., Koller, T., & Paraje, G. (2016). Healthy ageing: raising awareness of inequalities, determinants, and what could be done to improve health equity. *The Gerontologist, 56*(Suppl 2), S178–S193. doi: 10.1093/geront/gnw034.

Salamon, L. M., Sokolowski, S. W., & Haddock, M. A. (2011). Measuring the economic value of volunteer work globally: Concepts, estimates, and a roadmap to the future. *Annals of Public and Cooperative Economics, 82*(3), 217–252.

Selden, T. M., & Berdahl, T. A. (2020). COVID-19 And Racial/Ethnic Disparities In Health Risk, Employment, And Household Composition. *Health Aff (Millwood), 39*(9), 1624–1632. https://doi.org/10.1377/hlthaff.2020.00897

Schafer, M. H., Wilkinson, L. R., & Ferraro, K. F. (2013). Childhood (mis)fortune, educational attainment, and adult health: Contingent benefits of a college degree? *Social Forces, 91*(3), 1007–1034.

Shonkoff, J. P. (2010). Building a new biodevelopmental framework to guide the future of early childhood policy. *Child Development, 81*(1), 357–367. doi: 10.1111/j.1467-8624.2009.01399.x.

Staudinger, U. M., Finkelstein, R., Calvo, E., & Sivaramakrishnan, K. (2016). A global view on the effects of work on health in later life. *The Gerontologist, 56*(Suppl 2), S281–S292. doi: 10.1093/geront/gnw032

Teasley, M. L., McCarter, S., Woo, B., Conner, L. R., Spencer, M. S., & Green, T. (2021). *Elimintate Racism. Grand Challenges of Social Work.* Retrieved from https://grandchallengesforsocialwork.org/wp-content/uploads/2021/05/Eliminate-Racism-Concept-Paper.pdf

Towers, P. (2005). *The business case for workers age 50+: Planning for tomorrow's talent needs in today's competitive environment.* Washington, DC: AARP. Retrieved from http://assets.aarp.org/rgcenter/econ/workers_fifty_plus.pdf.

U.S. Department of Labor, Employment and Training Administration. (2015). *SCSEP nationwide participant satisfaction survey report for PY2014.* Retrieved January 12, 2023, from https://www.dol.gov/sites/dolgov/files/ETA/seniors/pdfs/PY2014%20Nationwide%20Host%20Agency%20Survey%20Report.pdf

Umberson, D., & Karas Montez, J. (2010). Social relationships and health: A flashpoint for health policy. *Journal of Health and Social Behavior, 51*(1 Suppl), 54–66.

Van Willigen, M. (2000). Differential benefits of volunteering across the life course. *The Journals of Gerontology Series B: Psychological Sciences and Social Sciences, 55*(5), S308–S318. doi: 10.1093/geronb/55.5.s308.

Wakabayashi, C., & Donato, K. M. (2006). Does caregiving increase poverty among women in later life? Evidence from the Health and Retirement Survey. *Journal of Health and Social Behavior, 47*, 258–274. doi: 10.1177/002214650604700305.

Walters, K. L., Spencer, M. S., Smukler, M., Allen, H. L., Andrews, C., Browne, T., . . . Uehara, E. (2016). *Health equity: Eradicating health inequalities for future generations* (Grand Challenges for Social Work Initiative Working Paper No. 19). Cleveland, OH: American Academy of Social Work and Social Welfare.

Williams, D. R., Lawrence, J. A., & Davis, B. A. (2019). Racism and health: Evidence and needed research. *Annual Review of Public Health, 40*, 105–125. https://doi.org/10.1146/annurev-publhealth-040218-043750

10

Racism and the Grand Challenge of Ending Family Violence among Black Families

Alan J. Dettlaff, Reiko Boyd, and Tricia Bent-Goodley

> *Where justice is denied, where poverty is enforced, where ignorance prevails, and where any one class is made to feel that society is an organized conspiracy to oppress, rob, and degrade them, neither persons nor property will be safe.*
>
> —Frederick Douglass

Racism is endemic to American society and must be recognized as a potent impetus for various forms of interpersonal violence that exist among Black families. Today, Black families continue to experience violence and oppression because they exist in a society that was founded on racism and White supremacy. As such, it is not enough to singularly focus on building healthy relationships as a solution to ending violence. In this chapter we center race and racism. We deem both to be critical foci necessary for responding to the call to action of this Grand Challenge in a manner that is in line with the social justice tenets that ground our profession. In this chapter, we focus on two forms of interpersonal violence—child maltreatment and intimate partner or domestic violence—and distinguish the prevalence and experience of such problems from the system/institutional reactions that are often generated as responses to these problems. Traditional approaches to conceptualizing and responding to racial disparities in child maltreatment and intimate partner violence have largely fixated on interpersonal and individual-level factors,

Alan J. Dettlaff, Reiko Boyd, and Tricia Bent-Goodley, *Racism and the Grand Challenge of Ending Family Violence among Black Families* In: *Social Work and the Grand Challenge to Eliminate Racism*. Edited by: Martell L. Teasley, Michael S. Spencer, and Melissa Bartholomew, Oxford University Press. © Oxford University Press 2023.
DOI: 10.1093/oso/9780197674949.003.0010

with minimal recognition of structural racism and related inequities in resources, opportunities, and conditions that shape experiences and outcomes of Black families. We also aim to advance understandings of disparities that exist in interpersonal violence by bringing structural racism to the forefront, and discussing it as a fundamental root cause that creates and perpetuates the inequitable conditions that generate these disparities. The focus of this chapter is on the occurrence of child maltreatment and intimate partner violence within Black families, and the reasons that these occur. However, this does not negate the real problems of racism and racial bias connected to the statistics that are used to document the occurrence of child maltreatment and intimate partner violence in the United States among Black families.

Black Families and Child Maltreatment

According to the U.S. Department of Health and Human Services (2020), Black children comprise 20.6% of all victims of child maltreatment. This represents a disproportionate rate of maltreatment, as Black children represent only 13.7% of the child population. Among all racial groups, Black children have the second highest rate of maltreatment at 14.0 per 1,000 children (Native American children have the highest rate at 15.2 per 1,000 children). These figures represent official rates of maltreatment, as they are calculated from child protective services (CPS) agencies' reports of children who have been identified as victims of maltreatment in child protection investigations. However, these figures may not be an accurate indicator of maltreatment due to significant problems of racial bias that have been documented for decades within CPS. Studies have consistently identified racial disparities in CPS agencies, with Black children more likely than White children to be reported for maltreatment (e.g., Putnam-Hornstein et al., 2013). Once reported to this system, Black children are significantly more likely to be confirmed as victims of maltreatment than White children (e.g., Font et al., 2012; Putnam-Hornstein et al., 2013). While it is possible this is a reflection of higher rates of maltreatment, studies have consistently documented biases among professional reporters, particularly among medical personnel, that increase the likelihood that Black children will be reported to CPS (e.g., Hymel et al., 2018; Jenny et al., 1999). Studies have also documented biases within CPS systems, demonstrating that even after controlling for poverty and related risk factors, Black children are more likely to be confirmed as victims than their White counterparts (e.g., Dettlaff et al., 2011). Thus, figures reported from CPS agencies cannot be viewed as actual or reliable rates of maltreatment.

Another indicator of maltreatment that seeks to provide a better indicator of *actual* rates of maltreatment is the National Incidence Studies of Child Abuse and Neglect (NIS). The NIS is a mandated effort of the U.S. Department of Health and Human Services and has been conducted at varying intervals since 1978. The goal of the NIS is to provide estimates of the incidence of child abuse and neglect in the United States and to report changes in incidence over time. In contrast to the *official* rates of maltreatment that are determined by CPS, the NIS attempts to estimate the *actual* incidence of maltreatment in the United States by collecting data from community professionals in sentinel agencies, in addition to data from CPS. Thus, the NIS estimates include children in the official CPS statistics and those who are not. In the most recent version of the NIS-4, published in 2010, rates of maltreatment for Black children were significantly higher than those for White or Hispanic children in several maltreatment categories. While there were differences according to maltreatment type, results of the NIS-4 found that Black children experienced significantly higher rates of overall maltreatment, overall abuse, physical abuse, and serious harm from their maltreatment (Sedlak et al., 2010).

Although estimates from the NIS are often used as more reliable indicators of *actual* maltreatment rates, the community professionals used by the NIS to identify child maltreatment, which include staff from law enforcement, public schools, day cares, hospitals, mental health agencies, and others, are still vulnerable to the biases that have been documented among mandated reporters who have made official reports to child abuse hotlines. Thus, the NIS is not free of bias, and its results cannot be considered any more accurate or reliable a reflection of actual maltreatment than those reported by CPS agencies.

Nonetheless, given the available data on child maltreatment in the United States, it is possible that child maltreatment occurs disproportionately among Black families, which, if true, is likely a reflection of the increased likelihood of Black families to experience many of the risk factors associated with maltreatment, particularly poverty, which has consistently been identified as one of the strongest predictors of maltreatment (Sedlak et al. 2010). As an example of this, findings from the NIS-4 found that children in low socioeconomic status households experienced some form of maltreatment at a

ENDING FAMILY VIOLENCE AMONG BLACK FAMILIES   261

rate more than 5 times the rate of other children, and Black children were significantly more likely to live in families with low socioeconomic status (Sedlak et al. 2010). However, this is then exacerbated by racial biases among mandated reporters and CPS agents that make it more likely that Black children will come to the attention of this system and be identified as victims of maltreatment.

Black Families and Intimate Partner Violence

These issues can also be seen as they relate to intimate partner violence. In the United States, 1 in 4 women and 1 in 10 men report experiencing some form of physical violence, sexual violence, or stalking. The reported statistics are even more grave in the Black community. Over 40% (41%) of Black women report experiencing domestic violence compared to 30% of White women, and over one-third (36%) of Black men report experiencing domestic violence compared to 26% of White men (Breiding et al., 2014). These statistics are consistent across other studies, including one that found a 40%–45% reported rate of domestic violence among Black and Caribbean Americans (Stockman et al., 2014). Considering then that Black women compose 13% of the U.S. population, they are over 3 times as likely to experience domestic violence (Blackmon et al., 2017). The numbers of reported cases of domestic violence exposure translate to what is seen in domestic violence homicide. Black women are 2.5 times more likely to be killed by an intimate partner compared to White women (Violence Policy Center, 2019). Domestic violence is the leading cause of death among Black women between the ages of 15 and 35 (Rice et al., 2020).

The reported numbers need to be taken into a context that is shaped in part by a history and current track record of discriminatory treatment and systemic racism. The systemic factors that have impacted help-seeking among Black survivors of domestic violence include disparate and abusive treatment among law enforcement, lack of cultural competence and discriminatory treatment by service providers, and inaccessible and poor systems of care for mental health (Al'Uqdah et al., 2016; Bent-Goodley, 2013; Ragavan et al., 2018; Valandra et al., 2019). This chapter will further explore the realities of these current lived experiences and a persistent historical context that pervades this experience.

Historical Overview of Racism and Violence against Black Families

Systemic racism continues to fuel the violence that has been inflicted upon Black families since this country's inception and significantly contributes to violence that occurs within Black families. Approaches that aim to stop violence must incorporate an understanding of the historic and current external assaults on Black family functioning in this society, which have resulted in Black families being disproportionately impacted by conditions that instigate risk and are inherently harmful to the family unit. Ahistorical conceptualizations of family violence are fundamentally flawed because they fail to take into account significant events, laws, policies, social dynamics, and economic influences that occurred in the past but continue to shape current social determinants of health for Black families in the United States. As such, we recognize that beginning with enslavement and dehumanization, racism against Black families has been a defining characteristic of society in the United States. Below, we apply a historical lens to demonstrate how forced family separation and laws and policies to maintain White supremacy reflect the roots of interpersonal violence and inequitable system involvement among Black families.

Forced Family Separation

The institutionalization of the forced separation of Black families is a damaging, yet often overlooked, feature of the legacy of the domestic slave trade in the United States. Enslaved people were denied the right to form stable families and to keep them intact (Billingsley, 1992; Franklin & Higginbotham, 2010). Kinship ties to parents, siblings, and extended family were not honored by enslavers or the courts. Enslaved people could not legally marry and had no claim to their own children, who could be bought, sold, and traded away at their owner's discretion (Bernard, 1966; Hannah-Jones, 2019).

Historical evidence suggests that the forced separation of children from parents was cruel, widespread, and devastating. Estimates indicate that about one-third of enslaved children in the upper South experienced family separation either by being sold themselves or from losing a parent or siblings (Williams, 2012). Within historic documents, formerly enslaved Black

ENDING FAMILY VIOLENCE AMONG BLACK FAMILIES   263

people who wrote the narratives of their lives described the shock and sense of loss that accompanied the separation they experienced as children. In their accounts, they tell of infants being beaten to death or given away simply because they had annoyed enslavers with their crying or impeded the sale of their Black mothers (Williams, 2012). Documented firsthand accounts also provide evidence of the tragic and enduring emotional toll of forced separation on both children and parents (Williams, 2012). Desperate pursuits to reunify with lost family members occurred during slavery and beyond. After the Civil War, thousands of "information wanted" ads were placed in Black newspapers across the South by those in search of family members who had been sold (Williams, 2012).

The institution of slavery, with all of its vicious facets, should be understood as a massive historical trauma that continues to shape the lives of Black children, families, communities, and the systems with which they interact (National Child Traumatic Stress Network, 2016). Given that the involuntary removal of children through foster care is not the first form of family separation to disproportionately impact Black families in this country, it should be understood that the trauma of current family separations by CPS agents can be heightened by the legacy of forced family separation. For Black families, the roots of legally sanctioned separation of children from parents by societal mandates and government institutions may be firmly embedded in the dismantling of families for profit that were integral to the brutal system of slavery.

The legacy of this trauma also cannot be separated from the domestic violence that exists today. Reports of domestic violence in the Black community were first reported following the Emancipation Proclamation (Franklin, 2000). Reports of domestic violence have not been reported in Early African culture (Martin & Martin, 2003). Prior to the legal end of slavery, enslaved Africans were focused on their survival as individuals, families, and communities (Billingsley, 1992; Franklin & Higginbotham, 2010). They were attempting to deal with forced separations, the rape of Black women by White slaveholders, daily trauma associated with the mental and physical turmoil of chattel slavery, fear of constant violence perpetrated against them, and the balance between a helplessness to stop the violence and a resilience to survive it. The remnants of this pervasive trauma are relevant to what is being experienced today (Al'Uqdah et al., 2016; Bent-Goodley, 2014a). Although they were forbidden to marry, Black males and females attempted to maintain relationships and family connections. These relationships were egalitarian whereby gender roles were blurred (Billingsley, 1992; Franklin, 2000; Gillum, 2019). The first records of domestic violence in Black relationships were recorded after the establishment of the Faustian Bargain—a policy created after the Emancipation Proclamation in 1863:

> The Faustian Bargain struck by white and black men—designating the black man as head of household, allocating him higher wages, and giving him authority over black women in exchange for their labor in the fields—was the first signal after emancipation of the erosion of gender relationships in the African American community. (Franklin, 2000, p. 51)

The Faustian Bargain resulted in reports of domestic violence and, for the first time, a decrease of Black women desiring marriage (Bernard, 1966; Franklin, 2000; Bent-Goodley, 2014a). This policy designated Black men as heads of household with authority over the labor of Black women—something unheard of and unnatural to these families. Prior to this policy, Black men and women did everything possible to marry and keep relationships together (Bernard, 1966). The interjection of White supremacy, ideas of the "cult of true womanhood," and economic distinguishing according to gender into Black families created a new dynamic that had not been part of the Black experience before it.

Laws and Policies to Maintain White Supremacy

Following the Emancipation Proclamation in 1863 and the legal abolishment of slavery in the United States by the passage of the Thirteenth amendment in 1865, a series of laws, policies, and systems were enacted to maintain White supremacy and reinforce inequity in the social order through the continued subjugation of Black people. Starting in 1865, Black codes were enacted after the Civil War in Southern states in order to restrict the freedom of Black people (Franklin & Higginbotham, 2010). They were strict local and state laws governing the conduct of Black people, meant to limit freedom and to ensure the availability of Black people as a cheap labor source. Black codes detailed when, where, and how formerly enslaved people could work, and for how much compensation. They appeared throughout Southern states as a legal method of putting Black citizens into indentured servitude. Many states required Black people to sign yearly labor contracts, and if they refused, they

ENDING FAMILY VIOLENCE AMONG BLACK FAMILIES 265

could be arrested, fined, or forced into unpaid labor (Middleton, 2020). For example, in Mississippi, Black people were required to have evidence of employment for the upcoming year each January, and if they left before their contract ended they could be arrested and forced to forfeit previously earned wages (Black Codes, 2022). In South Carolina, the law barred Black people from employment in any occupation other than a farmer or a servant unless they paid an annual tax of $10 to $100 (Black Codes, 2022). Black codes varied across states, but a consistent aspect was that heavy penalties were associated with vagrancy statutes that made it a crime for Black people to be unemployed. Through Black codes, many misdemeanors or trivial offenses were treated as felonies, with harsh sentences and fines applied. Black codes prohibited interracial marriage or cohabitation, restricted the practice of professions or trades outside of menial labor, and specified that Black people could only testify in court against other Black people (Black Codes, 2022). In addition, Black codes often denied voting rights, controlled where Black people lived, restricted how they traveled, and even included provisions to seize Black children for labor purposes (Franklin & Higginbotham, 2010).

Despite the guarantees of equality in the Fourteenth Amendment, White supremacy was protected and reinforced through subsequent U.S. Supreme Court decisions and legislation. Beyond Black Codes, additional laws, policies, and practices would continue sanctioned discrimination and subvert substantial improvement in the economic status of the formerly enslaved. Oppressive practices such as sharecropping and convict leasing perpetuated cycles of poverty, exploitation, and control of Black people, while benefiting White landowners. In 1873, in the *Slaughterhouse Cases*, the Supreme Court severely reduced the protections of the newly enacted Fourteenth Amendment, ruling that actions by states could not be struck down by federal courts because the protections only applied to federal government actions and did not apply to states. Further, the Supreme Court's landmark *Plessy v. Ferguson* decision in 1896 declared that the racial segregation of Black Americans was constitutional.

Between 1881 and 1964, a majority of states and local communities passed Jim Crow laws, which were statutes and ordinances that cemented a post-slavery racial caste system and continued the oppression of Black people (Franklin & Higginbotham, 2010). Jim Crow laws systematically denied Black people of dignity and worth. They were expected to jump off the sidewalk to let White people pass and to call all White people by an honorific (Hannah-Jones, 2019). They were prohibited from using Whites-only public pools, and White businesses regularly denied Black people service, often placing "Whites Only" signs in their windows. Jim Crow laws mandated "separate but equal" status for Black people, requiring that public schools, public facilities (e.g., water fountains, restrooms, and public transportation), churches, and restaurants have separate facilities for White and Black people. The most common Jim Crow laws prohibited interracial marriage, mandated that businesses separate their customers by skin color, and protected the rights of business owners to refuse service based on skin color (Tischauser, 2012). Jim Crow laws covered nearly every area of human interaction and segregated facets of everyday life across many states and jurisdictions, including the following:

- South Carolina prohibited White and Black textile workers from using the same doors.
- Oklahoma forced phone companies to segregate phone booths.
- Memphis had separate parking spaces for Black and White drivers.
- Baltimore passed an ordinance outlawing Black people from moving onto a block more than half White, and White people from moving onto a block more than half Black.
- Georgia made it illegal for Black and White people to be buried next to one another in the same cemetery.
- Louisiana required separate buildings in state institutions for Black and White people who were blind.
- Alabama barred Black people from using public libraries.
- In the North, White politicians implemented policies that segregated Black people into slum neighborhoods and into inferior all-Black schools.
- Local school boards in Illinois and New Jersey mandated segregated schools for Black and White children (Hannah-Jones, 2019; Tischauser, 2012).

Jim Crow laws were backed in full by the U.S. Supreme Court until 1964, when the Civil Rights Act outlawed all discriminatory legislation passed by any state body, county board, or city council. The battle to end Jim Crow segregation ended successfully, but took more than 80 years and involved severe casualties, including brutal lynchings, massacres, murders, humiliation, racist court opinions, racist police violence, and the loss of constitutional rights and privileges (Tischauser, 2012).

From the enslavement of African people to the wretchedness of Jim Crow laws, racial inequity continued to permeate systems connected to the Black community. Racial inequities, as evidenced in income and wealth disparities,

ENDING FAMILY VIOLENCE AMONG BLACK FAMILIES   267

housing discrimination, criminal punishment system involvement, health and mental health inaccessibility, and even discriminatory treatment within social service systems, had a profound impact on Black families (Davis & Bent-Goodley, 2004; Gary, 2008). The Moynihan Report was one such policy that pathologized Black people and was reinforced in disproportionately publicized negative media portrayals to reinforce bias and stereotypes (Billingsley, 1992; Davis & Bent-Goodley, 2004). At the point that Black families were finally allowed to receive public assistance, as an example, new policies were interjected that had a negative impact on these families. For example, the provision of the man-in-the-house rule stated that Black families could not receive public assistance if a man was in the home (Davis & Bent-Goodley, 2004). This provision was not in place when Black families were prohibited from receiving public assistance. This "racially regulatory feature" (Bent-Goodley, 2011, p. 33) caused instability of Black families and the demonization of Black men (Roschelle, 2017) as families had to decide between receiving needed support and keeping the family intact. Such discussions are often left undiscussed and disentangled from current realities, which creates a dishonest portrayal of what is seen today.

In sum, the history of enslavement and dehumanization of Black people in the United States, forced family separation, and policies to maintain White supremacy form an unjust foundation that continues to have a reverberating impact on social, legal, and political factors that shape the experiences of Black families. Evaluating why family violence exists requires connecting to these historical factors and recognizing the role of racism in creating and promoting disproportionate risk for interpersonal violence and inequitable system involvement. As such, this history provides a crucial context for understanding the relationship between racism and the factors that contribute to this disproportionate risk, including (a) poverty, (b) health and stress, and (c) geographic contexts, which are discussed in the following section.

The Role of Racism in Creating and Perpetuating Risk for Family Violence

Racism and Poverty

Current and historic racism continue to negatively impact the economic status of Black families and are the root causes of racial disparities in poverty. Enduring consequences of racism, including racial residential segregation, discrimination in labor markets and commerce, unequal access to quality education, implicit and explicit bias, and inequitable policies perpetuate the disproportionate concentration of Black families among the poor. As such, racial disparities in income, employment, educational attainment, home ownership, wealth, and economic mobility persist and often endure across generations (Bent-Goodley & Johnson-Eanes, 2014; Chetty et al., 2018).

Recent data consistently document inequitable outcomes for Black households across various measures of poverty and wealth. According to 2018 U.S. Census data, the Black poverty rate (20.8%) remains more than twice as high as the White poverty rate (8.1%). Gaps also persist in terms of income and wages. In 2018, the median income was $70,642 for White households, while Black households had a median income of $41,361 (Semega et al., 2019). The Black/White wage gap, which indicates how much less Black workers are paid relative to White workers, increased from 20.8% in 2008 to 26.7% in 2018. Further, the adjusted Black/White wage gap, which controls for education, age, and region, has become larger over time, increasing from 10.2% in 2000 to 16.2% in 2018 (Gould, 2019).

Notable and distinct differences in the conditions of poverty experienced by Black and White people have also been documented (Jargowsky, 2015). Prior research suggests that Black poverty is more isolating and concentrated than White poverty in that it is more likely to reach beyond the household context and extend through surrounding streets, neighborhoods, schools, grocery stores, parks, and infrastructure. Black families are more likely than White families to live in neighborhoods where many other families are also poor. In most major metropolitan areas, poor White families are spread out across space, but due to a legacy of racist policies and practices, Black families tend to be clustered geographically, living in areas of concentrated poverty (Jargowsky, 2015; Rothstein, 2017).

The wealth gap. Beyond income, the residual effects of racist legal statutes, inequities perpetuated by Jim Crow laws, suppressive violence, and systematic exclusion from homeownership have contributed to persistent disparities in wealth. The Black/White wealth gap exists at every income and education level, and is accelerating. On average, White families with college degrees have $300,000 more wealth compared to Black families with college degrees, and an estimated one-third of Black families have no assets at all (Baradaran, 2017). Over the past 30 years, the average rate of wealth for White families has grown at three times the rate for the average Black family. In 2019, less than half of Black families (42%) lived in owner-occupied housing, compared to 73% of White families (Rudden, 2019). Home ownership is particularly influential on the racial wealth gap, as home ownership helps families accumulate wealth and take advantage of substantial tax savings. By contrast, being forced into the rental market can exacerbate the challenges associated with exiting from poverty. Notably, approximately 1 in 6 Black households spend more than 50% of their income on housing, which increases financial strain and limits parents' ability to devote resources to their children's education, healthcare, and other basic needs. (Stanford Center on Poverty and Inequality, 2017).

The racialized nature of poverty in the United States is a direct consequence of racism, the evidence of which can be traced across decades through formal and informal policies that have intentionally and adversely targeted Black people. Poverty and associated economic hardships are well-established risk factors for interpersonal violence. Child maltreatment risk is associated with a variety of indicators of economic hardship, including unemployment, TANF (welfare receipt), single-parent household structure, income loss, food insecurity, difficulty paying for housing, utility shutoffs, and self-reported economic stress. Prior studies also confirm that poor families are overrepresented among those reported to CPS. While the link between poverty and child maltreatment risk is generally uncontested, the link between poverty and racism has been relatively unacknowledged and unaddressed in the discourse on the etiology of racial disparities within CPS agencies.

The connection between income and wealth disparities is also intricately linked to domestic violence. Diminished economic resources make it difficult and perceptually nearly impossible to escape an abusive relationship. It is important to highlight that intimate partner violence is not isolated to any particular income bracket (Bent-Goodley, 2011). In fact, the highest reported rates of domestic violence have been reported among those within income brackets making $15,000 to $24,000 (144.0 per thousand); however, immediately following were those making between $50,000 to $74,999 (112.0 per thousand) and $75,000 and more (108.9 per thousand) (The National Center for Victims of Crime, 2017). It has been found that when one isolates socioeconomic status from domestic violence statistics, the differential rates of domestic violence between Blacks and Whites are diminished (Al'Uqdah et al., 2016; Rice et al., 2020). This statement means that one's economic status plays an even more important role in understanding rates of domestic violence than race/ethnicity (Bent-Goodley, 2011). With Black people being disproportionately impacted by income and wealth disparities, the likelihood of being represented in domestic violence statistics is correspondingly increased. Poverty reduces perceived and actual options to escape violence, and being a victim of domestic violence decreases the likelihood of a woman escaping poverty (Goodman et al., 2009). The structural violence associated with poverty, such as food insecurity, lack of affordable and safe housing, homelessness, and violence within the neighborhood ecosystem, all combine to create an increase in social isolation and a decrease in the ability to leave an abusive situation (Goodman et al., 2009; Ragavan et al., 2018; Roschelle, 2017). The survivor's focus shifts to "survival-focused coping" (St. Vil et al., 2017, p. 307), which requires constant adjustments and negotiations of safety based on the realities of economic status. The double jeopardy of poverty and domestic violence creates negative impacts on help-seeking and enhanced vulnerability (Gillum, 2019). Due to wealth disparities, Black women in middle-class families also face decision-making based on economic realities, while different from those living in poverty (Bent-Goodley, 2014b). Their high income does not reduce their exposure to living in high debt and negotiating affordable housing options when trying to leave an abusive situation. Thus, the systemic inequities that exist around poverty, income, and wealth in the Black community create a nexus of barriers that are highly influential in the lives of Black families and survivors.

Racism, Health, and Stress

Racism is also intricately linked to the dramatic and persistent racial disparities across important indicators of health for Black Americans that have been documented in numerous studies. Health disparities include increased risk of serious conditions including heart disease, stroke, diabetes, certain cancers, low birth weight, and premature birth. Racism has explicitly been identified as a fundamental cause of adverse health outcomes and inequities in health for Black people (Williams & Mohammed, 2013). According to a meta-analysis focusing on the relationship between reported racism and mental and physical health outcomes, racism is associated with poorer general health, poorer physical health, and poorer mental health, including depression, anxiety, psychological stress, and various other outcomes (Paradies et al., 2015). Empirical evidence indicates that socioeconomic factors alone do not account for racial disparities in health. At every

ENDING FAMILY VIOLENCE AMONG BLACK FAMILIES   271

level of education and income, Black people have a lower life expectancy at age 25 than do White and Latinx populations. Black people with a college degree or more education have a lower life expectancy than do White and Latinx populations who graduated from high school (Braveman et al., 2010). Racism impacts health through a number of recognized pathways, including (a) socioeconomic status opportunities (reduced access to income, employment, housing, and education); (b) stress and increased allostatic load; (c) diminished participation in healthy behaviors (e.g., sleep and exercise) and increased engagement in unhealthy behaviors as a result of coping or reduced self-regulation; and (d) physical injury from racially motivated violence (Paradies et al., 2015; Williams & Mohammed, 2013).

Research on the relationship between racism and stress has also made clear that sustained stress stemming from racial discrimination can lead to significant wear and tear on the body. Repeated experiences of discrimination can be a chronic stressor that increases vulnerability to physical illness and physical sensitivity in stressful or potentially stressful social situations (Pascoe & Smart, 2009). The experience of racial stressors among Black Americans across the life-course may contribute to "weathering," or accelerated deterioration in health, as a consequence of the cumulative physiologic burden placed on biological systems by repeated experience with discrimination, social stigma, economic adversity, and political marginalization (Geronimus et al., 2006). Researchers have also suggested that chronic experiences of racism and racial microaggressions can result in "racial battle fatigue," which includes constant anxiety and worry, hypervigilance, intrusive thoughts, headaches, elevated heart rate and blood pressure, extreme fatigue, and other physical and psychological symptoms (Smith et al., 2007; Soto et al., 2011).

Notably, prior research demonstrates a strong link between various forms of parent/family stress and child maltreatment risk (Slack et al., 2004; Slack et al., 2011). For Black families, the experience of stress stemming from enduring racial discrimination and racist treatment (interpersonal and contextual) may have adverse consequences on parenting and stress-related maltreatment risk that go beyond general experiences of stress related to parenting or economic hardship.

While stress is not viewed as a cause of domestic violence (Bent-Goodley, 2011), the context of people's lives matters. Stress creates discord and enhances pressure. Stressors, such as financial insecurity, social isolation, navigating microaggressive environments, and systemic racism, all come together to reduce help-seeking and increase poorer health and mental health outcomes, such as post-traumatic stress disorder (PTSD), depression, cardiovascular, and chronic health conditions (Bent-Goodley, 2005; Gillum, 2019). Survivors experiencing stress are also often experiencing similar pressures and reduced social support from family members, reducing the communal support structures that are often relied upon to help manage mental health and emotional difficulties (Goodman et al., 2009; Roschelle, 2017).

Racism, Geographic Contexts, and Structural Inequities

Racism has shaped macro-level conditions (e.g., racial residential segregation, access to housing, neighborhood environments, areas of concentrated poverty) that are critical determinants of opportunities, resources, and well-being for people in the United States. Historically, racially discriminatory policies and practices across federal, state, and local levels have placed decisive restrictions on where Black people could live. The consequences of such actions continue to entrench inequality across geographic and community contexts today.

Racial residential segregation and housing. More than any other group, Black individuals and families continue to bear the burden of the legacy of racial residential segregation in the United States (Williams et al., 2019). Where one lives is a critical determinant of socioeconomic status, health, and well-being. It determines access to high-quality schools, educational institutions, job opportunities, safe, affordable, and healthy housing, fresh produce and nutritious food, surrounding safety (ability to safely walk, exercise, or play outside), proximity to nature/parks/green spaces, exposure to environmental pollution/toxins (highways, factories, hazardous waste sites), affordable and reliable public transit, quality of primary medical care, social cohesion, social capital, and life expectancy (Jones, 2008). For Black households, racial residential segregation has severely restricted access to quality resources and opportunities that have stifled widespread economic mobility. As a consequence of racism, Black families have been disproportionately subjected to adverse conditions; as a result, a range of risk factors associated with compromised well-being are disproportionately concentrated among Black communities.

Increasing attention has been directed to the explicit role that federal, state, and local governments played in creating and reinforcing residential racially segregated neighborhoods. Notably, throughout most of the twentieth century, federal, state, and local governments defined where Black and White people should live by enforcing racially explicit policies. Racial residential segregation was perpetuated by intentional government action, which was not de facto but de jure, amounting to segregation by law and public policy (Rothstein, 2017). These policies were not hidden or carried out covertly under disguise. Rather, overt federal public policy explicitly segregated every major metropolitan area in the United States through the following methods:

- The Federal Housing Authority and Veterans Administration refused to insure mortgages to Black people in designated "White" neighborhoods, and would not insure mortgages for White people in neighborhoods where Black households were present. State-regulated insurance companies adopted this same policy.
- Federal and local governments made purposeful use of public housing to segregate, using taxpayer funds to build public housing that was designated as either Black or White.
- Federally backed loans were awarded to private builders only if racial restrictions were included in their subdivision deeds.
- New Deal agencies imposed segregation on integrated communities through the Public Works Administration (Rothstein, 2017).

Without the government's intentional efforts, additional causes of segregation (e.g., private prejudice, White flight, real estate steering, bank redlining, and zoning) would have existed, but they would have had far less opportunity for expression (Rothstein, 2017). Still, segregation was firmly reinforced by local laws and customs that segregated schools, hospitals, hotels, restaurants, and parks (Eberhardt, 2019). Discrimination in housing was also rampant, as racially restrictive covenants were commonplace. These were written agreements that made it obligatory for White homeowners not to sell, rent, or transfer property to any person "not of the Caucasian race" (Eberhardt, 2019). Those who violated such covenants could be sued or forced to move. Across states, courts upheld the eviction of Black people from homes they had purchased, justifying such rulings by distinguishing restrictive covenants as voluntary private contracts. As a result of such practices, by the 1940s nearly 80% of neighborhoods in cities such as Chicago and Los Angeles were off-limits to Black families (Eberhardt, 2019).

Eventually, the Civil Rights Act of 1964 and the Fair Housing Act of 1968 were meant as remedies, but the cumulative effect of racially discriminatory policy and practices in the housing market had already taken their toll. Black families had been forced into undesirable areas, with limited amenities, inferior infrastructure and institutions, substandard housing, and industrial pollution. The racist policies that entrenched inequality across the nation's landscape were so systematic and forceful that effects continue to endure in the present. Sixty-two percent of Black Americans reside in highly segregated, inner-city neighborhoods that experience a high degree of violent crime, while the majority of White people live in "highly advantaged" neighborhoods that experience little violent crime (Krivo et al., 2009).

Most of the racist policies and practices that have concentrated Black families in racially segregated high poverty areas are no longer in place, but they have never been remedied. According to one national study, the elimination of residential segregation would erase Black–White differences in income, education, and unemployment and reduce racial differences in single motherhood by two-thirds (Cutler & Glaeser, 1997).

Intimate partner violence and housing. The connection between housing and intimate partner violence is inextricable. Domestic violence is the leading cause of homelessness for women (Sullivan et al., 2019). Survivors of domestic violence are four times more likely to experience housing instability and homelessness as compared to women who have not experienced such violence (Sullivan et al., 2019). Issues of increased trauma, PTSD, depression, and anxiety are magnified among women who are homeless, and chronic family violence and poverty go hand in hand with homelessness (Sullivan et al., 2019). Nearly half of Black children (47%) experience homelessness and are seven times more likely to experience homelessness compared to White children (Roschelle, 2017). As outlined earlier, there are a multitude of reasons for this; however, the lack of affordable housing (Rice et al., 2020), structural violence as experienced through discrimination in employment and income disparities (Gary, 2008), and the impact of losing one's job due to issues such as chronic absenteeism as connected to domestic violence (Gillum, 2019; Goodman et al., 2009) create a nearly impossible scenario for domestic violence survivors from the Black community. The importance of this lived experience cannot be overestimated (Ragavan et al., 2018).

Concentrated poverty and blight. Racist policies and practices have concentrated Black families in racially segregated high poverty areas. Sixty-two percent of Black Americans reside in highly segregated, inner-city neighborhoods that experience a high degree of violent crime, while the majority of White people live in "highly advantaged" neighborhoods that experience little violent crime (Krivo et al., 2009). Prior research indicates that among the largest 171 cities in the United States, there is not one city in which White people live under equivalent conditions to Black people, and that the worst urban context in which White people reside is considerably better than the average context of Black communities (Sampson & Wilson, 2013). Communities of concentrated poverty tend to have high levels of neighborhood disadvantage and low-quality housing stock, resulting in both government and the private sector disinterest and divestment, which contributes to elevated exposure to physical and chemical hazards, increased prevalence of psychosocial stressors, and reduced access to a broad range of resources that enhance health. Thus, the living conditions created by concentrated poverty and segregation hinder health and result in adverse health outcomes by making it more difficult for residents to practice healthy behaviors (Williams et al., 2019).

Over-policing, over-incarceration, and police violence. Racism in this country has contributed to a criminal punishment system and society in which race has been reflexively treated as a visible marker of criminality (Eberhardt, 2019). The problems of mass incarceration and racial disparity at every decision point of the criminal punishment system have been extensively documented, as have their disturbing consequences for individuals and families (Acker et al., 2019). Black people are incarcerated in state prisons at a rate that is 5.1 times the imprisonment of White people. In five states, the disparity is more than 10 to 1, and in 12 states, more than half of the prison population is Black. In 11 states, at least 1 in 20 adult Black males is in prison (Nellis, 2016).

Furthermore, over 700,000 people are released from prisons every year, and nearly two out of three are rearrested within a few years of being released. Most of such arrests are for breaking the rules of parole, not for new crimes (Eberhardt, 2019). Mandatory supervision and regulations of parole that govern those newly released from prison subject those individuals to years of routine surveillance and risk of reimprisonment for commonplace "offenses," such as failure to secure employment, inability to pay court fines and fees, missing appointments, or missing curfew (Eberhardt, 2019). People on parole can be stopped and searched by police at any time, even without a reasonable suspicion or probable cause, and Black people are disproportionately subject to these conditions. Consequences of mass incarceration also impact neighborhood dynamics. When Black people disproportionately make up the population of those on probation and of those arrested, racial disparities can serve to criminalize whole neighborhoods through indiscriminate law enforcement stops and over-policing (Eberhardt, 2019).

Numerous studies also document stark racial disparities in police maltreatment (Desmond et al., 2016). Black boys and men are disproportionately subject to excessive and deadly police force, even after accounting for situational factors of the encounter (e.g., resisting arrest) and officer characteristics (e.g., age, training) (Terrill & Reisig, 2003). Studies also show that police disproportionately use improper and deadly force on Black men (Matulia 1982; Worden, 2015).

According to research based on police stop data, Black people are disproportionately stopped by police, even adjusting for factors such as the crime rate and racial composition of residents in the areas where stops take place (Eberhardt, 2019). Not only are Black people more likely than White people to be stopped, they are also more likely to be searched, handcuffed, and arrested. A study of Oakland police stops indicated that across a 13-month period, 65% of police officers had conducted a discretionary search on a Black person, while only 23% had conducted such a search on a White person. In addition, 72% of police officers had handcuffed a Black person during the course of a stop, even when no arrest was made, while only 26% of officers had handcuffed a White person who was not arrested (Eberhardt, 2019). A U.S. Department of Justice report on contacts between police and the public, released in 2011, found that while White, Black, and Latinx people were stopped at similar rates nationwide, Black drivers were three times as likely to be searched during a stop as White drivers and twice as likely as Latinx drivers (Eith & Durose, 2011). Black drivers were also twice as likely to experience the use or threat of violent force at the hands of police officers compared to both White and Latinx drivers (Eith & Durose, 2011).

Furthermore, according to a meta-analysis of 18.5 million traffic stops across the country, when pulled over, Black drivers are more than twice as likely to have been stopped for high- discretion equipment violations as opposed to moving violations compared to other drivers. Discretionary stops involve stopping drivers for equipment-related issues such as a broken light, expired tag, faulty turn signal, or unfastened seat belt. In law enforcement, discretionary stops have traditionally been considered valid crime-fighting tools that give officers a way to investigate who drivers are and give wide latitude to follow up on the slightest suspicion. These types of practices can reinforce and activate biases that contribute to racial disparities across decision points in the criminal punishment system. For example, studies also document racial disparities in plea bargaining (Eberhardt, 2019). The institutional practice of plea-bargaining puts pressure on people to plead guilty to crimes, even ones they did not commit. Black defendants are more likely than those of any other background to be offered plea deals that require prison time, particularly for drug-related crimes.

Poor and unemployed Black women also experience higher rates of arrest compared to White women in the same status (Holland-Davis & Davis, 2014). Black women are two times as likely to be arrested compared to White women (Holland-Davis & Davis, 2014). The majority (68%) of Black women that are incarcerated report having experienced domestic violence (Gross, 2015; Richie, 2012). Black women who are survivors of domestic violence are more likely to experience dual arrest due to fighting the perpetrator back (Holland-Davis & Davis, 2014; St. Vil. et al., 2017) and negative perceptions and stereotypes of Black women such as being angry or combative (Hill-Collins, 2008; Richie, 1996). The negative experiences of Black men with the criminal punishment system, particularly as it connects to law enforcement, creates a mistrust of the criminal punishment system and the perception that it is not a viable option for help (Alexander, 2020; Bent-Goodley, 2004; Richie, 2012; St. Vil. et al., 2017). For these reasons, many survivors in the Black community avoid interactions with police, the criminal punishment system, and other formal provider systems (Bent-Goodley & Smith, 2017; Ragavan et al., 2018; Rice et al., 2020; Valandra et al., 2019).

This section has reviewed the relationship between racism and the societal factors that contribute to interpersonal violence among Black families, including poverty, health and stress, and geographic contexts including racial residential segregation and over-policing. Considered together, these factors demonstrate how racist laws, practices, and policies have concentrated various conditions of risk among Black families. As such, racism can be understood as a common denominator across systems and contexts that accounts for why Black families may disproportionately experience adverse conditions associated with family violence.

Evidence-Based and Evidence-Informed Strategies for Ending Family Violence

Throughout this chapter we have focused squarely on race and racism, demonstrating the structural roots of disparities in interpersonal violence. In discussing strategies for ending child maltreatment and intimate partner violence among Black families, we again argue that a structural lens is essential. We reject all notions and conclusions that normalize disparities and fail to apply an anti-racist lens to understanding the causes and potential responses to these issues.

In terms of evidence-based strategies, the field continues to direct the majority of resources and attention to interventions that center the problem on the individual and ignore the structural problems that create conditions of risk and reproduce systemic disadvantage. The limited state of evidence-based interventions that address family violence is a function of this tilted focus. In particular, the child maltreatment prevention evidence base is weighted heavily with studies that focus on individual- or family-level risks, as decades of research on the etiology of maltreatment and child welfare system involvement has produced a body of evidence that focuses overwhelmingly on parental deficits and individual-level risk factors.

In line with other scholars who have focused on racial disparities across sectors, we acknowledge that the standard frame that shapes most thinking about how to best correct racial inequality is incorrect (Darity, 2019). Specifically, emphasizing individual or group-based deficiencies in behavior as a root cause of adverse outcomes or conditions (e.g., low income, unemployment) presumes that improvements in key outcomes are inhibited by human capital or developmental deficits. This way of thinking posits education and training as "logical" responses to problems, making them all-purpose solutions for eliminating racial disparities. This standard frame pathologizes individuals and groups at the center of disparities and ignores, or at best grossly underestimates, the impact of both structural racism and interpersonal discrimination on outcomes that are plagued by persistent disparities. As a counter, Darity (2019) proposes an alternative frame for confronting racial inequality, which emphasizes linked deficiencies in resources and options rather than deficiencies in human capital, thus promoting the general principle that racial gaps are best removed by direct redistributive measures, rather than ineffective indirect measures such as increasing Black educational attainment. Applying this frame, Darity (2019) proposes a new agenda for eliminating racial inequality that aims to increase resources for Black Americans rather than "improve" Black Americans. This alternate frame stresses conditions of resources deprivation, structural racism, and the cumulative effects of anti-Black discriminatory policies as fundamental causes of racial inequality (Darity, 2019).

In agreement with Darity (2019), we echo the assertion that a new agenda for transformative change can only emerge when we fundamentally alter the frame that has traditionally been used for understanding disparities in family violence. As such, we call for a major shift in the current frame for thinking about racist inequities and hope to shine light on the glaring gaps in both the evidence base and in the range of responses that are currently in place.

To address interpersonal violence among Black families and to remediate conditions that disproportionately expose Black families to adverse conditions and risks, structural interventions must be considered and pursued as part of multi-sector, multi-level approaches. Structural interventions work by altering the context within which health and well-being are produced and reproduced (Blakenship et al., 2000). Structural interventions aim to change the social, physical, economic, or political environments that may shape or constrain individual, community, and social health and well-being outcomes, altering the larger social context in which disparities emerge and persist (Blakenship et al., 2000; Brown, et al., 2019). Examples of structural interventions have been detailed and reviewed in several prior works (Bailey et al., 2017; Brown et al., 2019; Thornton et al., 2017).

As explained by Bailey et al. (2017), approaches in structural interventions may include (1) using focused external forces that act on multiple sectors at once (e.g., place-based multisector initiatives such as Purpose Built Communities, Promise Neighborhoods, and Choice Neighborhoods); (2) disrupting leverage points within a sector that might have ripple effects in the system (e.g., reforming drug policy and reducing excessive incarceration); and (3) divorcing institutions from the racial discrimination system (e.g., by training the next generation of professionals about structural racism). Prior studies demonstrate that there is sufficient evidence to support policy interventions that focus on the social determinants of health, including interventions targeted at education and early childhood, urban planning and community development, housing, income enhancements and supplements, and employment interventions focused on upstream social determinants (Thornton et al., 2017). Though these show promise for achieving enduring improvements, it is notable that structural interventions also challenge firmly rooted political, social, and economic interests, and can also challenge deeply held beliefs in principles of individualism and individual autonomy (Blakenship et al., 2000).

Applying an Anti-Racist Framework
to Violence Prevention

Applying an anti-racist framework to the prevention of family violence begins by acknowledging that violence within Black families is the result of racial inequities within society. An anti-racist framework further acknowledges that these racial inequities are the result of racist policies that have been intentionally designed to produce and maintain this inequity. In this way, an anti-racist framework for ending family violence acknowledges and understands the racist origins of the United States and the means by which this country has oppressed Black families through its racist policies. An anti-racist framework acknowledges that these racist origins are so deeply rooted in our state and federal policies that they cannot simply be modified or revised. Rather, they have to be recreated with the specific goal of eliminating harm and racist inequities. Thus, applying an anti-racist framework to violence prevention begins by identifying and acknowledging the policies that produce and maintain the racist inequities that contribute to violence in Black families, and recreates those policies in a way that is designed to achieve racial equity as a means of reducing and eliminating violence.

Accordingly, an anti-racist framework isn't one of reform; it is one of abolition and re-creation. Policies need to be created that remedy the centuries of disadvantage Black families have experienced as a result of racist policies beginning with the Black Codes and extending through Jim Crow Laws, redlining, and decades of currently existing policies that contribute to racist inequities. These policies need to be specifically designed to remedy existing disparities in the wage and wealth gaps that persist between Black and White Americans, as well as disparities in home ownership and residential segregation.

These remedies also need to include divestment in the systems that oppress Black Americans and a complete reallocation of those funds to strengthen and support Black families and communities from a culturally centered and trauma-informed lens. These systems include the criminal punishment system and the family policing system, which includes CPS agencies. These systems of oppression are the source of many of the racist inequities that exist in society. These inequities will only be eliminated when these systems are dismantled and a fundamental shift occurs in the flow of resources that are designed to protect and promote public safety.

ENDING FAMILY VIOLENCE AMONG BLACK FAMILIES   281

Eliminating the racist inequities that contribute to family violence will require bold steps that completely reimagine our understanding of public safety. A future where family violence no longer exists requires a fundamental reimagining of how society responds to families in need, where families are strengthened and supported, rather than surveilled and separated. Ultimately, ending family violence will only be achieved when this vision for our future becomes our reality.

Study Questions

1. Why is a focus on building healthy relationships not sufficient for addressing violence among Black families?
2. This chapter suggests that official rates of child maltreatment reported by CPS agencies or the National Incidence Studies of Child Abuse and Neglect that report higher rates of maltreatment among Black families should be viewed with skepticism. Why is this?
3. Discuss the ways in which forcible family separations during the time of human chattel slavery in the United States are related to the current practice of forcible family separations conducted by state agents.
4. How has the historical development and implementation of policies in the United States contributed to the current experiences of violence among Black families? What are some of the policies that have resulted in a significant contribution to the experience of violence within Black families?
5. Risk for violence within families is often discussed at the individual or family level. Describe the ways in which the focus on individual- or family-level risk factors are an insufficient conceptualization and understanding of risk.
6. What are the ways in which police violence within communities may contribute to violence experienced within Black families?
7. The chapter suggests that current responses to child maltreatment and intimate partner violence that involve policing and punishment through the criminal punishment and family policing systems exacerbate the violence and oppression experienced by Black families. What are strategies to respond to child maltreatment and intimate partner violence that do not involve policing and punishment?

References

Acker, J., Braveman, P., Arkin, E., Leviton, L., Parsons, J., & Hobor, G. (2019). *Mass incarceration threatens health equity in America: Executive summary*. Princeton, NJ: Robert Wood Johnson Foundation.

Alexander, M. (2020). *The New Jim Crow: Mass incarceration in the age of colorblindness*. New York: The New Press.

Al'Uadah, S. N., Maxwell, C., & Hill, N. (2016). Intimate partner violence in the African American community: Risk, theory and interventions. *Journal of Family Violence, 31*, 877–884.

Bailey, Z. D., Krieger, N., Agénor, M., Graves, J., Linos, N., & Bassett, M. T. (2017). Structural racism and health inequities in the USA: Evidence and interventions. *The Lancet, 389*(10077), 1453–1463.

Baradaran, M. (2017). *The color of money: Black banks and the racial wealth gap*. Cambridge, MA: Harvard University Press.

Bent-Goodley, T. B. (2004). Policy implications of domestic violence for people of color. In K. E. Davis & T. B. Bent-Goodley (Eds.), *The color of social policy* (pp. 65–80). Alexandria, VA: Council on Social Work Education Press.

Bent-Goodley, T. B. (2005). An African centered approach to domestic violence. *Families in Society, 86*, 197–206.

Bent-Goodley, T. B. (2011). *The ultimate betrayal: A renewed look at intimate partner violence*. Washington, DC: NASW Press.

Bent-Goodley, T. B. (2013). Domestic violence fatality reviews and the African American community. *Homicide Studies, 17*, 375–390.

Bent-Goodley, T. B. (Ed). (2014a). *By grace: The challenges, strengths and promise of African American marriages*. Washington, DC: NASW Press.

Bent-Goodley, T. B. (2014b). An exploration of African American women's perceptions of the intersection of domestic violence and HIV/AIDS. *Journal of HIV/AIDS and Social Services, 13*, 97–116.

Bent-Goodley, T. B., & Johnson-Eanes, B. (2014). African American marriage and economics. In T. B. Bent-Goodley (Ed.), *By grace: The challenges, strengths and promise of African American marriages* (pp. 13–24). Washington, DC: NASW Press.

Bent-Goodley, T. B., & Smith, C. M. (2017). An African-centered approach to community policy. *Journal of Human Behavior and the Social Environment, 27*, 92–99.

Bernard, J. (1966). *Marriage and family among Negroes*. Hoboken, NJ: Prentice Hall.

Billingsley, A. (1992). *Climbing Jacob's ladder: The enduring legacy of African American families*. New York: Simon & Schuster.

Black Codes. (2022, January 26). History.com. Retrieved March 18, 2022, from https://www.history.com/topics/black-history/black-codes.

Blackmon, S. M., Owens, A., Geiss, M. L., Laskowsky, V., Donahue, S., & Ingram, C. (2017). Am I my sister's keeper? Linking domestic violence attitudes to Black racial identity. *Journal of Black Psychology, 43*, 230–258.

Blakenship, K. M., Bray, S. J., & Merson, M. H. (2000). Structural interventions in public health. *AIDS, 14*(S1), S11–S21.

Braveman, P. A., Cubbin, C., Egerter, S., Williams, D. R., & Pamuk, E. (2010). Socioeconomic disparities in health in the United States: What the patterns tell us. *American Journal of Public Health, 100*(S1), S186–S196.

ENDING FAMILY VIOLENCE AMONG BLACK FAMILIES   283

Breiding, M. J., Smith, S. G., Basile, K. C., Walters, M. L., Chen, J., & Merrick, M. T. (2014). Prevalence and characteristics of sexual violence, stalking, and intimate partner violence victimization: National Intimate Partner and Sexual Violence Survey, United States, 2011. *Morbidity and Mortality Weekly Report, 63*, 1–18.

Brown, A. F., Ma, G. X., Miranda, J., Eng, E., Castille, D., Brockie, T., . . . Trinh-Shevrin, C. (2019). Structural interventions to reduce and eliminate health disparities. *American Journal of Public Health, 109*(S1), S72–S78.

Chetty, R., Hendren, N., Jones, M., & Porter, S. (2018). *Race and economic opportunity in the United States: An intergenerational perspective.* Cambridge, MA: National Bureau of Economic Research.

Cutler, D. M., & Glaeser, E. L. (1997). Are ghettos good or bad? *The Quarterly Journal of Economics, 112*(3), 827–872.

Darity, W. (2019). A new agenda for eliminating racial inequality in the United States: The research we need. William T. Grant Foundation. Retrieved from https://wtgrantfou ndation.org/library/uploads/2019/01/A-New-Agenda-for-Eliminating-Racial-Ine quality-in-the-United-States_WTG-Digest-2018.pdf.

Davis, K. E., & Bent-Goodley, T. B. (Eds.). (2004). *The color of social policy.* Alexandria, VA: Cuncil on Social Work Education Press.

Desmond, M., Papachristos, A. V., & Kirk, D. S. (2016). Police violence and citizen crime reporting in the black community. *American Sociological Review, 81*(5), 857–876.

Dettlaff, A. J., Rivaux, S., Baumann, D., Fluke, J., Rycraft, J., & James, J. (2011). Disentangling substantiation: The influence of race, income, and risk on the substantiation decision in child welfare. *Children and Youth Services Review, 33*, 1630–1637.

Eberhardt, J. (2019). *Biased: Uncovering the hidden prejudice that shapes what we see, think, and do.* New York, NY: Viking.

Eith, C. A., & Durose, M. R. (2011). *Contacts between police and the public, 2008.* Washington, DC: US Department of Justice, Office of Justice Programs, Bureau of Justice Statistics.

Font, S. A., Berger, L. M., Slack, K. S. (2012). Examining racial disproportionality in child protective services case decisions. *Children and Youth Services Review, 34*, 2188–2200.

Franklin, D. L. (2000). *What's love got to do with it? Understanding and healing the rift between Black men and women.* New York: Simon & Schuster.

Franklin, J. H., & Higginbotham, E. (2010). *From slavery to freedom: A history of African Americans* (9th ed). New York: McGraw-Hill.

Gary, L. E. (2008). A social profile. In D. P. Aldridge (Ed.), *Our last hope: Black male-female relationships in change* (pp. 50–75). Bloomington, IN: Author House.

Geronimus, A., Hicken, M., Keene, D., & Bound, J. (2006). "Weathering" and age patterns of allostatic load scores among blacks and whites in the United States. *American Journal of Public Health, 96*, 826–833.

Gillum, T. (2019). The intersection of intimate partner violence and poverty in Black communities. *Aggression and Violent Behavior, 46*, 37–44.

Goodman, L. A., Smyth, K. F., Borges, A. M., & Singer, R. (2009). When crises collide: How intimate partner violence and poverty intersect to shape women's mental health and coping? *Trauma, Violence & Abuse, 10*, 306–329.

Gould, E. (2019, February 20). *State of working America wages 2018.* Washington, DC: Economic Policy Institute.

Gross, K. N. (2015). African American women, mass incarceration, and the politics of protection. *Journal of American History, 102*(1), 25–33.

Hannah-Jones, N. (2019, August 14). Introduction: 1619 Project. *New York Times Magazine*, pp. 14–22.

Hill-Collins, P. (2008). *Black feminist thought: Knowledge, consciousness and the politics of empowerment*. New York: Routledge.

Holland-Davis, L., & Davis, J. (2014). Victim arrest in intimate partner violence incidents: A multilevel test of Black's theory of law. *The Journal of Public and Professional Sociology, 6*, 3–24.

Hymel, K. P., Laskey, A. L., Crowell, K. R., Wang, M., Armijo-Garcia, V., Frazier, T. N., . . . Weeks, K. (2018). Racial and ethnic disparities and bias in the evaluation and reporting of abusive head trauma. *The Journal of Pediatrics, 198*, 137–143.

Jargowsky, P. (2015). *The architecture of segregation: Civil unrest, the concentration of poverty, and public policy*. New York, NY: The Century Foundation.

Jenny, C., Hymel, K. P., Ritzen, A., Reinert, S. E., Hay, T. C. (1999). Analysis of missed cases of abusive head trauma. *Journal of the American Medical Association, 282*, 621–626.

Jones, C. (2008). Unnatural causes: Is inequality making us sick? Edited Interview with Dr. Camara Jones Research Director on Social Determinants of Health, Centers for Disease Control, PBS California Newsroom. https://unnaturalcauses.org

Krivo, L., Peterson, R., & Kuhl, D. C. (2009). Segregation, racial structure, and neighborhood violent crime. *American Journal of Sociology, 114*(6), 1765–1802.

Martin, E. P., & Martin, J. M. (2003). *Spirituality and the Black helping tradition in social work*. Washington, DC: NASW Press.

Matulia, K. J. (1982). *A balance of forces*. Alexandria, VA: International Association of Chiefs of Police.

Middleton, S. (2020). Repressive legislation: Slave codes, northern black laws, and southern black codes. In J. Daily (Ed.), *Oxford Research Encyclopedia of American History*. https://oxfordre.com/americanhistory/view/10.1093/acrefore/9780199329175.001.0001/acrefore-9780199329175-e-634.

National Center for Victims of Crime (2017). Intimate partner violence. Washington, DC: National Center for Victims of Crime. https://www.ncjrs.gov/ovc_archives/ncvrw/2017/images/en_artwork/Fact_Sheets/2017NCVRW_IPV_508.pdf.

National Child Traumatic Stress Network. (2016). *Racial injustice and trauma: African Americans in the U.S.* Los Angeles, CA: National Child Traumatic Stress Center.

Nellis, A. (2016). *The color of justice: Racial and ethnic disparity in state prisons*. Washington, DC: The Sentencing Project.

Paradies, Y., Ben, J., Denson, N., Elias, A., Priest, N., Pieterse, A., Gupta, A., Kelaher, M., & Gee, G. (2015). Racism as a determinant of health: a systematic review and meta-analysis. *PloS One, 10*(9), 1–48.

Pascoe, E. A., & Smart Richman, L. (2009). Perceived discrimination and health: A meta-analytic review. *Psychological Bulletin, 135*(4), 531.

Putnam-Hornstein, E., Needell, B., King, B., & Johnson-Motoyama, M. (2013). Racial and ethnic disparities: A population-based examination of risk factors for involvement with child protective services. *Child Abuse & Neglect, 37*, 33–46.

Ragavan, M., Thomas, K. A., Fulambarker, A., Zaricor, J., Goodman, L. A., & Bair-Merritt, M. H. (2018). Exploring the needs and lived experiences of racial and ethnic minority domestic violence survivors through community-bsaed participatory research: A systematic review. *Trauma, Violence & Abuse, 20*, 1–18.

ENDING FAMILY VIOLENCE AMONG BLACK FAMILIES 285

Rice, J., West, C. M., Cottman, K., & Gardner, G. (2020). The intersectionality of intimate partner violence in the Black community. In R. Geffner, J. W. White, K. Hamberger, A. Rosenbaum, V. Vaughan-Eden, & V. I. Vieth's (Eds)., *Handbook of intimate partner violence across the lifespan* (pp. 1–29). Springer Publishing.

Richie, B. E. (1996). *Compelled to crime: The gender entrapment of battered black women*. Routledge.

Richie, B. E. (2012). *Arrested justice: Black women, violence and America's prison nation*. New York: NYU Press.

Rothstein, R. (2017). *The color of law: A forgotten history of how our government segregated America*. New York: Liveright.

Rudden, J. (2019). *Homeownership rate in the U.S. 2019, by ethnicity*. Available from www.statista.com.

Sedlak, A. J., Mettenburg, J., Basena, M., Petta, I., McPherson, K., Greene, A., & Li, S. (2010). *Fourth national incidence study of child abuse and neglect (NIS-4): Report to Congress*. Washington, DC: U.S. Department of Health and Human Services, Administration for Children and Families.

Semega, J., Kollar, M., Creamer, J., & Mohanty, A. (2019). *Current population reports, P60-266, income and poverty in the United States: 2018*. Washington, DC: U.S. Census Bureau.

Slack, K., Berger, L., DuMont, K., Yang, M., Kim, B., Ehrhard-Dietzel, S., & Holl, J. (2011). Risk and protective factors for child neglect during early childhood: A cross-study comparison. *Children and Youth Services Review, 33*, 1354–1363.

Slack, K. S., Holl, J. L., McDaniel, M., Yoo, J., & Bolger, K. (2004). Understanding the risks of child neglect: An exploration of poverty and parenting characteristics. *Child maltreatment, 9*(4), 395–408.

Smith, W. A., Allen, W. R., & Danley, L. L. (2007). "Assume the position . . . you fit the description": Psychosocial experiences and racial battle fatigue among African American male college students. *American Behavioral Scientist, 51*(4), 551–578.

Soto, J., Dawson-Andoh, N., & BeLue, R. (2011). The relationship between perceived discrimination and generalized anxiety disorder among African Americans, Afro Caribbeans, and non-Hispanic Whites. *Journal of Anxiety Disorders, 25*, 258–265.

Stanford Center on Poverty and Inequality. (2017). *State of the union: The poverty and inequality report*. Stanford, CA: Stanford Center on Poverty and Inequality.

Stockman, J. K., Lucea, M. B., Bolyard, R., Bertand, D., Callwood, G. B., Sharps, P. W., Campbell, D. W., & Campbell, J. C. (2014). Intimate partner violence among African American and Caribbean women: Prevalence, risk factors, and the influence of cultural attitudes. *Global Health Action, 7*, 1–9.

St. Vil, N. M., Sabri, B., Nwokolo, V., Alexander, K. A., & Campbell, J. C. (2017). A qualitative study of survival strategies used by low-income Black women who experience intimate partner violence. *Social Work, 62*, 63–71.

Sullivan, C. M., Lopez-Zeron, G., Bornsta, H., & Menard, A. (2019). "There's just all these moving parts": Helping domestic violence survivors obtain housing. *Clinical Social Work Journal, 47*, 198–206.

Terrill, W., & Reisig, M. D. (2003). Neighborhood context and police use of force. *Journal of Research in Crime and Delinquency, 40*(3), 291–321.

Thornton, R. L., Glover, C. M., Cené, C. W., Glik, D. C., Henderson, J. A., & Williams, D. R. (2016). Evaluating strategies for reducing health disparities by addressing the social determinants of health. *Health Affairs, 35*(8), 1416–1423.

Tischauser, L. V. (2012). *Jim crow laws*. Santa Barbara, CA: ABC-CLIO.

U.S. Department of Health & Human Services, Administration for Children and Families, Administration on Children, Youth and Families, Children's Bureau. (2020). *Child maltreatment 2018*. https://www.acf.hhs.gov/cb/research-data-technology/statistics-research/child-maltreatment.

Valandra, Murphy-Erby, Y., Higgins, B. M., & Brown, L. M. (2019). African American perspectives and experiences of domestic violence in a rural community. *Journal of Interpersonal Violence, 34*, 3319–3343.

Violence Policy Center. (2019). *When men murder women: An analysis of 2017 homicide data*. Washington, DC: Violence Poverty Center.

Williams, D., Lawrence, J., & and Davis, B. (2019). Racism and health: Evidence and needed research. *Annual Review of Public Health, 40*, 105–12.

Williams, D. R., & Mohammed, S. A. (2013). Racism and health I: Pathways and scientific evidence. *American Behavioral Scientist, 57*(8), 1152–1173.

Williams, H. (2012). *Help me to find my people: The African American search for family lost in slavery*. Chapel Hill: University of North Carolina Press.

Worden, R. E. (2015). *The causes of police brutality: Theory and evidence on police use of force* (Vol. 2, pp. 149–204). New York, NY: Routledge.

11

Beyond Colorism

The Impact of Racialization in U.S. Latinxs

Rocío Calvo, Jandel Crutchfield, and Jorge Delva

That the writing of this chapter coincides with two deadly epidemics, COVID-19 and racism, and a continuing broken immigration system, presents both a duty and opportunity to the social work profession. There is a duty for those steeped in social justice issues to magnify and lift how society's social fabric is currently failing its citizens in ways that result in death and grief. But more importantly, these pandemics present the opportunity to crystallize—for those who refuse or fail to acknowledge the negative impacts of White supremacy—that this mass grief and death are an ongoing experience for people of color. Hence, the disproportionate effect of COVID-19 in the Latinx community is the direct result of decades of unequal access to advancement opportunities. These disparities will continue long after the pandemic's end if we do not eradicate White supremacy.

This chapter argues that through symbolic indicators of colorism, immigration, and language, Latinxs have been racialized as non-White individuals unfit to become part of the American social fabric. We will dwell on the impact of this process of *otherism* on Latinxs' well-being to then provide an account of interventions that have shown promise in counteracting the harmful effects of White supremacy on Latinx communities.

Let's begin by clarifying frequently asked questions about terminology—namely, *who* is Latinx, and if Latinx is different from Hispanic or Latino/a. The short answer to the question of who is Latinx is "anybody that self-identifies as such" (Lopez et al., 2020). We recognize that this answer does not address the complex process of identity formation, especially one that stands at the crossroads of race and ethnicity. We also acknowledge that we tend to conduct our daily lives without considering the labels we utilize to classify

---

Rocío Calvo, Jandel Crutchfield, and Jorge Delva, *Beyond Colorism* In: *Social Work and the Grand Challenge to Eliminate Racism*. Edited by: Martell L. Teasley, Michael S. Spencer, and Melissa Bartholomew, Oxford University Press.
© Oxford University Press 2023. DOI: 10.1093/oso/9780197674949.003.0011

others into neatly established ethnoracial categories. Yet, it is vital to keep in mind that both terms—ethnicity and race—are socially constructed, and therefore far from simple. For example, the pan-ethnic qualifier "Hispanic" was created in 1976 by the U.S. Congress by the passage of Public Law 94-311, which mandates "the publication of economic and social statistics of Americans of Spanish origin descent" (Rumbaut, 2011, p. 3). Since then, "Hispanic" or "Latino"—the latter term was introduced in the 2000 Census—are used interchangeably to collect official statistics about individuals who self-identify as "Hispanic, Latino/a or Spanish origin," regardless of race (Rumbaut, 2011).

A more nuanced understanding of Latinx—a gender-neutral alternative to its predecessors Hispanic, Latino/a—denotes ethnicity or group belonging based on shared language, values, or culture (Cornell & Hartmann, 2007). Many dispute this shared heritage by pointing that while Mexicans, Cubans, and Puerto Ricans are considered Latinxs in the United States, others with similar cultural values, like Brazilians, are excluded from this qualifier (Marrow, 2003). Some question altogether the imposition of a pan-ethnic label to create a homogenous group that could not be further from uniform. The argument is that racializing nearly one-fifth of the U.S. population into a unique *Latinidad* identity minimizes striking differences within this group, and more importantly, masks vast inequities (Astrada & Astrada, 2017). It is essential to recognize that, despite common cultural and social characteristics, Latinx remains a socially constructed term that aggregates very different people into a single category. Other indicators, such as country of origin, socioeconomic factors, generations in the United States, and skin tone, have been proposed as better indicators of commonality than an assumed shared identity (Jones-Correa & Leal, 1996).

One way to test how well the Latinx label captures the ethnoracial identity of people from more than 20 nations, who speak a myriad of languages, and differ significantly by generations in the United States, socioeconomic circumstances, language, and racial self-identification, is to ask the so-called Latinxs themselves. A recent nationally representative survey from the Pew Research Center asked people what term—country of heritage, Hispanic/Latino, or American—they used most often to describe themselves. About half of respondents preferred their family's country of origin for self-identification. Forty percent of the sample used Latino/Hispanic interchangeably. The remaining participants identified themselves as Americans (Gonzalez-Barrera, 2020).

These findings suggest that Latinxs' racialization, or the process of ascribing meaning to a series of characteristics imposed on a group (Omi & Winant, 2015), is complex, context-specific, and occurs via multiple pathways in the United States, including colorism, immigration, and language. Colorism, or skin color stratification, places darker-skinned Latinxs at the bottom of the social hierarchy (Hunter, 2007, 2013). This racialization system is not unique to the United States. Chilean anthropologists coined the process used to determine access to opportunities in Latinoamerica "pigmentocracy" (Telles et al., 2015). In the United States, Latinx whose skin tones and phenotypic features (eye color, hair texture, and shape of nose and lips) indicate Black or Indigenous ancestries experience more discrimination and mental health disparities than Latinxs whose phenotypic features signal White descent. Using National Health survey data, Mena and colleagues (2019) found that Latinx who self-identified as Black experienced higher psychological distress levels than White Latinxs, even after adjusting for demographic and socioeconomic characteristics. The impact of colorism is also evident within Latinxs groups; Mexican Americans with darker skin experience more discrimination than peers who appear stereotypically Caucasian (Ortiz & Telles, 2012). Colorism also makes Black and Indigenous-presenting Latinxs more likely than lighter-skinned counterparts to fall victims to the criminal justice system. A study found that the likelihood of being arrested in Los Angeles was higher for darker skin color Mexicans than for White-passing counterparts (Alcala & Montoya, 2018).

In a White-supremacist society like the United States, colorism is essential to understand Latinxs' construction as a group placed at the bottom of the racial hierarchy. Yet, other elements—such as immigration and language—have also been used to racialize Latinxs as second-class citizens. Racialization in this context "signals the processes by which ideas about race are constructed, come to be regarded as meaningful, and are acted upon" (Murji & Solomos, 2005, p. 1). One of these ideas is that Latinxs are recent arrivals to the United States, while the reality is that almost 80% of Latinxs are U.S. citizens, many of whom have been Americans for generations (Noe-Bustamante, 2019). A significant proportion of Latinxs of Mexican descent never crossed the border. The border crossed them in 1848 when, to end the Mexican-American war, the United States annexed more than half of Mexico's territory with the Treaty of Guadalupe Hidalgo (Rumbaut, 2011). Yet, under the excuse of securing the nation from external threats, the United States has used immigration policies to make Latinxs "illegal," to then criminalize illegality as a primary mechanism to racialize Latinxs as a threat to the nation (Armenta, 2017; Stumfp, 2006). Thus, through public discourse, daily interactions with institutions, and everyday law enforcement practices, Latinxs are consistently signaled that they are not welcomed in the United States (Calvo et al., 2017). An example of such interactions can be found on the impact of immigration enforcement on Latinxs' access to social services. There is evidence that Latinxs have developed a profound mistrust toward health services, stemming from immigration laws that authorize local agencies to enforce federal immigration laws (Rhodes et al., 2015). Mallet and colleagues (2017) observed that undocumented Latinx youth who had grown up in the United States internalized messages of non-belonging to America after dealing with social services' bureaucrats. Using Census data, a recent study shows a steep decline of means-testing benefits among immigrant families after enacting the Public-Charge rule at the beginning of 2020. The rule gives immigration bureaucrats discretion to deny permanent residency to immigrants deemed a burden to the state because they participated in public-benefit programs (Capps et al., 2020). Within this deeply White-supremacist context, Spanish language is another symbolic indicator used to racialize Latinxs as not-belonging. Since the 1970s, English-only policies have been pushed as a mechanism to facilitate the incorporation of immigrants (Wiley & Wright, 2004), despite evidence that Spanish is a prime indicator of identity and culture and that bilingualism is beneficial for Latinx children. A study that followed Latinx children from kindergarten during elementary education found that in fifth grade, bilingual Latinxs surpassed their monolingual peers concerning innovative approaches to learning, self-control, and interpersonal skills (Han, 2010). In the U.S. White supremacist landscape, policies that discourage Latinxs from preserving their language reposition Latinx identity and culture as inferior.

Latinxs' racialization as not belonging in American society is present in its institutions and impacts their opportunities for advancement. We use a systems framework to show how oppressive practices based on ethnoracial discrimination contribute to disparate outcomes for Latinxs in healthcare, education, and housing, and to a disproportionate engagement with the criminal justice.

Healthcare

Compared to non-Latinx Whites, Latinxs are 1.9 times more likely to contract COVID-19, 2.8 times more likely to be hospitalized from complications of the virus, and 2.3 times more likely to die from COVID-19 (Centers for Disease Control and Prevention, 2021). These disparities stem, in part, from the structural racism embedded in the healthcare system that prevents Latinxs from accessing care. Structural racism manifests when discrimination in healthcare settings leads to adverse health outcomes. In their qualitative study of adherence to HIV antiretroviral therapy, Freeman and colleagues (2017) observed that Latinxs did not engage in medication maintenance because they perceived the health system care as dehumanizing and care providers as distrustful.

Systemic discrimination for U.S. Latinxs in the healthcare context is also present concerning access and quality. Latinxs are more likely to lack health insurance coverage than any other group in the United States (Findling et al, 2019). Even when insured, Latinxs receive worse healthcare than other groups (Guerrero et al., 2018). A systematic review of institutional racism and discrimination found that Latinxs received worse quality of care than any other ethnoracial group in the country (Shavers et al., 2012). Latinxs report that providers of care do not spend enough time with them and that they do not understand their values and culture (Calvo & Hawkins, 2015).

Access to mental healthcare is also fragmented and linked to poor outcomes (Guo et al., 2014), and Latinx populations with serious mental health issues are less likely to receive any treatment than non-Hispanic Whites (SAMHSA, 2019, 2020). An underlying structural contributor of this disparity in healthcare access is a shortage of bilingual/bicultural mental health professionals prepared to work with Latinxs (Calvo et al., 2018). There is evidence that Latinxs experience discrimination in behavioral healthcare settings due to providers' lack of understanding of cultural values such as familism, respect, and religiosity (Perreira et al., 2019). Discrimination against Latinxs has increased in the last decade, including in healthcare settings, which has been connected to increases in anxiety and substance use disorders (Cobb et al., 2020).

Housing

The pervasive effects of a White supremacist culture are also evident on social determinants of health. Latinxs tend to live in highly polluted neighborhoods (Tessum et al., 2019) and are more likely to face housing-related stress, including foreclosure, which have been linked to poor health outcomes, such as respiratory illnesses, cardiovascular disease, and substance abuse (Perreira et al., 2019).

Living in barrios, or co-ethnic neighborhoods with a high percentage of Latinx individuals, has cultural and economic advantages for Latinxs (Aranda et al., 2011; Onesimo et al., 2012; Robinette et al., 2018;). A study of Mexican American older adults living in a heavily dense Mexican American neighborhood showed improvements in self-reported health, cognitive functioning, and lower mortality rates (Robinette et al., 2018). Other benefits of living in high-density Latinx neighborhoods include access to informal employment networks (Elliotz & Sims, 2001). Living in barrios, however, can also entail restrictions on residential choice, employment, and educational options (Elliotz & Sims, 2001; Onesimo et al., 2012). A recent report about the impact of COVID-19 shows that barrios with a high concentration of Latinxs had a disproportionate impact of infections and mortality (Ford et al., 2020).

Education

Housing inequities pose serious consequences on the educational outcomes of Latinxs. The impact of discriminatory practices can be seen in graduation rates. While the dropout rate of Latinxs has decreased in the last decade, it is still almost 5% higher than for non-Latinx Whites, particularly among young males (U.S. Department of Education National Center for Education Statistics, 2019). Only 36% of Latinx enrolled in college in 2018. A disproportionately lower rate compared to Asian Americans (59%), non-Latinx-Whites (42%), and about the same as African American (37%) (U.S. Department of Education National Center for Education Statistics, 2018). Latinxs also have lower college graduation rates (54%) than Asian American (74%) and non-Latinxs White students (64%) (U.S. Department of Education National Center for Education Statistics, 2018).

The importance of educational achievement on an individual, family, and community's social and economic accomplishments cannot be overemphasized. Unfortunately, Latinx are disproportionately overrepresented among youth who do not graduate from high school and who do not pursue a college education (Merolla, 2017). The root factors contributing to negative educational achievements are many and complex, but considerable research has shown that youth of color in general, and Latinx in particular, experience extensive anti-Latinxs bias, discrimination, and disparate treatment due to negative biases and reduced expectations based on immigration status, being a Spanish-language speaker, and skin color, among others. Indirectly, youth education is impacted as a result of their caregivers experiencing strong anti-immigrant sentiments, as well as employment and housing segregation and discrimination, resulting in Latinx children experiencing chronic stress that impacts their ability to learn in school.

Latinxs who attend predominantly White institutions tend to experience implicit racial bias from educators. Implicit bias manifests, for instance, when schools with more Latinx students use harsh disciplines, such as expulsion and suspension, because of an implicit association between Latinx ethnicity and criminality (Welch & Payne, 2018). Bias is also present in terms of referrals to advanced educational programs. Latinx students are disproportionally referred to special education and remedial courses, rather than to advanced courses (Roach, 2006; Hardin et al., 2009). Latinxs made up 24% of the U.S. public school population in 2012, but only 17% of students in gifted and talented programs (McFarland et al., 2017).

While the gap in college enrollment has declined between Latinx and White college students in the past decade, White-supremacist institutional practices in higher education continue to deter Latinx students' success in higher education. Frequently experienced barriers to college enrollment and persistence include unaffordability, limited access to information and resources, and experiences of isolation (Solis & Duran, 2022). Advanced educational degrees are increasingly needed for upward mobility in the U.S. economy. As a result, this systemic challenge to education is linked to limited access to wealth generation for Latinxs (Carnevale & Fasules, 2017).

Criminal Justice

Whether pushed into the criminal justice system through school discipline or other routine experiences, criminal justice is a sector where Latinx people experience disparate treatment. Latinx youth are 65% more likely than their White counterparts to be detained or committed to the criminal justice system. Fifty-seven percent of adult Latinx respondents to a national criminal justice survey believed that the police were more likely to use deadly force on Latinos than whites (70% of those who identified as AfroLatino) (Couloute, 2018). According to the U.S. Bureau of Justice Statistics (2018), Latinxs make up 17.6% of the U.S. population but represent 23% of all police searches, 30% of arrests, and have a rate of police killings only second to African Americans.

Like the other areas discussed, scholars have explored the underlying structural and individual biases that contribute to such disparities. In a study of implicit bias in decisions to shoot potentially hostile targets in a multiracial context, Sadler and associates (2012) found that police officers demonstrate anti-Black racial bias toward Latinxs versus Asians and Whites. This manifested as a correlation between how much the officers estimated community violent crime among Latinxs and the amount of time it took to accurately shoot Latinx suspects in the simulation. Research on implicit bias demonstrates that all individuals, including police officers, are susceptible to explicitly or implicitly believing stereotypes about people of color that ultimately influence their actions (Goff et al., 2014).

Another form of bias in policing experienced by Latinx community in the United States is racial profiling of Latinx Americans who are racialized (identified as Mexican or foreign-looking based on skin color and phenotypic features like shape of eyes and nose). These Latinx U.S. citizens often become the subjects of immigration stops and searches, and experience increased racism within the criminal justice system (Romero, 2006). The history of immigration law enforcement in the United States must be understood to view these stops and searches as a legacy of White supremacy. After the Mexican-American war, special law enforcement patrols were sent out to round up Mexicans still living in claimed territories. These law enforcement agencies eventually became the Arizona and Texas Rangers, responsible for immigration raids and sweeps for decades (Romero, 2006).

Promising Practices to Counteract the Impact of Racism on Latinxs

Equal access to opportunities for advancement is the foundation of any thriving society. The United States is at the brink of the most significant demographic transformation of its history. If current demographic trends continue, by 2060, one in three Americans will be of Latinx descent (Vespa et al., 2020). Latinxs are also younger than the rest of the U.S. population and therefore can be thought of as cornerstone to the future of the country (Calvo, 2018)—a future that won't be as promising as it should, unless we dismantle the systemic racism that prevent Latinxs from achieve their full potential.

A place to start is by decriminalizing immigration. Studies show that providing undocumented Latinxs with access to employment through the Deferred Action for Childhood Arrivals (DACA) decreases unemployment and rises the income of immigrants at the bottom of the income distribution (Pope, 2016). One of the results of the Immigration Reform and Control Act of 1986 (IRCA)—which granted permanent residency or "green cards" to almost 3 million unauthorized immigrants—was that Latinxs filed tax returns at a comparable rate to non-Latinxs in California, a state with the vast majority of immigrants who benefited from IRCA (Cascio & Lewis, 2019). Allowing undocumented Latinxs immigrants to obtain driver's licenses decreases unemployment and gives access to better jobs by expanding employment options to car-dependent occupations (Cho, 2019).

The benefits of eliminating systemic barriers to Latinxs' advancement are also evident in the arenas of healthcare and education. The Affordable Care Act of 2010 (ACA) reduced national disparities in healthcare access and utilization between Latinxs and non-Latinx Whites (Alcalá et al., 2017; Buchmueller & Levy, 2020). Concerning education, at the national level, it is critical to ensure the support of educational institutions. The White House Hispanic Prosperity Initiative is an Executive Order that seeks to promote access to educational and economic opportunities to Latinx communities (U.S. Department of Education, 2020). At a school district and school level, implementing anti-racist policies is critical and may include training of teachers and administrators to enact programs and policies that eliminate discriminatory and racist practices (Kailin, 1998; Kohli et al., 2017), including hiring more diverse personnel (Quiocho & Rios, 2000). At the classroom level, initiatives may include the development of racial literacy by teachers and administrators (Rolón-Dow et al., 2020), the implementation of critical pedagogy to allow students to assess their lives within a structural lens and not with an individual, self-blaming internalized, perspective (Sarroub & Quadros, 2015), and development of positive racial identity and positive self-concept (Martinez-Fuentes et al., 2020; Prince & Nurius, 2014). At the individual youth level, culturally informed interventions such as motivational interviewing and cognitive behavioral therapy can effectively address academic challenges that youth may be experiencing as a result of psychosocial problems, thereby reducing the risk of dropping out of school for minority youth in general, and Latinxs in particular (Franklin et al., 2013).

As has been described earlier, the large number of structural factors that impact Latinxs' lives, such as housing and employment discrimination, among others, pose serious consequences on the educational outcomes of young people. The impact of discriminatory practices can be seen in graduation statistics. In order for graduate social work programs to succeed in recruiting more Latinx students, it is imperative that more programs be developed to increase the proportion of Latinx youth who graduate from high school, many of them needing to target middle school youth so that they are prepared to enter high school with the skills, knowledge, and confidence necessary to succeed when they are presented with more advanced material. Once students are in high school, more programs are needed to support Latinx students to ensure that they not only complete their high school education, but also enroll *and* graduate from college. A larger proportion of Latinx completing college will provide schools of social work with a larger population of Latinx students to recruit to their master of social work (MSW) programs.

There is a growing list of graduate social work programs that aim to increase the number of Latinx students who enroll in MSW programs. Some exceptional examples include Loyola University Chicago online bilingual (in Spanish) Master of Social Work program. An online MSW program offered in Spanish provides a unique opportunity to Latinx individuals who as a result of language barriers and family or work obligations would not be able to pursue a traditional MSW education, which includes full-time day classes all taught in English, for example. Another exceptional program is the Latinx Leadership Initiative (LLI) offered at Boston College School of Social Work. LLI seeks to increase the number of bilingual/bicultural social workers equipped to work with Latinx communities on sustainable solutions for complex problems.

Boston University's Building Refugee and Immigrant Degrees for Graduate Education Program (BRIDGE) and MSW Pathway are additional unique programs. Both are one-year programs that seeks to recruit and prepare immigrants and refugees (BRIDGE) and people of color (MSW Pathway) with a college degree who have shown leadership within their communities to pursue an MSW. While the programs are open to individuals of any background, it has served to recruit many Latinx. Students who complete the Programs have a higher chance of receiving more generous scholarships when applying to graduate programs because their professional backgrounds, commitment to working with underserved populations, and preparation for graduate schools make them more competitive applicants. At the University of Houston Graduate College of Social Work, their

MSW program offers a specialization called "Social Work Practice with Latinos" with courses specific to working with Latinx clients to inn Latino communities."

The importance of these programs cannot be overstated. In a country where nearly 60.6 million people (18.5%) are of Latinx backgrounds (U.S. Census Bureau, 2020), and who tend to be overrepresented among some of the most disenfranchised populations (Velasco-Mondagron et al., 2016), every school of social work should have some type of program that supports Latinx students. And while not every school offers such a program, there is a growing number of MSW programs that offer specific courses, concentrations, and even certificates focusing on working with Latinx populations, many with emphasis on bilingual practice. A result of the existence of these programs is that they serve to attract Latinx students who become interested in pursuing an MSW degree because they know they will encounter supporting services such as scholarships and a faculty, curricula, and field settings and community partnerships that speak to their unique experiences and desire to work with their corresponding Latinx communities.

As with immigration, healthcare, and education, several multifaceted and evidence-based approaches to stemming the racial and ethnic disparities in criminal justice have long been championed by civil rights organizations and nonprofits. One central solution for the Latinx community has been the inclusion of Latinx perspectives and narratives within criminal justice reform (UCLA LPPI, 2021). Much research on Latinx communities mirrors efforts to close racial disparities in criminal justice reform for African Americans, but there are still unique needs among the Latinx population that are increasingly being included in the narrative about criminal justice reform. In re sponse to the Black Lives Matter movement over the summer of 2020, there continue to be consistent calls for divestment from law enforcement and reinvestment in communities of color. For Latinx communities this solution has also been shown to increase investment in programs like drug and mental health treatment, in addition to education and health, rather than incarceration (Center for Popular Democracy Action, 2020). Additionally, efforts to support formerly incarcerated Latinx individuals have gained traction in places like California. In 2013, California began its support of individuals exiting jail by allocating medical coverage for these individuals to access both physical and mental health treatment. This, in turn, has decreased rates of recidivism. Another aspect of reducing recidivism among some agencies is to focus on the reintegration of those Latinx individuals with previous criminal convictions along with ending employment discrimination against those with conviction records (UCLA LPPI, 2021). Lastly, nonprofits like Homies Unidos engage Latinx individuals in drug and gang prevention, which ultimately decreases their likelihood of engagement with law enforcement and eventual push into the criminal justice system (Safe and Just, 2014).

Conclusion

Our goal is to eradicate the systemic racism that precludes Latinxs from equal opportunity for advancement. This is not a behavioral issue; thus changing the behaviors of those affected will not fix the problem. Rather, we need to dismantle the White-supremacist culture that permeates the systems in which groups are embedded. More specifically, if we are going to improve the lives of Latinx communities, we need to make the institutions that provide healthcare, education, housing, and immigration services, and the justice systems more responsive and accountable to Latinx populations.

Study Questions

1. The various terms utilized to describe the Latinx populations are socially constructed. What is the history behind the various labels or terms that are utilized, and what are the pros and cons of each?
2. How is colorism different than racism?
3. Colorism, Spanish language, and immigration status are used to racialize Latinxs in the U.S. How do these elements interact to construct the racialization of Latinxs?
4. Too often Latinxs are considered to be a homogeneous population. Please describe the diverse social, political, economic, cultural, historical, linguistic, phenotypical, and geographical characteristics, among others, that make these populations considerably heterogenous.
5. What are some of the social-structural factors that impact Latinxs' lives?
6. What social-political-economic interventions are needed to help improve the lives of Latinx populations?
7. What are initiatives that schools of social work can undertake to increase the number of Latinx students in their programs and to provide the necessary support to ensure high graduation rates?

8. What are common features of the initiatives discussed in this chapter aimed at reducing ethnic disparities in criminal justice, healthcare, housing, and education?
9. According to recent Pew Research, why is the term "country of heritage" more complicated and less inclusive of the term "Latinx" to describe ethnicity?
10. Explain how lacking access to equitable housing can impact access to education for Latinx families.

References

Alcalá, H. E., Chen, J., Langellier, B. A., Roby, D. H., & Ortega, A. N. (2017). Impact of the affordable care act on health care access and utilization among Latinos. *The Journal of the American Board of Family Medicine, 30*(1), 52–62.

Alcalá, H. E., & Montoya, M. F. L. (2018). Association of skin color and generation on arrests among Mexican-Origin Latinos. *Race and Justice, 8*(2), 178–193. doi:10.1177/2153368716670998.

Aranda, M., Ray, L., Snih, S., Ottenbacher, K., & Markides, K. (2011). The protective effect of neighborhood composition on increasing frailty among older Mexican Americans: A barrio advantage? *Journal of Aging Health, 23*(7), 1189–217. doi: 10.1177/0898264311421961.

Armenta, A. (2017). Racializing crimmigration: Structural racism, colorblindness, and the institutional production of immigrant criminality. *Sociology of Race and Ethnicity, 3*(1), 82–95.

Astrada, S. B., & Astrada, M. L. (2017). Being Latino in the 21st century: Reexamining politicized identity & the problem of representation. *University of Pennsylvania Journal of Law and Social Change, 20*(3), 245–272.

Buchmueller, T., & Levy, H. G. (2020). The ACA's impact on racial and ethnic disparities in health insurance coverage and access to care. *Health Affairs, 39*(3), 395–402.

Calvo, R. (2018). Introduction: The Latinx opportunity. *Journal of Teaching in Social Work, 38*(3), 246–250.

Calvo, R., & Hawkins, S. S. (2015). Disparities in quality of healthcare of children from immigrant families in the US. *Maternal and Child Health Journal, 19*, 2223–2232.

Calvo, R., Jablonska-Bayro, J. M., & Waters, M. C. (2017) Obamacare in action: how access to the health care system contributes to immigrants' sense of belonging. *Journal of Ethnic and Migration Studies, 43*(12), 2020–2036.

Calvo, R., Ortiz, L., Villa, P., & Baek, K. (2018). A call to action: Latinx in social work education. *Journal of Teaching in Social Work, 38*(3), 263–276.

Capps, R., Fix, M., & Batalova, J. (2020). Anticipated "chilling effects" of the public-charge rule are real: Census data reflects steep decline in benefits used by immigrant families. Commentary. Migration Policy Institute. https://www.migrationpolicy.org/news/anticipated-chilling-effects-public-charge-rule-are-real.

Carnevale, A. P., & Fasules, M. L. (2017). Latino education and economic progress: Running faster but still behind. Georgetown University, Center on Education and the workforce. Retrieved from: https://cewgeorgetown.wpenginepowered.com/wp-content/uploads/Latinos-FR.pdf

Cascio, E. U., & Lewis, E. G. (2019). Distributing the green (cards): Permanent residency and personal income taxes after the Immigration Reform and Control Act of 1986. *Journal of Public Economics, 172,* 135–150,

Centers for Disease Control and Prevention (2021). COVID-19 hospitalization and death by race/ethnicity (update July 2021). https://www.cdc.gov/coronavirus/2019-ncov/covid-data/investigations-discovery/hospitalization-death-by-race-ethnicity.html.

Cho, H. (2019). Driver's license reforms and job accessibility among undocumented immigrants. Available at SSRN: https://ssrn.com/abstract=3356102 or http://dx.doi.org/10.2139/ssrn.3356102.

Cobb, C. L., Salas-Wright, C. P., John, R., Schwartz, S. J., Vaughn, M., Martinez, Jr, C. R., Awad, G., Pinedo, M., & Cano, M. A. (2020). Discrimination trends and mental health among native- and foreign-born Latinos: Results from national surveys in 2004 and 2013. *Prevention Science, 22,* 397–407. https://doi.org/10.1007/s11121-020-01186-4.

Cornell, S., & Hartmann, D. (2007): *Making identities in a changing world.* Thousand Oaks, CA: Sage.

Couloute, L. (2018, January 24). New poll shows mass incarceration is a Latinx issue. *Prison Policy Initiative.* https://www.prisonpolicy.org/blog/2018/01/24/new-poll-shows-mass-incarceration-is-a-latinx-issue/.

Elliotz, J. R., & Sims, M. (2001). Ghettos and barrios: The impact of neighborhood poverty and race on job matching among Blacks and Latinos. *Social Problems, 48*(3), 341–361.

Findling, M. G., Bleich, S. N., Casey, L. S., Blendon, R. J., Benson, J. M., Sayde, J. M., & Miller, C. (2019). Discrimination in the United States: Experiences of Latinos. *Health Services Research, 54,* 1409–1418.

Ford, T., Reber, S., & Reeves, R. V. (2020, June 16). Race gaps in COVID-19 deaths are even bigger than they appear. Brookings Institution report. Retrieved June 21, 2020, from https://www.brookings.edu/blog/up-front/2020/06/16/race-gaps-in-covid-19-deaths-are-even-bigger-than-they-appear/.

Franklin, C., Harris M. B., & Allen-Meares, P. (2013). *The school services sourcebook: A guide for school-based professionals* (2nd ed.). Oxford: Oxford University Press.

Freeman, R., Gwadz, M., Silverman, E. Kutnik, A., Leonard, M., Riotchie, A., Reed, J., & Martinz, B. (2017). Critical race theory as a tool for understanding poor engagement along the HIV care continuum among African American/Black and Hispanic persons living with HIV in the United States: A qualitative exploration. *International Journal for Equity in Health, 16,* 54.

Goff, P. A., Jackson, M. C., Di Leone, B. A., Culotta, C. M., & DiTomasso, N. A. (2014). The essence of innocence: Consequences of dehumanizing Black children. *Journal of Personlaity and Social Psychology, 106,* 526–545.

Gonzalez-Barrera, A. (2020). The ways Hispanics describe their identity vary across immigrant generations. Pew Research Center. https://www.pewresearch.org/fact-tank/2020/09/24/the-ways-hispanics-describe-their-identity-vary-across-immigrant-generations/.

Guerrero, A. D., Zhou, X., & Chung, P. J. (2018). How well is the medical home working for Latino and Black children? *Maternal Child Health Journal, 22*(2), 175–183. doi: 10.1007/s10995-017-2389-6.

Guo, S., Kataoka, S. H., Bear, L., & Lau, A. S. (2014). Differences in school-based referrals for mental health care: Understanding racial/ethnic disparities between Asian

American and Latino youth. *School Mental Health: A Multidisciplinary Research and Practice Journal*, 6(1), 27–39.

Han, W. (2010). Bilingualism and socioemotional well-being. *Children and Youth Services Review*, 32, 720–731.

Hardin, B., Mereoiu, M., Hung, H.-F., & Roach-Scott, M. (2009). Investigating parent and professional perspectives concerning special education services for preschool Latino children. *Early Childhood Education Journal*, 37(2), 93–102.

Hunter, M. (2007). The persistent problem of colorism: Skin tone, status, and inequality. *Sociology Compass*, 1(1), 237–254.

Hunter, M. (2013). *Race, gender, and the politics of skin tone*. New York: Routledge.

Jones-Correa, M., & Leal, D. L. (1996). Becoming "Hispanic": Secondary panethnic identification among Latin American-origin populations in the United States. *Hispanic Journal of Behavioral Sciences*, 18, 214–254.

Kailin, J. (1998). Preparing urban teachers for schools and communities: An anti-racist perspective. *The High School Journal*, 82, 80–87.

Kohli, R., Pizarro, M., & Nevárez, A. (2017). The "new racism" of K–12 schools: Centering critical research on racism. *Review of Research in Education*, 41, 182–202.

Lopez, M. H., Krogstad, J. M., & Passel, J. S. (2020). Who is Hispanic? Pew Research Center. https://www.pewresearch.org/fact-tank/2019/11/11/who-is-hispanic/.

Mallet, M. L., Calvo, R., & M. C. Waters (2017). "I don't belong anymore": Undocumented Latino immigrants encounter social services in the United States. *Hispanic Journal of Behavioral Sciences*, 39(3), 267–282.

McFarland, J., Hussar, B., de Brey, C., Snyder, T., Wang, X., Wilkinson-Flicker, S., Gebrekristos, S., Zhang, J., Rathbun, A., Barmer, A., Bullock Mann, F., & Hinz, S. (2017). The Condition of Education 2017 (NCES 2017- 144). U.S. Department of Education. Washington, DC: National Center for Education Statistics. Retrieved from: https://nces.ed.gov/pubsearch/pubsinfo.asp?pubid=2017144.

Marrow, H., (2003).To be or not to be (Hispanic or Latino): Brazilian racial and ethnic identity in the United States. *Ethnicities*, 3(4), 427–464.

Martinez-Fuentes, S., Jager, J., & Umaña-Taylor, A. J. (2020). The mediation process between Latino youths' family ethnic socialization, ethnic–racial identity, and academic engagement: Moderation by ethnic–racial discrimination? *Cultural Diversity and Ethnic Minority Psychology, 27*(2), 296–306. https://doi.org/10.1037/cdp 0000349.

Mena, J. A., Durden, T. E., Bresette, S. E., & McCready, T. (2019). Black and White Self-identified Latinx respondents and perceived psychological distress and impairment. *Hispanic Journal of Behavioral Sciences*, 41(4), 504–522. doi: 10.1177/0739986319883827.

Merolla, D. M. (2017). Completing the educational career: High school graduation, four-year college enrollment, and bachelor's degree completion among Black, Hispanic, and White students. *Sociology of Race and Ethnicity*, 4, 281–297.

Murji, K., and Solomos, J. (Eds.) (2005). *Racialization: Studies in theory and practice*. New York: Oxford University Press.

Noe-Bustamante, L. (2019). Key facts about U.S. Hispanics and their diverse heritage. Fact Tank. Pew Research Center. Retrived January 25, 2023, from https://www.pewr esearch.org/fact-tank/2019/09/16/key-facts-about-u-s-hispanics/.

Omi, M., & Winant, H. (2014). *Racial Formation in the United States* (3rd Ed). New York: Routledge.

Onésimo Sandoval, J. S., & Jennings, J. (2012). Barrios and hyper barrios: How Latino neighborhoods changed the urban built environment. *Journal of Urbanism, 5*(2–3), 111–138.

Ortiz, V., & Telles, E. (2012). Racial identity and racial treatment of Mexican Americans. *Race and Social Problems, 4*(1), 41–56. https://doi.org/10.1007/s12552-012-9064-8.

Perreira, K. M., Marchante, A. N., Schwartz, S. J., Isasi, C. R., Carnethon, M. R., Corliss, H. L., Kaplan, R. C., Santisteban, D. A., Vidot, D. C., Van Horn, L., & Delamater, A. M. (2019). Stress and resilience: Key correlates of mental health and substance use in the Hispanic Community Health Study of Latino youth. *Journal of Immigrant & Minority Health, 21*(1), 4–13.

Pope, N. G. (2016). The Effects of DACAmentation: The impact of deferred action for childhood arrivals on unauthorized immigrants. *Journal of Public Economics, 143,* 98–114.

Prince, D., & Nurius, P. S. (2014). The role of positive academic self-concept in promoting school success. *Children & Youth Services Review, 43,* 145–152.

Quiocho, A., & Rios, F. (2000). The power of their presence: Minority group teachers and schooling. *Review of Educational Research, 70,* 485–528.

Roach, R. (2006). Jump starting Latino achievement. *Diverse: Issues in Higher Education, 23*(16), 26–27.

Rolón-Dow, R., Jill Ewing Flynn & Hilary Mead. (2021). Racial literacy theory into practice: Teacher candidates' responses. *International Journal of Qualitative Studies in Education, 34*(7), 663–679. doi: 10.1080/09518398.2020.1783013

Robinette, J., Boardman, J., & Crimmins, E. (2018). Perceived neighborhood social cohesion and cardiometabolic risk: A gene × environment study. *Biodemography Sociology Biology, 64*(3–4), 173–186. doi: 10.1080/19485565.2019.1579084.

Rhodes, S., Mann, L. Simán, F. M., Song, E., Alonzo, J., et al. (2015). The impact of local immigration enforcement policies on the health of immigrant Hispanic/Latinos in the United States. *American Journal of Public Health, 105,* 329–337.

Romero, M. (2006). Racial profiling and immigration law enforcement: Rounding up of usual suspect in the Latino community. *Critical Sociology, 32*(2–3), 447–473.

Rumbaut, R. (2011). Pigments of our imagination: The racialization of the Hispanic-Latino category. Migration Policy Institute. https://www.migrationpolicy.org/article/pigments-our-imagination-racialization-hispanic-latino-category.

Sadler, M. S., Correll, J., & Park, B. (2012). The world is not black and white: Racial bias in the decision to shoot in a multiethnic context. *Journal of Social Issues, 68*(2), 286–313.

Sarroub, L. K., & Quadros, S. (2015). Critical pedagogy in classroom discourse. In M. Bigelow & J. Ennser-Kananen (Eds.), *The Routledge handbook of educational linguistics* (pp. 252–260). New York and Abingdon: Routledge.

Shavers, V., Fagan, P., Jones, D., Klein, W., Boyington, J., Moten, C. & Rorie, E. (2012). The state of research on racial/ethnic discrimination in the receipt of health care. *American Journal of Public Health, 102,* 953–966. 10.2105/AJPH.2012.300773.

Stumpf, J. (2006). The crimmigration crisis: Immigrants, crime, and sovereign power. *The American University Law Review, 56*(2), 307–419.

Substance Abuse and Mental Health Services Administration (2019). *2018 National survey on drug use and health.* Rockville, MD: Substance Abuse and Mental Health Services Administration.

Substance Abuse and Mental Health Services Administration (2020). *2019 National survey on drug use and health.* Rockville, MD: Substance Abuse and Mental Health Services Administration.

Solis, B., & Durán, R. P. (2022). Latinx community college students' transition to a 4-year public research-intensive University. *Journal of Hispanic Higher Education, 21*(1), 49–66.

Telles, E., Flores, R. D., & Urrea-Giraldo, F. (2015). Pigmentocracies: Educational inequality, skin color and census ethnoracial identification in eight Latin American countries. *Research in Social Stratification and Mobility, 40,* 39–58. Open access: doi.org/10.1016/j.rssm.2015.02.002.

Tessum, C. W, Apte, J. S., Goodkind, A. L., Muller, N. Z, Mullins, K. A., et al. (2019). Inequity in consumption of goods and services adds to racial–ethnic disparities in air pollution exposure. *PNAS, 116*(13), 6001–6006.

UCLA Latino Policy & Politics Initiative. (2021). *Shaping a 21st Century Latino Agenda.* Retrieved January 25, 2023, from https://latino.ucla.edu/wp-content/uploads/2021/08/LPPI-Shaping-the-21st-Latino-Agenda.pdf.

U.S. Census Bureau (2020). *Hispanic Heritage Month 2020.* Retrieved January 25, 2023, from https://www.census.gov/newsroom/facts-for-features/2020/hispanic-heritage-month.html#:~:text=60.6%20million,of%20the%20nation's%20total%20population.

U.S. Department of Education, National Center for Education Statistics (2018). *Digest of education statistics.* Retrieved June 14, 2020, from https://nces.ed.gov/programs/digest/d18/foreword.asp.

U.S. Department of Education, National Center for Education Statistics. (2019). *The condition of education 2019 (NCES 2019-144), status dropout rates.* https://nces.ed.gov/programs/coe/indicator_coj.asp.

U.S. Department of Education (2020). Executive order on the White House Prosperity Initiative. Retrieved January 30, 2021, from https://sites.ed.gov/hispanic-initiative/.

U.S. Department of Education, Office of Civil Rights (2017). *2011–2012 state and national estimations.* http://ocrdata.ed.gov/StateNationalEstimations/Estimations_2011_12.

Velasco-Mondragon, E., Jimenez, A., Palladino-Davis, A. G., Davis, D., & Escamilla-Cejudo, J. A. (2016). Hispanic health in the USA: A scoping review of the literature. *Public Health Reviews, 37,* 31.

Vespa, J., Medina, L., & Armstrong, D. M. (2020). Demographic turning points for the United States: Population projections for 2020 to 2060. U.S. Census Bureau. https://www.census.gov/content/dam/Census/library/publications/2020/demo/p25-1144.pdf.

Welch, K., & Payne, A. A. (2018). Latino/a student threat and school disciplinary policies and practices. *Sociology of Education, 91*(2), 91–110.

Wiley, T. G., & Wright, W. E. (2004). Against the undertow: Language-minority education policy and politics in the "age of accountability." *Educational Policy, 18,* 142–168.

12

Confronting the History of Racism against Asian Americans in the United States

Meirong Liu

In fact, the racialization of Asian Americans as immigrants, foreigners, or as model minorities existing between black and white demonstrates that the failure to recognize racial differences results in racial injustice.
—Harvey Gee (1999)

Introduction

On March 16, 2021, six Asian American women were shot in a suburb of Atlanta, Georgia; the next morning in San Francisco, California, an 83-year-old Asian man was attacked. An hour later, the same person attacked Xiao Xie Chen, a 75-year-old Asian American woman. Chen picked up a stick nearby and fought off her attacker. Her eye was bleeding. Crying while defending herself, she kept on repeating, "You bum, why did you hit me?" (Peiser, 2021, para. 13).

During the COVID-19 pandemic, Asian Americans have been burdened by heightened racial tension and associated racist microaggressions and verbal attacks. From March 2020 to March 2021, Stop AAPI Hate received nearly 6,600 reported hate incidents, which represent both hate crimes and incidents of violence or discrimination against Asian American communities, including women and elders (Jeung et al., 2020). These events, as well as the spa shooting in the Atlanta area, represent, to many, the grim culmination of a year in which anti-Asian violence has increased across the United States, but this year is also part of a history that began long

Meirong Liu, *Confronting the History of Racism against Asian Americans in the United States* In: *Social Work and the Grand Challenge to Eliminate Racism*. Edited by: Martell L. Teasley, Michael S. Spencer, and Melissa Bartholomew, Oxford University Press. © Oxford University Press 2023. DOI: 10.1093/oso/9780197674949.003.0012

THE HISTORY OF RACISM AGAINST ASIAN AMERICANS   305

before 2020. Asian Americans have experienced persistent marginalizing stereotyping, physical and verbal attacks, hate crimes and harassments, and microaggressions motivated by individual-level racism and xenophobia from the time they arrived in America in the late 1700s to the present day. At the institutional level, the state (i.e., federal and state governments) has often implicitly or explicitly reinforced, encouraged, and perpetuated this violence through racist and xenophobic discriminatory rhetoric and exclusionary policies (Yung et al., 2006).

Asian Americans and Historical Experiences of Othering

Beginning in the 1850s, when young single men were recruited as contract laborers from China, Asian immigrants played a vital role in the development of the United States. Working as miners, railroad builders, factory workers, and fishermen, the Chinese represented 20% of California's labor force (Asian Americans Then and Now, n.d.). Almost immediately, the racist trope of "Asians coming to steal White jobs" was born (Brockell, 2021). Examples of such racism were reinforced by the State of California, which was seeing many people migrating to California for the Gold Rush in search of gold and related opportunities. The California court in 1854 reinforced racism against Asian immigrants in *People v. Hall*, ruling that people of Asian descent could not testify against a White person in court, virtually guaranteeing that Whites could escape punishment for anti-Asian violence (Brockell, 2021). Then, on October 24, 1871, a mob of 500 locals in Los Angeles, California, attacked innocent Chinese residents. At least 17 Chinese men and boys were lynched. In 1882, Congress passed the Chinese Exclusion Act, the country's first significant restrictive immigration law and the first to restrict a group of immigrants based on race and class (Lee, 2002). This law was largely successful in systematically denying Chinese Americans their civil rights and excluding them from the shores of the United States for decades (Fisher & Fisher, 2010) until it was repealed in 1943. A Chinese student, Saum Song Bo, described the irony of erecting a Statue of Liberty just after passing the law to exclude Chinese in his letter to the *New York Sun*:

> That statue represents Liberty holding a torch which lights the passage of those of all nations who come into this country. But are the Chinese allowed to come? As for the Chinese who are here, are they allowed to enjoy liberty

as men of all other nationalities enjoy it? Are they allowed to go about eve-rywhere free from the insults, abuse, assaults, wrongs and injuries from which men of other nationalities are free? (Bo, 1885, n.p.)

This xenophobic ban spread further to include later migrations from Japan, India, and Korea. The "Gentleman's Agreement" in 1907 restricted Japanese immigration, and the Immigration Act of 1924 further codified Asian exclusion. In the 1940s, the U.S. government forced people of Japanese descent into internment camps. Meanwhile, Chinese immigrants coming to the United States by boat were detained off the California coast and required to undergo humiliating medical examinations and detailed interrogations on Angel Island in San Francisco Bay. These actions were codified by both written laws and unwritten practices and occurred for over 30 years.

During the Civil Rights movements of the 1950s and 1960s, and later the Black Power movement, inspired Asian activists fought for the devel-opment of ethnic studies programs in universities and sought reparations for the forced incarceration of Asian American citizens in U.S. internment camps. As new waves of East Asian immigrants arrived in the United States throughout the mid- to late twentieth century and integrated into the society, a new stereotype proliferated alongside them: the myth of the "model mi-nority." In 1966, *New York Times Magazine* published "Success Story Japanese American Style," in which Asian Americans were framed as an embodiment of the ultimate American success story of meritocracy and hard work. The myth also implied that other minorities could also rise above the challenges of racism to succeed. Consequently, conservatives used the model minority myth as an ideological tool, dismissing civil rights activists' claims that racism was responsible for the struggles of people of color and delegitimizing challenges to racial oppression (Museus, 2013).

The Asian American civil rights movements ended by the 1980s. In 1981, as competition and tensions rose between local White and Vietnamese fishermen in Texas, the Ku Klux Klan burned the boats owned by Vietnamese fishermen (Smith, 2017). In 1982, Vincent Chin, a Chinese American, was beaten to death by two unemployed White autoworkers in Michigan who mistook him for Japanese who were "taking their auto-industry jobs." The subsequent lenient punishment—probation and a $3,000 fine—outraged the Asian American community (Wu, 2009). After September 11, 2001, South Asian, Sikh, Muslim, and Arab Americans have become the targets of nu-merous hate crimes, harassment, and profiling (Hing, 2001). As recently as

THE HISTORY OF RACISM AGAINST ASIAN AMERICANS 307

2017, an Indian American man was shot by a suspect who yelled, "Get out of my country." The suspect asked if he was a legal immigrant before shooting him (Morey, 2018).

In the wake of the coronavirus pandemic, racism and harassment toward Asian Americans have again spiked. Such racist attitudes were reinforced by institutional support. On March 16, 2020, former U.S. president Donald J. Trump referred to the coronavirus as the "Chinese Virus" from his Twitter account. Within a week, the number of anti-Asian hashtags on Twitter rose by 797% and 17,400% for #covid19 and #chinesevirus, respectively (Hswen et al., 2021). This growing chorus of hateful words contributed to the rise in hate incidents. Attacks on Asians in 16 of America's largest cities soared by an unprecedented 164% during the first quarter of 2021 compared with 2020, with women reporting incidents at twice the rate of men (Report to the Nation: Anti-Asian Prejudice & Hate Crime, 2021). A national survey found that a majority of nearly 80% of Asian Americans say they do not feel respected and are discriminated against in the United States (Daniller, 2021). Meanwhile, 37% of White Americans say they are not aware of an increase in hate crimes and racism against Asian Americans over the past year, with 24% saying anti-Asian American racism isn't a problem that should be addressed (Social Tracking of Asian Americans in the U.S. Index Report, 2021). Cheah et al. (2020) in their national survey found that three-fourths of parents and youth experienced at least one incident of COVID-19 related racism, either online or in person, with more than 4 out of 10 parents and 5 out of 10 youth reporting some form of direct or vicarious discrimination on a weekly basis. The COVID-19 Adult Resilience Experience Study found that two-thirds of Asian American participants reported experiencing COVID-19–related discrimination (Hahm et al., 2021).

These discriminations—situated in historically entrenched and intersecting individual-level and institutional-level racism and xenophobia—have operated to "other" Asian Americans and to reproduce inequality (Gover et al., 2020). It is important to note that, although Asian Americans now make up about 7% of the nation's overall population, they recorded the fastest population growth rate among all racial and ethnic groups in the United States between 2000 and 2019; the population nearly doubled during this period, and numbers are projected to surpass 46 million by 2060 (Budiman & Ruiz, 2021). In New York, Michigan, Illinois, and Rhode Island, increases in the number of Asian Americans between 2000 and 2019 exceeded the state's overall population growth (Budiman & Ruiz,

2021). Among other factors are the increasing political power of the Asian American community, unprecedented recognition of hate crimes against Asian Americans, growing solidarity across races, and increased determination to defeat White supremacy (Shah & Kauh, 2021).

Impact of Racism on the Health and Mental Health of Asian Americans

Previous studies have shown that racism is a chronic and acute stressor that elicits psychological, physiological, and behavioral responses within individuals (Karlsen & Nazroo, 2002; Gee et al., 2007). In response to racism, individuals can experience depression, intrusive thoughts, anger, hypervigilance, somatic symptoms, and physiological reactivity, decreased self-esteem, and avoidance or numbing (Carter & Pieterse, 2020). Further, the negative impacts of racism on mental health can be temporary and/ or long lasting, and racial trauma can be felt across generations (Nagata et al., 2015).

Experiences of discrimination are adversely related to a wide variety of mental, physical, and behavioral health outcomes among Asian Americans (Nagata et al., 2015; Phelan & Link, 2015; Samari, 2016). A meta-analysis of 23 studies found that, among Asian Americans, racial discrimination was associated with increased levels of depression, anxiety, suicidal ideation, overall distress, and lower well-being (Lee & Ahn, 2011).

Racism's contribution to increased mental health risk for Asian Americans may partially explain the higher rates of anxiety and depression in Asian Americans as compared to White European Americans, even when taking acculturation into account (Lau et al., 2013; Young et al., 2010). The awareness of the "perpetual foreigner" stereotype predicts a lower sense of belonging to the American culture and lower hope and life satisfaction (Huynh et al., 2011). Recent studies found that Asian Americans are experiencing unprecedented mental health issues brought about by the COVID-19 pandemic and anti-Asian hate, including increased anxiety, depression (Liu et al., 2021), and post-traumatic stress disorder (PTSD) symptoms (Hahm et al., 2021). A Stop AAPI Hate follow-up study with individuals who reported their anti-Asian hate incidents found that one in five Asian Americans who have experienced racism display racial trauma (Saw et al., 2021).

THE HISTORY OF RACISM AGAINST ASIAN AMERICANS   309

These problems are compounded by the fact that Asian American individuals are less likely than other racial groups to seek mental health treatment (U.S. Department of Health and Human Services, 2016, 2017, 2018, 2019). Trauma and fear of possible future experiences of racism also prevent Asian Americans from accessing needed resources (Le et al., 2020; Yee, 2021). For example, 25.4% of the Stop AAPI Hate follow-up study respondents reported access to healthcare, including mental healthcare, as a main source of stress, compared to 14.2% of the national needs assessment survey respondents. These challenges place Asian Americans at a greater risk for the development of long-term mental, physical, and behavioral health conditions (Saw et al., 2021).

Anti-Asian Racism and the Grand Challenges for Social Work

As a profession committed "to enhance human well-being and help meet basic needs of all people, with particular attention to those who are vulnerable, oppressed, and living in poverty" (National Association of Social Workers [NASW], 2020, para. 2), social work is deeply rooted in its social justice goals. Social workers have an ethical duty to dismantle racism, both personally and professionally, and to speak out against hatred, discrimination, and unjust systems that create hierarchies among marginalized racial minorities (NASW, 2020).

However, findings from original studies revealed that despite social work's articulated stance on racism, the profession is failing to address racism and White supremacy and the experiences of racially minoritized populations to build racial equity. McMachon and Allen-Meares (1992) systematically reviewed articles published in four major social work journals on Asian Americans, Native Americans, African Americans, and Hispanic Americans between 1980 and 1989 and found less than 6% of articles focused on racial and ethnic minorities. Corley and Young (2018) updated the 1992 study and found that only 7% of articles published between 2005 and 2015 focused on racial and ethnic minorities and suggested the profession is still failing to address institutional racism. Woo et al. (2018) conducted a content analysis of three major social work journals between 2006 and 2015 which showed that although race and ethnicity were referenced in many journal articles, there was a tendency among researchers to treat race and ethnicity as control variables rather than core constructs on which to center their inquiry. Social work research on race also focuses on Black and Brown communities, which excludes many ethnic groups experiencing racism and oppression (Choi & Lahey, 2006; Coley & Young, 2018). Further, the number of articles on Asian and Pacific Islander (API) Americans decreased significantly from 20 articles in the 1992 study to 14 articles in the 2018 study (Coley & Young, 2018). Such findings were especially surprising given the growing number of Asian families in the United States (Choi & Lahey, 2006; Ruiz et al., 2021).

The Grand Challenges for Social Work (GCSW) are a national initiative to campaign for social progress powered by science and a call for social work researchers and practitioners to tackle the most important social problems facing society (GCSW, 2020a). In 2013, the American Academy of Social Work and Social Welfare (AASWSW) led the process of identifying major challenges for social work that would guide practice and research over the next decade (Lubben et al., 2018). From over 80 concepts proposed by social work national organizations, academics, and a variety of stakeholders, 12 GCSW covering three domains (i.e., improving individual and family well-being, building a strong social fabric, and creating a just society) were selected based on their perceived importance, applicability, and potential for measurable improvement over a period of 10 years (GCSW, 2020a). However, although "ending racism" was initially proposed and considered, it was not selected as part of the initial GCSW (Lubben et al., 2018). Rather, ending racism was considered as inextricably linked to all of the GCSW and intersecting all other grand challenges and would thus be addressed within each of the selected GCSW, and therefore a stand-alone Grand Challenge was not necessary (Teasley et al., 2021).

A content analysis of the 21 concept papers published under the initial 12 GCSW found inadequate representation of certain racial and ethnic groups, which is consistent with previous findings of social work literature, with approximately four to five times as many studies mentioning African Americans and Latinxs compared with Asians and Native Americans (Woo et al., 2018; Rao et al., 2021). Against this background, the social work field needs to embrace a more explicit, renewed, and continued commitment to eradicating systemic racism (Rao et al., 2021).

As Davis (2016) asserted, racism has been and continues to be the grand challenge in the United States, and it is important to acknowledge racism in social work research because only then can social workers begin to address the underlying causes of social suffering experienced by the communities they serve. After a nationwide campaign by social work scholars, along with local and global support of Black Lives Matter following George Floyd's murder, the Grand Challenge to Eliminate Racism was announced by AASWSW in 2020. This key step explicitly focuses on racism and underscores the importance of racism in all the Grand Challenges, building on the values embodied in the aspiration of the Grand Challenges to achieve broad goals (GCSW, 2020). It makes it even more important to understand how the original 12 Grand Challenges have addressed racism, and highlights the gaps needed to be addressed in the context of the ongoing challenges; furthermore, it is important to underscore that the Grand Challenge to Eliminate Racism urges the social work profession to focus on eradicating systemic racism and White supremacy, both within the profession and within society (Teasley et al., 2021). Finally, it promotes innovative and effective ways to prevent or interrupt racism and provides both support and accountability to the profession in the quest to eliminate racism (Rao et al., 2021).

Moving Forward: Strategies to Eliminate Anti-Asian Racism

Evidence-based research and practice are instrumental in supporting efforts to eliminate racism and promote changes at the individual, organizational, community, professional, and societal levels to ultimately improve the well-being of the marginalized racial minorities who are impacted by racism and white supremacy (Teasley et al., 2021). The overall GCSW, and particularly the Grand Challenge to Eliminate Racism (GCSW, 2020b), are ideally positioned to provide leadership for racial justice at the macro, meso, and micro levels of social work (Teasley et al., 2021).

Disentangling the Model Minority Myth

The model minority myth was manufactured during the Civil Rights movement to weaponize Asian Americans against the Black Power movement and other racial justice movements in the 1960s and 1970s (Raju, 2021). The myth is problematic for a variety of reasons. First, it frames Asian Americans as universally successful minorities and therefore reinforces color-blind ideologies according to which racial barriers would not play a significant role in the lives of people of color (Museus, 2013). The discrimination experiences of Asian Americans are dismissed (Abrams, 2021). Second, it masks significant inequalities within the racial group and fuels the misconception that Asian Americans are problem-free and thus perpetuates assumptions that they do not require resources and support; further, it renders them invisible in research, policy, and practice (Museus & Kiang, 2009) and erases the needs of those who do not fit the stereotype. The myth constructs Asian Americans as honorary Whites who are not as good as individuals in the racial majority but are superior to other minority groups; it therefore fosters racial division, rather than solidarity, among people of color (Matsuda, 1990).

In fact, 23 million Asian Americans trace their roots to more than 20 counties in East and Southeast Asia and the Indian subcontinent, each with unique histories, cultures, languages, and other characteristics. Just as Black, Indigenous, and other people of color, Asian Americans suffer from many problems, including housing and employment discrimination, high rates of insurance, low access to mental health services, and immigration issues (Budiman & Ruiz, 2021). For example, although Asian Americans do well on measures of economic well-being compared with the overall U.S. population, this varies widely among Asian origin groups. The top 10% of households have 10 times the income of the bottom 10% (Budiman & Ruiz, 2021). Asian Americans also have a lower homeownership rate than the overall U.S. population (59% vs. 64%) (Budiman & Ruiz, 2021). People from Asia made up about 14% of the 10.5 million unauthorized immigrants in the United States in 2017 and are expected to make up 36% of all U.S. immigrants by 2055 (Budiman & Ruiz, 2021). In addition, only 72% of all Asian Americans are "proficient" in English, with nearly all U.S.-born Asians (95%) proficient in English, compared with 57% of foreign-born Asians (Budiman & Ruiz, 2021).

The model minority stereotype contributes to the misperception of Asian Americans' mental health status, which perpetuates the invisibility and possible neglect of this minority group's needs. The misperceptions also lead to inadequate resources and knowledge that are needed to work effectively with and meet the needs of this diverse group (Cheng et al., 2017). It is critical for social work researchers, educators, and practitioners to first dismantle the complexity of Asian American communities to hear and address the community's issues, including but not limited to poverty, health and mental health, immigration, and discrimination.

THE HISTORY OF RACISM AGAINST ASIAN AMERICANS   313

Fostering Racial Solidarity

It has long been recognized how vital is to create strong group solidarity among various racial minorities to battle racism (Chong & Rogers, 2005; Hoston, 2009). Racial minorities are empowered if different ethnic/racial groups support each other; building solidarity among racial minority groups is highly encouraged to overcome the current challenges. As xenophobia and White nationalism increase in the United States, it is more pressing than ever for the communities of color to be united to fight against racism. There have been many examples of powerful and moving coalitions between Asian and Black communities in the last 200 years that have led to major leaps forward in racial justice. For example, civil rights pioneer Frederick Douglass argued on behalf of Chinese and Japanese immigrants, urging Americans not to fear Asian languages or cultures. In his immigration lecture in 1867, Douglass declared that the people of the United States were not racially, ethnically, or religiously homogeneous:

> It is this great right I assert for the Chinese and Japanese, and for all other varieties of men equally with yourselves, now and forever. . . . Chinese immigration should be settled upon higher principles than those of a cold and selfish expediency. There are such things in the world as human rights. They rest upon no conventional foundation, but are eternal, universal, and indestructible. Among these, is the right of locomotion; the right of migration; the right which belongs to no particular race, but belongs alike to all and to all alike. . . . I want a home here not only for the Negro, the mulatto, and the Latin races; but I want the Asiatic to find a home here in the United States, and feel at home here, both for his sake and for ours. (Douglass, 1979, pp. 245–246)

During the Philippine-American War in 1898, the experiences of the Filipino people resonated with the Black community because of the shared histories of imperialism, racism, and economic exploitation. Many African American soldiers empathized and, along with prominent African American leaders, including Ida B. Wells and Henry M. Turner, supported Philippine's independence from the United States. During the 1960s, African American communities protested the Vietnam War under the leadership of Malcolm X, Muhammad Ali, and Martin Luther King Jr., who took strong stands against the war (Raju, 2021). Asian Americans activists include Grace Lee

Boggs, who spent much of her life advocating for civil rights and was a noted figure in Detroit's Black Power movement, and Yuri Kochiyama, who consistently raised the need for Black reparations to mend for the long legacy of anti-Black structures and practices that have harmed Black communities throughout 1960s and 1970s (Ahuja, 2014).

Following the racist murder of Vincent Chin, Black civil rights leaders like Rev. Jesse Jackson and leaders of the National Association for the Advancement of Colored People played a critical role in bringing attention to his case. The multicultural coalition that came together in that fight helped form the basis of the "Rainbow Coalition," which later became a prominent political organization that raised public awareness and pursued social justice, civil rights, and political activism. Many Asian American organizations, such as Asian Pacific Environmental Network and Organizing Asian Communities, have long histories of working in multi-racial solidarity with African Americans. During the summer of 2020, many Asian Americans made deep commitments to standing up for Black lives, including supporting Black Lives Matter (BLM) in protests, and providing multilingual resources to help Asian Americans talk about BLM within their families and communities (Jones, 2021). During the rise of hate crimes in the COVID-19 pandemic, African American leaders stepped up in solidarity with the Asian American community (Jones, 2021).

The remarkable examples of solidarity between African American and Asian American communities throughout U.S. history serve as testament to the power of communities of color when united. It is essential to continue to educate on shared histories and experiences. Some concrete steps that communities of color can take to show solidarity and be stronger allies to each other include consuming anti-racist literature, having conversations across races, recognizing their own racial biases, and engaging in community and policy initiatives (Raju, 2021).

Reflecting Racism within the Social Work Profession and Developing an Anti-Asian Racism Workforce

Issues of White privilege and the empathy gap between social workers and clients of color must be addressed (NASW, 2021). The inequality of power in conceptualizing, developing, analyzing, implementing, and disseminating

THE HISTORY OF RACISM AGAINST ASIAN AMERICANS   315

research and service delivery must be the start of the conversation (Coley & Young, 2018). Fundamental to opposing the dominant traditions of practice is the growth of a critical consciousness, in which social worker educators, researchers, and practitioners continuously reflect on our own biases, assumptions, and worldviews (Sakamoto, 2007). This state of awareness must also extend to the profession and institutions (Corley & Young, 2018). Such ongoing self-reflection, education, and professional training is the first step for social workers to address the challenges of anti-racism (NASW, 2020). Critical Race Theory (CRT) is valuable because it acknowledges that racism has been and continues to be a lasting fixture in the United States, one that is interwoven in dominant cultural norms and politics (Crenshaw et al., 1995). Therefore, issues of power, privilege, and oppression should play a critical role in the investigation of research topics. CRT helps expose the sociocultural and political processes that marginalize the minoritized groups. Moreover, it underscores that a social worker's racial privilege can act as blinders to the experiences of groups confronted by structural racism (Ortiz & Jani, 2010).

Pipelines within social work training programs that include more members of racial-ethnic groups are also critical (Yang et al., 2020). According to the Council on Social Work Education (CSWE), only 3.5% of master's degree and 2.2% of bachelor's degree graduates in social work in 2019 were Asian Americans (CSWE Annual Survey of Social Work Programs, 2019). This is significantly lower than the percentage of Asian Americans in the total population in the United States (Budiman & Ruiz, 2021). Kwong (2018) conducted surveys with Asian American social workers and confirmed the gap in recruiting and training adequate numbers of Asian American populations. More needs to be done to educate youth about social work career opportunities and to enhance the recruitment and retention, career development, and professional growth of Asian American social workers. Greater understanding of culture and career choice process among Asian American families is sorely needed. An emphasis on idealism and altruism of the profession can be provided during the career counseling process to motivate students to choose the social work profession to serve the population (Kwong, 2018). Scholarship opportunities or loan repayment programs could also be provided to encourage students from underserved Asian American communities to join the social work workforce and create a pipeline for social work practitioners who will in turn serve their communities, which often lack access to care.

Support Reporting and Bystander Intervention Training

Social workers should also look beyond traditional therapy and consider operating outside academic and healthcare settings. It is critical for social workers to study the roots and outcome of racist incidents, and design interventions to help both targets and bystanders fight racism. Bystander interventions, by which witnesses intercede to thwart harassment, have been proved effective and have positive downstream consequences for both individuals and society in terms of fostering inclusion and promoting equality for marginalized populations (Potter & Moynihan, 2011). Such training can help foster inclusive environments for racial/ethnic groups who may be targeted by abuse or harassment and support Asian Americans facing xenophobia (Ho et al., 2020).

Sue et al. (2012) identified four major anti-bias strategies that targets, allies, and bystanders can deploy when racist incidents occur in everyday life: educate the perpetrator, make the "invisible" visible, disarm the perpetrator, or seek outside support and help. Racism does not occur in isolation from others. If no one intervenes, it fosters a false consensus. Through bystander intervention, the targets who were intervened felt an increased sense of empowerment, health, and well-being, while bystanders who intervened felt that they were staying true to their moral values (Sue et al., 2012). Various organizations have hosted "anti-Asian racism" bystander intervention training. For example, Asian American Advancing Justice/Chicago, the Council on American Islamic Relations/Chicago, and Hollaback! have launched virtual trainings in which participants learn about the history of anti-Asian racism, how to identify situations of harassment, and how to intervene safely (Asian Americans Advancing Justice/Chicago, n.d.). The training also provides simple and effective instruction on bystander interventions with their approach of the "5 Ds": distract, delegate, document, delay, and direct. Social work organizations and social workers may actively engage in and disseminate such training and educate the public.

Meanwhile, it is important to recognize and further promote Asian Americans' healing and resistance practices, such as reporting and seeking social and community support. Survey results show that after reporting to Stop AAPI Hate, Asian Americans reported a reduction in racial trauma symptoms. This suggests that reporting is one important strategy for Asian Americans to cope with hate incidents (Saw et al., 2021). NASW has initiated work to get Congress to pass the NO HATE Act to prevent hate crimes, improve data reporting, and expand responses to better support those communities affected by hate crimes (NASW, 2021).

Policy Initiatives on Anti-Asian Racism

It is critical for social workers to note that racism operates at an institutional and individual level; thus, to address the negative impact of racism, social workers must consider interventions at multiple levels. In fact, scholars have called for urgent institutional changes that address structural inequalities (Coley & Young, 2018; McMahon & Allen-Meares). Macro-practice methods to address racial injustice include advocacy, social media activism, political activism, and organizational analysis of potentially racist policies and practices (Hohman, 2015). Policies to protect Asian Americans against racial hate crimes are necessary. More recently, we see greater attention focused on racist acts against Asian Americans. On February 22, 2021, California lawmakers passed legislation to allocate $1.4 million for tracking anti-Asian hate incidents; on May 18, 2021, the House of Representatives passed the COVID-19 Hate Crimes Act to expedite the review of hate crimes related to COVID-19 and directed resources toward making the reporting of hate crimes more accessible. Also, on July 9, 2021, Illinois passed the Teaching Equitable Asian American Community History Act and became the first state to mandate Asian American history in public schools, requiring "a unit of instruction studying the events of Asian American history" (Hauck, 2021). This legislation is a way to educate children and their families, create a more inclusive and comprehensive understanding of American history for students and their families, and thereby helps fight anti-Asian racism and xenophobia in Illinois and nationally. Social workers should advocate for such anti-racist policies/programs, participate in the policymaking process, and coordinate policy responses to anti-Asian racism.

National leadership is essential to speak out against anti-Asian stigma and coordinate an effective response (Misra et al., 2020). Actions and voices from political leaders are needed to change the current atmosphere against racial minorities, including Asian Americans. Social workers should coordinate with policymakers, communication experts, and media outlets to condemn racism and White supremacy, and xenophobia in all its forms and stand in unity with individual and communities who are targets of racial discrimination. In addition, efforts can be made to advocate government leaders to directly address anti-Asian racism and violence, provide targeted health, economic, and social assistance, and call on national, state, and local organizations to ensure investments in culturally appropriate services and community-based outreach to Asian communities that are targeted.

Social workers should also actively engage with national and local nonprofit organizations advocating for anti-Asian racism. Such organizations—for example, Asian Americans Advancing Justice, National Coalition for Asian Pacific American Community Development, and Asian Youth Center—provide various anti-Asian racism resources to better inform Asian American communities and individuals experiencing anti-Asian harassment. Equally important, social workers need to closely cooperate and engage with community organizations, private practices, and grassroot and activist agencies.

The Importance of Community-Based Solutions

For a pressing social problem such as racism, innovative, high-reward community-based solutions are needed. To further maximize their impact with the Asian American communities, social workers also need to collaborate with community leaders and engage the community on anti-racism advocacy and service delivery. Outreach conducted in Asian American communities could improve anti-racism discourse and make resources/care more accessible for those in need: for example, by collaborating with Asian American immigrant organizations to provide guidance on delivering trauma-informed care and culturally responsive services. Social workers can actively support a community-centered response and foster community care that prioritizes assessing and addressing community needs, for example, in language support for mental health, legal, employment, and immigration services.

Social workers can further coordinate with policymakers, communication experts, and media outlets to design counter-messaging strategies to stimulate the public discourse and a willingness to confront the reality of racism and inequality and reverse the harm that has already been done to Asian communities. Kwate et al. (2014) tested the effectiveness of an outdoor advertising media in validating racism experiences, reducing psychological distress, and improving neighborhood well-being. Such outdoor ad campaigns deliver bold messages and can serve as individual- and

THE HISTORY OF RACISM AGAINST ASIAN AMERICANS   319

community-level pathways, through which people stop, notice, and respond, to redress the negative health effects of racism and to stimulate public awareness. Topics can include the representation of Asian Americans in media, diversity of Asian Americans, anti-stigma and anti-discrimination campaigns, bystander interventions, and resources for reporting and care.

Addressing Access to Mental Healthcare

Asian Americans consistently display lower rates of utilization of mental health treatment compared to other racial/ethnic groups (U.S. Department of Health and Human Services, 2016, 2017, 2018, 2019). Literature has indicated that Asian Americans often have trouble accessing mental healthcare due to cultural, linguistic, structural, and societal barriers (Liu, 2009; Ngo-Metzger et al., 2003; Sue et al., 2012). Further, undocumented, low-income, elderly, and limited-English-proficient Asian Americans experience greater barriers to healthcare (Le et al., 2020). Feelings of shame, stigmatization, and an unwillingness to burden others are major contributors to the lack of help-seeking behavior among Asian Americans with mental illness. Non-cultural practical barriers to accessing care, such as cost, language barriers, and lack of knowledge of available resources, also contribute to low utilization rates among Asian Americans. A study examining perceived barriers to mental health treatment among Chinese Americans (Kung, 2004) found that practical barriers, including cost of treatment, time, knowledge of access, and language, were perceived as being more prohibitive than cultural barriers. Services improving the relevance and fit of mental healthcare and community-based outreach interventions increasing awareness of available services are needed to improve access to mental health treatment among Asian Americans (Yang et al., 2020).

Culturally Sensitive Evidence-Based Intervention

Evidence-based intervention is relevant to anti-racism and racial equity work. For example, research found that Korean American parents are keenly aware of xenophobia and racism and were clear about the importance of promoting strong ethnic identity and racial awareness; furthermore, American-born Asian American parents of school-age children felt more equipped to parent their children around issues of racial discrimination because of their own experience growing up in the United States (Okazaki, 2021). Park et al. (2022) found parental discrimination was associated with parental psychological distress. Based on such findings, social work educators and practitioners may help develop and distribute resources for Asian American families to talk about race and racism and to support healthy ethnic identity and imbue a sense of pride in cultural heritage; for example, videos, podcasts, and webinars to help parents learn how to talk to children about racist and xenophobic attacks against Asian Americans. Telehealth is a highly convenient form to provide appropriate mental/physical health services (Park et al., 2022). Social workers targeting immigrant parents can develop tailored programs to provide support in various forms, such as virtual support groups for parents or therapy sessions. Such virtual interventions can also target the children of immigrant parents (e.g., book clubs or social-emotional support groups for children). Reaching out to immigrant families with various virtual interventions can address and manage increased parental stress and psychological distress at the same time (Park et al., 2022).

In addition, having a higher level of a sense of belonging had a counter effect against the detrimental impact of racial microaggressions on the depressive symptoms (Choi et al., 2021). Service that fosters community belongings to improve the mental health of immigrants could be provided as ways to address issues of ethnocultural diversity and discrimination. Supporting programs in immigrant service agencies and cultural and religious institutions to increase social participation and engagement also would help strengthen community belonging and improve immigrant mental health (Salami et al., 2019).

Research has also suggested the heterogeneity of Asian Americans and its implications for services for this population. For example, first-generation Asian Americans display a higher risk of anxiety and depression, and experience lower rates of mental health service utilization due to stigma and lack of access than second-generation counterparts (Takeuchi et al., 2007); friend networks and relative groups play different roles in influencing depression for different generations of Asian Americans. Further, the relationships between immigration-related factors and mental disorders were different for men and women (Takeuchi et al., 2007). In their prevention and treatment efforts, social workers need to be aware of the complicated sociocultural contexts and nuanced association between social relational factors and depression.

THE HISTORY OF RACISM AGAINST ASIAN AMERICANS   321

Research also found that Asian Americans who experienced racism display racial trauma that can be felt across generations (Hahm et al., 2021; Nagata et al., 2015; Saw et al., 2021). Therefore, social workers can use trauma-informed approaches and contribute to more healing (Abrams, 2021). Based on the findings on stigma as an important factor to explain the lack of mental health services of Asian Americans, suggestions have been made for social work interventions that may carry less stigma than one-on-one therapy, such as workshops and support groups (Abrams, 2021).

Directions for Future Anti-Asian Racism Research

Asian Americans, comprising several diverse cultures, remain one of the most under-researched racial groups; yet they are the fastest-growing minority population in the United States today (Choi et al., 2006; Ruiz et al., 2021). The lack of research makes it difficult to understand the impact of discrimination, as well as develop effective micro-, meso-, and macro-level interventions.

Scholars have emphasized that within-group heterogeneity is a key characteristic of the Asian American population. This heterogeneity is based not only on culture but also on language, national origin, social class, gender, religion, immigration status, and experiences with discrimination. Estimates that aggregate across Asian American populations may lose information about high-risk groups and lead to missed opportunities for intervention. Hence, future studies should oversample Asian subgroups and disaggregate their data to better understand the experience of specific ethnic groups (Coley & Young, 2018; Gee et al., 2009; Mokuau et al., 2008; Pelczarski & Kemp, 2006). Breaking out the data into subcategories allows a closer look at the data and thus reveals patterns that would otherwise be masked (Shah & Kauh, 2021). Such disaggregated data are needed to thoroughly explore internal or cultural factors, the meaning and measurements of mental health, stigma reduction, coping strategies, and support mechanisms in different Asian subcultures in the United States and to develop evidence-based intervention models based on these findings (Yang et al., 2020).

The research to date has mostly focused on the racism experiences of Asian Americans at the individual level, and there is a shortage of studies that have examined structural discrimination (Coley & Young, 2018; McMahon & Allen-Meares, 1992). Little attention has been paid to how societal conditions (e.g., institutional policies) may disadvantage the Asian American population. Future research should study discrimination at multiple levels and develop new methods to assess structural discrimination. For example, it would be important to understand whether geographic locations—such as living in areas with more negative media coverage, stringent immigration policies—is associated with increased levels of racism and negative health outcomes, and coping strategies.

In addition, nearly all studies of Asian Americans and discrimination are based on cross-sectional data. Such reliance on cross-sectional designs prevents the evaluation of causal relations and the study of the potential cumulative adverse effects of discrimination. Hence, longitudinal studies are needed to examine the long-term impacts of discrimination on Asian American communities (Gee et al., 2009).

Future research should also focus on mediating and moderating factors that may reduce discrimination or its impact. This could include individual-level factors, such as social connectedness and social support, or macro-level factors, such as anti-Asian racism policies, programs, and legislations. Such studies would greatly extend the current body of research and identify ways to promote resilience and support, and to help social work educators, service providers, and policymakers to proactively provide services and implement policies that promote well-being of the targeted marginalized groups and educate the larger public groups (Corley & Young, 2018).

Lastly, more research is needed to develop and test the effectiveness of innovative anti-Asian racism interventions. For example, as Asian Americans have experienced the largest single year-over-year rise in severe online harassment in comparison to other groups from 2020 to 2021 (ADL, 2021), it would be important to understand the effects of increasing incidents of online racism, particularly on adolescents (Hswen et al., 2021) and give important considerations for the use of online platforms, such as Reddit and Twitter, as future sites for interventions (Silberman & Record, 2021).

Conclusion

Asian Americans have long experienced a history of racism and discrimination in the United States. Social work cannot fully maximize its mission and pursue social justice without advocating for dismantling systemic racism. Social workers must continue to address their own biases within the profession, and challenge the model minority myth to hear Asian American

THE HISTORY OF RACISM AGAINST ASIAN AMERICANS   323

communities' needs and address their issues; equally important, social workers must actively promote solidarities among people of color to build racial justice. Eradicating systemic racism requires practitioners', educators', and researchers' efforts at the individual, organizational, community, professional, and societal levels. Last but not least, there is an urgent need for anti-racism research to focus on the examinations of within-group heterogeneity of Asian Americans, structural racism, the long-term impacts of discrimination, mediating and moderating factors of racial discrimination, as well as on developing innovative and effective anti-Asian racism interventions.

Study Questions

1. What is the history of the interpersonal and structural anti-Asian American racism and oppression in the U.S.?
2. How has systemic racism negatively impacted Asian American communities?
3. Why does addressing anti-Asian American racism fit the mission and core value of the social work profession, and why is the "Grand Challenge to Eliminate Racism" a key step in providing support and leadership in the efforts to eliminate anti-Asian racism?
4. What are the possible strategies social workers can use to address anti-Asian racism at the individual, organizational, community, professional, and societal levels?
5. How has the myth of the "model minority" fostered invisibility and racial erasure of Asian Americans' experiences?
6. How in U.S. history have Asian Americans fostered solidarity, and what can be learned from such examples to fight racism and promote racial justice?
7. How can future social work research address and contribute to eliminate anti-Asian racism?

References

Abrams, Z. (2021). The mental health impact of anti-Asian racism. *Monitor on Psychology*, 52(5), 22. doi: 10.1037/a0031547.
Asian-Americans Experience Rise in Severe Online Hate and Harassment, ADL Survey Finds. (2021). Anti Defamation League. https://www.adl.org/resources/press-release/asian-americans-experience-rise-severe-online-hate-and-harassment-adl

324 MEIRONG LIU

Ahuja, K. (2014, June 6). Honoring the Legacy of Yuri Kochiyama. https://obamawhiteho use.archives.gov/blog/2014/06/06/honoring-legacy-yuri-kochiyama

Asian Americans Then and Now. Asia Society. Retrieved Jan 19, 2023, from https://asia society.org/education/asian-americans-then-and-now.

Asian Americans Advancing Justice/Chicago (n.d.). As COVID-19 cases surge, nonprofit organizations launch local bystander intervention training to combat anti-Asian harassment. *Asian Americans Advancing Justice/Chicago.* https://www.advancingjustice-chicago.org/as-covid-19-cases-surge-nonprofit-organizations-launch-local-bystan der-intervention-trainings-to-combat-anti-asian-harassment/.

Asian-Americans Experience Rise in Severe Online Hate and Harassment, ADL Survey Finds. (2021). Anti Defamation League. https://www.adl.org/resources/press-release/ asian-americans-experience-rise-severe-online-hate-and-harassment-adl

Bo, S. (1885). A protest against the Statue of Liberty. *Digital History.* https://www.digital history.uh.edu/disp_textbook_print.cfm?smtid=3&psid=31.

Brockell, G. (2021, March 18). The long, ugly history of anti-Asian racism and violence in the U.S. *Washington Post.* https://www.washingtonpost.com/history/2021/03/18/hist ory-anti-asian-violence-racism/

Budiman, A., & Ruiz, N. (2021). Key facts about Asian Americans, a diverse and growing population. *Pew Research Center.* https://www.pewresearch.org/fact-tank/2021/04/29/ key-facts-about-Asian Americans/.

Carter, R. T., & Pieterse, A.L. (2020). *Measuring the effects of racism: Guidelines for the assessment and treatment of race-based traumatic stress injury.* New York: Columbia University Press.

Cheah, C. S. L., Wang, C., Ren, H., Zong, X., Cho, H. S., & Xue, X. (2020). COVID-19 racism and mental health in Chinese American families. *Pediatrics (Evanston), 146*(5), e2020021816. doi:10.1542/peds.2020-021816.

Cheng, A. W., Chang, J., O'Brien, J., Budgazad, M., & Tsai, J. (2017). Model minority stereotype: Influence on perceived mental health needs of Asian Americans. *Journal of Immigrant and Minority Health, 19*(3), 572–581. https://doi: 10.1007/s10903-016-0440-0.

Choi, S., Weng, S., Park, H., Lewis, J., Harwood, S. A., Mendenhall, R., & Huntt, M. B. (2021). Sense of belonging, racial microaggressions, and depressive symptoms among students of Asian descent in the United States. *Smith College Studies in Social Work, 91*(2), 115–141. https://doi.org/10.1080/00377317.2021.1882922.

Choi, Y., Harachi, T., Gilmore, M. R., & Catalano, R. F. (2006). Are multiracial adolescents at greater risk? Comparisons of rates, patterns, and correlates of substance use and violence between monoracial and multiracial adolescents. *American Journal of Orthopsychiatry, 6*(1), 86–97. doi: 10.1037/0002-9432.76.1.86.

Choi, Y., & Lahey, B. (2006). Testing the model minority stereotype: Youth behaviors across racial and ethnic groups. *Social Service Review, 80*(3), 419–452. doi: 10.1086/ 505288.

Chong, D., & Rogers, R. (2005). Racial solidarity and political participation. *Political Behavior, 27*(4), 347–374. https://www.jstor.org/stable/4500204.

Corley, N. A., & Young, S. M. (2018). Is social work still racist? A content analysis of recent literature. *Social Work (New York), 63*(4), 317–326. doi: 10.1093/sw/swy042.

Crenshaw, K., Gotanda, N., Peller, G., & Thomas, K. (1995). *Critical Race Theory: The key writings that formed the movement.* New York: New Press.

CSWE Annual Survey of Social Work Programs. (2019). *Statistics on social work education in the United States: Summary of the CSWE Annual Survey of Social Work Programs.* https://cswe.org/getattachment/Research-Statistics/2019-Annual-Statistics-on-Social-Work-Education-in-the-United-States-Final-(1).pdf.aspx.

Davis, L. E. (2016). Race: America's grand challenge. *Journal of the Society for Social Work and Research, 7,* 395–403. doi: 10.1086/686296.

Daniller, A. (2021). Majorities of Americans see at least some discrimination against Black, Hispanic, and Asian people in the U.S. *Pew Research Center.* https://www.pewresearch.org/fact-tank/2021/03/18/majorities-of-americans-see-at-least-some-discrimination-against-black-hispanic-and-asian-people-in-the-u-s/.

Douglass, F. (1979). Our composite nationality: An address delivered in Boston, Massachusetts, on 7 December 1869. In J. W. Blassingame & J. R. McKivigan (Eds.), *The Frederick Douglass Papers, Series One: Speeches, Debates and Interviews, Vol. 4: 1864–80* (pp. 240–259). New Haven: Yale University Press.

Fisher, F., & Fisher, F. (2010) Congressional passage of the Chinese exclusion act of 1882. *Immigrants & Minorities, 20*(2), 58–74. doi: 10.1080/02619288.2001.9975015.

Gee, G. C., Spencer, M., Chen, J., Yip, T. & Takeuchi, D. T. (2007). The association between self-reported racial discrimination and 12-month DSM-IV mental disorders among Asian Americans nationwide. *Social Science & Medicine, 64*(10),1984–1996.

Gee, H. (1999). Beyond Black and White: Selected writings by Asian Americans within the Critical Race Theory movement (comments). *St. Mary's Law Journal, 30,* 759–800.

Gee, G. C., Ro, A., Shariff-Marco, S., & Chae, D. (2009). Racial discrimination and health among Asian Americans: evidence, assessment, and directions for future research. *Epidemiologic Reviews, 31,* 130–151. https://doi.org/10.1093/epirev/mxp009

Gover, A. R., Harper, S. B., & Langton, L. (2020). Anti-Asian hate crime during the COVID-19 pandemic: Exploring the reproduction of inequality. *American Journal of Criminal Justice, 45*(4), 647–667. doi: 10.1007/s12103-020-09545-1.

Grand Challenges for Social Work. (2020a). About. https://grandchallengesforsocialwork.org/about/.

Grand Challenges for Social Work. (2020b). Eliminate racism. https://grandchallengesforsocialwork.org/eliminate-racism/.

Hauck, G. (2021). "A watershed moment": Illinois becomes first state to mandate Asian American history in public schools. *USA Today.* https://eu.usatoday.com/story/news/nation/2021/07/09/illinois-mandates-asian-american-history-public-schools-teaach-act/7472690002/.

Hahm, H., Ha, Y., Scott., J., Wongchai., V., Chen, J., & Liu, C. (2021). COVID-19 Adult resilience Experience Study, Stop AAPI Hate Mental Health report. *Stop AAPI Hate.* https://stopaapihate.org/wp-content/uploads/2021/05/Stop-AAPI-Hate-Mental-Health-Report-210527.pdf.

Hing, B. O. (2001). Vigilante racism: The de-Americanization of immigrant America. *Michigan Journal of Race, 7,* 441.

Ho, C. P., Chong, A., Narayan, A., Cooke, E. A., Deng, F., Agarwal, V., DeBenedectis, C. M., Deitte, L. A., Jay, A. K., & Kagetsu, N. J. (2020). Mitigating Asian American bias and xenophobia in response to the Coronavirus pandemic: How you can be an upstander. *Journal of the American College of Radiology: JACR, 17*(12), 1692–1694. https://doi.org/10.1016/j.jacr.2020.09.030

Hohman, M. (2015). Racial justice: Moving from macro to micro and back again. https://socialwork.sdsu.edu/insitu/diversity/racial-justice-moving-from-macro-to-micro-and-back-again-by-melinda-hohman-ph-d/.

Hollaback! Training to stop anti-asian/american and xenophobic harassment. (n.d.). https://www.ihollaback.org/bystanderintervention/.

Hosten, W. T. (2009). Black solidarity and racial context: An exploration of the role of Black solidarity in U.S. cities. *Journal of Black Studies, 39*(5), 719–731. https://doi.org/10.1177/0021934707299642.

Hswen, Y., Xu, X., Hing, A., Hawkins, J. B., Brownstein, J. S., & Gee, G. C. (2021). Association of "#covid19" versus "#chinesevirus" with anti-Asian sentiments on Twitter: March 9–23, 2020. *American Journal of Public Health, 111*, 956–964. https://doi.org/10.2105/AJPH.2021.306154.

Huynh, Q. L., Devos, T., & Smalarz, L. (2011). Perpetual foreigner in one's own land: Potential implications for identity and psychological adjustment. *Journal of Social and Clinical Psychology, 30*, 133–162. 10.1521/jscp.2011.30.2.133.

Jeung, R., Kulkarni, M. P., & Choi, C. (2020, April 1). Epidemic of hate: Asian xenophobia amid coronavirus. *Los Angeles Times*. https://www.latimes.com/opinion/story/2020-04-01/coronavirus-anti- asian-discrimination-threats.

Jones, V. (2021, March 19). Black-Asian solidarity has a long and storied history in America. *CNN Commentary*. https://search.proquest.com/docview/2502925825.

Karlsen, S., & Nazroo, J. Y. (2002). Relation between racial discrimination, social class, and health among ethnic minority groups. *American Journal of Public Health, 92*(4), 624–631.

Kung, W. (2004). Cultural and practical barriers to seeking mental health treatment for Chinese Americans. *Journal of Community Psychology, 32*, 27–43. 10.1002/jcop.10077.

Kwate, N. O. (2014). "Racism still exists": A public health intervention using racism "countermarketing" outdoor advertising in a Black neighborhood. *Journal of Urban Health, 91*(5), 851–872. https://doi.org/10.1007/s11524-014-9873-8.

Kwong, K. (2018). Career choice, barriers, and prospects of Asian American social workers. *International Journal of Higher Education, 7*(6), 1. doi: 10.5430/ijhe.v7n6p1.

Lau, A. S., Tsai, W., Shih, J., Liu, L. L., Hwang, W. C., & Takeuchi, D. T. (2013). The immigrant paradox among Asian American women: Are disparities in the burden of depression and anxiety paradoxical or explicable? *Journal of Consulting and Clinical Psychology, 81*, 901–911. 10.1037/a0032105.

Le, T. K., Cha, L., Han, H. R., & Tseng, W. (2020). Anti-Asian xenophobia and Asian American COVID-19 disparities. *American Journal of Public Health, 110*(9), 1371–1373.

Lee, D. L., & Ahn, S. (2011). Racial discrimination and Asian mental health: A meta-analysis. *The Counseling Psychologist, 39*(3), 463–489. https://doi.org/10.1177/0011000010381791.

Lee, E. (2002). The Chinese exclusion example: Race, immigration, and American gatekeeping, 1882–1924. *Journal of American Ethnic History, 21*(3), 36–62. http://www.jstor.org/stable/27502847.

Liu, C., Liu, T., Chang, J., Koh, A., Huang, L., Fu, R., Noh., R., & Yang., A. (2021). The National Anti-Asian American Racism Survey: Stop AAPI Hate health report. *Stop AAPI Hate*. https://stopaapihate.org/wp-content/uploads/2021/05/Stop-AAPI-Hate-Mental-Health-Report-210527.pdf.

Liu, M. (2009). Addressing the mental health problems of Chinese international college students in the United States. *Advances in Social Work, 10*(1), 69–86.

Lubben, J. E., Barth, R. P., Fong, R., Flynn, M. L., Sherryden, M., & Uehara, E. (2018). Grand challenges for social work and society. In R. Fong, J. E. Lubben, & R.P. Barth (Eds.), *Grand challenges for social work and society* (pp. 1–17). Oxford: Oxford University Press.

Matsuda, G. (1990). "Only the beginning": Continuing the fight for empowerment. *Amerasia Journal, 16*(1): 159–169.

McMahon, A., & Allen-Meares, P. (1992). Is social work racist? A content analysis of recent literature. *Social Work, 37*, 533–539. doi: 10.1093/sw/37.6.533.

Misra, S., Le, P. D., Goldmann, E., & Yang, L. H. (2020). Psychological impact of anti-Asian stigma due to the COVID-19 pandemic: A call for research, practice, and policy responses. *Psychological Trauma: Theory, Research, Practice and Policy, 12*(5), 461–464. https://doi.org/10.1037/tra0000821.

Mokuau, N., Garlock-Tuialii, J., & Lee, P. (2008). Has social work met its commitment to Native Hawaiians and other Pacific Islanders? A review of the periodical literature. *Social Work, 58*, 115–121.

Morey, B. N. (2018). Mechanisms by which anti-immigrant stigma exacerbates racial/ethnic health disparities. *American Journal of Public Health, 108*(4), 460–463.

Museus, S. D. (2013). Asian Americans and Pacific Islanders: A national portrait of growth, diversity, and inequality. In S. D. Museus, D. C. Maramba, & R. T. Teranishi (Eds.), *The misrepresented minority: New insights on Asian Americans and Pacific Islanders, and their implications for higher education* (pp. 11–41). Virginia, Sterling: Stylus.

Museus, S. D., & Kiang, P. N. (2009). The Model Minority myth and how it contributes to the invisible minority reality in higher education research. *New Directions for Institutional Research, 142*, 5–15.

Nagata, D. K., Kim, J. H., & Nguyen, T. U. (2015). Processing cultural trauma: Intergenerational effects of the Japanese American incarceration. *Journal of Social Issues, 71*(2), 356–370.

NASW (2020, August 21). Social workers must help dismantle systems of oppression and fight racism within the social work profession. *National Association of Social Workers.* https://www.socialworkers.org/News/News-Releases/ID/2219/Social-Workers-Must-Help-Dismantle-Systems-of-Oppression-and-Fight-Racism-Within-Social-Work-Profession.

NASW (2021, March 18.) NASW calls for an end to hate, racism and gun violence against Asian Americans. *National Association of Social Workers.* https://www.socialworkers.org/News/News-Releases/ID/2298/NASW-Calls-for-an-End-to-Hate-Racism-and-Gun-Violence-Against-Asian Americans.

Ngo-Metzger, Q., Massagli, M. P., Clarridge, B. R., Manocchia, M., Davis, R. B., Iezzoni, L. I., & Phillips, R. S. (2003). Linguistic and cultural barriers to care. *Journal of General Internal Medicine, 18*(1), 44–52.

Okazaki, S. (2023). *Asian American Experiences of Racism during COVID-19.* New York University. Retrieved Jan 19, 2023, from https://steinhardt.nyu.edu/ihdsc/on-the-ground/asian-american-experiences-racism-during-covid-19

Ortiz, L., & Jani, J. (2010). Critical race theory: A transformational model for teaching diversity. *Journal of Social Work Education, 46*(2), 175–193. https://doi.org/10.5175/JSWE.2010.200900070

Park, H., Choi, S., Noh, K., & Hong, J. Y. (2022). Racial discrimination as a cumulative risk factor affecting parental stress on the psychological distress of Korean Americans (both US- and foreign-born) amid COVID-19: Structural equation modeling. *Journal of Racial and Ethnic Health Disparities, 9*(5), 1670–1679. https://doi.org/10.1007/s40 615-021-01106-4.

Peiser, J. (2021, March 19). Asian woman, 75, beats back man who punched her in San Francisco: "I am amazed by her bravery." *Washington Post*. https://www.washingtonp ost.com/nation/2021/03/19/san-francisco-asian-attack-arrest/.

Pelczarski, Y., & Kemp, S. P. (2006). Patterns of child maltreatment referrals among Asian and Pacific Islander families. *Child Welfare, 85*, 5–31.

Phelan, J. C., & Link, B. G. (2015). Is racism a fundamental cause of inequalities in health? *Annual Review of Sociology, 41*, 311–330.

Potter, S. & Moynihan, M. (2011). Bringing in the bystander in-person prevention program to a U.S. military installation: Results from a pilot study. *Military Medicine, 176*(8), 870–875. doi: 10.7205/MILMED-D-10-00483.

Raju, A. (2021, February 5). Black and Asian solidarity in American history: The power of unity exemplified by 5 major events. *Medium.com*. https://medium.com/advanc ing-justice-aajc/black-and-asian-solidarity-in-american-history-the-power-of-unity-exemplified-by-5-major-events-391025bbf228.

Ruiz, N., Edwards, K., Lopez, M. (2021). One-third of Asian Americans fear threats, physical attacks and most say violence against them is rising. *Pew Research Center*. threats-physical-attacks-and-most-say-violence-against-them-is-rising/.

Sakamoto, I. (2007). An anti-oppressive approach to cultural competence. *Canadian Social Work Review / Revue Canadienne de Service Social, 24*(1), 105–114. http://www. jstor.org/stable/41669865.

Salami, B., Salma, J., Hegadoren, K., Meherali, S., Kolawole, T., & Díaz, E. (2019). Sense of community belonging among immigrants: Perspective of immigrant service providers. *Public Health, 167*, 28–33. 10.1016/j.puhe.2018.10.017.

Samari, G. (2016). Islamophobia and public health in the United States. *American Journal of Public Health, 106*(11), 1920–1925. https://doi.org/10.2105/AJPH.2016.303374.

Saw, A., Horse, A. J. Y., & Jeung, R. (2021). Stop AAPI Hate mental health report. Stop AAPI Hate. https://stopaapihate.org/wp-content/uploads/2021/05/Stop-AAPI-Hate-Mental-Health-Report-210527.pdf.

Shah, M., & Kauh, T. (2021, June 23). How do we advance health equity for Asian Americans? (Blog). *Robert Wood Johnson Foundation*. https://www.rwjf.org/en/blog/ 2021/06/how-do-we-advance-health-equity-for-asian-americans.html.

Silberman, W. & Record, R. (2021). We post it, U Reddit: Exploring the potential of Reddit for health interventions targeting college populations. *Journal of Health Communication, 26*(6), 381–390. https://doi.org/10.1080/10810730.2021.1949648.

Smith, L. (2017). The war between Vietnamese fishermen and the KKK signaled a new type of White supremacy. *Timeline*. https://timeline.com/kkk-vietnamese-fishermen-beam-43730353df06.

Social Tracking of Asian Americans in the U.S. Index Report 2021 (2021). *LAAUNCH*. https://uploadsssl.webflow.com/5f629e7e013d961943d5cec9/6098a7be3d627168e03 054 da_staatus-index-2021.pdf.

Sue, S., Cheng, J. K. Y., Saad, C. S., & Chu, J. P. (2012). Asian American mental health: A call to action. *American Psychologist, 67*(7), 532–544.

THE HISTORY OF RACISM AGAINST ASIAN AMERICANS   329

Takeuchi, D. T., Zane, N., Hong, S., Chae, D. H., Gong, F., Gee, G. C., Walton, E., Sue, S., & Alegría, M. (2007). Immigration-related factors and mental disorders among Asian Americans. *American Journal of Public Health, 97*(1), 84–90. https://doi.org/10.2105/AJPH.2006.088401.

Teasley, M., McCarter, S., Woo, B., Conner, L. R., Spencer, M. S., & Green, T. (2022). *Grand Challenges for Social Work and Society* (Second ed.). Oxford University Press. 10.1093/oso/9780197608043.003.0014

Yang, K. G., Rodgers, C. R. R., Lee, E., & Lê Cook, B. (2020). Disparities in mental health care utilization and perceived need among Asian Americans: 2012–2016. *Psychiatric Services (Washington, D.C.), 71*(1), 21–27. doi: 10.1176/appi.ps.201900126.

Yee, A. (2021, May 6). COVID's outsize impact on Asian Americans is being ignored. *Scientific American.* https://www.scientificamerican.com/article/covids-outsize-impact-on-Asian Americans-is-being-igno red/.

Young, C. B., Fang, D. Z., & Zisook, S. (2010). Depression in Asian American and Caucasian undergraduate students. *Journal of Affective Disorders, 125,* 379–382. 10.1016/j.jad.2010.02.124.

Yung, J., Chang, G., & Lai, H. (Eds.). (2006). *Chinese American voices: From the gold rush to the present.* Berkeley: University of California Press.

U.S. Department of Health and Human Services (2016). National Survey on Drug Use and Health 2016 (NSDUH-2016-DS0001). https://datafiles.samhsa.gov.

U.S. Department of Health and Human Services (2017). National Survey on Drug Use and Health 2017 (NSDUH-2017-DS0001). https://datafiles.samhsa.gov.

U.S. Department of Health and Human Services (2018). National Survey on Drug Use and Health 2018 (NSDUH-2018-DS0001). https://datafiles.samhsa.gov.

U.S. Department of Health and Human Services (2019). National Survey on Drug Use and Health 2019 (NSDUH-2019-DS0001). https://datafiles.samhsa.gov.

Woo, B., Figuereo, V., Rosales, R., Wang, K., & Sabur, K. (2018). Where is race and ethnicity in social work? A content analysis. *Social Work Research, 42,* 180–186. doi: 10.1093/swr/svy010.

Wu, F. H. (2009). Embracing mistaken identity: How the Vincent Chin case unified Asian Americans. *Asian American Policy Review, 19,* 17.

PART III
ELIMINATING RACISM THROUGH STRENGTHENING THE SOCIAL FABRIC

Creating a strong social fabric is central to the health and well-being of a democratic society. Within the profession of social work, practitioners and researcher strive to address both social and environmental factors that confront society and impact the human condition. When the role of race and racism is not made explicit, members of the profession have an ethical responsibility as practitioners to view their work through the critical lens with professional values in mind. When racism in excluded in our analysis, there is a tendency to focus on individual-level behaviors and solutions, rather than the social environment that produces inequities. These include both policies and practices that were historically developed for the benefit of the dominant White population and not those who are marginalized. The historical context of racist practices and policies continues to have major implications for contemporary inequities in policies and practices.

As discussed throughout Part I, although race is a social construct, it has acquired meaningful substance though ideological, legal, institutional, structural, and interpersonal reification. As a result, race has primarily been used to differentiate people based on physical characteristics and as a tool for oppression and violence. Though not biologically based, the impact of racism socially and politically on populations of color is real. The social work profession is in need of strategies and intervention that address the root of racial injustice, which results from structural and institutional racism inherent in our society. To this end, Part III continues to focus on the role of racism within three specific Grand Challenges for Social Work: "Create Social Responses to a Changing Environment" (Chapter 13), "End Homelessness" (Chapter 14), and "Eradicating Social Isolation" (Chapter 15). Content

332 ELIMINATING RACISM

within these chapters accentuates the need to examine the role of race and racism in responding to the need to create a strong social fabric.

In Chapter 13, Forbes and colleagues identify environmental racism as source for promoting a wide range of inequitable and unjust outcomes for BIPOC communities in the United States. Environmental racism is environmental policy, practice, or directive that differently affects or disadvantages, whether intentionally or not, individuals, groups or communities based on their race, ethnicity, or color. Environmental racism perpetuates an inequitable and unjust society, through environmental circumstances that contribute to producing and maintaining health disparities among historically underrepresented racial and ethnic communities. Specifically, the health implications of pesticide exposure, food insecurity, and extractive energy development, as well as the disproportionate impacts of extreme weather events like hurricanes, flooding, and tornadoes are explored. Padgett and colleagues (Chapter 14) discuss race and racism in relation to the homelessness crisis in the United States. The decades-long crisis of homelessness that began in the 1980s was not an accident of history. The upstream factors that converged to produce this crisis—the sharp decline in federal spending on public housing, the loss of affordable low-cost housing to gentrification, the decline in household income relative to rising rents—were rarely brought up in public policy discourses focused on temporary solutions such as soup kitchens and shelters. Meanwhile, public opinion focused on the deficiencies and pathologies of homeless individuals. Amidst the volumes that have been written about homelessness, the role of race and racism has received surprisingly little attention—despite the ongoing disproportionate representation of African Americans among the homeless, whether single adults or families. This chapter traces the history of housing discrimination and segregation in the United States and describes best practices in ending homelessness with a focus on Housing First and its success with veterans in particular. It is proposed that racial equity be centered in all housing and homelessness policies moving forward. The chapter concludes with potential solutions for centering racial equity in homelessness research and practice. In Chapter 15, Crewe and colleagues demonstrate the ways that racism acts as a persistent factor in perpetuating social isolation that results in social exclusion for BIPOC communities. Social isolation is well documented for its detrimental effects on health and well-being across the life span. In short, the quality of our social networks influences the quality of life. While there are many underlying contributors to social isolation, macro factors such as social exclusion play a significant role. Racism is a persistent factor in perpetuating social isolation that results in social exclusion for African Americans, Latinx, and other racial and ethnic minorities. These authors assert that eradicating social isolation inherently calls for the eradication of racism and provide examples of this work. In general, chapters in this section represent solutions to pressing problems that have race and racism as instrumental factors to eliminating in creating a strong social fabric.

13

Strengthening the Social Responses to the Human Impacts of Environmental Change

Rachel Forbes, Dorlisa J. Minnick, Amy Krings, Felicia M. Mitchell, Samantha Teixeira, and Shanondora Billiot

> *Mother Nature—militarized, fenced-in, poisoned—demands that we take action.*
> —Berta Cáceres, leading Lenca indigenous and environmental activist in Honduras, who was assassinated in her home in March 2016 for her activism to protect indigenous lands from a hydroelectric project

Environmental racism forces people of color, including Indigenous, Black, and Latinx communities, to bear the brunt of environmental degradation and climate change. BIPOC (Black, Indigenous, and People of Color) communities are disproportionately affected by the climate crisis as they breathe more polluted air, live in hotter temperatures, experience more natural disasters, are displaced at higher rates, and often have limited resources to respond to crises (Fernandez Rysavy & Lloyd, 2016). *Environmental racism* is defined as environmental policy, practice, or directive that differently affects or disadvantages, whether intentionally or not, individuals, groups, or communities based on their race, ethnicity, or color (Bullard, 1993, 2003; Taylor, 2000). In the occupied lands now known as the United States, environmental racism has deep roots, embedded in economic and racial inequities including, but not limited to, genocide, segregation, immigration, and racial discrimination in practically all aspects of life for communities of color (Bullard, 1999; Taylor, 2000). We have intentionally described the United States as a collective of occupied lands to affirm that the land which comprises the United States was stolen from Indigenous

---

Rachel Forbes, Dorlisa J. Minnick, Amy Krings, Felicia M. Mitchell, Samantha Teixeira, and Shanondora Billiot, *Strengthening the Social Responses to the Human Impacts of Environmental Change* In: *Social Work and the Grand Challenge to Eliminate Racism*. Edited by: Martell L. Teasley, Michael S. Spencer, and Melissa Bartholomew, Oxford University Press. © Oxford University Press 2023. DOI: 10.1093/oso/9780197674949.003.0013

communities throughout the violent colonial history of the country's initial and ongoing settlement. Environmental racism is a form of institutionalized discrimination and is reinforced by government, legal, economic, social, political, and military institutions, and can take a multitude of forms (Bullard, 1999, 2003; Taylor, 2000). Environmental racism perpetuates an inequitable and unjust society, through environmental circumstances that contribute to and maintain health disparities among historically marginalized racial and ethnic communities.

Climate change disproportionately impacts BIPOC communities. The world is in a global environmental crisis as a result of anthropocentric climate change, human-induced destruction, environmental injustice, and ecological devastation of land, air, water, and living beings (Gray et al., 2018). The consequences are now being felt across generations, with BIPOC communities experiencing the disproportionate impacts of environmental injustice and climate change. The exponential rate at which the planet is warming and the subsequent damaging impacts are repeatedly described by scientists as greatly outpacing their predictions among BIPOC communities around the world. Importantly, the brunt of the initial environmental crises are borne by the poorest countries and most vulnerable communities (Intergovernmental Panel on Climate Change [IPCC], 2018). They are usually hit the hardest by ecological destruction and subsequent disasters, which is exacerbated by the fact that these populations have the fewest resources for combating them. Often those who are currently impacted the greatest are not those who created the problem. Following these principles, environmental justice organizing attends to the fair distribution of both environmental amenities and hazards (distributive justice), the use of inclusive decision-making processes (procedural justice), and is dedicated to creating safe and welcoming spaces for those who have been traditionally marginalized (interactional justice) (Krings & Copic, 2020; Schlosberg, 2007).

Chapter Overview

This chapter begins with a discussion on the intersections of health equity and environmental justice within a racialized context. Specifically, the health implications of pesticide exposure, food insecurity, and extractive energy development will be explored. After examining health equity, the chapter illustrates the disproportionate impacts of extreme weather events like hurricanes, flooding, and tornadoes upon BIPOC communities and the implications of these phenomena upon climate migration. Lastly, the chapter draws attention to global pandemics such as COVID-19 within the context of increasing environmental degradation and species loss, citing the ways that BIPOC communities are more vulnerable to COVID-19 as an example of environmental injustice. The chapter concludes with social work–specific solutions to address these great inequalities, including activism and advocacy, and key mechanisms for creating lasting systemic change.

Intersection of Health Equity and Environmental Justice

Understanding the effects of climate change and environmental racism on human health and well-being is of great importance to the social work profession. Unprecedented environmental changes threaten human health and well-being in communities worldwide. Urbanization and population growth are on the rise, and extreme weather events are increasing in frequency and severity (The Grand Challenges for Social Work, 2018). The Social Work Grand Challenge to Create Social Responses to a Changing Environment seeks to address linkages between environmental and social inequity with children, older adults, historically marginalized racial and ethnic populations, and those living with mental illness being vulnerable to escalating environmental threats (Kemp et al., 2015; Kemp et al., 2018; Kemp et al., 2022; Mason et al., 2021). Understanding how this challenge impacts racialized communities across systems remains the focal point of this chapter.

Environmental hazards adversely affect humans and the environment and are commonly transmitted through elements of air, water, and soil (Billiot et al., 2019). Environmental harm and resultant health inequities are distributed inequitably along lines of poverty, race, and ethnicity (McDonald et al., 2015). Scholars have called for more complex analysis to understand how exposure disparities are associated with health disparities, calling attention to groups that experience environmental hazard exposure at high levels or in the multiplicity of exposure pathways (Burger & Gochfeld, 2011). Here, we briefly describe a few examples of disparate exposure to environmental harm, including pesticide exposure, exposures within food systems, water, and extreme weather events.

Pesticide Exposure

Pesticide exposure, which carries risks to human health, is high among migrant farmworkers, as they provide a substantial portion of labor to the fruit and vegetable industry in the United States (Pfeifer, 2016). The majority of migrant farmworkers are Latinx, and these farmworkers and their children experience higher rates of diabetes, heart disease, asthma, and living in overcrowded housing, which can lead to increased respiratory illnesses and infectious diseases (Flocks, 2012; Schwartz et al., 2015). Birth defects among babies born to farmworkers can happen during early pregnancy (Desrosiers et al., 2012). Also, because healthcare access is limited in the farmworker population, pregnant farmworkers may not seek prenatal care, and when they do, pesticide toxicity symptoms like headaches and nausea are often attributed to pregnancy and not pesticide toxicity by both pregnant patients and their physicians (Flocks, 2012). Barriers to reporting acute occupational pesticide-related illness among farmworkers, in general, include job insecurity, language, fear of deportation with increased anti-immigrant sentiment, fear of retaliation by an employer, high cost of health insurance, distance to clinics, and mistrust of healthcare providers, to name a few (Prado et al., 2017; Flocks, 2012). Flocks (2012) cites that in spite of many of the fears listed, it was a social worker who encouraged three pesticide-exposed farmworker women who delivered babies with serious birth defects to sue the company for damages. The social worker also located a lawyer who was willing to provide pro bono services. The lawyer was successful, and the company settled out of court. Social workers use science and interpersonal skills to advocate for communities.

Food Systems and Food Security

Social workers also remain engaged in food security and food justice work across BIPOC communities. The unjust working conditions that farmworkers must face is part of a larger food system that is rooted in inequity and racism. Food systems are composed of "all the processes involved in getting food from farm to table to disposal . . . and . . . involve people, farms, businesses, communities, interventions, policies, and politics" (Neff et al., 2009, p. 283). As chemicals enter the soil, water, and food sources, health disparities follow into food systems. High rates of obesity are associated with food insecurity across America, referred to as the food insecurity obesity paradox (Dhurandhar, 2016), often associated with high-calorie intake of low-nutrient food bought from corner stores, bodegas, and fast-food restaurants in low-income communities that are identified as food deserts (Ludwig et al., 2011). It is considered a paradox because of the assumption that less food should mean weighing less. Obesity often results in negative health outcomes such as high blood pressure, heart disease, and diabetes, with Black and African Americans dying from stroke, heart disease, and diabetes at much higher rates than White Americans (Neff et al., 2009).

Given their close connection with land and water, Indigenous peoples are disproportionately susceptible to and affected by climate change, though they have contributed little to its causes (Dominelli, 2011; Krakoff, 2008; Lynn et al., 2013; Trainor et al., 2007). Climate change has affected traditional subsistence living activities that have, in turn, affected Indigenous health through changes in diet and the physical activity exerted during subsistence activities. Indigenous communities have reported adaptations in their hunting and fishing activities due to climate change events that include a decline in wildlife/aquatic habitats and the flooding and erosion of land (Billiot et al., 2019; Cochran et al., 2013; Dittmer, 2013). Climate change events are altering streamflow in the U.S. Pacific Northwest that has affected salmon populations. Many tribes in this region depend on salmon for cultural, subsistence, and commercial reasons (Dittmer, 2013). Climate change is connected to the spiritual health of Indigenous people and can compromise the transmission of cultural knowledge and related subsistence customs that are part of traditional food systems. As access to traditional food sources is changed due to shifting aquatic environments, tribal elders may have fewer opportunities to transmit cultural teachings to the next generation. Less engagement between relatives can result in a loss of traditional practices or incomplete transmission of cultural knowledge that is vital to sustaining subsistence living practices for future generations (Kuhnlein & Receveur, 1996; Lynn et al., 2013; Nabhan, 2010). Climate change, in conjunction with other stressors, can affect Indigenous peoples' connection to traditional foods, including access and availability, harvesting methods, and the ability to store, process, and consume foods in traditional ways (Lynn et al., 2013). Climate change affects water temperatures and water availability, which is a primary concern for growing and harvesting corn, wild rice, and other traditional foods (Lynn et al., 2013; NRC, 2010). Reduced options to grow and consume traditional foods can result in a reliance on a Western diet that can increase the risk for a range of chronic diseases such as diabetes, heart disease, and obesity (Lynn et al., 2013). Thus, the evidence demonstrates the importance of including macro factors in change work related to food systems to move the dialogue from personal faults to examining how systemic structures like poverty, settler-colonialism, and racism influence disease risk in marginalized communities due to "broad social, economic, and political forces that impact food supply, nutrient quality, and affordability" (Neff et al., 2009, p. 283).

Social work scientists are addressing food insecurity and building racially just and decolonized alternative food systems by building participatory strategies with residents to build ecologically and socially just sustainable food systems (Kaiser, 2017), leading county-wide food system alliances (Center for Land Use and Sustainability, 2019), continuing deep university-community partnerships that tackle systemic racism by building the capacity of low-income, food desert communities of color through community gardens (Booth et al., 2018), highlighting collective survival strategies of Black Detroit farmers (Bell et al., 2019), calling on culturally relevant ways to work with Indigenous communities grounded in Indigenous Ways of Knowing to strengthen social responses to food systems change and the changing environment (Billiot et al., 2019), and creating modules or courses on food justice in social work education that examine the social and environmental justice implications of food insecurity (Kaiser et al., 2015).

Water

Clean drinking water is imperative to healthy communities, but on tribal lands and across occupied lands of the United States of America, marginalized communities are often subjected to contaminated water. In their work, Balazs, Morello-Frosch, Hubbard, and Ray (2011) concluded that community water systems supporting larger percentages of Latinx residents and renters result in drinking water with higher nitrate levels, documenting environmental racism. Balazs and Ray (2014) went on to develop and test a multifaceted, multi-tiered Drinking Water Disparities framework to explain which infrastructural factors shape disparities, and include the role of social and political factors such as the mutually constitutive (intersectional) factors of race and poverty, giving focus to how specific decisions at different levels drive drinking water disparities; and "extends the classic exposure–disease paradigm to show the water system and household coping mechanisms, intended to alleviate exposure, create a feedback loop through which disparities in drinking water quality may be exacerbated" (p. 604). This framework, applied to the San Joaquin Valley, an area that was previously designated as labor camps, demonstrates the capacity to examine historical and contemporary practices, structures, and agency in developing what they term "composite drinking water burden" defined by feedback cycles and resulting in exposure and coping costs which are unevenly distributed. The source and concentration of water pollution trigger coping mechanisms, albeit differently based on social location and household agency, and these coping mechanisms are cyclical in environmental exposure. This framework embedded race and poverty throughout the model and found poor Latinx communities and other BIPOC communities experiencing a greater composite drinking water burden.

Water is a relative to Indigenous peoples and under constant threat due to environmental degradation from settler-colonialism erasure (Norman, 2017) through "exposure to environmental toxins and changes primarily through natural resource extraction" (Billiot et al., 2019, p. 300). Using community-based participatory research methods, Mitchell (2018) engaged participants in Photovoice to document perspectives on the health impact of water insecurity in a Midwestern tribal community. The community relies on the river for its water, but damming upstream off sovereign territory has resulted in political and legal campaigns but more readily is experienced as little water availability and poor water quality. Climate change has resulted in increased floods and stormwater runoff, which ends up in creeks that run into this river on the reservation, leaving the Indigenous community with contaminated water in spite of being stewards of the Earth, caring for relatives.

The Flint water crisis provides another example. The crisis was created by the unilateral decision by an appointed emergency manager who transferred the city's water source to the Flint River, despite concerns about its quality and safety (Krings, Kornberg, et al., 2018). Further, the city did not use appropriate safeguards to monitor the water's quality, and over time, this highly corrosive water eroded resident pipes, leading to water contamination and a variety of human health impacts, including lead poisoning. Lee et al. (2016) report on the racially disproportionate application of emergency management laws in times of austerity that further reduce investment and local accountability in Black communities in urban areas, a form of structural racism. In examining the emergent Latinx capacity building that occurred during the government-induced Flint water crisis, Duntley-Matos et al. (2017) used Critically Intersubjectively Engaged Ethnography (CIEE) to create space for Latinx youth and families to engage in the broader community discussions and decisions taking place. While all community residents were exposed to water contamination, children and older adults were particularly vulnerable to the impact of lead poisoning, including skin rashes, hair loss, and increased reports of blindness. Latinx communities were exposed to a dual crisis, experiencing both the water crisis and a family separation crisis when Immigration and Customs Enforcement (ICE) officers initiated raids on community members who were undocumented under the guise of delivering bottled water and assistance (Duntley-Matos et al., 2017). Finally, fertility was another poor health outcome from the Flint water crisis. Grossman and Slusky (2019), using natural experiment modeling, found a significant 12% reduction in women's fertility overall.

Extractive Energy and Natural Resource Development

Water is a key resource in extractive energy development, including processes surrounding hydraulic fracturing, or "fracking," which involves injecting highly pressurized water mixed with chemicals into the Earth to release natural gases that are then harvested for energy development. Fracking, which requires an inordinate amount of water, often occurs in marginalized communities due to a perception of cheap land and limited resources, including limited political power to challenge fracking permits (Brady et al., 2019; Fry et al., 2015; Johnston et al., 2016). Some studies have found rurality to be a significant factor in marginalization because of its often associated poverty status (Fry et al., 2015; Johnston et al., 2016). Johnston, Werder, and Sebastian (2016) examined the intersection of race and poverty on proximity to fracking injection wells in southern Texas, finding that geographical areas with a higher proportion of people of color communities comprising poor Latinx, Black, and American Indian residents were granted a disproportionate number of fracking permits compared to White and more affluent communities, demonstrating racism along dimensions of poverty and rurality. Moreover, in examining patterns of state inspections, Spina (2015) reported significantly fewer inspections of fracking wastewater in low-income communities of color. Thus, not only are BIPOC communities more likely

HUMAN IMPACTS OF ENVIRONMENTAL CHANGE 343

to be located near oil and gas wastewater wells, but pathways to exposure are greater because of lackluster state monitoring and inspection. Poor management of wastewater leads to increased exposure to respiratory and endocrine illnesses and cancer (Burgos et al., 2017).

In addition to harmful fracking and damming practices on BIPOC communities, radiation from uranium mining tailings has contaminated water resources in tribal communities in the Southwest (Lehtinen, 1998) and the North (Eggers et al., 2015) for decades. Natural resource extraction by non-Indigenous peoples on Indigenous peoples' lands contributes to the changes in subsistence, livelihood, migration, and cultural practices, further contributing to the suffering among Indigenous and marginalized communities worldwide. For instance, uranium mining on the Navajo Nation depleted an already limited water supply and contaminated the remainder of the tribe's water resources with uranium runoff (Sharder-Frechette, 2006). In 1979, a flash flood rushed through a Navajo community that contained radioactive water that Navajo children were later playing in (Lehtinen, 1998; Woody et al., 1981). In testing home wells on the Crow Reservation, the Apsaalooke Tribal Research Group confirmed that 68% of tested wells exceeded the acceptable levels of uranium in drinking water (Eggers et al., 2015). Environmental impacts such as these extend further than uranium mining sites and degrade adjacent communities by contaminating the soil, vegetation, and water, as well as the animals (i.e., livestock) that drink polluted water and eat plants grown in contaminated soil (Markstrom & Charley, 2003). Environmental hazards that release wastewater can have numerous impacts on the physical and psychological health of communities that can extend for generations. The Agency for Toxic Substances and Disease Registry (ATSDR) (2013) reports kidney damage as the most common health effect from uranium exposure through water sources in adulthood. The intersection of natural resources such as water and land within food and energy systems is important to understanding the ways in which racialized communities have come to bear the brunt of environmental injustices within White supremacy culture.

Extreme Weather Events

Extreme weather events such as flooding, wildfires, temperature, hurricanes, tornadoes, and earthquakes are happening more frequently due to environmental degradation and climate change and exert devastating and disparate effects on human health (Balbus et al., 2016). The social work profession has a tradition of providing disaster intervention (Rosen et al., 2010; Bauwens & Naturale, 2017; Stamm, 2017; Zakour & Harrell, 2004), including addressing deep socio-emotional needs through clinical first aid in the aftermath of disasters, as well as systems-level interventions to mitigate and prevent future harm. In fact, nearly one-third of published social work research on environmental topics focuses on natural disasters (Krings, Victor, et al., 2018; Mason, Shires, et al., 2017). For example, Mason and colleagues have examined the perceptions and protective factors of Tennessee residents on extreme weather events of flooding, temperature, and tornadoes (Mason, Ellis, et al., 2019; Ellis et al., 2019; Mason, Erwin, et al., 2018; Mason, Ellis, et al., 2018; Mason, Ellis, et al., 2017). In the following section, we describe their findings related to urban heat islands and extreme weather events.

Urban Heat Islands (UHI)

Starting in 2014, the interdisciplinary team of Mason (social work), Ellis (geography), and Hathaway (civil & environmental engineering) began collecting original data on urban microenvironments by surveying neighborhood residents and installing weather monitors in four economically and racially diverse Knoxville, Tennessee, neighborhoods (Ellis et al., 2017). Mason, Ellis, and Hathaway (2017) found disparities based on neighborhood locations where low- and lower-income communities of color report more vulnerability than wealthier and whiter neighborhoods. With more impervious surfaces and less tree coverage, neighborhoods with higher proportions of Black and Latinx residents experience hotter microclimates than residents in the whiter and wealthier neighborhoods. These residents reported socially isolating inside due to difficulty breathing in hot temperature days and not being able to walk the distance to the nearest bus stop. Additionally, participants rationed air conditioning due to the expense of utility bills. These experiences were amplified for older adults on fixed incomes, who expressed more concern than younger participants of falling in winter conditions. About 50% of the residents in the two most racially diverse and low-income neighborhoods also expressed concerns regarding local air quality.

To move examination of urban heat islands in Knoxville beyond descriptive surveying, Mason, Erwin, Brown, Ellis, and Hathaway (2018) used a capitals theoretical framework—human (general health), social (social cohesion), financial (income), and physical (homeownership)—to explain factors that can protect households from extreme temperature events. They found participants reporting higher categorization of human and social capital had decreased odds of reporting physical or mental health impact when experiencing extreme summer heat, but financial and physical capitals were not significant.

Tornadoes

Mason and colleagues have also published original research pertaining to local tornado knowledge and perceptions (Ellis et al., 2019; Walters et al., 2019; Mason, Ellis, et al., 2018). Using random sampling from three Tennessee regions to either a nighttime or daytime tornado warning scenario, Mason, Ellis, Winchester, and Schexnayder (2018) found that residents self-report they currently are not signed up for nighttime alerts. This is a public health issue, particularly in Tennessee where 46% of tornadoes happen after dark, with 61% of them resulting in casualties. Black residents were more likely to report receiving daytime tornado warnings than White residents; however, this protective factor of more likely to receive tornado warnings during daytime hours did not carry over to receiving nocturnal tornado warnings, where there were no statistical differences across race and ethnicity.

Hurricanes and Flooding

Flooding from rising sea levels, more frequent intense precipitation, hurricanes, and storm surge will expose more of the population to contaminated water, debris, and disruptions to essential infrastructure, with negative health impacts from drowning, injuries, gastrointestinal illnesses, and increased mental health distress, according to *The Impacts of Climate Change on Human Health in the United States* (2016). Yet the report also identifies that social determinants of health (SDoH) influence one's adaptive capacity and, like Mason, Erwin, Brown, Ellis, and Hathaway's (2018) research on using a capitals framework for explaining protective factors to experiencing extreme weather events, the report points to social capital and social cohesion as increasing adaptive capacity to climate change. However, being forced to adapt due to structural racism and settler-colonialism upheld by White supremacy only increases vulnerability of historically marginalized populations.

Racism exacerbates vulnerability during extreme weather events like Hurricane Katrina (Levy, 2012). Although the sample and statistical power were small, Levy (2012) found that the most significant factors associated with Hurricane Katrina damage were a parish's elevation and concentration of Black residents. In exploring disaster response to Hurricane Maria, Hayward, Morris, Ramos, and Díaz (2019), using a single case design, describe how "Puerto Ricans were highly susceptible to [Hurricane Maria's] impact due to a combination of geographic, economic, and political factors" (p. 250), forcing neighbors to organize in making their own recovery intervention because they knew that mainland intervention would come too late, failing them in their critical time of need.

Understanding the ways in which extreme weather events such as flooding, wildfires, temperature, hurricanes, and tornadoes impact BIPOC communities is critical to the social work profession (Rao, Doherty, & Teixeira, 2022) . Because extreme weather events are ever-increasing as sea levels and temperatures rise worldwide, critical knowledge of social work interventions to support diverse communities is important to competent and ethical practice. One of the most important phenomena caused by extreme weather events is climate migration, which is the forced movement of peoples due to climate change.

Climate Migration

Climate change is a significant factor precipitating environmental degradation, deteriorating political and economic systems, and forcing increased migration internationally and within national borders. Often vulnerable and marginalized prior to migration, individuals and families seeking refuge through passage too often face additional challenges as their safety and status are further marginalized on the journey. The crisis is global in nature and complex in its multidimensionality, requiring a holistic response that crosses disciplines.

As recognized by the International Office for Migration, environmental migrants are individuals or groups who, because of environmental change negatively changing the ecology, "have to leave their habitual homes, or choose to do so, either temporarily or permanently, and who move either within their territory or abroad" (IOM, 2015, p. 13). Estimates of the magnitude vary widely from 25 million to 1 billion; 200 million is the one most widely accepted (IPCC, 2022; International Organization for Migration, n.d.)

Environmental migrants are situated at the intersection of climate change and natural disasters, violent conflict, and historic marginalization. In their countries of origin, the efforts to rebuild and continue surviving amidst the ongoing crisis in the aftermath of a natural disaster or the slow degradation of the environment are daunting. The role of community building in remediating ecological restoration, healing, and development fall in the hands of those left behind without the needed resources and supportive structures and systems. Interdisciplinary processes of engagement expand the lens for analysis and intervention. Social workers are engaged with helping environmental migrants in deteriorating environments, while in transition, and as they resettle/rebuild (Drolet, 2017; Powers & Nsonwu 2020). When trained to work across disciplines and within a global context, social workers bring a unique lens to practice in communities struggling with rapid change, fear of change, and inadequate resources. For displaced migrant communities, resilience becomes more a form of resistance, as some will never be able to return to a home that has ceased to exist. The complexity of starting a life in the host country is exacerbated by the ongoing trauma of being unable to cope with the aftermath of the forcible displacement and removal from the land. Responses to natural disasters, including the recent Hurricane Maria in Puerto Rico, have evolved into a large-scale exodus of families. Many of these citizens of the United States will likely never return to the island.

Climate-induced displacement has become a growing concern for Indigenous groups unable to respond to climate change events in-place. The effects of climate change are expected to displace millions of people around the globe, as peoples' lands become either temporarily or permanently uninhabitable. At present, the effects of climate change have impacted Indigenous people, with tribal communities in Alaska, Louisiana, Washington, and the Pacific Islands being forced to consider relocation due to increasing sea levels, erosion, extreme weather events, and an overall lack of resources to cope with such circumstances in-place (Callaway et al., 1999; Cozzetto et al., 2013; Billiot et al., 2019). Relocation due to climate-induced displacement can disrupt physical ties and the rights of Indigenous peoples to their land and its resources, and influence their spiritual and cultural connection with the earth (UN, 2007). As climate change events are expected to continue, the far-reaching consequences of climate change and climate-induced displacement for Indigenous people across the globe have yet to be completely understood.

COVID-19

The phenomenon of climate migration illustrates the importance of the connection between people and places in understanding environmental justice issues. A place-based perspective to exploring health inequities, including global public health issues such as pandemics, is a critical way to explore the disproportionate ways in which health systems are built upon racial inequities.

The Coronavirus disease 2019 (COVID-19) pandemic, like any major disaster, affects environmental justice communities at alarming rates as these communities are typically some of the poorest, most polluted, and at-risk due to preexisting health disparities (Wilson et al., 2020). Correspondingly, these communities are primarily composed of BIPOC who are experiencing a high burden of COVID-19 infection and subsequent complications and death (Anyane-Yeboa et al., 2020; Mitchell, 2020; Wilson et al., 2020). Consequently, the COVID-19 pandemic has once again exposed, and likely exacerbated, racial and ethnic health disparities in the United States on a national scale.

Air Quality

Air quality, which is related to housing quality, indoor air pollution, and poor ventilation, can be a factor in the spread of COVID-19 (Wilson et al., 2020). Recent studies conclude that air pollution, specifically exposure to fine particulate matter, is associated with an increased risk of COVID-19 infection and death (Miyashita et al., 2020). These findings help explain at least part of the reason racial and ethnic minorities have been more affected by the virus; they are more likely to live in proximity to toxic land uses. Thus, some

HUMAN IMPACTS OF ENVIRONMENTAL CHANGE   349

public officials have advocated for keeping air pollution at low levels to help prevent another wave of coronavirus infections, while scientists suggest encouraging the use of extra precautions and resources in high-risk areas (Carrington, 2021).

Food Systems

COVID-19 has worsened preexisting issues in the global food system that may have been minimized or overlooked pre-pandemic. COVID-19 is causing disruptions in food supplies and increasing food waste when hunger is widespread and growing globally (Fleetwood, 2020). Complicating the U.S. food supply, there have been considerable outbreaks of COVID-19 among essential workers (often BIPOC) in meat-processing plants in the United States. In response to COVID-19 infections in meat-processing plants, and their subsequent closures, millions of chickens, pigs, and cattle have been slaughtered and not processed for food, but as waste. Similarly, access to produce, dairy, and other perishable foods has been impacted by COVID-19 due to their short shelf life and reliance upon essential workers for harvesting and processing (Fleetwood, 2020). Many communities are experiencing changes in food availability, and people may be consuming more canned or packaged foods (CDC, 2020). Access to fresh, nutritious foods helps support a healthy immune system to guard against COVID-19 and its intensity. However, immunity-boosting foods are often the foods that are absent from communities of color. Climate change also contributes to changes in agricultural yields and further affects the availability of food choices in communities (Wilson et al., 2020). Climate change's impact on agriculture, in combination with the COVID-19 pandemic, creates further strain on the U.S. food supply, particularly when considering access to fresh, nutritious food in communities of color.

Water

Frequent hand washing is recommended as one of the key ways to prevent the spread of COVID-19. However, regular hand washing requires access to adequate, safe, and affordable water in addition to water that is needed for cooking, hydration, and general sanitation (Armitage & Nellums, 2020). In communities with inadequate or untrusted residential water supplies, many community members depend on bottled water retrieved from outside the home to meet their daily water needs (Hyde, 2020). Without access to safe water, COVID-19 disproportionality impacts people living in water insecure settings. A poignant example from the frontlines of the pandemic is the Navajo Nation. At the time of this writing, approximately 30%–40% of the Navajo households do not have running water (Dikos Ntsaaígíí-19 [COVID-19], n.d.). About one-third of Navajo households haul water home every day, and Navajo people pay 67 times more for water they haul versus piped water. Additionally, one in three Navajo people does not have a sink or toilet (Navajo Water Project, n.d.). According to Dikos Ntsaaígíí-19 (n.d.), water insecurity presents a notable risk for residents and challenges for Navajo leaders as they try to stop the spread of COVID-19. On the reservation, lack of access to clean and secure water sources forces the Navajo people to reuse dirty water for cooking and cleaning, which further increases risk of the COVID-19 spread. The Navajo Nation is one of the hardest-hit communities; in a population of nearly 400,000 tribal members, as of 2021, with 173,000 living on the reservation, the Navajo Nation had a total of 80,539 positive COVID-19 cases and 2,009 confirmed deaths as of January 19, 2023 (Dikos Ntsaaígíí-19 [COVID-19], n.d.). Though not the only factor linked to increased COVID-19 rates, water insecurity is a major concern in combating the virus. COVID-19 has highlighted the urgency for water infrastructure and policy reform to ensure equitable, safe water access for those who need it most now, and who will continue to need it after the pandemic subsides. Though water insecurity is not a new issue for poor, rural, and BIPOC communities in the United States, safe and sustainable water resources are a necessity for health, and health equity is a prerequisite for social and environmental justice (Mitchell, 2019; 2020; Billiot et al., 2021).

The COVID-19 pandemic continues to expose the unforgiving reality of structural and environmental inequalities that BIPOC face in the United States (Mitchell, 2020). Institutional change and policy reform were needed before the pandemic to address environmental justice and the social determinants of health that underlie racial and ethnic health disparities in the United States, but now it is needed more than ever.

Activism and Advocacy

The philosophy of environmental justice embraces the idea that all people and all communities are entitled to equal protection under environmental health laws and regulations (Bullard, 1996; Teixeira & Krings, 2015). Human responses to environmental degradation are most frequently traced back to the Progressive era in the United States, during which unsanitary conditions in cities drove movements to promote public health and improve human and environmental conditions in cities (Daniels, 2009). A number of movements cropped up with a focus on improving aesthetics and place-making through the creation of urban parks and playgrounds, including the garden city movement that worked to find a balance between nature and urban life (Daniels, 2009). These efforts were followed by movements related to wilderness protection and conservation of natural resources, implemented at the federal level, exemplified by the advocacy of John Muir and the founding of the Sierra Club in 1892. While the work of Muir, Gifford Pinchot, and other contemporary advocates for wilderness protection has been lauded, it should be noted that their views and legacy are tarnished by their expressions of anti-Indigenous sentiments and White supremacy (DeLuca & Demo, 2001). After the world wars, environmental issues came back to the forefront as part of the anti-toxic movement.

Though the anti-toxic movement of the 1960s and beyond, spurred by Rachel Carson's Silent Spring, is credited as the predecessor to the environmental justice movement, movements by people of color were taking shape on a similar timeline, if not well before. Examples of such efforts include the 1960s United Farm Workers' anti-pesticide campaign and 1970s advocacy for Black Ecology and Apartheid Ecology, which called for an approach to environmentalism that highlighted pressing issues in Black communities (Berman Santana, 2002; Hare, 1970). Both of these are examples of well-organized, deliberate environmental work led by communities of color, leading to the formalization of the environmental justice movement.

The environmental justice movement emerged because of systemic racial discrimination in the siting of hazardous facilities like dumps and disparate exposure to toxic chemicals in the settings in which people of color live and work, unfair enforcement of environmental and public health laws, and exclusion from land-use decision-making processes (Bryant & Mohai, 1992; Mohai et al., 2009). The environmental justice movement was formalized at the 1991 First National People of Color Environmental Leadership Summit, which consisted of Black, Indigenous, and other people of color (BIPOC) coming together to reimagine the environmental movement, which had been critiqued for excluding people of color, as well as issues that mattered most to them (Krings & Copic, 2020; Pezullo & Sandler, 2007; Taylor, 2014). Leaders at the Summit developed a set of environmental justice principles and defined the environment broadly, incorporating social, racial, and economic justice as tenets of environmentalism. Environmental justice has moved beyond traditional environmentalism through its use of a critical lens that incorporates power, inclusion, and representation.

Anguelovski (2016) describes the environmental justice movement as having evolved through three waves of organizing. These "waves" are not always chronological or mutually exclusive, as neighborhoods may experience the impacts associated with one or more of these categories at the same time. Yet, we describe each to illustrate the rich history of goals, strategies, and tactics employed by environmental justice activists and organizations.

The first wave focused on identifying and dismantling systemic environmental racism wherein racial and ethnic minorities were excluded in the development, implementation, and enforcement of environmental laws; this wave established the modern environmental justice movement. Many early environmental justice campaigns were instrumental in the creation of environmental and public health protections by building power through locally representative community organizations (Gibbs, 2002). Exemplar first-wave campaigns responded to the environmental health impacts of exposure to contamination, toxins, and other neighborhood and workplace-based hazards, including those related to waste facilities, heavy transportation, and contaminated waterways (Pellow, 2004; Sze, 2006; Teixeira & Krings, 2015). For example, in 1982, in a campaign considered by many to be the birth of the environmental justice movement, residents and activists in Warren County, North Carolina, organized protests and broad social action strategies to oppose the siting of a toxic waste dump in a largely Black and low-income community (McGurty, 2000; Teixeira et al., 2019). Though this example occurred in a rural setting, many first-wave efforts involved broad efforts to improve life in urban areas that had been divested through structurally racist policies and programs including deindustrialization, redlining, White flight, and cuts to state and federal spending in cities (Anguelovski, 2016).

The water crisis in Flint, Michigan, is a contemporary example of this first wave. Flint residents, who are majority Black and living within one of the most impoverished metropolitan areas in the United States, became sick as a result of lead contamination and bacteria in their drinking water. Yet, they did not enjoy the same degree of protection, or political recourse, as other communities and, as a result, many became sick and the lead content in children's blood spiked (Agyeman et al., 2016). Despite their politically and socially marginalized status, residents organized grassroots groups that partnered with academic researchers whose evidence bolstered their claims, thus inspiring national media attention, philanthropic support, and, ultimately, the decision to change back to a safer, but more expensive source of water (Krings, Kornberg, et al., 2018).

While the first wave focused on reducing environmental hazards, the second wave of environmental justice organizing took on issues of access to environmental amenities (Anguelovski, 2016). Relevant campaigns worked to improve access to green space, public parks, healthy food, clean water, and safe affordable housing. A contemporary example of this second wave includes efforts to create community gardens as a tool to promote health and financial security, and as community-building sites (Draper & Freedman, 2010). Community agriculture and conservation initiatives have also been found to contribute to the revitalization of distressed areas (Ohmer et al., 2009; Teixeira & Sing, 2016).

The first and second waves of environmental justice organizing were grounded in the assumption that residents, particularly those who are poor or people of color, struggle to move away from contaminated and divested neighborhoods for many reasons, including structural barriers such as segregation or limited access to credit. Thus, the typical response was that environmental justice organizations worked on place-based improvements to reduce contamination (first wave) or to improve access to environmental amenities (second wave). In contrast, the third wave of environmental justice organizing emerged to address issues related to self-determination, the defense of place and culture, and resistance of environmental gentrification (Anguelovski, 2016). The process of greening, land revaluation, and displacement is known as *environmental gentrification* and can result in a loss of social and racial equity (Checker, 2011; Krings & Schusler, 2020; Melstrom et al., 2021; Thurber et al., 2019). As gentrification becomes a more pressing problem, contributing to the shortage of affordable housing in the United States and globally (Aurand et al., 2017; Thurber & Krings, 2021), many environmental justice organizations are placed in the challenging, counterintuitive position of opposing local investments to prevent the displacement that may follow (Checker, 2011; Dale & Newman, 2009; Krings & Copic, 2020).

In their analysis of how contemporary environmental justice organizations are responding to threats of environmental gentrification, Krings and Schusler (2020) identified several practice principles that community practitioners, including social workers, can employ to reduce contamination and improve environmental amenities without displacing people who are poor or people of color. First, practitioners need to recognize that not all developments or projects labeled as "sustainable" or "green" include principles of ecological, social, and economic justice. In fact, many projects are branded as sustainable because doing so can prevent opposition or resistance (Swyngedouw, 2007). Thus, in order to equitably distribute environmental amenities (including access to land, clean air, and safe drinking water), practitioners should ask critical questions that politicize planning processes (Markus & Krings, 2020), such as: Who decides? Who participates? Who is considered an expert? Who is burdened and who benefits? This is needed not only in urban developments but also in rural areas, such as the hydrofracturing examples provided previously.

Second, environmental justice advocacy is about more than reducing contamination or securing green spaces; it is about broader questions of place, identity, and culture (Mathias et al., In press). Therefore, rather than taking on campaigns that narrowly attend to nature (e.g., bringing wildlife back to the city), practitioners should use an intersectional approach that integrates social concerns, including the risk of rising rent and displacement due to environmental gentrification. Among youth organizing to advance environmental justice, this holistic approach may include attention to environmental hazards (e.g., lead paint) and amenities (e.g., green spaces) in their schools, neighborhoods, and transportation systems (Schusler et al., 2019).

Third, a core assumption and practice principle of environmental justice organizing is that the people who are most impacted by land-use decisions, particularly BIPOC and people who are poor, must have power and influence in deciding how to balance social, economic, and environmental imperatives within their natural and built environments. Social workers and community practitioners can use community organizing principles to assist residents in collectively organizing, securing resources that facilitate participation and amplify the voices of politically marginalized groups, or facilitating citizen-led research on environmental impacts—all of which can help to redistribute power and resources (Teixeira et al., 2019; Mason et al., 2021).

Finally, although social work researchers and practitioners have many skill sets that can contribute to environmental justice organizing at a local level, it is important to remember that many environmental problems that are experienced locally are driven by global political and economic systems. For this reason, in addition to working at a local level, pro-poor and anti-racist policies are needed to confront policies and economic systems that produce environmental injustices and climate change. This begins with understanding both how austerity politics shape environmental regulations and social welfare provision and extends to better understanding alternative economic systems (Matthies et al., 2020; Peeters, 2012; Powers et al., 2019) or policy tools such as community benefits agreements (Krings et al., 2014; Krings & Thomas, 2018).

Conclusion and Moving Forward

The intersections of race and a changing environment are more pressing than ever for social workers. Understanding how environmental racism is apparent in all systems and structures is critical to social work research, advocacy, education, and practice. The challenge of meeting community needs while addressing racial inequalities at all levels should remain at the forefront of the social work international agenda. Global environmental change and degradation, along with climate change, cause widespread harm to oppressed groups, including BIPOC communities. Addressing these complex and systemic inequities requires centering the voices of the communities who are most impacted, cultivating a deep understanding of the needs of local communities, and challenging White supremacy and settler colonialism in all of its manifestations. In sum, for social workers to truly advance environmental justice, they must apply and develop skills that support impacted communities, working to ensure fair outcomes, inclusive decision-making processes, and cultural representation.

Study Questions

1. What are some extreme weather events in your area (region, state, county)? Where do people go for disaster-related services or evacuations?
2. What services are offered publicly (e.g., staying in a shelter), and what services are offered privately (e.g., staying in a hotel)? What does this mean for people without savings?
3. How accessible and affordable are these services?
4. Go online and review the air and water quality near your home. https://www3.epa.gov/myem/envmap/find.html.
5. What are the water and air quality ratings for your area?

6. What are the major greenhouse gas emissions sectors in your area?
7. What are some of the projected health concerns based on these ratings?
8. Would these be similar or different for your future clients?
9. What does the history of colonization look like in the community where you live as it relates to the built and natural environments?
10. How possible is it to understand and assess the linkages between one's air or water quality and one's health?
11. How are people of different races and ethnicities affected by environmental degradation in your home community?
12. Who in your community is working to protect the environment? Consider both individuals and organizations or companies. What are they doing, and how can social workers be allies in this work?
13. What have you learned about the global environmental crisis as it intersects with the COVID-19 pandemic and racism? How might we address the issues raised?

References

Agency for Toxic Substances and Disease Registry (ATSDR). 2013. *Toxicological profile for uranium*. Atlanta, GA: U.S. Department of Health and Human Services, Public Health Service.

Agyeman, J., Schlosberg, D., Craven, L., & Matthews, C. (2016). Trends and directions in environmental justice: From inequity to everyday life, community, and just sustainabilities. *Annual Review of Environment and Resources, 41*, 321–340.

Anguelovski, I. (2016). From toxic sites to parks as (green) LULUs? New challenges of inequity, privilege, gentrification, and exclusion for urban environmental justice. *Journal of Planning Literature, 31*(1), 23–36.

Anyane-Yeboa, A., Sato, T., & Sakuraba, A. (2020). Racial disparities in COVID-19 deaths reveal harsh truths about structural inequality in America. *Journal of Internal Medicine, 288*(4), 479–480. https://doi.org/10.1111/joim.13117. Epub 2020 Jun 15. PMID: 32452046.

Armitage, R., & Nellums, L. B. (2020). Water, climate change, and COVID-19: Prioritising those in water-stressed settings. *The Lancet Planetary Health, 4*(5), e175. https://doi.org/10.1016/S2542-5196(20)30084-X.

Aurand, A., Emmanuel, D., Yentel, D., & Errico, E. (2017). *The gap: A shortage of affordable homes*. Washington, DC: National Low Income Housing Coalition. Retrieved from https://nlihc.org/sites/default/files/Gap-Report_2017.pdf.

Balazs, C., Morello-Frosch, R., Hubbard, A., & Ray, I. (2011). Social disparities in nitrate-contaminated drinking water in California's San Joaquin Valley. *Environmental Health Perspectives, 119*(9), 1272–1278. doi: 10.1289/ehp.1002878.

Balazs, C. L., & Ray, I. (2014). The drinking water disparities framework: On the origins and persistence of inequities in exposure. *American Journal of Public Health*, *104*(4), 603–611. doi: 10.2105/AJPH.2013.301664.

Balbus, J., Crimmins, A., Gamble, J. L., Easterling, D. R., Kunkel, K. E., Saha, S., & Sarofim, M. C. (2016). Chapter 1: Climate change and human health. In *The Impacts of Climate Change on Human Health in the United States: A Scientific Assessment* (pp. 1–18). Washington, DC: U.S. Global Change Research Program. Retrieved from https://hea lth2016.globalchange.gov/downloads#climate-change-and-human-health.

Bauwens, J., & Naturale, A. (2017). The role of social work in the aftermath of disasters and traumatic events. *Clinical Social Work Journal*, *45*(2), 99–101. doi: 10.1007/s10615-017-0623-8.

Bell, F. M, Dennis, M. K., & Krings, A. (2019). Collective survival strategies and anti-colonial practice in ecosocial work. *Journal of Community Practice*, *27*(3–4), 279–295. doi: 10.1080/10705422.2019.1652947.

Billiot, S., Beltrán, R. Brown, D., Mitchell, F. M., & Fernandez, A. (2019). Indigenous perspectives for strengthening social responses to global environmental changes: A response to the social work grand challenge on environmental change. *Journal of Community Practice*, *27*(3–4), 296–316. doi: 10.1080/10705422.2019.16558677.

Billiot, S., & Parfait, J. (2019). Reclaiming land: Adaptation activities and challenges to global environmental changes within indigenous communities: Indigenous. In M. Sherraden, J. Riggs, & L. Mason (Eds.), *People and Climate Change: Vulnerability, Adaptation, Social Justice*.

Billiot, S., Duran, B., & Jolivette, A. (2021). Take Me To The Water: Wi hokišak kuš in Louisiana Kinship Models of Healing and Thrivance. In L. Pihama & L. Tuhiwai Smith (Eds.) *ORA: Healing Ourselves Indigenous Knowledge, Healing and Wellness*.

Billiot, S., *Kwon, S., Burnette, C. E. (2019). Repeated disasters through generations impede transmission of cultural knowledge. *Journal of Family Strengths*, *19*(1). Available at: https://digitalcommons.library.tmc.edu/jfs/vol19/iss1/11

Booth, J. M., Chapman, D., Ohmer, M. L. & Wei, K., (2018). Examining the relationship between level of participation in community gardens and their multiple functions. *Journal of Community Practice*, *26*(1), 5–22. doi: 10.1080/10705422.2017.1413024.

Brady, S., Krings, A., & Sawyer, J. (2019). Hydraulic fracturing and Indigenous rights in the Heartland of the USA: Lessons for environmental social workers. In M. Rinkel and M. Powers (Eds.), *Social work promoting community and environmental sustainability: A workbook for social work practitioners and educators (Vol. 3)* (pp. 155–171). Rheinfelden, Switzerland: International Federation of Social Work (IFSW).

Bryant, B., & Mohai, P. (Eds.). (1992). *Race and the incidence of environmental hazards: A time for discourse*. Boulder, CO: Westview.

Bullard, R. D. (1996). Environmental justice: It's more than waste facility siting. *Social Science Quarterly*, *77*(3), 493–499.

Burger, J., & Gochfeld, M. (2011). Conceptual environmental justice model for evaluating chemical pathways of exposure in low-income, minority, Native American, and other unique exposure populations. *American Journal of Public Health*, *101*(S1), S64–S73. doi: 10.2105/AJPH. 2010.300077.

Burgos, W. D., Castillo-Meza, L., Tasker, T. L., Geeza, T. J., Drohan, P. J., Liu, X., . . . Warner, N. R. (2017). Watershed-scale impacts from surface water disposal of oil and gas wastewater in Western Pennsylvania. *Environmental Science Technology, 51*(15), 8851–8860. doi: 10.1021/acs.est.7b01696.

Bullard, R. D. (1999). Dismantling environmental racism in the USA. *Local Environment, 4*(1), 5–19.

Bullard, R. D. (Ed.). (1993). *Confronting environmental racism: Voices from the grassroots.* South End Press.

Callaway, D., Eamer, J., Edwardsen, E., Jack, C., Marcy, S., Olrun, A., Patkotak, M., Rexford, D., & Whiting, A. (1999). Effects of climate change on subsistence communities in Alaska. In: G. Weller, P. Anderson (Eds.), *Assessing the consequences of climate change for Alaska and the Bering Sea Region.* Center for Global Change and Arctic System Research, University of Alaska Fairbanks.

Carrington, K., Morley, C., Warren, S., Ryan, V., Ball, M., Clarke, J., & Vitis, L. (2021). The impact of COVID-19 pandemic on Australian domestic and family violence services and their clients. *The Australian Journal of Social Issues, 56*(4), 539–558. https://doi.org/10.1002/ajs4.183

CDC. (2020, February 11). Coronavirus Disease 2019 (COVID-19). Centers for Disease Control and Prevention. https://www.cdc.gov/coronavirus/2019-ncov/index.html.

Center for Land Use and Sustainability (CLUS). (2019). *2018–2019 CLUS annual report.* Retrieved February 9, 2020, from https://centerforlanduse.org/resources/documents/.

Checker, M. (2011). Wiped out by the greenwave: Environmental gentrification and the paradoxical politics of urban sustainability. *City and Society, 23,* 210–229.

Cochran, P., Huntington, O. H., Pungowiyi, C., Tom, S., Chapin, F. S, III, Huntington, H. P., . . . Trainor, S. F. (2013). Indigenous frameworks for observing and responding to climate change in Alaska. *Climate Change, 120,* 557–567. doi: 10.1007/s10584-013-0735-2.

Cozzetto, K., Chief, K., Dittmer, K., Brubaker, M., Gough, R., Souza, K., . . . Chavan, P. (2013). Climate change impacts on the water resources of American Indians and Alaska Natives in the U.S. *Climatic Change, 120*(3), 569–584. doi: 10.1007/s10584-013-0852-y.

Dale, A. & Newman, L. L. (2009). Sustainable development for some: Green urban development and affordability. *Local Environment, 14*(7), 669–681.

Daniels, T. L. (2009). A trail across time: American environmental planning from city beautiful to sustainability. *Journal of the American Planning Association, 75*(2), 178–192. doi: 10.1080/01944360902748206.

DeLuca, K., & Demo, A. (2001). Imagining nature and erasing class and race: Carleton Watkins, John Muir, and the construction of wilderness. *Environmental History, 69*(7), 541–560.

Desrosiers, T. A., Lawson, C. C., Meyer, R. E., Richardson, D. B., Daniels, J. L. Waters, M. A. . . . Olshan, A. (2012). Maternal occupational exposure to organic solvents during early pregnancy and risks of neural tube defects and orofacial clefts. *Occupational & Environmental Medicine, 69*(7), 493–499. doi: 10.1136/oemed-2011-100245.

Dhurandhar, E. J. (2016). The food-insecurity obesity paradox: A resource scarcity hypothesis. *Physiology & Behavior, 162,* 88–92. doi: 10.1016/j.physbeh.2016.04.025.

Dikos Ntsaaígíí-19 [COVID-19]. (n.d.). Retrieved June 29, 2020, from https://www.ndoh.navajo-nsn.gov/COVID-19.

Dittmer, K. (2013). Changing streamflow on Columbia basin tribal lands: Climate change and salmon. *Climatic Change, 120*(3), 627–641. doi: 10.1007/s10584-013-0745-0.

Dominelli, L. (2011). Climate change: Social workers' roles and contributions to policy debates and interventions. *International Journal of Social Welfare, 20*(4), 430–438. doi: 10.1111/j.1468-2397.2011.00795.x.

HUMAN IMPACTS OF ENVIRONMENTAL CHANGE 359

Draper, C. & Freedman, D. (2010). Review and analysis of the benefits, purposes, and motivations associated with community gardening in the United States. *Journal of Community Practice, 18*(4), 458–492.

Drolet, J. (2017). Forced Migration and the Lived Experiences of Refugees. In M. Rinkel & M. Powers (Eds.), *Social work promoting community and environmental sustainability: A workbook for social work practitioners and educators* (pp. 192–201). Switzerland: International Federation of Social Work (IFSW). http://ifsw.org/prod uct/books/social-work-promoting-community-and-environmental-sustainabil ity-free-pdf/

Duntley-Matos, R., Arteaga, V., García, A., Arellano, R., Garza, R., & Ortega, R. M. (2017). "We always say: And then came the water. . . ": Flint's emergent Latinx capacity building journey during the government-induced lead crisis. *Journal of Community Practice, 25*(3–4), 365–390. doi: 10.1080/10705422.2017.1384422.

Eggers, M. J., Moore-Nall, A. L., Doyle, J. T., Lefthand, M. J., Young, S. L., Bends, A. L., . . . Camper, A. K. (2015). Potential health risks from Uranium in home well water: An investigation by the Apsaalooke (Crow) Tribal Research Group. *Geosciences, 5*, 67–94. doi: 10.3390/geosciences5010067.

Ellis, K. N., Hathaway, J. M., Mason, L. R., Howe, D., Epps, T., & Brown, V. M. (2017). Summer temperature variability across four urban neighborhoods in Knoxville, Tennessee, USA. *Theoretical and Applied Climatology, 127*, 701–710. doi: 10.1007/ s00704-015-1659-8.

Ellis, K. N., Mason, L. R., & Gassert, K. N. (2019). Public understanding of local tornado characteristics and perceived protection from land-surface features in Tennessee, USA. *PLoS One, 14*(7), e0219897. doi: 10.1371/journal.pone.0219897.

Fernandez Rysavy, T., & Floyd, A. (2016). People of color are on the front lines of the climate crisis. *Green American.* Spring 2016. https://www.greenamerica.org/climate-just ice-all/people-color-are-front-lines-climate-crisis

Fleetwood, J. (2020). Social justice, food loss, and the Sustainable Development Goals in the era of COVID-19. *Sustainability, 12*(12), 5027. https://doi.org/10.3390/su1 2125027.

Flocks, J. D. (2012). The environmental and social injustice of farmworker pesticide exposure. *Georgetown Journal on Poverty Law & Policy, 19*(2), 255–282.

Fry, M., Briggle, A., & Kincaid, J. (2015). Fracking and environmental (in)justice in a Texas city. *Ecological Economics, 117*, 97–107. doi: 10.1016/j.ecolecon.2015.06.012.

Gibbs, L. (2002). Citizen activism for environmental health: The growth of a powerful new grassroots health movement. *Annals of the American Academy of Political and Social Science, 584*, 97–109.

Grand Challenges for Social Work. (2018). Create social responses to a changing environment. Retrieved from https://grandchallengesforsocialwork.org/wp-content/uploads/ 2015/12/GC-one-pager-Environment-final.pdf.

Gray, M., Coates, J., & Yellow Bird, M. (2018). *Indigenous social work around the world: Towards culturally relevant education and practice.* New York: Routledge.

Grossman, D. S., & Slusky, D. J. G. (2019). The impact of the Flint water crisis on fertility. *Demography, 56*, 2005–2031. doi: 10.1007/s13524-019-00831-0.

Hare, N. (1970). Black ecology. *The Black Scholar, 1*(6), 2–8. doi: 10.1080/ 00064246.1970.11728700.

Hayward, R. A., Morris, Z., Ramos, Y. O., Díaz, A. S. (2019). "Todo ha sido a pulmón": Community organizing after disaster in Puerto Rico. *Journal of Community Practice, 27*(3–4), 249–259. doi: 10.1080/10705422.2019.1649776.

Hyde, K. (2020). Residential water quality and the spread of COVID-19 in the United States. Available at SSRN: https://ssrn.com/abstract=3572341 or http://dx.doi.org/10.2139/ssrn.3572341.

Intergovernmental Panel on Climate Change [IPCC]. (2022). Cambridge University Press. Cambridge, UK and New York, NY. https://report.ipcc.ch/ar6/wg2/IPCC_AR6_WGII_FullReport.pdf

International Organization for Migration [IOM]. (2015). *Migration, environment, and climate change: Evidence for policy glossary.* Geneva: International Office for Migration. Retrieved from https://publications.iom.int/system/files/pdf/meclep_glossary_en.pdf?language=en.

Johnston, J. E., Werder, E., & Sebastian, D. (2016). Wastewater disposal wells, fracking, and environmental injustice in southern Texas. *American Journal of Public Health, 106*(3), 550–556. doi: 10.2105/AJPH.2015.303000.

Kaiser, M. L. (2017). Redefining food security in a community context: An exploration of community food security indicators and social worker roles in community food strategies. *Journal of Community Practice, 25*(2), 213–234. doi: 10.1080/10705422.2017.1308897.

Kaiser, M. L., Himmelheber, S., Miller, S., & Hayward, R. A. (2015). Cultivators of change: Food justice in social work education. *Social Work Education, 34*(5), 544–557. doi: 10.1080//02615479.2015.1063599.

Kemp, S. P., Palinkas, L. A., Mason, L. R., Billiot, S., Mitchell, F. M., & Krings, A. (2022). Creating Social Responses to a Changing Environment. In R. P. Barth, T. R. Shanks, J. Messing, & J. H. Williams (Eds.), *Grand challenges for social work and society* (2nd Edition). London, Oxford: Oxford University Press.

Kemp, S. P., Palinkas, L. A., Wong, M., Wagner, K., Mason, L. R., Chi, I., . . . Rechkemmer, A. (2015). Strengthening the social response to the human impacts of environmental change (Grand Challenges for Social Work Initiative Working Paper No. 5). Cleveland, OH: American Academy of Social Work and Social Welfare.

Kemp, S. P., Palinkas, L. A., & Mason, L. R. (2018). Responding to global environmental change: A grand challenge for social work. In R. Fong, J. Lubben, & R. Barth (Eds.), *Grand challenges for social work and society* (pp. 140–160). New York: Oxford University Press.

Krakoff, S. (2008). American Indian tribes, climate change, and ethics for a warming world. *Denver Law Review, 85*(865), 1–26.

Krings, A., & Copic, C. (2020.) Environmental justice organizing in a gentrifying community: Navigating dilemmas of representation, recruitment, and issue selection. *Families in Society: The Journal of Contemporary Social Services, 102*(2), 154–166. https://doi.org/10.1177/1044389420952247.

Krings, A., Kornberg, D., & Lane, E. (2018). Organizing under austerity: How residents' concerns became the Flint water crisis. *Critical Sociology, 45*(4-5), 583–597. doi: 10.1177/08969205187570531.

Krings, A., & Schusler, T. (2020). Equity in sustainable development: Integrating social work and environmental justice to prevent environmental gentrification. *International Journal of Social Welfare, 29*(4), 321–334. https://doi.org/10.1111/ijsw.124.

Krings, A., Spencer, M. S., & Jimenez, K. (2013). Organizing for environmental justice: From bridges to taro patches. In S. Dutta & C. Ramanathan (Eds.), *Governance, development, and social work* (pp. 186–200). London: Routledge. https://doi.org/10.4324/9780203796009.

Krings, A., & Thomas, H. (2018). Integrating green social work and the U.S. environmental justice movement: An introduction to community benefits agreements. In L. Dominelli (Ed.), *The Routledge handbook of green social work* (pp. 397–406). London: Routledge. https://doi.org/10.4324/9781315183213.

Krings, A., Victor, B., Mathias, J, & Perron, B. (2018). Environmental social work in the disciplinary literature, 1991–2015. *International Social Work, 63*(3), 275–290. https://doi.org/10.1177/0020872818788397.

Kuhnlein, H. V., & Receveur, O. (1996). Dietary change and traditional food systems of Indigenous peoples. *Annual Review Nutrition, 16*, 417–442. 10.1146/annurev.nu.16.070196.002221.

Lee, S. J., Krings, A., Rose, S., Dover, K., Ayoub, J., & Salman, F. (2016). Racial inequality and the implementation of emergency management laws in economically distressed urban areas. *Children and Youth Services Review, 70*, 1–7. doi: 10.1016/j.childyouth.2016.08.016 0190-7409.

Lehtinen, U. (1998). Eco-justice: Environmental racism; the US nuclear industry and Native Americans. *Abya Yala News, 11*(1), 20.

Levy, B. (2012). Bayou blues: The social structure of Hurricane Katrina's damage. *Sociological Spectrum, 32*(5), 424–435. doi: 10.1080/02732173.2012.694796.

Ludwig, J., Sanbonmatsu, L., Gennetian, L., Adam, E., Duncan, G. J., Katz, L. F., Kessler, R. C., Kling, J. R., Lindau, S. T., Whitaker, R. C., & McDade, T. W. (2011). Neighborhoods, Obesity, and Diabetes—A Randomized Social Experiment. *New England Journal of Medicine, 365*(16), 1509–1519. https://doi.org/10.1056/NEJMsa1103216

Lynn, K., Daigle, J., Hoffman, J., Lake, F., Michelle, N., Ranco, D., . . . Williams, P. (2013). The impacts of climate change on tribal traditional foods. *Climate Change, 120*, 545–556. doi: 10.1007/s10584-013-0736-1.

Markus, G. B., & Krings, A. (2020). Planning, participation, and power in a "shrinking city": The Detroit Works Project. *Journal of Urban Affairs, 42*(8), 1141–1163. https://doi.org/10.1080/07352166.2020.1779009.

Markstrom, C. A., & Charley, P. H. (2003). Psychological effects of technological/human-caused environmental disasters: Examination of the Navajo and uranium. *American Indian & Alaska Native Mental Health Research: The Journal of the National Center, 11*(1), 19–45.

Mason, L., Kemp, S., Palinkas, L., & Krings, A. (2021). Responses to Environmental Change. In *Encyclopedia of Social Work*. Oxford University Press.

Mason, L. R., Ellis, K. N., & Hathaway, J. M. (2017). Experiences of urban environmental conditions in socially and economically diverse neighborhoods. *Journal of Community Practice, 25*(1), 48–67. doi: 10.1080/10705422.2016.1269250.

Mason, L. R., Ellis, K. N., & Hathaway, J. M. (2019). Urban flooding, social equity, and "backyard" green infrastructure: An area for multidisciplinary practice. *Journal of Community Practice, 27*(3-4), 334–350.

Mason, L. R., Ellis, K. N., Winchester, B., & Schexnayder, S. (2018). Tornado warnings at night: Who gets the message? *Weather, Climate, and Society, 10*(3), 561–568. doi: 10.1175/WCAS-D-17-0114.1.

Mason, L. R., Erwin, J., Brown, A., Ellis, K. N., & Hathaway, J. M. (2018). Health impacts of extreme weather events: Exploring protective factors with a capitals framework. *Journal of Evidence-Based Social Work, 15*, 579–593. doi: 10.1080/23761407.2018.1502115.

Mason, L. R., Shires, M. K., Arwood, C., & Borst, A. (2017). Social work research and global environmental change. *Journal of the Society for Social Work and Research, 8*(4), 645–672.

Mathias, J., Krings, A., & Teixeira, S. (In press). Which environmental social work? Environmentalisms, social justice, and the dilemmas ahead. *Social Service Review*.

Matthies, A. L., Peeters, J., Hirvilammi, T., & Stamm, I. (2020). Ecosocial innovations enabling social work to promote new forms of sustainable economy. *International Journal of Social Welfare, 29*(4), 378–389. https://doi.org/10.1111/ijsw.12423.

McDonald, Y. J., Grineski, S. E., Collins, T. W., & Kim, Y.-A. (2015). A scalable climate health justice assessment model. *Social Science & Medicine, 133*, 242–252. doi: 10.1016/j.socscimed.2014.10.032.

McGurty, E. M. (2000). Warren County, NC, and the emergence of the environmental justice movement: Unlikely coalitions and shared meanings in local collective action. *Society & Natural Resources, 13*(4), 373–387.

Melstrom, R., Mohammadi, R., Schusler, T., & Krings, A. (2021). Who benefits from brownfield cleanup and gentrification? Evidence from Chicago. *Urban Affairs Review, 58*(6), 1622–1651. doi: 10780874211041537.

Mitchell, F. M. (2018). "Water is life": Using Photovoice to document American Indian perspectives on water and health. *Social Work Research, 42*(4), 277–289. doi: 10.1093/swr/svy025.

Mitchell, F.M. (2019). Water (in)security and American Indian health: Social and environmental justice implications for policy, practice, and research. *Public Health, 176*, 98–105. doi: doi: 10.1016/j.puhe.2018.10.010.

Mitchell, F. M. (2020). American Indian water insecurity in the era of COVID-19. *Journal of Indigenous Social Development, 9*(3), 67–75. https://journalhosting.ucalgary.ca/index.php/jisd/article/view/71067.

Miyashita, L., Foley, G., Semple, S., & Grigg, J. (2020). Traffic-derived particulate matter and angiotensin-converting enzyme 2 expression in human airway epithelial cells. *BioRxiv*.

Mohai, P., Pellow, D. N., & Roberts, J. T. (2009). Environmental justice. *Annual Review Environmental Resources, 34*, 405–430.

Nabhan, G. P. (2010). Perspectives in ethnobiology: Ethnophenology and climate change. *Journal of Ethnobiology, 30*, 1–4. doi: 10.2993/0278-0771-30.1.1.

National Research Council [NRC]. (2010). *Advancing the science of climate change*. Washington, DC: The National Academies Press.

Navajo water project. (n.d.). Retrieved June 25, 2020, from https://www.navajowaterproject.org/.

Neff, R. A., Palmer, A. M., McKenzie, S. E., & Lawrence, R. S. (2009). Food systems and public health disparities. *Journal of Hunger & Environmental Nutrition, 4*, 282–314. doi: 10.1080/19320240903337041.

Norman, E. S. (2017). Standing up for inherent rights: The role of Indigenous-led activism in protecting sacred waters and ways of life. *Society & Natural Resources, 30*(4), 537–553. doi: 10.1080/08941920.2016.1274459.

Ohmer, M. L., Meadowcroft, P., Freed, K., & Lewis, E. (2009). Community gardening and community development: Individual, social and community benefits of a community conservation program. *Journal of Community Practice, 17*(4), 377–399.

Peeters, J. (2012). The place of social work in sustainable development: Towards ecosocial practice. *International Journal of Social Welfare, 21*(3), 287–298.

Pellow, D. N. (2004). *Garbage wars: The struggle for environmental justice in Chicago*. Cambridge, MA: MIT Press.

HUMAN IMPACTS OF ENVIRONMENTAL CHANGE 363

Pezzullo, P. C., & Sandler, R. (2007). Introduction: Revisiting the environmental justice challenge to environmentalism. In R. Sandler & P. C. Pezzullo (Eds.), *Environmental justice and environmentalism: The social justice challenge to the environmental movement* (pp. 1–25). Cambridge, MA: MIT Press.

Pfeifer, G. M. (2016). Pesticides, migrant farm workers, and corporate agriculture: How social work can promote environmental justice. *Journal of Progressive Human Services, 27*(3), 175–190. doi: 10.1080/10428232.2016.1196428.

Powers, M. C., Rambaree, K., & Peeters, J. (2019). Degrowth for transformational alternatives as radical social work practice. *Critical and Radical Social Work, 7*(3), 417–433.

Powers, M. C., & Nsonwu, C. (2020). Environmental injustices faced by resettled refugees: Housing policies and community development. In R. Hugman, J. Drolet, & S. Todd (Eds.), *Community practice and social development in social work: Major research works* (pp. 385–389). Singapore: Springer Nature. doi.org/10/11007/978-981-13-1542-8_20-1.

Prado, J., Mulay, P. R., Kasner, E. J., Bojes, H. K., & Calvert, G. M. (2017). Acute pesticide-related illness among farmworkers: Barriers to reporting to public health authorities. *Journal of Agromedicine, 22*(4), 395–405. doi: 10.1080/1059924X.2017.1353936.

Rao, S., Doherty, F., & Teixeira, S. (2022). Are You Prepared? Self-efficacy, social vulnerability, and disaster readiness. *International Journal of Disaster Risk Reduction, 77*(103072). https://doi.org/10.1016/j.ijdrr.2022.103072.

Rosen, C. S., Greene, C. J., Young, H. E., & Norris, F. H. (2010). Tailoring disaster mental health services to diverse needs: An analysis of 36 crisis counseling projects. *Health & Social Work, 35*(3), 211–220. doi: 10.1093/hsw/35.3.211.

Santana, D. B. (2002). Review: Untitled. [Review of the book *Where we live, work, and play: The environmental justice movement and the struggle for a new environmentalism*, by Patrick Novotny]. *Contemporary Sociology, 31*(1), 63. doi: 10.2307/3089428.

Schlosberg, D. (2007). *Defining environmental justice: Theories, movements, and nature.* Oxford: Oxford University Press.

Schusler, T., Krings, A., & Hernández, M. (2019). Integrating youth participation and ecosocial work: new possibilities to advance environmental and social justice. *Journal of Community Practice, 27*(3-4), 460–475. https://doi.org/10.1080/10705 422.2019.1657537.

Schwartz, N. A., von Glascoe, C. A., Torres, V., Ramos, L., & Soria-Delgado, C. (2015). "Where they (live, work and) spray": Pesticide exposure, childhood asthma and environmental justice among Mexican-American farmworkers. *Health & Place, 32*, 83–92. doi: 10.1016/j.healthplace.2014.12.016.

Shrader-Frechette, K. (2006). *Environmental justice: Creating equality, reclaiming democracy.* New York: Oxford University Press.

Spina, F. (2015). Environmental justice and patterns of state inspections. *Social Science Quarterly, 96*(2), 417–429. doi: 10.1111/ssqu.12160.

Stamm, B. (2017). A personal-professional experience of losing my home to wildfire: Linking personal experience with the professional literature. *Clinical Social Work Journal, 45*(2), 136–145. doi: 10.1007/s10615-015-0520-y.

Swyngedouw, E. (2007). Impossible "sustainability" and the postpolitical condition. In R. Krueger & D. Gibbs (Eds.), *The sustainable development paradox* (pp. 13–40). New York: Guilford.

Sze, J. (2006). *Noxious New York: The racial politics of urban health and environmental justice.* Cambridge, MA: MIT Press.

Taylor, D. E. (2000). The rise of the environmental justice paradigm: Injustice framing and the social construction of environmental discourses. *American Behavioral Scientist, 43*(4), 508–580.

Taylor, D. E. (2014). *The state of diversity in environmental organizations.* Ann Arbor, MI: Green 2.0.

Teixeira, S., & Krings, A. (2015). Sustainable social work: An environmental justice framework for social work education. *Social Work Education, 34*(5), 513–527.

Teixeira, S., Mathias, J., & Krings, A. (2019). The future of environmental social work: Looking to community initiatives for models of prevention. *Journal of Community Practice, 27*(3–4), 414–429. https://doi.org/10.1080/02615 479.2015.1063601.

Teixeira, S., & Sing, E. (2016). Reclaim Northside: An environmental justice approach to address vacant land in Pittsburgh. *Family and Community Health, 39*(3), 207–215. doi: 10.1097/FCH.0000000000000107

Thurber, A., & Krings, A. (2021). Gentrification. In *Encyclopedia of Social Work* (pp. 1–24). Oxford University Press. https://doi.org/10.1093/acrefore/9780199975839.013.1413

Thurber, A., Krings, A., Martinez, L. S., & Ohmer, M. (2019). Resisting gentrification: The theoretical and practice contributions of social work. *Journal of Social Work, 21*(2), 26–45. https://doi. org/10.1177/1468017319861500.

Trainer, S. F., Chapin, S., Huntington, H. P., Natcher, D. C., & Kofinas, G. (2007). Arctic climate impacts: Environmental injustice in Canada and the United States. *Local Environment, 12*(6), 627–643. doi: 10.1080/13549830701657414.

United Nations. (2007). *Declaration on the rights of Indigenous peoples.* New York: United Nations.

Walters, J. E., Mason, L. R., & Ellis, K. N. (2019). Examining patterns of intended response to tornado warnings among residents of Tennessee, United States, through a latent class analysis approach. *International Journal of Disaster Risk Reduction, 34*, 375–386. doi: 10.1016/j.ijdrr.2018.12.007.

Wilson, S. M., Bullard, R., Patterson, J., & Thomas, S. B. (2020). Roundtable on the pandemics of racism, environmental injustice, and COVID-19 in America. *Environmental Justice, 13*(3), 56–64. https://doi.org/10.1089/env.2020.0019.

Woody, R. L., Jack, B., & Bizahaloni, V. (1981). *Social impact of the uranium industry on two Navajo communities.* Tsaile, AZ: Navajo Community College.

Zakour, M. J., & Harrell, E. B. (2004). Access to disaster services. *Journal of Social Service Research, 30*(2), 27–54. doi: 10.1300/J079v30n02_03.

14

Race and Racism in the Homelessness Crisis in the United States

Historic Antecedents, Current Best Practices, and Recommendations to End Racial Disparities in Housing and Homelessness

Deborah K. Padgett, Benjamin F. Henwood, and James Petrovich

The roots of African-American housing exclusion go back to the post-Civil War Reconstruction period, when millions of former slaves lived in a hostile white-dominated South where planters and landowners ensured that the promise of "40 acres and a mule" was never met.

—Ta-Nehisi Coates, 2014

Foreword: A Brief Comment on the Authors' Positionality

We three authors begin this chapter by acknowledging that we have expertise in research on homelessness and that we are white and not persons of color. The latter obviously means that we do not have the lived experience of racial discrimination, which may result in deficiencies or limitations in the content of this chapter. While writing this chapter required assuming a stance of being anti-racist with which we were (and are) comfortable, we also acknowledge that it reflects, to varying degrees, opportunities afforded to us by white privilege.

Deborah K. Padgett, Benjamin F. Henwood, and James Petrovich, *Race and Racism in the Homelessness Crisis in the United States* In: *Social Work and the Grand Challenge to Eliminate Racism.* Edited by: Martell L. Teasley, Michael S. Spencer, and Melissa Bartholomew, Oxford University Press. © Oxford University Press 2023. DOI: 10.1093/oso/9780197674949.003.0014

Racism in Plain Sight: From Slavery to Jim Crow to Post–World War II Housing Exclusion

The decades-long crisis of homelessness in the United States that began in the 1980s was not an accident of history, nor was it inevitable. The upstream factors that converged to produce this crisis—the sharp decline in federal spending on public housing, the loss of affordable low-cost housing to gentrification, the decline in household income relative to rising rents—were rarely brought up in public policy discourses focused on temporary solutions such as soup kitchens and shelters. Meanwhile, public opinion focused on the deficiencies and pathologies of homeless individuals.

Amidst the volumes that have been written about homelessness over the past three decades—its prevalence, putative causes, and potential solutions—the role of race has received surprisingly little attention, despite the obvious and ongoing disproportionate representation of non-White racial and ethnic groups among the homeless, whether single adults or families. According to the 2018 Point-in-Time (PIT) count (Department of Housing and Urban Development [HUD], 2019), the most overrepresented non-White racial or ethnic group is African Americans, who comprise 40% of all homeless (and 51% of homeless family members) while representing 13% of the U.S. population. Nationally, African Americans are homeless in all but two of 461 federally defined geographic Continnums of Care, and they are overrepresented in every state (National Alliance to End Homelessness, 2019). Only among street-dwelling homeless do Whites outnumber African Americans (60%) (HUD, 2018). PIT data also indicate that Native Americans and people identifying as Hispanic/Latinx are overrepresented among people experiencing homelessness, with Native Americans representing less than 1% of the U.S. population but comprising 4% of all people experiencing homelessness. The overrepresentation of Hispanic/Latinx is less dramatic, with members of this ethnic subgroup representing 18% of the total U.S. population but comprising 22% of all people experiencing homelessness. Among all non-white racial and ethnic groups, only Asian Americans are not overrepresented among people experiencing homelessness (HUD, 2018).

While one could argue that the overrepresentation of African Americans among people experiencing homelessness stems from the high rate of poverty affecting this subgroup, the proportion of African Americans experiencing homelessness significantly exceeds their disproportionality in household poverty (Center for Social Innovation, 2018). Why is homelessness a fate far more likely for African Americans? We argue that a pernicious history of racist exclusion of African Americans from housing (Rothstein, 2017) has uniquely heightened their risk of homelessness by excluding their access to a primary source of wealth in the United States (equity in home ownership).

The roots of African-American housing exclusion go back to the post–Civil War Reconstruction period, when millions of former slaves were left to fend for themselves in a hostile White-dominated South, where planters and landowners ensured that the promise of "40 acres and a mule" was never met (Coates, 2014). Living in debt peonage as sharecroppers or impelled to migrate to an industrializing North, African American men and women endured deplorable living conditions—renting run-down cabins or living in teeming slums in Northern cities (Wilkerson, 2010). As White control was consolidated politically and economically in the late nineteenth century, Jim Crow laws were promulgated to legally enforce segregation and racist exclusion. Enforcement by formal legal means was supplemented by widespread violence and the terrorism of lynchings and Ku Klux Klan attacks.

Most Americans are familiar with these injustices, and historians point to the civil rights reforms of the 1960s as helping to reverse (or at least ameliorate) the racism and segregation rooted in the previous century. But fair housing laws and other Great Society programs arrived long after racial housing segregation had been firmly put into place.

The link between racism and homelessness requires spotlighting the post–World War II period when, as Richard Rothstein points out in *The Color of Law* (2017), government and private sectors conspired to enforce and institutionalize racial segregation throughout the nation. Prior to the 1940s, de facto integration was not uncommon in many parts of the country where African Americans lived among Whites in small towns as well as large cities. The rapid growth of factory jobs, in the absence of formal zoning or other race-based policies (at least outside of the Jim Crow South), led to a degree of de facto residential mixing of the races. Of course, housing segregation remained widespread, but it was less a matter of overt governmental policies than a combination of long-standing tradition combined with income barriers and racialized decisions by local authorities (city and county officials, bank loan policies, etc.).

Any semblance of de facto integration was undone by federal, state, and local policies instituted after the end of World War II. In the postwar construction boom in housing intended for veterans and the baby boom generation, the federal government actively incentivized home ownership through low-interest loans and mortgage guarantees. Yet the Federal Housing Administration and the Veterans Administration refused loans and mortgage insurance to African Americans seeking to buy in designated "White" neighborhoods (likewise for Whites seeking to buy in designated "Black" neighborhoods). Local zoning ordinances forbade residential integration. Housing prices were high in Black neighborhoods, forcing residents to double up, reducing local taxes and infrastructure supports and thus contributing to crowding and slum-like conditions (Rothstein, 2017). Similarly, public housing was racially segregated by federal decree.

The pervasive enforcement of housing segregation was promoted by the National Association of Real Estate Boards (whose realtors blatantly encouraged "White flight" from integrating neighborhoods) and by banks whose "redlining" practices denied loans to African Americans seeking to buy homes in White neighborhoods. Regardless of their income level, African Americans were forced to live in low-income areas (Rothstein, 2017).

In Chicago, unscrupulous speculators sold "contract" housing at inflated prices (promising eventual ownership), then quickly repossessed and re-sold the property if the owner fell behind in payments. As these speculators became wealthy, their tenants and properties grew poorer (Coates, 2014). The resulting "concentration of disadvantage" (Sampson et al., 2008) can be found in cities from Palo Alto to St. Louis to Boston—the enduring legacy of segregation and discrimination.

As mentioned earlier, home ownership is a prime source of wealth accumulation in American society as equity (value) grows over time and can be passed on to the next generation. Rothstein (2017) gives a telling explanation for why African Americans earn 60% of White income in the United States but have cumulative wealth only 5%–7% of White wealth. While the roots of such a wealth disparity emerge from a number of race-related discriminations, housing is pivotal to understanding this phenomenon.

A prime example comes from the massive tract house developments like Levittown (Long Island) that were built for returning World War II veterans. African Americans were excluded from purchasing these homes, which originally sold for $7,000. Ultimately, these same African American families ended up paying more in rent (in less desirable neighborhoods) than White homeowners paid in mortgage and other costs (Rothstein, 2017). Today, Levittown homes sell on average for $300,000, an enormous bounty of equity wealth that can be passed down to future generations of one's family. The origins of a vast racial "wealth gap" can now be envisioned as a consequence of racism in access to housing, lasting for decades. Lacking a financial safety net, it is no surprise that losing one's home is catastrophic for an African American person or family (Coates, 2014). Pathways into homelessness are more open to some Americans than to others, and African Americans had a uniquely historical shortcut imposed upon them.

The housing boom of the 1950s gradually slowed down and the stock of affordable housing shrank in the wake of 1960s urban renewal and gentrification, followed by overt government abnegation during the Reagan administration. In this context, a rise in homelessness became almost inevitable by the 1980s. Exacerbating preexisting racial disparities was the sharp rise in incarceration among African Americans, subject to disproportionately longer sentences for drug and other nonviolent offenses (Alexander, 2010). As prison release is a major risk for homelessness, once again racial biases played out. Moreover, having a criminal record barred many ex-prisoners from access to public housing and private rentals, as well as job opportunities.

The above historic antecedents may interact with individual risk factors for homelessness, including discrimination based upon sexual or gender orientation, severe substance abuse, and domestic violence. Clearly, the vast majority of African Americans do not become homeless. Rarely is homelessness the result of a single cause; instead it is a cascade of events that propel a person or family into losing their home (Shinn & Khadduri, 2020). Nevertheless, we know of no comparable confluence of legal and illegal barriers placed before a racialized group of citizens seeking to buy or rent a home in the neighborhood of their choice.

Research on Homelessness: The Missing Significance of Race

In an insightful book on homelessness in the United States, anthropologist Kim Hopper (2002) noted the visible disproportion in the number of African Americans among the homeless crowding the shelters in big cities in the 1980s. Historically, the American discourse on homelessness had been largely confined to the plight of White America—families displaced during the Great Depression, the Dust Bowl exodus to California, and the predominantly White men found in a city's Skid Row, typically heavy drinkers referred to as bums, vagrants, and derelicts (Hopper, 2002).

With the sharp and continued rise in homelessness in the 1980s, researchers pursued a number of tacks including surveys of shelter users (Barrow et al., 1999) as well as ethnographies of homeless persons such as Liebow's sensitive portrayal of Black homeless women in *Tell Them Who I Am* (1993). In a meta-synthesis review of the role of race in homelessness research, Bond (2019) noted the rarity with which race was considered as salient beyond being one of many demographic variables. The fact that African Americans were consistently overrepresented among the homeless population, upwards of 3 or 4 times, was viewed as a descriptive rather than explanatory factor.

To date, there has also been limited consideration of racial disparities in access to homeless services. The introduction of a federal requirement that all local providers cooperate in using a Coordinated Entry (CE) system in 2009, which inhibited prior tendencies to "cherry pick" the more favorable (and less problematic) homeless persons for access to care, was viewed as more equitable. Developing CE systems, communities are required to identify priority populations based on greatest need for Continuum of Care assistance (Department of Housing and Urban Development, 2017). It appears, most often, that communities defined vulnerable populations based on age (especially youth aged 18–24 and older adults), whether individuals met criteria for chronic homelessness, whether children were present in the household, and whether individuals were veterans of military service. Because the identification of vulnerable populations rarely appears to have been based on race, the CE system has had little direct effect on ameliorating racial disparities that may exist within homeless services. However, when communities focus on priority populations that disproportionately include African Americans, such as veterans of military service, a secondary effect is that racial disparities are mitigated.

Another racial disproportion in homeless research that has received little attention is the racial/ethnic breakdowns of homeless service providers, where senior managers are 66% White (13% Black) and all other staff are 52.3% White (22.1% Black) (Center for Social Innovation, 2018). Thus, while the prototypical homeless adult or family is African American, their service providers are predominantly White. This disproportion obviously reflects racial preferences in hiring practices. But it also poses clear implications in perpetuating a White power structure having authority over Black lives.

A final area of racial disparities unexamined in the research literature lies in the locations of shelters, supportive housing units, and other programs serving homeless persons. With the possible exception of the nonprofit's corporate headquarters, local offices as well as housing options are located in low-income areas dominated by populations of African American, Latinx, and other low-income groups. Given housing costs, it is reasonable to assume that homeless persons fortunate enough to find housing (either independently through possession of a federal housing voucher or through placement by a service program) would be forced to seek apartments in low-income neighborhoods (and NIMBY responses ensure this state of affairs to continue despite efforts to equalize community involvement in homeless housing programs) (Wong & Stanhope, 2009). Somewhat more successful have been mixed-income developments that set aside units for low-income families or vouchers that allow families to move to lower-poverty neighborhoods (Chetty et al., 2016). Unfortunately, the portion of such units allocated to homeless families is very small, and they are often excluded altogether from mixed-income housing (National Low Income Housing Coaltion, 2019).

Current Best Practices in Ending Homelessness: Housing First

The emphasis in the Grand Challenges has been to bring forward evidence-based practices (EBPs) and policies and to situate them as part of social work's overarching commitment to science-based advocacy led by the American Academy for Social Work and Social Welfare (https://aaswsw.org/). The most prominent EBP related to ending homelessness is Housing First (HF). In this section we describe HF and how it emerged as a proven alternative to the status quo (which has had little to no effect in stemming the tide of homelessness over the years). As we will see, HF was developed and disseminated with no overt attention to racial inequality. However, to the extent that HF targets people who are chronically homelessness and disproportionately African American, it can be viewed as a possible means to begin to address the consequences of racism as it effectively ends homelessness.

The most widely embraced and influential best practice in terms of federal, state, and local policies has been the adoption and promulgation of HF, known initially as Pathways to Housing (PTH) (Padgett et al., 2016). Since its origin in New York City in 1992, HF has been subsequently adopted by many U.S. cities as well as government authorities in Canada, Western Europe, Australia, and New Zealand. In its earliest days in New York City,

PTH readily accepted and housed homeless persons who had long been rejected by traditional services—those with criminal justice histories in particular. Thus, by countering the status quo, PTH de facto offered services more readily to African Americans.

HF has garnered a consistent and robust record of evidence demonstrating significant improvements in housing stability for the vast majority of clients. Bolstered by a randomized trial in New York City (Tsemberis et al., 2004), a national five-city trial in Canada (the AtHome/ChezSoi experiment) (Goering et al., 2014), and numerous other controlled studies in Western Europe, HF has emerged as having system-wide transformational influence in ending homelessness for those served. Reversing the usual "staircase" order of requiring homeless persons to obey rules, participate in supportive services, take their medications, and become clean and sober before attaining housing, HF emphasizes consumer choice, harm reduction, and access to one's own apartment without such preconditions (Padgett et al., 2015). HF has been endorsed by HUD, the U.S. Inter-Agency Council on Homelessness (USICH), the U.S. Department of Veterans Affairs (VA), the National Alliance to End Homelessness, and virtually all advocacy groups, as it promotes the human right to housing even as it brings cost savings relative to reduce jail, hospital, and medical care utilization (National Alliance to End Homelessness, 2015). Resistance to HF arises from a status quo mentality threatened by such a shift (changes in program values, in program staff practices favoring client empowerment, acceptance of harm reduction, etc.). In particular, faith-based organizations and substance abuse providers have been critical of HF's embrace of harm reduction as it directly challenges their abstinence-only mandates.

There is growing consensus that a "housing industry" has emerged in which—however well-intentioned—stakeholders from top executives to the myriad of workers (case managers, van drivers, security personnel, messengers, office staff, janitors, house managers, etc.) stand to lose if HF is implemented. Private landlords would benefit in providing scatter-site rentals, but the profits from renting units temporarily to city homeless agencies far exceed market rents.

With respect to attention to race in the literature on HF, African Americans are typically the largest single group in HF studies in the United States—as would be expected. In the Canadian HF experiment, one of the sites (Toronto) opted to include a racial equity component (the Winnipeg site included a First Nations cultural component). In Toronto, this meant incorporating Anti-Racist/Anti-Oppressive (AR/AO) principles into support services delivered by a local provider. In addition, fidelity assessments of HF implementation used AR/AO measures to ensure these tenets were supported in practice (Goering et al., 2014). Findings from the Toronto site (as well as the other four sites) showed too few Black participants to find significant effects for race (Nelson, personal communication).

The scarcity of other EBPs designed to end homelessness is due, in part, to the growing consensus that dissemination of such a strongly supported EBP (HF) should take priority over a search for new approaches. Meanwhile, new avenues of research have sprung up around the implementation and challenges of adapting HF for homeless families, youths, rural clients, and older adults (Shinn & Khadduri, 2020). Another EBP related to homelessness is known as Critical Time Intervention (CTI) (Susser et al., 1997). In CTI, an array of social support services are provided to psychiatric patients, shelter users, or other institutionalized groups facing likely homelessness upon discharge. CTI has proven successful in preventing homelessness once discharged to the community (Susser et al., 1997). As with HF, many of the recipients of CTI were disproportionately African American, but the origins or impact of such differences did not receive attention in subsequent reports.

The larger movement toward providing permanent supportive housing (PSH) for homeless persons with disabilities (primarily psychiatric) has gained momentum in recent years. Though encompassing a much broader approach than HF (the latter a type of PSH), PSH was largely unexamined empirically until a recent report was released by the National Academies of Science, Engineering and Medicine (NASEM, 2018). The report examined the effectiveness and relative costs of PSH in improving health outcomes of chronically homeless persons. The NASEM panel noted a number of problems, including a lack of clarity in definitions of PSH and the absence of data and research on PSH. Given this situation, the report's authors admitted that solid conclusions regarding health could not be drawn except for persons with HIV/AIDS, who had improved health outcomes (NASEM, 2018). Notably, the report did not address racial disparities as influencing these health outcomes.

In considering non-health-specific outcomes, we note that HF was not originally designed to improve health but to end homelessness for its clients. In terms of housing stability, HF has no peer in succeeding in this regard. However, further research is needed to address lingering questions about its impact on mental health, substance use, health, and social integration (Padgett et al., 2015).

We end this section by reiterating that research on homelessness has, by and large, remained silent on the disproportionality of race and the significance of this phenomenon. Absent a historic perspective, one might be inclined to consider race solely as one of many demographic variables. We suggest that the salience of race—and its absence from the homelessness research literature—is an oversight that should be remedied in moving forward.

The HUD-VASH Program for Homeless Veterans: A Rare Success Story and Lessons Learned

African Americans among Homeless Veterans

Throughout American history, veterans of military service have experienced homelessness due to service-related medical, mental health, and substance abuse problems, post-service reintegration challenges, as well as economic depressions and recessions and the deinstitutionalization movement (Tsai, 2018). African Americans are overrepresented among veterans experiencing homelessness, currently comprising one-third (33%) of this subpopulation but only 12% of all U.S. veterans (Department of Housing and Urban Development [HUD], 2019).

Research examining this racial disparity is lacking, but African American veterans appear to possess fewer psychiatric problems, maintain more extensive social contacts, and are longer-term residents of their home cities compared to White veterans. Social disadvantages and racial discrimination have been identified as contributing to African American veteran homelessness, suggesting that residential treatment and culturally competent clinical services play an important role in serving this vulnerable population (Rosenheck et al., 1997). This finding, however, also confirms that racial disparities due to historical racism and structural discrimination have gone unaddressed.

The U.S. Department of Veterans Affairs (VA) has created a number of programs to assist veterans experiencing homelessness. Permanent supportive housing is provided through HUD-VASH, a collaboration combining HUD housing vouchers with VA supportive services. Initially created as a demonstration project in 1992 with approximately 1,700 vouchers (U.S.

Department of Housing and Urban Development, 2017b), the program now supports just over 100,000 HUD-VASH housing vouchers.

In 2010, the U.S. Interagency Council on Homelessness announced a goal to end veteran homelessness by 2015 (U.S. Interagency Council on Homelessness, 2015). When 2015 arrived, it was clear the plan did not achieve this goal, but the number of veterans experiencing homelessness had decreased 36%, dropping from 74,087 to 47,725. This decrease has continued, with 37,085 veterans being identified as homeless in 2019, an overall reduction of 51% compared to 2010 (U.S. Department of Housing and Urban Development, 2019).

The Success of HUD-VASH

A key contributor to reducing veteran homelessness has been the HUD-VASH program. When the federal goal to end veteran homelessness was announced in 2010, program funding supported 29,968 vouchers. Over the next nine years, 70,128 vouchers were added, with each voucher being found to increase the local supply of affordable housing units by 0.9 and decrease the number of homeless veterans by 1.0 (Evans et al., 2019). Other positive outcomes of the program include greater stability in housing, reductions in substance and alcohol use, higher overall quality of life, and a greater sense of safety (O'Connell & Rosenheck, 2018).

In addition to reducing homelessness among all veterans, HUD-VASH appears to be successfully correcting for the overrepresentation of African American veterans experiencing homelessness. An exit study of HUD-VASH programs in Houston, Los Angeles, Palo Alto, and Philadelphia indicates that 56% of 7,115 veterans served were African American (U.S. Department of Housing and Urban Development, 2017), a rate exceeding national estimates of African Americans among homeless veterans (33%) (U.S. Department of Housing and Urban Development, 2019). The study also found that African Americans were more likely than other racial groups to remain housed in the program or to exit the program to stable housing. Other studies of HUD-VASH indicate that African American participants experience better social, clinical, and functional outcomes, including being housed in higher quality neighborhoods compared to White veterans and African American non-veterans housed through the mainstream Housing Choice voucher program (Patterson et al., 2014).

The success of HUD-VASH in housing African American veterans can be attributed to the program's implementation of HF and substantial fiscal resources allocated to the program. Additionally, because HUD-VASH does not require that homeless veterans possess a mental illness or chronic substance abuse disorder, the program reaches a broader cross section of veterans. A final key strength of HUD-VASH is that applicants are screened using less-restrictive VA criteria, instead of more restrictive Public Housing Authority criteria, which may deny assistance based on prior criminal activity and substance use-related challenges (Section 8 Housing Choice Vouchers, 2012).

Structural and Institutional Changes Needed to Address Racial Inequities in Housing Access and Housing Security

This chapter considers HF as the most consonant corrective mechanism for targeting the disproportionate number of African Americans in the U.S. homeless population. This assumes, however, that HF programs end homelessness for African Americans at rates that reflect their overrepresentation in the homeless population. As noted, this evidence is not yet clear, as homelessness researchers have not focused on racial disparities. According to a recent report, African Americans in Los Angeles County are placed in PSH through an HF approach at rates proportionate to their numbers within the homeless population (LAHSA 2018). Yet this report also states that these individuals have higher rates of returning to homelessness, perhaps for some of the same structural reasons that caused them to become homeless in the first place, or because of inequities within homeless services. It is not clear the extent to which this is the case nationally.

This uncertainty underlines the importance of making sure that homeless services are monitored and do not perpetuate racial inequities or make things worse. In terms of HUD-VASH, evidence suggests the program is serving African American veterans at rates similar to their representation among all veterans experiencing homelessness. The small number of programs included in the analysis, however, precludes generalization of these results to the broader HUD-VASH program. Future research should leverage the VA's integrated medical records system to examine racial inequities across the HUD-VASH program.

Focused on the day-to-day amelioration of homelessness, the homeless service system does not have the capacity or mission to address all the structural factors that conspired to create racial inequity (Stanhope & Dunn, 2011). However, organizations such as the National Alliance to End Homelessness have recently developed "racial equity toolkits" (https://endh omelessness.org/resource/the-alliances-racial-equity-network-toolkit/) to assist local homeless service providers in addressing racial inequities in housing the homeless in their jurisdictions. Because HF is ultimately a downstream approach that does not change the racist structures that have created disproportionate homelessness among African Amercans, it is inherently a limited tool for addressing racial equity and has been critiqued as part of a neoliberal agenda that perpetuates existing structures (Hennegan, 2017). This highlights the need to better understand homelessness prevention and likely cannot be accomplished without broader structural reform, including addressing income and wealth accumulation inequality, fair housing law enforcement, decarceration, zoning law changes (allowing more multi-family dwellings), and much broader funding of public housing and rental vouchers. While such reforms would help reduce the numbers of people experiencing homelessness across all races, they would likely have a disproportionately positive impact on African Americans.

With respect to changes specific to assisting African Americans as uniquely victimized by housing discrimination (Rothstein, 2017), recent discourses around paying some form of reparations to Black Americans have become increasingly mainstream (Coates, 2014; Ray and Perry, 2020). Relatedly, Rothstein (2017) refers to "remedies," suggesting the repeal of exclusionary zoning ordinances, subsidization of African American home ownership, and greater investment in Black communities. Though racist legal and policy changes cannot erase centuries of discrimination and housing exclusion, they may help to erode the structural conditions that place African Americans at greater risk of losing their homes.

Conclusion and Recommendations

Despite having effective interventions such as HF, the Grand Challenge to End Homelessness cannot be achieved without addressing the effects of racism in the United States. Built into the institutional structures that result in disproportionately high numbers of African Americans among the homeless (and incarcerated) populations are racist policies dating to distant as well as recent history. We conclude this chapter with three recommendations with regard to improving access to safe, affordable housing and preventing homelessness. The third recommendation addresses specific changes needed to address racism as a fundamental cause of homelessness and its perpetuation.

Recommendation #1: Increase the stock of affordable housing. Increasing the stock of affordable housing requires the creation of new units and the preservation of existing ones. Currently, there is no state in the United States that has enough affordable housing, with a gap of over 7 million units (National Low Income Housing Coaltion, 2020). Many more existing affordable housing units may be lost over the next five years through the expiration of affordability requirements, deteriorating physical conditions, and inadequate federal funding (Public and Affordable Housing Research Corporation & National Low Income Housing Coalition, 2020). Expanding the National Housing Trust Fund, which provides federal grants to states to produce and preserve affordable housing for low-income families, should be a top priority (Grand Challenge to End Homelessness, 2020). There is also a need to change zoning laws in many local areas to increase housing density favoring multi-family dwellings over single-family dwellings (Grand Challenge to End Homelessness, 2020). Within homeless service systems, it is worth examining whether funding designated solely for short-term and emergency shelters can be diverted to increase the number of units of permanent supportive housing (for persons with physical and mental disabilities) as well as single-room occupancies (SROs) for single adults.

Recommendation #2: Increase access to affordable housing. Government-funded rental vouchers such as housing choice vouchers (HCVs) have proven to be a vital safety net for low-income Americans (Shinn & Khadduri, 2020). The success of the HUD-VASH program is testimony to the redemptive power of rental assistance when combined with judicious use of support services.

According to the Congressional Budget Office (CBO), the cost of making HCV an entitlement (i.e., providing HCV to everyone who qualifies financially) would be $41 billion per year; this cost could be offset by reductions in housing subsidies to home-owning affluent Americans (CBO, 2015). A more flexible option suitable for some individuals is to provide shallow subsidies that would allow recipients to pool their subsidies to live together or to pay family members directly in exchange for housing. More funding for rapid re-housing for individuals and families who only need "bridge" funds to stay

RACE AND RACISM IN THE HOMELESSNESS CRISIS 379

housed can also have a positive impact. Finally, increasing legal assistance to prevent evictions is critical to helping people stay housed (Desmond, 2016).

Recommendation #3: Reduce and eliminate racial barriers to housing, whether through purchasing or renting. Although the Fair Housing Act was originally enacted as Title VIII of the Civil Rights Act of 1968 to combat racial discrimination, enforcement has been uneven at best. African Americans are disproportionately targeted in high-cost, high-risk mortgage markets and are frequently discriminated against in their pursuit of rental units (Steil et al., 2018). Increased enforcement of Fair Housing Laws with stronger penalties against discriminating landlords and rental agents will help address some of these inequities. Banks must also be held accountable to make available low-interest home loans to low-income Black families and to prevent "redlining" neighborhoods, thereby enforcing and exacerbating longstanding segregation that dates back decades. Ensuring fair hiring practices in banking and the financial services sectors, as well as in homeless service sectors, is an important step to reducing notable racial imbalances in employment opportunities.

Taken together, these recommendations constitutate a clarion call for vastly increased federal investment in housing and in enforcing fair access to housing. For too long, African Americans have paid an extraordinary price in lost income and lost accumulated wealth, paired with far greater exposure to blatant discrimination, living in poor neighborhoods, and descending into homelessness. Ending homelessness is a Grand Challenge that cannot be achieved without addressing the racial inequities that contributed to the problem to begin with.

Study Questions

1. How does a knowledge of post–World War II housing trends help to understand the disproportionate number of African Americans among homeless persons in the United States today?
2. What factors caused the stock of affordable housing to shrink dramatically in the late twentieth century?
3. This chapter describes a number of racial disparities that are reflected in research on homelessness and in the delivery of homeless services. Choose two of these and discuss further.

4. Describe how the "Housing First" approach aligns closely to social work professional values.
5. Discuss some of the reasons why the HUD-VASH program was so successful in housing homeless veterans.
6. What barriers might exist to replicating the HUD-VASH program for non-veterans who are experiencing homelessness?
7. How can assistance providers support structural changes needed to address racial disparities among people experiencing homelessness?

References

Alexander, M. (2010). *The New Jim Crow: Mass incarceration in the age of color-blindness.* New York: New Pess.

Barrow, S., Herman, D., Cordova, P., & Struening, E. (1999). Mortality among homeless shelter residents in New York City. *American Journal of Public Health, 89,* 529–534.

Bond, L. (2019). *Examining racial dispariies in homelessness services research.* Unpublished paper.

Center for Social Innovation (2018). Race and homelessness. Retrieved June 3, 2020, from https://center4si.com/race-and-homelessness/.

Chetty, R., Hendren, N., & Katz, L. F. (2016). The effects of exposure to better neighborhoods on children: New evidence from the Moving to Opportunity experiment. *American Economic Review, 106*(4), 855–902.

Coates, T. N. (2014, May 21). The case for reparations. *Atlantic Magazine.* Retrieved July 12, 2020, from https://www.theatlantic.com/magazine/archive/2014/06/the-case-for-reparations/361631/.

Congressional Budget Office. (2015). *Federal housing assistance for low-income households.* Retrieved from https://www.cbo.gov/publication/50782.

Desmond, M. (2016). *Evicted: Poverty and profit in the American city.* New York: Broadway Books.

Evans, W. N., Kroeger, S., Palmer, C., & Pohl, E. (2019). Housing and Urban Development-Veterans Affairs supportive housing vouchers and veterans' homelessness, 2007–2017. *American Journal of Public Health, 109*(10), 1440–1445.

Goering, P., Veldhuizen, S., Watson, A., Adair, C., Kopp, B., Latimer, E., Nelson, G., MacNaughton, E., Streiner, D., & Aubry, T. (2014). *National at home/chez soi final report.* Calgary, AB: Mental Health Commission of Canada. Retrieved from: http://www.mentalhealthcommission.ca.

Department of Housing and Urban Development. (2019). The 2018 Annual Homelessness Assessment Report (AHAR) to Congress—Part 1: Point-in-time estimates of homelessness. Accessed online: https://files.hudexchange.info/resources/documents/2019-AHAR-Part-1.pdf.

Grand Challenge to End Homelessness. (2020). Policy proposals for the 2020 U.S. presidential election. Accessed online: https://a82940b1-6726-4847-84f4-80859ccc329e.filesusr.com/ugd/2a8466_37f1e1e18c694f44b112d41d04272cfa.pdf.

Hennigan, B. (2017). House broken: Homelessness, housing first, and neoliberal poverty governance. *Urban Geography, 38*(9), 1418–1440.

Hopper, K. (2002). *Reckoning with homelessness.* Ithaca, NY: Cornell University Press.

Interagency Council on Homelessness. (2015). Opening doors: Federal strategic plan to prevent and end homelessness. Accessed online: https://www.usich.gov/resources/uploads/asset_library/USICH_OpeningDoors_Amendment2015_FINAL.pdf.

Liebow, E. (1993). *Tell them who I am: The lives of homeless women.* New York: Penguin.

Los Angeles Homeless Services Authority (LAHSA) (2018). Report and recommendations of the ad-hoc committee on Black people experiencing homelessness. Accessed online: https://www.lahsa.org/documents?id=2823-report-and-recommendations-of-the-ad-hoccommittee-on-black-people-experiencing-homelessness.

National Academic of Sciences, Engineering and Medicine (2018). *Permanent supportive housing: Evaluating the evidence for improving health outcomes for people experiencing chronic homelessness.* Washington, DC: National Academies Press.

National Alliance to End Homelessness (2015). *Study data shows that housing chronically homeless people saves money, lives.* Retrieved from https://endhomelessness.org/study-data-show-that-housing-chronically-homeless-people-saves-money-lives/.

National Alliance to End Homelessness. (2019). Demographic data project; Part III: Race, ethnicity, and homelessness. Retrieved from https://endhomelessness.org/wp-content/uploads/2019/09/DDP-Race-brief-09272019-byline-single-pages-2.pdf.

National Low Income Housing Coaltion (2019). *Opportunities to end homelessness and housing poverty in the 116th Congress.* Washington, DC: NLIHC.

National Low Income Housing Coaltion (2020). *The gap: A shortage of affordable homes.* Washington, DC: NLIHC. Retrieved from https://reports.nlihc.org/sites/default/files/gap/Gap-Report_2020.pdf.

O'Connell, M. J., & Rosenheck, R. A. (2018). Supported housing: Twenty-five years of the Housing and Urban Development-Veterans Affairs Supported Housing (HUD-VASH) program. In J. Tsai (Ed.), *Homelessness among U.S. veterans: Critical perspectives* (pp. 77–108). Oxford: Oxford University Press.

Padgett, D. K., Henwood, B. F., & Tsemberis, S. (2016). *Housing First: Ending homelessness, transforming systems and changing lives.* New York: Oxford University Press.

Patterson, K. L., Nochajski, T., & Wu, L. (2014). Neighborhood outcomes of formerly homeless veterans participating in the HUD-VASH program. *Journal of Community Practice, 22,* 324–341.

Public and Affordable Housing Research Corporation & National Low Income Housing Coalition. (2020). *2020 picture of presentation.* Retrieved from https://preservationdatabase.org/wp-content/uploads/2020/05/NHPD_2020Report.pdf.

Ray, R. and Perry, A. (2020). Why we need reparations for Black Americans. Brookings Institute. Accessed online: https://www.brookings.edu/policy2020/bigideas/why-we-need-reparations-for-black-americans/.

Rosenheck, R., Leda, C., Frisman, L., & Gallup, P. (1997). Mentally ill homeless veterans: Race, service use, and treatment outcomes. *American Journal of Orthopsychiatry, 67*(4), 632–638.

Rothstein, R. (2017). *The color of law.* New York: W. W. Norton.

Sampson, R., Sharkey, P., & Raudenbush, S. (2008). Durable effects of concentrated disadvantage on verbal ability among African American children. *PNAS, 105,* 845–851.

Section 8 Housing Choice Vouchers. (2012). Revised implementation of the HUD-VA Supportive Housing Program. *Federal Register, 77*, 17086–17090.

Shinn, M. B., & Khadduri, J. (2020). *In the midst of plenty: Homelessness and what to do about it.* New York: Wiley Blackwell.

Stanhope, V., & Dunn, K. (2011). The curious case of Housing First: The limits of evidence based policy. *International Journal of Law and Psychiatry, 34*(4), 275–282.

Steil, J. P., Albright, L., Rugh, J. S., & Massey, D. S. (2018). The social structure of mortgage discrimination. *Housing Studies, 33*(5), 759–776.

Susser, E., Valencia, E., Conover, S., Felix, A., Tsai, W., & Wyatt, R. (1997). Preventing recurrent homelessness among mentally ill men: A "critical time" intervention after discharge from a shelter. *American Journal of Public Health, 87*(2), 256–262.

Tsai, J. (2018). Introduction and history of veteran homelessness. In J. Tsai (Ed.), *Homelessness among veterans: Critical perspectives* (pp. 1–12). New York: Oxford University Press.

Tsemberis, S., Gulcur, L., & Nakae, M. (2004). Housing first, consumer choice and harm reduction for individuals with dual diagnoses. *American Journal of Public Health, 94*, 651–656.

Wilkerson, I. (2010). *The warmth of other suns.* New York: Vintage.

Wong, Y. L. I., & Stanhope, V. (2009). Conceptualizing community: A comparison of neighborhood characteristics of supportive housing for persons with psychiatric and developmental disabilities. *Social Science & Medicine, 68*(8), 1376–1387.

15

Eradicating Social Isolation

Focus on Social Exclusion and Racism

Sandra Edmonds Crewe, Claudia Thorne, and Natalie Muñoz

A person is a person through other persons; you can't be human in isolation; you are human only in relationships.

—Desmond Tutu

Introduction

Sadly, W. E. B. Du Bois's well-known 1903 proposition that "the problem of the twentieth century is the problem of the color-line" is also today's reality; the problem of the twenty-first century remains the problem of the color-line. As this chapter is being finalized, painful twenty-first century encounters with racism flashed before the world and force fed many to digest the racial disparities in the COVID-19 pandemic and the social unrest related to the horrific murder by police excessive force of George Floyd, another Black man in America killed by racism. And there are many more examples of lost lives and lost opportunities that make racism a continuing crisis that begs for attention through the Social Work Grand Challenges.

Each of the 12 challenges (Fong et al., 2018) finds race and racism associated with its etiology, and the investment in eradicating racism is inextricably bound to addressing the challenge. Yet, none of them has an explicit statement that addresses eliminating racism. Racism, while often subdivided into scientific racism, strategic racism, and structural racism, is generally defined as a system of advantage that results in negative and unfair treatment toward a group based on their ethnicity or race. Fish and Syed (2020) add that a more complete definition of racism must also include power and privilege, resulting in a social science definition of racism "as a system of power entwined with practices and beliefs that produce and maintain an ethnic and

Sandra Edmonds Crewe, Claudia Thorne, and Natalie Muñoz, *Eradicating Social Isolation* In: *Social Work and the Grand Challenge to Eliminate Racism*. Edited by: Martell L. Teasley, Michael S. Spencer, and Melissa Bartholomew, Oxford University Press. © Oxford University Press 2023. DOI: 10.1093/oso/9780197674949.003.0015

384 CREWE, THORNE, AND MUÑOZ

racial hierarchy" (p. 5). Racism is a persistent factor in perpetuating social isolation that results in social exclusion for African Americans, Latinx, First Americans, and other continuously oppressed groups. Thus, the grand challenge, eradicating social isolation, inherently calls for addressing racism that contributes to social isolation and its subset of cases causing social exclusion. Social isolation is a potent killer (Lubben et al., 2018). Racism is a potent killer. When considered together, they are a lethal combination.

Social Isolation and Social Exclusion

Social Isolation

Models of social isolation include both objective social contact and subjective perceived adequacy of contact. Mills, Zavaleta, and Samuel (2014, p. 6.) define social isolation "as the inadequate quality and quantity of social relations with other people at the different levels where human interaction takes place (individual, group, community and the larger social environment)." Social isolation, according to AARP, occurs when individuals withdraw and become disconnected from networks such as family, friends, work, and community (Frank, 2018). Subjective isolation refers to the sense of loneliness and perceived belonging, as contrasted with objective isolation, that is quantifiable and addresses the structure of social work networks, as well as areas such as frequency of contacts and more. Social isolation is well documented for its detrimental effects on health and well-being across the life span (Lubben et al., 2018). For over 30 years, the health effects of social isolation have been described as just as deadly as smoking 15 cigarettes a day (Holt-Lunstad et al., 2015), and these negative effects influence the quality of life. The effects of social isolation are reported to be as damaging to health and well-being as obesity. Despite these serious effects, the severity of social isolation is not always recognized by practitioners and included in assessment tools.

Social isolation harms across the life course. For older persons, some researchers posit that up to 50% are at risk and almost one-third in later life will have some experience with social isolation of loneliness (Landeiro et al., 2017). The National Academy of Sciences (2020) also affirm the impact of social isolation and loneliness in older age. The AARP Foundation (2016) reported that more than 8 million older adults in America are socially isolated

(Lubben et al, 2018). Similarly, social isolation is a problem among children and youth (Lubben et al., 2018), and the research has largely focused on peer relationships and experiences in school. Additionally, prisoners are another sanctioned neglected group in society who experience social isolation. Among the most egregious criminal justice practices is solitary confinement, which is documented to have profound impact on health and well-being (Shalev, 2008). Additionally, despite evidence that there is "nothing redemptive, reformative, disciplinary or productive" (Zurn, 2015, p. 156), it is still widely practiced. And given the racial disparities in the criminal justice system, it is no surprise that African Americans, Latinx, and other populations of color are sentenced to this cruel treatment. There are many more examples of social isolation that beg our attention. Social isolation often is hidden because those impacted are marginalized and easily missed or misdiagnosed by mainstream society.

Social Exclusion

Like social isolation, social exclusion is a public health problem in the United States. It is a complex and multidimensional process. The World Health Organization (WHO) describes it as "dynamic, multi-dimensional processes driven by unequal power relationships interacting across four main dimensions—economic, political, social and cultural—and at different levels including individual, household, group, community, country and global levels. It results in a continuum of inclusion/exclusion characterized by unequal access to resources, capabilities and rights which leads to health inequalities" (Pompay et al., 2008, p. 7). This definition moves the focus from the individual to the structural inequalities that create many of the challenges in society. Social exclusion is caused by and results from the denial of rights, goods, and services that promote quality of life. Social exclusion is closely aligned with marginalization of groups based upon characteristics like race, ethnicity, and sexual orientation that are often deemed undesirable by segments of society, including the power structure. "Social exclusion is not just a concept or a complex of rules. Social exclusion is a set of decisions and actions" (Razza, 2018, p. 2). The dynamics of social exclusion include social deprivation, economic disadvantage, and democratic disqualification, according to Razza. Omidvar and Richmond (2003) also associate social isolation with voicelessness:

Whether the source of exclusion is poverty, racism, fear of difference or lack of political clout, the consequences are the same: a lack of recognition and acceptance; powerlessness and "voicelessness"; economic vulnerability; and diminished life experiences and limited life prospects. For society, the social exclusion of individuals and groups can become a major threat to social cohesion and economic prosperity. (p. viii)

Literature on social exclusion uses social isolation interchangeably. In seminal research by William Julius Wilson (1987) on urban poverty, social isolation is identified as a critical dimension in continuing the disadvantages of African Americans and other marginalized groups. For example, Wilson asserts that survival strategies such as reliance on kinship care reinforced social exclusion by creating encapsulated networks that, while necessary, contributed to the generational poverty among African American and other minority groups. The deleterious effects of social exclusion have been central to explaining the devastation of the community, as well as fostering adaptive behaviors that often further promote isolation (Rankin & Quane, 2000). Furstenberg (1993), Rainwater (1970), and Stack (1974) state that fear of victimization and distrust of the system lead to bonding with relatives/kin and trusted resources and avoiding outside contact. While often cited as strengths of the Black community, there is also evidence that the bonds make poverty self-perpetuating because of the closed networks (Tigges et al., 1998). The limited diversity of social networks in impoverished communities contributes to self-reliance and an over-reliance on resilience to overcome structural barriers. This too often has the unintended consequence of ignoring structural inequalities because individuals use inner strength to overcome barriers created by racism. They are perceived as overcomers rather than victims of a racist system that has elevated allostatic loads (Dura et al., 2012). Ohm (2019, p. 50) describes allostatic load as the "physiological consequences of repeated chronic exposure to environmental stressors" and has associated it with enhanced resilience factors that result in wear and tear on the body caused by stressors such as poverty and racism. This harmful allostatic load is associated with health disparities that negatively impact quality of life for African Americans.

The history of enslavement and immigration biases is a painful case study of social exclusion based on race and ethnicity. Thus, dismantling social exclusion requires the dismantling of long-standing policies that promoted exclusion, such as separate but equal school systems, redlining, gentrification, and more. To understand contemporary social exclusion and social isolation of racial and ethnic groups, it is important to understand the history of the United States. First Americans resisted the seizure of their lands by White Europeans and were subsequently displaced to live on reservations. They continue the resistance and are making incremental gains in economic development (Nies, 1996). Black Africans were captured, involuntarily brought to the United States, and enslaved to provide a free labor force for a growing agricultural society. Following the Emancipation of formerly enslaved persons in 1865 and the period of Reconstruction to build an economic base, Jim Crow Laws were enacted to keep Blacks in separate and unequal political, economic, educational, and social systems (Du Bois, 2012). Blacks have resisted oppression since they arrived in the United States through numerous movements, including initial resistance, abolition, Reconstruction, anti-lynching, Progressive era, Civil Rights movement (Robinson, 1997), and the Black Lives Matter movement. When the United States won the Mexican-American War and received land that formerly belonged to Mexico, the United States gained a Mexican population that provided a cheap labor supply for a growing U.S. economy (Greenberg, 2012). Subsequent immigrations from Spanish-speaking countries for nearly two centuries has resulted in discrimination, the creation of negative stereotypes, and the perception of a foreign Latinx underclass. Latinx, who have immigrated from numerous countries, have consistently resisted oppression as they grow into a social, cultural, and political force (Salomon, 2017). Thus, an understanding of social exclusion requires the grasp of legislated structural inequalities that persist, despite organized resistance and resulting legislation.

Theories: Racism and Social Exclusion

There are theories that help us to understand racism and how it underpins social isolation and social exclusion. The authors have selected Critical Race Theory, intersectionality, and Racialized Organizations Theory to provide important contexts for discussion and critical analysis of the topic. Critical Race Theory, intersectionality, and Racialized Organization Theory help the profession of social work to approach social exclusion through a person-in-environment lens that does not overly attribute the isolation or the exclusion to personal shortcomings. A person-in-environment perspective "views the individual and their multiple environments as a dynamic, interactive system,

388   CREWE, THORNE, AND MUÑOZ

in which each component simultaneously affects and is affected by the other" (Weiss-Gal, 2008, p. 65). Collectively they provide a context for understanding social exclusion, stigma, and racism and guide evidence-based programs and initiatives that rely upon the known, but also recognize the lack of attention given to race in the examination of many social problems (challenges) that confront society today. Eradication of social isolation and social exclusion requires critical examination of the underlying policies and practices that are grounded in racism.

Critical Race Theory

Critical Race Theory (CRT) challenges the dominant discourse on race and racism by examining how theory, policy, and practice are utilized to marginalize certain racial and ethnic groups (Solórzano, 1998). According to Zamudio et al. (2011), CRT matters, especially in education. "[I]t challenges the dominant discourse on race and racism as they relate to education by examining how educational theory, policy, and practice are used to subordinate certain racial and ethnic groups" (Solórzano, 1998, p. 122). The intersectionality of race and racism, the challenge of the dominant ideology, the commitment to social justice, the centrality of experiential knowledge, and the interdisciplinary perspective are what makes the CRT framework so unique (Solórzano, 1998). It promises to not only affect how "race discrimination is conceived and discussed but also litigated and adjudicated, thereby helping to make the sort of practical difference that is a key aim of activist scholars" (Valdes, 2015, p. 3). "Critical race theories argue that it is not enough to simply produce knowledge, but to dedicate this work to the struggle for social justice" (Zamudio et al., 2011, p. 6). CRT challenges the ahistoricism and meritocracy that are often associated with social policy (Gilborn, 2015) and that result in social exclusion. Crewe and Gourdine (2019) also assert that CRT can be used in conjunction with other frequently used theories in social work, such as ecological theory, life course perspective, restorative justice, and intersectionality.

Intersectionality

Intersectionality further highlights how discrimination is compounded by intersecting systems of oppression, such as homophobia, classism, sexism, xenophobia, and racism (Carasthasis, 2014). The term was introduced by Kimberlé Crenshaw, an African American lawyer and civil rights scholar, in 1989 (Carasthasis, 2014). Her work aims to demolish White supremacy (Carasthasis, 2014). The tenets of intersectionality call for an understanding of experiences of privilege and oppression assigned to multiple social identities (Gillborn, 2015). It also helps to facilitate an understanding of how race inequity is created, perpetuated, and reinforced at the macro level, and how it impacts various subsets of society such as healthcare, housing, and/or incarceration (Gillborn, 2015). Crenshaw (2020, para 5) states, "intersectionality is an analytic sensibility, a way of thinking about identity and its relationship to power." Intersectionality is important in the examination of race and social exclusion because social exclusion is associated with many of the intersecting systems of oppression that create environments that cultivate exclusion. Derek Bell cautions that when using intersectionality, care must be taken to not be silenced and fail to call out the too often "unsayable" racism (Bell, 1992, p. 111) that serves as a driving force for the other oppressions. Focusing on the intersectionality of oppressions also helps to understand how people of color both respond to and resist racism (Lewis & Grzanka, 2016) at both individual and organizational levels.

Racialized Organizations Theory

Racialized Organizations Theory provides a powerful perspective when examining racial stratification within organizations (Ray, 2019). From a race-based perspective, it certainly affirms the Black experience, as it alleviates the notion that racism is only perpetuated at the individual level and examines how racism is institutionalized through hiring practices, laws, politics and cultural norms (Ray, 2019). From a social justice perspective, it alleviates some of the unfair burdens of Blacks to be more resilient and allows organizations to take accountability and better understand the roles they play in perpetuating racism within the organization and the community at large (Ray, 2019).

Ray (2019) developed a framework for Racialized Organizations Theory around four main tenets: "(1) racialized organizations enhance or diminish the agency of racial groups; (2) racialized organizations legitimate the unequal distribution of resources; (3) Whiteness is a credential; and (4) the decoupling of formal rules from organizational practice is often racialized" (Ray, 2019, para. 1). Some of the philosophical underpinnings of Racialized

Organizations Theory are that organizations have the power to socially construct race on a micro and macro level and that racial inequality is intentional, in that organizations can construct, maintain, resist, and perpetuate patterns of racial hierarchy (Jewel, 2017).

Ray (2019) draws on the work of previous scholars such as Bonilla-Silva (1997), Sewell (1992), and Jung (2015) to better understand how social structures are formed, how they become stable, and how structures limit or enable human agency in systems where they are often taken for granted. For example, Ray, Ortiz, and Nash (2018) utilized Racialized Organizations Theory to analyze social exclusion in the workplace. They critiqued the recruitment, hiring, promotion, and organizational contexts in police forces. Their research advocated for police departments to be seen as racialized organizations whose operations both reflect and reinforce widespread schemas about the appropriate place of people of color within organizations (Ray, Ortiz, & Nash, 2018). Like Ray (2019), this article illuminates how organizations can influence racial inequalities within departments, but also more broadly in terms of state-level racial dynamics.

Because Racialized Organizations Theory was published so recently (in 2019 by Victor Ray), there are very few outcomes studies that demonstrate its application. With that said, there is a great need, especially during this violent political climate, for more social scientists to utilize Racialized Organizations Theory as a lens to analyze the impact of race on access to an equitable education and healthcare, housing accessibility, diversity and inclusion workplace policies, and small business/mortgage loan approval processes. This research is critical to the future health of Black and Brown communities, as we know through research that lack of socioeconomic resources, combined with social exclusion due to racial trauma, mass incarceration, and segregated neighborhoods, has had detrimental impacts on the health of people within those communities, compared to people within White communities (Brown, 2016, Williams & Mohammed, 2013, Massey, 2007, Elo, 2009, as cited by Brown, 2018).

Social Exclusion, Stigma, and Racism

As is noted in the above referenced theories, humans are social beings existing within a complex ecological system that shapes the health and mental health of individuals, families, groups, and communities over time and place

(Bailey et al., 2017). Our individual and collective health and mental health are dependent on how well this system functions to care for, affirm, and support its members. Research has demonstrated that racism has a detrimental effect on the well-being of racial and ethnic groups (Williams & Mohammed, 2013) and is related to health disparities in Blacks, Latinx, First Americans, immigrants of color, and other racial and ethnic groups (National Academies of Sciences, Engineering and Medicine, 2017). The cumulative and interactive effects of racism, social exclusion, and social isolation over the life course and across generations have over-relied on individual/group resiliency to overcome structural inequalities. Racialized organizations can diminish the ability of systems to respond to needs because the needs become secondary to maintaining the status quo that they represent.

Relationship of Racism to Social Exclusion and Stigma

According to Hoyt (2012), the fundamental assumption of racism is that one race is superior to a race of people who are considered inferior. This mantle of racial superiority provides a framework for White privilege, to take and withhold resources, and to oppress racial and ethnic groups that are perceived as inferior. Feagin (2006) states, ". . . oppression has included the exploitive and other oppressive practice of whites, the unjustly gained socioeconomic resources and assets of whites, and the long-term maintenance of major socio-economic inequalities across what came to be defined as a rigid color line" (p. 2). The history of colonialism in the United States gave rise to the system of racism, based on the assumption that Whites are biologically superior, dominant, privileged, and they are entitled to first-class citizenship and power over groups they perceive as inferior and subservient. These assumptions support a multifaceted and pervasive system of racism, including structural, individual, and institutional racism and the related assaults on health, mental health, and overall well-being (Kendi, 2019). Structural racism, a system of White supremacy, is embedded in multiple institutions and cultural norms and manifests as political power restrictions, inequality of economic opportunity and access, and limitations to accessing social capital networks for upward mobility (Razza, 2018). Outward manifestations of racism and social exclusion are evident in employment, entrepreneurship, housing, education, and physical and mental health (Bailey et al., 2017).

Income and Wealth

While the Civil Rights movement did not eradicate discrimination and disparities, it allowed African Americans greater access to educational and economic opportunities, increased the numbers of African Americans entering professional, business, and white-collar employment, and expanded the African American middle class (Landry & Marsh, 2011). Social exclusion results in vast income, net worth, and generational wealth transfer differential between Blacks, Latinx, and Whites. According to Semega et al. (2020), the 2019 median income for all U.S. households was $68,703. For Whites (non-Hispanic), income was reported as $76,057, Blacks $46, 073, and Hispanic (any race) $56,113. The poverty rate for Whites is 7.3% compared to Blacks (18.8%) and Hispanics (15.7%). According to the Children's Defense Fund, Black and Hispanic children continued to face the highest poverty rates—31% of Black children and 23.7% of Hispanics under age 18 lived below the poverty level in 2018 compared to White children (10.3%) (Children's Defense Fund, 2020).

The economic disadvantage of Black families is associated with long-term inequality and the lack of generational transfer of wealth, with Black families being less wealthy, and downwardly mobile in household wealth (Pfeffer & Killewald, 2019), even in college-educated households (Meschede et al., 2017). Wealth accumulates through real estate in a housing market that appreciates over time (Herring & Henderson, 2016). Redlining, prominent during the 1930s through the 1960s, was a federal government practice that restricted Blacks from purchasing homes, or allowed them to buy homes only in Black neighborhoods where homes appreciate less. From the 1930s through the 1960s, White wealth accumulated through real estate that allowed the accumulation of equity to fund businesses, education, and investments (Rothstein, 2017).

Education

Holding assets, including homeownership, relieves stressors related to poverty and is associated with favorable educational outcomes for children (Grinstein-Weiss et al., 2014). Homeownership is tied to the quality of public education. The quality of public education that children and youth receive is often linked to the location of the school and the tax revenue generated to fund public schools—equipment, facilities, teacher salaries, and extracurricular activities. Students attending schools in higher-income neighborhoods tend to outperform students residing in lower-income communities (Baker, 2017). Public schools in higher-income communities are better funded and have more resources to support quality education. Quality education is related to the ability to access higher education, which is correlated with increased income and a network of privilege and access. The career earnings premium from a four-year college degree (relative to a high school diploma) for persons from low-income backgrounds is considerably less than it is for those from higher-income backgrounds (Bartik & Hershbein, 2018). Social networks have been shown to be effective in providing access to knowledge and business opportunities that can increase income and employment status (Pedulla & Pager 2019). Yet, ethnic minorities continue to face discrimination in the workplace and in having access to capital for entrepreneurship. The exclusion also relates to health and mental health outcomes.

Physical and Mental Health Outcomes

Racism impacts health through social and economic deprivation, exposure to toxic substances and hazardous conditions, socially inflicted trauma and violence, targeted marketing of commodities, and inadequate medical care (Bailey et al., 2017). The association of perceived racism with adverse psychological outcomes is well documented in the literature (Lamont 2010; Pieterse et al., 2012). The daily experience of racism is a potent stressor, activating responses that contribute to depression and negative mood states associated with health disparities (Williams, 2018). In addition to health disparities, the quality of physical and mental healthcare provided to racial and ethnic groups is not of the same quality that is provided to Whites (Williams et al., 2015).

Witnessing the preferential treatment, privilege, and power of White people can create internalized racism among people of color and taking in the negative perceptions about one's race (David et al., 2019). The constant exposure to racism is a continuous attack on the mind, body, emotions, and spirit, resulting in psychological trauma for the person experiencing prejudice and discrimination. (Carter et al., 2019). Internalized racism is related to depression and psychological distress (Mouzon & McLean, 2017) and adverse health outcomes (Lamont, 2010; Pieterse et al., 2012). Members of stigmatized groups ask themselves the following questions to try to make sense of the world from which they are excluded as they experience micro and overt aggressions daily: Who fits in? Who doesn't and why? Who is worthy and who is unworthy? (Lamont, 2010) What is happening here? I'm playing by the rules, but I don't fit in.

According to Bivens (2005), White people have the following privileges that elude racial and ethnic groups: the ability to define reality, decision-making power and the ability to enforce decisions, resource access, and setting standards for appropriateness. Exposure to White privilege can lead to people of color experiencing internalized racism, which can manifest in the following ways: believing White people know more; not supporting one's own race and cultural peers in leadership positions; barriers to resource access and control; not knowing one's own cultural values and standards; and blaming the person of color for racism and not the racist structural system. Bivens (2005) further explains that internalized racism can cause isolation and exclusion by:

- Feeling inferior and feeling like a victim
- Not having a clear sense of self
- Focusing on understanding and trying to change White people
- Raging and not being able to engage and mediate conflict
- Not trusting and supporting persons of color in leadership.

Mental, spiritual, emotional, economic, and political strength is necessary to build resiliency as a protective factor against racism and to build social connections and networks (Karenga & Karenga 2007).

Case Vignettes (Racism and Social Exclusion)

Case vignettes or case studies have long been used in social work education to stimulate critical thinking and culturally sound approaches to practice. Case studies are an active learning approach based on real-life scenarios to support theory application, critical reflection, and practice integration (LeCroy, 2014; Patil et al., 2020). They support an inductive reasoning learning style where students learn more effectively through examples rather than logic and theory. Case studies provide students with a lens to view the complex constructs of social isolation, exclusion, and racism and support the application of the social work problem-solving method to complex constructs. Gorski and Pothini (2018) describe case studies as a pedagogical framework to present diversity and equity in a way that examines the complexities of real life situations. The case methods approach to learning is a discussion-based versus lecture-based format that has been historically integrated into social work education (Jones, 2003). Charlotte Towle (1957) advocated for the case method in teaching social work, and this early guidance continues to have primacy in building critical thinking and problem-solving skills for social workers. Two of the core competencies (CSWE, 2015) in social work education focus on the ability to engage difference and diversity in practice and advancing human rights at individual and systems levels—these directly relate to eradication of social exclusion caused by racism. A case-method or case-study approach supports skills building, leading to attainment of the competencies. Thus, the following vignettes are offered to support engagement of social work education in the Grand Challenges focused on eradicating social isolation and social exclusion and eliminating racism.

Case Vignette # 1: Ms. Jones

Ms. Jones is a 64-year-old African American woman. She is single, and she has legal custody of her 15-year-old grandson. She works in the hospitality industry at a major hotel chain as a front desk receptionist, where she has held the same position for more than 25 years. Ms. Jones has legal custody of her 15-year-old grandson because his mother was killed in a domestic dispute with her husband, who is now incarcerated. Ms. Jones is grateful for her grandson, and she views his presence as a gift and a blessing to her. Her grandson attends the local charter school, where he is reading at the third-grade level even though he is promoted each year. He is not involved in any activities in the city because his grandmother doesn't feel that it is safe for him to be traveling after school hours. Since the COVID-19 pandemic, he has not been able to continue with his studies because their home does not have computer and internet access. Most recently, with the number of increased demonstrations, her grandson saw a White nationalist group openly marching with white hoods. He was visibly upset and is anxious about going out. Ms. Jones has been telling him to pray and that God has everything under control.

Ms. Jones has lived the same rent-controlled apartment building for more than 15 years. She is worried about gentrification and being displaced from her neighborhood where many of her family members and friends live. She would like to retire when she turns 65, but she is concerned that she will not have enough income. She has contributed to her employer-based retirement plan, and when she decides to retire, the amount she would receive each month will be approximately $400. Combined with social security income of $1,000 per month, she would not have enough income to live on. Ms. Jones has the health challenges of hypertension and diabetes, which are controlled with medication. However, because of the concerns about the COVID-19 pandemic, she has been more anxious, and her blood pressure has been going up.

Critical Context

- *COVID-19 pandemic*: The social isolation and exclusion of Blacks, Latinx, and First American populations have been further impacted by COVID-19. According to the Centers for Disease Control and Prevention (CDC), as of January 23 2023 t here had been 101,873,730 cases of COVID-19 and 1,099,866 (Corona Virus 2023 [COVID 19], 2023). According to the CDC, the living conditions placing certain racial and ethnic groups at risk include: living in densely populated areas; racial segregation; living farther from grocery stores and medical facilities; multigenerational households; and overrepresentation in jails, prisons, and detention centers. Racial and ethnic groups are overrepresented as critical care workers, and they have a lack of paid sick leave, which requires them to continue to work, resulting in exposure to COVID-19. Underlying serious health conditions and barriers to care increase the vulnerability of racial and ethnic groups to contracting and/or passing COVID-19 (Centers for Disease Control and Prevention [CDC], 2020, June 12). During the period of social isolation imposed by local and state governments, reliance on the internet and computers have kept people connected. However, low-income households have less internet and computer access in their homes. Additionally, race/ethnicity data is not always collected. This could reflect an under reporting.
- *Gentrification* shifts the residential and commercial makeup of low-income and working-class communities, often composed of racial and ethnic groups, to more affluent middle- and upper-middle-class residents. Through a combination of rehabilitation and new

development of residential and commercial properties and the creation of stores and other businesses that attract a more affluent base, the composition and dynamics of neighborhoods change. In the process of gentrification, long-time working-class residents of communities are displaced, not only geographically. As a result of having to move because of affordability, a sense of community and social connections to friends, families, social, cultural, and religious institutions are lost. If the person can stay in the gentrified neighborhood, there may be conflict and hostilities with the new, more affluent residents (Richardson et al., 2019).

Case Vignette Questions

- How does social isolation or social exclusion contribute to a social worker's understanding of the situation?
- How does structural racism contribute to a social worker's understanding of the situation?
- What other structural factors are at work in the life of Ms. Jones and her grandson?
- What theories help to understand and address the situation?

Case Vignette #2: Julissa

Julissa is a dark-skinned Afro-Boricua (a Puerto Rican who is predominantly/partially of African descent) who has struggled with mental health challenges since she was a teenager. Julissa was adopted at 3 months alongside her sister, and welcomed into the arms of her Puerto Rican mother and African American father. Her journey of self-discovery and ethnic/racial identity development included phases of self-hate, self-discovery, and self-love. Her experiences with abandonment, child-abusive discipline at home, discrimination, colorism, and challenges with belonging to both Blackness and Latinidad often left her feeling angry and would lead to social isolation.

Julissa was diagnosed with depression and anxiety in high school and was subscribed medication. Despite exhibiting behavioral concerns in middle school, it was not until after 20 school suspensions and an expulsion from high school that she was first offered mental health services. While Julissa grew up with some privilege due to her father's socioeconomic position as an architect, she experienced social isolation and exclusion because of her phenotype throughout her youth in familial, social, and educational settings.

Julissa's most prominent memory of familial exclusion was as a little girl, when Julissa's uncle married a white-passing Cuban woman. In Latinx culture, specifically in countries that were colonized, whiteness as property was ingrained in the community. Whiteness as property is a tenet of Critical Race Theory and references how historically and presently whiteness serves as status of racialized privilege (Harris, 1993)—a status of power that, despite racial progress over time, the laws continue to protect. As her aunt and uncle began planning their wedding, her aunt made it clear that she embodied a Eurocentric ideology of beauty. She purposefully excluded Julissa and her sister from the wedding due to their dark skin, while other light-skinned nieces and nephews were included.

Julissa didn't experience a sense of belonging in Latinx spaces until college, where she was able to explore her Afro-Latino history through coursework and joined a Latinx student dance troupe. The president was a dark-skinned Dominican whose presence and leadership made her feel welcomed. However, initially, not everyone in the club made her feel a sense of belonging. One dark-skinned young girl approached her and stated, "Just so you know I'm Dominican, I'm not Black." Statements such as these are not uncommon in the Dominican Republic.

As she began developing friendships in the troupe, she realized that many of the Dominican and Puerto Rican students shared similar experiences of discrimination and exclusion. Julissa's discovery of self-love and pride for her Afro-Latinidad identity emerged while receiving mental health support and access to culturally relevant pedagogy, and continued as she began to see representation of Afro-Latinidad in pop culture through Amara La Negra's character on *Love & Hip Hop*. Today she is proud to be Afro-Latina and has gained a strong love for her culture. While she recognizes that discrimination will continue in some White and Latinx spaces, she no longer feels she must choose between her Blackness and her Latinidad. She is proudly both.

Critical Context
- *Mental health stigma*: Julissa's experience in K–12 is not uncommon. as the mental health stigma within the Black and Latinx community leaves many youth unsupported and unseen (NWLC, 2019). According to the CDC. 46.8% of high school Latinas in the United States expressed feelings of hopelessness and sadness which led to social isolation

(NWLC, 2019). Additionally, research shows that Latinas struggling with mental health in school settings are often labeled as "crazy" and thus receive less mental health support than White girls (NWLC, 2019).

- *Anti-blackness*: The Dominican Republic has a long history of anti-Blackness which reaches back to the Haitian revolution (Garcia-Peña, 2016). Denying Blackness was utilized as a form of self-preservation to separate themselves from the global social and economic isolation that Haiti would experience as a result of them being the first Black republic (Garcia-Peña, 2016).

Case Vignette Questions
- How does social isolation or social exclusion contribute to Julissa's identified problems?
- What theories help social workers to understand and address Julissa's situation?
- How can we better equip school social workers to address the mental health needs of Black and Latinx youth experiencing social exclusion?

Case Vignette #3: Michael

Michael is a Black male. He is very social, active in sports, hard worker, a solid "B" student in high school and in college. He grew up in a single-parent household; his mother is an educator. At the end of his junior year in high school, he had a three-week summer experience at an HBCU (historically black colleges and universities) to provide business exposure. A family friend from church told him about the HBCU summer business school experience (social network). His mother insisted that he dress business casual, as was stated on the application. Following a heated debate on what qualifies as business casual, which included a phone call to a male relative, he had a successful summer experience at the HBCU business program, appropriately dressed for success.

During his senior year in high school, a donor, who was a principal at an investment banking firm, came to his school for a tour. Michael happened to be in the hallway, and the director of development, who was a friend of the family (social network), casually asked Michael to provide a tour of the school. Michael is very personable and he gave an excellent tour. The principal of the investment banking firm offered him an internship at the firm following his graduation from high school.

Michael had a very successful summer and continued to work at the investment banking firm. His early experience taught him a lot about wealth and investing and opened his eyes to a different way of living. He continued working at the investment banking firm throughout college. He started investing and used his income to partially pay for college. Following graduation from the HBCU, he started a career as a trader at the investment banking firm. The principal of the firm was his mentor and supervisor. His income in his first year of working exceeded his mother's.

Twenty years since that chance meeting with the principal of the investment banking firm, Michael has a very successful career in financial planning and is married to a CPA he met while a student at the HBCU he attended. She works for one of the major accounting firms.

Critical Context

- *HBCU*: Historically black colleges and universities (HBCUs) were established in the mid-1800s to provide education to formerly enslaved Black people. They were mission driven and had the intent of tackling racism (Crewe, 2017). The Freedmen's Bureau supported this initiative, as well as other self-help initiatives of formerly enslaved persons (Bowles et al., 2016). According to the U.S. Department of Labor (2023), there are approximately 107 HBCUs, which include both private and public institutions. Over 150 years after their establishment, HBCUs continue to embrace the legacy of the racial uplift ideology and make extraordinary contributions to local and global communities.
- *Social networks*: Social networks are essential to establishing an employment trajectory as business opportunities are shared through social contacts. Well-connected individuals with high employment status share business opportunities through their networks (Calvo-Armengol & Jackson, 2004). Within social networks is social capital, an asset one can mobilize or access for a purpose (Lin et al., 2017). Small or nonexistent social networks can lead to social isolation.

Case Vignette Questions

- How does this case relate to social isolation/social exclusion?
- How is social connectedness related to racism?
- How can Michael's experience be used to inform a strengths-based versus deficit approach to social work practice?

Conclusion: The Way Forward

Crewe and Gourdine (2019) assert that it is an ethical responsibility for social workers to address social justice issues such as racism in tackling the Grand Challenges that disrupt the quality of lives of those we serve. It is essential that African Americans, Latinx, Native Americans, and other oppressed/marginalized ethnic groups create an empowering cultural framework as a protective factor to sustain resilience in the face of constant racist structural, institutional, and individual attacks. Every ethnic group must know and own the strength of their experience and practice this at every level of the ecosystem: micro, meso, and macro levels simultaneously. At the level of the micro and meso system, individuals and families can be equipped with knowledge of resilient cultural values through the study of history and the application of principles to enhance living. Black clients who are provided a framework through which to understand and make sense of the psychological toll associated with exposure to racism might also ameliorate the sense of powerlessness and shame that is often experienced by individuals who encounter various forms of race-based oppression (Franklin et al., 2006). However, resilience alone is inadequate to eradicate the racism that undergirds social exclusion.

Eradicating social isolation/social exclusion requires investment in social cohesion. This in turn requires an examination of the systems that perpetuate race-based social isolation and social exclusion. This includes advocating to remove workplace barriers, housing discrimination, access to affordable healthcare, reform in criminal justice, education justice, access to technology, transportation equity, and more. As the work takes place to eradicate social isolation at the micro level, it must be accompanied by campaigns for social justice across domains of power and privilege. Social work must assume its role in the eradication of social isolation/social exclusion by examining our practices and acceptance of policies that maintain the structure for the continuation of social exclusion on the basis of proxies for race such as income, poverty, residency, and more. It is critical that social work programs nationwide re-examine their curricula to ascertain that their pedagogy is inclusive of content that values all persons and gives primacy to those impacted by racism. Howard University's School of Social Work's guiding philosophy, the Black Perspective, is an exemplar. The Black Perspective uses six principles, including diversity and social justice, to ensure that their graduates are adequately prepared to engage and work with diverse Black communities (Gourdine & Brown, 2016; HUSSW, 2022).

Returning to the assertion of Razza (2018) that "social exclusion is a set of decisions and actions" (p. 2) gives us a way forward. This means that our informed decisions and actions as social workers related to social injustice can eradicate the lethal outcomes associated with social isolation and social exclusion. This offers every social worker the opportunity to disrupt business as usual and stray from street-level bureaucracy (Lipsky, 2010) which includes strategies to make their jobs manageable, including withholding information, stereotyping, screening, and rubber stamping, making access difficult, and requiring clients to wait for services. Rather than using the power relationship to continue the status quo, workers have an opportunity to dismantle racism that drives social exclusion.

There is no absence of opportunities to address racism and social isolation/social exclusion. Whether the focus is the aging network, child welfare system, criminal justice, mental health, education, or other systems, the important thing is for the social work profession to take ownership of the impact that racism has in the promotion of social exclusion and to start somewhere. The only wrong door is the door that is not taken to end the lethal combination of racism and social exclusion that is destroying lives and communities. The evidence of the pervasive harm is abundant—what is needed is a collective agenda that includes practice innovations that embrace radical social justice aimed at breaking down silos and building inclusive communities that celebrate diversity and that recognize the dignity and worth of all.

References

AARP Foundation. (2012). *Framework for isolation in adults over 50*. Retrieved from http://www.aarp.org/content/dam/aarp/aarp_foundation/2012_PDFs/AARP-Foundation-Isolation-Framework-Report.pdf.

AARP Foundation. (2016). AARP Foundation Draws Attention to Social Isolation with the Launch of Connect2Affect. https://press.aarp.org/2016-12-07-AARP-Foundation-Draws-Attention-to-Social-Isolation-with-the-Launch-of-Connect2Affect

Bailey, Z., Krieger, N., Agenor, M. J., & Linor, N. (2017). Structural racism and health inequalities in the USA: Evidence and interventions. *The Lancet, 389*(10077), 1453–1463. doi: https://doi.org/10.1016/S0140-6736(17)30569-X.

Baker, B. D. (2017). *How money matters for schools*. Palo Alto, CA: Learning Policy Institute. Retrieved January 11, 2021, from https://learningpolicyinstitute.org/product/how-money-matters-schools.

Bartik, T., & Hershbein, B. (2018). Degrees of poverty: The relationship between family income background and the returns to education. Upjohn Institute Working Paper 18-284. Kalamazoo, MI: W.E. Upjohn Institute for Employment Research. doi: doi.org/10.17848/wp18-284.

Bell, D. (1992). *Faces at the bottom of the well: The permanence of racism.* New York: Basic Books.

Bivens, D. (2005). What is internalized racism? In M. Potapchuk, S. Leiderman, D. Bivens, & B. Major (Eds.), *Flipping the script: White privilege and community building* (pp. 43–49). Silver Spring, MD: MP Associates. Retrieved June 8, 2020, from https://www.racial equitytools.org/resourcefiles/potapchuk1.pdf.

Bonilla-Silva, E. (1997). Rethinking racism: Toward a structural interpretation. *American Sociological Review, 62*(3), 465–480.

Bowles, D. D, Hopps, J. G., & Clayton, O. (2016). The impact and influence of HBCUs on the social work profession. *Journal of Social Work Education,* 118–132.

Brown, K. D. (2016). *After the at-risk label: Reorienting educational policy and practice.* United States: Teachers College Press.

Brown, K. D. (2018). Race as a durable and shifting idea: How Black millennial preservice teachers understand race, racism, and teaching. *Peabody Journal of Education, 93*(1), 106–120. doi: 10.1080/0161956X.2017.1403183

Calvo-Armengol, A., & Jackson, M. A. (2004). The effects of social networks on employment. *American Economic Review, 94*(3), 426–454.

Carastathis, A. (2014). The concept of intersectionality in feminist theory. *Philosophy Compass, 9*(5), 304–314. https://doi.org/10.1111/phc3.12129.

Carter, R. T., Johnson, V. E., Kirkinis, K., Roberson, K., Muchow, C., & Galgay, C. (2019). A meta-analytic review of racial discrimination: Relationships to health and culture. *Race and Social Problems, 11*(1), 15–32. https://doi-org.proxy-cs.researchport.umd. edu/10.1007/s12552-018-9256-y.

Centers for Disease Control and Prevention (CDC). (2020, June 12). *Corona virus disease 2019 (COVID 19) cases in the US.* Retrieved from Centers for Disease Control and Prevention (CDC): https://www.cdc.gov/coronavirus/2019-ncov/cases-updates/cases-in-us.html.

Centers for Disease Control and Prevention (CDC). (20, June 20). *Corona virus disease (COVID-19) racial and ethnic minority groups.* Retrieved from Centers for Disease Control and Prevention (CDC): https://www.cdc.gov/coronavirus/2019-ncov/need-extra-precautions/racial-ethnic-minorities.html.

Children's Defense Fund (2020). *State of America's children.* Washington, DC: Children's Defense Fund. https://www.childrensdefense.org/wp-content/uploads/2020/02/The-State-Of-Americas-Children-2020.pdf.

Crewe, S. E. (2017). Education with intent: The HBCU experience. *Journal of Human Behavior in the Social Environment, 27*(5), 360–366.

Crewe, S. E., & Gourdine, R. M. (2019). Race and social policy: Confronting our discomfort. *Social Work in Public Health, 34*(1), 1–11. doi: 10.1080/19371918.2018.1562397.

Crenshaw, K. (2020). *Opinion: Why intersectionality can't wait.* Washington Post. https://www.washingtonpost.com/news/in-theory/wp/2015/09/24/why-intersectionality-cant-wait/

David, E. J. R., Schroeder, T. M., & Fernandez, J. (2019). Internalized racism: A systematic review of the psychological literature on racism's most insidious consequence. *Journal of Social Issues, 75,* 1057–1086. https://doi.org/10.1111/josi.12350.

Du Bois, W. E. B. (1903). *Souls of Black folk*. New York: Oxford University Press.

Du Bois, W. (2012). *Black reconstruction in America: Toward a history of the part in which Black folk played in an attempt to reconstruct democracy*. New York: Transaction.

Duru, O. K., Harawa, N. T., Kermah, D., & Norris, K. C. (2012). Allostatic load burden and racial disparities in mortality. *Journal of the National Medical Association, 104*(1–2), 89–95. https://doi.org/10.1016/s0027-9684(15)30120-201.

Fish, J., & Syed, M. (2020). Racism, discrimination, and prejudice. In S. Hupp & J. Jewll (Eds.), *Encyclopedia of Child and Adolescent Development*. San Francisco: Wiley-Blackwell. 10.1002/9781119171492.wecad464

Feagin, J. (2006). *A theory of oppression*. New York: Routlege.

Fong, R., Lubben, J. E., & Barth, R. P. (2018). *Grand challenges for social work and society*. New York: Oxford University Press.

Frank, D. (2018, July 3). *The Danger of Social Isolation*. Retrieved Jan 19, 2023, from AARP: https://www.aarp.org/health/conditions-treatments/info-2018/social-isolation-symptoms-danger.html

Franklin, A., Boyd-Franklin, N., & Kelly, S. (2006). Racism and invisibility: Race related stress, emotional abuse, and psychological trauma for people of color. *Journal of Emotional Abuse, 6*(2–3), 9–30. doi: https://psycnet.apa.org/doi/10.1300/J135v06n02_02.

Furstenberg, F. F., Jr. 1993. How families manage risk and opportunity in dangerous neighborhoods." In W. J. Wilson (Ed.), *Sociology and the public agenda* (pp. 231–258). Thousand Oaks, CA: Sage Publications.

Lorgia García-Peña. (2016). *The Borders of Dominicanidad. Race, Nation, and Archives of Contradiction*. Durham: Duke University Press.

Gillborn, D. (2015). Intersectionality, Critical Race Theory, and the primacy of racism: Race, class, gender, and disability in education. *Qualitative Inquiry, 21*(3), 277–287. https://doi.org/10.1177/1077800414557827.

Gorski, P. C., & Pothini, S. G. (2018). *Case Studies on Diversity and Social Justice Education* (2nd ed.). Routledge. https://doi.org/10.4324/9781351142526

Gourdine, R. M., & Brown, A. W. (2016). *Social action, advocacy and agents of change: Howard University School of Social Work in the 1970s*. Baltimore, MD: Black Classic Press.

Greenberg, A. (2012). *A wicked war: Polk, Clay, Lincoln, and the 1846 U.S. Invasion of Mexico*. New York: Random House.

Grinstein-Weiss, M., Shanks, T., & Beverly, S. (2014). Family assets and child outcomes: Evidence and directions. *Helping Parents, Helping Children: Two Generation Mechanisms, 24*(1), 147–170.

Harris, C. (1993). Whiteness as property. *Harvard Law Review, 106*(8), 1707–1791. https://doi.org/10.2307/1341787.

Herring, C., & Henderson, L. (2016). Wealth inequality in black and white: Cultural and structural sources of the racial wealth gap. *Race and Social Problems, 8*(1), 4–17. doi: 10.1007/s12552-016=9159-8.

Holt-Lunstad, J., Smith, T., Baker, M., Harris, T., & Stephenson, D. (2015). Loneliness and social relationships as risk factors for mortality: A meta-analytic review. *Perspectives on Psychological Science, 10*(2), 227–237. doi: 10.1177/1745691614568352.

Howard University's School of Social Work (HUSSW) (2022). *Six principles of the Black perspective*. Howard University. https://socialwork.howard.edu/about-us.

Hoyt, C., Jr. (2012). The pedagogy of the meaning of racism: Reconciling a discordant discourse. *Social Work, 57*(3), 225–234. doi: 10.1093/sw/sws009.

ERADICATING SOCIAL ISOLATION   405

Jones, K. A. (2003). Making the case for the case method in graduate social work education. *Journal of Teaching in Social Work, 23*(1–2), 183–200. https://doi-org.proxyhu.wrlc.org/10.1300/J067v23n01_12.

Jung, M. K. (2015). *Beneath the surface of white supremacy: Denaturalizing U.S. racisms past and present.* Stanford, CA: Stanford University Press.

Karenga, M., & Karenga, T. (2007). Nguzo Saba and the Black family: Principles and practices of well being and flourishing. In H. McAdoo (Ed.), *Black family* (pp. 7–28). Thousand Oaks, CA: Sage Publications.

Kendi, I. (2019). *How to be an antiracist.* New York: One World.

Lamont, M. (2010). Responses to racism, health, and social inclusion as a dimension of successful societies. In P. Hay & M. Lamont (Eds.), *Successful societies: How institutions and culture affect health* (pp. 151–168). New York: Cambridge University Press.

Landeiro, F., Barrows, P., Nuttall Musson, E., Gray, A. M., & Leal, J. (2017). Reducing social isolation and loneliness in older people: A systematic review protocol. *BMJ Open, 7*(5), e013778. https://doi.org/10.1136/bmjopen-2016-013778

Landry, B., & Marsh, K. (2011). The evolution of the new black middle class. *Annual Review of Sociology, 37*, 373–394.

LeCroy, C. (2014). *Case studies in social work practice.* New York: Wiley.

Lewis, J. A., & Grzanka, P. R. (2016). Applying intersectionality theory to research on perceived racism. In A. Alvarez, C. T. H. Liang, & H. A. Neville (Eds.), *Cultural, racial, and ethnic psychology book series. The cost of racism for people of color: Contextualizing experiences of discrimination* (pp. 31–54). Washington, DC: American Psychological Association.

Lin, N., Cook, K., & Burt, R. (2017). *Social capital theory and research.* London:Routledge Press.

Lipsky, M. (2010). *Street level bureaucracy: Dilemmas of the individual in public services.* 30th anniversary expanded edition. New York: The Russell Sage Foundation.

Lubben, J., Tracy, E., Crewe, S. E., Sabbath, E., Gironda, M., Johnson, C., Kong, J., Munson, M., & Brown, S. (2018). Social isolation. In R. Fong, J. Lubben, and R. P. Barth (Eds.), *Eradicate social isolation in Grand Challenges for social work and society: Social progress powered by science.* (pp. 1–22).New York: Oxford University Press.

Massey, D. (2007). *Categorically Unequal: The American Stratification System.*

Meschede, T., Taylor, J., Mann, A., & Shapiro, T. (2017). "Family achievements?": How a college degree accumulates wealth for Whites and not for Blacks. *Federal Reserve Bank of St. Louis Review, 99*(1), 121–137.

Mills, C., Zavaleta, D., & Samuel, K. (2014). Shame, humiliation and social isolation: Missing dimensions of poverty and suffering analysis. *OPHI Working Paper* 71, University of Oxford.

Mouzon, D., & McLean, J. (2017). Internalized racism and mental health among African-Americans, US-born Caribbean Blacks, and foreign-born Caribbean Blacks. *Ethnicity & Health, 22*(1), 36–48. doi: 10.1080/13557858.2016.1196652.

National Academies of Sciences, Engineering, and Medicine (2017). *Communities in action: Pathways to health equity.* Washington, DC: The National Academies Press. doi: 10.17226/24624.

National Academies of Sciences, Engineering, and Medicine (2020). *Social isolation and loneliness in older adults: Opportunities for the health care system.* Washington, DC: The National Academies Press. https://doi.org/10.17226/25663.

National Women's Law Center (NWLC). (2019). We are not invisible/No somos invisibiles: Latina girls, mental health and Philadelphia schools. https://nwlc.org/wp-content/uploads/2019/04/We-Are-Not-Invisible-Final-Report-1.pdf

Nies, J. (1996). *Native American history*. New York: Random House.

Ohm, J. E. (2019). Environmental exposures, the epigenome, and African American women's health. *Journal of Urban Health, 96*(1), 50–56. doi: 10.1007/s11524-018-00332-2.

Omidvar, R., & Richmond, T. (2003). Immigrant settlement and social inclusion in Canada. January 2003, Laidlaw Foundation Working Paper Series.

Patil, T., Hunt, M., Cooper, K., & Townsend, R. (2020). Developing a case-based experiential learning model at a program level in a regional university: Reflections on the developmental process. *Australian Journal of Adult Learning, 60*(2), 225–244.

Pedulla, D. S., & Pager, D. (2019). Race and networks in the job search process. *American Sociological Review, 84*(6), 983–1012. https://doi-org.proxy-cs.researchport.umd.edu/10.1177/0003122419883255.

Pfeffer, F. K., & Killewald, A. (2019). Intergenerational wealth mobility and racial inequality. *Socius, 5*, 10. doi: https://doi.org/10.1177/2378023119831799. Epub 2019 Mar 21. PMID: 31312720; PMCID: PMC6634987.

Pieterse, A., Todd, N., Neville, H., & Carter, R. (2012). Perceived racism and mental health among Black American adults: A meta-analytic review. *Journal of Counseling Psychology, 59*(1), 1–9. doi: 10.1037/a0026208.

Popay, J., Escorel, S., Hernández, Johnston, H., Mathieson, J., & Rispel, L. (February 2008). *Understanding and tackling social exclusion*. Final Report to the World Health Organization (WHO) Commission on Social Determinants of Health from the Social Exclusion Knowledge Network. Geneva, Switzerland: WHO Press.

Rainwater, L. (1970). *Behind ghetto walls*. Chicago: Aldine Publishing.

Rankin, B. H. & Quane, J.M. (2000). Neighborhood poverty and the social isolation of inner-city African American families. *Social Forces, 79*(1), 139–164.

Ray, V. (2019). A theory of racialized organizations. *American Sociological Review, 84*(1), 26–53. https://doi.org/10.1177/0003122418822335.

Ray, V., Ortiz, K., & Nash, J. (2018). Who is policing the community? A comprehensive review of discrimination in police departments. *Sociology Compass, 12*(1). https://doi.org/10.1111/soc4.12539.

Razza, C. M. (2018) Social exclusion: The decisions and dynamics that drive racism: How social exclusion blocks Black people from full participation and power in the United States. Demos Organization. https://www.demos.org/sites/default/files/publications/Social%20Exclusion%20The%20Decisions%20and%20Dynamics%20that%20Drive%20Racism.pdf.

Richardson, J., Mitchell, B., & Franco, J. (2019). *Shifting Neighborhood: Gentrification and cultural displacement in American cities*. National Community Reinvestment Coalition. doi:10.13140/RG.2.2.25432.85764

Robinson, C. (1997). *Black movements in America*. New York: Routledge.

Rothstein, R. (2017). *The color of law: A forgotten history of how our government segregated America*. New York: Liveright.

Salomon, C. (2017). *The Routledge history of Latin American culture*. London: Taylor & Francis.

Semega, J., Kollar, M., Shrider, E. A., & Creamer, J. F. (2020). *U.S. Census Bureau, current population reports, P60-270, income and poverty in the United States: 2019*. Washington, DC: U.S. Government Publishing Office.

Sewell, W. H. (1992). A theory of structure: Duality, agency, and transformation. *American Journal of Sociology, 98*(1), 1–29. The University of Chicago Press.

ERADICATING SOCIAL ISOLATION 407

Shalev, S. (2008). *A sourcebook on solitary confinement*. London: Mannheim Centre for Criminology, London School of Economics.

Solórzano, D. G. (1998). Critical race theory, race and gender microaggressions, and the experience of Chicana and Chicano scholars. *Qualitative Studies in Education, 11*(1), 121–136.

Stack, C. (1974). *All our kin: Strategies for survival in a Black community*. New York: Harper and Row.

Tigges, L. M., Browne, I., & Green, G. (1998). Social isolation of the urban poor: Race, class and neighborhood effects on social resources. *The Sociological Quarterly, 39*(1), 53–77.

Towle, C. (1957). The case method in teaching social work. In *Proceedings of the Institute of the Use of the Case Method in Teaching Psychiatric Social Work* (pp. 1–78). New York: National Association of Social Workers.

Tutu, D. (n.d.). Quotes: Goodreads. Retrieved from: https://www.goodreads.com/author/quotes/5943.Desmond_Tutu

U.S. Department of Labor. (2023, Jan 20). *Office of Federal Contract Compliance Programs*. Retrieved from U.S. Department of Labor. https://www.dol.gov/agencies/ofccp/compliance-assistance/outreach/hbcu-initiative/about

Valdes, F. (2015). Latina/o ethnicities, critical race theory, and post-identity politics in postmodern legal culture: From practices to possibilities. *Berkeley La Raza Law Journal, 9*(1), 1–31.

Weiss-Gal, I. (2008). The person-in-environment approach: Professional ideology and practice of social workers in Israel. *Social Work, 53*(1), 65–75. https://doi.org/10.1093/sw/53.1.65

Williams, D. R., & Mohammed, S. A. (2013). Racism and Health I: Pathways and Scientific Evidence. *American Behavioral Scientist*. doi: 10.1177/0002764213487340.

Williams, D. R., & Wyatt, R. (2015). Racial bias in health care and health: Challenges and opportunities. *JAMA, 314*(6), 555–556. doi: 10.1001/jama.2015.9260.

Williams, D. R. (2018). Stress and the mental health of populations of color: Advancing our understanding of race-related stressors. Journal of Health and Social Behavior, 59(4), 466–485. https://doi.org/10.1177/0022146518814251.

Wilson, W. J. (1987). *The truly disadvantaged*. Chicago: University of Chicago Press.

Zamudio, M., Russell, C., Rios, F., & Bridgeman, J. (2011). *Critical Race Theory matters*. New York: Routledge. Retrieved from https://doi.org/10.4324/9780203842713.

Zurn, P. (2015). Lisa Guenther. Solitary confinement: Social death and its afterlives. *Philosophia, 5*(1), 155–160.

PART IV

PROGRESSIVE APPROACHES TO ELIMINATING INSTITUTIONAL, SOCIAL POLICY, AND ECONOMIC RACISM

Part IV contains six chapters which underscore the need to undo systemic policy, economic, and child welfare practices that reduce well-being and life chances. In a straightforward manner, the authors of these chapters deal with some of the most irretractable, racialized topics within the social work profession and the broader society. In many ways, the content within these chapters provides a direct illustration as to why this textbook is dedicated to eliminating racism within social work education and practice, before moving toward a concerted focus on racism in the broader society. At the heart of racism are social class and economic problems that beset individual and group interaction through systemic structures and functions. Such practices are the product of institutional practices set in motion and reinforced over time. Public schools, the juvenile justice system, and the prison industrial complex are well known for poor outcomes and less than optimal treatment of African American and Latino youth. In many ways, these social welfare problems are the product of economic inequality and approaches to social welfare policy that hinder educational opportunities and social mobility for minoritized groups.

In Chapter 16, "Juvenile Justice for Achieving Equal Opportunity and Justice," the authors examine the role of assessment, evidence-based programs, promising practices, services in correctional settings, and re-entry/probation for juvenile justice in the United States. Despite steadily declining juvenile justice system involvement, the U.S. juvenile justice custody rate remains the highest in the world at approximately 26.9 for every 1,000

410 PROGRESSIVE APPROACHES

persons younger than the age of majority. In 2018, for every 1,000 American Indian youth in the United States, 22.8 had an active delinquency case; the delinquency rate was 4.4 for Asian youth, 55.5 for Black youth, 18.0 for Latinx youth, and 19.3 for White youth (Hockenberry & Puzzanchera, 2020). (The National Center for Juvenile Justice classifies American Indian and Alaska Native together; Asian includes Asian, Native Hawaiian, and Other Pacific Islander; and persons who identify as Hispanic/Latinx are treated as a distinct racial group.) This disproportionality cannot be explained by youth behavior alone but is a combination of differential offending, differential treatment, structural racism, and both legal and extra-legal factors. Contributing to structural racism is the fact that the juvenile justice system does not equitably define, arrest, adjudicate, or incarcerate youth; and often the most vulnerable and disadvantaged youth in the United States bear the largest burden of justice involvement, which can lead to worsened outcomes for youth across development, educational attainment, employment, and the transition to adulthood. This chapter includes a current overview of racial and ethnic disparities in juvenile justice, policy changes following the reauthorization of the Juvenile Justice and Delinquency Prevention Act, trend data on disparities across micro, meso, and macro social domains for youth in juvenile justice, and strategies to reduce racial/ethnic disparities in the juvenile justice system.

Chapter 17, "From Mass Incarceration to Smart Decarceration," includes a current overview of mass incarceration and the racial and ethnic disparities, trend data on disparities across micro, meso, and macro social domains for incarcerated adults, and strategies to reduce RED/DMC (Racial and Ethnic Disparities/Disproportionate Minority Contact) in the criminal justice system. Unfortunately, investment capitalism has secured a foothold in the carceral state and its structural tentacles, which fan out to public schools and other child welfare systems. The Promote Smart Decarceration Grand Challenge suggests that social work employ a proactive, transdisciplinary, cross-sector, and empirically driven approach to transform the criminal justice system and reduce mass incarceration in the United States. Disrupting the status quo and creating new opportunities through appropriate investment means divestment from pernicious government intervention through investment in prosocial early child welfare programs and schooling.

Chapter 18, "Reducing Racialized Barriers to School Success for All Children and Youth," outlines the many problems experienced by minoritized children and youth as they relate to disproportionality in school-based disciplinary outcomes. School success is a key factor in potential lifetime earnings, family formation, and career opportunities and satisfaction. Young adults who graduate from high school are less likely to make use of social welfare programs, particularly in early adult years, and are less likely to be involved in the criminal justice system. School suspension and expulsion are associated with delinquency and referral to juvenile justice. In every state, minoritized populations are disproportionately suspended and expelled from the nation's public-school systems. The juvenile justice system is notorious for harsh and biased treatment and outcomes for minoritized youth. The struggle for change in systemic factors that outline the problems identified for racialized populations within this chapter is central to creating opportunity and reducing extreme inequality.

Chapter 19, "Reversing Extreme Inequality," focuses on how the intersection of capitalism and White supremacy create, maintain, and further economic inequality generally and between racial groups. Analysis focuses on American experiences beginning with the colonialist appropriation of Native land, destruction of Indigenous culture, and enslavement of Native peoples alongside the trade and enslavement of Africans. We will overview events from our country's full history, including the location of the U.S.–Mexico border, policy failures in the Reconstruction era, and twentieth–twenty-first-century events including redlining, wealth stripping, welfare reform, and the rise of the incarceration state.

Chapter 20, "White Supremacy and American Social Policy: Implications for Racism-Centered Policy Practice," examines a racism-centered perspective of policy practice to do the following: (1) discuss the reasons for American social policy's reluctance to grapple with the problem of White supremacy; (2) provide specific policy practice recommendations as to how social workers can render social policies more responsive to White supremacy; and (3) offer ideas as to how policy practice against White supremacy can be integrated in the social policy sequence of schools of social work to reinforce CSWE's core competency of "engaging in policy practice."

Authors of Chapter 21, "Policy, Practice, and Institutional Barriers to FCAB for All Related to Race (Racism) in the United States," posit that because race permeates every aspect of our social fabric, when it comes to society's response to people experiencing financial issues, there is no difference; race is a major factor. This chapter examines the intersection between race/racism in making the other Grand Challenges that much harder for African Americans and other people of color. In the end, the authors of

412   PROGRESSIVE APPROACHES

this chapter demonstrate pathways to progress and much needed reform. It is possible to tackle and ameliorate income inequality though a reversal of entrenched economic inequality and change in child welfare policies. Opportunity breeds achievement and create synergy toward success.

As the authors make clear within the content of these chapters, the Grand Challenges laid out with this final part must be approached by an investment in understanding the historical antecedents that fostered the current state of affairs, leading to present-day economic inequality and low opportunity for social mobility among minoritized groups. Untangling mass incarceration from the vested interest of Wall Street profit margins, in a movement toward smart decarceration, will require fortitude, tenacity, and the display of strategic commitment and willingness to go the distance. The inappropriate treatment of minoritized children in many public-school systems, inattention to their community needs, and neglect through educational policy and school funding mechanisms requires a pivot from normative approaches. The problems are magnified for racialized groups, operating with little guidance, and perhaps strengthened through longevity. Therefore, astute attention to policy formation, including the examination of intended and unintended consequences, is required, along with close scrutiny and policy advocacy.

16

Juvenile Justice for Achieving Equal Opportunity and Justice

Susan A. McCarter, Bo-Kyung Elizabeth Kim, Patricia Logan-Greene, and Vanessa Drew

> *We are willing to spend the least amount of money to keep a kid at home, more to put him in a foster home and the most to institution-alize him.*
>
> —Marian Wright Edelman, *Psychology Today* (June 1975)

Since 2008, the number of youth in the United States who become involved in the juvenile justice system has been declining (Hockenberry & Puzzanchera, 2020). Yet, the U.S. juvenile justice custody rate remains the highest in the world at approximately 26.9 for every 1,000 persons younger than the age of majority. African American/Black youth receive approximately three times (61.8) the rate (per 1,000 Black youth at risk of juvenile justice involvement) of referrals to the juvenile justice system as do Hispanic/Latinx (19.9) and White (21.0) youth. Delinquency cases are more likely to be petitioned for formal processing for Black youth (64%) as compared to Latinx (55%) or White (52%) youth. Then, once in juvenile court, cases involving Black youth are slightly less likely to be adjudicated (49%) than cases involving Latinx (57%) and White (52%) youth, and more likely to be waived to criminal court (1.1%) than Latinx (0.6%) and White youth (0.7% each). Once adjudicated, cases involving Black or Latinx youth are more likely to result in residential placement (both 32%) than cases involving White youth (23%). Finally, adjudicated cases involving White youth were more likely to result in

---

Susan A. McCarter, Bo-Kyung Elizabeth Kim, Patricia Logan-Greene, and Vanessa Drew, *Juvenile Justice for Achieving Equal Opportunity and Justice* In: *Social Work and the Grand Challenge to Eliminate Racism*. Edited by: Martell L. Teasley, Michael S. Spencer, and Melissa Bartholomew, Oxford University Press. © Oxford University Press 2023. DOI: 10.1093/oso/9780197674949.003.0016

probation (65%) than cases involving Black or Latinx youth (61% and 64%, respectively) (Hockenberry & Puzzanchera, 2020).

The Office of Juvenile Justice and Delinquency Prevention (OJJDP) suggests that youth of color are overrepresented in the juvenile justice system because of differential opportunity for prevention and treatment, mobility effects, indirect effects, differential offending/behavior, differential processing by the juvenile justice system, justice by geography, and legislation that advantages some while disadvantaging others (Leiber et al., 2009). The theory of differential offending suggests that racial and ethnic disparities (RED) in juvenile justice occur because youth of color act differently than White youth and there are slight differences in offending by race/ethnicity. For example, in most jurisdictions White youth commit more arson and Black youth commit more petit larceny (Hockenberry & Puzzanchera, 2020). However, the empirical evidence suggests that differential offending cannot explain the current and sustained racial and ethnic disparities in juvenile justice, and the majority of justice scholars suggest that differential treatment is a more significant predictor of RED, as youth of color are systematically treated differently than White youth (Bishop, 2005; National Research Council, 2013; Piquero et al., 2005; Tracy 2005). A 2013 National Research Council study concludes that RED "exists in the broader context of a 'racialized society' in which many public policies, institutional practices, and cultural representations operate to produce and maintain racial inequities" (p. 239).

Juvenile Justice and Delinquency Prevention Act

The Juvenile Justice and Delinquency Prevention Act of 1974 (JJDPA; P.L. 93-415) made addressing overrepresentation a core requirement in 1992 (McCarter, 2011). This requirement, then called disproportionate minority contact (DMC), compels states participating in the Formula Grants Program to reduce the disproportionate number of BIPOC (Black, Indigenous, and Other People of Color) youth who come into contact with the juvenile justice system or risk losing federal funding (see §223(a)(22)). On December 21, 2018, the JJDPA was reauthorized for five years through the Juvenile Justice Reform Act (JJRA; H.R. 6964), which changed the language to racial and ethnic disparities (RED) (indicated if a specific racial/ethnic group's rate of involvement at a specific juvenile justice contact point is different than the rate of contact for non-Hispanic Whites or other racial/ethnic groups) (see §103(41)). The JJRA also requires that states report how they have reduced RED to the Office of Juvenile Justice and Delinquency Prevention every three years (H.R. 6964).

Disparate Impacts of Juvenile Justice System Involvement

The U.S. juvenile justice system does not equitably define, arrest, adjudicate, or incarcerate youth, but, instead, the most vulnerable and disadvantaged youth bear a disproportionate burden of justice involvement. Youth growing up with neglect, maltreatment, abuse, and trauma; those living in poverty; those facing mental, emotional, and behavioral health (MEB) problems and physical/other forms of disability; as well as those experiencing discrimination, including on the basis of race, ethnicity, culture, sex, gender identity, and sexual orientation, are overrepresented in juvenile justice. We explore just a few of the examples of the micro-, meso-, and macro-level impacts of these disparities and juvenile justice involvement.

Micro-Level Impacts

Both juvenile justice involvement and outcomes vary by legal and extra-legal factors. Very few jurisdictions classify youth by gender but instead categorize juveniles by biological sex using a binary female/male, denying the experience of other gender identities; and even fewer jurisdictions ask about juveniles' sexual orientation (Irvine & Canfield, 2016). Yet, cis-gender boys are more likely than cis-gender girls to become juvenile justice-involved (Hockenberry & Puzzanchera, 2020) and a burgeoning literature is finding that lesbian, gay, bisexual, gender-expansive, and non-cisgender youth are overrepresented in the juvenile justice system (Himmelstein & Brückner, 2011; Majd et al., 2009).

Youth who have experienced neglect or abuse are more likely than children who have not to be affected by the juvenile justice system (Courtney & Heuring, 2005; Ryan et al., 2007; Ryan et al., 2008). National estimates indicate that approximately 22% of the overall population under age 18 years experience psychiatric disorders but that the rate is approximately 70% for court-involved youth (Cocozza & Shufelt, 2006; Teplin et al., 2012). Such mental, emotional, and behavioral problems can increase the risk of aggression or displays of anger, self-regulatory challenges, substance use, and trauma symptoms (Kim et al., 2019; Wasserman et al., 2002). Juvenile justice-involved youth are also more likely to have a learning disability (Sedlak & McPherson, 2010) and exposure to childhood adversity (Baglivio et al., 2014; Logan-Greene et al., 2016).

Moreover, incarceration for juveniles interrupts typical processes of psychosocial development and can hamper attainment of developmental tasks such as social integration and autonomy (Dmitrieva et al., 2012), and solitary confinement can have even more detrimental effects (Lewis, 2006). Incarceration also increases the risk of victimization (Ahlin, 2018) and suicide (Campaign for Youth Justice, 2018). Finally, the stigma associated with justice involvement can significantly challenge positive adolescent development (Mears & Travis, 2004; Wiley et al., 2013). For example, youth who experience arrest and adjudication must try to make sense of their experiences and what it means about them and their future (Bernburg et al., 2006; Kroska et al., 2017). Anticipated stigma (the expectation of being discriminated against because of one's identity) during out-of-home placements/incarceration predicted social withdrawal three months after an individual's release, which then predicted elevated mental health challenges one year after an individual's release (Moore & Tangney, 2017). Additionally, and contrary to popular belief, arrest records of youth crimes are often not sealed or destroyed at age 18, meaning that justice-involved youth can face continuous legal discrimination when seeking housing, employment, or even educational opportunities (Shah et al., 2014). Keene, Smoyer, and Blankenship's (2018) study found that criminal justice stigma is enacted by both individuals and institutions/the state, can be regarded as a more "legitimate" reason than racism, for example, for housing denial, and can reproduce power to justify inequality.

Meso-Level Impacts

Youth from impoverished backgrounds are at increased risk of court involvement (Birkhead, 2012). And many of the options for exit from the system or from formal legal proceedings (e.g., diversion, community service) require time, resources (e.g., restitution, fees), transportation, and a stable mailing address to receive court communications, which can disadvantage low-income children (Birkhead, 2012; Harris, 2016).

Exposure to other delinquent peers can exacerbate problem behaviors via peer contagion, thereby amplifying instead of rehabilitating negative sequelae (Mennis & Harris, 2011). And evidence shows that instruction in juvenile detention facilities is often inferior (Altschuler & Brash, 2004; Hogan et al., 2010), and youth who return to the community are frequently shunned from the normative school setting (Mears & Travis, 2004). It is unsurprising that few youth—approximately 20%—with detention histories graduate high school or complete a GED (Osgood et al., 2010) and fewer continue for secondary education (Chung et al., 2011). Subpar education affects future employment opportunities as youth then lack important skills and educational qualifications for jobs (Abrams & Snyder, 2010), which compounds employers' unwillingness to hire those with criminal/juvenile records (Nellis, 2011). Moreover, given the multiple disruptions and barriers, many justice-involved youth reoffend within a short period of time (e.g., Trulson et al., 2005), increasing not only their likelihood of participating in criminal behavior as an adult, but also the likelihood of incarceration during adulthood (Gilman et al., 2015).

Macro-Level Impacts

The same structural racism and White supremacy that are evident across all systems and institutions in the United States are also impacting youth in our juvenile justice system. White youth are disproportionately selected for gifted and talented education programs (Grissom & Redding, 2016) whereas youth of color are disproportionately suspended, expelled, and arrested at school (Fabelo et al., 2011; McCarter, 2017). Scholars suggest that the overrepresentation of youth of color in school discipline reflects cultural bias embedded in school discipline practices (Monroe, 2005). Studies (e.g., Skiba et al., 2002; Wallace et al., 2008) note that Black youth, for example, are more likely to receive suspension or expulsion for subjective reasons (e.g., disruptive behavior) compared to White youth, who are suspended or expelled for objective reasons (e.g., carrying a weapon). Moreover, Bradshaw et al. (2010) found that if two students—one Black and one White—had identical ratings on all other measures in the study, the Black student had a 24%–80% increase in the odds of receiving an office disciplinary referral compared to their White counterpart.

Despite the overall decline in the number of youth entering the juvenile justice system starting in 2008, racial and ethnic disparities have been worsening (Hockenberry & Puzzanchera, 2020). For example, in 1997, Black youth were held in detention at a rate 5 times that of White youth, and by 2015, the difference had risen to 6.1 times (OJJDP, 2017). For American Indian youth, the 1997 rate was 2.3 times the White rate, and in 2015, 3.0 times the White rate. For Hispanic youth, the 1997 rate was 2.4 times the White rate, and in 2015, 2.0 times the White rate. And Asian youth are detained at a lower rate than White youth—in 1997, .9 times the White rate, and in 2015, .3 times the White rate (OJJDP, 2017).

Assessing Racial and Ethnic Disparities in Juvenile Justice

As with all complex phenomenon, a combination of research paradigms and methods are most effective for studying racial and ethnic disparities in juvenile justice (Leiber et al., 2009). One established quantitative method used to assess RED is a relative rate index (RRI). RRIs provide mathematical context by dividing occurrences at specified decision points by the number of youth in the jurisdiction's general population. Any RRI less than 1.0 suggests underrepresentation, whereas those greater than 1.0 indicate overrepresentation. Until 2019, OJJDP required that states collect these data from at least nine decision or contact points, typically: arrest, complaint, diversion/no approval for court, detention, approval for court, adjudication, disposition, placement, and transfer to adult/criminal justice. Starting in fiscal year 2019, OJJDP reduced the number of contact points evaluated from nine to five: arrest, diversion/no approval for court, detention, placement, and transfer to adult/criminal justice (OJJDP, n.d.).

Recommendations presented in the Juvenile Justice Working Paper within the Achieving Equal Opportunity and Justice Grand Challenge suggest that all nine contact points be used to measure RED and that RRIs be used to contextualize multiple intersectional identities (Kim et al., 2020). Finally, any authentic evaluation of these disparate outcomes also requires qualitative input from justice-involved youth and their families, as well as various system stakeholders (Leiber et al., 2009). Moreover, these data are best collected by researchers who are guided by a race lens/analysis (McCarter et al., 2017).

JUVENILE JUSTICE   419

Reducing Racial and Ethnic Disparities in Juvenile Justice

In our racialized society, policies and practices generate and maintain different systems of "justice" for Black and Brown youth compared to White youth (NRC, 2013). To date, no jurisdictions have completely eliminated RED, but the evidence base is growing. In 2014, Elizabeth Spinney and her colleagues published a study of nine juvenile justice jurisdictions (in Alabama, Connecticut, Nevada, New Hampshire, New Jersey, New Mexico, Oklahoma, Pennsylvania, and Utah) that had some level of success reducing RED. Eight recommendations based on their findings are: (1) disaggregate data by race and ethnicity and use data to inform policy and practice; (2) collaborate with state and local agencies, police, judges, and community stakeholders; (3) change culture from punitive/procedural focus toward what's best for the youth, family, and community; (4) affiliate with national juvenile justice reform initiatives; (5) create alternatives to detention, secure confinement, and formal system involvement; (6) develop an intentional focus on RED reduction; (7) cultivate leadership at both state and local levels; and (8) make reducing RED a long-term priority.

More recently, Spinney, Cohen, Feyerherm, Stephenson, Yeide, and Shreve (2018) examined 107 state assessments/research studies on RED in juvenile justice across the United States from January 2001 to December 2014 to explore the role that race and ethnicity play in juvenile justice processing. They compared the current research on racial/ethnic groups included, justice decision points investigated, stages extracted, race effects, and results. Their findings largely echo the eight earlier recommendations: data (Richetelli et al., 2009); stakeholder collaboration (Rodriguez, 2008); culture change/community involvement (Motes et al., 2004); juvenile justice reform initiatives and alternatives (Hobbs et al., 2012; Rodriguez, 2010); intentional focus on RED (Leiber et al., 2006a, 2006b; leadership (Motes et al., 2004); and prioritizing RED (Richetelli et al., 2009).

Conclusion and Implications

Now more than ever, it is important to recognize and begin to authentically address the systemic racism and White supremacy that prohibits youth from achieving equal opportunity and justice across all U.S. institutions (e.g., education, child welfare, healthcare, employment, housing, banking/finance, juvenile and criminal justice). Racial and ethnic disparities in juvenile justice are:

> a consequence of U.S. history, of the biases and stereotypes created by that history, and of the still-strong divisions in lived experience between groups that we call "races." . . . Regrettably, our history also left us with pervasive and false ideas about "races" that have shaped our perceptions of who is valued and who is not, who is capable and who is not, and who is "safe" and who is "dangerous." (Carter et al., 2014, p. 2)

As social workers, we can use the Grand Challenge to Eliminate Racism to champion difference, dismantle the current racial hierarchy, eliminate structural racism, realize racial equity, and achieve equal opportunity and justice for all youth in our justice systems. The addition of the 13th Grand Challenge provides a mechanism to explicitly highlight racial and ethnic disparities in the juvenile justice system. Considerations for social work include the need to:

- Focus resources on prevention and diversion programs that address areas that influence involvement, such as poverty-related community issues;
- Support local community leaders who are invested in positive youth outcomes for members of their communities;
- Provide an evidence-based counternarrative demonstrating that explicit and implicit bias and systemic racism are driving factors in the disproportionate numbers of Black and Brown justice-involved youth;
- Shift away from only providing micro-level interventions toward including meso and macro spheres of interventions, policy, and practice change;
- Decrease the stigma placed on youth who are justice-involved, especially those with marginalized identities;
- Effect change beyond reducing racial/ethnic disparities and move toward achieving racial/ethnic equity in juvenile justice through continued accountability mechanisms required by laws and policies (e.g., 2018 Juvenile Justice and Delinquency Prevention Act, H.R. 6964 The Juvenile Justice Reform Act of 2018);
- Acknowledge and work to address the influence of the systemic impact of racism and root causes when reforming the juvenile and adult justice systems.

Although the intent may have been to address racism and White supremacy in each of the Grand Challenges, that is not the reality (Rao et al., 2021). The profession, therefore, continues to be complicit in perpetuating a juvenile justice system that disproportionately advantages White youth while it disadvantages youth of color. As we collaborate in support of the Grand Challenge to Eliminate Racism, social work must be actively anti-racist and require reform that dismantles White supremacy and replaces it with racial equity.

Study Questions

1. What are the current U.S. trends in juvenile delinquency?
2. What factors contribute to disparities in the juvenile justice system?
3. What is the difference between differential offending and differential treatment? What is the difference between legal factors and extra-legal factors in juvenile justice?
4. Consider your own race/ethnicity. Have you ever been treated better or worse in school, at a hospital, by the police, etc., because of your identity?
5. Juvenile justice involvement has different micro-, meso-, and macro-level impacts. Did any of these surprise you?
6. Why is context important when assessing disproportionality/disparities?
7. Inherent in any discussion of racial/ethnic disparities is the topic of racism. How might racism be addressed explicitly in the juvenile justice system?

References

Abrams, L. S., & Snyder, S. M. (2010). Youth offender reentry: Models for intervention and directions for future inquiry. *Children and Youth Services Review, 32*(12), 1787–1795. doi: 10.1016/j.childyouth.2010.07.023.

Ahlin, E. M. (2018). Risk factors of sexual assault and victimization among youth in custody. *Journal of Interpersonal Violence, 36*(3-4), 1–24. doi: 10.1177/0886260518757226.

Altschuler, D. M., & Brash, R. (2004). Adolescent and teenage offenders confronting the challenges and opportunities of reentry. *Youth Violence and Juvenile Justice, 2*(1), 72–87. doi: 10.1177/1541204003260048.

Baglivio, M. T., Epps, N., Swartz, K., Huq, M. S., Sheer, A., & Hardt, N. S. (2014). The prevalence of adverse childhood experiences (ACE) in the lives of juvenile offenders.

Journal of Juvenile Justice, 3(2), 1–23. Retrieved from https://www.ncjrs.gov/pdffiles/246951.pdf.

Bernburg, J. G., Krohn, M. D., & Rivera, C. J. (2006). Official labeling, criminal embeddedness, and subsequent delinquency: A longitudinal test of labeling theory. *Journal of Research in Crime & Delinquency, 43*(1), 67–88.

Birckhead, T. R. (2012). Delinquent by reason of poverty. *Washington University Journal of Law & Policy, 38*, 53–107. Retrieved from https://openscholarship.wustl.edu/law_journal_law_policy/vol38/iss1/4.

Bishop, D. M. (2005). The role of race and ethnicity in juvenile justice processing. In D. F. Hawkins & K. Kempf-Leonard (Eds.), *Our children, their children: Confronting racial and ethnic differences in American juvenile justice* (pp. 23–82). Chicago: University of Chicago Press.

Bradshaw, C. P., Mitchell, M. M., O'Brennan, L. M., & Leaf, P. J. (2010). Multilevel exploration of factors contributing to the overrepresentation of black students in office disciplinary referrals. *Journal of Educational Psychology, 102*(2), 508.

Campaign for Youth Justice. (2018). Mandatory transfer and reverse waiver fact sheets. Retrieved from: http://www.campaignforyouthjustice.org/images/factsheets/Mandatory_Transfer_FINAL_1.pdf

Carter, P., Skiba, R. J., Arredondo, M. I., & Pollock, M. (2014). You can't fix what you don't look at: Acknowledging race in addressing racial discipline disparities. *Urban Education, 52*(2), 207–235. https://doi.org/10.1177/0042085916660350

Chung, H. L., Mulvey, E. P., & Steinberg, L. (2011). Understanding the school outcomes of juvenile offenders: An exploration of neighborhood influences and motivational resources. *Journal of Youth Adolescence, 40*, 1025–1038. doi: 10.1007/s10964-010-9626-2.

Cocozza, J. J., & Shufelt, J. L. (2006, June). *Juvenile mental health courts: An emerging strategy* (National Center for Mental Health and Juvenile Justice Research and Program Brief). Retrieved from IssueLab website: https://www.issuelab.org/resources/9972/9972.pdf.

Courtney, M. E., & Heuring, D. H. (2005). The transition to adulthood for youth "aging out" of the foster care system. In D. W. Osgood, E. M. Foster, C. Flanagan, & G. R. Ruth (Eds.), *On your own without a net: The transition to adulthood for vulnerable populations* (pp. 27–67). Chicago: University of Chicago Press.

Dmitrieva, J., Monahan, K. C., Cauffman, E., & Steinberg, L. (2012). Arrested development: The effects of incarceration on the development of psychosocial maturity. *Development and Psychopathology, 24*(3), 1073–1090. doi: 10.1017/S0954579412000545.

Fabelo, T., Thompson, M. D., Plotkin, M., Carmichael, D., Marchbanks, M. P., III, & Booth, E. A. (2011). *Breaking schools' rules: A statewide study of how school discipline relates to students' success and juvenile justice involvement* (Report). New York: Council of State Governments Justice Center and Public Policy Research Institute.

Gilman, A. B., Hill, K. G., & Hawkins, J. D. (2015). When is a youth's debt to society paid? Examining the long-term consequences of juvenile incarceration for adult functioning. *Journal of Developmental and Life-Course Criminology, 1*(1), 33–47. doi: 10.1007/s40865-015-0002-5.

Grissom, J. A., & Redding, C. (2016). Discretion and disproportionality: Explaining the underrepresentation of high-achieving students of color in gifted programs. *AERA Open, 2*(1), 1–25. doi: 10.1177/2332858415622175.

Harris, A. (2016). *A pound of flesh: Monetary sanctions as punishment for the poor.* New York: Russell Sage Foundation.

JUVENILE JUSTICE 423

Himmelstein, K. E. W., & Brückner, H. (2011). Criminal-justice and school sanctions against nonheterosexual youth: A national longitudinal study. *Pediatrics, 127*(1), 49–57. doi: 10.1542/peds.2009-2306.

Hobbs, A., Neeley, E. M., Behrens, C., & Wulf-Ludden, T. (2012). *Nebraska state DMC assessment*. Omaha: UNO Juvenile Justice Institute.

Hockenberry, S., & Puzzanchera, C. (2020). *Juvenile court statistics, 2018*. Pittsburgh, PA: National Center for Juvenile Justice. ISSN 0091-3278.

Hogan, K. A., Bullock, L. M., & Fritsch, E. J. (2010). Meeting the transition needs of incarcerated youth with disabilities. *Journal of Correctional Education, 61*(2), 133–147. Retrieved from https://www.jstor.org/stable/23282636.

Irvine, A., & Canfield, A. (2016). The overrepresentation of lesbian, gay, bisexual, questioning, gender nonconforming and transgender youth within the child welfare to juvenile justice crossover population. *American University Journal of Gender, Social Policy & the Law, 24*(2), 243–261.

Keene, D. E., Smoyer, A. B., & Blankenship, K. M. (2018). Stigma, housing and identity after prison. *The Sociological Review, 66*(4), 799–815. doi: 10.1177/0038026118777447.

Kim, B. K. E., Gilman, A. B., Kosterman, R., & Hill, K. G. (2019). Longitudinal associations among depression, substance abuse, and crime: A test of competing hypotheses for driving mechanisms. *Journal of Criminal Justice, 62*, 50–57. doi: 10.1016/j.jcrimjus.2018.08.005.

Kim, B. E., McCarter, S., & Logan-Greene, P. (2020). *Achieving equal opportunity and justice in juvenile justice (Grand Challenges for Social Work Initiative Working Paper No. 25)*. Baltimore, MD: Grand Challenges for Social Work. https://grandchallengesforsoc ialwork.org/wp-content/uploads/2020/06/Achieving-Equal-Opportunity-and-Just ice-in-Juvenile-Justice-3.pdf

Kroska, A., Lee, J. D., & Carr, N. T. (2017). Juvenile delinquency and self-sentiments: Exploring a labeling theory proposition. *Social Science Quarterly, 98*(1), 73–88.

Leiber, M. J., Johnson, J. D., & Fox, K. C. (2006a). *An examination of the factors that influence justice decision-making in Anchorage and Fairbanks, Alaska: An assessment study*. Prepared for Alaska Department of Health and Social Services, Division of Juvenile Justice. Richmond, VA: Wilder School of Government and Public Affairs, Virginia Commonwealth University.

Leiber, M. J., Johnson, J. D., & Fox, K. C. (2006b). *An examination of the factors that influence juvenile justice decision-making in the jurisdictions of Black Hawk, Johnson, Linn, and Scott, Iowa: An assessment study*. Des Moines: Prepared for the Iowa Division of Criminal and Juvenile Justice Planning.

Leiber, M. J., Richetelli, D. M., & Feyerherm, W. (2009). Assessment. In *Disproportionate Minority Contact Technical Assistance Manual* (4th ed.). pp. 2.1-41. Washington, DC: Office of Juvenile Justice and Delinquency Prevention, U.S. Department of Justice.

Lewis, M. (2006). Conditions of confinement: Abusive treatment. In *Custody and control: Conditions of confinement in New York's juvenile prisons for girls* (pp. 44–80). New York: Human Rights Watch & American Civil Liberties Union.

Logan-Greene, P., Kim, B. K. E., & Nurius, P. S. (2016). Childhood adversity among court-involved youth: Heterogeneous needs for prevention and treatment. *Journal of Juvenile Justice, 5*(2), 68–84.

Majd, K., Marksamer, J., & Reyes, C. (2009). *Hidden injustice: Lesbian, gay, bisexual, and transgender youth in juvenile courts*. Retrieved from the Center for HIV Law & Policy website: http://www.hivlawandpolicy.org/sites/default/files/hidden_injustice.pdf.

McCarter, S. A. (2011). Disproportionate minority contact in the American juvenile justice system: Where are we after 20 years, a philosophy shift, and three amendments? *Journal of Forensic Social Work*, *1*(1), 96–107. https://doi.org/10.1080/19369 28X.2011.541217

McCarter, S. A. (2017). The school-to-prison pipeline: A primer for social workers. *Social Work*, *62*(1), 53–61. https://doi.org/10.1093/sw/sww078.

McCarter, S. A., Chinn-Gary, E., Trosch, L. A., Jr., Toure, A., Alsaeedi, A., & Harrington, J., (2017). Bringing racial justice to the courtroom and community: Race matters for juvenile justice and the Charlotte model. *Washington and Lee Law Review*, *73*(2), 641–686. https://scholarlycommons.law.wlu.edu/wlulr-online/vol73/iss2/6/.

Mears, D. P., & Travis, J. (2004). Youth development and reentry. *Youth Violence and Juvenile Justice*, *2*(1), 3–20. doi: 10.1177/1541204003260044.

Mennis, J., & Harris, P. (2011). Contagion and repeat offending among urban juvenile delinquents. *Journal of Adolescence*, *34*(5), 951–963.

Monroe, C. R. (2005). Why are "bad boys" always black?: Causes of disproportionality in school discipline and recommendations for change. *The Clearing House: A Journal of Educational Strategies, Issues and Ideas*, *79*(1), 45–50.

Moore, K. E. & Tangney, J. P. (2017). Managing the concealable stigma of criminal justice system involvement: A longitudinal examination of anticipated stigma, social withdrawal, and post–release adjustment. *Journal of Social Issues*, *73*(2), 322–340. https://doi.org/10.1111/josi.12219

Motes, S., Patricia, T. A., Payne, J. P., Rivers, A. B., MacDonald, J. M., & Smith, C. O. (2004). *Minorities in South Carolina's Juvenile Justice System: Understanding the Disparities and Assessing Community Readiness for Change*. Institute for Families and Society, University of South Carolina. Retrieved from http: llwww. ojjdp. govldmclpdflexecsummary_aug2004. pdf.

National Research Council. (2013). *Reforming juvenile justice: A developmental approach*. Washington, DC: The National Academies Press.

Nellis, A. (2011, July–August). Addressing the collateral consequences of convictions for young offenders. *The Champion*, 20–27. Retrieved from https://www.sentencingproj ect.org/wp-content/uploads/2016/01/Addressing-the-Collateral-Consequences-of-Convictions-for-Young-Offenders.pdf.

Office of Juvenile Justice and Delinquency Prevention. (2017). Statistical briefing book. Retrieved from https://www.ojjdp.gov/ojstatbb/special_topics/qa11802.asp?qaDate=2017.

Office of Juvenile Justice and Delinquency Prevention. (n.d.). Disproportionate minority contact. Retrieved from https://ojjdp.ojp.gov/programs/disproportionate-minority-contact-summary.

Osgood, D. W., Foster, E. M., & Courtney, M. E. (2010). Vulnerable populations and the transition to adulthood. *Future Child*, *20*(1), 209–229. doi: 10.1353/foc.0.0047. PMID: 20364628.

Piquero, A. R., Moffitt, T. E., & Lawton, B. (2005). Race and crime: The contributions of individual, familial, and neighborhood-level risk factors to life-course-persistent offending. In D.F. Hawkins & K. Kempf–Leonard (Eds.), *Our children, their children* (pp. 202–244). Chicago: University of Chicago Press.

Rao, S., Woo, B., Maglalang, D. D., Bartholomew, M., Cano, M., Harris, A., & Tucker, T. B. (2021). Race and ethnicity in the Social Work Grand Challenges. *Social Work*, *66*(1), 9–17. doi: 10.1093/sw/swaa053.

Richetelli, D., Eliot, M., Hartstone, C., & Murphy, K. L. (2009). *A second reassessment of disproportionate minority contact in Connecticut's juvenile justice system*. Avon, CT: Spectrum Associates Market Research.

JUVENILE JUSTICE 425

Rodriguez, N. (2008). Multilevel analysis of juvenile court processes: The importance of community characteristics. Submitted to the National Institute of Justice. NCJ 223465. https://nij.ojp.gov/library/publications/multilevel-analysis-juvenile-court-processes-importance-community

Rodriguez, N. (2010). The cumulative effect of race and ethnicity in juvenile court outcomes and why preadjudication detention matters. *Journal of Research in Crime and Delinquency, 47*(3), 391–413. doi: 10.1177/0022427810365905.

Ryan, J. P., Herz, D., Hernandez, P. M., & Marshall, J. M. (2007). Maltreatment and delinquency: Investigating child welfare bias in juvenile justice processing. *Children and Youth Services Review, 29*(8), 1035–1050.

Ryan, J. P., Testa, M. F., & Zhai, F. (2008). African American males in foster care and the risk of delinquency: The values of social bonds and permanence. *Child Welfare, 87*(1), 115–140.

Sedlak, A. J., & McPherson, K. S. (2010). *Youth's needs and services: Findings from the survey of youth in residential placement*. Washington, DC: Office of Juvenile Justice and Delinquency Prevention.

Shah, R. S., Fine, L., & Gullen, J. (2014). Juvenile records: A national review of state laws on confidentiality, sealing and expungement. Juvenile Law Center. Retrieved from https://jlc.org/sites/default/files/publication_pdfs/national-review.pdf.

Skiba, R. J., Michael, R. S., Nardo, A. C., & Peterson, R. L. (2002). The color of discipline: Sources of racial and gender disproportionality in school punishment. *The Urban Review, 34*(4), 317–342.

Spinney, E., Cohen, M., Feyerherm, W., Stephenson, R., Yeide, M., & Shreve, T. (2018). Disproportionate minority contact in the U.S. juvenile justice system: a review of the DMC literature, 2001–2014, Part I. *Journal of Crime & Justice, 41*(5), 573–595. https://doi.org/10.1080/0735648X.2018.1516155.

Teplin, L. A., Welty, L. J., Abram, K. M., Dulcan, M. K., & Washburn, J. J. (2012). Prevalence and persistence of psychiatric disorders in youth after detention: A prospective longitudinal study. *Archives of General Psychiatry, 69*(10), 1031–1043. doi: 10.1001/archgenpsychiatry.2011.2062.

Tracy, P. E. (2005). Race, ethnicity, and juvenile justice: Is there bias in postarrest decision-making? In D. F. Hawkins and K. Kempf-Leonard (Eds.), *Our children, their children* (pp. 300–348). Chicago: University of Chicago Press. https://doi.org/10.7208/chicago/9780226319919.003.0010

Trulson, C. R., Marquart, J. W., Mullings, J. L., & Caeti, T. J. (2005). In between adolescence and adulthood: Recidivism outcomes of a cohort of state delinquents. *Youth Violence and Juvenile Justice, 3*(4), 355–387. doi: 10.1177/1541204005278802.

Wallace, J. M., Jr., Goodkind, S., Wallace, C. M., & Bachman, J. G. (2008). Racial, ethnic, and gender differences in school discipline among US high school students: 1991–2005. *The Negro Educational Review, 59*(1–2), 47.

Wasserman, G. A., McReynolds, L. S., Lucas, C. P., Fisher, P., & Santos, L. (2002). The voice DISC-IV with incarcerated male youths: Prevalence of disorder. *Journal of the American Academy of Child & Adolescent Psychiatry, 41*(3), 314–321. doi: 10.1097/00004583-200203000-00011.

Wiley, S. A., Slocum, L. A., & Esbensen, F. A. (2013). The unintended consequences of being stopped or arrested: An exploration of the labeling mechanisms through which police contact leads to subsequent delinquency. *Criminology, 51*(4), 927–966. https://doi.org/10.1111/1745-9125.12024

17

From Mass Incarceration
to Smart Decarceration

Susan A. McCarter, Camille R. Quinn, Charles H. Lea, III,
and Laura S. Abrams

> *The mass incarceration of poor people of color, particularly Black men,*
> *has emerged as a new caste system, one specifically designed to address*
> *the social, economic, and political challenges of our time.*
>
> —Michelle Alexander, 2010

The latest Bureau of Justice Statistics reports suggest that there were 1,583,602 individuals in U.S. prisons in 2018 (1,285,260 in state, 179,898 in federal, and 118,444 in private prisons) (Carson, 2020) and approximately 631,000 in local jails, for an incarceration rate of 655 prisoners per every 100,000 U.S. residents (Sawyer & Wagner, 2020). This means that despite only comprising 5% of the world's population, the United States has 25% of all those incarcerated. Meanwhile, incarceration figures have been declining in the United States since 2009, but the racial and ethnic disparities (RED) in the criminal justice system have remained significant. Black adults are 5.6 times more likely to be imprisoned as compared to Whites, and the rate is 1.9 times more likely for Latinx adults. Current incarceration trend data for racial and ethnic groups highlight social and economic disparities across micro, meso, and macro levels. Although RED and disproportionate minority contact (DMC) policies have been legislated in the juvenile justice system, similar efforts have yet to occur in the criminal justice system.

The Promote Smart Decarceration Grand Challenge suggests that social work employ a proactive, transdisciplinary, cross-sector, and empirically

Susan A. McCarter, Camille R. Quinn, Charles H. Lea, III, and Laura S. Abrams, *From Mass Incarceration to Smart Decarceration* In: *Social Work and the Grand Challenge to Eliminate Racism.* Edited by: Martell L. Teasley, Michael S. Spencer, and Melissa Bartholomew, Oxford University Press. © Oxford University Press 2023. DOI: 10.1093/oso/9780197674949.003.0017

driven approach to transform the criminal justice system and reduce mass incarceration in the United States. However, promoting smart decarceration as a goal has not been well attuned, thus far, to the numerous racialized factors that contribute to rearrest, incarceration, and offense rates. To date, policy strategies to reduce mass incarceration (such as sentencing reform laws, release laws, and prison reforms) have largely been ineffective at reducing RED, and in some cases, can even exacerbate RED in the criminal justice system. This chapter includes a current overview of mass incarceration and the racial and ethnic disparities, trend data on disparities across micro, meso, and macro social domains for incarcerated adults, and strategies to reduce RED/DMC in the criminal justice system. And the chapter concludes with explanations of the role of social workers and interdisciplinary professionals to address RED/DMC while promoting smart decarceration at all practice levels to maximize public safety and the well-being of restored citizens as they reenter their communities.

Mass Incarceration

Mass incarceration, also known as the carceral state or prison boom, refers to "the current American experiment in incarceration which is defined by comparatively and historically extreme rates of imprisonment" (Wildeman, 2018, p. 1). According to the Bureau of Justice Statistics, in 1972, there were approximately 200,000 individuals incarcerated in the United States, and today there are more than 2 million (Carson, 2020; Zeng, 2020). Moreover, the United States comprises 5% of the world's population but has 25% of all those incarcerated, for a rate of 655 per 100,000 residents. This compares to England/Wales rate of 134; China, 121; Canada, 107; Japan, 39; and India, 34 (World Prison Brief, 2020).

In 2018, there were 1,583,602 individuals in American prisons in 2018 (1,285,260 in state, 179,898 in federal, and 118,444 in private prisons) (Carson, 2020) and 738,400 in county and city jails (Zeng, 2020). In 2016 (the latest data available) an estimated 6,613,500 adults were supervised by adult correctional systems (prison, jail, probation, or parole), meaning that approximately 1 out of every 38 adults in the United States is under correctional supervision via prison, jail, probation, or parole (Kaeble & Cowhig, 2018).

428 MCCARTER, QUINN, LEA, AND ABRAMS

Racial and Ethnic Disparities in the Criminal Justice System

Unfortunately, the Bureau of Justice Statistics does not consistently disaggregate correctional population data by race/ethnicity, but triangulating other sources, it is obvious that the more than 6 million adults under correctional supervision are largely people of color. Despite declining incarceration statistics in the country since 2009, RED remain significant. African American/Black adults are imprisoned at a rate of 1,501 per every 100,000 Black adults in the United States as compared to a rate of 797 for Latinx adults and 268 for White adults (Carson, 2020). In criminal justice, RED exist when the outcomes experienced by one racial or ethnic group(s) differ at any contact point within the system from another group's outcomes. Criminal justice scholars suggest that RED in the criminal justice system result from differential behaviors and differential treatment, explicit and implicit bias at the micro-, meso-, and macro-levels, and structural racism (Ghandnoosh, 2015).

Promote Smart Decarceration Grand Challenge

The Promote Smart Decarceration (PSD) Grand Challenge for Social Work requires policy innovations that substantially reduce the use of incarceration in jails and prisons, redress the racial, economic, and behavioral health disparities among the incarcerated, and maximize public safety and community well-being (Epperson & Pettus-Davis, 2016). To that end, four policy recommendations are outlined for the PSD Grand Challenge: (1) use incarceration primarily for incapacitation of the most dangerous, (2) make reduction of disparities a key outcome in decarceration efforts, (3) remove civic and legal exclusions, and (4) reallocate community resources to community-based supports. Although all of these recommendations could impact people of color, this chapter focuses on policy recommendation 2, the shortest of the four recommendations.

Epperson and Pettus-Davis (2016) suggest that PSD make reduction of disparities a key outcome in decarceration efforts, but do not offer any specific tactics to accomplish this. The authors state that decarceration efforts should include a commitment to reduce racial, economic, and behavioral-health disparities and that emerging decarceration policies must be evaluated as to whether they improve or exacerbate disparities, but the only strategy offered is that legislation articulate racial equity goals such as racial impact statements. Articulating goals and commitments and analyzing data, though necessary elements, fall short of actually reducing racial and ethnic disparities in the criminal justice system (Eaglin & Solomon, 2015; Mauer, 2011; The Sentencing Project, 2008).

Similar to the efforts to address mass incarceration using smart decarceration, the Juvenile Detention Alternatives Initiative (JDAI) was very successful in reducing the number of juveniles detained, but unfortunately the initiative exacerbated disparities for detained youth of color in the process (AECF, 2017). This chapter emphasizes the recommendation that the reduction of disparities should be a key outcome of the PSD Grand Challenge by examining smart decarceration using a critical race lens to identify micro-, meso-, and macro-level factors related to racial and ethnic group outcomes, including the myriad of racialized factors that contribute to rearrest, incarceration, and parole violations, for example. It highlights the fact that to date, many policy strategies to reduce mass incarceration, such as sentencing reform laws, release laws, and prison reforms, have either maintained RED or have worsened the disparities (Gotsch, 2019). The chapter concludes by introducing six specific strategies for forensic practitioners, social workers, justice stakeholders, and legislators to reduce RED in criminal justice as efforts continue to address mass incarceration.

Micro, Meso, and Macro Contributors to RED

A host of factors contribute to racial disparities in the carceral continuum, including disparities at the critical junctures of policing, arrest, prosecution, conviction, sentencing, and incarceration (for a comprehensive review, see The Sentencing Project, 2008). These disparities, which affect Black people and communities most harshly, have roots in implicit and explicit biases on the part of criminal legal actors, as well as legacies of institutional and structural racism (The Sentencing Project, 2008). It is important to identify these factors and critical junctures in order to design interventions and systemic reforms to reduce these disparities. Indeed, the Promote Smart Decarceration Grand Challenge focuses on the use of data-driven and evidence-based strategies for reducing the numbers of people who are incarcerated and safely returning them to communities, thus breaking cycles of incarceration (Epperson & Pettus-Davis, 2016). Yet still this Grand

430 MCCARTER, QUINN, LEA, AND ABRAMS

Challenge has not explicitly considered how racism or anti-Blackness shapes the state of incarceration, practices within the system, or areas for criminal legal reform or abolition.

In this section, we will we focus on what is known about RED in rates of incarceration as well as recidivism, which is the most common metric of criminal justice outcomes. Policymakers and academics typically measure recidivism using rates of rearrest, re-conviction, or re-incarceration. Though we acknowledge that recidivism is imperfect and even racially problematic as a criminal justice outcome (Goldstein, 2014), it is indeed the most commonly used metric across jurisdictions. Hence in this section, we will scan the literature to identify the key the micro, meso, and macro factors that contribute to RED in criminal justice outcomes.

Micro Factors

Micro factors can be defined as the host of factors viewed and measured at an individual level (i.e., person level) that are known to be related to criminal justice data and outcomes, which are also often viewed as "risks." Whereas the discussion of risks often reinforces a deficit model and tends to pathologize individuals, including in correctional research (Starr, 2014), it is also the reality that many scholars use a risk framework in viewing incarceration rates and risk outcomes.

The first key micro factors related to disparities in the criminal justice population are race and gender. We acknowledge that these terms are socially constructed, often eclipsing individuals' intersectional identities and/or the ways that individuals identify themselves (Golash-Boza, 2016). For example, an African immigrant and a Black American would be classified as the same race in the United States' criminal justice system. We use "race" to refer to the classifications employed by the Office of Management and Budget (that sets the racial classifications for the federal government): American Indian or Alaska Native, Asian, Black or African American, Native Hawaiian or Other Pacific Islander, Multi-racial, and White; and "ethnicity" as: Hispanic/Latinx.

We use "gender" to refer to those classified as male or female within the criminal justice system, recognizing that most jurisdictions do not ask about gender identity and only about biological sex and that trans* individuals are often misclassified and that statistics often are not reflective of the trans* experience.

MASS INCARCERATION TO SMART DECARCERATION 431

Among the incarcerated population, both in jails and prisons, the lifetime incarceration rate for all men is 1 in 9, but for Black men it is 1 in 3, and for Latino men, 1 in 6 (The Sentencing Project, 2019b). Substantial racial disparities also exist among women, in that 1 in 111 White women are imprisoned in their lifetime, compared to 1 in 18 Black women and 1 in 45 Latina women (The Sentencing Project, 2019b). Overall, race in itself—particularly being Black—is a salient risk factor for incarceration due to factors beyond self-reported criminal activity (Ghadnoosh, 2015; The Sentencing Project, 2008). Race stands out as a risk factor for incarceration even when considering other related factors, such as education level and poverty (Petit & Western, 2004). And race remains a unique risk factor for recidivism even after controlling for related factors such as poverty and concentrated disadvantage (Jung et al. 2010; Wehrman, 2010).

Despite the fact that substance use rates are almost equal for African Americans/Blacks and Whites, and Whites are more likely than Blacks to sell drugs, Black individuals are twice as likely to be arrested for possession and four times as likely to be arrested for selling drugs (Rothwell, 2014). Nationally, African Americans/Blacks comprise approximately 12% of the country's population, but the Bureau of Justice Statistics reports that of the 1,561,231 individuals arrested for possessing or selling drugs in 2014, African Americans comprised 30% of the arrests (454,960; Snyder et al., 2015). Current federal data suggest that 68% of all jail inmates are dependent on or have abused alcohol or drugs (Karberg & James, 2005). Moreover, substance use disorders (SUD) are frequently associated with recidivism, particularly when drug treatment is not offered in prison or continued upon reentry or when co-occurring with mental health disorders (Huebner & Cobbnna, 2007). Research suggests that even above and beyond drug use, being Black still results in a higher likelihood of rearrest immediately following release (Link & Hamilton, 2017), which may be related to differential probation supervision and surveillance of formerly incarcerated people of color.

The latest data suggest that 56% of state prisoners, 45% of federal prisoners, and 64% of those in local jails have mental health diagnoses (James & Glaze, 2006). Yet, in regard to mental health disorders, the literature is unclear regarding if having a unique mental health disorder, separate from an SUD, is a risk factor for recidivism (Baillargeon et al., 2010). Yet still, research shows that people of color are often underdiagnosed and/or misdiagnosed. Many of the screening tools used to diagnose are also racially biased, which results in fewer people of color screening positive for mental health needs (Bronson

432 MCCARTER, QUINN, LEA, AND ABRAMS

& Berzofsky, 2017; Prims et al., 2012). The role that trauma plays in micro-level effects is also noteworthy. Studies indicate that 77% to 90% of female offenders with histories of drug dependence were more likely to report traumatic experiences of emotional, physical, and sexual abuse (Jordan et al., 1996; Langan & Pelissier, 2001; Messina et al., 2007; Messina et al., 2006), and experiences of childhood adversity have been associated with criminal behavior as adults among some men (Reavis et al., 2013). Research suggests that trauma symptoms are more pronounced in offenders because of their past childhood traumatic experiences, which are linked to adult physical and mental health problems, as well as substance abuse (Bloom et al., 2004; Chesney-Lind & Pasko, 2004; Messina et al., 2007). The high correlation between trauma and contact with the criminal justice system experienced by impoverished and minority populations in the United States points to the fact that victims and perpetrators of crime often share the same physical environment (Jäggi et al., 2016). Further, trauma exposure and trauma-associated psychopathology have been linked to greater likelihood of arrest and incarceration in adulthood among Black Americans (Jäggi et al., 2016).

Meso Factors

Criminological research focuses on the causes, types, and correlates of behavior (Baskin-Sommers et al., 2013) and social work research reiterates that persons are within their environment; thus, criminal justice research must include a perspective beyond the micro level to include meso and macro levels as well. Examinations of individuals' environments, as well as their engagement with different systems, are needed to analyze the kinds of problems associated with recidivism. The meso level consists of the community level, which is affected by both the absence of the individual while incarcerated, but also upon reentry and return home (Dodd, 2016). "Concentrated disadvantage" (Anderson, 1999; Wehrman, 2010), also referred to as "racial concentration" (Clear, 2007; Sampson & Wilson, 1995), has been noted as a structural barrier to reentry for African Americans and Latinos (Bowman et al., 2012). Specifically, these communities experience a scarcity of resources and chances to create edifying capital for themselves and their families (Hagan, 1994). Further, communities with elevated concentrated disadvantage are less likely to offer opportunities for financial or scholastic success for those involved in crime, which is reasonably low compared to those residing in more privileged communities. The structural and systemic obstacles in the settings where most restored citizens (those formerly incarcerated) live and return to are challenging for most individuals to overcome, especially people with criminal backgrounds (Wehrman, 2010). Accordingly, a considerable proportion of incarceration is the result of socioeconomic and political factors, and structural causes, including the shortcomings of communities, versus that of hardened criminal behavior alone (Baillargeon et al., 2010; Dumont et al., 2013; Lamb et al., 2005). Prisons serve as warehouses for impoverished individuals with mental illness and substance misuse problems, whereas those from wealthier communities are much more likely to obtain needed treatment versus incarceration (Baillargeon et al., 2010; Dumont et al., 2013; Lamb et al., 2005). The community also reflects the carceral state, e.g., an extension into the community based on the number of individuals on probation and parole supervision. Thus, these communities that reintegrate former prisoners returning to them are also home to several inhabitants on community supervision (Morenoff & Harding, 2014; Wacquant, 2001).

Macro Factors

Macro level policy, laws, and practice impact incarceration rates for adults, especially adults of color, and their risk of offending and re-offending. For example, habitual offender laws, also known as "Three Strikes Laws," work against individuals with arrest histories which are both a result of differential behavior and differential treatment (Chen, 2008). Mears et al., (2014) found that formerly incarcerated men are more directly impacted by societal forces such as declines in the labor market that increase recidivism than are those without incarceration histories. Recent reform efforts, such as the First Step Act, attempt to tackle the systems and structures that perpetuate racial disparities in the criminal justice system (The Urban Institute, 2019). Specific improvements include funding in-prison rehabilitation programs, continuing reentry programs, expanding early release programs, and adjusting long mandatory minimums for repeat drug offenses—collateral consequences of the War on Drugs (Moore & Elkavich, 2008; Gotsch, 2019). However, the reduction of sentences alone will not correct or decrease racial disparities and could worsen the issue for Black, Latino and Indigenous people who are disproportionately incarcerated (The Urban Institute, 2019). In addition, the act does not address issues of racial bias or the obstacles that individuals, especially Black people, experience that lead to harsh and unequal treatment (The Opportunity Agenda, n.d.).

Macro implications for adults of color certainly include profiling and high levels of police contact (Quinn et al., 2019; Weitzer & Tuch, 2005). Media coverage and disturbing statistics about policing behaviors, police brutality, and racism are pervasive throughout the country (Quinn et al., 2019). Further, increased police contact in communities of disadvantage can feed into the deeper end of the criminal justice system. Recognizing the role of racialized legislation, impact of police, systemic and structural racism, and the need to address explicit barriers omitted from the First Step Act should include racial profiling, discriminatory practices in prosecutorial decision-making, and racially biased sentencing outcomes (The Opportunity Agenda, n.d.). Changing policies and practices that promote and reinforce disparities requires intentional and deliberate social, economic, racial/ethnic, and civil strategies for reform (The Urban Institute, 2019).

Although some laws are regarded as racially neutral, they are enforced in a manner that systematically disadvantages BIPOC (Black, Indigenous, and People of Color) (Eaglin & Solomon, 2015). Criminalization of substance abuse, possession, and trafficking creates a host of social and environmental barriers that not only complicate access to substance abuse treatment on micro and meso levels, but also impede the resolution of public health and safety issues on the macro level (Bishop et al., 2017; Mennis et al., 2019). One specific outcome of this is that people with addiction do not consistently or universally receive evidence-based treatment while detained or incarcerated, and may be exposed to painful withdrawal if they received medication-assisted treatment in the community prior to their incarceration (Begun et al., 2016; Gallo, 2019). Referrals to outside treatment providers differ across facilities and are often significantly overlooked, which leads to significant numbers of substance-dependent individuals in American jails and prisons (Begun et al., 2016; Gallo, 2019). Moreover, people of color are less likely to receive treatment due to their mental health and/or substance misuse disorders being underdiagnosed and/or misdiagnosed and are more likely to be criminalized (Bronson & Berzofsky, 2017; Prims et al., 2012).

Finally, macro systems exist relative to the micro- and meso-level factors associated with individuals and communities, including racial and ethnic minority populations living in the middle of police scrutiny, financial relegation, and political exclusion (Brewer et al., 2008). Scholars identify an overreliance on social justice versus civil justice, based on current laws that

MASS INCARCERATION TO SMART DECARCERATION   435

are designed to protect those in power at the expense of the most vulnerable (Brewer et al., 2008, Coates, 2004; hooks, 1992). Moreover, some argue that civil justice has been used "to enslave, to segregate, to mete out unequal punishments for comparable crimes on the basis of race" (Brewer et al., 2008, p. 626). The role of criminal justice in policing, indicting, incarcerating, and electrocuting people of color has deep historical roots, especially among Black Americans (Brewer et al., 2008). Racial structures inform mass incarceration but have not been named or identified, and remain virtually untouched despite reform efforts and propositions (Epperson & Pettus-Davis, 2017). Smart decarceration efforts should try to target solutions that recognize and center racial and ethnic minoritized groups to reduce disparities as they are disproportionately affected by the problems of mass incarceration and recidivism.

Strategies to Redress Racial and Ethnic Disparities in the Criminal Justice System

The PSD Grand Challenge suggests that social work employs a proactive, transdisciplinary, cross-sector, and empirically driven approach to transform the criminal justice system and reduce mass incarceration in the United States (Pettus-Davis & Epperson, 2015). However, to ensure the PSD Grand Challenge is attuned to the multilevel factors that drive RED in the criminal justice system, improvements to existing policies and practices, as well as the development, implementation, and testing of innovative science-driven approaches, are necessary. In this section, we present six evidence-based policy and practice strategies that can help redress racial and ethnic disparities in the criminal justice system.

Increase the Availability of and Access to Culturally Congruent Reentry Programs

With approximately one-half of formerly incarcerated people ($N = 404,638$) returning to prison within five years of being released (Durose et al., 2014), connecting them to correctional and community-based multimodal, singular-focused, and comprehensive prisoner reentry programs is central to improving their post-release success and redressing RED in the criminal justice system (Mauer, 2011; The Sentencing Project, 2008). Yet, to date, most reentry programs are designed to reduce recidivism, and no consistent reentry model or manual exists (Johnson & Cullen, 2015, Petersilia, 2003, Visher & Travis, 2011). The 5-Key Reentry Model, a theory-based, adaptive intervention designed around five well-being facilitators (i.e., healthy thinking patterns, meaningful work trajectories, effective coping strategies, positive social engagement, and positive interpersonal relationships) that promote successful reentry (i.e., increased well-being and reduced recidivism) was therefore developed (Pettus-Davis et al., 2019). Currently being tested in four states (Florida, Kentucky, Texas, Pennsylvania), preliminary findings indicate that 5-Key study participants (N = 1,543; Black/African American = 48%) are experiencing improved employment and behavioral health-related outcomes approximately eight months post-release as compared to non-program participants (Pettus-Davis & Prost, 2020; Pettus-Davis et al., 2020). For example, in Texas, 77% of participants were employed full or part-time, 87% participated in a substance abuse support group, and 54% received psychotherapy services. Though focusing on facilitators of well-being offers a promising approach to address the economic and behavioral health impacts of incarceration for individuals of color (Ginwright, 2018), the 5-Key Reentry Model is not guided by a critical race lens, nor does it include stated equitable outcomes by race and ethnicity, which raises questions about its ability to redress RED in the criminal justice system. Moreover, existing micro-level programs aimed at reducing recidivism and underlying mechanisms for re-offending, such as substance abuse, are modest and mixed (Duwe, 2012; Lattimore et al., 2012; Lipsey & Cullen, 2007), and they have not been widely tested or proven for effectiveness with specific cultural, ethnic, or racial groups.

Given this knowledge gap and the racialized structures and processes that fuel and sustain RED in the criminal justice system, reentry programs that are culturally congruent must be developed, implemented, and tested with incarcerated and formerly incarcerated individuals of color (Oliver et al., 2004; Stepteau-Watson et al., 2014). Culturally congruent interventions are those that integrate sociocultural factors (e.g., cultural norms, values and beliefs, language, religion, etc.) and address historical, structural, and systemic barriers (e.g., racial discrimination) that hinder and support "successful reentry" for racial and ethnic groups and individuals (Abrams & Lea, 2016; Freire, 1983; Ginwright, 2018; Paris & Alim, 2017; Williams et al., 2010). Although integrating cultural and contextual factors into reentry programs can promote post-release success among minoritized individuals, rigorous, longitudinal research and evaluation studies that use a research-to-practice approach are critical to determining their effectiveness at redressing RED in the criminal justice system (Pettus-Davis & Kennedy, 2019). Community-based participatory research can also help to produce counter-hegemonic knowledge that informs racially equitable policies and practices (Atkins & Duckworth, 2019; Branom, 2012). Additionally, because recidivism as an outcome is insufficient and racially problematic (Goldstein, 2014; Petersilia, 2004), research and evaluation studies of culturally congruent reentry programs should examine promotive factors and seek to better understand subjective meanings of "successful reentry."

Increasing the availability of and access to culturally congruent reentry programs is an important strategy to redressing RED in the criminal justice system, and screening/assessment tools must also be developed and modified to ensure reentry interventions effectively respond to the risks and needs of incarcerated and formerly incarcerated people of color (The Sentencing Project, 2008). The Risk, Need, and Responsivity (RNR) Model, often used by judicial and correctional agencies to guide assessment and treatment options, suggests that targeting change factors or criminogenic needs associated with criminal behavior (e.g., employment, education) will promote successful reentry (Bonta & Andrews, 2007; Turner & Petersilia, 2012). A qualitative study with racial and ethnic minority men ($N = 295$; African American: 65%; Latino: 33%) found preliminary support for the Fresh Start Reentry Program, a strengths-based RNR intervention that provides pre- and post-reentry services based on a participants' evaluated risks, needs, strengths and goals (Hunter et al., 2016). Hunter and colleagues (2016) therefore recommend that reentry programs "move from a risk-evaluation framework towards a strengths-based assessment approach, coordinate with family and community resources, and build a flexible and responsive program" (pp. 12–13). However, because not all change factors associated with successful reentry and criminal desistance have a direct relationship with recidivism (Taxman et al., 2013), and can influence the reentry process at different times and in different stages (Durnescu, 2018), Taxman et al. (2013) suggest the RNR Model be revised to include facilitators of well-being (e.g., mental health, housing stability, substance abuse) to ensure people are assigned to reentry programs that effectively respond to their different and intersecting risks and needs. Appropriate training of professionals implementing screening

Address Collateral Consequences through Racial and Ethnic Equity-Informed Policies and Practices

Although the risk of re-offending ceils after six or seven years following a period of incarceration (Kurlycheck et al., 2006), civil and disability policies and practices that revoke and restrict individuals' legal rights and privileges (e.g., education, employment, housing, voting) because of their criminal history and/or race and ethnicity continue to perpetuate RED in the criminal justice system (Epperson & Pettus-Davis, 2016; Pinard, 2010). To address these stigmatizing and racially discriminatory policies, various stakeholders advocate for states to ban policies that deny housing and federal cash assistance and food stamp benefits for people with a criminal record (Ghandoosh, 2015). Some jurisdictions are also addressing voter disenfranchisement by registering people in jails to vote and increasing ballot access (Porter, 2020). Ban-the-Box policies and sealing or expunging criminal records are additional strategies being implemented to address employment discrimination, as well as facilitate employment and prevent rearrest and recidivism among formerly incarcerated individuals (Agan & Star, 2018; Johnson, 2020). With employment being a key predictor of successful reentry and desistence (Decker et al., 2015; Pager, 2003, 2008), several studies find that implementing strategies that remove information about job applicants' criminal histories increases their employment opportunities and outcomes and reduces repeat offending (e.g., Agan & Star, 2018; D'alessio et al., 2015; Doleac & Hansen, 2016; Henry & Jacobs, 2007; Pager, 2003, 2008). However, even when these strategies are implemented, racial differences in post-release employment outcomes can increase, especially among young, low-skilled Black and Hispanic men (Agan & Start, 2018; Doleac & Hansen, 2016; Holzer et al., 2006). Thus, to ensure these strategies are racial equity-informed, they must include components, such as implicit bias training, that can help to address stigmatizing and racially discriminatory hiring practices (Eaglin & Solomon, 2015; Ghandnoosh, 2015; Nellis, 2016; The Sentencing Project, 2008). Moreover, because ignoring a job applicant's past criminal history can pose both real and perceived risk for employers (Kurlycheck et al., 2006), which can perpetuate racially discriminatory hiring practices, Pager (2006) suggests that intermediaries, such as staffing agencies, be considered to address the concerns and needs of formerly incarcerated people and employers simultaneously.

Removing barriers to post-release success is important to redress RED in the criminal justice system, and we must also focus efforts on the front end of the carceral continuum. In particular, racial and ethnic equity-informed policy and practice strategies that limit and prevent pretrial monetary sanctions (i.e., cash bail system) for vulnerable individuals (e.g., limited financial resources) who interface with the criminal justice system are needed (Eaglin & Solomon, 2015; Ghandnoosh, 2015; Harris et al., 2017; Miller et al., 2018). For example, following the dissemination of a local report on fines and fees that show a disproportionate impact on low-income and people of color (Harvey et al., 2014), a court in Missouri issued an order to allow people with limited or no financial resources to pay their court fees in installments (Martin et al., 2018). A year following this court order, Senate Bill 5 was passed in Missouri to cap the general operating funds coming from traffic fines at 20%, prevent cities from adding monetary sanctions for those who fail to appear in court, and prohibit jail time for minor traffic offenses (Kramer, 2020; Martin et al., 2018). Missouri's steps have been encouraging, but additional research is needed to better understand the multilevel factors influencing monetary sanctions and the impact of these strategies on redressing RED in the criminal justice system.

Decriminalize Low-Level Offenses and Invest in Alternatives to Incarceration

Using the criminal justice system to incarcerate the most dangerous is commonly cited as a key strategy to reduce jail and prison populations (Eaglin & Solomon, 2015; Epperson & Pettus-Davis, 2016; Ghandnoosh, 2015; Mauer, 2011; The Sentencing Project, 2008). Policy and practice strategies that seek to prevent arrest and repeat involvement with the criminal justice system and respond to the needs of the most vulnerable are therefore important to redressing RED in the criminal justice system. Decriminalizing low-level offenses, such as traffic, marijuana possession, and public order offenses, limiting driver license suspensions, reducing failure-to-appear warrants, and referring people to pre-booking diversion programs such as Seattle's Law Enforcement Assisted Diversion (LEAD) Program, are key strategies to prevent arrest and contact with the criminal justice system, especially among low-income individuals of color (Altman, 2017; Aykanian & Lee, 2016; Baumer & Adams, 2006; Bornstein et al., 2013; Clifasefi et al., 2017; Collins et al., 2017; Crozier & Garrett, 2020; Howat et al., 2016; Natapoff, 2015; Woods, 2015). In many jurisdictions, marijuana possession and use, for example, has been reclassified as a civil offense, wherein individuals may receive a citation or be referred to social services as opposed to being arrested and receiving jail time (e.g., Illinois HB1438; New York SB657A). One study that examined the extent to which marijuana decriminalization in Philadelphia County reduced arrest rates between 2009 and 2018 found a 35% reduction in arrests for all marijuana-related crimes, 43% for possession, and 15% for sales/manufacturing (Tran et al., 2020). Although the absolute and relative reduction in arrest rates for marijuana possession was greater for African Americans than Whites, relative arrest rates for marijuana sales/manufacturing increased for African Americans. Additional planning and analyses are needed to ensure that decriminalization and diversion strategies effectively prevent arrest and criminal justice contact for people of color.

As a result of the cost savings from decriminalization and diversion efforts (e.g., Collins et al., 2019), some jurisdictions reinvest in community-based expansion of prevention and treatment services to respond to the underlying mechanisms for incarceration and recidivism (e.g., substance abuse) (Austin et al., 2013; Clement et al., 2011). Commonly referred to as problem-solving courts (e.g., drug courts, mental health courts, human trafficking courts, community courts), alternatives to incarceration programs, which can intervene at pre- or post-adjudication, are often used to prevent arrest and repeat involvement with the criminal justice system (Canada et al., 2019; Ghandnoosh, 2015; Zozula, 2018). These programs have been found to significantly reduce substance use/abuse and recidivism (Carey et al., 2012; Remple et al., 2012; Rossman et al., 2011) and modestly improve socioeconomic well-being (e.g., school enrollment, employment, annual income) and family relationship outcomes (e.g., conflict, emotional support) (Green & Rempel, 2012). Yet, their impacts on mental health outcomes are dismal (Epperson et al., 2014; Green & Rempel, 2012; Sarteschi et al., 2011; Skeem et al., 2011), and they are less effective with Black, Indigenous, and people of color (Dannerbeck et al., 2006; Finigan, 2009; Marlow et al., 2016; Marlow, 2013; especially young adult Black men (Butzin et al., 2002; Marlowe et al., 2003; Shannon et al., 2015). To address the limited effects of existing drug and mental health courts on individuals from racial and ethnic minority groups, different models that are culturally congruent are needed.

According to O'Hear (2009), drug courts are ineffective with racial and ethnic minority groups and can even exacerbate racial disparities in the criminal justice system, because they do not respond to group stigmatization or focus on (re)building trust among criminal justice professionals and communities of color. The author, therefore, proposes a restorative justice drug court model that directly responds to issues of stigma, trust, and collective problem-solving. Burns (2013) also proposes a restorative justice model for mental health courts that recognizes people with mental illness who interface with the criminal justice system as "(1) the victim of the offender's acts and (2) the offender, as a victim of circumstances" (p. 429). This victim-based restorative justice mental health court emphasizes the importance of services being delivered in community-based settings where the harm occurred, along with a dedicated restorative justice team, and mental health training for criminal justice professionals assigning alternatives to incarceration programs. In addition to restorative justice approaches, offering drug court programs and materials in racial and ethnic minority individuals' native language, such as Maricopa County's Spanish-Speaking Driving Under the Influence (DUI) court, are other examples of culturally congruent alternatives to incarceration programs (Ghandnoosh, 2015; The Sentencing Project, 2008). Other jurisdictions, such as Atlanta, Georgia, which formed a task force to transform the Atlanta City Detention Center into a center for justice and equity, are also using a cross-sector approach to repurpose jail and prison settings into community-based prevention and treatment centers that provide mental health services, reentry programs, and other legal, education, and financial services (City of Atlanta, 2020; Design Justice + Design Spaces, 2020). Nevertheless, additional testing is needed to determine the effectiveness of these programs and their impact, alongside intentional efforts to address racialized legislation and policies (O'Hear, 2009).

Repeal Racialized Criminal Justice Legislation and Policies

Over the past two decades, several policy strategies, such as the Fair Sentencing Act, the Second Chance Act, California Senate Bill 136, and the recent First Step Act have been implemented to address the deleterious effects of mandatory minimum sentencing laws and policies for drug-related offenses (e.g., Ghandnoosh, 2015; Porter, 2020; Samuels et al., 2019). As a result, the American correctional population has decreased by 18% (Kaeble & Cowig, 2018), and states such as Alaska, Connecticut, California, New Jersey, New York, and Vermont reduced their carceral populations by 30% or more (Porter, 2020). Although these policy strategies have helped to reduce jail and prison populations nationwide, RED persists and in some jurisdictions is worsening. New Jersey, for instance, has implemented several policy strategies since 2000 and reduced its carceral population by 28%, yet the state still has one of the.highest differences in incarceration rates by race (Nellis, 2016). The Urban Institute also created the *Prison Population Forecaster* to model how criminal justice reform might impact the size of state prison populations by 2025. The forecaster shows that even dramatic decreases in state carceral populations barely move the needle in addressing RED, and in some cases, increase them (Pelletier et al., 2018). Intentional efforts to address mandatory minimum sentencing laws and policies are still needed, because racial and ethnic minorities are still released under sentencing reform legislation and policies, but simultaneous efforts to reduce RED must also be implemented (Ghandnoosh, 2015; Porter, 2020).

Adopt Racial Impact Statements as a Policy Priority

One strategy to ensure that criminal justice legislation and policies are racially and ethnically informed is for racial impact statements to become a policy priority at federal, state, and local levels (Erickson, 2014; London, 2011; Mauer, 2011; Smith, 2017). According to London (2011), "A racial impact statement is a predictive report summarizing the effects that legislation may have on minority groups" (p. 212). The goal of these statements is to force lawmakers to confront the potential racial consequences of criminal sentencing policies prior to enacting new legislation and to raise public awareness for RED. Currently, four states, Connecticut, Iowa, New Jersey, and Oregon, have adopted racial impact statement requirements, and in 2019, seven states (i.e., Illinois, Kentucky, Minnesota, Mississippi, New York, Oklahoma, Vermont) introduced racial impact legislation (The Sentencing Project, 2019a). However, because this strategy is still evolving, as in the case of New Jersey, even when such mechanisms are implemented, racial disparities remain. Thus, a proactive approach to addressing racialized legislation and policies through racial impact statements is to attach them automatically to legislation, include specific data collection standards, and require legislators to take additional steps to address predicted disproportionate impact (Erickson, 2014, p. 1459; London, 2011).

Address Explicit and Implicit Bias along the Carceral Continuum

Given the inhumane treatment of people of color, especially Black men, who interface with the criminal justice system (Butler, 2018; Vansickle & Villa, 2019), and because racism is an endemic feature of American society and its institutions (Delgado & Stefancic, 2017), efforts to redress RED in the criminal justice system should intentionally work to end racial and ethnic bias along the carceral continuum. As discussed throughout this section, mandating implicit bias training for all criminal justice professionals (e.g., police officers, jurors, prosecutors, correctional officers, probation officers, social workers, judges) is central in addressing the stigmatizing and racially discriminatory structures and processes that fuel and sustain racial differences in criminal justice outcomes (McCarter et al., 2017; Nellis, 2016; The Sentencing Project, 2008). Few implicit bias trainings, however, provide empirical evidence or demonstrate sustained change. Those that do provide such evidence combine education with values assessment and skill-building and have institutional support and accountability (Devine et al., 2012; King et al., 2010). Passing laws that require transparency and accountability regarding excessive use of force in policing, such as requiring body cameras and investigating police misconduct using special prosecutors, is another strategy to address racial bias (Eaglin & Solomon, 2015; Ghandnoosh, 2015, The Sentencing Project, 2008). To ensure prosecutorial decision-making processes are fair and racially equitable, some jurisdictions might consider tools, such as the Judicial Bench Card Checklist (McCarter et al., 2017), which help to address racial bias in deciding appropriate placements for first appearances in juvenile justice and for young people in the foster care system, or the asset-driven Wise Feedback tool (Godsil & Jiang, 2018). Participatory decision-making models of community-based supervision that facilitate empowerment among formerly incarcerated people of color are also highlighted as effective strategies at addressing racially differential supervision and surveillance of formerly incarcerated people of color (Bell, 2019; Miller, 2017; Sakala & Vigne, 2019; Taxman, 2009). Lastly, considering racial and ethnic data as essential metrics and developing cross-sector and research-to-practice partnerships and task forces to help collect, share, analyze, interpret, and disseminate the findings from such data are indispensable to inform improvements to the criminal justice system that help to redress RED (Atkins & Duckworth, 2019; Branom, 2012; Eaglin & Solomon, 2015; Pettus-Davis & Kennedy, 2019).

In sum, whereas these six strategies lay an important foundation to redressing RED in the criminal justice system, it is important to understand that some individuals and groups engaged in promoting smart decarceration pursue strategies and solutions, such as sentencing reform, and some take an abolitionist approach by focusing on issues of safety, healing, and accountability solutions that exist outside the criminal justice system, and many pursue a blend of these approaches. In this section, we have offered a blend of strategies across micro, meso, and macro levels that can help to redress RED along the carceral continuum.

Conclusion/Implications

The juvenile justice system is legislatively guided by the Juvenile Justice and Delinquency Prevention Act (JJDPA), which includes four core requirements that carry federal financial penalty for noncompliance (P.L. 93-415). The fourth requirement was called Disproportionate Minority Contact (DMC) but was revised to Racial and Ethnic Disparities (RED) in Juvenile Justice in December 2018 through the reauthorization of the JJDPA (H.R. 6964). The RED requirement mandates that states reduce the overrepresentation of youth of color in their juvenile justice systems and report their progress every three years. States must participate in five sustained efforts: (1) identify whether RED exists; (2) assess the contributing factors for RED (if it exists); (3) develop an intervention to address the contributing factors; (4) evaluate the effectiveness of the RED reduction efforts; and (5) monitor the RED trends over time (OJJDP, 2012). No corresponding requirement exists in the adult justice system. Yet, justice scholars contend that parallel incentives and metrics must be established in the adult criminal justice system. Thus, it would behoove all social workers, especially those committed to smart decarceration, to learn from JDAI and include steps to redress the rife disparities within the system as they implement policy and practice change (e.g., First Step Act) (Eaglin & Solomon, 2015; Ghandnoosh, 2015; Gotsch, 2019).

A plethora of national evidence suggests that RED exists in the adult criminal justice system from stops and arrests, charges, pre-trial detentions, convictions, sentences, incarceration, and probation/parole (Eaglin & Solomon, 2015; Mauer, 2011; National Research Council, 2014), but there is no consistent mechanism designed for disaggregated data collection, analysis, and reporting. A data-driven approach to reducing RED should include more rigorous research and assessment at the law enforcement, pre-trial, prosecution, defense, judiciary, probation, jail and prison custody, and parole/reentry contact points (The Sentencing Project, 2008). "Despite substantial progress in achieving racial justice in American society over the past half century, racial disparities in the criminal justice system have persisted and worsened in many respects" (Ghandnoosh, 2015, p. 27).

Factors that contribute to RED in criminal justice include differential behaviors and differential treatment, explicit and implicit bias at the micro, meso, and macro levels, and structural racism (Ghandnoosh, 2015). Many of these factors have a cumulative effect since disparities accrue at each contact point within the justice system, starting with police contact, then arrest, and extending through probation and parole, with little regard for their amassed implications on individuals and communities (The Sentencing Project, 2008). The National Research Council (2014) contends:

> Blacks are more likely than whites to be confined awaiting trial (which increases the probability that an incarcerative sentence will be imposed), to receive incarcerative rather than community sentences, and to receive longer sentences. Racial differences found at each stage are typically modest, but their cumulative effect is significant. (pp. 93–94)

Using the extant empirical evidence, we present six strategies to redress racial and ethnic disparities in the criminal justice system: (1) increase the availability of and access to culturally congruent reentry programs; (2) address collateral consequences through racial and ethnic equity-informed policies and practices; (3) decriminalize low-level offenses and invest in alternatives to incarceration; (4) repeal racialized criminal justice legislation and policies; (5) adopt racial impact statements as a policy priority; and (6) address explicit and implicit bias along the carceral continuum.

To evaluate the effectiveness of RED strategies in the criminal justice system, the Brennan Center for Justice suggests, in *Reducing Racial and Ethnic Disparities in Jails*, that redressing RED while reducing the number of those incarcerated requires clearly defined criteria and measurable goals. However, they recognize that political will and resources to address the drivers of racial disparities will vary among jurisdictions, and thus stakeholders should identify specific drivers of racial disparities and then create measures of success (Eaglin & Solomon, 2015). Creating these measures and setting actionable goals should be conducted by a diverse group of justice stakeholders, including formerly incarcerated individuals, all with their own sense of agency as well as social responsibility, and should center the work and voices of BIPOC (McCarter et al., 2017).

In order to monitor the strategies implemented to redress RED in criminal justice over time, scholars and practitioners conclude that stakeholders need to regularly evaluate whether the recommended policy and practice changes are advancing the desired racial equity goals (Eaglin & Solomon, 2015). This consistent, periodic assessment employs quantitative and qualitative data collection and reporting to clients, stakeholders, and the public, which assures the effort's accountability and sustainability (Leiber et al., 2009).

To date, the majority of factors contributing to RED in criminal justice have been identified at the micro level with interventions focused on "fixing" the individuals (e.g., anger management initiatives, mentoring programs, substance abuse treatment, GED courses) using the punishment philosophy for lower-level offenses (punish the offenders to disincentivize re-offending), and the incapacitation philosophy for violent offenses (to protect public safety) (Mauer, 2011; Starr, 2014). The micro-level response from service providers has been to identify the racist police officers or judges or prosecutors—the bad apples—and send them to additional training (McCarter et al., 2017). These reactions, however, largely overlook the meso- and macro-level contributors to RED and have done nothing to address the root causes. Frank Baumgartner analyzed over 20 million traffic stops with demographic data (undergirding work referred to as "disproportionate risks of driving while Black") and was able to identify the officers with the highest rates of stopping and searching drivers of color (Baumgartner et al., 2018). When he removed their data from the analysis, the findings remained unchanged—suggesting that addressing individual acts of bigotry and explicit/implicit bias at the micro level will not ultimately affect outcomes, but that reducing RED requires meso- and macro-level change. We must look beyond "fixing" individuals and begin "fixing" policies, practices, and systems. It is our hope that forensic practitioners and social workers will use the new Grand Challenge to Eliminate Racism (Teasley et al., 2021), in concert with efforts to promote smart decarceration such that we finally begin to seriously redress racial and ethnic disparities in the United States' criminal justice system. "Practitioners, policymakers, academics and advocates in the criminal justice field have a duty to challenge themselves to lead a national conversation on the role of race in crime and punishment" (The Sentencing Project, 2008, p. 62).

Study Questions

1. What is racism, and how does it influence America's rate of incarceration in comparison to the rest of the world?
2. What are some ways that racial and ethnic disparities (RED) in the criminal justice system result from differential behaviors and differential treatment, explicit and implicit bias at the micro, meso, and macro levels, and structural racism?
3. What is anti-Blackness, and how does it contribute to RED in the American criminal justice system?
4. Could a strengths-based perspective replace the current risk-assessment typology that tends to pathologize individuals? Why or why not?
5. Provide an example of how historical trauma, poverty, mental health, and substance abuse influence involvement with the criminal-legal system. What are the best ways to address the impact of these cumulative factors?
6. What are the potential elements of a culturally congruent reentry program that can promote health and well-being among formerly incarcerated Black and Indigenous people of color?
7. Will marijuana policy reform (decriminalization/legalization) contribute to redressing RED in the criminal justice system? Why or why not?
8. In addition to racial impact statements, what other types of system accountability for RED reduction should be implemented as we promote smart decarceration?
9. What are some of the best ways to address explicit and implicit bias at each stage of the criminal-legal system?

References

Abrams, L. S., & Lea, C. H., III (2016). Becoming employable: An ethnographic study of life skills courses in a men's jail. *The Prison Journal, 96*(5), 667–687. https://doi.org/10.1177%2F0032885516662627.

Agan, A., & Starr, S. (2018). Ban the box, criminal records, and racial discrimination: A field experiment. *The Quarterly Journal of Economics, 133*(1), 191–235. https://doi.org/10.1093/qje/qjx028.

Alexander, M. (2010). *The New Jim Crow: Mass Incarceration in the Age of Colorblindness.* New York: The New Press.

Altman, B. (2017). Improving the indigent defense crisis through decriminalization. *Arkansas Law Review, 70,* 769.

Anderson, E. (1999). *Code of the Street: Decency, Violence, and the Moral Life of the Inner City.* New York: W.W. Norton.

Annie E. Casey Foundation. (2017). JDAI at 25: Juvenile Detention Alternatives Initiative = Insights from the annual results reports. Retrieved from AECF: https://www.aecf.org/resources/jdai-at-25/.

Atkins, L., & Duckworth, V. (2019). *Research methods for social justice and equity in education.* London: Bloomsbury Academic.

Austin, J., Cadora, E., Clear, T. R., Dansky, K., Greene, J., Gupta, V., . . . Young, M. C. (2013). *Ending mass incarceration: Charting a new justice reinvestment.* Washington, DC: The Sentencing Project. Retrieved from https://www.sentencingproject.org/wp-content/uploads/2015/12/Ending-Mass-Incarceration-Charting-a-New-Justice-Reinvestment.pdf.

Aykanian, A., & Lee, W. (2016). Social work's role in ending the criminalization of homelessness: Opportunities for action. *Social Work, 61*(2), 183–185. https://doi.org/10.1093/sw/sww011.

Baillargeon, J., Penn, J. V., Knight, K., Harzke, A. J., Baillargeon, G., & Becker, E. A. (2010). Risk of reincarceration among prisoners with co-occurring severe mental illness and substance use disorders. *Administration and Policy in Mental Health and Mental Health Services Research, 37*(4), 367–374.

Baskin-Sommers, A. R., Baskin, D. R., Sommers, I. B., & Newman, J. P. (2013). The intersectionality of sex, race, and psychopathology in predicting violent crimes. *Criminal Justice and Behavior, 40*(10), 1068–1091.

Baumer, T. L., & Adams, K. (2006). Controlling a jail population by partially closing the front door: An evaluation of a "summons in lieu of arrest" policy. *The Prison Journal, 86*(3), 386–402. https://doi.org/10.1177/0032885506291036.

Baumgartner, F. R., Epp, D. A., & Shoub, K. (2018). *Suspect citizens: What 20 million traffic stops tell us about policing and race.* New York: Cambridge University Press.

Begun, A. L., Early, T. J., & Hodge, A. (2016). Mental health and substance abuse service engagement by men and women during community reentry following incarceration. *Administration and Policy in Mental Health and Mental Health Services Research, 43*(2), 207–218.

Bell, M. C. (2019). The community in criminal justice: Subordination, consumption, resistance, and transformation. *Du Bois Review: Social Science Research on Race, 16*(1), 197–220. https://doi.org/10.1017/S1742058X1900016X.

Bishop, D., Borkowski, L., Couillard, M., Allina, A., Baruch, S., & Wood, S. (2017). Bridging the divide white paper: Pregnant women and substance use: Overview

MASS INCARCERATION TO SMART DECARCERATION 449

of research & policy in the United States. *Jacobs Institute of Women's Health*. Paper 5. https://hsrc.himmelfarb.gwu.edu/sphhs_centers_jacobs/5

Bloom, B., Owen, B., & Covington, S. (2004). Women offenders and gendered effects of public policy. *Review of Policy Research, 21*, 31–48.

Bonta, J., & Andrews, D. A. (2007). Risk-need-responsivity model for offender assessment and rehabilitation. *Rehabilitation, 6*(1), 1–22.

Bornstein, B. H., Tomkins, A. J., Neeley, E. M., Herian, M. N., & Hamm, J. A. (2013). Reducing courts' failure-to-appear rate by written reminders. *Psychology, Public Policy, and Law, 19*(1), 70. https://doi.org/10.1037/a0026293

Bowman, S. W., & Travis, R., Jr. (2012). Prisoner reentry and recidivism according to the formerly incarcerated and reentry service providers: A verbal behavior approach. *The Behavior Analyst Today, 13*(3–4), 9.

Branom, C. (2012). Community-based participatory research as a social work research and intervention approach. *Journal of Community Practice, 20*(3), 260–273. https://doi.org/10.1080/10705422.2012.699871.

Brewer, R. M., & Heitzeg, N. A. (2008). The racialization of crime and punishment: Criminal justice, color-blind racism, and the political economy of the prison industrial complex. *American Behavioral Scientist, 51*(5), 625–644.

Bronson, J., & Berzofsky, M. (2017, June). Indicators of mental health problems reported by prisoners and jail inmates, 2011–12. *Bureau of Justice Statistics*, NCJ 250612, 1–16.

Burns, J. (2013). A restorative justice model for mental health courts. *Southern California Review of Law & Social Justice, 23*, 427.

Butler, P. (2018). *Chokehold: Policing Black men*. New York: The New Press.

Butzin, C. A., Saum, C. A., & Scarpitti, F. R. (2002). Factors associated with completion of a drug treatment court diversion program. *Substance Use & Misuse, 37*(12-13), 1615–1633. https://doi.org/10.1081/JA-120014424

Canada, K., Barrenger, S., & Ray, B. (2019). Bridging mental health and criminal justice systems: A systematic review of the impact of mental health courts on individuals and communities. *Psychology, Public Policy, and Law, 25*(2), 73. https://doi.org/10.1037/law 0000194.

Carey, S. M., Mackin, J. R., & Finigan, M. W. (2012). What works? The ten key components of drug court: Research-based best practices. *Drug Court Review, 8*(1), 6–42.

Carson, A. (2020, April). *Prisoners in 2018*. (Office of Justice Programs NCJ Publication No. 253516). Retrieved from the Bureau of Justice Statistics website: https://www.bjs. gov/content/pub/pdf/p18.pdf.

Chen, E. Y. (2008). Impacts of "three strikes and you're out" on crime trends in California and throughout the United States. *Journal of Contemporary Criminal Justice, 24*(4), 345–370.

Chesney-Lind, M., & Pasko, L. (2004). *The female offenders: Girls, women, and crime* (2nd ed.). Thousand Oaks, CA: Sage.

City of Atlanta. (2020). *Mayor Keisha Lance Bottoms announces the reimagining Atlanta city detention center task force recommendations*. City of Atlanta, GA. Retrieved from https://www.atlantaga.gov/Home/Components/News/News/13378/672.

Clear, T. R. (2007). *Imprisoning Communities: How Mass Incarceration Makes Disadvantaged Neighborhoods Worse*. New York: Oxford University Press.

Clement, M., Schwarzfeld, M., & Thompson, M. (2011). *The national summit on justice reinvestment and public safety: Addressing recidivism, crime, and corrections spending*. Justice Center, the Council of State Governments. Retrieved from https://bja.ojp.gov/sites/g/files/xyckuh186/files/Publications/CSG_JusticeReinvestmentSummitReport.pdf.

Clifasefi, S. L., Lonczak, H. S., & Collins, S. E. (2017). Seattle's Law Enforcement Assisted Diversion (LEAD) program: Within-subjects changes on housing, employment, and income/benefits outcomes and associations with recidivism. *Crime & Delinquency, 63*(4), 429–445. https://doi.org/10.1177/0011128716687550.

Coates, R. (2004). If a tree falls in the wilderness: Reparations, academic silences, and social justice. *Social Forces, 83*(2), 841–864.

Collins, S. E., Lonczak, H. S., & Clifasefi, S. L. (2017). Seattle's Law Enforcement Assisted Diversion (LEAD): Program effects on recidivism outcomes. *Evaluation and Program Planning, 64*, 49–56. https://doi.org/10.1016/j.evalprogplan.2017.05.008.

Collins, S. E., Lonczak, H. S., & Clifasefi, S. L. (2019). Seattle's Law Enforcement Assisted Diversion (LEAD): Program effects on criminal justice and legal system utilization and costs. *Journal of Experimental Criminology, 15*(2), 201–211. https://doi.org/10.1007/s11292-019-09352-7.

Crozier, W. E., & Garrett, B. L. (2019). Driven to failure: An empirical analysis of driver's license suspension in North Carolina. *Duke Law Journal, 69*, 1585.

D'alessio, S. J., Stolzenberg, L., & Flexon, J. L. (2015). The effect of Hawaii's ban the box law on repeat offending. *American Journal of Criminal Justice, 40*(2), 336–352. 10.1007/s12103-014-9251-9.

Dannerbeck, A., Harris, G., Sundet, P., & Lloyd, K. (2006). Understanding and responding to racial differences in drug court outcomes. *Journal of Ethnicity in Substance Abuse, 5*(2), 1–22. https://www.tandfonline.com/doi/abs/10.1300/J233v05n02_01.

Decker, S. H., Ortiz, N., Spohn, C., & Hedberg, E. (2015). Criminal stigma, race, and ethnicity: The consequences of imprisonment for employment. *Journal of Criminal Justice, 43*(2), 108–121. https://doi.org/10.1016/j.jcrimjus.2015.02.002.

Delgado, R., & Stefancic, J. (2017). *Critical race theory: An introduction* (Vol. 20). New York: New York University Press.

Design Justice + Design Spaces. (2020). Radically reimagining Atlanta's city jail. *Medium.* Retrieved from https://medium.com/@designingjustice/radically-reimagining-atlan tas-justice-architecture-71aa643a49ca.

Devine, P. G., Forscher, P. S., Austin, A. J., & Cox, W. T. (2012). Long-term reduction in implicit race bias: A prejudice habit-breaking intervention. *Journal of Experimental Social Psychology, 48*(6), 1267–1278. doi: 10.1016/j.jesp.2012.06.003.

Dodd, M. A. (2016). Perceptions of factors affecting recidivism and recovery (Masters thesis). California State University – Fresno.

Doleac, J. L., & Hansen, B. (2016). *Does "ban the box" help or hurt low-skilled workers? Statistical discrimination and employment outcomes when criminal histories are hidden (No. w22469).* National Bureau of Economic Research. Retrieved from https://www.nber.org/papers/w22469.

Dumont, D. M., Allen, S. A., Brockmann, B. W., Alexander, N. E., & Rich, J. D. (2013). Incarceration, community health, and racial disparities. *Journal of Health Care for the Poor and Underserved, 24*(1), 78–88.

Durnescu, I. (2018). The five stages of prisoner reentry: Toward a process theory. *International Journal of Offender Therapy and Comparative Criminology, 62*(8), 2195–2215. https://doi.org/10.1177/0306624X17706889.

Durose, M. R., Cooper, A. D., & Snyder, H. N. (2014). *Recidivism of prisoners released in 30 states in 2005: Patterns from 2005 to 2010 (Vol. 28).* Washington, DC: U.S. Department of Justice, Office of Justice Programs, Bureau of Justice Statistics. Retrieved from https://intranet.americansforthearts.org/sites/default/files/recidivism0510.pdf.

MASS INCARCERATION TO SMART DECARCERATION 451

Duwe, G. (2012). Evaluating the Minnesota comprehensive offender reentry plan (MCORP): Results from a randomized experiment. *Justice Quarterly, 29*(3), 347–383. https://doi.org/10.1080/07418825.2011.555414.

Eaglin, J. M., & Solomon, D. (2015). *Reducing racial and ethnic disparities in jails: Recommendations for local practice.* Brennan Center for Justice. Retrieved from https://www.brennancenter.org/sites/default/files/201908/Report_Racial%20Disparit ies%20Report%20062515.pdf.

Eperson, M. W., & Pettus-Davis, C. (Eds.) (2017). *Smart decarceration: Achieving criminal justice transformation in the 21st century.* Oxford University Press.

Epperson, M., & Pettus-Davis, C. (2016). *Policy recommendations for meeting the grand challenge to promote smart decarceration (Grand Challenges for Social Work Initiative Policy Brief No. 9).* Cleveland, OH: American Academy of Social Work & Social Welfare. doi: 10, K7DJ5F50. Retrieved from: https://openscholarship.wustl.edu/cgi/ viewcontent.cgi?article=1792&context=csd_research.

Epperson, M. W., Wolff, N., Morgan, R. D., Fisher, W. H., Frueh, B. C., & Huening, J. (2014). Envisioning the next generation of behavioral health and criminal justice interventions. *International Journal of Law and Psychiatry, 37*(5), 427–438. https://doi. org/10.1016/j.ijlp.2014.02.015.

Erickson, J. (2014). Racial impact statements: Considering the consequences of racial disproportionalities in the criminal justice system. *Washington Law Review, 89*, 1425.

Finigan, M.W. (2009). Understanding racial disparities in drug courts. *Drug Court Review, 7*(2), 135–142.

Freire, P. (1983). *Pedagogy of the oppressed.* New York: Continuum.

Gallo, A. (2019). Legal and behavioral health service responses to substance abuse and addiction in the United States (Doctoral dissertation, University of Pittsburgh).

Ghandnoosh, N. (2015). *Black lives matter: Eliminating racial inequality in the criminal justice system.* Washington, DC: The Sentencing Project. Retrieved from https://senten cingproject.org/wp-content/uploads/2015/11/Black-Lives-Matter.pdf.

Ginwright, S. (2018, May 31). The future of healing: Shifting from trauma informed care to healing centered engagement. Kinship Carers Victoria, *Occasional Paper, 25.* Retrieved from: https://kinshipcarersvictoria.org/wp-content/uploads/2018/08/OP-Ginwright-S-2018-Future-of-healing-care.pdf

Godsil, R. D., & Jiang, H. C. (2018). Prosecuting fairly: Addressing the challenges of implicit bias, racial anxiety, and stereotype threat. *CDAA Prosecutor's Brief, 40*(2), 142–157. Retrieved from https://mlac.org/wp-content/uploads/2019/07/Godsil-2018-Pros ecuting-Fairly.pdf.

Golash-Boza, T. (2016). A critical and comprehensive sociological theory of race and racism. *Sociology of Race and Ethnicity, 2*(2), 129–141. https://doi.org/10.1177/23326 49216632242.

Goldstein, D. (2014). The misleading math of recidivism. The Marshall Project. Retrieved from: https://www.themarshallproject.org/2014/12/04/the-misleading-math-of-rec idivism.

Gotsch, K. (2019, December 17). *One year after the First Step Act: Mixed outcomes.* Washington, DC: The Sentencing Project. Retrieved from https://www.sentencingproj ect.org/publications/one-year-after-the-first-step-act/.

Green, M., & Rempel, M. (2012). Beyond crime and drug use: Do adult drug courts produce other psychosocial benefits? *Journal of Drug Issues, 42*(2), 156–177. https://doi. org/10.1177/0022042612446592.

452 MCCARTER, QUINN, LEA, AND ABRAMS

Hagan, J. (1994). *Crime and disrepute*. Thousand Oaks, CA: Pine Forge Press.

Harris, A., Huebner, B., Martin, K., Pattillo, M., Pettit, B., Shannon, S., . . . Fernandes, A. (2017). *Monetary sanctions in the criminal justice system*. Houston, TX: Laura and John Arnold Foundation. Retrieved from http://www.monetarysanctions.org/wp-content/uploads/2017/04/Monetary-Sanctions-Legal-Review-Final.pdf.

Harvey, T., McAnnar, J., Voss, M. J., Conn, M., Janda, S., & Keskey, S. (2014). *ArchCity defenders: Municipal courts white paper*. St. Louis, MO: ArchCity Defenders. http://www.archcitydefenders.org/wp-content/uploads/2014/11/ArchCity-Defenders-Municipal-Courts-Whitepaper.pdf.

Henry, J. S., & Jacobs, J. B. (2007). Ban the box to promote ex-offender employment. *Criminology & Public Policy*, 6, 755.

Holzer, H. J., Raphael, S., & Stoll, M. A. (2006). Perceived criminality, criminal background checks, and the racial hiring practices of employers. *The Journal of Law and Economics*, 49(2), 451–480.

hooks, b. (1992). *Black looks*. Boston: South End.

Howat, H., Forsyth, C. J., Biggar, R., & Howat, S. (2016). Improving court-appearance rates through court-date reminder phone calls. *Criminal Justice Studies*, 29(1), 77–87. https://doi.org/10.1080/1478601X.2015.1121875.

Huebner, B. M., & Cobbina, J. (2007). The effect of drug use, drug treatment participation, and treatment completion on probationer recidivism. *Journal of Drug Issues*, 37(3), 619–641. https://doi.org/10.1177/002204260703700307.

Hunter, B. A., Lanza, A. S., Lawlor, M., Dyson, W., & Gordon, D. M. (2016). A strengths-based approach to prisoner reentry: The fresh start prisoner reentry program. *International Journal of Offender Therapy and Comparative Criminology*, 60(11), 1298–1314. https://doi.org/10.1177/0306624X15576501.

Jäggi, L. J., Mezuk, B., Watkins, D. C., & Jackson, J. S. (2016). The relationship between trauma, arrest, and incarceration history among black Americans: Findings from the National Survey of American Life. *Society and Mental Health*, 6(3), 187–206.

James, D. J., & Glaze, L. E. (2006, September). *Mental Health Problems of Prison and Jail Inmates* (Office of Justice Programs NCJ Publication No. 213600). Retrieved from the Bureau of Justice Statistics website: https://www.bjs.gov/content/pub/pdf/mhppji.pdf.

Johnson, K. (2020). One mistake does not define you: Why first-time felony drug convictions should be automatically expunged after five years. *Mitchell Hamline Law Journal of Public Policy and Practice*, 41(2), 2. Retrieved from https://open.mitchell hamline.edu/cgi/viewcontent.cgi?article=1029&context=policypractice.

Jonson, C. L., & Cullen, F. T. (2015). Prisoner reentry programs. *Crime and Justice*, 44(1), 517–575.

Jordan, B. K., Schlenger, W. E., Fairbank, J. A., & Caddell, J. M. (1996). Prevalence of psychiatric disorders among incarcerated women. II. Convicted felons entering prison. *Archives of General Psychiatry*, 53, 513–519.

Jung, H., Spjeldnes, S., & Yamatani, H. (2010). Recidivism and survival time: Racial disparity among jail ex-inmates. *Social Work Research*, 34(3), 181–189.

Kaeble, D., & Cowhig, M. (2018, April). *Correctional populations in the United States, 2016* (Office of Justice Programs NCJ Publication No. 251211). Retrieved from the Bureau of Justice Statistics website: https://www.bjs.gov/content/pub/pdf/cpus16.pdf.

Karberg, J. C., & James, D. J. (2005, July). *Substance dependence, abuse, and treatment of jail inmates, 2002* (Office of Justice Programs NCJ Publication No. 209588). Retrieved from the Bureau of Justice Statistics website: https://www.bjs.gov/content/pub/pdf/sdatji02.pdf.

King, E., Gulick, L., & Avery, D. (2010). The divide between diversity training and diversity education: Integrating best practices. *Journal of Management Education*, 34(6), 891–906. doi: 10.1177/1052562909348767.

Kramer, D. (2020). Bail reform: A possible solution to Missouri's broken public defender system? *Missouri Law Review*, 85(1), 12.

Kurlychek, M. C., Brame, R., & Bushway, S. D. (2006). Scarlet letters and recidivism: Does an old criminal record predict future offending? *Criminology & Public Policy*, 5(3), 483–504. https://doi.org/10.1111/j.1745-9133.2006.00397.x.

Lamb, H. R., & Weinberger, L. E. (2005). The shift of psychiatric inpatient care from hospitals to jails and prisons. *Journal of the American Academy of Psychiatry Law*, 33(4), 529–534.

Langan, N., & Pelissier, B. (2001). Gender differences among prisoners in drug treatment. *Journal of Substance Abuse*, 13, 291–301.

Lattimore, P. K., Barrick, K., Cowell, A., Dawes, D., Steffey, D., Tueller, S., & Visher, C. A. (2012). *Prisoner reentry services: What worked for SVORI evaluation participants*. Washington, DC: National Institute of Justice. Retrieved from https://www.ncjrs.gov/pdffiles1/nij/grants/238214.pdf.

Leiber, M. J., Richetelli, D. M., & Feyerherm, W. (2009). Assessment. In *Disproportionate minority contact technical assistance manual* (4th Ed., pp. 2.1–41). Washington, DC: Office of Juvenile Justice and Delinquency Prevention, U.S. Department of Justice.

Link, N. W., & Hamilton, L. K. (2017). The reciprocal lagged effects of substance use and recidivism in a prisoner reentry context. *Health & Justice*, 5(1), 8.

Lipsey, M. W., & Cullen, F. T. (2007). The effectiveness of correctional rehabilitation: A review of systematic reviews. *Annual Review of Law and Social Science*, 3, 297–320.

London, C. (2011). Racial impact statements: A proactive approach to addressing racial disparities in prison populations. *Law & Inequality*, 29, 211.

Marlowe, D. B. (2013). Achieving racial and ethnic fairness in drug courts. *Court Review*, 49(1), 40–47.

Marlowe, D. B., Hardin, C. D., & Fox, C. L. (2016, June). *Painting the current picture: A national report on drug courts and other problem solving courts in the United States*. Alexandria, VA: National Drug Court Institute. Retrieved from http://www.ndcrc.org/sites/default/files/pcp_final_version.pdf.

Marlowe, D. B., Patapis, N. S., & DeMatteo, D. S. (2003). Amenability to treatment of drug offenders. *Federal Probation*, 67, 40–46.

Martin, K. D., Sykes, B. L., Shannon, S., Edwards, F., & Harris, A. (2018). Monetary sanctions: Legal financial obligations in US systems of justice. *Annual Review of Criminology*, 1, 471–495.

McCarter, S. A. (2011). Disproportionate minority contact in the American juvenile justice system: Where are we after 20 years, a philosophy shift, and three amendments? *Journal of Forensic Social Work*, 1(1), 96–107. doi: 10/1080/1936928X.2011.541217.

McCarter, S. A., Chinn-Gary, E., Trosch, L. A., Jr., Toure, A., Alsaeedi, A., & Harrington, J. (2017). Bringing racial justice to the courtroom and community: Race Matters for Juvenile Justice and the Charlotte Model. *Washington and Lee Law Review*, 73(2), 641–686. https://scholarlycommons.law.wlu.edu/wlulr-online/vol73/iss2/6/.

Mears, D. P., Wang, X., & Bales, W. D. (2014). Does a rising tide lift all boats? Labor market changes and their effects on the recidivism of released prisoners. *Justice Quarterly*, 31(5), 822–851.

Mennis, J., Stahler, G. J., Abou El Magd, S., & Baron, D. A. (2019). How long does it take to complete outpatient substance use disorder treatment? Disparities among Blacks, Hispanics, and Whites in the US. *Addictive Behaviors*, 93, 158–165.

Messina, N., Burdon, W., Hagopian, G., & Prendergast, M. (2006). Predictors of prison TC treatment outcomes: A comparison of men and women participants. *American Journal of Drug and Alcohol Abuse, 32,* 7–28.

Messina, N., Grella, C., Burdon, W., & Prendergast, M. (2007). Childhood adverse events and current traumatic distress: A comparison of men and women drug-dependent prisoners. *Criminal Justice and Behavior, 34*(11), 1385–1401.

Miller, R. 2017. Rethinking reentry: Reimagining community corrections in an age of mass supervision. In M. Epperson and C.A. Pettus (Eds.), *Smart decarceration: Achieving criminal justice transformation in the 21st century* (pp. 101–114). Oxford: Oxford University Press.

Miller, R. J., Kern, L. J., & Williams, A. (2018). The front end of the carceral state: Police stops, court fines, and the racialization of due process. *Social Service Review, 92*(2), 290–303.

Moore, L. D., & Elkavich, A. (2008). Who's using and who's doing time: Incarceration, the War on Drugs, and public health. *American Journal of Public Health, 98,* 782–786. doi: 10.2105/AJPH.2007.126284.

Morenoff, J. D., & Harding, D. J. (2014). Incarceration, prisoner reentry, and communities. *Annual Review of Sociology, 40,* 411–429.

Natapoff, A. (2015). Misdemeanor decriminalization. *Vanderbilt Law Review, 68,* 1055.

National Research Council (2014). *The growth of incarceration in the United States: Exploring causes and consequences, 57.* Washington, DC: The National Academies Press. Available at: https://nap.nationalacademies.org/catalog/18613/the-growth-of-incarceration-in-the-united-states-exploring-causes

Nellis, A. (2016). *The color of justice: Racial and ethnic disparity in state prisons.* Washington, DC: The Sentencing Project. Retrieved from https://www.sentencingproj ect.org/wp-content/uploads/2016/06/The-Color-of-Justice-Racial-and-Ethnic-Dispar ity-in-State-Prisons.pdf.

O'Hear, M. M. (2009). Rethinking drug courts: Restorative justice as a response to racial injustice. *Stanford Law & Policy Review, 20,* 463.

Office of Juvenile Justice and Delinquency Prevention (OJJDP) (2012). Disproportionate minority contact. Retrieved from the OJJDP website: https://ojjdp.ojp.gov/sites/g/files/xyckuh176/files/pubs/239457.pdf.

Oliver, W., Willliams, O. J., Hairston, C. F., & Crowder, L. (2004). Prisoner reentry and intimate partner violence in the African American community: The case for culturally competent interventions. *Journal of the Institute of Justice and International Studies, 4,* 147.

Pager, D. (2003). The mark of a criminal record. *American Journal of Sociology, 108*(5), 937–975. https://doi.org/10.1086/374403.

Pager, D. (2006). Evidence-based policy for successful prisoner reentry. *Criminology & Public Policy, 5*(3), 505–514. https://doi.org/10.1111/j.1745-9133.2006.00391.x.

Pager, D. (2008). *Marked: Race, crime, and finding work in an era of mass incarceration.* Chicago: University of Chicago Press.

Paris, D., & Alim, H. S. (2017). *Culturally sustaining pedagogies: Teaching and learning for justice in a changing world.* New York: Teachers College Press.

Pelletier, E., Peterson, B., King, R., & Sakala, L. (2018). *The prison population forecaster.* Washington, DC: Urban Institute. Retrieved from: https://apps.urban.org/features/pri son-population-forecaster/.

Petersilia, J. (2003). *When prisoners come home: Parole and prisoner reentry.* Oxford: Oxford University Press.

MASS INCARCERATION TO SMART DECARCERATION 455

Petersilia, J. (2004). What works in prisoner reentry: Reviewing and questioning the evidence. *Federal Probation, 68*, 4.

Pettit, B., & Western, B. (2004). mass imprisonment and the life course: Race and class inequality in U.S. incarceration. *American Sociological Review, 69*(2), 151–169. https://doi.org/10.1177/000312240406900201.

Pettus-Davis, C., & Epperson, M. W. (2015). *From mass incarceration to smart decarceration.* Center for Social Development. *CSD Working Papers* (14-312014). Retrieved from https://aaswsw.org/wp-content/uploads/2015/03/From-Mass-Incarceration-to-Decarceration-3.24.15.pdf.

Pettus-Davis, C., & Kennedy, S. (2019). *Accelerating science using the research-to practice feedback loop: Early findings from a multi-state trial.* Florida State University Institute for Justice Research and Development. Retrieved from https://ijrd.csw.fsu.edu/sites/g/files/upcbnu1766/files/media/images/publication_pdfs/5key_QR3_Feedback_Loop_FINAL.pdf.

Pettus-Davis, C., & Prost, S. (2020). Early lessons from the multistate study of the 5-key model for reentry. *The Journal of the American Probation and Parole Association, 44*(1), 18–31. Retrieved from https://www.appa-net.org/eweb/docs/APPA/pubs/Perspectives/Perspectives_V44_N1/index.html#page=18.

Pettus-Davis, C., Renn, T., & Veeh, C. (2020). *Employment and behavioral health: 5-key model preliminary results for policy stakeholders.* Institute for Justice Research and Development. Retrieved from https://ijrd.csw.fsu.edu/sites/g/files/upcbnu1766/files/media/images/publication_pdfs/5Key_Preliminary_results_for_policy_stakeholders.pdf.

Pettus-Davis, C., Renn, T., Veeh, C. A., & Eikenberry, J. (2019). Intervention development study of the five-key model for reentry: An evidence-driven prisoner reentry intervention. *Journal of Offender Rehabilitation, 58*(7), 614–643.

Pinard, M. (2010). Collateral consequences of criminal convictions: Confronting issues of race and dignity. *NYU Law Review, 85*, 457.

Porter, N. D. (2020). *Top trends in state criminal justice reform, 2019.* Washington, DC: The Sentencing Project. Retrieved from https://www.sentencingproject.org/publications/top-trends-in-state-criminal-justice-reform-2019/.

Prins, S. J., Osher, F. C., Steadman, H. J., Robbins, P. C., & Case, B. (2012). Exploring racial disparities in the brief jail mental health screen. *Criminal Justice and Behavior, 39*(5), 635–645.

Quinn, C. R., Hope, E. C., & Cryer-Coupet, Q. R. (2019) Neighborhood cohesion and procedural justice in policing among Black adults: The moderating role of cultural race-related stress. *Journal of Community Psychology, 48*, 124–141. https://doi.org/10.1002/jcop.22251.

Reavis, J. A., Looman, J., Franco, K. A., & Rojas, B. (2013). Adverse childhood experiences and adult criminality: How long must we live before we possess our own lives? *The Permanente Journal, 17*(2), 44.

Rempel, M., Green, M., & Kralstein, D. (2012). The impact of adult drug courts on crime and incarceration: Findings from a multi-site quasi-experimental design. *Journal of Experimental Criminology, 8*(2), 165–192. doi: 10.1007/s11292-012-9143-2.

Rossman, S. B., Roman, J. K., Zweig, J. M., Rempel, M., & Lindquist, C. H. (2011). *The multi-site adult drug court evaluation: The impact of drug courts.* Washington, DC: Urban Institute. Retrieved from https://www.urban.org/sites/default/files/alfresco/publication-pdfs/412357-The-Multi-site-Adult-Drug-Court-Evaluation-The-Impact-of-Drug-Courts-Pre-Production-.PDF.

456   MCCARTER, QUINN, LEA, AND ABRAMS

Rothwell, J. (2014, September 20). *How the War on Drugs damages Black social mobility.* Brookings Institution. http:// www.brookings.edu/blogs/social-mobility-memos/posts/2014/09/30-war-on-drugs-black-social-mobility-rothwell.

Sakala, L., & La Vigne, N. (2019). Community-driven models for safety and justice. *Du Bois Review: Social Science Research on Race, 16*(1), 253–266.

Sampson, R. J., & Wilson, W. J. (1995). Towards a theory of race, crime, and urban inequality. In J. Hagan and R.D. Peterson (Eds.), *Crime and inequality* (pp. 37–56). Stanford, CA: Stanford University Press.

Samuels, J., La Vigne, N., & Thomson, C. (2019). Next steps in federal corrections reform: Implementing and building on the first step act. *Federal Sentencing Reporter, 32*(2), 92–101.

Sarteschi, C. M., Vaughn, M. G., & Kim, K. (2011). Assessing the effectiveness of mental health courts: A quantitative review. *Journal of Criminal Justice, 39*(1), 12–20. https://doi.org/10.1016/j.jcrimjus.2010.11.003.

Sawyer, W., & Wagner, P. (2020, March 24). Mass incarceration: The whole pie 2020. Prison Policy Initiative. https://www.prisonpolicy.org/reports/pie2020.html.

Shannon, L. M., Jackson, A., Newell, J., Perkins, E., & Neal, C. (2015). Examining factors associated with treatment completion in a community-based program for individuals with criminal justice involvement. *Addiction Science & Clinical Practice, 10*(Suppl 1), A60–A61. https://doi.org/10.1186/1940-0640-10-S1-A60.

Skeem, J. L., Manchak, S., & Peterson, J. K. (2011). Correctional policy for offenders with mental illness: Creating a new paradigm for recidivism reduction. *Law and Human Behavior, 35*(2), 110–126. doi: 10.1007/s10979-010-9223-7.

Smith, J. M. (2017). Racial impact statements, knowledge-based criminology, and resisting color blindness. *Race and Justice, 7*(4), 374–397. https://doi.org/10.1177/2153368716661223.

Snyder, H. N., Cooper, A. D., & Mulako-Wangota, J. (2015). Arrests by race and age in the U.S., 2014. Generated using the Arrest Data Analysis Tool at www.bjs.gov. https://www.bjs.gov/index.cfm?ty=datool&surl=/arrests/index.cfm# (06/29/20).

Starr, S. B. (2014). Evidence-based sentencing and the scientific rationalization of discrimination. *Stanford Law Review, 66*, 803.

Stepteau-Watson, D., Watson, J., & Lawrence, S. K. (2014). Young African American males in reentry: An Afrocentric cultural approach. *Journal of Human Behavior in the Social Environment, 24*(6), 658–665. https://doi.org/10.1080/10911359.2014.922801.

Taxman, F. (2009). Effective community punishments in the United States: probation: Faye Taxman outlines a radical "shared decision" model of probation that operates to empower offenders. *Criminal Justice Matters, 75*(1), 42–44. https://doi.org/10.1080/09627250802699830.

Taxman, F. S., Pattavina, A., Caudy, M. S., Byrne, J., & Durso, J. (2013). The empirical basis for the RNR model with an updated RNR conceptual framework. In F. S. Taxman & A. Pattavina (Eds.), *Simulation strategies to reduce recidivism* (pp. 73–111). New York: Springer.

Teasley, M., McCarter, S., Woo, B., Conner, L. R., Spencer, M., & Green, T. (2021). Eliminate racism (Grand Challenges for Social Work Initiative Working Paper No. 26). Baltimore, MD: Grand Challenges for Social Work. https://grandchallengesforsocialwork.org/wp-content/uploads/2021/05/Eliminate-Racism-Concept-Paper.pdf.

MASS INCARCERATION TO SMART DECARCERATION 457

The Opportunity Agenda (n.d.). *Talking about race and the First Step Act.* Retrieved from https://www.opportunityagenda.org/explore/resources-publications/talking-about-race-and-first-step-act.

The Sentencing Project. (2008). *Reducing racial disparities in the criminal justice system: A manual for practitioners and policymakers.* Washington, DC: The Sentencing Project. Retrieved from: https://www.sentencingproject.org/wp-content/uploads/2016/01/Reducing-Racial-Disparity-in-the-Criminal-Justice-System-A-Manual-for-Practitioners-and-Policymakers.pdf.

The Sentencing Project (2013). *Report of the Sentencing Project to the United Nations Human Rights Committee: Regarding racial disparities in the United States criminal justice system.* Washington, DC: The Sentencing Project. Retrieved from: https://www.sentencingproject.org/publications/un-report-on-racial-disparities/.

The Sentencing Project (2019a). *State advocacy news: Expanding racial impact statements.* Washington, DC: The Sentencing Project. Retrieved from https://www.sentencingproject.org/news/7002/.

The Sentencing Project (2019b). *Trends in U.S. corrections.* Washington, DC: The Sentencing Project. Retrieved from: https://sentencingproject.org/wp-content/uploads/2016/01/Trends-in-US-Corrections.pdf.

The Urban Institute (2019). Reducing mass incarceration is not enough to end racial disparities. Retrieved from https://www.urban.org/evidence-and-ideas-change/reducing-mass-incarceration-is-not-enough-to-end-racial-disparities.

Tran, N. K., Goldstein, N. D., Purtle, J., Massey, P. M., Lankenau, S. E., Suder, J. S., & Tabb, L. P. (2020). The heterogeneous effect of marijuana decriminalization policy on arrest rates in Philadelphia, Pennsylvania, 2009–2018. *Drug and Alcohol Dependence, 212*(108058). https://doi.org/10.1016/j.drugalcdep.2020.108058.

Turner, S., & Petersilia, J. (2012). Putting science to work: How the principles of risk, need, and responsivity apply to reentry. In J. A. Dvoskin (Ed.), *Using social science to reduce violent offending* (pp. 179–198). Oxford: Oxford University Press.

Vansickle, A., & Villa, M. (2019). California's jails are so bad some inmates beg to go to prison instead. *Los Angeles Times.* Retrieved from https://www.latimes.com/local/lanow/la-me-california-jails-inmates-20190523-story.html.

Visher, C. A., & Travis, J. (2011). Life on the outside: Returning home after incarceration. *The Prison Journal, 91*(Suppl 3), 102S–119S. https://doi.org/10.1177/0032885511415228.

Wacquant, L. (2001). Deadly symbiosis: When ghetto and prison meet and mesh. *Punishment & Society, 3*(1), 95–133.

Wehrman, M. M. (2010). Race, concentrated disadvantage, and recidivism: A test of interaction effects. *Journal of Criminal Justice, 38*(4), 538–544.

Weitzer, R., & Tuch, S. A. (2005). Racially biased policing: Determinants of citizen perceptions. *Social Forces, 83*(3), 1009–1030.

Wildeman, C. (2018). Mass incarceration. *Oxford Bibliographies.* doi: 10.1093/OBO/9780195396607-0033.

Williams, J. K., Wyatt, G. E., & Wingood, G. (2010). The four Cs of HIV prevention with African Americans: Crisis, condoms, culture, and community. *Current HIV/AIDS Reports, 7*(4), 185–193. doi: 10.1007/s11904-010-0058-0.

Woods, J. B. (2015). Decriminalization, police authority, and routine traffic stops. *UCLA Law Review, 62,* 672.

World Prison Brief. (2020). *World Prison Brief data.* Retrieved from the World Prison Brief website: https://www.prisonstudies.org/highest-to-lowest/prison_population_rate?field_region_taxonomy_tid=All.

Zeng, Z. (2020). *Annual survey of jails (AJS).* Bureau of Justice Statistics. U.S. Department of Justice. https://bjs.ojp.gov/data-collection/annual-survey-jails-asj.

Zozula, C. (2018). Courting the community: Organizational flexibility and community courts. *Criminology & Criminal Justice, 18*(2), 226–244. https://doi.org/10.1177/1748895817709864.

18

Reducing Racialized Barriers to School Success for All Children and Youth

Terence Dwight Fitzgerald, Martell L. Teasley, Tasha Seneca Keyes, and Schnavia Hatcher

If we are kind, the children of others will become our children.
—Maulana Karenga

In the United States, exclusionary discipline practices in schools in the forms of suspension and expulsion have become a major impediment to school success for many children and youth. Studies have indicated that almost one-third of all students in the United States may experience school exclusion (in the form of suspension or expulsion) at some point at their school years (Fabelo et al., 2011). Racial disproportionality is defined as "the difference between a racial group's representation in a service population and its representation in the general population, often signals unfairness or non-responsiveness to the needs of a minority racial group" (Teasley et al., 2016, p. 2). Data from the U.S. Department of Education (2016) demonstrates that rates of school suspension have increased dramatically for all grade levels, with more than 3.4 million students experiencing in-school suspensions and 3.5 million experiencing out-of-school suspension. School suspension refers to a disciplinary action involving the short-term removal of a student from school (Skiba et al., 2009). School expulsion refers to the removal of a student from school for a longer period of time and may involve decision-making by school superintendents or school boards (Skiba & Sprague, 2008).

Terence Dwight Fitzgerald, Martell L. Teasley, Tasha Seneca Keyes, and Schnavia Hatcher, *Reducing Racialized Barriers to School Success for All Children and Youth* In: *Social Work and the Grand Challenge to Eliminate Racism*. Edited by: Martell L. Teasley, Michael S. Spencer, and Melissa Bartholomew, Oxford University Press.
© Oxford University Press 2023. DOI: 10.1093/oso/9780197674949.003.0018

Race, Gender, and Disproportionality in School Suspension and Expulsion

In the 1980s and 90s there was exaggerated and speculated concern, at the federal, state, and local levels, of increased violence and drug usage in U.S. schools leading to "zero tolerance" legislation that affected students as early as pre school (Gilliam, 2005; Skiba, 2014). Said legislation affected students as early as pre-kindergarten. Malik (2005) estimated that 50,000 preschoolers were suspended at least once and 17,000 were removed from the school setting. This occurrence has been coined the "discipline gap" by education experts and scholars (Gregory, Skiba, & Noguera, 2010). In relations to demographics, Black and Latinx students were the recipients of discipline more often than their White counterparts were. Further, a majority of these were males of color who were also involved in school-related arrests and/or referrals to local law enforcement agencies.

Studies indicated that teacher bias, discriminatory practices, and a lack of cross-cultural understanding are associated with the disproportionality of school suspension and expulsion for racial and ethnic minorities. Race is a salient factor, as minority students are suspended and expelled more often than White students (Gregory & Weinstein, 2008; Nicholes, 2004; Gottfredson & Gottfredson, 2001; Losen & Martinez, 2013). For example, in the 2009–2010 school year, rates of suspension doubled for African American (11.8% to 24.3%) and Latinx (6.1% to 12.0%) students, whereas rates did not increase significantly for White students (6.0% to 7.1%) (Losen & Martinez, 2013). African American students from K–12 are two to three times more likely to be suspended than White students (Meek & Gilliam, 2016; Wallace et al., 2008; Kinsler, 2011).

There is also inequity existing within school corporal punishment, ("the use of physical force with the intention of causing a child to experience pain, but not injury, for the purpose of correction or control of a child's behavior") (Straus, 1994, p. 4). Currently and legally operating within largely 19 Southern states, research has indicated that Black children were physically struck by public school personnel more often than all other racial groups (Gregory, 1995). Within 286,539 recorded discipline reports, Black male students were disproportionately hit more often in school than others for "simple" acts of misbehaving. Gershoff and Font (2016) found that Black males were also the highest overall group in schools to receive corporal punishment. Ward et al. (2019) argue that the use of violence to control Black students in schools is connected the history of violence directed toward chattel slaves and Blacks during the era of Jim Crow.

In schools that allow corporal punishment, studies have argued that students demonstrate lower levels of executive functioning, math scores, repetitive vocabulary, and intrinsic motivation (Talwar et al., 2011). Children who attend these schools also want to avoid attending due to their fear of being physically harmed (Ogando Portela & Pells, 2015). Consequently this can lead to an increase in the school dropout rate among those most affected by the act of physical violence.

African American students experience higher rates of school suspension and expulsion than any other ethnic group. African American males experience higher rates of suspension and expulsion than females, and African American females experience higher rates than White females (Hemplill et al., 2014). A study by Yang, Harmeyer, Chen, and Lofaso (2018) demonstrated that risk factors contributing to school suspension in elementary school differ based on gender. Data indicate that although boys and girls make up equal public-school enrollment, boys account for 70% of suspensions (U.S. Department of Education, Office of Civil Rights, 2004). Boys having behavioral problems as assessed by teachers were more likely to experience suspension, whereas girls who had a lack of parental supervision were more likely to experience suspension (Yang et al., 2018).

In relations to American Indian and Alaskan Natives (AIAN) the rate of disproportionality exists within these areas as well. However, AIAN students make up only 1 percent of the public school population but comprise up to 2 percent of the out school suspensions and 3 percent of expulsions (Tribal Leaders Toolkit, 2018). During the academic year of 2015–2016, in Jefferson County 509J School District in Oregon, Native students made up only one-third of the student population. However, approximately a third of 6th–12th grade AIAN students were suspended (Clarren, 2017). A graduate of the district reported to InvestigateWest, a nonprofit investigative news organization, "The administrators 'don't see us as people deserving the same sort of education and opportunities. . . . I felt worthless—like I wasn't worth the effort or patience to understand who I am and my history. This school district has failed us my entire lifetime, and it continues to do this today'" (Clarren, 2017). In comparison to the White students, AIAN students were twice as likely to be suspended. At the same time, two-thirds of them were expelled. In Montana, Native students are four times more likely to be expelled and in Utah they are 7.5 times more likely to be expelled than their White counterparts (Tribal Leaders Toolkit, 2018, online). Further, Sprague et al. (2013, p. 452), examining the 2009–2010 discipline and juvenile state data of an unnamed Northwestern U.S. state, reported that AIAN students were overrepresented in all exclusionary discipline school practices in comparisons to their White peers. Moreover, AIAN special education students are also more likely to be given out-of-school suspensions/expulsions, and are less likely to be assigned to in-school suspension than their White counterparts who commit the same school infractions (Whitford & Levine-Donnerstein, 2014). As research has noted, the rate of suspension and expulsion increases the likelihood of students interacting with the criminal justice system—the school-to prison pipeline.

Potential Outcomes of School Suspension and Expulsion

Researchers have recognized that school suspension and expulsion create disparities regarding loss of instruction time. Middle and high school loss of instruction time is five times higher than at the elementary level. Black, Latinx, and AIAN students experience higher loss of instruction than White students do (Losen & Martinez, 2020). This has contributed to the current academic achievement gap that exists within education.

Studies indicate that school suspension and expulsion are associated with lower academic achievement at the school level (Rausch & Skiba, 2005) and the individual level (Mendez et al., 2002). Welch and Payne (2012) suggested that cross-school variations in disciplinary matters affect student behavior, student achievement, and the school environment in general. School suspension is also associated with increased risks of negative behavior over time (Tobin et al., 1996). The impact of the suspension on students in the long run may hinder graduation and increases the potential for youth to drop out of high school (Suh & Suh, 2007). Children who are suspended in elementary years are more likely to experience subsequent suspension in middle and high school and drop out of school by the 10th grade (Skiba et al., 2014).

This rise of the school-to-prison pipeline has become a major concern (Skiba et al., 2014). Studies indicate that students experiencing suspension and expulsion are more likely to be transferred to the juvenile and criminal justice system. This progression is commonly known as the school-to-prison pipeline (Na & Gottfredson, 2013; Fabelo et al., 2010). Krezmien, Leone, and Wilson (2014) addressed two pathways, direct and indirect routes of suspension and expulsion, that may lead students to enter the justice system. An example of a direct pathway would be schools referring students who have experienced suspension or expulsion directly to law enforcement and the courts (Kupchik & Monahan, 2006; Krezmien et al., 2010). An indirect pathway would be when students who experience exclusionary discipline practices become disconnected from school, become involved with delinquent activity and/or are incarcerated (Krezmien et al., 2014).

Existing Approaches for Tackling Disproportionality

The U.S. Department of Justice and the U.S. Department of Education have put forth recommendations to reduce racial and ethnic disparities in exclusionary discipline practices in schools (U.S. Department of Education/ Department of Justice 2014). There has been considerable momentum in policy discussions on alternatives to school suspension and expulsion. These discussions focus on improving school climate as well as understanding factors that contribute to disproportionality in school suspension and expulsion (Skiba et al., 2014). For example, research studies have demonstrated that restorative justice has helped to change school climate and has reduced need for exclusionary discipline practices in schools (Teasley et al., 2016).

Funded by the U.S. Department of Education's Office of Special Education Programs, the Positive Behavioral Interventions and Supports (PBIS) program is an evidence-based approach that initiated a guide for school districts and school teams based on seven key elements of effective policies for reducing discipline disproportionality (Green et al., 2015). These seven key elements are: (1) specific commitment to equity, (2) family partnerships, (3) focus on implementing positive and proactive behavior support practices, (4) clean and objective discipline procedures, (5) removal or reduction of exclusionary practices, (6) graduated discipline systems with instructional alternatives to exclusion, and (7) procedures with accountability for equitable student outcomes (Green et al., 2015, p. 3).

Welch and Payne (2012) have argued that it is critical to understand what leads to the sanctions of suspension and expulsion at schools. In addition to understanding how student behaviors and characteristics are associated with exclusionary punishment, it is important to examine the potential impact of school-level influences on youth educational success. Studies suggest that for the majority of students, suspension and expulsion did not prevent

464 FITZGERALD, TEASLEY, KEYES, AND HATCHER

the ongoing behavioral problems beyond the initial behavioral infraction (Green et al., 2018; Skiba, 2006; McFadden et al., 1992). Reports produced by professional associations such as the American Academy of Pediatrics (2013) and the American Psychological Association (2008) indicate the ineffectiveness of and risks associated with such disciplinary exclusions and recommend using these measures only as last resorts. Given the concerns of the use of exclusionary disciplinary practices in schools, there is a need for effective evidence-based initiatives to reduce/eliminate disproportionality in school suspension and expulsion.

Current Approaches

Concerning the reduction of discipline disproportionalities, varieties of evidence-based approaches are in use today within school settings. This chapter discusses two of the most popular approaches, Response to Intervention (RtI) and Schoolwide Positive Behavioral Interventions and Supports (SWPBIS). Both are widely used by school practitioners who seek to confront the current state of the discipline gap and the overrepresentation of children of color in special education. Although not legislatively delegated, the reauthorization of Individuals with Disabilities Education Improvement Act of 2004 allowed the use of RtI as a viable option for schools to use in order to identify students with emotional, behavioral, and or academic disabilities (Berkeley et al., 2009). Concerning special education, previous approaches relied mainly on discrepancies between students' IQ and their achievement to determinate special education eligibility. Educators and researchers heavily criticized this method of eligibility due to its inability to provide copious student and assessment information. Further, by relying largely upon discrepancy criteria, educators were unable to capture successfully all eligible students early in their academic career.

Concerning RtI, schools that implement the three-tier approach/steps do so in various means. Currently there is no single or universal method of implementation and delivery across public school settings (RTI Action Network). Regardless, RtI consists of both an early identification and evidence-based approach that targets both academically struggling general and special education students (Vaughn & Fuchs, 2003). Initially, RtI provided appropriate evidence-based services/interventions to students presenting academic worry. The educational decision to vary the degree of interventions/services provided to students in need were either increased or decreased in terms of intensity (Mellard & Johnson, 2007). Today, behavior is included in the RtI ethos. Within the process, assigned school personnel watchfully observe and document the academic and or behavioral progress or decline exhibited by students receiving interventions. Overall, the instructional process is rooted in a process guided by collected student outcome data. Educators and researchers argue that this approach creates a well-integrated system of instruction and intervention.

Critics, on the other hand, have argued that RtI approaches utilize interventions that are void of strong empirical confirmation (Kavale, 2005). Moreover, there is currently no well-researched model of the RtI approach (RTI Network). Next, RtI has been criticized for not allowing for differentiation between students with specific learning disabilities (SLD) from those students categorized as exhibiting disorders such as intellectual disabilties, behavioral disorders, etc. (Mastropieri & Scruggs, 2005).

Schools have also adopted the use of the Schoolwide Positive Behavioral Interventions and Supports (SWPBIS). Like RtI, it is also an evidence-based intervention and support system consisting of a three-tier framework that utilizes student behavioral data to improve student outcome. The Center on Positive Behavioral Interventions & Supports argues that "it is a commitment to addressing student behavior through systems change. When it's implemented well, students achieve improved social and academic outcomes, schools experience reduced exclusionary discipline practices, and school personnel feel more effective" (Center on PBIS, n.p.). Similar to RtI, schools that incorporate SWPBIS utilize evidence-based strategies, methods of monitoring, and evaluation of student outcomes.

In relation to its impact on students of color and the current discipline gap, findings indicate a divided conclusion. On one hand, an array of small studies indicate that SWPBIS implementation decreased, but not eliminated, the discipline gap in their school setting (Tobin & Vincent, 2011; Vincent et al., 2011). Other scholars and educators argue that SWPBIS has no significant effect on the discipline gap (Sandomierski, 2011; Vincent et al., 2015).

Regardless of the above-mentioned approaches and others employed by schools across the United States, as research associate professor Michael Pullman at the University of Washington in Seattle stated, "So far, we've found no intervention has evidence of significantly reducing disproportionate discipline and bias, . . . and this problem has been around 50, 60 years" (Sparks, 2018, online). Instead of using a single approach such as RtI or SWPBIS to address the issues related to excessive discipline and the consequential possible thwarted path to the criminal justice system, researchers argue that a multifaceted approach and/or strategy is required (Gregory & Mosley, 2004; Skiba et al., 2008). Schools that rely upon a single approach process, policy, or procedure can never produce the equality needed to address school discipline concerns. It is safe to consider that when one takes into account the multifaceted ramification of race in the United States that seeps into public schools, a multifaceted approach to the issue of discipline is in need. Hence, approaches such as the School Success Project (SSP) are imperative to eliminating the ramifications of the current approaches to discipline that public schools across the country are guilty of pursuing.

Restorative justice (RJ) approaches to school suspension and expulsion demonstrate promise. "RJ is a broad term that encompasses a growing social movement to institutionalize peaceful and non-punitive approaches for addressing harm, responding to violations of legal and human rights, and problem solving" (Fronious et al., 2016, p. 1). It has been defined as an innovative approach to correct offensive and inappropriate behavior by repairing harm to people and relationships, rather than approaches that blame and call for punishment. In order to be appropriately implemented, RJ practices require a change in school culture to include a buy-in from school administrators, teachers, parents, and schoolchildren. It is a form of conflict resolution, as well as having youth understand the gravity of their offense. Moreover, RJ is an alternative to zero-tolerance policies and the use of school resource officers. "RJ is viewed as a remedy to the negative consequences of exclusionary punishment and its disproportionate application" (Fronious et al., 2016, p. 10). Although gaining in popularity and utilization, RJ studies are still in their infancy, but have demonstrated effectiveness in the reduction of undesirable behaviors and school suspension and expulsion when implemented system-wide (see Fronious et al. (2016) for an overview of research on RJ).

Launching the School Success Project (SSP)

The School Success Project (SSP) seeks to eliminate disproportionality in school suspension and expulsion. As a watchdog group interested in successful academic outcomes for K–12 children and youth, the SSP is part of the Grand Challenges for Social Work, which seeks to create innovative methods for reducing social welfare problems in society. In drafting district, state, and regional reports, members of the SSP make use of evidence-based methods in suggesting to school systems how to eliminate disproportionality in school suspension and expulsion. Knowing that there are evidence-based approaches to reducing disproportionality in school suspension and expulsion, the authors launched the School Success Project (SSP) in the summer of 2019 (https://schoolsuccessproject.com). The goal of this project is to eliminate disproportionality of school suspension and expulsion for all minority groups. As a watchdog group interested in successful academic outcomes for K–12 children and youth, our purpose is to raise awareness and promote school success by reducing disproportionate suspension and expulsion of school-aged youth.

In order to promote the SSP, we developed the Suspension/Expulsion Tracking and Rating System (STARS) as a method to rate disproportionality as well as progress toward reducing disproportionality within a given school district. The STARS was developed as an objective and an easily replicable method, which consists of two main indices: (1) a disproportionality index, and (2) a progress index. The disproportionality index determines the level of disproportionality in a local school or district level by race and ethnicity. The index should include Pre-K and K–12 data, when available. The progress index determines how far schools are in addressing and reducing disproportionality.

We present disproportionality using the concept of relative risk ratios, which is a comparison of risk indices for two groups, with one group remaining constant for comparison—which is usually the White student population (Lewis, Goodman, & Barrett, 2021). When risk indices are presented in a ratio, the resulting number indicates the extent of disproportionality, which can be compared across groups (Coutinho & Oswald, 2004). For example, a relative risk ratio value between 0 and 1 indicates underrepresentation, and greater than 1 indicates overrepresentation. A relative risk ratio of 1, on the other hand, characterizes equal representation.

The change in risk ratio and STARS over time will represent the progress index. Progress index is the representation of the amount of change from one point in time to another in terms of school disciplinary outcomes. In other words, it helps us understand how well schools are doing in their efforts to reduce disproportionality. Both indices (disproportionality index and progress index) will then be assigned a 1 (Extreme challenges) to 5 (Excellent) STAR rating. Hence, the more STARS, the better a school is doing in reducing

468   FITZGERALD, TEASLEY, KEYES, AND HATCHER

school discipline disproportionality. Following the STARS method, a progress index should be determined approximately one year after an initial report on a local school or district level.

The SSP set several objectives to address and reduce/eliminate disproportionality in school suspension and expulsion: (1) collaborate and capacity-build with school districts, academic institutions, existing and new advocacy groups and organizations, individuals, and communities; (2) make use of existing evidence-based and innovative methods; (3) gather data to complete our interactive map; (4) galvanize interest at local, state, and national levels to actively participate in the SSP; (5) significantly reduce disproportionality in school suspensions and expulsions by 2025; and (6) develop a dissemination strategy for outreach, advocacy, and capacity building.

Collaboration and Capacity-Building

In order to execute the SSP, it will be necessary to bring together teachers, school administrators, related school-services personnel, and community-based advocates and organizations as part of a collaborative effort. This will require coalition building, outreach, and collaboration with scholars from the disciplines of social work, criminal justice, law, education, psychology, anthropology, communications, urban studies, and school counseling. A great deal of collaboration needs to take place at the local level, consisting of interested individuals and organizations, dedicated to removing disproportionality. Interested individuals and organizations should visit our website and fill out the participation form to join us. Making use of this website can foster important collaborations and can help people to identify local interest. The website will be a repository for sharing information about the progress toward the reduction of disproportionality in school suspension and expulsion.

Utilizing Evidence-Based and Innovative Methods

Several innovative approaches to reducing school suspensions and expulsions have demonstrated promise. However, there is no one-size-fits-all approach to reducing disproportionality in school suspension and expulsion. Evidence-based practices such as restorative justice practices, Positive

Behavioral Interventions and Supports model (PBIS), behavioral health-service teams (BHTs) and other data-driven decision-making approaches have shown promise. The use of innovative, evidence-informed approaches can facilitate the elimination of disciplinary disproportionality and its effects on African American children and youth.

The SSP reports created by local teams will be available on the website, as well as additional research information on innovative practices. As part of these reports, local teams will make evidence-based recommendations to local school districts who may be struggling with high rates of disproportionality in school suspensions and expulsions. Prior to making these suggestions, it is important for local teams to be aware of the existing approaches in addressing this problem. Lastly, this will require an in-depth study of approaches attempted by local school systems to reduce disproportionality.

Completing the Interactive Map

The interactive map serves as an exciting visual representation of the current situation and ongoing progress as the project unfolds using the STARS. It allows people to easily access reports based on location. One goal is to fill up the map with several reports in areas of high disproportionality. Over time, we want to foster a high volume of traffic using that map, with the hope that it attracts potential collaborators to join the SSP. Our suggestion is that local teams update their reports annually and that they distribute their findings broadly to stakeholders and all interested parties. After initial contact with the SSP team through the website, interested parties will receive systematic directions on how to gather data and create a report. They will also be provided a sample report and instructions on how to provide a STARS. The SSP team will also accept existing reports that rate disproportionality in a given school district for placement on the map.

Developing a Dissemination Strategy

After the development of the reports, dissemination is necessary to highlight findings and promote advocacy for change and greater accountability within school systems. At local and state levels, a strategy for dissemination

470 FITZGERALD, TEASLEY, KEYES, AND HATCHER

will target media outlets as a form of advocacy, outreach, and coalition building to promote change in school disciplinary practices using evidence-based approaches. This will consist of announcements and distribution to news media outlets, local advocacy groups, policy think tanks, and major professional organizations for school-based professionals, including related school-services personnel. "Planned political advocacy is central to our efforts; it is necessary to promote greater awareness, generate program implementation, advance policy recommendations, and place a continuous spotlight on the challenge of school suspension and expulsion disproportionality in urban America" (Teasley et al., 2016, p. 17).

Conclusion

The development of the SSP is a response to the far-reaching challenges caused by the use of disproportionate exclusionary discipline practices in schools, particularity their negative effects on African American children and youth. The SSP is a long-term project that will, through the use of identified goals and recommendations using evidence-based approaches, serve as a measurement of progress to eliminate excessive exclusionary discipline practices in schools. The primary goal of this project is to hold school districts accountable, as well as highlight progress toward equity in school disciplinary practices, toward the promotion of successful school-based outcomes. In order to make the SSP a success, it is necessary to galvanize interest at local, state, and national levels and to have interested individuals actively participate. Our ultimate goal is to significantly reduce disproportionality in school suspensions and expulsions by 2025. Because of the long-term consequences of exclusionary discipline practices, including the cost to society, it is important that headway is made to foster healthy educational outcomes for all children and youth.

Study Questions

1. Reflecting on your own school experience, were there suspensions and expulsions from school? And if so, which groups where more likely and less likely to be suspended or expelled?

2. In your opinion, what is the effect of school suspension on preschoolers?
3. Identify and discussion residential racial and ethnic and gender rates of school suspension and expulsion within your local community and state school systems.
4. What role should state, local, and federal governments play in reducing disproportionality in school suspension and expulsion? What can social workers do to assist in any possible solution?
5. Discuss the problem of educators in the over-identification of minoritized children and youth for school suspension and expulsion.
6. Discuss the link between school suspension and participation in the juvenile justice system.
7. How can school-based social workers help to reduce disproportionality in school suspension and expulsion?
8. In your opinion, why have school social workers not been effective in reducing school suspension and expulsion?
9. What are the costs to individuals, families, communities, and society in general from the school-to-prison pipeline?
10. What is your opinion on the use of Restorative Justice in schools as a remedy to reduce school suspension and expulsion?

References

American Academy of Pediatrics. (2013). *Out-of-school suspension and expulsion.* Elk Grove Village, IL: Author.

American Psychological Association. (2008). Are zero tolerance policies effective in the schools? An evidentiary review and recommendations. *American Psychologist, 63,* 852–862.

Berkeley, S., Bender, W. N., Gregg Peaster, L., & Saunders, L. (2009). Implementation of Response to Intervention: A snapshot of progress. *Journal of Learning Disabilities, 42*(1), 85–95. https://doi.org/10.1177/0022219408326214.

Clarren, R. (2017, July 24). How America is failing Native American students: Punitive discipline, inadequate curriculum, and declining federal funding created an education crisis. The Nation. Retrieved from: https://www.thenation.com/article/archive/left-behind/

Coutinho, M. J., & Oswald, D. P. (2004). Disproportionate representation of culturally and linguistically diverse students in special education: measuring the problem. National Center for Culturally Responsive Education Systems. Retrieved from: https://www.ldonline.org/ld-topics/research-reports/disproportionate-representation-culturally-and-linguistically-diverse

472 FITZGERALD, TEASLEY, KEYES, AND HATCHER

Fabelo, T., Thompson, M. D., Plotkin, M., Carmichael, D., Marchbanks, M. P., & Booth, E. A. (2010). *Breaking schools' rules: A statewide study of how school discipline relates to students' success and juvenile justice involvement*. New York: Council of State Governments Justice Center and Public Policy Research Institute.

Fronius, T., Persson, H., Guckenburg, S., Hurley, N., & Petrosine, A. (2016, February). *Restorative justice in U.S. schools: A research review*. WestEd Justice & Prevention Research Center. Retrieved from file:///C:/Users/Martel/Dropbox/My%20PC%20(DESKTOP-518GGAM)/Documents/Research/Restorative%20Justice%20and%20Schools.pdf.

Gershoff, E., & Font, S. 2016. Corporal punishment in US public schools: Prevalence, disparities in use, and status in state and federal policy. *Social Policy Report, 30*(1), 1–26.

Gilliam, W. S. (2005). *Prekindergarteners left behind: Expulsion rates in state prekindergarten systems*. New York: Foundation for Child Development.

Gottfredson, G. D., & Gottfredson, D. C. (2001). What schools do to prevent problem behavior and promote safe environments. *Journal of Educational and Psychological Consultation, 12*, 313–344.

Green, A. L., Maynard, D. K., & Stegenga, S. M. (2018). Common misconceptions of suspension: Ideas and alternatives for school leaders. *Psychology in the Schools, 55*, 419 428. https://doi.org/10.1002/pits.22111

Green, A., Nese, R., McIntosh, K., Nishioka, V., Eliason, B., Delabra, A. C. (2015). Key elements of policies to address discipline disproportionality: A guide for district and school teams. *Positive Behavioral Interventions & Supports OSEP Technical Assistance Center*. Retrieved from https://www.pbis.org/resource/key-elements-of-policies-to-address-discipline-disproportionality-a-guide-for-district-and-school-teams.

Gregory, A., & Mosely, P. M. (2004). The Discipline Gap: Teachers' Views on the Over-Representation of African American Students in the Discipline System. *Equity & Excellence in Education, 37*(1), 18–30. https://doi.org/10.1080/10665680490429280

Gregory, A., Skiba, R. J., & Noguera, P. A. (2010). The achievement gap and the discipline gap: Two sides of the same coin? *Educational Researcher, 39*(1), 59–68. https://journals.sagepub.com/doi/10.3102/0013189X09357621.

Gregory, A., & Weinstein, R. S. (2008). The discipline gap and African Americans: Defiance or cooperation in the high school classroom. *Journal of School Psychology, 46*, 455–475.

Gregory, J. F. (1995). The crime of punishment: Racial and gender disparities in the use of corporal punishment in U.S. public schools. *The Journal of Negro Education, 64*(4), 454–462. https://doi.org/10.2307/2967267.

Hemphill, S. A., Plenty, S. M., Herrenkohl, T. I., Toumbourou, J. W., & Catalano, R. F. (2014). Student and school factors associated with school suspension: A multilevel analysis of students in Victoria, Australia and Washington state, United States. *Children and Youth Services Review, 36*, 187–194.

Karenga, M. (1999). *Odu Ifa: The ethical teachings*. University of Sankore Press: Los Angeles.

Kavale, K. A. (2005). Identifying specific learning disability: Is responsiveness to intervention the answer? *Journal of Learning Disabilities, 38*(6), 553–562. https://doi.org/10.1177/00222194050380061201.

Kinsler, J. (2011). Understanding the black-white school discipline gap. *Economics of Education Review, 30*, 1370–1383.

Krezmien, M. P., Leone, P. E., & Wilson, M. G. (2014). Marginalized students, school exclusion, and the school-to-prison pipeline. In W. T. ChurchII, D. W. Springer, &

RACIALIZED BARRIERS TO SCHOOL SUCCESS 473

A. R. Roberts (Eds.), *Juvenile justice sourcebook* (pp. 267–288). New York: Oxford University Press.

Krezmien, M. P., Leone, P. E., Zablocki, M. S., & Wells, C. S. (2010). Juvenile court referrals and the public schools: Nature and extent of the practice in five states. *Journal of Contemporary Criminal Justice, 26*, 273–293.

Kupchik, A., & Monahan, T. (2006). The new American school: Preparation for post-industrial discipline. *British Journal of Sociology of Education, 27*, 617–631.

Lewis, T. J., Goodman, S., & Barrett, S. (May, 2021). *Leveraging short term funding to build long term capacity.* Eugene, OR: Center on PBIS. www.pbis.org

Losen, D., & Martinez, P. (2020, October). *Lost opportunities: How disparate school discipline continues to drive differences in the opportunity to learn.* The Center for Civil Rights Remedies. Retrieved from: https://files.eric.ed.gov/fulltext/ED608537.pdf

Losen, D. J., & Martinez, T. E. (2013). *Out of school & off track: The overuse of suspensions in American middle and high schools.* Los Angeles, CA: The UCLA Center for Civil Rights Remedies at The Civil Rights Project. Retrieved from: https://files.eric.ed.gov/fulltext/ED541731.pdf

Malik, R. (2017). *New data reveal 250 preschoolers are suspended or expelled every day.* Center for American. Retrieved from: https://www.americanprogress.org/article/new-data-reveal-250-preschoolers-suspended-expelled-every-day/

Mastropieri, M. A., & Scruggs, T. E. (2005). Feasibility and consequences of response to intervention: Examination of the issues and scientific evidence as a model for the identification of individuals with learning disabilities. *Journal of Learning Disabilities, 38*(6), 525–531. https://doi.org/10.1177/00222194050380060801.

McFadden, A. C., Marsh, G. E., Price, B. J., & Hwang, Y. (1992). A study of race and gender bias in the punishment of school children. *Education & Treatment of Children, 15,* 140–146.

Meek, S. E., & Gilliam, W. S. (2016). *Expulsion and suspension as matters of social justice and health equity.* Washington, DC: National Academy of Medicine.

Mellard, D. F., & Johnson, E. S. (2007). *RTI: A practitioner's guide to implementing response to intervention.* Thousand Oaks, CA: SAGE Publications.

Na, C., & Gottfredson, D. C. (2013). Police officers in schools: Effects on school crime and the processing of offending behaviors. *Justice Quarterly, 30*(4), 619–650.

Nichols, J. D. (2004). An exploration of discipline and suspension data. *Journal of Negro Education, 73*, 408–423.

Ogando Portela, M. J., & Pells, K. (2015). *Corporal punishment in schools: Longitudinal evidence from Ethiopia, India, Peru, and Viet Nam* (Innocenti Discussion Paper No. 2015-02). Florence: UNICEF Office of Research. Retrieved from https://www.unicef-irc.org/publications/series/22/.

Raffaele Mendez, L. M., Knoff, H. M., & Ferron, J. M. (2002). School demographic variables and out-of-school suspension rates: A quantitative and qualitative analysis of a large, ethnically diverse school district. *Psychology in the Schools, 39*, 259–277.

Rausch, M. K., & Skiba, R. J. (2005, April). The academic cost of discipline: The contribution of school discipline to achievement. Paper presented at the Annual Meeting of the American Educational Research Association, Montreal, Canada.

RTI Action Network. *What is RTI?* Retrieved from http://www.rtinetwork.org/learn/what/whatisrti.

Sandomierski, T. (2011). *Disciplinary Outcomes by race and gender in schools implementing positive behavior support: Does fidelity of implementation reduce disproportionality?*

University of Florida Scholar Commons. ProQuest Dissertations Publishing. Retrieved from: https://digitalcommons.usf.edu/cgi/viewcontent.cgi?article=4524&context=etd

Skiba, R. J. (2006). Zero tolerance, suspension, and expulsion: Questions of equity and effectiveness. In C. M. Evertson (Ed.), *Handbook of classroom management: Research, practice, and contemporary issues* (pp. 1063–1092). Mahwah, NJ: Erlbaum.

Skiba, R. J. (2014). The failure of zero tolerance. *Reclaiming Children and Youth, 22*(4), 27.

Skiba, R. J., Arredondo, M. I., & Williams, N. T. (2014). More than a metaphor: The contribution of exclusionary discipline to a school-to-prison pipeline. *Equity & Excellence in Education, 47*, 546–564.

Skiba, R. J., Chung, C., Trachok, M., Baker, T. L., Sheya, A., & Hughes, R. (2014). Parsing disciplinary disproportionality: Contributions of infraction, student, and school characteristics to out-of-school suspension and expulsion. *American Educational Research Journal, 51*, 640–670.

Skiba, R. J., Eckes, S. E., & Brown, K. (2009). African American disproportionality in school discipline: The divide between best evidence and legal remedy. New *York Law School Law Review, 54*(4), 1071–1112.

Skiba, R. J., Simmons, A. B., Ritter, S., Gibb, A. C., Rausch, M. K., Cuadrado, J., & Chung, C.-G. (2008). Achieving equity in special education: history, status, and current challenges. *Exceptional Children, 74*(3), 264–288. https://doi.org/10.1177/0014402 90807400301

Skiba, R. J., Trachok, M., Chung, C., Baker, T. L., Sheya, A., & Hughes, R. (2014). Where should we intervene? How infractions, students, and schools all contribute to out-of-school suspensions. In Losen, D. (Ed.), *Closing the school discipline gap: Equitable remedies for excessive exclusion* (pp. 132–146). New York: Teachers College.

Skiba, R. J., & Sprague, J. (2008). The positive classroom. Safety without suspensions. *Educational Leadership, 66*(1), 38–43.

Sparks, S. (2018, April 24). Discipline gaps and ways to close them get researchers' attention. *Education Week* (n.p.). Retrieved from https://www.edweek.org/leadership/dis cipline-gaps-and-ways-to-close-them-get-researchers-attention/2018/04

Sprague, J., Vincent, C., Tobin, T., & CHiXapkaid. (2013). Preventing disciplinary exclusions of students from American Indian/Alaska Native backgrounds. *Family Court Review, 51*(3), 452–459. https://doi.org/10.1111/fcre.12042.

Straus, M., & Donnelly, D. (1994). *Beating the devil out of them: Corporal punishment in American families.* Lexington, MD: Lexington Books.

Suh, S., & Suh, J. (2007). Risk factors and levels of risk for high school dropouts. *Professional School Counseling, 10*, 297–306.

Talwar, V., Carlson, S. M., & Lee, K. (2011). Effects of a punitive environment on children's executive functioning: A natural experiment. *Social Development, 20*, 805–824. doi: 10.1111/j.1467-9507.2011.00617.x.

Teasley, M. L., McRoy, R. G., Joyner, M., Armour, M., Gourdine, R. M., Crewe, S. E., Kelly, M., Franklin, C. G. S., Payne, M., Jackson, J., & Fong, R. (2017). *Increasing success for African American children and youth (Grand Challenges for Social Work initiative Working Paper No. 21).* Cleveland, OH: American Academy of Social Work and Social Welfare.

Tobin, T., Sugai, G., & Colvin, G. (1996). Patterns in middle school discipline records. *Journal of Emotional and Behavioral Disorders, 4*, 82–94.

Tobin, T., & Vincent, C. G. (2011). Strategies for preventing disproportionate exclusions of African American Students. *Preventing School Failure, 55*(4), 192–201. https://doi. org/10.1080/1045988X.2010.532520.

Tribal Leaders Toolkit. (2018.). *Education choice for Indian country: Supporting tribal decision making for schools and students.* National Congress of American Indians. Retrieved from http://www.ncai.org/NCAI_Tribal_Leader_Toolkit_Education_Choice_2018.pdf

U.S. Department of Education/Department of Justice (2014). *U.S. Departments of Education and Justice release school discipline guidance package to enhance school climate and improve school discipline policies/practices.* Washington, DC: Author.

U.S. Department of Education (2016). *School climate and discipline: Know the data.* Washington, DC: U.S. Department of Education Office for Civil Rights.

U.S. Department of Education, Office for Civil Rights. (2004). Elementary and secondary school survey (2004). Retrieved from http://ocrdata.ed.gov/.

Vaughn, S., & Fuchs, L. S. (2003). Redefining learning disabilities as inadequate response to instruction: The promise and potential problems. *Learning Disabilities Research and Practice, 18*(3), 137–146. https://doi.org/10.1111/1540-5826.00070.

Vincent, C. G., Sprague, J. R., Pavel, M., Tobin, T., & Gau, J. (2015). Effectiveness of schoolwide positive behavior interventions and supports in reducing racially inequitable disciplinary exclusion. In D. J. Losen (Ed.), *Closing the school discipline gap: Equitable remedies for excessive exclusion* (pp. 207–221). New York: Teachers College Press.

Vincent, C. G., Swain-Bradway, J., Tobin, T. J., & May, S. (2011). Disciplinary referrals for culturally and linguistically diverse students with and without disabilities: Patterns resulting from school-wide positive behavior support. *Exceptionality, 19*(3), 175–190.

Wallace, J. M., Goodkind, S., Wallace, C., & Bachman, J. G. (2008). Racial, ethnic, and gender differences in school discipline among U.S. high school students: 1991–2005. *Negro Educational Review, 59,* 47–62.

Ward, G., Petersen, N., Kupchik, A., & Pratt, J. (2019). Historic lynching and corporal punishment in contemporary southern schools. *Social Problems, 61,* 41–62. https://doi.org/10.1093/socpro/spz044.

Welch, K., & Payne, A. N. (2012). Exclusionary school punishment: The effect of racial threat on expulsion and suspension. *Youth Violence and Juvenile Justice, 10,* 155–171.

Whitford, D. K., & Levine-Donnerstein, D. (2014). Office disciplinary referral patterns of American Indian students from elementary school through high school. *Behavioral Disorders, 39*(2), 78–88. https://doi.org/10.1177/019874291303900204.

Yang, M., Harmeyer, E., Chen, Z., & Lofaso, B. M. (2018). Predictors of early elementary school suspension by gender: A longitudinal multilevel analysis. *Children and Youth Services Review, 93,* 331–338.

19

Reversing Extreme Inequality

The Legacy and Persistence of Racism Economic Inequality

Trina R. Shanks, Jennifer Romich, Stephanie C. Boddie,
Laura Lein, and Dominique S. Crump

The Legacy and Persistence of Racism: Implications and Possibilities for Extreme Economic Inequality

The Significance of the Racial Income and Wealth Gaps

Economic inequality, while related to the prevalence of poverty, is a different and distinct aspect of our economy and society. Inequality has a significant impact on the overall health of the economy (Bivens, 2017), and on an array of other social variables, such as health (Matthew & Brodersen, 2018) and education (Noguera, 2017). This chapter explores the nature and trajectory of economic inequality and its intersection with race. We will also explore policies that have exacerbated inequality, and the kinds of policies and practices that could mediate our growing racial inequality. This introduction lays the groundwork—briefly establishing the comparative strength of inequality in the United States, compared to other countries, and introducing the importance of understanding how race and economic inequality intersect.

A well-known measure of economic inequality, the Gini Coefficient (Bellu, 2006) allows us to track the level of inequality over time in the United States, and to compare it to inequality and the track of inequality in other countries. The Gini Coefficient scales the level income difference between the highest earners and that of the lowest earners in an economy. A Gini coefficient of 0 indicates that income is the same for everyone in the population, while a factor of 1 indicates that income all goes to a single person.

Trina R. Shanks, Jennifer Romich, Stephanie C. Boddie, Laura Lein, and Dominique S. Crump, *Reversing Extreme Inequality* In: *Social Work and the Grand Challenge to Eliminate Racism*. Edited by: Martell L. Teasley, Michael S. Spencer, and Melissa Bartholomew, Oxford University Press. © Oxford University Press 2023.
DOI: 10.1093/oso/9780197674949.003.0019

Research at the Pew Research Center and other organizations (Schaefer, 2020; Duffin, 2020) indicates that the Gini Coefficient for United States income has increased over the last three decades. The top group of earners in the United States are receiving an increasing proportion of all earnings. Indeed, while the growth of the bottom quintile of earners has stagnated, that of the highest earnings has grown substantially. While the Gini Coefficient is limited in the kinds of comparison that can be made among and within groups in the United States, it is useful as a general assessment tool, and allows us to track changes in United States inequality over time.

This type of analysis also indicates that the United States has the highest Gini Coefficient among the G7 countries (in order of size of Gini Coefficient: United States, United Kingdom, Italy, Japan, Canada, Germany, France) (Schaefer, 2020). Among the OECD (Organisation for Economic Co-operation and Development) countries, the United States' Gini Coefficient is exceeded only by Bulgaria, Turkey, Mexico, Chile, Costa Rica, and South Africa (OECD, 2020).

A similar analysis can be used to explore the inequality in wealth, as well as income. In the United States the inequality in wealth is considerable and is increasing rapidly (Horowitz et al., 2020). Most recently (2001–2016) only upper income families saw their wealth grow. In comparison with other countries, the United States has an extreme degree of wealth inequality. In comparison with European countries, the percentage of wealth owned by the top 1% far outstrips that of any European nation. The top 1% of the population owns 41.8% of the wealth, and the top 10% owns 77.2% of the wealth (Zucman, 2016).

The Gini Coefficient gives us an important overview. However, it does not highlight the particular condition of the lower 40%–50% income group of the population, nor does it illuminate the strong role played by race in creating and reinforcing economic inequality. In the United States, the massive differences in wealth and income across the population are intertwined with the also massive differences in income and wealth by racial groups. Since the Great Recession, the racial gaps continue for income (Wilson, 2018) and wealth (Kochhar & Fry, 2014). Furthermore, as we shall see in the following section, the beliefs, policies, and other practices that laid the groundwork for these inequities in the United States have continued for centuries.

There have been several efforts to undertake national comparative studies using available data (Lonnghi, 2017) or experiments (Quillan et al., 2019). These studies explore wage differentials by countries for ethnic/racial minorities. However, they face enormous problems in discovering comparable materials and identifying definitions and rubrics that are meaningful across different countries. On the other hand, recent cross-national analysis explores the relationship among social beliefs that underlie social policies, punitive policies, and the dependence on individualism and personal responsibility (Kornhauser, 2015). This study further explores the relationship between racism and punitive policy approaches, leading to social policy preferences. The interdependence of these concepts in formulating public policy leaves some countries with policies more oriented toward personal responsibility, punishment, and selective and limited social supports. This constellation of beliefs and outcomes appears to be related to the ideas and concepts around race and ethnicity and what these concepts imply.

Only a few countries have undertaken regular public analyses of income and wealth by race in their own country. However, several industrialized countries besides the United States have given attention to the intersection of race with economic inequality, and the ramifications of that inequality. For instance, Canada has undertaken such studies with an emphasis on the economic status and health consequences of their Indigenous populations (e.g., Brennenstuhl, 2018). Studies exploring countries previously part of the British Empire have similarly taken on health and other areas and have explored policies to address the economic inequality that has been identified (e.g., Martinson & Reichman, 2016). Not only studies like these, but also the policies and practices they have inspired in other countries, provide valuable insight into possible next steps in the United States for research, policy, and practice.

Canadian research, for example, revealed that more Black Canadian children were living in low-income households in 2006 than other Canadian children (Livingstone & Weinfeld, 2015). Additionally, the study showed that the economic state of Black Canadian households declined from 1986 to 2006 while it improved for other Canadian families (Livingstone & Weinfeld, 2015). This study controlled for family structure, and their research showed that, while two-parent households slightly reduced inequality for Black Canadian families, it did not eliminate it (Livingstone & Weinfeld, 2015). Finally, the authors suggested that racial discrimination in the workplace and immigrant integration impediments played a role in further disadvantaging Black Canadian households (Livingstone & Weinfeld, 2015). Still, while Canadian researchers, and many other scholars worldwide, have published numerous studies that analyze how race impacts socioeconomic status, much of the research available is related to health outcomes of respective disadvantaged racial and ethnic groups. The kinds of policies and practices developed in other countries in response to such findings can present possibilities for the United States.

The United States and other countries have concentrated on the inequalities in income, but the gap in wealth (or assets) is of enormous significance and has powerful impacts across generations. In this chapter we focus on high-level mechanisms whereby racist policies create economic inequalities in assets and income. Land and real property (homes and other buildings) comprise important sources of wealth and income generation. America's racial disparities related to real property began with the first European incursions into and claims on Native American land and continue through to the current day with pro-White mortgage policies.

Similarly, the conditions of work and compensation for one's market labor matter for income and, as income accumulates, for wealth. Again, from the earliest days of American chattel slavery, a system defined in part by unpaid forced labor, race-specific policies and practices concerning the right to and nature of compensation create racial inequalities in the United States. Inequalities in assets and income get reinforced by social institutions, including the educational system and the criminal legal system. Whether via unequal access to education or mass incarceration through race-specific crime policy, these social institutions create unequal outcomes and prevent groups of people from earning or accumulating assets.

This chapter begins with an overview of the historic policies of wealth exclusion that have barred racial and ethnic groups from entering the American economy. We then discuss both wealth and income discrepancies in greater detail. We include in each discussion ideas for policies and approaches that could bridge the gaps in income and wealth among these groups.

The History of Exclusionary Policies in the United States

We present below an outline of the history of wealth and income discriminatory policies in the United States. This presentation is, as might be expected, limited in that no one image can capture all of the national and more local policies that impinged on the opportunities available to Native Americans, Black Americans, Latino-Hispanic Americans, and Asian Americans, as compared to White Americans. However, this timeline and the following discussion indicate the powerful barriers to and drags on the financial success for each group.

While each group has felt the impact of repeated policies that prevent the accrual of stable income and assets, the history of each group includes

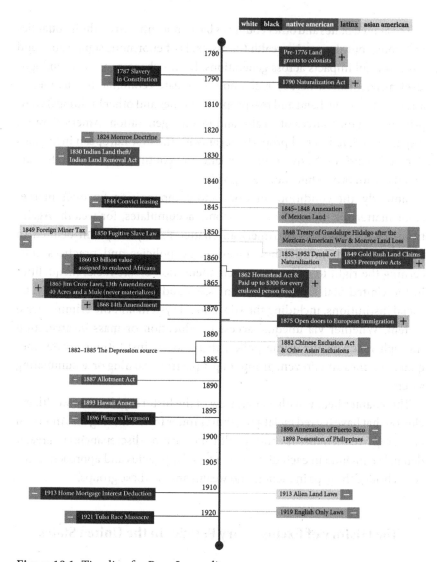

Figure 19.1 Timeline for Race Inequality
Sources: Harmon, 2010; Lui et al., 2006; Oliver & Shapiro, 2006; Rothstein, 2017.

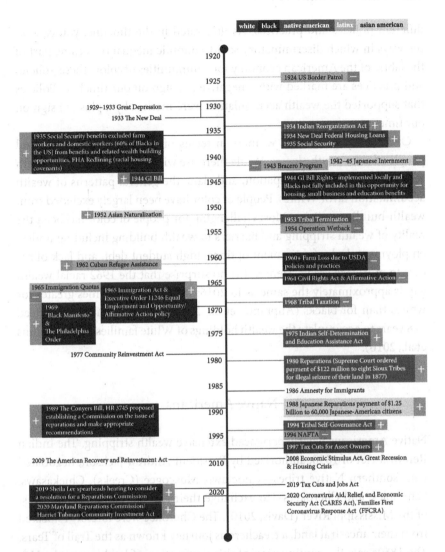

Figure 19.1 Continued

482 TRINA R. SHANKS ET AL.

different policies and practices. As illustrated in the timeline, you can see the ways in which discriminatory socioeconomic inequality became part of the fabric of the American economy for communities of color. These policies and practices are marked with a negative (−) sign on our timeline. Policies that supported the wealth accumulation were marked by a plus (+) sign on our timeline.

Overall, Whites are the winners in terms of wealth accumulation, and people of color are the losers. While there are within-group differences with respect to education, occupation, and class, the general patterns of wealth accumulation favor Whites. People of color have been largely excluded from wealth-building policies. Most challenging for people of color has been the reality of wealth stripping and barriers to wealth building including under-employment, lack of retirement options, high student debt, and lack of access to mortgage credit. Hence, it is no surprise that the 1962 racial wealth gap is approximately the same as in 2016; that is, about 7 times greater for whites than for blacks (Aliprantis et al., 2019). Black families would need 228 years to accumulate the wealth holdings of White families today (Collins et al., 2016).

Native Americans

Native Americans have experienced extensive wealth stripping. The Indian Removal Act of 1830, authorized by President Andrew Jackson, negotiated with southern Native tribes—Choctaws, Muscogee (Creeks), Chickasaws, Seminoles, and Cherokees—to exchange their ancestral land for land west of the Mississippi River (Davis, 2010). The Cherokee were forcibly relocated from their ancestral land, a treacherous journey known as the Trail of Tears. The 1850s saw the continuation of this devastation of land loss as the U.S. Army waged war against Indian tribes, including those in California during the Gold Rush (Lui et al., 2006; Trafzer & Hyer, 1999). In 1851, the Sioux tribe relinquished Iowa to the United States. It is impossible to completely restore the wealth taken from the original people on this land.

The 1975 Indian Self-Determination and Education Assistance Act and Tribal Self-Governance Act of 1994 have allowed Native Americans to gain control over their lands. While Native Americans have the highest poverty rate, there are also many examples of wealth. In the 1920s, the Osage Indians profited from oil found on their reservation. Since the 1990s, Native

American people have accrued wealth through gaming from lucrative tribal casinos. Some tribes have received reparations. For example, the U.S. Supreme Court ordered payment of $122 million to eight Sioux Tribes for illegal seizure of their land in 1877 (Harmon, 2010). In *Rich Indians: Native People and the Problem of Wealth in America*, Alexandra Harmon (2010) outlines seven cases of Native wealth building and affluence.

Black Americans

Black Americans in the United States were enslaved people, used as tools for wealth leveraging for White slave owners. Hence, Blacks Americans were unable to accrue their own wealth for over two centuries in any systematic way. The Reconstruction era proposal to grant freed slaves 40 acres and a mule was great in theory but never materialized. The era of Jim Crow segregation lasted from the 1870s until the 1950s, legally disenfranchising most Black Americans while vastly expanding White wealth. Accordingly, Black Americans lived segregated lives and created their own institutions, including businesses, and built their own communities out of necessity (Lui et al., 2006). This kind of wealth building was viewed as a threat and often those who amassed any substantial assets were the targets of terror, including property confiscation, house burning, lynching, and other violence. Oklahoma's Greenwood district, the Black Wall Street, represented the height of wealth accumulation among Black people in the 1920s. Two days of rioting destroyed 35 city blocks, including businesses and homes (Johnson, 2007).

It was not until the Civil Rights movement that opportunities for wealth building, including homeownership and business ownership, become more widely available for Black Americans (Baradaran, 2017). Before this time, wealth-building strategies that included Black Americans were partial and limited in scope (e.g., New Deal era policies, the GI Bill). The Fair Housing Act of 1968 was among several measures to prohibit discrimination; however, it did little to reverse residential patterns (Rothstein, 2017). A "separate and unequal" world of credit ushered in new forms of discriminatory and predatory practices. Such practices kept many Black Americans from achieving the American dream (Baradaran, 2017, p. 146; Fergus & Shanks, 2022; Taylor, 2019).

In 1969, James Forman of the National Black Economic Development presented a demand for reparations from White churches and synagogues, known as the "Black Manifesto" (Dye, 2007; George, 2013; Lechtreck, 2012). Though this demand was not addressed, the call for reparations continues in various forms. Black wealth building continues to be complicated by wealth stripping through predatory lending and wealth minimizing with limited values on homes owned compared to Whites. Africans and Caribbeans have immigrated to the United States in larger numbers after the 1965 Immigration Act. These new immigrants are accruing higher levels of education and increasing wealth. See Oliver and Shapiro's (2006) *Black Wealth/White Wealth: A New Perspective on Racial Inequality*, as well as Thomas Shapiro's (2017) *Toxic Inequality*, for more details on the relationship between wealth disparities and racial inequities.

Latinx/Hispanic

The Latinx community has had a varied history regarding wealth building in the United States. This is largely due to their varied national origins—Mexico, Central America, South America, and much of the Caribbean. The most significant story related to wealth can be traced back to the Monroe Doctrine, the policy used to justify military interventions in Latin American that ultimately led to the cessation of Mexican territory (that is, modern-day southwestern United States). The 1848 Treaty of Guadalupe Hidalgo that ended the U.S.-Mexican War resulted in the transfer of land from Mexico to the United States. This land loss has been one of the most significant barriers to wealth accumulation for this population.

In 1924, the US Border Control was created and began to allow deportation of Mexican Americans. However, the Cuban Refugee Assistance program of 1962 began the support of Cuban refugees relocating to the United States from a "dictatorial regime." During the 1980s and 1990s, Guatemalans, Salvadorans, and Nicaraguans fled the political unrest dominating their countries (Lui et al., 2006). The Latinx community is now the fastest growing racial/ethnic group though one of the most economically insecure (Macias, 2018). Latinx wealth continues to lag behind White wealth, though continuing to rise as education increases, family sizes decrease, and more saving and more asset-building strategies are implemented by this population (Lui et al., 2006).

Asian Americans

Asian Americans immigrated to the United States around 1850 in an inhospitable environment. The Chinese were first underpaid employees of the Central Pacific Railroad and later became cheap labor for agriculture and other industries. However, in California, Chinese were expected to pay a $3 per month Foreign Miner's Tax (an example of taxation without representation). By 1853, Chinese were not acknowledged as White and were still denied citizenship. In 1882, the Chinese Exclusion Act was passed to curb the influx of Chinese immigrants for 10 years. The Geary Act extended this exclusion another 10 years. The Immigration Act of 1924 restricted the immigration of other Asians, including Japanese and East Indians. In reaction to Pearl Harbor and World War II, Japanese residents were considered a national security threat and were relocated to internment camps to "prevent espionage" (Lui et al., 2006; Yamamoto et al., 2014). Forty years later, Japanese Americans regained a portion of their losses through the Evacuations Claim Act of 1948. It was not until 1988 that the United States made a formal statement acknowledging this injustice and issued a payment of $20,000 to each survivor.

The Immigration Act of 1965 brought a new wave of Asian immigrants from varied places of origin, including the Philippines and Laos. Overall, since the 1960s, certain Asians have moved closer to the economic status of Whites and are considered a "model minority" (Lui et al., 2006). While a few Asians, namely Chinese, Indians, and Japanese, have achieved significant wealth, others like Filipino, Korean, and Vietnamese have lower net worth than White households (Runes, 2018).

White Americans

For White Americans, wealth building has largely been facilitated through land acquisition and wealth extraction of Native American ancestral land, Black American labor, and Mexican territories. Hence, the significantly higher net wealth of Whites is primarily due to their historic legacy of wealth accumulation at the expense of other groups (Oliver & Shapiro, 2019). The Homestead Act of 1862 is a policy which enabled close to 1.5 million European immigrants to claim hundreds of acres of land at minimal cost (Williams Shanks, 2005). During the Gold Rush years, White Americans made substantial progress accumulating land west of the Mississippi River as well as mining for precious metals (Trafzer & Hyer, 1999). Other policies, including the Federal Housing Act of 1934 and the GI Bill, were created to give White Americans a wealth-building advantage by providing opportunities in business ownership, homeownership, and higher education (Oliver & Shapiro, 2019; Rothstein, 2017; Taylor, 2019). Tax policies like the Tax Cut and Jobs Act of 2019 also provided benefits to White Americans who already possessed assets. Similar trends can be found with relief aid during the COVID-19 pandemic (Gross, 2020). Ultimately, the following four components perpetuate White wealth: family income, family savings, family wealth, and community context (Mock, 2020). The community context provides social networks that facilitate employment opportunities and access to credit for homes and businesses. These are deeply entrenched advantages that help White Americans outpace most groups in wealth building.

The legacy of most of these policies and practices and many of the policies themselves are with us still. We discuss many of these in the sections below on labor and income, on the one hand, and wealth and assets, on the other.

Labor and Income

How does race matter for income? Income is the money coming into a household over time, whether from a job, from transfers, or from assets. This section focuses on earnings from employment and business ownership, as well as income from social insurance or other public programs; passive income from assets such as stock dividends or rental income stem from the assets covered in the section on wealth in this chapter. Racialized practices in the labor market disproportionately support the employment and earnings of White workers, processes which are reinforced by other social institutions. For most households, earnings from market work are the primary source of income, but social insurance and other public programs provide important stabilizing effects during periods of unemployment or for those who cannot work.

Racial inequalities arise in the labor market due to racialized patterns in the overall valuing of labor and because of how the job market works. While neoclassical economic theory holds that workers are paid the marginal value of their productivity, in practice, a long and complex set of institutional relations govern how much a given job will pay. These institutional factors can lead to discriminatory outcomes regardless of the intent or preferences of the actors involved (Small & Pager 2020). Whether someone is paid a salary or an hourly wage and the level of that wage depend in part on history and perceived value (Wallerstein 1999).

Historically, jobs occupied by persons of color are perceived as less valuable, even when other characteristics of the job such as difficulty or risk are considered. Early railroad work provides but one example; brakemen who had the challenging and dangerous job of manually pulling brakes on each train car were primarily Black but were paid less than White engineers with less risky positions (Darity & Mullen, 2020). More recently, occupations with larger percentages of Black men pay less than occupations in which Black men are underrepresented, even accounting for different levels of educational credentials necessary (Hamilton et al., 2011). When more Black and Latino men move into an occupation within a city, wages in that industry fall and disparities between men of color and similarly educated White men increase (von Lockette & Spriggs, 2015).

The processes whereby a potential worker finds—or does not find—a specific job also create or amplify racial inequalities. Many jobs are found through referrals—in which current employees alert potential employees about job opportunities. Collecting job applicants through referrals tends to maintain an employer's racial structure because of the homogeneity of social networks. Job seekers similarly rely on social network ties, which also vary by race and gender. White men use contacts in ways hypothesized to help them find jobs, and the use of these ties explains some of their earnings advantages (Smith 2000). Strong experimental evidence also points to discrimination in formal hiring processes. Employers are less likely to schedule an interview with potential employees whose name or résumé signifies that they are Black relative to equally qualified White applicants (Pager et al., 2009; Bertrand & Mullainthan, 2004).

When individuals are not able to work in the market or when jobs are not available, social welfare policy can provide crucial income supports. However, as is the case with the U.S. labor market, core elements of the U.S. income safety net exacerbate rather than eliminate racial inequalities. The foundation document of the U.S. social welfare state, the Social Security Act of 1935 (SSA), created a social pension system that provided income support for older Americans; established unemployment insurance and disability insurance systems; and set out state programs for cash assistance for the poor. But many features of the SSA and its subsequent revisions benefited

White Americans to the exclusion of others, maintaining the racial caste system that characterized the U.S. labor market. Racialized aspects show up in both the broad social insurance programs (old age and unemployment insurance) and the "secondary" programs that targeted the poor.

The Act excluded agricultural workers and domestic servants from the social insurance programs. One theory holds that this exclusion was political, designed to secure the support of Southern legislators whose constituencies would have been harmed if Black sharecroppers and laborers would have had viable alternatives to low-paid labor (Quadagno, 1994). Other explanations focus on administrative or policy diffusion explanations (Rodems & Shaefer, 2016), but the end result was the same: the program by design disproportionately benefited White workers. For instance, 60% of Native Americans workers, close to half of all Black workers, and over 40% of workers of Mexican, Japanese, and Filipino descent were excluded from the newly established Unemployment Insurance (UI) system (Lovell, 2002). These exclusions applied most heavily to women; almost three-quarters of Black women were ineligible. Although these exclusions were rolled back in the 1950s, racial differences in coverage and claims for UI remain today. Relative to White, non-Hispanic workers, Black and Hispanic workers are less likely to apply for unemployment benefits when unemployed. Contingent on unemployment, Hispanic workers are less likely than White workers to receive benefits (Gould-Werth & Shaefer, 2012). During the Great Recession, unemployed Black and Hispanic workers were less likely than White workers to receive unemployment insurance (Nichols & Simms, 2012).

The Social Security Act also established a framework for anti-poverty programs for elders and women with children, including the Aid to Dependent Children (ADC) program, which later became Aid to Families with Dependent Children (AFDC). Unlike the social insurance programs which were designed as broad-based, fully funded programs to secure citizens' social rights (albeit primarily White citizens), these "secondary" programs targeted politically weaker groups (the poor) and lacked the stable funding of the primary programs. Additionally, the authority and responsibility for much of the design and funding of these programs fell to the states, which were given considerable leeway in designing and enforcing rules. This state-level discretion allowed for racialized policies, such as "suitable home" requirements that allowed public officials to monitor mothers' private behavior and Southern states' policies that limited welfare access during cotton-picking season (Gordon, 1994; Neubeck & Cazenave, 2002).

REVERSING EXTREME INEQUALITY   489

From this unequal foundation, the income support system continued to evolve. Conservative political rhetoric drew on American anti-Black sentiment in building a case against AFDC. Political actors used racially coded language that associated welfare receipt with Blackness. President Ronald Reagan's invocation of the "welfare queen" stereotype most famously associated failures of the economic system with character flaws or behavioral deviance of Black women. While such "welfare racism" (Neubeck & Cazenave, 2002) extends to other populations of color in some instances, anti-Blackness pervades the social construction of the welfare system, providing useful cover for social neglect of poverty. As scholar Emilie Townes notes:

> The images of the Black Matriarch and the Welfare Queen allow us to feel better about cutting back the help that we, as a society, give to poor people. . . . These two stereotypes divert our attention from structural inequalities—economic, political, and social—that affect not only Black mothers and their children but all of us. (2010, pp. 64–65)

Trends of using anti-Black coded rhetoric continued in the 1996 welfare reforms, which replaced AFDC with Temporary Assistance to Needy Families (TANF), which gave states even more freedom in designing income support programs. States with larger percentages of Black populations instituted stricter TANF rules—such as family caps which did not increase benefits when recipients had more children (Soss et al., 2008). Over time, the value and availability of TANF benefits have further eroded, meaning the program has all but disappeared as a source of support for any poor families. Thus, income inequality by race not only has strong historical roots, but also is sustained and continues to evolve in the present.

Assets and Wealth

Although related, wealth is distinct from income. Wealth is defined as net worth, or the value of all assets minus all debts (Leigh 2006). Focusing on assets, these are the "rights or claims related to property," particularly tangible assets that include financial wealth and physical property (Nam et al., 2008). It is possible to earn little income from labor and earnings, yet still maintain high levels of wealth and thus receive sizable income from capital interests and assets. In addition, wealth is even more concentrated and unequal than income, and racial disparities in wealth are much greater than disparities in income. Earnings inequality is one factor that contributes to higher wealth inequality, yet earnings alone cannot account for the extreme concentrations at the top of the wealth distribution in the United States (Benhabib et al., 2017). Bequests and high returns to wealth (including private business and capital income) are additional key contributors.

Wealth inequality is almost as high now as in the 1920s before the stock market crash and the Great Depression. The share of wealth held by the top tenth of a percent (0.1%) hit a high of almost 25% in 1929, declined to a low of 7% in 1978, but persistently increased over the next three decades, rising up to 22% in 2012 following the recent Great Recession of 2007–2009 (Saez & Zucman, 2016). Only the top 20% of the wealth distribution has fully recovered from the Great Recession as the middle class has seen modest growth, but has not returned to pre-2007 levels. To put this in context, a Brookings report notes that if all the wealth held by U.S. households were distributed equally, it would equate to $343,000 per person (Sawhill & Pulliam, 2019). Black and Hispanic households have median net worth about a tenth that of White households and are more likely to be in the bottom of wealth distributions, with zero or negative net worth (Dettling et al., 2017). Thus, as wealth becomes more concentrated at the top, households of color fall further behind.

How does race relate to wealth? The answers that immediately come to mind are often not the best predictors of racial wealth gaps. One key reason is that wealth can be passed along from generation to generation, so individual economic mobility can rarely compensate for family wealth that has been built over decades. One study intentionally highlights incorrect ideas that people offer about why Blacks and Latinos have less wealth than Whites that don't hold up to empirical scrutiny. Some of these "myths" are that greater educational attainment, increased employment, more savings, greater financial literacy, increased entrepreneurship, or higher marriage rates would decrease racial wealth disparities (Darity et al., 2018). But in fact, Whites who are high school dropouts and unemployed have greater median wealth than their Black counterparts with a college degree who are working full-time (Hamilton et al., 2015). Given the timeline noted above and the fact that White children have always grown up in families with significantly greater wealth than Black children and most other children of color (Oliver & Shapiro 2006; Shanks et al., 2011), they by definition start from a better financial position to build wealth. The following paragraphs offer a description of racial trends in three key areas that impact wealth: land, homeownership, and wealth stripping through fines and fees.

Land Loss

While Native Americans were being forced off their lands and the 4 million newly freed slaves were denied their promised 40 acres and a mule following the Civil War, large numbers of immigrants from Europe were given 160-acre plots through the Homestead Act (Oubre, 1978; Williams 2003; Williams Shanks 2005). Despite such unequal treatment, Blacks owned 15 million acres of farmland by 1910. Almost a century later, however, Blacks owned only about 1.1 million acres of farmland and were part owners of another 1.07 acres (Lewan & Barclay, 2001). This land loss was typically involuntary. Much of this land was taken by cheating, intimidation, and violence (Lewan & Barclay, 2001). One recent practice used by unscrupulous lawyers and speculators is to locate "heir property" owned in common by multiple people, buy interest in a portion of the land, and then force a partition sale to purchase the rest, often at a price below market value (Lewan & Barclay, 2001; Mitchell, 2000, 2005). It is estimated that about half of the 4.4 million acres lost since 1969 was a result of such forced partition sales (Lewan & Barclay, 2001). About a quarter of U.S. household assets is in the form of non-financial assets, which is primarily real estate (Sawhill & Pulliam, 2019). If those 13 million acres of land lost since 1910 were still controlled by Black landowners, tens of thousands more Black families would have valuable assets to grow and invest.

In addition to providing a stable place to live, homeownership comprises a significant portion of the wealth portfolio and growth of low- to moderate-income households. The forced savings and increasing equity position via a fixed mortgage provide a predictable path to asset accumulation. After the Civil War, Blacks were eager to have a place of their own. Even during a time of great uncertainty, lack of access to credit, and persistent violence, they still managed to move up the ladder from tenancy to ownership. Thus, the period between 1870 and 1910 represents the time of largest growth, with owner occupancy increasing from 8% to 24%. Between 1910 and 1940, with the Great Migration and people moving from rural areas and farms to urban cities, contested spaces and segregation led to a stagnation in Black home ownership (Collins & Margo, 2011). Between 1940 and 2007, there were positive

492 TRINA R. SHANKS ET AL.

changes in mortgage terms, the GI Bill, and the Fair Housing Act of 1968. Over these years, the rate of homeownership increased for both Whites and Blacks—but the racial gap didn't decrease much (Collins & Margo, 2011).

After all-time highs in home ownership, the Great Recession of 2007–2009 led to a collapse of the housing market and a record number of foreclosures where many lost their homes. Losses in wealth were greatest among communities of color (Kochhar & Fry, 2014). In addition to pre-recession racially motivated structural barriers to homeownership, new post-recession barriers emerged, such as more stringent lending criteria, including requiring larger down payments (Famighetti & Hamilton, 2019). By the second quarter of 2020, home ownership rates had begun to rise across the board and reached 76% for non-Hispanic Whites, 47% for Blacks, 61% for Asians, and 51% for Hispanics (U.S. Census Bureau, 2020). Policies that eliminate disparities in homeownership rates and returns could substantially reduce racial wealth gaps for Black and Latino households (Sullivan et al., 2015).

Wealth Stripping through Fees and Fines

Three legislative acts passed in the 1980s (Depository Institutions Deregulation and Monetary Control Act, Garn-St. Germain Act, and the Tax Reform Act of 1986) paved the way for financial deregulation and usurious fees that have led to egregious wealth stripping among low- to moderate-income households (Fergus, 2014). With these legal changes, choices that under other circumstances would lead to greater economic security are now becoming a source of increasing debt and reductions in wealth. There are four examples of this phenomenon. In homeownership there was a rise in subprime mortgages and predatory lending. In higher education, changes in fees and student aid have led to crippling levels of student debt. With employment in the face of stagnating wages, there has been a rise in payday lending. In transportation, auto insurance rates based on zip codes have led to higher rates among the poorest residents (Fergus, 2014). An erosion of consumer protections and these increases in disparate rates, fines, and fees mean that families have even less discretionary income to build assets. Households of color are those most hurt by these financial shifts and complexities (Fergus & Shanks, 2022).

Student loan debt is a good illustrative example of how the changing costs of funding higher education has helped strip wealth and has led to greater disparities. On average, Black college graduates owe $25,000 more in student loan debt than White college graduates, and Black student borrowers are most likely to struggle financially with high monthly payments of $350 or more (Hanson, 2020). Four years after graduation, the Black-White student loan debt gap nearly triples—mostly due to graduate school debt (Hanson, 2020; Scott-Clayton & Li, 2016). Thus, student loan debt hampers economic progress and further exacerbates existing racial wealth gaps (Hanson, 2020; Mishory et al., 2019). Student debt is also an issue of concern among master of social work (MSW) graduates, with the mean level of debt at $66,000 in 2019, with even higher average amounts for Black and Latinx/Hispanic students (Salsberg et al., 2020).

Policy to Mitigate Economic Inequality by Race

Eliminating the racial inequalities in income and wealth will require different policies than the United States has tried over the past several decades. After civil rights demonstrators of the late 1950s and 1960s brought attention to the social and economic struggles of Black, Latino, and Indigenous Americans, the federal government responded with the Civil Rights Act of 1964, the Economic Opportunity Act of 1964, and other programs of the War on Poverty. Five decades later, these programs have proven inadequate to counter the historic and ongoing trends that have been noted. Going forward, we believe that making real progress requires more than tepid investments in universal programs in hopes that communities of color will disproportionately benefit. Instead, policy should focus on intentional race-based reparations (discussed below) and designing universal programs with explicit equity goals. This section discusses the latter—how to use a targeted universalism approach (Powell et al., 2019) in which policies are established with universal goals but are designed with evidence-based and possibly population-specific strategies for ensuring equitable outcomes.

Income supplements—whether in the form of a child allowance, basic income, or similar transfer schemes—hold the potential to reduce the racial income gap. The logic of such proposals is that they would equalize income through providing some level of guaranteed incomes to all households. Unlike means-tested benefits that phase out as earnings increase, unconditional income supplements are often designed to be universal, although subject to progressive taxation. For instance, one proposal for a universal child allowance of \$250–\$300 per child with possible reductions for multiple children, is forecast to reduce child poverty overall by about 40% (Shaefer et al., 2018). Poverty among Black and Hispanic children would fall slightly more (projected reductions of 41.5% and 40.6%, respectively) than poverty among White children (reduction of 39.8%), but the differences are slight (Shaefer et al., 2018). While other experiments underway in Stockton, California, Jackson, Mississippi, and elsewhere may yield more equitable outcomes, universal income supplements will likely be more powerful programs if designed with a race-conscious addition or in conjunction with reparations.

Inclusive asset building strategies—whether innovation in the provision of shelter/housing, cooperative and small business support, or debt-free higher education—can help reduce racial wealth gaps. At a minimum, they can ensure that the incentives and tax breaks to promote savings and wealth accumulation also benefit low-income populations and communities of color, not just those already well-off. Raising the floor so everyone has some financial assets can provide greater economic security for all. One specific proposal is for universal progressive child development accounts (CDAs) that automatically enroll newborns and provide financial incentives for financially vulnerable populations. There is already experimental evidence of the benefits for parents and children of opening such accounts with an initial deposit of \$1,000 (Huang et al., 2017). If CDAs are targeted in such a way that poor children and children of color receive additional endowments over time, they would enter young adulthood with greater wealth and less racial disparity (Kijakazi & Carther, 2020).

Reparations

Much of what we have discussed so far can be examined through the lens of ongoing discussions on reparations. However, the U.S. history of reparations has been complicated. On the one hand, the United States assisted with reparation for Jews impacted by the Holocaust through the Marshall Plan. Japanese and some Native Americans tribal nations have received partial reparations. However, the promise of reparations to formerly enslaved Black Americans and their descendants has never been realized. Though the slave owners were compensated for their losses, the significant loss of life and wages has never been addressed nationally. The "Black Manifesto" marks the most notable proposal for reparations (Dye, 2007; George, 2013; Lechtreck,

2012). Over the past 30 years there has been new interest in developing a Reparations Commission and developing recommendations for a national reparations plan. The Conyers House Bill and the Booker Senate Bill represent other proposals to consider ways to redress the wealth inequity that exists for Black Americans. Sandy Darity and Mullen (2020) even suggest using the racial wealth gap as a barometer to calculate how much is owed to the African descendants of slaves (#ADOS) and to measure over time whether reparations are working sufficiently to remedy past harms.

What Can Social Workers Do?

Social workers play an integral role in progressing policies and values that protect the rights and dignity of the most vulnerable populations in the United States. Our code of ethics demands that social workers challenge injustice with a particular focus on poverty, unemployment, discrimination, and oppression (National Association of Social Workers [NASW], 2017). Social work practitioners, researchers, and educators need to develop anti-racist skills and work for racial justice (McCoy, 2020). We need social workers in positions of power in public office to give voice to the facts. As our timeline depicts, Black, Indigenous, and People of Color in the United States have endured a myriad of policies that intentionally barred each respective community from the same access to economic upward mobility and security. Moreover, many of these policies were enacted to further disadvantage marginalized communities while benefiting White Americans. These facts must be taken into account when discussing macro-level interventions. In addition to improving the United States' safety net programs, targeted interventions for our most vulnerable groups must be seriously considered and fought for, not just on social media and the streets, but also in local, state, and federal legislatures.

Social workers who are not policymakers still have a responsibility to arm their communities with factual information regarding the policies that affect their daily lives. It can be difficult to encourage eligible voters who have lost hope in democracy in the United States to become engaged, and this is why it is critical to energize communities consistently, rather than every two to four years. Social workers who practice one-on-one therapy can utilize health models that emphasize holistic well-being, which include discussing environmental factors that cause clients to feel unsafe in their communities (Yocum & Lawson, 2019).

Emphasizing the areas where clients do have power can create a powerful shift in government where the voices of constituents are appropriately represented by lawmakers. Finally, social workers practicing community organizing can empower communities on a larger scale through hosting non-partisan events that address issues that are important to community members. These suggestions are not exhaustive, but rather a launching point for practitioners to consider how to leverage our influence for the betterment of our most vulnerable populations.

Conclusion

Economic inequality in the United States has been growing over the past three decades in both income and wealth. Black, Indigenous, and People of Color (BIPOC) have been the groups hardest hit by these trends. Although our country promotes its founding values of liberty and justice for all, these have not been realized in the economic lives experienced across race and ethnicity. There is economic largess at the top of income and wealth distributions, but deprivation and struggle at the bottom. There are periods in our history when things were not quite so unequal as today, or at least were trending in the opposite direction. Changing these trajectories is the next frontier for civil rights.

Study Questions

1. Why is it important to understand the difference between wealth and income when considering economic inequality?
2. How do economic inequality and its social impacts differ from poverty? What kinds of programs and policies specifically address inequality? Which policies specifically address economic inequality due to race?
3. What implications can you draw from the finding that the United States has the highest level of economic inequality among developed industrial countries?
4. To what extent could changes to labor laws reduce racial gaps in earnings? What parts of the labor market are more easily changed? Less easily changed?

5. How do racialized policies of the early twentieth century show up in modern safety net programs? What kind of changes could reduce the racial gap in support provided by programs such as Unemployment Insurance or Social Security?
6. Which policies contributed to the extraction of wealth from Black/African Americans? Native Americans?
7. Is the racial wealth gap roughly the same in 2016 as it was in 2002, 1982, or 1962? Why is this the case?

References

Aliprantis, D., Carrol, D. R., & Young, E. (2019). *The dynamics of the racial wealth gap.* Cleveland, OH: Federal Reserve Bank of Cleveland.

Baradaran, M. (2017). *The color of money: Black banks and the racial wealth gap.* Cambridge, MA: Harvard University Press.

Bellu, G. (2006). Inequality analysis, the Gini Index. Food and Agriculture Organization of the United Nations. Retrieved September 30, 2020, from http://www.fao.org/3/a-am352e.pdf%20.

Benhabib, J., Bisin, A., & Luo, M. (2017). Earnings inequality and other determinants of wealth inequality. *American Economic Review, 107*(5), 593–97.

Bertrand, M., & Sendhil, M. (2004). Are Emily and Greg more employable than Lakisha and Jamal? A field experiment on labor market discrimination. *American Economic Review, 94*(4), 991–1013.

Bivens, J. (2017). Inequality is slowing US economic growth: Faster wage growth for low- and mid-income workers is the solution. Economic Policy Institute. Retrieved September 30, 2020, from https://www.epi.org/publication/secular-stagnation/.

Brennenstuhl, S. (2018). Health of mothers of young children in Canada: Identifying dimensions of inequality based on socio-economic position, partnership status, race, and region. *Canadian Journal of Public Health, 109*(1), 27–34.

Collins, C., Asante-Muhammed, D., Hoxie, J. & Nieves, E. (2016). Ever growing gap: Without change African American and Latino families won't match White families for centuries. Institute for Policy Studies. Retrieved October 8, 2020, from https://ips-dc.org/report-ever-growing-gap/.

Collins, W. J. & Margo, R. A. (2011). Race and home ownership from the end of the Civil War to the present. *American Economic Review, 101*(3), 355–359.

Darity, W. A., & Mullen, K. A. (2020). *From here to equality: Reparations for Black Americans in the twenty-first century.* Chapel Hill: University of North Carolina Press.

Darity, W., Jr., Hamilton, D., Paul, M., Aja, A., Price, A., Moore, A., & Chiopris, C. (2018). *What we get wrong about closing the racial wealth gap.* Samuel DuBois Cook Center on Social Equity and Insight Center for Community Economic Development. Durham, NC (DuBois Cook Center) and Oakland, CA (Insight).

David, E. (2010). An administrative Trail of Tears: Indian removal. *American Journal of Legal History, 50*(1), 49–100. https://doi.org/10.1093/ajlh/50.1.49.

Dettling, L. J., Hsu, J. W., Jacobs, L., Moore, K. B., & Thompson, J. P. (2017). *Recent trends in wealth-holding by race and ethnicity: Evidence from the Survey of Consumer·Finances.* Washington, DC: Board of Governors of the Federal Reserve System (US).

Duffin, E. (2020). U.S. household income distribution, by Gini-coefficient 1990–2019. *Statista*. Retrieved September 30, 2020, from https://www.statista.com/statistics/219 643/gini-coefficient-for-us-individuals-families-and-households/.

Dye, K. (2007). *The Detroit beginnings of the Black Manifesto for reparations controversy, 1968–1969.* ProQuest. Toledo, OH: University of Toledo. Retrieved October 1, 2020, from https://search.proquest.com/openview/d8f07c0be9fa4c1b034d037f01d1bde1/1?pq-origsite=gscholar&cbl=18750&diss=y.

Famighetti, C., & Hamilton, D. (2019). The Great Recession, education, race, and home-ownership. Economic Policy Institute Working Economics Blog. Retrieved October 8, 2020, from https://www.epi.org/blog/the-great-recession-education-race-and-homeownership.

Fergus, D. (2014). Financial fracking in the Land of the Fee, 1980–2008. In R. Cramer & T.R. Williams Shanks (Eds.), *The assets perspective: The rise of asset building and its impact on social policy* (pp. 67–95). London: Palgrave Macmillan.

Fergus, D., & Shanks, T. R. (2022). The long afterlife of slavery in asset stripping, historical memory, and family burden: Toward a third reconstruction. *Families in Society, 103*(1), 7–20.

George, M. E. (2013). The Black Manifesto and the churches: The struggle for Black Power and reparations in Philadelphia [M.A., Temple University]. Retrieved September 30, 2020, from http://search.proquest.com/docview/1411316371/abstract/ED738A5 7A8CF41F2PQ/1.

Gordon, L. (1994). *Pitied but not entitled: Single mothers and the history of welfare.* New York: Free Press.

Gould-Werth, A., & Shaefer, H. L. (2012). Unemployment insurance participation by education and by race and ethnicity. *Monthly Labor Review, 135*(10), 28–41.

Gross, T. (2020). How the CARE Act became a tax-break bonanza for the rich explained. Retrieved October 8, 2020, from https://www.npr.org/2020/04/30/848321204/how-the-cares-act-became-a-tax-break-bonanza-for-the-rich-explained.

Hamilton, D., Austin, A. & Darity, W., Jr. (2011). Whiter jobs, higher wages: Occupational segregation and the lower wages of black men. *Economic Policy Institute Briefing Paper 268*, 1–13.

Hamilton, D., Darity, W., Jr, Price, A. E., Sridharan, V., & Tippett, R. (2015). *Umbrellas don't make it rain: Why studying and working hard isn't enough for Black Americans.* New York: The New School.

Hanson, M. (2020). Student loan debt by race. EducationData.org. Retrieved March 12, 2021, from https://educationdata.org/student-loan-debt-by-race#student-loan-debt-by-race-and-ethnicity.

Harmon, A. (2010). *Rich Indians: Native people and the problem of wealth in America.* Chapel Hill: University of North Carolina Press.

Horowitz, J. M., Igielnik, R., & Kochhar, R. (2020). *Most Americans say there is too much economic inequality in the U.S. but fewer than half call it a top priority.* Pew Research Center. Retrieved September 30, 2020, from https://www.pewsocialtrends.org/2020/01/09/trends-in-income-and-wealth-inequality/.

Huang, J., Sherraden, M. S., Clancy, M. M., Sherraden, M., & Shanks, T. R. (2017). *Start lifelong asset building with universal and progressive Child Development Accounts.*

Retrieved October 9, 2020, from https://grandchallengesforsocialwork.org/wp-cont
ent/uploads/2017/03/PAS.11.1-v2.pdf.

Johnson, H. (2007). *Black Wall Street: From riot to renaissance in Tulsa's Historic Greenwood District*. Fort Worth, TX: Eakin Press.

Kijakazi, K., & Carther, A. (2020). *How Baby Bonds could help Americans start adulthood strong and narrow the racial wealth gap*. Urban Institute. Retrieved October 10, 2020, from https://www.urban.org/urban-wire/how-baby-bonds-could-help-americans-start-adulthood-strong-and-narrow-racial-wealth-gap.

Kochhar, R., & Fry, R. (2014). Wealth inequality has widened along racial, ethnic lines since end of Great Recession. *Pew Research Center, 12*(104), 121–145.

Kornhauser, R. (2015). Economic individualism and punitive attitudes. *Punishment & Society 17*(1), 27–53. https://doi/10.1177/1462474514560393.

Lechtreck, E. A. (2012). We are demanding $500 million for reparations: The Black Manifesto, mainline religious denominations, and black economic development. *The Journal of African American History, 97*(1–2), 39–71. https://doi.org/10.5323/jafria merhist.97.1-2.0039.

Leigh, W. (2006). Wealth measurement: Issues for people of color in the United States. In Jessica Gordon Nembhard & Ngina Chiteji (Eds.), *Wealth accumulation and communities of color in the United States* (pp. 23–66). Ann Arbor: University of Michigan Press.

Lewan, T. & Barclay, D. (2001). Torn from the land: Black Americans' farmland taken through cheating, intimidation, even murder. *Associated Press*. Retrieved October 8, 2020, from http://muckrakerfarm.com/2001/12/torn-land-black-americans-farml and-taken-cheating-intimidation-even-murder/.

Livingstone, A., & Weinfeld, M. (2015). Black families and socio-economic inequality in Canada. *Canadian Ethnic Studies, 47*(3), 1–23. https://doi.org/10.1353/ces.2015.0026.

Lonnghi, S. (2017). Racial wage differential in developed countries. IZA World of Labor. Retrieved September 20, 2020, from https://wol.iza.org/articles/racial-wage-differenti als-in-developed-countries/long.

Lovell, V. (2002). Constructing social citizenship: The exclusion of African American women from unemployment insurance in the US. *Feminist Economics, 8*(2), 191–197.

Lui, M., Robles, B., Leondar-Wright, B, Brewer, R., & Adamson, R., with United for a Fair Economy (2006). *The color of wealth: The story behind the U.S. racial wealth divide*. New York: The New Press.

Macias, J. (2018). Racial wealth snapshot: Latino Americans. *Prosperity Now*. Retrieved October 8, 2020, from https://prosperitynow.org/blog/racial-wealth-snapshot-latino-americans.

Martinson, M. L., & Reichman, N. E. (2016). Socioeconomic inequalities in low birth weight in the United States, the United Kingdom, Canada, and Australia. *American Journal of Public Health, 106*(4), 748–754.

Matthew, P., & Brodersen, D. M. (2018). Income inequality and health outcomes in the United States: An empirical analysis. *The Social Science Journal, 55*(4), 432–442. https://doi.org/10.1016/j.soscij.2018.05.001.

McCoy, Henrika. 2020. Black Lives Matters, and yes, you are racist: The parallelism of the twentieth and twenty-first centuries. *Child and Adolescent Social Work Journal, 37*, 463–475. https://doi.org/10.1007/s10560-020-00690-4.

Mishory, J., Huelsman, M., & Kahn, S. (2019). How student debt and the racial wealth gap reinforce each other. The Century Foundation. Retrieved March 12, 2021, from https://

tcf.org/content/report/bridging-progressive-policy-debates-student-debt-racial-wea
lth-gap-reinforce/?agreed=1&agreed=1.

Mitchell, T. W. (2000). From reconstruction to deconstruction: Undermining black
landownership, political independence, and community through partition sales of
tenancies in common. *Northwestern University Law Review, 95*, 505.

Mitchell, T. W. (2005). Destabilizing the normalization of rural black land loss: A critical
role for legal empiricism. *Wisconsin Law Review, 2*, 557–615.

Mock, B. (2020). Why black businesses and home ownership won't close the wealth gap.
Bloomberg City Lab. Retrieved February 28, 2021, from https://www.bloomberg.com/
news/articles/2020-02-25/how-to-actually-close-the-racial-wealth-gap.

Nam, Y., Huang, J., & Sherraden, M. (2008). Asset definitions. In Signe-Mary McKernan
& Michael Sherraden (Eds.), *Asset building and low-income families* (pp. 1–31).
Washington, DC: Urban Institute Press.

National Association of Social Workers (2017). NASW code of ethics. Retrieved
September 30, 2020, from https://www.socialworkers.org/About/Ethics/Code-of-Eth
ics/Code-of-Ethics-English.

Neubeck, K. J., & Cazenave, N. A. (2002). *Welfare racism: Playing the race card against
America's poor*. New York: Routledge.

Nichols, A., & Simms, M. (2012). Racial and ethnic differences in receipt of unemployment insurance benefits during the Great Recession. Urban Institute. Unemployment
and Recovery Project Brief 4 (June). https://www.urban.org/sites/default/files/publ
ication/25541/412596-Racial-and-Ethnic-Differences-in-Receipt-of-Unemployment-
Insurance-Benefits-During-the-Great-Recession.PDF

Noguera, P. A. (2017). Introduction to "Racial inequality and education: Patterns and
prospects for the future." *The Educational Forum, 81*(2), 129–135. doi: 10.1080/
00131725.2017.1280753. Received September 30, 2020, from https://www.tandfonline.
com/doi/full/10.1080/00131725.2017.1280753.

OECD (2020). Income inequality (indicator). Received on September 30, 2020, from
https://data.oecd.org/inequality/income-inequality.htm.

Oliver, M. L., & Shapiro, T. M. (2006). *Black wealth, white wealth: A new perspective on racial inequality*. London: Taylor & Francis.

Oliver, M. L., & Shapiro, T. M. (2019). Disrupting the racial wealth gap. *Contexts, 18*(1),
16–21. https://doi.org/10.1177/1536504219830672.

Oubre, C. F., & Mooney, K. C. (1978). *Forty acres and a mule: The Freedmen's Bureau and
Black land ownership* (p. 178). Baton Rouge, LA: Louisiana State University Press.

Pager, D., Bonikowski, B., & Western, B. (2009). Discrimination in a low-wage labor
market: A field experiment. *American Sociological Review, 74*(5), 777–799.

Powell, j. a., Menendian, S., & Ake, W. (2019). *Targeted universalism: Policy and practice*.
Haas Institute for a Fair and Inclusive Society. Berkeley, CA: University of California.

Quadagno, J. (1994). *The color of welfare*. Oxford University Press.

Quillian, L, Heath, A, Pager, D, Midtbøen, A. H., Fleischmann, F. & Hexel, O. (2019). Do
some countries discriminate more than others? Evidence from 97 Field Experiments
of Racial Discrimination in Hiring. *Sociological Science, 6*(18), 467–496. Received
September 20, 2021, from https://www.sociologicalscience.com/download/vol-6/
june/SocSci_v6_467to496https://wol.iza.org/articles/racial-wage-differentials-in-
developed-countries/long

Rodems, R., & Shaefer, H. L. (2016). Left out: Policy diffusion and the exclusion of black workers from unemployment insurance. *Social Science History, 40*(3), 385–404.

Rothstein, R. (2017). *The color of law: A forgotten history of how our government segregated America*. New York: Liveright.

Runes, C. (2018). *What's behind the wealth gap in Asian American and Pacific Islander communities?* The Urban Institute. Retrieved October 8, 2020, from https://www.urban.org/urban-wire/whats-behind-wealth-gap-asian-american-and-pacific-islander-communities.

Saez, E., & Zucman, G. (2016). Wealth inequality in the United States since 1913: Evidence from capitalized income tax data. *The Quarterly Journal of Economics, 131*(2), 519–578.

Salsberg, E., Quigley, L., Richwine, C., Sliwa, S., Acquaviva, K. D., & Wyche, K. (2020). The Social Work profession: Findings from three years of surveys of new social workers. CSWE. Retrieved March 12, 2021, from https://cswe.org/CSWE/media/Workforce-Study/The-Social-Work-Profession-Findings-from-Three-Years-of-Surveys-of-New-Social-Workers-Dec-2020.pdf.

Sawhill, I. V., & Pulliam, C. (2019). *Six facts about wealth in the United States*. Brookings Institute (June 25). Retrieved October 9, 2020, from https://www.brookings.edu/blog/up-front/2019/06/25/six-facts-about-wealth-in-the-united-states.

Schaefer, K. (2020). 6 facts about economic inequality in the U.S. Pew Research Center. Received September 30, 2020, from https://www.pewresearch.org/fact-tank/2020/02/07/6-facts-about-economic-inequality-in-the-u-s/.

Scott-Clayton, J., & Li, J. (2016). Black-white disparity in student loan debt more than triples after graduation. Brookings. *Evidence Speaks Reports, 2*(3). http://hdl.handle.net/10919/83265.

Shaefer, H. L., Collyer, S., Duncan, G., Edin, K., Garfinkel, I., Harris, D., Smeeding, T. M., Waldfogel, J., Wimer, C., & Yoshikawa, H. (2018) A universal child allowance: A plan to reduce poverty and income instability among children in the United States. *The Russell Sage Foundation Journal of the Social Sciences, 4*(2), 22–42.

Shanks, T., Price, A., Lui, M., & Corral, V. (2011). *Diverging pathways: How wealth shapes opportunity for children*. Insight Center for Community Economic Development. Oakland. Retrieved October 9, 2021, from http://ww1.insightcced.org/uploads/CRWG/DivergingPathways.pdf.

Shapiro, T. (2017). *Toxic inequality: How America's wealth gap destroys mobility, deepens the racial divide, and threatens our future*. New York: Basic Books.

Small, M. L. & Pager, D. (2020). Sociological perspectives on racial discrimination. *Journal of Economic Perspectives, 34*(2), 49–67.

Smith, S. S. (2000). Mobilizing social resources: Race, ethnic, and gender differences in social capital and persisting wage inequalities. *The Sociological Quarterly, 41*(4), 509–537.

Soss, J., Fording, R. C., & Schram, S. F. (2008). The color of devolution: Race, federalism, and the politics of social control. *American Journal of Political Science, 52*(3), 536–553.

Sullivan, L., Meschede, T., Dietrich, L., & Shapiro, T. (2015). *The racial wealth gap*. Institute for Assets and Social Policy, Brandeis University. Waltham, MA (Brandeis) and New York (DEMOS).

Taylor, K. (2019). *Race for profit: How banks and the real estate industry undermined black homeownership*. Chapel Hill: The University of North Carolina Press.

Townes, E. M. (2010). From mammy to welfare queen: Images of Black women in public-policy formation. In B. J. Brooten (Ed.), *Beyond slavery* (pp. 61–74). London: Palgrave Macmillan.

Trafzer, C. E. & Hyer, J. E. (1999). *Exterminate them: Written accounts of the murder, rape, and enslavement of Native Americans during the California Gold Rush.* East Lansing, MI: Michigan State University Press.

U.S. Census Bureau. (2020). *Quarterly residential vacancies and homeownership, first quarter 2020 (CB20-58).* Social, Economic & Housing Statistics Division. Washington, DC: U.S. Government Printing Office.

Von Lockette, N. D., & Spriggs, W. E. (2015). Wage dynamics and racial and ethnic occupational segregation among less-educated men in metropolitan labor markets. *Review of Black Political Economy, 43,* 35–56.

Wallerstein, M. (1999). Wage-setting institutions and pay inequality in advanced industrial societies. *American Journal of Political Science, 43*(3), 649–680.

Williams, T. R. (2003). Asset-building policy as a response to wealth inequality: Drawing implications from the Homestead Act of 1862. *Social Development Issues, 25,* 47–58.

Williams Shanks, T. (2005). The Homestead Act: A major asset-building policy in American history. In M. Sherraden (Ed.), *Inclusion in the American dream: Assets, poverty, and public policy* (pp. 20–41). Oxford: Oxford University Press.

Wilson, V. (2018). *10 years after the start of the Great Recession Black and Asian households have yet to recover lost income.* Economic Policy Institute. Retrieved September 30, 2020, from https://www.epi.org/blog/10-years-after-the-start-of-the-great-recession-black-and-asian-households-have-yet-to-recover-lost-income/.

Yamamoto, E. K., Chon, M., Izumi, C. L., & Kang, J. (2014). *Race, rights, and reparations: Law and the Japanese American interment.* Boston, MA: Wolters Kluwer Law & Business.

Yocum, S., & Lawson, K. (2019). Health coaching case report: Optimizing employee health and wellbeing in organizations. *Journal of Values-Based Leadership, 12*(2), Article 8. Retrieved October 1, 2020 from https://scholar.valpo.edu/jvbl/vol12/iss2/8/.

Zucman, G. (2016). *Wealth inequality.* The Stanford Center on Poverty and Inequality. Received September 30, 2020, from https://inequality.stanford.edu/sites/default/files/Pathways-SOTU-2016-Wealth-Inequality-3.pdf.

20

White Supremacy and American Social Policy

Implications for Racism-Centered Policy Practice

Jerome H. Schiele, Denise McLane-Davison, and Christopher Maith, Sr.

White supremacy has been a persistent social problem that has challenged America's promise of racial equality since the 1619 landing (Hope-Franklin & Higginbotham, 2010; Kendi, 2016). Because of its ubiquitous effects, White supremacy can be conceived as a meta grand challenge that has contributed significantly to inequality in America (Feagin, 2019).

Although White supremacy has been well documented as a grand challenge in thwarting America's potential toward racial justice, American social policy has not sufficiently addressed nor remedied White supremacy's intergenerational consequences (Neubeck & Cazenave, 2001; Quadagno, 1994). Social policy's ability to contest White supremacy should not be underestimated. As a major form of social intervention, and with the authority and resources of the state, social policy can influence sweeping and substantive social change. However, by tending to deny, deflect, or downplay racism as a comprehensive challenge to democracy, American social policy's attempt at grappling with the problem of White supremacy has been piecemeal, reluctant, and often hypocritical.

This chapter uses a racism-centered perspective of policy practice to analyze American social policy's reluctance at effectively addressing White supremacy and to provide examples of how this perspective can be applied in policy practice and in social work curricula. A racism- centered perspective of policy practice views racism as the fulcrum of American social policy and allows a racially true consciousness, rather than a racially false consciousness, to guide social policy development, implementation, and analysis

---

Jerome H. Schiele, Denise McLane-Davison, and Christopher Maith, Sr, *White Supremacy and American Social Policy* In: *Social Work and the Grand Challenge to Eliminate Racism.* Edited by: Martell L. Teasley, Michael S. Spencer, and Melissa Bartholomew, Oxford University Press. © Oxford University Press 2023. DOI: 10.1093/oso/9780197674949.003.0020

(Schiele, 2020). Applying this perspective is important for social policy analysis because although racism Applying this perspective is important for social policy analysis because although racism is examined in most social policy texts used in social work, it frequently is not the exclusive or even primary focus (Schiele, 2020). Thus, the study of racism has experienced a kind of marginalization even in a profession, like social work, that purports to care deeply about social justice issues. For the purpose of this chapter, white supremacy is defined as the systematic normalization and institutionalization of the belief that people of European descent are superior to other groups and, therefore, should dominate the political, economic, and cultural domains of life. It essentially is the system of white racism, especially in the United States, that bestows unearned power and privileges to white people relative to people of color (DiAngelo, 2018). Thus, this chapter uses the term "racism" to imply white supremacy in that American racism was created and exist to protect and advance the collective interests of white or European-Americans (Feagin, 2019; Katznelson, 2005).

The Reluctance to Address White Supremacy

American social welfare policy has been reluctant at grappling with the problem of racism/white supremacy since the start of the Republic. Evidence of this unwillingness can be observed in two important ways. First, there is an absence of a coherent and explicit federal social policy that specifically addresses the needs of people of color (Neubeck & Cazenave, 2001). Although there are and have been various civil rights legislation, these policies rely heavily on race neutral terms that affirm the immorality and illegality of racism. Thus, terms such as "all citizens," "all persons" or "prohibit discrimination on the basis of . . . " are used but references to specific groups of color, such as African-Americans or Latinx Americans are generally not found, unless, for example, those that speak to Native or First Nation Americans. This phenomenon reinforces the entrenchment of white supremacy in American social policy in that, historically, people of color have disproportionately experienced poverty and economic, employment, and educational disadvantage (Schiele, 2020), which would justify the need to address these groups explicitly.

The second indicator of this reluctance is that when anti-discriminatory or anti-racist policies have been established, they are enacted in the context of a national crisis or social upheaval, rather than being developed during normal times (Day & Schiele, 2013). Indeed, the two major periods—the 1860s and the 1960s—when anti-discriminatory policies were passed were both characterized by tremendous social unrest. Regarding the 1860s, the Thirteenth, Fourteenth, and Fifteenth Amendments to the U.S. constitution (see Chapter 10) each advanced the cause of racial justice (Hope-Franklin & Higginbotham, 2010). Societal and political adjustments to these constitutional amendments buttressed the promotion of White supremacy and its political and economic domination (see Chapter 10).

Along with the Civil Rights Act of 1866, these amendments emerged from the aftermath of the Civil War that produced sudden and significant social change, and that placed the former confederacy under federal control until the 1877 Hayes Tilden Compromise (Hope-Franklin & Higginbotham, 2010). Similarly, the Civil Rights Act of 1964, which prohibited discrimination based on race, sex, and other factors, and subsequent civil rights legislation of that decade emerged from the social upheaval of the Civil Rights movement (Day & Schiele, 2013). The Civil Rights movement of the 1950s and 1960s forced America to re-examine its legacy of structural racism by unearthing the atrocities of racial injustice that were frequently displayed on the new medium of television (Hope-Franklin & Higginbotham, 2010).

Identifying a few examples of this reluctance is important, but it is equally important to examine the reasons for the unwillingness of American social policy to seriously and substantively address White supremacy. There at least three reasons for this reluctance: (1) White supremacy's firm foundation when the nation was established; (2) social welfare policy as a form of racial regulation; and (3) the denial of racism.

White Supremacy's Foundation

The United States was founded on the value of White supremacy. Although the founders were concerned about the injustices levied against them by the British, they nonetheless used the British model as a way to incorporate themes of White supremacy to establish a new White nation (Hope-Franklin & Higginbotham, 2010; Kendi, 2016). The themes of White supremacy essentially dehumanized people of color by concluding that they were objects of exploitation and subjugation (Akbar, 1996; Kendi, 2016). The themes that justified this exploitation and subjugation were as follows: (a) the notion that people of color were dominated by their emotions and that reasoning was beyond their ability, and, thus, people of color were thought to be intellectually inferior to Whites; (b) because they were assumed to be dominated by their emotions, people of color were characterized as subhuman and immoral; and (c) characterizations of intellectual and moral inferiority also were extended to describe the culture of people of color as "uncivilized" (Schiele, 2020).

These themes were codified very early in law and in social practices. For African Americans, these themes were codified in the slave codes of the mid-seventeenth century that designated that a person's bondage was linked to the race of the individual's birth mother (Hope-Franklin & Higginbotham, 2010). In other words, one's race was increasingly legalized as a marker of one's perpetual bondage. The legalization of slavery would last until 1865, and would lay the foundation for the stigmatization and victimization of African Americans thereafter (Day & Schiele, 2013; Kendi, 2016). Moreover, American slavery provided White supremacy with further ammunition in that it provided evidence to support the notion that White people were born to rule and regulate African Americans. American slavery also provided the poorest White American with a benchmark for personal comparison that positioned him or her in a higher social/racial status. As Du Bois (1935) intimated years ago, whiteness produced psychological "wages" that were independent of a White person's socioeconomic status. Thus, regardless of status, the privileges associated with being White protected White Americans and ensured their power base relative to people of color.

The themes of White supremacy were also codified in stigmatizing and subjugating other groups of color. For Native Americans, for example, White supremacy was expressed by considering the Native peoples as poor stewards of property and having a "savage" way of life (Schiele, 2020). Regarding the latter, White supremacy justified the taking of land from Native peoples and displacing them ultimately on reservations. This displacement and forced acquisition of land was guided by the principle of "manifest destiny," the belief that White Christian America was ordained by God to settle, conquer, and civilize the new land and native peoples (Day & Schiele, 2013). In this sense, Native Americans, like African Americans, were viewed as property that could be not only bought and sold, but also easily removed. The Indian Removal Act of 1930 was the legal manifestation of this belief (Day & Schiele, 2013).

Social Policy as Racial Regulation

The examples of the enslavement of African Americans and the removal and displacement of Native Americans demonstrate the racial control or regulatory features of White supremacy. The slave codes and the Indian Removal Act were models of how the regulatory aspects of White supremacy were implemented. Thus, the slave codes and the Indian Removal Act were social policies that represented what several authors refer to as the "social control" function of social policy development and implementation (Blau & Abramovitz, 2014; Piven & Cloward, 1993). Socially controlling the behavior of people of color would help ensure that they would not threaten the political, economic, and cultural domination Whites had over the American landscape (Feagin, 2019; Kendi, 2016; Zinn, 2005). In this way, the social control feature of social policy can be understood as racial regulation for people of color (Neubeck & Cazenave, 2001; Schiele, 2020).

In this racial regulation, social policy serves to protect, maintain, and advance White supremacy, or what Neubeck and Cazenave (2001) refer to as "white racial hegemony," which they conceptualize as "European Americans' systematic exercise of domination over racially subordinate groups" (Neubeck & Cazenave, 2001, p. 23). They moreover maintain that from a racism-centered perspective, the state becomes a racialized state and "is the political arm of white racial hegemony" (Neubeck & Cazenave, 2001, p. 23). Here, the state is assumed to protect and promote the political, economic, and cultural interests of White Americans relative to people of color. Walters (2003) refers to this White bias in state affairs as "white nationalism" and argues that a major outcome of this form of nationalism is "policy racism" (p. 250), which engenders a racialized ideology that institutionalizes racism within all branches of government.

Protecting the interests of White Americans through White nationalism has been enhanced since the election of former president Donald J. Trump. His 2016 campaign theme of "Make America Great Again," which some believed was a dog whistle for "Make America White Again" (Thompson, 2016; Perez-Huber, 2016), spoke in large part to the racial anxiety many non-Hispanic White Americans have over the growing population of people of color. Former president Trump tapped into this fear and used the topic of immigration to exploit it. From a racism-centered framework, Trump's immigration enforcement proposals and policies were a political strategy to reduce White racial anxiety over demographic and cultural changes that threaten the advantages White Americans have had over people of color (Schiele, 2020). Therefore, Trump's policies and political agenda affirmed and reinforced this racial desperation, as overt expressions of White nativism and nationalism appear to be rising (Perez-Huber, 2016; Shear & Davis, 2017). Primary examples of these overt actions were the 2020 police killings of unarmed Black men by White police officers, such as the appalling murder of George Floyd in Minnesota (Klemko & Dennis, 2020), and the domestic terrorist attack on the U.S. Capitol building in January 2021 (Ray, 2021).

The Denial of Racism

The denial of racism is a third reason for American social policy's reluctance to address White supremacy. Throughout American history, a critical feature of the system of White supremacy has been to deny racism as a motive and outcome for its existence (Hope-Franklin & Higginbotham, 2010; Kendi, 2016). Denying racism has essentially been a strategy to deflect attention away from the privileges and control that White Americans have had and continue to have (Bonilla-Silva, 2001, 2013). This deflection strategy has been manifested in divergent ways but basically relies heavily on religious and scientific justifications, cultural oppression, and the value of individualism.

Regarding religious justifications, White supremacy has relied heavily on biblical interpretations to dehumanize and victimize people of color (Hope-Franklin & Higginbotham, 2010; Kendi, 2016). These interpretations use biblical texts and scriptures to demonstrate God's preference for whiteness or White people and God's mandate that non-Whites be subservient. Martin and Martin (2002) refer to these misinterpretations as "religious mythomania," because they distort and misrepresent scriptural meanings to support Eurocentric domination. The "mania" aspect of this concept implies that the creation and application of these myths are a form of pathology, similar to what Wright (1985) referred to as racial psychopathology. In this pathology, the racist thrives on ego inflation that distorts his or her self-image and concept so that "others" can be systematically objectified and then set up for exploitation that advances the racist's political and economic interests. In this way, religion has been used to provide the ultimate rationale for subjugation and violence because God's word is viewed as universally unquestionable.

The scientific community, especially social science, also has contributed to the denial of racism in that its use of so-called objective methods and measures is purported to advance the truth. For people of color, the "truth" was thought and "found" to be that people of color, especially African Americans, were less intelligent, more prone to criminal behavior, and members of pathological families (Gould, 1996; Moynihan, 1965; Terman, 1916). The fallout of this historic scientific racism is the portrayal of the culture of people of color as uncivilized and the projection of the belief that people of color have contributed nothing to world development and human history (Ani, 1994). Thus, how could people of European descent be racist if indeed science demonstrates the inferiority of people of color as a consistent finding and observation?

Finally, cultural oppression and the value of individualism also have contributed to the denial of racism. Young (1990) defines cultural oppression as "the universalization of a dominant group's experience and culture and its establishment as the norm" (p. 59). In this universalization, the dominant group regulates values and interpretations, creating inequality in the worth assigned to divergent interpretations and life experiences. Because White Americans have had more power relative to other racial groups, their experiences and interpretations have dominated the American sociocultural landscape (Day & Schiele, 2013). White supremacy is a major cultural value and experience that has significantly shaped social relationships and the distribution of material and symbolic resources. However, because White Americans benefit from its existence and continuation, it is in their collective self-interest to deny White supremacy as the reason for their racial domination.

A primary way racism is denied in America is through the culturally imposed value of individualism (Day & Schiele, 2013). Individualism is the belief that all success and failure experienced by a person are attributed to his or her work ethic, intelligence, genetic proclivities, and resiliency. Ignored is the person in his or her situation or environment, and how this context significantly facilitates or hinders individual growth and development. In this cultural model, the assumption is that people should be strong enough to deal with life adversities, and that human misery and societal inequities are independent of one another (Day & Schiele, 2013). Thus, racism is denied because the individual person of color should be resilient enough to overcome life obstacles that all people, regardless of race, are assumed to experience equally.

From a racial oppression perspective, the use of individualism as a strategy to deny and deflect racism conceals the systemic privileges and inequities produced by White supremacy (Bonilla-Silva, 2001, 2013). To the extent that people internalize the value of individualism and repudiate the power of the context, they participate in the perpetuation of White supremacy. A major principle of racism-centered policy practice and analysis is, as Mills (1959) posited, that all personal problems are essentially public issues. Racism is an American public issue, and the next section applies the racism-centered perspective to examine a few roles that policy practitioners can assume when advocating for policies that address White supremacy.

Policy Practice to Address White Supremacy

Policy practice is an important strategy to address the problem of White supremacy. Cummins et al. (2011) define policy practice as advocacy in the political arena aimed at preventing, reducing, and eliminating shared human problems. For the purpose of this chapter, racism-centered policy practice can be understood as a process and method aimed at influencing political/ policy change to eliminate and offset the nefarious consequences of White supremacy. Racism-centered policy practitioners can assume many different roles in combating injustices that people of color face daily. We offer a few below.

Policy Practitioner Roles

The roles that policy practitioners can assume to advocate for social policy change continue to evolve (Cummins et al., 2011). However, there are three roles that can be very important in combating racism/White supremacy: (1) protester, (2) legislative advocate, and (3) social media influencer. Advocacy is the underlying activity in these roles and is defined as championing the rights of individuals or communities through direct intervention or through empowerment. Each assumed policy practice role has its level of importance in the overall fight against racial inequality and eliminating White supremacy.

Protester. The role of protestor is the most visible that a policy practitioner can assume to address racial injustice and White supremacy. Protestors are often those who mobilize and gather around a common cause to address social inequities. Thus, protest requires what Martin Luther King Jr. (1963)

viewed as nonviolent direct action to unearth the oppressive features of a community. For King (1963), a primary goal of nonviolent direct action was to compel an oppressive regime to deal with its injustice: "Nonviolent direct action seeks to create such a crisis and foster such a tension that a community which has constantly refused to negotiate is forced to confront the issue. It seeks so to dramatize the issue that it can no longer be ignored" (p. 81).

The major activities of racism-centered policy practitioners who engage in protests are organizers and planners (Cummins et al., 2011; Morris, 1984). Organizers engage community members around policies that impact the community and generate support from the community (Cummins et al., 2011; Morris, 1984). Organizers work with and develop community leaders to empower them to speak out against the policies and mobilize community members. Politically, organizers work to research and analyze policies to discover their adverse consequences on affected communities (Cummins et al., 2011; Morris, 1984). This information is then shared with members of the community to sound the alarm against the policy. Policy practitioners who engage in planning focus on empowering community members to express and strategically promote their voices to address a policy (Cummins et al., 2011; Morris, 1984). They facilitate opportunities for the community to come together through advocacy events, such as protests, to express their voices and narratives about a policy (Cummins et al., 2011; Morris, 1984).

Using youth crime as an example, racism-centered policy practitioners can utilize the protester role as a way to bring attention to the problem of youth crime and the racial disparities associated with this problem. These racial disparities are well documented and adversely affect communities of color, especially young African American men (Teasley, 2020). Practitioners can begin the process of organizing others through grassroots efforts to educate community members on youth crime, its impact on juveniles, and its overall short- and long-term economic and social implications. The practitioner can also solicit additional advocates to help advance the agenda of addressing the racial disproportionality of youth crime and ultimately organize visible protests. The most powerful display of protesting could also include the mobilization of large numbers of youth of color and others who could peacefully protest against the racial disproportionality of youth crime. Educating and mobilizing youth of color as protesters could provide a more authentic critique of policies that regulate youth crime, similar to when the Parkland Florida students organized to protest school gun shootings (see Grinberg & Muaddi, 2018).

Legislative advocate. The second role that is important for racism-centered policy practice is that of legislative advocate. Cummins et al. (2011) view legislative advocacy as occurring through eight stages of policymaking. Although all of the stages are relevant, only the first four will be used here as examples for racism-centered policy practice, and the problem of crime among youth of color will be used to illustrate the four stages. For the first stage, *Problem Identification and Case Findings*, utilization of racism-centered policy practice would examine youth crime as a problem that disproportionately impacts communities of color. During this first stage, legislative advocates would confirm the problem of youth violence and determine its pervasiveness.

Questions such as who are specifically affected by the problem, and how it affects communities of color and the broader society, are considered. During the second stage, *Data Collection and Analysis*, the legislative advocate would use racism-centered policy practice to determine how the social problem of youth crime emerged by collecting data from various sources, including members of communities of color. Here, the legislative advocate seeks to determine how youth crime varies by different communities of color so that prospective recommendations to resolve the problem can be tailored to each group. In this stage, the advocate endeavors to understand the role that racism plays in the emergence and manifestation of youth crime and how racism exerts both common and differential effects on young people of color. The third stage, *Informing the Public and Identifying Stakeholders*, requires that the legislative advocate use racism-centered policy practice to identify those who would benefit from, and who would have a genuine interest in, reducing or eliminating youth crime. Racism-centered policy practice is vital in this stage because this is where formulating a team of advocates to address the policy begins. Thus, the legislative advocate will need to incorporate divergent voices from communities of color to obtain their explanations of and solutions to the problem. These voices become the face of the movement and thus have the responsibility to influence policy change.

The fourth stage that Cummins et al. (2011) discuss is *Selecting Policy Options and Developing Policy Goals*. Legislative advocates, during this stage, use racism-centered policy practice to incorporate all of the prior three stages. During this stage, legislative advocates, with the assistance of the public and stakeholders identified in stage 3, begin to formulate policy options to address youth crime in communities of color. This stage incorporates the use of the first two stages through the utilization of data collection and analysis of youth crime to establish the goals of the proposed policy options. Legislative advocates would then work with their stakeholders, especially those from the affected communities, to develop anti-racist policy language that can be included in the policy options to ensure that the problem of youth crime is adequately and appropriately addressed.

A related role of the legislative advocate is that of the lobbyist, which is a person who formally advocates on behalf of an organized interest or numerous organized interests (Cummins et al., 2011). These organized interests usually manifest as coalitions that collaborate to advance a specific legislative agenda. Lobbying can be either "proactive" or "defensive."

Proactive lobbying involves activities aimed at promoting a specific bill or legislation, whereas defensive lobbying works to arrest or prevent the bill or legislation from becoming law (Cummins et al., 2011). There are several national organizations that specifically lobby to advance racial justice, a few of which are Black Lives Matter, Dream Defenders, The National Association for the Advancement of Colored People (NAACP), and Color of Change. Racism-centered policy practitioners should connect with organizations like these to help eliminate the deleterious consequences of White supremacy.

Social media influencer. The final racism-centered policy practitioner role is the social media influencer. Because of the proliferation of social media, this role has quickly become a major activity that policy practitioners can engage in when advocating for social justice issues. Social media platforms have become the most efficient way to reach enormous numbers of people instantaneously (Lane et al., 2019), which can significantly facilitate the dissemination of social justice messages and expose racist and White supremacist ideas. Racism-centered policy practitioners can utilize social media platforms to reach and mobilize mass amounts of individuals around the world and expose racial injustices on a global scale.

Within the role of social media influencer, the practitioner can educate, enlighten, motivate, and ultimately attempt to eradicate racist and White supremacist sentiments instantaneously. The significance of this role can be observed in the recent mobilization efforts against police shootings of unarmed African Americans. According to Valinote (2020), activists mobilized on social media, with scores of images, videos, and written messages shared, to highlight the May 2020 killing of George Floyd. Valinote goes on to say that social media gives those who face injustice a chance to control the narrative: "If it weren't for technology and social media, [the protests] would not have happened. That's why it's so important that we have those outlets. That's going to help catapult change" (Valinote, 2020, n.p.).

Finally, in the role of social media influencer, racism-centered policy practitioners should rely heavily on the #hashtag method used in social media platforms, such as Twitter, Facebook, and Instagram. The #hashtag method is a great way for racism-centered policy practitioners to organize around a racial justice issue and mobilize for change through social policy development.

The roles of protester, legislative advocate, and social media influencer are just a few ways in which racism-centered policy practitioners can advocate for policy changes that reduce and eliminate racism. We next offer an example of how social work educators can incorporate the themes of racism-centered policy practice in their social welfare policy classes.

Racism-Centeredness in a Social Welfare Policy Course

This section provides some specific examples of how the racism-centered perspective can be applied in a social welfare policy course taught by the second author. The graduate course *Social Welfare & Urban Economics* explores historical dynamics of race, class, and other oppressions impacting U.S. social welfare policy. This foundation course focuses on the dynamics and complexities of urban communities as the basis for urban social work research and practice. Race and culture are centered as a part of a critical discourse for understanding public social welfare historical formulation and the impact of its implementation. In alignment with the Council on Social Work Education's (CSWE's) Education Policy and Accreditation Standards (CSWE, 2015), students are engaged in structural immersion assignments that advance human rights and social, economic, and environmental justice. The course relies heavily on a racism-centered framework augmented significantly by womanist educational theory (Marr, 2015) to achieve the social work competencies and objectives.

Womanist Pedagogy and Racism-Centeredness

Both racism-centered and womanist educational theory are undergirded by tenets of critical pedagogies which critique interlocking power structures and agency (Schiele, 2020; McLane-Davison, 2017; Marr, 2015). Through a synergy of these concepts, knowledge production and truth are validated from the inter- and intragenerational collective life experiences and narratives. Race is interrogated as both a form of oppression and position of collective action toward liberation (Gilbert, 1974; McGee & Stovall, 2015). Thus, centering racism represents an oppression-resistance interchange which is dynamically fluid and consistently stagnant as White racial hegemony fights to maintain its hold.

Womanist pedagogy builds from critical epistemologies and methodologies and provides a tool to disrupt the strongholds of White domination in teaching, research, and praxis (McLane-Davison, 2017; Nash, 2019). Womanist pedagogy intentionally centers the racialized voices of historically marginalized populations, and promotes equity of resources of disenfranchised communities by validating their lived experiences as truth that celebrates resilience (Espino, 2012; Bent-Goodley et al., 2017; Marr, 2015), and honors their cultural ontology. Womanist pedagogy engages the student-faculty relationship in transformative practices of collective intellect which are inclusive of rituals, traditions, and cultural practices which produce knowledge.

The reciprocity of knowledge offers a freedom standpoint (McLane-Davison, 2017) that transcends time and space as it interrogates and exposes covert agendas and power imbalances. The utilization of womanist pedagogy evokes agency through narratives of storytelling and using proverbs, affirmations, idioms, lyrics, and indigenous forms of communication to "talk back" to the dehumanization of Black bodies and "othering" of Black intellect (Marr, 2015; McLane-Davison, et al., 2019). Womanist pedagogy is thus a complementary method of instruction for the racism-centered framework as disruptive tools of White hegemonic education. The course assignments reinforce both frameworks and help students to gain experiential learning around real world problems.

Course Assignments

Case Study Model: Freddie Gray's Life
In 2015, a young unarmed African American man, Freddie Gray, was found dead after the Baltimore police had arrested and transported him to a police station. Gray's death sparked major protests and rioting in Baltimore for a

number of days and placed the Baltimore Police Department under considerable scrutiny (Tkacik, 2018). This prompted Baltimore mayor Stephanie Rawlings-Blake to request that the U.S. Department of Justice (2016) provide a thorough investigation of the Baltimore Police Department, which revealed a historical and systemic pattern of structural racism and police brutality. The report also provided evidence that the Baltimore City Police Department (BPD) participated in pervasive violations of Black citizen's civil and human constitutional rights (U.S. Department of Justice, 2016; West Baltimore Commission on Police Misconduct, 2016).

The course uses the death of Freddie Gray as a historical marker for understanding decades of structural inequities based on race (West Baltimore Commission on Police Misconduct, 2016; Brown, 2015). Freddie Gray was an unarmed Black male who died in the custody of the Baltimore Police Department (U.S. Department of Justice, 2016). The community outcry of resistance demanded accountability for Freddie's detainment and subsequent death (Brown, 2015; McLane-Davison et al., 2019). On the heels of the death of Travon Martin (February 2012), Jordan Davis (November 2012), Michael Brown (August 2014), and Tamir Rice (November 2014), the death of Freddie Gray (April 2015) was symptomatic of the social ills of Black and Brown youth in Baltimore and across the United States (DeKosnik & Feldman, 2019). A closer examination of Freddie Gray's life revealed a childhood of poverty, lead poisoning, special education, public housing, and inconsistent employment. His life story is a perfect storm of race-based public policies which legalized the residential segregation and divestment of public funding in his community of Sandtown-Winchester in Baltimore (Brown, 2015; McLane-Davison et al., 2019; Roberts, 2011).

In the course, a system known as Results-Based Accountability (RBA), which is a performance measurement tool that uses data-driven decision-making (McLane-Davison et al., 2019), is employed to examine the degree of community safety in Baltimore. At the height of the 2015 Baltimore uprising in response to Gray's death, there was a call for public and community safety. Throughout the course, the professor underscores the complexity of "community safety." Students are asked to imagine being residents of Freddie Gray's community and are posed the following question: What are the necessary indicators needed to ensure safety in that community? Data from multiple sources are used to comparatively analyze data between Gray's community in Baltimore and the rest of Maryland. RBA is used to examine the impact of social policy at the intersection of race and place, starting with the desired outcome that "Baltimore communities are safe." In the course, students are required to use the RBA to examine the safety issues in Gray's community and offer community-based and social policy recommendations to improve safety.

Cyberactivism through Syllabi Development

For this assignment, students are required to develop a social/racial justice syllabus using the resources of the internet. The first hashtag syllabus, #Ferguson Syllabus, initiated by Marcia Chatelain, emerged in 2014 after the fatal shooting of Michael Brown Jr. Through Twitter crowdsourcing, the collective input of the greater community has curated a variety of syllabi which functioned as a form of activist research correcting popular narratives about power, gender, and race (Gipson, 2019). Technology is engaged as a tool of activism, consciousness raising, and affirmation for communities seeking representation and power. Hashtag syllabi promote the collective intellect of intergenerational knowledge production through a multidimensional "living document" (McLane-Davison et al., 2019).

Related to the development of the students' hashtag syllabi, Cyberwomanism is used as concept to critique and condemn the patriarchal structuring of technology as a masculine and cis- gendered space alienating women and non-White powered institutions (Everett, 2004).

Cyberwomanism is utilized to circumvent agencies that have sought to disenfranchise voices from the margins. As an integral part of community organizing and political engagement, cyberwomanism expands womanist pedagogy to include advocacy leadership that deconstructs structural systems and policies, thus moving from passive to active learning and agency.

Through this form of storytelling, there are three main components: collaboration, critical dialogue, and transformative research. A few examples of syllabi developed by students are as follows: #TheFeddrieGraySyllabus: An Unlikely Case Study; #ToPimpAButterflySyllabus: Intergenerational Trauma in African American Communities; and #ThisIsAmericaSyllabus: Developing Critical Narratives from the Streets.

Anti-Gentrification and Ethnic Displacement

In this course, students also focus on the problems of gentrification and ethnic displacement, which are major contemporary urban social problems. This residential displacement of people of color, primarily African Americans, disrupts their existing social networks and resource accessibility and can cause many other social problems. One assignment that highlights some of the consequences of this displacement is the #FightBlightBmore's Hood Hike (Fight Blight Bmore, 2018). #FightBlightBmore is a local non-profit agency founded by Nneka N'Nambi, a Black woman civic engineer. The agency provides a cultural immersion into the neighborhoods of West Baltimore where Freddie Gray lived for most of his life.

A two-mile guided walk by the organization's founder focuses on the visual representation of structural racism. On the Hood Hike, community stakeholders are encouraged to focus on cracked sidewalks, community dumping, exposed water hoses, and vacant and decaying buildings. Baltimore's community demolition and rehabilitation project has left old buildings with asbestos, mold, and exposed lead and other environmental hazards (Brown, 2015). #FightBlightBaltimore indicates that because of the lack of green space, along with the decaying buildings, it creates a "hot spot" where temperatures are artificially elevated during the summer months. The high levels of heat, combined with the toxins of decaying buildings, spread this poison throughout the community (Brown, 2015).

Focusing on the assumptive outcome, "Baltimore communities are safe," students are asked to look for visual indicators that tell a story of the impact of their selected social policy for the course. For instance, one student focused on the overrepresentation of Black youth from this zip code who had police contact or arrest. As the class walked through the community, there was notably an overgrown area which was once used for recreation, including eating tables and a basketball court. There were also numerous surveillance devices designed to record voices and photos of community residents. Because of these observations, the student indicated that even if the youth wanted to play in the community, the air and land had been polluted with toxins.

Another observation of this particular Hood Hike was the impact of lead poisoning and poor air quality on the youth and their families' education outcomes, and mental and physical health, especially the high rates of asthma. The conclusion, although there was no visible presence of an arrestable crime, was that the community is not safe.

Congressional Black Caucus Foundation (CBCF) Annual Conference

For the past 40 years the U.S. Congressional Black Caucus Foundation has hosted an Annual Legislative Conference in Washington, D.C., during the third week of September (Congressional Black Caucus Foundation, 2020). This event offers a National platform that examines the impact of various social policies that affect communities of color. Students are required to attend the conference, which provides them with access to decision-makers and community stakeholders, as well as elected officials, grassroot organizers, celebrities, and the global Black community. The four-day event includes think tanks and special topic sessions that address priority issues in Black America. The evenings are networking opportunities that include invitational and open access receptions, banquets, and regional or special interest events. Attendance provides an opportunity to influence national and local discussions about key issues/policy priorities.

The policy tracks include health and wellness, education and labor, community and civic engagement, criminal justice, business, economic development and wealth creation, beauty, fashion and lifestyle, and foreign affairs. When attending the conference, students are asked to remember the RBA framework and the desired outcome of "Baltimore communities are safe." Before attending the conference, students will have identified a specific federal social policy of interest. During the conference, they attend sessions that they feel are important in helping them make the case for how their particular social policy is relevant to the lives of Baltimore residents. The students are generally overwhelmed with excitement as they listen to content experts debate the same social policy and social problems which have been reviewed in the class. The students are often amazed at the accessibility of national power brokers and feel confident contributing to the discourse and networking. After returning from the conference, students submit reflection papers and are encouraged to utilize their new knowledge as a primary source for their policy analysis final paper.

Conclusion

White supremacy is a grand challenge for America and the social work profession, and there is considerable hesitancy to address it head on. The reluctance to grapple with White supremacy can be especially discerned in American social policy. Because of White supremacy's firm national foundation, social policy's racial regulatory function, and the denial of racism, White supremacy has not received the attention it deserves in American social policy practice and analysis. Using a racism-centered policy practice framework, this chapter has analyzed the reasons for social policy's reluctance to effectively address White supremacy, has offered a few roles that policy practitioners can assume when advocating for policies to reduce and eliminate White supremacy, and has provided an example of how racism-centeredness can be integrated in social welfare policy courses.

With its emphasis on understanding micro-level problems through macro-level lenses, social policy practice and advocacy are great ways to allow a broad interrogation of White supremacy. Social policy practitioners and analysts are encouraged to focus more on the singular problem of racism and White supremacy in America instead of the popular paradigm of intersectional oppressions. Although the popularity and application of intersectionality offers much for policy practitioners and analysts, a major shortcoming of intersectionality is that it can be viewed as a form of human identity reductionism that slices and dices the individual into micro components without linking them to a broader and more overarching form of human identity and experience. Racism continues to be a major overarching problem that enormously shapes the identities and experiences associated with privilege and oppression in the United States (Kendi, 2019). Thus, racism deserves to be designated as a "Grand Challenge" for social work to take on, and its significance in generating multiple and interlocking problems of inequality warrants much more attention.

Study Questions

1. Define White supremacy and discuss why U.S. social policies are reluctant to focus exclusively and comprehensively on this form of injustice.
2. Why is it important for social workers to focus on White supremacy and its role in social policy development and implementation?
3. Why and how has U.S. social policy promoted racial regulation?
4. What are some important strategies that social workers can utilize to address White supremacy in social policy development and implementation?
5. Of the policy practitioner roles discussed in the chapter, which one do you believe can most effectively advocate for social policy change that challenges White supremacy?
6. What are some additional policy practitioner roles, not identified in the chapter, that can be employed to resist White supremacy?

WHITE SUPREMACY AND AMERICAN SOCIAL POLICY   521

7. Why should more attention be given to White supremacy in social policy courses in social work?
8. What are some factors that prevent greater focus on White supremacy in social work education generally, but especially in social policy courses?
9. What are some additional assignments, not included in the chapter, that can be integrated in social policy courses in social work to highlight the problem of White supremacy?
10. How can U.S. social policies be used to address the ascendency of explicit White supremacy groups that promote and engage in racial violence?

References

Akbar, N. (1996). *Breaking the chains of psychological slavery*. Tallahassee, FL: Mind Productions and Associates.

Ani, M. (1994). *Yurugu: An African-centered critique of European cultural thought and behavior*. Trenton, NJ: Africa World Press.

Bent-Goodley, T., Fairfax, C., & Carlton-LaNey, I., (2017). The significance of African-centered social work for social work practice. *Journal of Human Behavior in the Social Environment, 27*, 1–14.

Blau, J., with Abramovitz, M. (2014). *The dynamics of social welfare policy* (4th ed.). New York: Oxford University Press.

Bonilla-Silva, E. (2001). *White supremacy and racism in the post-civil rights era*. Boulder, CO: Lynne Rienner.

Bonilla-Silva, E. (2013). *Racism without racists: Color-blind racism and the persistence of racial inequality in the United States* (4th ed.). Lanham, MD: Rowman and Littlefield.

Brown, L. (2015, October 29). Down to the wire: Displacement and disinvestment in Baltimore city. *The 2015 State of Black Baltimore*. Still separate, still unequal. Greater Baltimore Urban Leagues. 71–89. Retrieved from: https://www.academia.edu/8619 756/Down_to_the_Wire_Displacement_and_Disinvestment_in_Baltimore_City

Congressional Black Caucus Foundation, (2020, September, 29). 2020 Annual Report: Lifting up, leading up. Retrieved from: https://issuu.com/congressionalblackc aucusfoundation/docs/2021_cbcf_annualreport2020_final_single_pages

Council on Social Work Education. (2015). *Educational policy and accreditation standards*. Alexandria, VA: Council on Social Work Education.

Cummins, L. K., Byers, K., & Pedrick, L. (2011). *Policy practice for social workers: New strategies for a new era*. Boston: Allyn and Bacon.

Day, P. J., & Schiele, J. H. (2013). *A new history of social welfare* (7th ed.). Boston, MA: Pearson.

De Kosnik, A., & Feldman, K. (2019). Introduction: The hashatags we've been forced to remember. In A. DeKosnick & K. P. Feldman (Eds.), *#Identity hashtagging: Race, gender, sexuality, and nation* (pp. 1–19). Ann Arbor: University of Michigan Press.

Du Bois, W. E. B. (1935). *Black reconstruction in America: An essay toward a history of the part black folk played in the attempt to reconstruct democracy in America, 1860–1880.* Reprinted in 1966. London: Frank Cass.

Espino, M. (2012). Seeking the "truth" in stories we tell: The role of critical race epistemology in higher education research. *The Review of Higher Education, 36*(1) 31–67.

Everett, A (2004). On cyberfeminism and cyberwomanism: High-tech mediations of feminism's Discontents. *Signs: Journal Women in Culture and Society, 30,* 1278–1286.

Feagin, J. R. (2019). *Racist America: Roots, current realities, and future reparations* (4th ed). New York: Routledge.

#Fight Blight Bmore's Hood Hikes (2018, June 18). Retrieved from: https://www.fightblig htbmore.com/fight-blight-bmore-blog/2018/6/20/fightblightbmore-hood-hikes

Gilbert, G. (1974). The role of social work in black literature. *The Black Scholar, 6,* 16–23.

Gipson, G. (2019). Creating and imagining Black futures through Afrofuturism. In A. De Kosnik & K. P. Feldman (Eds.), *#identity: Hashtagging race, gender, sexuality, and nation* (pp. 84–103). Ann Arbor: University of Michigan Press.

Gould, S. J. (1996). *The mismeasure of man* (revised and xxpanded ed.). New York: W. W. Norton.

Grinberg, E., & Muaddi, N. (2018). How the Parkland students pulled off a massive national protest in only 5 weeks. https://www.cnn.com/2018/03/26/us/march-for-our-lives/index.html.

Hope-Franklin, J., & Higginbotham, E. (2010). *From slavery to freedom: A history of African Americans* (9th ed.). New York: McGraw-Hill.

Kendi, Ibram X. (2016). *Stamped from the beginning: The definitive history of racist ideas in America.* New York: Bold Type Books.

Kendi, Ibram X. (2019). *How to be an antiracist.* New York: One World.

King, M. L., Jr. (1963). *Why we can't wait.* New York: Harper & Row.

Klemko, R., & Dennis, B. (2020, May 29). Former Minneapolis police officer charged in George Floyd's death as protests continue nationwide. *Washington Post.* Retrieved from https://www.washingtonpost.com/national/former-minneapolis-police-officer-char ged-in-george-floyds-death-as-protests-continue-nationwide/2020/05/29/d20b76e6-a1cd-11ea-81bb-c2f70f01034b_story.html

Lane, D. S., Lee, S. S., Liang, F., Kim, D. H., Shen, L., Weeks, B. E., & Kwak, N. (2019). Social media expression and the political self. *Journal of Communication, 69,* 49–72.

Marr, V. L. (2015). Ditchin' the master's gardening tools for our own: Growing a womanist methodology from the grassroots. *Feminist Teacher, 24,* 99–109.

Martin, E. P., & Martin, J. M. (2002). *Spirituality and the black helping tradition in social work.* Washington, DC: National Association of Social Workers.

McGee, E.O. & Stovall, D. (2015). Reimagining critical race theory in education: Mental health, healing, and the pathway to liberatory praxis. *Educational Theory, 65,* 491–511.

McLane-Davison, D. (2017). Emancipatory engagement: An urban womanist social work pedagogy. *Journal of Human Behavior in the Social Environment, 27,* 474–486.

McLane-Davison, D., Allen-Milton, S., Archibald, P., & Holmes, R. (2019). Of common bonds: Accounting for intergenerational culture competency in community policing. *Race and Justice, 9,* 8–21.

Mills, C. W. (1959). *The sociological imagination.* New York: Oxford University Press.

Morris, A. D. (1984). *The origins of the civil rights movement.* New York: The Free Press.

Moynihan, D. P. (1965, March). *The Negro family: The case for national action.* Washington, DC: The U.S. Department of Labor, Office of Policy Planning and Research.

Nash, J. C. (2019). *Black feminism reimagined: After intersectionality.* Durham, NC: Duke University Press.

Neubeck, K. J., & Cazenave, N. A. (2001). *Welfare racism: Playing the race card against America's poor*. New York: Routledge.

Perez-Huber, L. (2016). Make America great again: Donald Trump, racist nativism and the virulent adherence to White supremacy amid US demographic change. *Charleston Law Review, 10*, 215–248.

Piven, F. F., & Cloward, R. (1993). *Regulating the poor: The functions of public welfare* (updated ed.). New York: Vintage Press.

Quadagno, J. (1994). *The color of welfare: How racism undermined the war on poverty*. New York: Oxford University Press.

Ray, R. (2021, January 12). What the Capitol insurgency reveals about white supremacy and law enforcement. Brookings Institution. Retrieved from https://www.brookings.edu/blog/how-we-rise/2021/01/12/what-the-capitol-insurgency-reveals-about-white-supremacy-and-law-enforcement/.

Roberts, D. (2011). *Fatal invention: How science, politics, and big business re-crate race in the twenty-first century*. New York: The New Press.

Schiele, J. H. (Ed.). (2020). *Social welfare policy: Regulation & resistance among people of color* (2nd ed.). San Diego, CA: Cognella.

Shear, M. D., & Davis, J. H. (2017). Trump moves to end DACA and calls on Congress to act. *New York Times*, September 5. Retrieved from https://www.nytimes.com/2017/09/05/us/politics/trump-daca-dreamers-immigration.html.

Teasley, M. (2020). Black male education and criminalization in the United States: Racial regulation and resistance In J. H. Schiele, *Social welfare policy: Regulation & resistance among people of color* (2nd ed., pp. 209–223). San Diego, CA: Cognella.

Terman, L. M. (1916). *The measurement of intelligence*. Boston: Houghton Mifflin.

Thompson, D. (2016, May 13). Donald Trump and the twilight of White America. *The Atlantic*. Retrieved from https://www.theatlantic.com/politics/archive/2016/05/donald-trump-and-the-twilight-of-white-america/482655/

Tkacik, C. (2018, April 27). Remembering the Baltimore riots after Freddie Gray's death, 3 years later. *The Baltimore Sun*. Retrieved from https://www.baltimoresun.com/maryland/baltimore-city/bs-md-ci-riots-three-years-later-20180426-story.html

U.S. Department of Justice (DOJ), Civil Rights Division (2016). Investigation of the Baltimore City police department. Retrieved from https://www.justice.gov/crt/file/883296/download.

Valinote, N. (2020, June 19). George Floyd protests: How activists are using social media to call for change. *KCCT-TV*. Retrieved from https://medium.com/dfrlab/how-activists-used-social-media-to-organize-during-the-george-floyd-protests-3bb3b527ff36.

Walters, R. W. (2003). *White nationalism, black interests: Conservative public policy and the black community*. Detroit, MI: Wayne State University Press.

West Baltimore Commission on Police Misconduct (2016). Over-policed yet underserved: The people's findings regarding police misconduct in west Baltimore. Retrieved from https://www.noboundariescoalition.com/wp-content/uploads/2016/03/No-Boundaries-Layout-Web-1.pdf

Wright, B. E. (1985). *Psychopathic racial personality and other essays* (2nd ed). Chicago: Third World Press.

Young, I. M. (1990). *Justice and politics of difference*. Princeton, NJ: Princeton University Press.

Zinn, H. (2005). *A people's history of the United States: 1492–present*. New York: Harper Perennial.

21

Policy, Practice, and Institutional Barriers to Financial Capability and Asset Building Related to Race (Racism) in the United States

Jenny L. Jones, Julie Birkenmaier, Lissa Johnson, Gena G. McClendon, Yunju Nam, Jin Huang, and Eyitayo Onifade

> *Every man is our brother, and every man's burden is our own. Where poverty exists, all are poorer. Where hate flourishes, all are corrupted. Where injustice reins, all are unequal.*
>
> —Whitney M. Young, Jr.

This chapter centers on the impact that race has on African Americans and other people of color as it relates to asset building. For years past, African Americans have had fewer assets than their White American counterparts (Aliprantis & Carroll, 2019), thus necessitating the re-emergence of race-based public policy and race-selective interventions from nongovernmental organizations centered on the historical and current conditions of African Americans, separate and above other types of identity politics, who have been historically marginalized from building wealth.

The chapter provides a historical overview of race and its impact on financial inclusion, including the economics of race, its effect on people of color's ability to access financial institutions, and address initiatives specific to financial capability and asset building (FCAB). Moreover, the chapter includes information on the basic understanding of financial inclusion and policy.

Jenny L. Jones, Julie Birkenmaier, Lissa Johnson, Gena G. McClendon, Yunju Nam, Jin Huang, and Eyitayo Onifade, *Policy, Practice, and Institutional Barriers to Financial Capability and Asset Building Related to Race (Racism) in the United States* In: *Social Work and the Grand Challenge to Eliminate Racism.* Edited by: Martell L. Teasley, Michael S. Spencer, and Melissa Bartholomew, Oxford University Press. © Oxford University Press 2023. DOI: 10.1093/oso/9780197674949.003.0021

The chapter also discusses training curricula such as FCAB, techniques used in social work research and education, and their impact on race as it relates to social workers' training and professional practice; asset-building research, innovation, and practice/policy impact are included. We end with lessons learned and the potential of FCAB in overcoming structural racism and addressing racial economic inequality.

The Economics of Racism

Racism in America persists across all races and cultures, beginning as early as 1605 when Native Americans were enslaved; the loss of wealth (land) that occurred is just one example of economic racism in the United States (Newell, 2015). This loss of wealth would persist for hundreds of years, including the economic disparity of Blacks. In 1619 Africans were brought to this country and were denied personhood, basic education, homeownership opportunities, and access to any level of true financial empowerment. Those challenges are based solely on both race and racism (Reich, 1971). For example, before the Civil Rights Act (1964), public policy explicitly excluded people of color for opportunities like the Homestead Act of 1862, access to Home Owners Loan Corporation (HOLC) starting in 1933, or coverage under the Social Security Act of 1935 (Davies & Derthick, 1997).

More than 200 years after slavery, the result is that the annual median income of African American households in 2018 was $41,361, which is far lower than the national average of $60,293, while non-Hispanic White households' annual median income was $70,672 (U.S. Census, 2018). In terms of wealth, the difference between what a person owes and owns makes the racial wealth gap more pronounced. White median household wealth is $140,055, compared to Black median household wealth of $3,400 (Gould, 2017). Contributing factors to the disparity in median household wealth include the lack of homeownership, as housing is acknowledged to make up two-thirds of a typical household's wealth (Mishel et al., 2012).

The Challenges of Economics and Race/Racism

Race is reified as a unified framework though the intersection between race and racism, which then necessitates the re-emergence of race-based public policy and race-selective interventions. This focus on race acknowledges that differential impact between racial groups does not require malicious intent to warrant specific redress at macro-intervention level. It follows that such a practice centers the conditions of African Americans, separate and above other types of identity politics, as is the case when we use the term "minorities" as a catchall for groups that have been historically marginalized. There are a number of examples currently offered as part of a "Black Policy Agenda," like the Magnolia Mother's Trust project in Jackson, Mississippi, that provides a guaranteed income specifically to African American mothers in Jackson and has demonstrated some poverty-alleviating effects for that population.

The lack of financial education, knowledge, access to financial services, and asset-building strategies related to institutional discrimination/exclusion (by government and financial institutions) speaks to the importance of policies and financial education knowledge/literacy that addresses historical economic oppression. Such examples include redlining, tax-based asset-building policies, mortgage interest rate discrimination, lack of language services, and enhanced identification requirements at financial institutions. The consequences of institutional racism and racial wealth disparity on vulnerable populations and wealth disparity on immigration status are all a part of the issues that must be addressed.

Race and Financial Education

Most Americans are financially illiterate, as measured by tests of financial knowledge (Lusardi, 2008; Yakaboski et al., 2019). On average, persons of color score the lowest (Yakaboski et al., 2019). Why is that? And why does it matter? Financial education can contribute to improved financial knowledge and skills and positive financial behavior (Robb & Woodyard, 2011; Lusardi, 2008). We would expect such improvements to lead to greater financial well-being (Sherraden, 2013; Lusardi, 2008; Robb & Woodyard, 2011), suggesting opportunities for bridging the racial wealth divide.

But what comprises financial education? And what should be measured in determining one's ability to make good financial decisions and achieve economic well-being? In assessing the impact of financial education on well-being, terms such as "financial literacy" are often used as a form of measurement. Some define financial literacy as "knowledge and understanding

POLICY, PRACTICE, AND INSTITUTIONAL BARRIERS 527

that enable sound financial decision-making and effective management of personal finances" (Yakaboski et al., 2019, p. 2).

In our model of financial capability, we use the term "ability to act" to reflect a broader concept of financial education that incorporates learning through socialization processes and experiences, as well as through more structured forms of financial education and guidance. This "ability to act" also suggests an expanded measure of "financial literacy"—the accumulation of "knowledge and skills, attitudes, habits, motivation, confidence, and self-efficacy related to his/her finances" (Sherraden et al., 2018, p. 395). Applying this definition in assessing the effectiveness of financial education adds complexity to the measure and has implications for strategies to achieve our goal of building financial capability and assets for all.

These complexities may help to explain differences in financial literacy outcomes for historically marginalized subpopulations, such as women and persons of color.

In the following sections, we address elements of one's "ability to act" through (1) financial socialization, (2) financial education, and (3) financial guidance (Sherraden, 2013). We conclude by discussing strategies that can enhance financial education's impact on financial behaviors and well-being for persons of color.

Financial Socialization

Financial socialization is largely defined as ". . . the process of acquiring and developing values, attitudes, standards, norms, knowledge, and behaviors that contribute to the financial viability and wellbeing of the individual . . ." (Schuchardt et al., 2009, p. 86). Examples include parental attitudes about money and modeling of financial behaviors, and early interactions with financial institutions (Fulk & White, 2018). As such, the socialization process begins early in life and can be a very different experience depending on the community and culture in which one is raised (Robles, 2014). Families, regardless of income or ethnicity, vary widely in their approach to money and economic decision-making. Some involve their children in money matters or saving at a young age, perhaps taking their children to the bank, while others may shield their children from any financial concerns or conversations. Regardless of which approach parents may take, they are the primary socialization agents for their children, modeling values, attitudes, and behaviors (Clarke et al., 2005; Mitchell et al., 2009).

Though perhaps difficult to measure, for those who have been systematically excluded from participating in social, financial, political, and economic institutions across generations, financial socialization may be limited. Positive financial experiences and financial knowledge and skills are less likely to be passed on to the next generation. Lack of financial socialization results in financial knowledge and skill deficits, limited exposure to financial systems, and lack of confidence in mainstream financial institutions and associated products and services. As studies on gender and ethnicity have shown, this gap in financial socialization can have a lasting negative impact on future financial well-being (Shapiro et al., 2013; Shapiro et al., 2011; Dewees & Mottola, 2017). For example, women and persons of color tend to be less confident in money management, and less likely to use the stock market, obtain quality loans, or use formal financial products (Chang, 2010; Dewees & Mottola, 2017; FDIC, 2018; Morrin et al., 2009). Some research suggests that financial socialization is a key component in building financial capability, but the extent to which it does and the particular influences deserve further research. Though socialization processes continue over the course of human development, it is clear that the residual effects of financial exclusion remain entrenched for many.

Financial Education

Financial education typically occurs through formal classroom instruction and various types of workshops. For young people, elementary, secondary, and post-secondary educational institutions are increasingly offering personal finance or economic education in their classrooms. As of 2020, 21 states require high school students to take a course in personal finance, and 25 states require a high school course in economics (Council for Economic Education, 2020). The benefit of including such education through the public school system is that the content is taught to everyone who attends. If state or federally mandated, then theoretically all young people will receive the content, regardless of whether they attend a public or private school, or are home-schooled.

Some high school financial education studies show outcomes associated with improved credit management, higher credit scores, and lower use of

POLICY, PRACTICE, AND INSTITUTIONAL BARRIERS 529

payday loans (Harvey, 2019; Urban et al., 2020). However, such instruction's quality may still be uneven because of differences in community resources in the district where a school is located. Schools located in communities comprised largely of low-income or persons of color tend to be lower resourced and unable to afford higher quality technology, equipment, and curricular materials. Financial education in such schools may not offer the same opportunities, exercises, and connections to community resources as the same course taught in a higher-resourced school. Financial literacy measures do not account for such variation and can disguise the financial literacy gap's true nature.

For example, some schools

can offer in-school banking programs to heighten the experiential learning process. Findings from research on these programs show improved financial knowledge, skills, and attitudes about financial institutions and saving, as well as greater likelihood of having a savings account, than if the program was not available (FDIC, 2017; Sherraden et al., 2011). As part of the financial education learning process, these enhanced opportunities to use their new financial knowledge with real saving accounts starting early in life are particularly relevant for persons of color as one strategy in bridging the financial literacy gap created by historical barriers to financial access and participation.

For adults, financial education varies widely in method and focus, ranging from general personal finance classes and workshops to more specific topics, such as repairing debt, purchasing a home, choosing a health insurance product, and investing for retirement. These "teachable moments" (or "just-in-time" education) can be especially effective because they are particularly relevant to the current circumstances of the individual (Kaiser & Menkhoff, 2017, p. 15; Fernbach & Sussman, 2018). They are also, by definition, experiential—learning in the process of doing, and connecting knowledge with access to products and services.

Access to and the cost of financial education and guidance provided by individuals and institutions covers a wide range—from free services offered by schools, government agencies, and social service organizations to banks, credit unions, and paid financial advisors. The quality of instruction and subsequent outcomes in skills, knowledge, and behaviors are dependent on a number of variables, including the preparation, training, and experiences of the instructor (CFPB, 2019; Urban et al., 2020; Lusardi, 2019). Research findings show that those who typically teach such content—teachers, social workers, agency case workers—are not necessarily confident or well-prepared to teach the subject matter (Hageman et. al, 2019; Huang et Al., 2021). Thus, positive outcomes may be biased toward individuals who have absorbed financial knowledge and skills through other means and not necessarily from the material being taught.

Financial Guidance

Financial guidance refers to resources and persons who advise or offer guidance on financial issues or use of financial products and services. People may need financial guidance and mentoring, especially when family members and friends cannot provide such support (Collins & O-Rourke, 2010). Financial guidance has been shown to be effective for the least financially literate (Lusardi & Mitchell, 2009).

Such guidance can be particularly effective when the client initiates contact and the guidance focuses on the client's individual goals. For example, a study of financial coaching programs comprising a majority of Black and Hispanic clients, most of whom were seeking credit counseling, found positive outcomes in money management, paying down debt, saving, and perceptions of financial well-being (Theodos et al., 2015). Conklin's (2017) study highlights the importance of face-to-face interaction in working with persons of color who have low financial literacy. The study revealed that face-to-face interaction in financial guidance prior to receipt of loan funds results in a lower mortgage default incidence.

Those who offer financial guidance and counseling tend to be more experienced and better trained in the topic. But more experience tends to come at a higher cost, and in a field dominated by White males. For example, paid financial advisors, such as Certified Financial Planners (CFPs) and investment brokers, are particularly skilled in helping their clients achieve financial goals and improve the value of their investments (Winchester & Huston, 2015). For example, one study finds that comprehensively managed middle-class clients are over three times more likely to be prepared for retirement and twice as likely to have adequate emergency funds than those who do not purchase such advice (Winchester & Huston, 2015). Further, an analysis of the increasing wealth gap across income shows that a key factor in the past several years has been the increase in investment portfolios' value (Batty et al., 2019).

Unfortunately, significantly fewer persons of color benefit from this type of financial education, and indeed, investment portfolios show smaller participation in financial markets by minority households (Choudhury, 2002). For example, only 15% of clients served by certified financial planners (CFPs) are Black or Latino, and less than 3.5% of CFPs are Black or Latino themselves (CFP Board Center for Financial Planning, 2018; Eisenberg, 2018)). When they do participate, persons of color are more likely to be risk averse. For example, Blacks tend to favor conservative investments such as real estate and insurance. Lusardi and Mitchell (2011) posit that this may be due to lack of understanding about risk diversification and compound interest, as reflected in incorrect responses to survey questions on the subject. In terms of financial impact, lower risk investments tend to draw a lower return than corporate stocks, and thus their participation is more likely to result in slower wealth accumulation (Choudhury, 2002).

Impacts of Financial Education on Financial Behaviors and Well-Being

In each element of one's ability to act, whether socialization, financial education, or guidance, we note gaps in financial literacy. Common across these elements are lack of opportunity to build one's ability through education and experience. Such lack of opportunity across one's lifetime may be an underlying reason for studies that show lower financial literacy scores at both younger and older ages (Fulk & White, 2018; Lusardi & Mitchell, 2007). Given that financial literacy does contribute to financial well-being (Lusardi & Mitchell, 2011; Sherraden, 2013), is it possible to attribute the racial wealth gap to low financial literacy? And therefore, can financial literacy reduce the racial wealth gap?

Generally, the results of research on the effectiveness of financial education on financial well-being are mixed. Much of the literature tests effects on financial knowledge and behaviors, but not on overall financial well-being. In addition, measures are not standardized and do not fully account for the variety of socialization and experience an individual may have (Al-Bahrani, Weathers, & Patel, 2018; Fernandes, Lynch, & Netemeyer, 2014; Kaiser &

532   JENNY L. JONES ET AL.

Menkhoff, 2017; Miller et al., 2014). While it is not clear what financial education elements are particularly impactful, evidence of effective pedagogy and practices may help inform strategies for increasing financial literacy and well-being, and perhaps even begin to reduce the racial wealth gap.

One example shown to be effective is experiential or participatory learning methods (CFPB, 2013, Kolb & Kolb, 2009; Batty et al., 2015). "Learning by doing" is a theory of education espoused by John Dewey (1938), who maintained that people know best when they can apply what they learn. Applied to financial education, the process bridges financial knowledge and skills with access to financial products and services. Research on programs that offer this combination of education and opportunities to apply knowledge with affordable and secure financial products and services has shown positive results in financial behaviors and asset accumulation for young children, youth, and adults (Johnson et al., 2018; Lee et al., 2017; Sherraden et al., 2011, 2005; Langholz et al., 2019). Findings from research with Native American communities, for example, show that offering financial education along with financial products and services are more effective in raising credit scores and increasing savings than offering them independently (Langholz et al., 2019). As noted earlier, just-in-time education is another effective form of building and applying knowledge simultaneously (Fernandes et al., 2014).

These programs also reflect another critical and fundamental component of financial socialization, education, and guidance—institutional partnerships. Quality institutions and the partnerships among them— between schools, social service agencies, government entities, and financial institutions—are critical for building knowledge and skills and ensuring access to resources, products, and services.

Many minority-serving higher educational institutions, including historically black colleges and universities (HBCUs), Hispanic serving institutions (HSIs), Asian and Pacific Islands (APIs), and Tribal colleges and universities (TCUs), have taken a strong role in building access to financial education and experiences into their curricula and campus programs. They consider financial education an essential tool for increasing student retention and school completion and reducing loan default. "Successful financial literacy strategies and initiatives not only promote stronger student and institutional outcomes, they also promote a more responsive and responsible postsecondary system" (Looney, 2011, p. 7). These schools offer a variety of models and examples that could be adapted for use at other higher education institutions that are interested in reaching and retaining students of color. For example, Florida A&M

University, an HBCU, integrated modules from the FCAB curriculum into several social work classes, including Introduction to Social Work, Policy Practice, and Community Organizations. The Institute for Higher Education Policy has supported Minority Serving Intuitions by expanding financial education and outcome assessments across their campuses. Valencia College, for example, has developed an integrated cross-departmental approach that includes embedding financial education into existing campus programs as well as training peer student financial learning ambassadors. Savannah State University has embedded financial literacy into its "Pathways to Success" program (Looney, 2011). Similarly, a number of HBCUs have partnered with the Society for Financial Education & Professional Development (SFEPD) to participate in SFEPD's "student ambassador program" that trains college students to teach their peers about personal finance (Society for Financial Education & Professional Development, 2020). In 2021, for example, three HBCUs in the Washington, D.C., area (Howard University, Medgar Evers College, and the University of the District of Columbia) have established a pilot program involving SFEPD and Minority Depository Institution Carver Federal Savings Bank, which will broaden the students' training through tools and engagement from Carver's leadership (Bloomberg, 2021).

University administration at all schools should identify opportunities and encourage career paths for persons of color in business and finance to raise the percentage of those who become financial advisors and leaders in the financial market. Field education with initiatives like the Wall Street Project, and the Family Financial Planning Certificate program offered through an online collaboration of six HBCUs (1890s Family and Consumer Science Distance Instructional Alliance institutions), can help to increase participation of persons of color in the corporate sector (Choudhury, 2002). Many of these examples involve partnerships with the business departments at the universities. Given the high level of engagement that financially vulnerable families have with social workers, such programs would be appropriate for implementation through social work or human services departments as well.

Based on the above examples and other research, the timing of financial education should begin early, and continue through primary, secondary, and post-secondary school (CFPB, 2019; Kasman et al., 2018; Lusardi & Mitchell, 2014, 2019). While research shows that the racial literacy gap exists even with higher levels of financial education (Al-Bahrani et al., 2018), early and sustained positive experiences and education may go a long way toward bridging the divide. The research suggests a missing variable which may well be the socialization process: a history of exclusion has created a financial literacy gap, not because of some inaptitude but because of the lack of accumulated experiences, in contrast to the design and use of structures favoring White and upper-class populations. In trying to understand the racial wealth gap, Emmons and Rickets (2016) come to a similar conclusion that there are ". . . deeper causes: structural, systemic or historical factors related to race or ethnicity that affect educational and/or wealth outcomes" (p. 2). Overcoming these factors will necessitate augmenting community resources in areas where families live, and starting early with children and their parents in order for the next generation to get a more equal start in building financial capability and assets.

Race and Household Financial Access

Access to basic affordable and accessible household financial products and services is essential for financial well-being and full participation in today's economy. Owning and using checking, savings, and money market accounts, having a strong credit report and score, and accessing consumer credit products from mainstream financial institutions, such as banks, credit unions, and insurance companies, are foundational to financial well-being. Saving in designated retirement accounts is also key to long-term financial stability in older years. However, racial and ethnic disparities to access exist, making it difficult for some populations to manage their daily financial life as well as build assets toward financial security and wealth (Apaam et al., 2018; Dewees & Mottola, 2017; Jorgensen & Akee, 2017).

Basic Financial Access: Banked Status

The utilization of an affordable bank account is imperative in today's economy. Yet, many households struggle to transact funds or borrow funds from a formal financial institution, without or even with a bank account. Households without a savings, checking, or money market account at a federally insured depository institution are considered "unbanked," while those who supplement their banked relationship with use of alternative financial service (AFS) (discussed next) are considered "underbanked." While nearly a quarter of all Americans are either un- or underbanked, these populations are disproportionately racial and ethnic minorities (Apaam et al., 2018). Despite declining over the past several years, un- and underbanked rates are still substantially higher among Black and Hispanic households than among White households (Kim et al., 2015). Almost 17% of Black households and 14% of Hispanic households were unbanked in 2017, compared to 6.5% overall. Almost one-third of the unbanked state that they "don't trust banks" as the reason they do not have an account, the second most common reason after "do not have enough money to keep in account" (Apaam et al., 2018). For older Black adults, neighborhood-level sociodemographic factors substantially contribute to their unbanked status, while for Hispanics, language barriers contribute most to their status (Blanco et al., 2018). About one-third of Black and Hispanic households were underbanked in 2017, as compared to 15% of White households. Even though declines occurred in the un- and underbanked rates for the overall population and minority populations in recent years, these groups' rates remain substantially higher than the overall rate (Apaam et al., 2018).

Alternative Financial Service (AFS) Use

Alternative financial services (AFS) are non-bank financial transactions (e.g., money order, prepaid debit card) and credit products (e.g., pawnshop and rent-to-own loans). The AFS industry is massive—Americans currently spend over $30 billion annually just on AFS credit products (Pew Charitable Trusts, 2018). Minority households have easier access to AFS providers than White households: majority Black or Latino neighborhoods have, on average, twice as many AFS providers as majority-White neighborhoods, while mainstream banks and credit unions are less common (Shrider et al., 2021). AFS use is more common among Black and Hispanic households, and working age-disabled, younger, less-educated, and lower-income households (Apaam et al., 2018). Over one-third of Native, Black, and Hispanic Americans have used at least one non-bank, higher cost form of transacting or borrowing within the past five years, at much higher rate than Asian Americans and Whites (Apaam et al., 2018; Dewees & Mottola, 2017). While transaction AFS products are the most commonly used, credit AFS products raise the most concern because they typically are more costly and provide a way for borrowers to get into a cycle of increasing debt (Pew Charitable Trusts, 2018).

Policy and Practice Suggestions to Increase Rate of Banked Products and Services Use

There are a number of practices and policy suggestions to decrease the differential rates of un- and underbanked for Black, Hispanic, and Native American households and to lower AFS use. First, meaningful regulatory changes or other types of incentives for banks to physically locate branches in and serve minority communities with affordable products and services may influence the number of minorities with accounts and their usage of bank financial products and services. Research has demonstrated that financial providers' physical location is associated with the likelihood of consumer use (Celerier & Matray, 2019; Goodstein & Rhine, 2017) and consumer financial well-being. Second, expanding the capacity of current community-based institutions, such as credit unions, minority deposit institutions (MDIs), and community development financial institutions (CDFIs), could enable these institutions to increase their outreach and expand their account product offerings to meet a wider need. Providing more incentives to banks to offer accounts that are affordable through the Community Reinvestment Act is needed for banks to respond to community efforts, such as the "Bank On" effort sponsored by the Cities for Financial Empowerment Fund (Cities for Financial Empowerment Fund, 2020) to expand the number of accounts that meet standardized affordability and functionality guidelines. Third, increasing access to affordable, reliable, high-speed internet connectivity would assist minority communities to expand their use of financial technology ("fintech"), which would enable these communities to utilize mobile and online banking (Friedline, Chen, & Morrow, 2021).

Credit Reports, Credit Scores, and Credit Use

Lenders, such as banks, typically rely on credit reports and scores to make lending decisions. Without a positive credit record with a strong score, lenders are unlikely to either offer credit or offer credit with reasonable terms. Racial disparities in credit scores exist at the community level. Radcliffe and Brown (2017) found 100 credit point differences in median credit scores between predominantly non-White and White communities in 38 of 60 cities. Minority households, other than Asians, are more likely to experience challenges with their credit. Across all age categories, Blacks and Hispanics

POLICY, PRACTICE, AND INSTITUTIONAL BARRIERS   537

have unequal access to consumer credit because of their insufficient credit history or lack of recent history of usage. About 15% of Blacks and Hispanics, compared to 9% of Whites, have no credit record. Another 13% of Blacks and 12% of Hispanics have a record that is unscored because of low current credit usage, compared to 7% of Whites. Both groups experience limited access to credit from mainstream providers and must turn to alternatives, such as higher-cost AFS products, when they need credit (Brevoort et al., 2015). One way that limited access is manifested is through home mortgage loans. In 2018, Black and Hispanic-White borrowers had higher mortgage denial rates compared to other racial and ethnic groups. In 2018, almost 61% of Blacks and 50% of Hispanic-Whites took out more expensive nonconventional home-purchase loans as first-time homeowners than almost 30% of non-Hispanic Whites and only 12% of Asians (Dietrich et al., 2018).

Black and Hispanic households and lower-income, less-educated, working-age disabled households are less likely to have or use most mainstream credit products. Mainstream credit products include credit cards, a personal loan or line of credit from a bank, store credit card, student loan, mortgage, home equity loan, or credit line. Over one-third of all Black and Hispanic households have no mainstream credit, compared to 14% of White households (Apaam et al., 2018). While 77% of Americans have credit cards, 36% of Native Americans, 33% of Blacks, and 23% of Hispanics have no credit cards. (Dewees & Mottola, 2017). Much larger percentages of Native American, Black, and Hispanic Americans than Whites report feeling worried that they have too much debt. Similarly, the same groups have the highest percentage who reported that they have been contacted by a debt collection agency in the past year, as compared to Whites (Dewees & Mottola, 2017). A recent investigation found that debt collectors sued households in Black communities at twice the rate of mostly White neighborhoods in three metropolitan areas (Waldman & Kiel, 2015).

Policy and Practice Suggestions Regarding Consumer Credit

Advocates can help households seek and use credit from formal financial institutions that can help them build a positive credit history (Apaam et al., 2018). First, expanding the opportunity to access small-dollar consumer credit through banks and credit unions could help borrowers save billions of dollars annually by avoiding AFS credit products (Pew Charitable Trusts, 2018). Fully utilizing and expanding the capacity of CDFIs and MDIs to deliver mainstream credit in underserved communities could expand the supply of available, affordable credit to minority communities. Second, supporting the use of alternative data, such as rent, cell phone, utility payments, and other types of payments historically excluded from credit reports, is increasingly being used in newer scoring products (Brevoort & Kambara, 2017). Although consumer advocates express some caution about using these types of data, their use has helped people gain a scorable credit report and produce a score. More widespread use of the newer scoring models by lenders in their lending decisions could be helpful.

Retirement Savings

Minorities face more significant challenges than Whites in preparing for retirement (Rhee, 2013). Nearly two-thirds of minority households do not have any retirement savings, as compared to over one-third of White households. The amount saved is also significantly different. Most minority households have inadequate savings—less than $10,000 in retirement savings, and a median of $30,000 for near-retirees (Li & Dalaker, 2019), as compared to $130,000 for White households (Urban Institute, 2017).

Policymakers designed the Social Security system to supplement employer-sponsored pensions and other savings, yet due to lack of retirement savings to supplement, more than half of older adults rely only on Social Security for their income (Rhee, 2013). The amount of income replaced by Social Security is an estimated 35%, which leaves a significant gap (Rhee, 2013; Shrider et al., 2021). Social Security and Supplemental Security Income (SSI) provide almost 90% of total income for Americans age 65 and older who had incomes below the poverty line (Li & Dalaker, 2019). Latinos and Blacks are less likely to receive Social Security income than Whites during retirement due to the current Social Security rules and immigration status challenges.

Access to retirement saving instruments is crucial to promote saving. Black, Hispanic, and Native American households are significantly less likely than White workers to be covered by an employer-sponsored retirement plang. Only about half of Black (Rhee, 2013) and 31% of Latino employees of working age (Brown & Oakley, 2018) have such a retirement account, compared to 62% of White employees (Rhee, 2013). Minorities are much less likely than Whites to have access to a job-based retirement plan in the private sector, as compared to the public sector. While 24% of White households have a defined benefit plan (pension) that guarantees income for life, only 16% of Blacks and 12% of Latinos have pensions (Rhee, 2013). Black and Hispanic workers also have lower participation and contributions in employer-sponsored retirement plans than do White workers (Tamborini & Kim, 2020). Thus, the poverty rate for Americans age 65 and older is the highest for Blacks (18.7%) and Hispanics (17.3%), as compared to 7% of Whites (Shrider, et al., 2021).

Policy and Practice Suggestions Regarding Retirement Accounts

Both Social Security and employer-sponsored retirement plans are vital tools for supplying adequate retirement income for older adult years. Strengthening Social Security by stabilizing its financing and increasing benefits for lower-wage workers could play a critical role in retirement security, such as raising the income ceiling on which Federal Insurance Contributions Act taxes are levied (Miller et al., 2014; Rhee, 2013). In addition, Black and Latinos are less likely than Whites to work in industries and occupations that provide higher wages and workplace benefits, including retirement benefits. Policy proposals that facilitate higher wages in industries where Black and Hispanic workers are likely to be employed would assist minority workers to have adequate income for saving (Raphael, 2016). Making it more difficult to exclude workers and incentivizing private employers to offer retirement plans for workers, or ensuring universal retirement plan coverage, would help these workers and their families (Brown & Oakley, 2018). For some Hispanics, citizenship and immigration status issues are also connected to "take up" rates of retirement benefits, and must be addressed (Rhee, 2013). Automatic savings in retirement plans, rather than "opt-in" plans, would enable more workers to grow their savings over their working years (Urban Institute, 2017).

Racism as a Barrier to Achieving Financial Capability and Asset Building for All

Throughout U.S. history, racial wealth disparity has been maintained. White wealth has been transmitted from one generation to another, while minority

540 JENNY L. JONES ET AL.

groups are being trapped in the vicious cycle of asset poverty. That is to say, the initial wealth gap built on slavery, Jim Crow, and redlining has been perpetuated through the transmission of wealth from parents' generations to children's generations (Martin, 2019; Nam, 2021; Shapiro, 2004). In addition, U.S. society still maintains various de facto barriers to asset building against racial and ethnic minority groups (Conley, 1999, 2001; Hamilton & Darity, 2017; Sullivan et al., 2016). Accordingly, we should understand both the historical legacy of past exploitations and institutionalized racism's ongoing practices to obtain a comprehensive view of the wide and tenacious wealth disparities.

Early history clearly shows that public policies promoted Whites' wealth building while sacrificing other groups' economic interests (Martin, 2019). The Indian Removal Act of 1830 forced Native Americans living east of the Mississippi River to move west of the Mississippi River. The 1862 Homestead Act gave public land and opportunities to accumulate wealth almost exclusively to Whites, while the Southern Homestead Act of 1866 failed to offer the same opportunities to newly freed African Americans (Martin, 2019; Oliver & Shapiro, 1995). The enactment of the National Housing Act (NHA) of 1934 offered Whites another opportunity to boost their wealth through homeownership, while people of color were systematically excluded from the American dream of homeownership. While promoting homeownership among White families by providing government-backed low-interest long-term mortgages, the Federal Housing Authority (FHA) excluded minority families from these government programs through redlining (Herring & Henderson, 2016; Oliver & Shapiro, 1995). Only 1% or fewer mortgages were issued to African Americans under these programs before the enactment of the Civil Rights Act of 1964 (Herring & Henderson, 2016).

Racial Wealth and Disparity

Initial wealth disparity generated by racist public policies has been maintained through intergenerational transmissions of socioeconomic resources. Lower levels of wealth and other resources among parents of color hindered their investment in their children's future. Without parents' investments at critical life stages, children of color are often stuck in the vicious cycle of low economic achievement. On the contrary, White children often receive financial assistance for education, homeownership, and other long-term developments, which usually lifted their position beyond their own innate abilities (Conley, 1999; Killewald et al., 2017; Nam, 2021; Shapiro, 2004). Existing empirical studies support the roles of intergenerational transmission of socioeconomic resources in persistent racial wealth disparity. Blacks' chance of receiving parents' resources is lower than Whites for inheritances and inter vivo transfers (Jayakody, 1998; Sarkisian & Gerstel, 2004), for college (Meschede et al., 2017; Nam, 2021), and for homeownership (Charles & Hurst, 2002; Graves et al., 2019). Racial disparities in parents' financial assistance are mainly due to low socioeconomic resources among parents of color (Charles & Hurst, 2002; Nam, 2021). Parental financial assistance is estimated to be one source of persistent Black-White wealth disparity (Avery & Rendall, 2002; Nam et al., 2015; Scholz & Levine, 2004).

However, it should be noted that intergenerational transmission of socioeconomic resources does not fully explain racial wealth disparity: the Black-White wealth gap remains significant even after controlling for parents' social and economic resources (Conley, 2001; Killewald, 2013). Existing literature clearly shows that various forms of institutional racism—covert or explicit— still bar members of minority groups from building wealth.

Although the Fair Housing Act of 1968 and the Equal Credit Opportunity Act of 1974 officially outlawed redlining and other race-based discrimination in the credit market, people of color are still systematically excluded from access to mortgages and other credits (Killewald et al., 2017; Sullivan & Meschede, 2018; Sullivan et al., 2016). Under anti-discriminatory laws, mainstream financial institutions have developed so-called objective measures of creditworthiness without considering the consequences of discrimination and exclusion in the past (Reid, 2019). For example, financial institutions' use of debt-to-income ratio and down-payment amount for mortgage approval and interest rates may place people of color in disadvantaged positions: people of color tend to have heavier education loans, higher debt-to-income ratios, and lower down payments than Whites because of their lower chances of receiving assistance from parents (Addo et al., 2016; Charles & Hurst, 2002; Hamilton & Darity, 2017). Furthermore, mainstream financial institutions still employ discriminatory practices against communities of color, as revealed by recent investigations by the Consumer Financial Protection Bureau and the Department of Justice. For example, mainstream financial institutions avoid mortgage brokers working in African American or Hispanic neighborhoods and exclude these neighborhoods from marketing strategies (Consumer Financial Protection

Bureau, 2015; U.S. Department of Justice, 2012). Existing empirical evidence also shows that mortgage applications by African Americans and Hispanics are more likely to be rejected and to be charged with higher fees and interest rates than Whites with comparable credit histories and household economic conditions (Charles & Hurst, 2002; Sullivan et al., 2016).

Excluded from the mainstream credit market and targeted by the subprime mortgage industry's marketing, people of color and those living in minority communities are often driven to the subprime mortgage market (Herring & Henderson, 2016). Defined as modern-day redlining (Shapiro, 2006), subprime mortgages impose excessive fees, high interest rates, and steep prepayment penalties (Herring & Henderson, 2016; Shapiro, 2006; Sullivan et al., 2016). As a result, African American and Hispanic homeowners are significantly more likely to lose their home through foreclosures (Hamilton & Darity, 2017; Reid, 2019; Sullivan et al., 2016).

In addition to restricted opportunities for homeownership, minority neighborhoods have limited access to financial services in general. Deregulation in the 1980s and 1990s resulted in a high bank closure rate in low-income, minority neighborhoods (Figart, 2013). Alternative financial services fill the void by offering transaction services (e.g., check cashing) and credit services (e.g., a payday loan). These alternative services often trap minority users in a vicious cycle of never-ending debt (Figart, 2013; Sullivan et al., 2016).

In recent years, the digital divide and gaps in access to fintech (financial technology) have emerged as a new mechanism of perpetuating racial wealth disparity, as access to digital technology and fintech is not equally distributed across races (Friedline & Chen, in press; Friedline et al., 2019). The rates of high-speed internet service access, smartphone ownership, and online and mobile banking utilization rates are significantly lower in minority neighborhoods than White neighborhoods with comparable characteristics (Friedline & Chen, in press).

Institutionalized racism in the labor market and unfair tax systems also contribute to the persistent wealth disparity. Although the Civil Rights Act of 1964 prohibited racial discrimination in the labor market, and the Employment Equality Act of 1998 introduced affirmative actions to promote racial equity, racial disparities in employment, occupation prestige, and wages remain substantial in the current economic system (Hamilton & Darity, 2017; Tsang & Dietz, 2001). Furthermore, minority groups' progress since the Civil Rights movement has stalled as attacks against affirmative action have intensified (Hamilton & Darity, 2017; Margo, 2016). As income, especially labor income, is a primary source of saving and asset building for the majority of Americans (Beverly et al., 2008), labor market discrimination is likely a source of persistent racial wealth disparity.

The direct consequence of this racist structuring of U.S. systems and institutions is a persistent wealth gap between Whites and Black and Brown families. Black households have fewer tax-advantaged savings. Discrimination in the housing market makes these households less likely to be homeowners, and Black and Brown families are less likely to pass wealth between generations (Daly et al., 2017). The median wealth for African American and Hispanic households was less than $21,000 in to 2016, compared to $171,000 in White households (Traub and Ruetschin, 2016). Black retirees have less than 10% of the wealth of Whites in the same age group.

The current tax system also contributes to racial wealth disparities by unequally distributing federal asset-building subsidies (Hamilton & Darity, 2017; Sullivan et al., 2016). Although tax benefits are introduced to facilitate asset-building by assisting homeownership, saving for retirement, and economic investment, these tax policies benefit mostly high-income, high-wealth families by design: mortgage interest deductions benefit only homeowners with incomes high enough to pay the federal income tax, and reduced tax rates on long-term capital gains advance the economic interests of rich investors (Hamilton & Darity, 2017). As a result, about 50% of federal asset-building subsidies go to the wealthiest 5%, while almost no subsidies are allocated to the bottom 20%. Few African Americans and Hispanics receive these asset-building tax benefits (Sullivan et al., 2016), widening wealth gaps between races.

Race and FCAB and Social Work Education

"Financial capability is a central concern for social work because lack of financial knowledge, ability, opportunity, and assets are key contributors to poverty and inequality" (Sherraden et al., 2015, p. 4). A growing area in social work professional education to address these financial complexities and inequities is financial capability and asset building (FCAB). The theoretical framework of financial capability builds on Amartya Sen's theory of capability (Sen, 1999). It articulates the intersection of an individual's own "ability to act" through financial socialization, education, and guidance, with "opportunities to act," through access to affordable, safe, and easy to use financial products and services, resulting in financial stability and well-being (Sherraden, 2013). Stated more broadly, it is the freedom to learn and develop financial knowledge and skills and apply them through full participation in social, political, and economic institutions.

From the initial practices of the profession in the early twentieth century, social workers have focused on issues of social and economic development, embracing both individual concerns and tackling the larger socioeconomic issues and constraints under which an individual lives. Today, in returning to these roots, a key strategy is to better prepare social work students through social work education and practice to improve families' financial lives (Frey et al., 2017). Preparation ranges from direct practice, such as budgeting, credit repair, saving, and home purchasing—to meso and macro practice through community programming, coalition-building, and policy reform.

One example of educational efforts is the FCAB curriculum project developed and tested with faculty and students in 16 minority-serving universities, including HBCUs, TCUs, and Hispanic-serving institutions (Rochelle et al., 2015). This curriculum was one of the first of its kind to explicitly focus on financial practice with low-income, low-wealth, and financially vulnerable groups, including persons of color. The curriculum was subsequently published as a textbook for social workers (Sherraden et al., 2018). The content is based on four family case studies that describe how their life experiences intersected with financial issues. They represent a Black widow and her family, a Hispanic couple and their immigrant mother, a Native American father who is a recovering alcoholic, and a White mother living in a domestic violence shelter. Material includes education on non-biased and ethical approaches to client-centered values and goals, and concrete information about financial management, such as how to read a credit report, develop an income statement and balance sheet, and deal with problem debt. Each substantive set of information includes examples of related research, policy, programs, and organizations to help students understand the importance of connecting micro to macro practice in creating social change.

An increasing number of social work programs offer full courses and continuing education certification, such as the Financial Social Work Initiative, housed in the School of Social Work at the University of Maryland, Baltimore. The goal is to develop a pipeline of professional social workers equipped to improve all households' financial well-being. A bold but achievable measure of success will be the extent to which the profession can contribute to narrowing the racial wealth gap.

Conclusion

The racial wealth divide is well documented in history and continues to impact the lives of Black and Brown people more so than any other racial group. This is well documented in the literature, and the consequences of this fact are reflected in the inability of Black and Brown people to access affordable, safe, and easy to use financial products and services that would result in financial stability and well-being (Johnson & Sherraden, 2007; Sherraden, 2013). These unfair and biased policies date back as far as Jim Crow laws, lack of affordable housing practice policies and practice, to current-day lack of affordable healthcare. All of these issues are linked to financial ability and access. We believe that one way to impact this is through financial education, to include capability and asset-building training. Financial education can contribute to improved financial knowledge and skills and positive financial behavior (Robb & Woodyard, 2011; Lusardi, 2019). We would expect such improvements to lead also to greater financial well-being (Sherraden, 2013; Lusardi, 2019; Robb & Woodyard, 2011), which suggests opportunities for bridging the racial wealth divide.

Financial capability is a developmental process that occurs at every life stage (Sherraden et al., 2018). Strategies to bridge the racial wealth gap should include opportunities to learn and to apply financial knowledge and skills at every life stage. But effective financial education must be relevant and must be directly applied through opportunities to use the knowledge and skills. The FCAB curriculum is an example of that developmental process. The curriculum starts with one's "ability to act" to reflect a broader concept of financial education that incorporates learning through socialization processes and experiences and through more structured forms of financial education and guidance. This "ability to act" suggests an expanded measure of financial literacy, which is the accumulation of self-efficacy based on knowledge and skills, motivation, attitudes, habits, confidence, and self-efficacy related and individual's finances (Sherraden et al., 2018).

The FCAB curriculum was tested with faculty and students in 16 minority-serving universities, including HCBUs, TCUs, and Hispanic-serving institutions (Rochelle et al., 2015). This curriculum was one of the first of its kind to explicitly focus on financial practice with low-income, low-wealth, and financially vulnerable groups, including persons of color. Today, the curriculum is being taught and integrated in social work courses across the South and Mid-Atlantic states. Using FCAB within social work education curriculum can facilitated students' understanding of asset-building, policy formation, and their impact on racial and ethnic groups of different income strata asset-building research, innovation, and practice/policy impact are included. Teaching FCAB as a grand challenge would contribute to the social work profession knowledge base specific to income inequality, race-based public policy, and race-selective interventions. The curriculum has been scientifically tested and is designed to increase human efficacy. This model has a proven track record with social workers at the wheel. At the community-based level, knowledge and education about FCAB and the intersection with race/racism, and understanding the importance of race-based financial policies and practices, will assist social work professionals when working with low-income Black and Brown families and is critical to being effective in helping to build knowledge.

Study Questions

1. What impact does race play in the ability of people of color, specifically African Americans, to access financial institutions?
2. What public policies are needed to break the vicious cycle of intergenerational transmission of asset poverty among members of racial and ethnic minorities and to reduce racial wealth disparity?
3. How does financial capability differ from financial literacy?
4. In this chapter, we have provided a broad definition of financial literacy. What factors are included in this definition, and why?
5. What are the components of basic, affordable, and accessible household financial products and services?
6. In general terms, describe the differences between White and non-White un- and underbanked rates.
7. Describe three policy/practice ideas to increase the use of banked products and services among those who are un- and underbanked.
8. What role can social work education play in the integration of FCAB curriculum into social work education?

POLICY, PRACTICE, AND INSTITUTIONAL BARRIERS   547

9. What are some reasons why Black and Brown families are less likely to have asset growth, even with higher level incomes?

10. What are some strategies MSIs are using to bridge the financial literacy and wealth gap?

References

Apaam, G., Burhouse, S., Chu, K., Ernst, K., Fritzdixon, K., Goodstein, R., Lloro, A., Opoku, C., Osaki, Y., Sharma, D., & Weinstein, J. (2018, October, 2018). 2017 FDIC National Survey of Unbanked and Underbanked Households: Executive Summary. Federal Deposit Insurance Corporation. Retrieved from https://www.fdic.gov/hous eholdsurvey/2017/2017execsumm.pdf

Addo, F. R., Houle, J. N., & Simon, D. (2016). Young, Black, and (still) in the red: Parental wealth, race, and student loan debt. *Race and Social Problems, 8*(1), 64–76. doi: 10.1007/s12552-016-9162-0.

AFL-CIO Labor Commission on Racial and Economic Justice (2017). A brief history of labor, race and solidarity. Retrieved from https://racial-justice.aflcio.org/blog/est-aliq uid-se-ipsum-flagitiosum-etiamsi-nulla.

Al-Bahrani, A., Weathers, J., & Patel, D. (2019). Racial differences in the returns to financial literacy education. *Journal of Consumer Affairs, 53*, 572–599. https://doi.org/10.1111/joca.12205

Aliprantis, D., & Carroll, D. R. (2019, 28 February). What is behind the persistence of the racial wealth gap? *Economic Commentary,* Federal Reserve Bank of Cleveland. Retrieved from: https://ideas.repec.org/a/fip/fedcec/00095.html (2019-03).

Avery, R. B., & Rendall, M. S. (2002). Lifetime inheritances of three generations of Whites and Blacks. *American Journal of Sociology, 107*(5), 1300–1346.

Batty, M., Collins, J. M., O'Rourke, C., & Odders-White, E. (2016). *Experiential Financial Capability Education: A Field Study of My Classroom Economy.* Center. for Financial Security. University of Wisconsin-Madison. Research Brief 2016-9.1.

Batty, M., Bricker, J., Briggs, J., Holmquist, E., McIntosh, S., Moore, K., Nielsen, E., Reber, S., Shatto, M., Sommer, K., Sweeney, T., & Henriques Volz, A. (2019). *Introducing the Distributional Financial Accounts of the United States.* Finance and Economics Discussion Series 2019-017. Washington: Board of Governors of the Federal Reserve System, https://doi.org/10.17016/FEDS.2019.017

Batty, M., Collins, J. M., O'Rourke, C., & Odders-White, E. (2015). Experiential financial education: A field study of my classroom economy in elementary schools. *Economics of Education Review, 49*(1), 69–96.

Bloomberg (2021, February 8). Society for Financial Education & Professional Development and Carver bank partner to reduce financial literacy gap for student. Press release. Retrieved from https://www.bloomberg.com/press-releases/2021-02-08/society-for-financial-education-professional-development-and-carver-bank-partner-to-reduce-financial-literacy-gap-for-student.

Blanco, L., & Rodriguez, L. (2018, October 16). Delivering information about retirement saving among hispanic women: A facebook experiment. *Behavioural Public Policy, 4*(3), 343–369. doi: 10.1017/bpp.2018.33

Brevoort, K. P., & Kambara, M. (2017, November 27). CFPB Data Point: Becoming Credit Visible. The Consumer Financial Protection Bureau Office of Research Reports FPD Office of Research. Data Point Research Reports Series No. 17-2. Retrieved from: https://papers.ssrn.com/sol3/papers.cfm?abstract_id=3288830

Kearney, M. S., & Haskins, R. (2020). How cultural factors shape children's economic outcomes. *The Future of Children*, *30*(1), 3–8 https://www.brookings.edu/events/how-cultural-factors-shape-economic-outcomes/.

Bureau of Consumer Financial Protection (CFPB) (2019). Financial literacy annual report (2019). Retrieve from: https://files.consumerfinance.gov/f/documents/bcfp_financial-literacy_annual-report_2019.pdf

Celerier, C., & Matray, A. (2019). Bank-branch supply, financial inclusion and wealth accumulation. *Review of Financial Studies*, *32*(12), 1–43. http://dx.doi.org/10.2139/ssrn.2392278

Cities for Financial Empowerment Fund (2020). New York. Retrieved from: https://cfefund.org/

CFP Board Center for Financial Planning (2018). Racial diversity in financial planning: Where we are and where we must go. [Report]. Washington DC: Certified Financial Planner Board of Standards. Retrieved from: https://www.cfp.net/-/media/files/cfp-board/knowledge/reports-and-research/racial-diversity-in-financial-planning/racial-diversity-in-financial-planning.pdf?la=en&hash=AF448519B74AFB8ED7C74FB4B511E36F

Chang, M. (2010). *Shortchanged: Why women have less wealth and what can be done about it*. New York: Oxford University Press.

Charles, K. K., & Hurst, E. (2002). The transition to home ownership and the Black-White wealth gap. *Review of Economics and Statistics*, *84*(2), 281–297.

Choudhury, S. 2002 Racial and ethnic differences in wealth holdings and portfolio choices. Working Paper Series No. 95. Washington, DC: Social Security Administration, Office of Policy, Office of Research, Evaluation, and Statistics.

Clarke, M. C., Heaton, M. B., Israelsen, C. L., & Eggett, D. L. (2005). The Acquisition of Family Financial Roles and Responsibilities. *Family and Consumer Sciences Research Journal*, *33*(4), 321–340.

Conklin, J. N. (2017). Financial literacy, broker–borrower interaction and mortgage default. *Real Estate Economics*, *45*, 376–414. https://doi.org/10.1111/1540-6229.12140

Conley, D. (1999). *Being Black, living in the red*. Berkeley and Los Angeles: University of California Press.

Conley, D. (2001). Decomposing the Black-White wealth gap: The role of parental resources, inheritance, and investment dynamics. *Sociological Inquiry*, *71*(1), 39–66.

Consumer Financial Protection Bureau (2013, July). *CFPB Financial Literacy Annual Report*. https://files.consumerfinance.gov/f/201307_cfpb_report_financial-literacy-annual.pdf

Consumer Financial Protection Bureau (2015). *CFPB and DOJ order Hudson City Savings Bank to pay $27 million to increase mortgage credit access in communities illegally redlined*. Retrieved from http://www.consumerfinance.gov/about-us/newsroom/cfpb-and-doj-order-hudson-city-savings-bank-to-pay-27-millionto-increase-mortgage-credit-access-in-communities-illegallyredlined/.

Council for Economic Education (2020). *2020 Economic and personal finance education in our nation's schools*. https://www.councilforeconed.org/wp-content/uploads/2020/02/2020-Survey-of-the-States.pdf

POLICY, PRACTICE, AND INSTITUTIONAL BARRIERS 549

Consumer Financial Protection Bureau (2013, July). CFPB Financial Literacy Annual Report. https://files.consumerfinance.gov/f/201307_cfpb_report_financial-literacy-annual.pdf

Davies, G., & Derthick, M. (1997). Race and social welfare policy: The Social Security Act of 1935. *Political Science Quarterly, 112*(2), 217–235.

Dewees, S., & Mottola, G. (2017, April). *Race and financial capability in America: Understanding the Native American experience* [Insights Issue Brief]. FINRA Investor Education Foundation. https://www.usfinancialcapability.org/downloads/NativeAmerican-Experience-Fin-Cap.pdf

Dewey, J. (1938). *Experience and education*. New York: Macmillan.

Dietrich, J., Liu, F., Parrish, L., Roell, D., & Skhirtladze, A. (2018, May). Data point: 2017 Mortgage Market Activity and Trends: A look at the 2017 HMDA Data. Bureau of Consumer Financial Protection. Retrieved from: https://files.consumerfinance.gov/f/documents/bcfp_hmda_2017-mortgage-market-activity-trends_report.pdf

Eisenberg, R. (2018, June 12). Why minority financial planners are nearly nonexistent—and how to fix it. Forbes. https://www.forbes.com/sites/nextavenue/2018/06/12/minority-financial-planners-nearly-nonexistent/?sh=242acefed9cb

Emmons, W. R., & Rickets, L. R. (2016, October). Unequal degrees of affluence: Racial and ethnic wealth differences across education levels. The Regional Economist. Federal Reserve Bank of St. Louis. https://www.stlouisfed.org/-/media/project/frbstl/stlouisfed/Publications/Regional%20Economist/2016/October/degrees_of_influence.pdf

Federal Deposit Insurance Corporation (2018, October). 2017 FDIC national survey of unbanked and underbanked households. Retrieved from https://www.fdic.gov/householdsurvey/2017/2017report.pdf.

Federal Deposit Insurance Corporation (2017, February). *Linking youth savings with financial education: Lessons from the FDIC pilot.* [FDIC Report] https://www.fdic.gov/consumers/assistance/protection/depaccounts/youthsavings/documents/lessons-from-the-fdic-pilot.pdf

Fernandes, D., Lynch, J. G., Jr., & Netemeyer, R. G. (2014). Financial literacy, financial education, and downstream financial behaviors. *Management Science, 60*(8), 1861–1883. https://doi.org/10.1287/mnsc.2013.1849

Fernbach, P., & Sussman, A. (2018, October 27). Teaching people about money doesn't seem to make them any smarter about money-here's what might. MarketWatch. https://www.marketwatch.com/story/financial-education-flunks-out-and-heres-whats-being-done-about-it-2018-10-10

Figart, D. M. (2013). Institutionalist policies for financial inclusion. *Journal of Economic Issues, 47*(4), 873–893. doi: 10.2753/jei0021-3624470404.

Friedline, T., & Chen, Z. (2021). Digital redlining and the fintech marketplace: Evidence from U.S. zip codes. *The Journal of Consumer Affairs, 55*(2), 366–388. doi: 10.1111/joca.12297.

Friedline, T., Naraharisetti, S., & Weaver, A. (2019). Digital redlining: Poor rural communities' access to fintech and implications for financial inclusion. *Journal of Poverty, 24*(6), 517–541. doi: 10.1080/10875549.2019.1695162.

Frey, J. J., Sherraden, M. S., Birkenmaier, J., & Callahan, C. (2017). Financial capability and asset building in social work education. *Journal of Social Work Education, 53*(1), 79–83. doi: 10.1080/10437797.2016.1256170.

Fulk, M., & White, K. (2018). Exploring racial differences in financial socialization and related financial behaviors among Ohio college students. *Cogent Social Sciences, 4*, 1.

Gould, E. (2017). Racial gaps in wages, wealth, and more. Economic Policy Institute. Retrieved from https://www.epi.org/blog/racial-gaps-in-wages-wealth-and-more-a-quick-recap/.

Goodstein, R. M., & Rhine, S. L. W. (2017). The effects of bank and nonbank provider locations on household use of financial transaction services. *Journal of Banking & Finance, 78*(2). doi: 10.1016/j.jbankfin.2017.01.016.

Graves, E., Muñoz, A. P., Hamilton, D., Darity, W. A., & Nam, Y. (2019). Non-Hispanic White versus Black parental wealth and wealth transfers to enable homeownership in five metropolitan areas. In A. K. B., M. T. Nguyen, & D. P. Varady (Eds.), *The Routledge handbook of housing policy and planning* (pp. 54–67). New York: Routledge.

Hageman, S. A., Sherraden, M.S., Birkenmaier, J. M., & Loke, V. (2021). Economic and financial well-being in the social work curriculum: Faculty perspectives. *Journal of Social Work Education, 57*(2), 251–263. doi: 10.1080/10437797.2019.1661919

Hamilton, D., & Darity, W. A., Jr. (2017). The political economy of education, financial literacy, and the racial wealth gap. *Federal Reserve Bank of St. Louis Review, 99*(1), 59–76.

Harvey, M. (2019). Impact of financial education mandates on younger consumers' use of alternative financial services. *Journal of Consumer Affairs, 53,* 731–769. https://doi.org/10.1111/joca.12242

Herring, C., & Henderson, L. (2016). Wealth inequality in Black and White: Cultural and structural sources of the racial wealth gap. *Race and Social Problems, 8*(1), 4–17. doi: 10.1007/s12552-016-9159-8.

Huang, J., Yunju Nam, Y., Michael Sherraden, M., Margaret, M., & Clancy, M. M. (2019). Impacts of child development accounts on parenting practices: Evidence from a randomised statewide experiment. *Asia Pacific Journal of Social Work and Development, 29*(1), 34–47. https://doi.org/10.1080/02185385.2019.1575270.

Huang, J., Sherraden, M. S., Johnson, L., Birkenmaier, J., Loke, V., & Hageman, S. (2021). Preparing social work faculty to teach financial capability: Where we stand. *Journal of Social Work Education, 57*(4), 688–706. https://doi.org/10.1080/10437 797.2020.1714524

Jayakody, R. (1998). Race differences in intergenerational financial assistance: The needs of children and the resources of parents. *Journal of Family Issues, 19*(5), 508–533. doi: 10.1177/019251398019005002.

Johnson, L., Lee, Y., Njenga, G., Kieyah, J., Osei-Akoto, I., Rodriguez, C. O., . . . Zou, L. (2018). School banking as a strategy for strengthening youth economic participation in developing countries: Lessons from YouthSave. *Global Social Welfare, 5*(4), 265–275. doi: 10.1007/s40609-017-0109-1

Johnson, E., & Sherraden, M. S. (2007). From financial literacy to financial capability among youth. *Journal of Sociology and Social Welfare, 34*(3), 119 Article 7.

Jorgensen, M., & Akee, R. (2017, January). Accessing capital and credit in native communities: A data review. University of Arizona, Native Nations Institute, 1–62. doi: 10.13140/RG.2.2.16560.87049

Kaiser, T., & Menkhoff, L. (2017). Does financial education impact financial literacy and financial behavior, and if so, when? *The World Bank Economic Review, 31*(3), 611–630. https://doi.org/10.1093/wber/lhx018

Kasman, J. L. M., Heuberger, B., & Hammond, R. A. (2018). *A review of large-scale youth financial literacy education policies and programs.* The Brookings Institution.

POLICY, PRACTICE, AND INSTITUTIONAL BARRIERS 551

Waldman, A., & Kiel, P. (2015, October 8). Racial disparity in debt collection lawsuits: A study of three metro areas. White Paper. Retrieved from: https://static.propublica.org/projects/race-and-debt/assets/pdf/ProPublica-garnishments-whitepaper.pdf

Killewald, A. (2013). Return to being Black, living in the red: A race gap in wealth that goes beyond social origins. *Demography*, *50*(4), 1177–1195. doi: 10.1007/s13524-012-0190-0.

Killewald, A., Pfeffer, F. T., & Schachner, J. N. (2017). Wealth inequality and accumulation. *Annual Review of Sociology*, *43*, 379–404. doi: 10.1146/annurev-soc-060116-053331.

Kim, Y., Sherraden, M., Huang, J., & Clancy, M. M. (2015). Child development accounts and parental educational expectations for young children: Early evidence from a statewide social experiment. *Social Service Review*, *89*(1), 99–137. http://doi.org/10.1086/680014.

Kolb, A. Y., & Kolb, D. A. (2009). The learning way: Meta-cognitive aspects of experiential learning. *Simulation & Gaming*, *40*(3), 297–327. https://doi.org/10.1177/1046878108325713

Langholz, K., Selby, C., & Marks, B. (2019). Promoting Financial empowerment through building Native communities: Financial skills for families. Longmont, CO: First Nations Oweesta Corporation. https://www.oweesta.org/wp-content/uploads/2019/10/Oweesta-Key-Bank-Report-2019-Digital-Edition.pdf

Lee, Y. S., Johnson, L., Ansong, D., Osei-Akoto, I., Masa, R., Chowa, G., & Sherraden, M. (2017). "Taking the Bank to the Youth": Impacts on savings from the Ghana YouthSave Experiment. *Journal of International Development*, *29*(7), 936–947. doi:10.1002/jid.3315

Looney, S. M. (2011). *Financial literacy at Minority-Serving Institutions*. Washington DC: The Institute for Higher Education Policy. https://files.eric.ed.gov/fulltext/ED527709.pdf

Li, Z., & Dalaker, J. (2019, July 1). Poverty Among Americans Aged 65 and Older. Congressional Research Service. Retrieved from: https://www.everycrsreport.com/files/20190701_R45791_e0cd165614a677c58c608ef6dd5ad2e55484120e.pdf

Lusardi, A. (2008, February). *Household saving behavior: The role of financial literacy, information, and financial education programs* (No. w13824). National Bureau of Economic Research: Cambridge, MA Retrieved from: https://www.nber.org/papers/w13824#:~:text=Household%20Saving%20Behavior%3A%20The%20Role%20of%20Financial%20Literacy%2C,charge%20of%20their%20own%20financial%20security%20after%20retirement.

Lusardi, A. (2019). Financial literacy and the need for financial education: Evidence and implications. *Swiss Journal of Economics and Statistics*, *155*, 1. https://doi.org/10.1186/s41937-019-0027-5

Lusardi, A., & Mitchell, O. S. (2014). The economic importance of financial literacy: Theory and evidence. *Journal of Economic Literature*, *52*(1), 5–44.

Lusardi, A., & Mitchell, O. S. (2011). Financial literacy and planning: Implications for retirement wellbeing. [Working paper 17078]. NBER Working Paper Series. Cambridge, MA: National Bureau of Economic Research.

Lusardi, A., & Mitchell, O. S. (2009). Financial literacy: Evidence and implications for financial education. *Trends and Issues*, 1–10.

Lusardi, A., & Mitchell, O. S. (2007). Financial Literacy and Retirement Planning: New Evidence from the Rand American Life Panel. Michigan Retirement Research Center

Research Paper No. WP 2007-157. Available at SSRN: https://ssrn.com/abstract=1095 869 or http://dx.doi.org/10.2139/ssrn.1095869

Martin, L. L. (2019). Race, wealth, and homesteading revisited: How public policies destroy(ed) Black wealth and created the wealth feedback loop. In J. Grimm & J. Loke (Eds.), *How public policy impacts racial inequality* (pp. 140–165). Baton Rouge: Louisiana State University Press.

Meschede, T., Taylor, J., Mann, A., & Shapiro, T. (2017). "Family achievements?": How a college degree accumulates wealth for Whites and not for Blacks. *Federal Reserve Bank of St. Louis Review, 99*(1), 121–137. doi: 10.20955/r.2017.121-137.

Miller, M., Reichelstein, J., Salas, C., & Zia, B. (2014, January 1). Can You Help Someone Become Financially Capable? A Meta-Analysis of the Literature. World Bank Policy Research Working Paper No. 6745. Available at SSRN: https://ssrn.com/abstract= 2380391

Mishel, L., Bivens, J., Gould, E., & Shierholz, H. (2012). *The state of working America.* Ithaca, NY: Cornell University Press.

Mitchell, O. S., Lusardi, A., & Curto, V. (2009, August 21). Financial Literacy Among the Young: Evidence and Implications for Consumer Policy. Pension Research Council WP 2009-09. SSRN: https://ssrn.com/abstract=1459141 or http://dx.doi.org/10.2139/ssrn.1459141

Morrin, M., Broniarczyk, S. M., & Inman, J. (2009, June 1). *Fund assortments and 401(K) plan participation: The moderating effect of gender.* Networks Financial Institute Working Paper No. 2009-WP-06. Available at SSRN: https://ssrn.com/abstract=1432 510 or http://dx.doi.org/10.2139/ssrn.1432510

Nam, Y. (2021). Parents' financial assistance for college and black-white wealth disparity. *Children and Youth Service Review. 128,* 1–8. *https://doi.org/10.1016/j.childyo uth.2021.106159*

Newell, M. E. (2015). *Brethren by nature: New England Indians, colonists, and the origins of American slavery.* Ithaca, NY: Cornell University Press.

Oliver, M. L., & Shapiro, T. (1995/2006). *Black wealth/White wealth: A new perspective on racial inequality.* London: Taylor & Francis.

Pew Charitable Trusts (2018). Family Finances. https://www.pewtrusts.org/en/topics/family-finances

Ratcliffe, C., & Brown, S. (2017). Credit scores perpetuate racial disparities, even in America's most prosperous cities. *Urban Wire-the Blog of the Urban Institute.*

Rhee, N. (2013, December). Race and Retirement Insecurity in the United States. National Institute on Retirement Security (pp. 1–22). Washington, DC. Retrieved from: https://www.nirsonline.org/wp-content/uploads/2017/07/race_and_retirement_insecurity_final.pdf

Reich, M. (1971). The economics of racism. In D. M. Gordon (Ed.), *Problems in Political Economy: An urban perspective* (pp. 107–112). Lexington: Better World Books.

Reid, C. K. (2019). Homeownership and the racial and ethnic wealth gap in the United States. In A. K. B., M. T. Nguyen, & D. P. Varady (Eds.), *The Routledge handbook of housing policy and planning* (pp. 37–53). New York: Routledge.

Robb, C. A., & Woodyard, A. S. (2011). Financial knowledge and best practice behavior. *Journal of Financial Counseling and Planning, 22*(1), 60–70.

Robles, T. F. (2014). Marital quality and health: Implications for marriage in the 21st century. *Current Directions in Psychological Science, 23*(6), 427–432.

POLICY, PRACTICE, AND INSTITUTIONAL BARRIERS   553

Rochelle, M., McClendon, G., Brackett, M., Wright, M., & Sherraden, M. S. (2015). *Adopting a financial capability and asset building curriculum at historically Black colleges and universities* (CSD Working Paper No. 15-36). St. Louis, MO: Washington University, Center for Social Development.

Sarkisian, N., & Gerstel, N. (2004). Kin support among blacks and whites: Race and family organization. *American Sociological Review, 69*(6), 812–837. doi: 10.1177/000312240406900604.

Scholz, J. K., & Levine, K. (2004). U.S. Black-White wealth inequality. In K. M. Neckerman (Ed.), *Social inequality* (pp. 895–929). New York: Russell Sage Foundation.

Schuchardt, J., Hanna, S., H, Tahira, Lyons, A., Palmer, L., & Xiao, J. (2009). Financial literacy and education research priorities. *Journal of Financial Counseling and Planning, 20*(1), 84–95.

Sen, A. (1999). *Development as freedom.* New York: Anchor Books.

Shapiro, T. M. (2004). *The hidden cost of being African-American: How wealth perpetuates inequality.* Oxford and New York: Oxford University Press.

Shapiro, T. M. (2006). Race, homeownership and wealth. *Washington University Journal of Law & Policy, 20,* 53.

Shapiro, Meschede, T., Cronin, M., & Sullivan, L. (2011). Rising economic insecurity among senior single women. Institute on Assets and Social Policy, Heller School for Social Management, Brandeis University; Demos.org. https://www.demos.org/sites/default/files/publications/senior-single-women_final%20%281%29.pdf

Shapiro, T. M., Meschede, T., & Osoro, S. (2013). *The roots of the widening racial wealth gap: Explaining the black-white economic divide.* New York: Institute on Assets and Social Policy. https://drum.lib.umd.edu/bitstream/handle/1903/24590/racialwealthg apbrief.pdf

Sherraden, M. (1991). *Assets and the poor: A new American welfare policy.* Armonk, NY: M. E. Sharpe.

Sherraden, M. S. (2013). Building blocks of financial capability. In J. Birkenmaier, M. S. Sherraden, & J. Curley (Eds.), *Financial capability and asset development: Research, education, policy, and practice* (pp. 3–43).Oxford University Press: New York.

Sherraden, M. S., Birkenmaier, J., & Collins, J. M. (2018). *Financial capability and asset building in vulnerable households: Theory and practice.* New York: Oxford University Press.

Sherraden, M., Clancy, M. M., Nam, Y., Huang, J., Kim, Y., Beverly, S. G., Mason, L. R., Wikoff, N. E., Schreiner, M., & Purnell, J. Q. (2015). Universal accounts at birth: Building knowledge to inform policy. *Journal of the Society for Social Work and Research, 6*(4), 541–64. https://doi.org/10.1086/684139.

Sherraden, Michael, Clancy, M. M., Nam, Y., Huang, J., Kim, Y., Beverly, S. G., Mason, L. R., Wikoff, N. E., Schreiner, M., Purnell, J. Q., & Margaret M. Clancy, Yunju Nam, Jin Huang, Youngmi Kim, Sondra G. Beverly, Lisa Reyes Mason, Nora Ellen Wikoff, Mark Schreiner, & Jason Q. Purnell. (2015). Society for Financial Education & Professional Development (2020). Student ambassador program. Retrieved from https://sfepd.org/student-ambassador-program/.

Sherraden, M. S., Huang, J., Frey, J. J., Birkenmaier, J., Callahan, C., Clancy, M. M., & Sherraden, M. (2015). *Financial capability and asset building for all* (Grand Challenges for Social Work Initiative Working Paper No. 13). Cleveland, OH: American Academy of Social Work and Social Welfare.

Sherraden, M. S., Johnson, L., Guo, B., & Elliott III, W. (2017). Financial capability in children: Effects of participation in a school-based financial education and savings program. *Journal of Family and Economic Issues, 32*, 385–399. https://doi.org/10.1007/s10 834-010-9220-5

Sherraden, M. S., McBride, A. M., Johnson, E., Hanson, S., Ssewamala, F. M., & Williams Shanks, T. R. (2005). *Saving in low-income households: Evidence from interviews with participants in the American Dream Demonstration.* CSD Report No. 05-02. St. Louis, MO: Washington University, Center for Social Development.

Shrider, E. A., Kollar, M, Chen, F., & Semega, J. (2021, September). Income and Poverty in the United States: 2020. Current Population Reports. U.S. Department of Commerce, U.S. Census Bureau. Washington, DC. Retrieved from: https://www.census.gov/cont ent/dam/Census/library/publications/2021/demo/p60-273.pdf

Society for Financial Education & Professional Development (2020). Student Ambassador Program. Retrieved from https://sfepd.org/student-ambassador-program/

Sullivan, L., & Meschede, T. (2018). How Measurement of Inequalities in Wealth by Race/Ethnicity Impacts Narrative and Policy: Investigating the Full Distribution. *Race and Social Problems, 10*(1), 19–29. doi:10.1007/s12552-017-9217-x

Sullivan, L., Meschede, T., Dietrich, L., Shapiro, T., Traub, A., & Ruetschlin, C. (2016). *The Racial Wealth Gap: Why Policy Matters.* New York, NY. Retrieved from: https://www.demos.org/research/racial-wealth-gap-why-policy-matters

Tamborini, C. R., & Kim, C. (2020). Are you saving for retirement? Racial/Ethnic differences in contributory retirement savings plans. *The Journals of Gerontology, 75*, 4, 837–848. https://doi.org/10.1093/geronb/gbz131

Theodos, B., Simms, M., Treskon, M., Stacy, C., Brash, R., Emam, D., . . . Collazos, J. (2015). An evaluation of the impacts and implementation approaches of financial coaching programs. Washington, DC: Urban Institute. https://www.fdic.gov/analysis/cfr/consu mer/2015/presentations/theodos.pdf

Traub, A., Catherine & Ruetschlin, C. (2016). *The racial wealth gap: Why policy matters.* New York: Demos. Available at: http://www.demos.org/publication/racial-wealth-gap-why-policy-matters.

Tsang, C.-W. R., & Dietz, T. L. (2001). The unrelenting significance of minority statuses: Gender, ethnicity and economic attainment since Affirmative Action. *Sociological Spectrum, 21*(1), 61–80. doi: 10.1080/02732170117961.

Urban, C., Schmeiser, M., Collins, J. M., & Brown, A. (2020). The effects of high school personal financial education policies on financial behavior. *Economics of Education Review, 78*. https://doi.org/10.1016/j.econedurev.2018.03.006

Urban Institute (2017, October 5). Nine Charts about Wealth Inequality in America (Updated). Retrieved from: https://apps.urban.org/features/wealth-inequality-charts/

U.S. Census (2018). https://www.census.gov/newsroom/press-releases/2019/income-poverty.html.

U.S. Department of Justice (2012). *Justice department reaches settlement with Wells Fargo.* Retrieved from http://www.justice.gov/opa/pr/2012/July/12-dag-869.html.

Winchester, D., & Huston, S. (2015). All financial advice for the middle class is not equal. *Journal of Consumer Policy, 38.* doi: 10.1007/s10603-015-9290-8.

Yakoboski, P., Lusardi, A., & Hasler, A. (2019). Financial literacy and wellness among African Americans. New insights from the Personal Finance (P-Fin) Index. TIAA Institute and the Global Financial Literacy Excellence Center *Special Report* (October 2019).

Young, W. M. (n.d.). QuotesGuy.com. https://www.quotesguy.com/every-man-is-our-brother/

Index

For the benefit of digital users, indexed terms that span two pages (e.g., 52–53) may, on occasion, appear on only one of those pages.

Tables and figures are indicated by *t* and *f* following the page number

AARP's Experience Corps, 244–45, 247–48
ability to act, 527, 543–44
Abrams, L. S., 39–40
ACA (Affordable Care Act), 295
acceptance and commitment therapy, 110–11
Action Plan to Reduce Racial and Ethnic Health Disparities, 130
activism
  cyberactivism, 517
  environmental justice, 350–55
  social justice, 115
Addams, J., 33–34
advocacy, 115, 318, 350–55, 510
Affordable Care Act (ACA), 295
affordable housing, access to, 378–79
African Americans. *See* Black Americans
AFS (alternative financial services), 535
Aid to Families with Dependent Children (AFDC), 488–89
air quality, role in COVID-19 pandemic, 348–49
Alexander, M., 102–3, 426
Allen, D. G., 85
Allen-Meares, P., 309–10
alliance building, 114
allostatic loads, 386
alternative financial services (AFS), 535
alternative healing strategies, 115
American Psychological Association (APA), 6
Anguelovski, I., 352
anti-Blackness, 399
anti-gentrification, 517–18

anti-oppressive practice (AOP), 114–15, 116
anti-racism practice. *See also* productive aging framework
  addressing structural and interpersonal racism, 109–16
  anti-oppression practices combined with, 114–15
  building practice and theory narrative, 101–6
  critique of, 116
  interpersonal efforts, 86
  mindfulness and, 110–11
  need for focus on, 45–51, 52
  prevention of Black family violence, 280–81
  prioritizing, 97–98
  structural and policy approaches to, 107–9
anti-racist projects, 45
anxiety due to racism, 308–9, 320
APA (American Psychological Association), 6
apology for racialized practices, 105–6
Armfield, F. L., 33
Asante, M. K., 17–18
Asian Americans
  bystander intervention training, 316–17
  community-based solutions for, 318–19
  culturally sensitive evidence-based interventions for, 319–21
  developing anti-Asian racism workforce, 314
  future research, 321–22
  Grand Challenges for Social Work and, 309–11

556   INDEX

Asian Americans (*cont.*)
  hate crimes against, 304, 305, 306–7, 316–17
  historical racism against, 34–35, 81–82, 305–8
  impact of racism on health and mental health of, 308–9
  mental healthcare access, 319
  model minority myth, 311–12
  overview, 304–5
  policy initiatives on anti-Asian racism, 317–18
  racial stereotypes of, 16
  reporting racism against, 316–17
  solidarity with African Americans, 313–14
  strategies to eliminate racism against, 309–21
  wealth building, 485
assessment of psychosis risk, 171–75, 178–86
asset building, 489–91, 494. *See also* financial capability and asset building
Association of Social Work Boards (ASWB), 47–51
authenticity, 62–63

bachelor of social work (BSW) degree, 47–51
Balazs, C. L., 340–42
Baldwin, J., 3, 9, 18, 51–52
Ball, A., 69–70
banked status, 534–35, 536
barrios, 291–92
BASICS (Brief Alcohol Screening and Intervention for College Students), 141*f*
Baumgartner, F. R., 446–47
behavioral analysis, 109, 110, 111–12
behavioral contingency theory of racism, 103–4
behavioral health problems in young people, preventing, 127–29, 154–55. *See also* equity-enhancing interventions; psychosis prevention
Bell, D., 95, 100–1, 388–89
Bell, J. M., 13–14, 36–39
Bennefield, Z., 17–18

BIPOC (Black and indigenous people of color). *See* Black Americans; Native Americans
Bivens, D., 394
Black Americans. *See also* family violence in Black families
  child welfare among, 43–44
  civil rights movement, 36–39
  climate change impact on, 336
  COVID-19 pandemic and, 348–50
  culturally relevant health-promotion interventions, 213–21
  early study of effects of systemic racism on, 95–96
  extractive energy and natural resource development and, 342–43
  extreme weather events and, 343–48
  food systems/security and, 338–40
  health effects of racism in, 201–3
  in history of social work and racism, 33–35, 79–83
  homelessness among, 366–67
  household financial access, 534–37
  housing inequities, 367–69, 376–79
  HUD-VASH program for veterans, 374–76
  inequities among older adults, 238*t*
  juvenile justice involvement, 413–14
  land loss and, 491
  legal and policy infrastructure affecting, 99–101, 102–3
  mass incarceration of, 430–31
  pesticide exposure in, 338
  poverty rates, 392
  racial commonsense thinking, 19–20
  racial stereotypes of, 16
  recruitment into health-serving professions, 213
  reparations for, 494–95
  school suspensions and expulsions among, 460, 461
  serious mental illness in, 175–77, 178–81, 184–85
  social exclusion of, 386–87, 395–400
  solidarity with Asian Americans, 313–14
  urban heat islands, 344–45
  wage gap, 268, 543

INDEX

water insecurity and, 340–42
wealth inequality, 268–69, 482, 483–84, 490–91
White supremacist social practice foundation, 506
Black and indigenous people of color (BIPOC). *See* Black Americans; Native Americans
Black codes, 264–65
Black Lives Matter (BLM), 4–5, 63–64, 105, 314
Black Manifesto, 483–84, 494–95
Black Perspective principles, 66, 401–2
Black Task Force, 37–39
Blaisdell, R. K., 204
Blueprints for Healthy Youth Development, 139–48, 141*f*, 143*t*
Blues Program, 141*f*
Bo, S. S., 305–6
Body Project, 141*f*, 145–46
Boston College School of Social Work, 296
Bowles, D. D., 36
Bowser, B. P., 102–5
Bradshaw, C. P., 39–40
Brandt, J. A., 109–12
Brennan Center for Justice, 446
Brief Alcohol Screening and Intervention for College Students (BASICS), 141*f*
Briggs, H. E., 32–33, 38–39, 40
Brown, A., 345
Brown, K. S., 109
Brown v. Board of Education, 101
BSW (bachelor of social work) degree, 47–51
Building Refugee and Immigrant Degrees for Graduate Education Program (BRIDGE), Boston University, 296–97
Burghardt, S., 5
bystander intervention training, 316–17

CAARMS (Comprehensive Assessment of At-Risk Mental States), 172
Cáceres, B., 335
CaFI (Culturally-adapted Family Intervention), 183
calling out racism, 102

Canada, studies of economic inequality and race in, 478
capitalism, 12, 205
caregiving by older adults, 243–45, 248
Carle, S. D., 33–34
Carlton-LaNey, I., 33
Carter, P., 420
case studies
 personal-professional narratives, 148–49
 social exclusion, 395–400
 value of, 394–95
Catagnus, R., 109–12
Caucasian Americans. *See* White Americans
Cazenave, N. A., 507
CBCF (Congressional Black Caucus Foundation) Annual Conference, 518–19
CBPH. *See* Coalition for the Promotion of Behavioral Health
CBPR (community-based participatory research), 221, 223–24
CBT (cognitive behavioral therapy), 7–8, 173, 181–82
CDAs (child development accounts), 494
CDFIs (community development financial institutions), 536, 537–38
CE (Coordinated Entry) systems, 370
centering approach to equity-enhancing interventions, 135–36
Centers for Medicare & Medicaid Services, 212–13
centers of excellence, 174
centrality of race and racism, 6–9
Certified Financial Planners (CFPs), 530–31
CFI (cultural formulation interview), 180, 184
CHamoru healers, 201
Chicano communities, 81–82
child development accounts (CDAs), 494
child maltreatment in Black families
 evidence-based strategies for ending, 277–79
 poverty and, 269
 rates of, 259–61
 stress and, 271

558 INDEX

child protective services (CPS), 259–60, 269
child welfare system
  personal-professional narratives, 68–69
  racialized problems in, 42–45
Chin, M. H., 213–14
Chinese Americans. *See* Asian Americans
Choctaw people, culturally tailored interventions for, 220
Chomsky, N., 23–24
chronic illness, disparities in, xxvi
CIEE (Critically Intersubjectively Engaged Ethnography), 341–42
CIT-S (Culturally Informed Treatment for Schizophrenia), 183
Civil Rights Act of 1866, 96
Civil Rights Division of the Department of Justice (DOJ), 117
civil rights movements
  African American, 36–39
  Asian American, 306–7
client narratives, 62
climate change, 336, 339–40
climate migration, 346–48
clinical interviews for psychosis risk, 172–73, 180–81, 184
Close the Health Gap Grand Challenge, 222–24
Coalition for the Promotion of Behavioral Health (CBPH), 128, 130–34. *See also* equity-enhancing interventions
Coates, T. N., 365
cognitive behavioral therapy (CBT), 7–8, 173, 181–82
Cohen, M., 419
Cole, N. L, 14
college education among Latinx, 292–93, 295–96
colonialism, settler, 203–5, 210
colorblindness, 63–64, 78–79
colorism, 289–90
committed actions, 111
commonsense thinking, racial, 18–21, 37
Communities That Care, 130–32
community-based financial institutions, 536, 537–38
community-based participatory research (CBPR), 221, 223–24
community belonging, role of, 320

community development financial institutions (CDFIs), 536, 537–38
community empowerment, 223–24
Comprehensive Assessment of At-Risk Mental States (CAARMS), 172
concentrated disadvantage, 432–33
concentrated poverty, 273–75
Congressional Black Caucus Foundation (CBCF) Annual Conference, 518–19
conspiracy of silence, 99
consumer credit, 537–38
Coordinated Entry (CE) systems, 370
Corley, N. A., 309–10
Corneau, S., 114–15
corporal punishment in schools, 460–61
Council on Social Work Education (CSWE)
  diversity standards, 35, 38–39
  nondiscriminatory practices, 36–38
  requirements for anti-racism practices, 106
  role in eradicating racism, 87, 88–89
COVID-19 Hate Crimes Act, 317
COVID-19 pandemic
  anti-Asian racism during, 304, 307
  environmental racism and, 348–50
  impact on Latinx Americans, 290–91
  impact on older workers, 247
  prevention paradox, 154
  racial disparities in, xxv–xxvii, 117
  social exclusion and, 395–97
CPS (child protective services), 259–60, 269
crack-cocaine epidemic, 20
credit reports and scores, 536–37
credit unions, 536, 537–38
Crenshaw, K., 388–89
criminal history, policies regarding, 438–39
criminal justice system. *See also* juvenile justice
  contributors to disparities in, 429–35
  culturally congruent reentry programs, 435–38
  decriminalizing low-level offenses, 439–40
  equity-informed policies and practices, 438–39

evidence-based practices for addressing disparities in, 435–44
explicit and implicit bias along continuum of, 443–44
investment in alternatives to, 440–41
Latinx Americans and, 293–94, 297–98
Promote Smart Decarceration Grand Challenge, 428–29
racial and ethnic disparities in, 428
racial impact statements, 442–43
repealing racialized legislation and policies, 441–42
solitary confinement, 384–85
Critically Intersubjectively Engaged Ethnography (CIEE), 341–42
Critical Race Theory (CRT), 87–88, 314–15, 388
Critical Time Intervention (CTI), 373
CSWE. See Council on Social Work Education
cultural competence, 39–41, 86, 208–9
cultural coping, 215–19
cultural formulation interview (CFI), 180, 184
cultural historical trauma, 204
cultural humility, 86, 208–9
Culturally-adapted Family Intervention (CaFI), 183
Culturally Informed Treatment for Schizophrenia (CIT-S), 183
culturally relevant interventions
for Asian Americans, 319–21
health-promotion interventions, 213–21
reentry programs, 435–38
cultural oppression, 509
cultural racism, 103–4
cultural resilience, 215–19
cultural responsiveness, in psychosis prevention, 178–87
cultural values and practices, 218–19
Curry, T., xxii
cyberactivism, 517
cyberwomanism, 517

DACA (Deferred Action for Childhood Arrivals), 294–95
Dale, T., 48
Darity, W., 278

David, E. J. R., 83–84
Davis, L., 28–29
deaths of despair, 21
DeCarlo, M. P., 51
decolonization of organizational cultures, 105–6
decriminalizing low-level offenses, 439–40
deep structure fit efforts, 150–51
Deferred Action for Childhood Arrivals (DACA), 294–95
DEI (diversity, equity, and inclusion), 213
de jure practices, 99–101
denial of racism, 113–14, 508–10
Department of Veterans Affairs (VA), 374–76
depression in Asian Americans, 308–9, 320
Detroit Head Start neighborhoods, 202
DeVylder, J. E., 170–71
Díaz, A. S., 346
differential offending, 414
digital infrastructure, social determinant, 211
"dindu nuffin" memes, 65
discipline gap, 460
discretionary police stops, 276–77
disproportionate minority contact (DMC), 414–15, 426–27, 444–45
dissemination strategy, School Success Project, 469–70
diversity
commitment of social work profession to, 32–33
CSWE standards, 35, 38–39
in social work education, 39–41
diversity, equity, and inclusion (DEI), 213
DOJ (Civil Rights Division of the Department of Justice), 117
domestic violence in Black families
evidence-based strategies for ending, 277–79
housing and, 274
poverty and, 269–70
rates of, 261
stress and, 271–72
Douglass, F., 20, 258, 313
Drapetomania, 175–76
drinking water, 340–42

560 INDEX

Drinking Water Disparities
framework, 340–42
drug abuse, possession, and trafficking,
431, 434, 439–40, 441–42
drug courts, 440–41
Du Bois, W. E. B., 95–96
Duntley-Matos, R., 341–42

Early College High School Initiative
(ECHS), 141*f*, 145–46
early psychosis interventions, 170–75
Eaton, I., 95–96
economic inequality, xxvi. *See also*
financial capability and asset building
assets and wealth, 489–91
history of exclusionary policies, 479–86
labor and income, 486–89
land loss, 491–92
mitigating policies for, 493–94
racial income and wealth gaps, 476–79
reparations, 494–95
social exclusion and, 392
social work practice and, 495
wealth stripping through fees and
fines, 492–93
economics of racism, 525
Edelman, M. W., 413
education. *See also* school suspensions and
expulsions
financial, 526–27, 528–30, 531–34
impact of juvenile justice involvement
on, 417–18
impact of social isolation/exclusion
on, 392–93
of Latinx Americans, 292–93, 295–96
education, social work. *See* social work
education
Education Policy Accreditation Standards
(EPAS), 46–47
electronic medical records, 210–11
Ellis, K. N., 344–45
Emancipation Proclamation, 263–64
emotional health, impact of racism on, 201
employer-sponsored retirement
plans, 538–39
employment of older adults, 242–
43, 246–47
empowerment, 114

ending racism
overview, 95–99
practice approaches for, 109–16
race consciousness-raising and anti-
racism practice, 101–6
racism by legislative fiat and de
jure, 99–101
structural and policy approaches, 107–9
sustainability of racism in America, 99
environmental gentrification, 353–54
environmental justice, 336, 337, 350–55
environmental racism, 202–3
activism and advocacy, 350–55
COVID-19 pandemic and, 348–50
extractive energy and natural resource
development, 342–43
extreme weather events, 343–48
food systems and food security, 338–40
intersection of health equity and
environmental justice, 337
overview, 335–37
pesticide exposure, 338
water insecurity, 340–42
EPAS (Education Policy Accreditation
Standards), 46–47
Epperson, M., 428–29
equal justice, 95, 97–98, 102, 105–6
equitable access, 206*t*, 212
equity-enhancing interventions
anti-racism practice and, 154–55
approaches to, 135–37
case study, 148–49
impact on marginalized groups, 139–
48, 141*f*, 143*t*
innovative service-delivery
models, 152–53
participatory processes in, 149–50
re-examining goal to establish, 134–39
science-based prevention
versus, 130–32
tailoring to cultures, contexts, and
conditions, 150–52
*Unleashing the Power of
Prevention*, 130–32
equity-informed policies and
practices, 438–39
eradicating racism
conceptualization of racism, 78–79

history of social work and racism, 79–83
institutional efforts, 86–89
interpersonal efforts, 85–86
intrapersonal efforts, 83–85
overview, 76–78
Erwin, J., 345
ethical standards, 83
ethnic displacement, 517–18
ethnic/racial identity, 8, 216–17
ethnic-racial socialization, 217–18
eugenics, 80–81
evidence-based practice
for Asian Americans, 319–21
culturally tailored, 219–21
for ending Black family
violence, 277–79
for homelessness, 371–74
for mass incarceration
disparities, 435–44
for psychosis prevention, 181–83, 186
School Success Project, 468–69
experiential learning methods, 532
explicit bias along carceral
continuum, 443–44
expulsions from school. *See* school
suspensions and expulsions
extractive energy development, 342–43
extreme weather events, 343–48

Fair Housing Laws, 379
Family Focused Therapy (FTT), 182
family violence in Black families
applying anti-racist framework to
prevention of, 280–81
child maltreatment, 259–61
evidence-based interventions
for, 277–79
forced family separation, 262–64
geographic contexts and structural
inequities in, 272–77
health disparities and stress in, 270–72
historical racism and violence against
Black families, 262–67
intimate partner violence, 261
laws and policies maintaining White
supremacy, 264–67
overview, 258–59
poverty and, 267–70

farmworkers, pesticide exposure
among, 338
Faustian Bargain, 263–64
FCAB. *See* financial capability and asset
building
Feagin, J., xxiv–xxv, 17–18, 391
Feldman, D. C., 244
Feyerherm, W., 419
FFT (Functional Family Therapy), 141f
#FightBlightBaltimore, 517–18
financial capability and asset
building (FCAB)
consumer credit, 537–38
curriculum based on, 543–45
economics of racism, 525
financial education, 526–27, 528–
30, 531–34
financial guidance, 530–31
financial socialization, 527–28
household financial access, 534–37
overview, 524–25
racial wealth and disparity, 540–43
racism as barrier to achieving, 539–40
retirement accounts, 539
retirement savings, 538–39
financial education, 526–27, 528–
30, 531–34
financial guidance, 530–31
financial literacy, 526–34
financial socialization, 527–28
financing systems, 206t, 212–13
Fire Next Time, The (Baldwin), 8, 18
First Step Act, 433–34
first wave of environmental justice, 352–53
5-Key Reentry Model, 435–36
Flint water crisis, 341–42, 352–53
flooding, 345–46
Floyd, G., 4, 513–14
food systems and food security, 338–
40, 349
forced separation of Black families, 262–64
foster care system, racialized problems
in, 42–43
Fourteenth Amendment, 100–1
fracking, 342–43
Franklin, D. L., 264
Freire, P., 82–83
Fronius, T., 466

562 INDEX

FTT (Family Focused Therapy), 182
Functional Family Therapy (FFT), 141*f*

Galton, F., 80–81
Garran, A., 61
GCSW (Grand Challenges for Social
  Work), xxi–xxii, xxiv, 77, 309–11
gender
  in criminal justice disparities, 430–31
  in school suspensions and
    expulsions, 460–63
GenerationPMTO, 141*f*
gentrification, 242, 396–97, 517–18
geographic context, impact on Black
  family violence, 272–77
geographic racism, xxvi
Gini Coefficient, 476–77
global social contract, 11
governance in health systems, 213
graduation rates of Latinx, 292, 295–96
Gramlich, J., 100
Grand Challenge of Preventing Serious
  Mental Illness, 170–71
Grand Challenges for Social Work
  (GCSW), xxi–xxii, xxiv, 77, 309–11
Grand Challenge to Create Social
  Responses to a Changing
  Environment, 337
Grand Challenge to Ensure Healthy
  Development for Youth, 127, 129
Gray, F., 515–17
Griffith, D. M., 108

Hamilton-Mason, J., 46–47
Hardeman, R. R., 108
#hashtag method, 514
hashtag syllabus, 517
hate crimes
  against Asian Americans, 304, 305,
    306–7, 316–17
  individual racism, 104
  upsurge of, 76–77
Hathaway, J. M., 344–45
Hayward, R. A., 346
HBCUs (historically black colleges and
  universities), 399–400, 532–33, 544
HCVs (housing choice
  vouchers), 378–79

healing-centered engagement
  framework, 214–15
health
  association between racism, settler
    colonialism, and, 203–5
  holistic view of, 201–3
  as a human right, 222
  overview, 200–201
health disparities
  in Asian Americans, 308–9
  association between racism, settler
    colonialism, and health, 203–5
  in behavioral health, 130–34, 154–55
  in Black Americans, 270–72
  creating structural change, 222–24
  cultural coping and cultural
    resilience, 215–19
  culturally tailored and culturally
    grounded interventions, 219–21
  equitable access, 212
  financing systems, 212–13
  health information systems, 210–12
  health service delivery, 207–10
  in Latinx Americans, 290–91, 295
  leadership and governance, 213
  overview, 200–201
  racial healing, 214–15
  social isolation/exclusion and, 384–
    85, 393–94
  workforce development, 210
health equity. *See also* productive aging
  framework
  defined, 237
  intersection of environmental justice
    and, 337
  Unleashing the Power of Prevention, 130
health information systems, 206*t*, 210–12
health service delivery, 206*t*, 207–10
health systems
  building blocks of, 205, 206*t*
  equitable access, 212
  financing systems, 212–13
  health information systems, 210–12
  health service delivery, 207–10
  Latinx discrimination in, 290–91, 295
  leadership and governance, 213
  overview, 205
  workforce development, 210

INDEX 563

healthy development of youth, 127–29. *See also* equity-enhancing interventions; psychosis prevention

helping relationship, racism in, 61–63

Hepworth, D. H., 62–63

Heywood, J. S., 21

HF (Housing First) program, 371–74, 376

high school financial education, 528–29

hiring process, discrimination in, 487

Hispanic Americans. *See* Latinx Americans

historically black colleges and universities (HBCUs), 399–400, 532–33, 544

history of social work and racism, 33–35, 79–83

holistic outcomes in psychosis prevention, 173–74

holistic view of health, 201–3

homelessness, 274

history of housing exclusion, 366–69

Housing First, 371–74

HUD-VASH program for veterans, 374–76

racial lens lacking in research on, 369–71

recommendations to end racial disparities, 376–79

homeownership, 367–69, 392–93, 483, 491–92, 540, 541–42

Hopper, K., 369

household financial access, 534–37

housing. *See also* homelessness

among Black families, 272–75

among Latinx Americans, 291–92

history of housing exclusion, 366–69

homeownership, 367–69, 392–93, 483, 491–92, 540, 541–42

Housing First, 371–74

HUD-VASH program for veterans, 374–76

recommendations to end racial disparities, 376–79

housing choice vouchers (HCVs), 378–79

Housing First (HF) program, 371–74, 376

Hoyt, C., Jr., 78–79

HUD-VASH program for veterans, 374–76

human right, health as, 222

Hunter, B. A., 437–38

hurricanes, 345–46, 347

Hymans, D., 49–50

identity formation, 11

identity politics of race, 16–17

ideology, racist, 13–14

immigration

Asian exclusion, 305–6

decriminalization of, 294–95

Flint water crisis and, 341–42

law enforcement, 294

racialization of Latinx Americans, 289–90

racial projects, 15–16

Immigration Reform and Control Act of 1986 (IRCA), 294–95

implicit bias, 207, 293, 294, 443–44

imposition of racism, 13–14

incarceration. *See* mass incarceration

income disparities

history of exclusionary policies, 479–86

impact on Black family violence, 269–70

labor market inequalities and, 486–89

social isolation/exclusion and, 392

income supplements, 493–94

Indigenous people. *See* Native Americans

individualism, 509–10

individual racism, 104, 177

institutional efforts to eradicate racism, 86–89

institutional racism, 13–14, 40–41, 104

integrated framework of productive aging, anti-racism, and health equity. *See* productive aging framework

interactive map, School Success Project, 469

intergenerational trauma, xxvii

intergroup dialogue, 209–10

internalized domination, 83–84

internalized racism, 83–84, 393–94

internalized stigma related to psychosis, 172–73

International Center for Transitional Justice (ITCJ), 223

International Office for Migration, 347

interpersonal efforts to eradicate racism, 85–86

564 INDEX

interpersonal racism, practice approaches for, 109–16
interpreters, in equity-enhancing interventions, 152–53
interprofessional education, 210
intersectionality, 388–89
intimate partner violence in Black families
evidence-based strategies for ending, 277–79
housing and, 274
poverty and, 269–70
rates of, 261
stress and, 271–72
intrapersonal efforts to eradicate racism, 83–85
invisible hand of racism, 14
IRCA (Immigration Reform and Control Act of 1986), 294–95
ITCJ (International Center for Transitional Justice), 223

Jani, J. S., 39–40
Japanese Americans. See Asian Americans
JDAI (Juvenile Detention Alternatives Initiative), 429
Jim Crow laws, 265–67, 367, 483
JJDPA (Juvenile Justice and Delinquency Prevention Act), 414–15, 444–45
job demands, 243
Jones, C. P., 107–8
Jones, E. K., 34
Judicial Bench Card Checklist, 443–44
Juvenile Detention Alternatives Initiative (JDAI), 429
juvenile justice
assessing disparities in, 418
Juvenile Justice and Delinquency Prevention Act, 414–15, 444–45
macro-level impacts, 417–18
meso-level impacts, 416–17
micro-level impacts, 415–16
overrepresentation of minoritized youth, 44
overview, 413–14
personal-professional narratives, 67–68
reducing disparities in, 419

Juvenile Justice and Delinquency Prevention Act (JJDPA), 414–15, 444–45

Kā-HOLO project, 221
Kānaka Maoli (Native Hawaiian) culture, 200, 221
Karenga, M., 11, 13–14, 23–24, 459
Kendi, I. X., 45–46, 78–79
Kijakazi, K., 109
Kim, J. J., 47
King, M. L., Jr., 76, 510–11
King County Public Health, Washington State, 211
Koh, H. K., 129
Kozhimannil, K. B., 108
Kumpfer, K. L., 139

labor force participation of older adults, 242–43, 246–47
labor market inequalities, 486–89, 542–43
land, health of, 202–3
land loss, 491–92
language
in anti-racism culture, 114–15
in equity-enhancing interventions, 152–53
racialization of Latinx Americans, 289–90
Larson, K. E., 39–40
Latinx Americans
colorism, 289–90
criminal justice disparities, 293–94
culturally competent interventions with, 39–40
educational achievement, 292–93
Flint water crisis and, 341–42
health disparities, 290–91
history of social work and racism, 81–82
homelessness among, 366
household financial access, 534–37
housing inequities, 291–92
inequities among older adults, 238t
juvenile justice involvement, 413–14
mass incarceration of, 430–31
overview, 287
pesticide exposure among farmworkers, 338

poverty rates, 392
practices counteracting impact of
  racism on, 294–98
racialized problems in child
  welfare, 43–44
racial projects, 15–16
school suspensions and expulsions
  among, 460
social exclusion of, 386–87, 397–99
terms used to describe Latinx
  populations, 287–88
urban heat islands, 344–45
wealth building, 484
Latinx Leadership Initiative (LLI), Boston
  College School of Social Work, 296
Law Enforcement Assisted Diversion
  (LEAD) Program, 439–40
leadership in health systems, 206t, 213
legal infrastructure of structural racism,
  99–101, 117
legal segregation, 101, 106
legislation
  maintaining White supremacy, 264–67
  racial impact statements, 442–43
  repealing racialized criminal
    justice, 441–42
  zero-tolerance, 43–44, 460
legislative advocates, 510, 512–13
Levittown, Long Island, 368–69
Levy, B., 346
licensure testing, racially biased, 47–51
life expectancy, racial disparities
  in, 270–71
LifeSkills Training (LST), 141f, 142–45
Lincoln, A., 20
Lipsitz, G., xxvi
Liu, K., 69–70
LLI (Latinx Leadership Initiative), Boston
  College School of Social Work, 296
lobbying, 513
locus of control, 65
London, C., 442–43
Longres, J., 28, 31–32, 35, 37
low-level offenses,
  decriminalizing, 439–40
Loyola University Chicago online
  bilingual Master of Social Work
  program, 296

LST (LifeSkills Training), 141f, 142–45
Lytle, A., 127

macro factors, 22t, 34–35, 41, 433–35
macro-level impacts of juvenile justice
  involvement, 417–18
ma'i, 200–201
manifest destiny, 506
man-in-the-house rule, 266–67
Mann, A. B., 17
marijuana decriminalization, 439–40
Markle, M., 16–17
Maryland Ignition Interlock License
  Restriction, 141f
Mason, L. R., 344–45
mass incarceration
  culturally congruent reentry
    programs, 435–38
  decriminalizing low-level
    offenses, 439–40
  equity-informed policies and
    practices, 438–39
  evidence-based practices for disparities
    in, 435–44
  explicit and implicit bias along
    continuum, 443–44
  general discussion, 427
  impact on Black family violence, 275–77
  investment in alternatives to, 440–41
  of Latinx Americans, 297–98
  macro factors, 433–35
  meso factors, 432–33
  micro factors, 430–32
  overview, 426–27
  Promote Smart Decarceration Grand
    Challenge, 428–29
  racial and ethnic disparities in, 100, 428
  racial impact statements, 442–43
  repealing racialized legislation and
    policies, 441–42
master of social work (MSW) degree, 47–
  51, 296–97
material needs of participants, providing
  in interventions, 152–53
Matsuda, K., 109–12
McCoy, H., 154–55
McCurdy, J., 20
McMahon, A., 309–10

566 INDEX

MDIs (minority deposit institutions), 536, 537–38
Medina, E. M., 108
mental health. *See also* psychosis
  prevention
  in Asian Americans, 308–9, 319
  disparities in illness identification and treatment, 176–77
  evidence-based practices for, 181–83
  history of social construction of race and, 175–76
  impact of social isolation/exclusion on, 393–94
  in Latinx Americans, 291
  mass incarceration and, 431–32
  racism in healthcare, 175–78
  stigma and social exclusion, 398–99
mental health courts, 440–41
meso factors, 22t, 34–35, 41, 432–33
meso-level impacts of juvenile justice involvement, 416–17
Metal, J. M., 169, 176
micro factors, 22t, 34–35, 41, 430–32
micro-level impacts of juvenile justice involvement, 415–16
migrant farmworkers, pesticide exposure among, 338
Miller, J. L., 61
Miller, R., 69–70
Mills, C., 384
Mills, C. W., 7–8
mindfulness, 110–11
minority deposit institutions (MDIs), 536, 537–38
Mirelowitz, S., 37–38
mixed-income housing, 370–71
Moch, M., 82–83
model minority myth, 306, 311–12, 485
Moio, J. A., 39–40
Morris, Z., 346
Morrow, D. F., 50–51
Moynihan Report, 36
MSW (master of social work) degree, 47–51, 296–97
Multisystemic Therapy (MST), 141f
Multisystemic Therapy-Problem Sexual Behavior (MST-PSB), 141f, 142–46

Nadimpalli, S. B., 218–19

naming racism, 107
Nash, J., 390
National Association of Black Social Workers (NABSW), 36
National Association of Deans and Directors of Schools of Social Work (NADD), 48–49, 88–89
National Association of Social Workers (NASW)
  apology for racialized practices, 42
  criticism of, 5
  racial diversity in workforce, 35
  role in eradicating racism, 88–89
National Conference of Social Work (NCSW), 34
National Incidence Studies of Child Abuse and Neglect (NIS), 260
National Research Council, 445
National Stakeholder Strategy for Achieving Health Equity, 130
Native Americans
  climate change and, 336, 347–48
  COVID-19 pandemic and, 348–50
  culturally relevant health-promotion interventions for, 213–21
  effect of racism on health of, 201–3
  extractive energy and natural resource development, 342–43
  extreme weather events and, 343–48
  food security and, 338–40
  in history of social work and racism, 82
  homelessness among, 366
  land loss, 491
  pesticide exposure, 338
  racialized problems in child welfare, 43–44
  recruitment into health-serving professions, 213
  school suspensions and expulsions among, 461–62
  water insecurity and, 340–42, 349–50
  wealth building by, 482–83
  White supremacist social practice foundation and, 506
Native Hawaiian (Kānaka Maoli) culture, 200, 221
naturalization laws, 11–12
natural resource development, 342–43

INDEX 567

NCSW (National Conference of Social Work), 34
Neff, R. A., 338–40
neighborhood capacity, 242
Neubeck, K. J., 507
New Beginnings, 141*f*, 146–47
NFP (Nurse-Family Partnership), 141*f*
Ng, T. W. H., 244
NIS (National Incidence Studies of Child Abuse and Neglect), 260
Nurse-Family Partnership (NFP), 141*f*

Obama, B., 60
Obama, M., 59
obesity rates, 338–39
Office of Immigrant and Refugee Affairs (OIRA), Seattle, 148–53
Office of Juvenile Justice and Delinquency Prevention (OJJDP), 414, 418
Ohm, J. E., 386
ola, 200–201
older adults. *See* productive aging framework
Omi, M., 14–16
Omidvar, R., 385–86
opioid epidemic, 20–21
Ortiz, K., 390
othering of Asian Americans, 305–8
outdoor advertising media, 318–19
overdiagnosis of mental illness, 175–78
over-policing, 275–77

paranoid thinking, 181, 184–85
ParentCorps, 145–46
participatory learning methods, 532
participatory processes in equity-enhancing interventions, 149–50
Pathways to Housing (PTH), 371–72
PBIS (Positive Behavioral Interventions and Supports) program, 463
"people of color," 17
People v. Hall, 305
permanent supportive housing (PSH), 373, 374–76
personal-professional narratives
case study, 67–69
discussing racism with students, 63–65
evaluating outcomes, 69–70
implications for practice, 71

overview, 59–61
racism in the helping relationship, 61–63
use of, 66–67
pesticide exposure, 338
Pettus-Davis, C., 428–29
PIER (Portland Identification and Early Referral) program, 174–75
PIT (Point-in-Time) count, 366
Pitts, C. S., 179–80
Plessy v. Ferguson, 101
Point-in-Time (PIT) count, 366
police
macro factors in incarceration, 434
racial disparities in stops by, 276–77, 446–47
violence by, 184–85, 276, 293–94
policy practice
policy practitioner roles, 510–14
social welfare policy course on, 514–19
Popay, J., 385
Portland Identification and Early Referral (PIER) program, 174–75
Positive Action program, 142–45
Positive Behavioral Interventions and Supports (PBIS) program, 463
poverty. *See also* economic inequality
impact on Black family violence, 260–61, 267–70
social exclusion and, 392
presidential election of 2020, 105
prevention of behavioral health problems in young people, 127–29, 154–55. *See also* equity-enhancing interventions; psychosis prevention
Prime Screen self-report tool, 179–80
prisoner reentry programs, 435–38
Prison Population Forecaster, 441–42
proactive lobbying, 513
problem-solving courts, 440–41
productive aging framework
contributions of, 245–49
individual capacity, 241–42
inequities among older adults, 238*t*
institutional capacity, 242–43
neighborhood capacity, 242
outcomes among older adults, 243–44
overview, 235
productive activities, 243

568 INDEX

Progressive era, 80–81
Project Toward No Drug Abuse, 142–45
Promote Smart Decarceration (PSD)
  Grand Challenge, 426–27, 428–
  29, 435
promoting approach to equity-enhancing
  interventions, 136–37, 148–49
protecting approach to equity-enhancing
  interventions, 136
protesters, 510–11
*Protest Psychosis: How Schizophrenia
  Became a Black Disease, The*
  (Metzl), 176
PSH (permanent supportive housing),
  373, 374–76
psychiatric functioning, racism and, 117
psychosis prevention
  assessments and interventions
    in, 171–75
  cultural responsiveness in, 178–
    81, 183–87
  early, 170–75
  evidence-based practices for, 181–
    83, 186
  Grand Challenge of Preventing Serious
    Mental Illness, 170–71
  history of social construction of mental
    illness and race, 175–76
  overview, 169–70
  race and mental illness, 175–78
  racial and ethnic disparities in, 178
  risk assessment in, 178–81
  service provision, 186–87
  strategies for reducing racism
    in, 183–87
PTH (Pathways to Housing), 371–72
Public-Charge rule, 289–90
Public Health Association's campaign
  against racism, 107–8
public policy
  advocacy, 512–13
  anti-Asian racism initiatives, 317–18
  productive aging framework, 237–41
  racial residential segregation, 272–74
Pullman, M., 465

race
  centrality of racism and, 6–9

history of social construction of mental
  illness and, 175–76
meaning and function of, 9–12
race consciousness, 106
race work, 96–97
racial amnesia, 19–20
racial and ethnic equity-informed policies
  and practices, 438–39
racial battle fatigue, 271
racial bias
  acceptance and commitment
    treatment, 110–11
  addressing along carceral
    continuum, 443–44
  behavioral analysis, 110
  in child maltreatment
    assessment, 259–61
  in health service delivery, 207
  reducing in psychosis
    prevention, 183–87
  in youth psychosis-risk
    assessment, 178–83
racial capitalism, 205
racial commonsense
  thinking, 18–21, 37
racial concentration, 432–33
Racial Contract, The (Mills), 7–8
racial discrimination in workplace,
  addressing, 112–13
racial disproportionality, 459
racial healing, 214–15
racial impact statements, 442–43
racialized identity, 17–18
Racialized Organizations
  Theory, 389–90
racialized trauma, 12–13, 203–4, 308–
  9, 321
racializing people, 16–17
racial justice ambassadors, 88
racial profiling, 294, 434
racial projects, 14–16
racial regulation features of White
  supremacy, 507–8
racial residential segregation, 272–
  75, 367–68
racial solidarity,
  fostering, 313–14
racial stereotypes, 16

INDEX 569

racial violence
against Asian Americans, 304, 305,
306–7, 316–17
individual racism, 104
upsurge of, 76–77
racism
behavioral analysis, 110
against Black families, 262–67
centrality of race and, 6–9
civil rights movement, 36–39
conceptualization of, 78–79
denial of, 113–14, 508–10
discussing with students, 63–65
effect on health, 201–3
in the helping relationship, 61–63
history of social work and, 79–83
institutional efforts to eradicate, 86–89
interpersonal efforts to eradicate, 85–86
intrapersonal efforts to eradicate, 83–85
by legislative fiat and de jure, 99–101
meaning and function of, 9–12
micro, meso, and macro factors, 22t
overview, 12–13
practice approaches for reducing, 109–16
racial commonsense thinking, 18–21
racialized identity, 17–18
racializing people, 16–17
racial projects, 14–16
settler colonialism, health, and, 203–5
in social work, 33–35, 42–45
social work education and, 39–41
sustainability of, 99
systemic, 14, 99–101, 102–3
three-pronged theory of, 102–5
racism-centered perspective, 45–46
racism-centered policy practice
overview, 503–5
policy practitioner roles, 510–14
social welfare policy course on, 514–19
Rainbow Coalition, 314
Rakhshan Rouhakhtar, P., 179–80
Ramos, Y. O., 346
Ray, I., 340–42
Ray, V., 389–90
Razza, C. M., 385, 402
RBA (Results-Based
Accountability), 516–17
recidivism, 430, 431–32

reconciliation, 222–23
redlining, 242, 368, 379, 392, 542
reducing approach to equity-enhancing
interventions, 136
reentry programs, culturally
congruent, 435–38
reflexivity, fostering, 115
regulatory features of White
supremacy, 507–8
Reid, W. J., 112–13
Reid-Merritt, P., xxii
relative rate index (RRI), 418
religious justifications for White
supremacy, 508
reparations, 494–95
repealing racialized criminal justice
legislation and policies, 441–42
reporting racism against Asian
Americans, 316–17
residential segregation, 272–75, 367–68
resilience, 401
Response to Intervention (RtI), 464–65
responsive service delivery, 152–53
restorative justice approaches, 441, 466
Results-Based Accountability
(RBA), 516–17
retirement, delaying, 243–44
retirement accounts, 539
retirement savings, 538–39
Richmond, T., 385–86
Risk, Need, and Responsivity (RNR)
Model, 437–38
RRI (relative rate index), 418
RtI (Response to Intervention), 464–65
Runes, C., 109

Samuel, K., 384
Sandler, I., 146–47
Schexnayder, S., 345
Schiffman, J., 179–80, 185–86
schizophrenia
evidence-based practices for, 181–83
racialization of diagnosis of, 176–
77, 178–81
Schneider, S., 46–47
school corporal punishment, 460–61
school social work practice, 43–44
School Success Project (SSP), 466–70

570 INDEX

school suspensions and expulsions
approaches for tackling
disproportionality in, 463–66
overview, 459
race, gender, and disproportionality
in, 460–63
School Success Project, 466–70
school-to-prison pipeline, 44, 461–63
Schoolwide Positive Behavioral
Interventions and Supports
(SWPBIS), 464, 465–66
science-based prevention, 130–32, 139
scientific racism, 508–9
screening for psychosis risk, 171–
73, 178–80
SCSEP (Senior Community Service and
Employment Program), 247
Seattle Office of Immigrant and Refugee
Affairs (OIRA), 148–53
second wave of environmental
justice, 353
segregated neighborhoods, 242, 272–
75, 367–68
segregation, legal, 101, 106
self-as-context, 111
self-consciousness-building strategy, 108
self-disclosure, 62–63
self-reflection, 8–9, 83–85, 115, 314–15
self-report measures of psychosis risk,
171–72, 178–80
semi-structured interviews for psychosis
risk, 172–73, 184
Semlow, A. R., 108
Senior Community Service and
Employment Program (SCSEP), 247
Senreich, E., 48
serious mental illness. See also psychosis
prevention
in Black Americans, 175–77, 178–
81, 184–85
disparities in identification and
treatment of, 176–77
evidence-based practices for, 181–83
Grand Challenge of Preventing Serious
Mental Illness, 170–71
history of social construction of race
and, 175–76
in Latinx Americans, 291

structural and individual racism in
mental healthcare, 177
service-delivery models for equity-
enhancing interventions, 152–53
settlement houses, 33, 80, 81–82
settler colonialism, 203–5, 210
SFEPD (Society for Financial Education &
Professional Development), 532–33
SFP. See Strengthening Families 10–14
Program
Shaia, W. E., 187
Sherraden, M. S., 527, 543–44
Shreve, T., 419
SIPS (Structured Interview for Psychosis
Risk Syndromes), 172
skin color, 16
Slaughterhouse Cases, 265
slavery, 262–64, 483, 506
social cohesion, 401–2
social construction of mental illness and
race, 175–76
social determinant digital
infrastructure, 211
social isolation/exclusion
case vignettes, 394–400
Critical Race Theory and, 388
educational outcomes, 392–93
income and wealth disparities, 392
intersectionality and, 388–89
overview, 383–84
physical and mental health
outcomes, 393–94
Racialized Organizations
Theory, 389–90
relationship of racism to stigma
and, 391
social exclusion, discussion of, 385–87
social isolation, discussion of, 384–85
theories linking race to, 387–90
socialization, financial, 527–28
social justice activism, 115
social media influencers, 510, 513–14
social networks, 400
social policy
racial regulation features of White
supremacy, 507–8
racism-centeredness in course
on, 514–19

wealth exclusion and, 487–88
Social Security, 237–41, 487–88, 538, 539
Social Welfare & Urban Economics
    graduate course, 514–19
social work education. *See also* personal-
    professional narratives
    in anti-racism practice, 114
    Asian Americans in, 315
    core competencies, 59
    curricular efforts to eradicate
        racism, 87–88
    decolonization of organizational
        cultures, 105–6
    discussing racism with students, 63–65
    diversity and cultural competence
        in, 39–41
    FCAB curriculum, 543–45
    Latinx Americans in, 296–97
    overview, 30
    in productive aging, 248–49
    in psychosis prevention, 174–75
    strategies for reducing racism and
        increasing cultural responsiveness
        in, 183–87
    value of case studies, 394–95
social work organizations, 88, 112–13
social work practice
    anti-racist, 45–51
    civil rights movements and, 36–39
    developing anti-Asian racism
        workforce, 314
    economic inequality and, 495
    eliminating anti-Asian racism
        in, 309–21
    overview, 28–33
    racism, diversity, and education, 39–41
    racism in, 33–35, 42–45
    reducing racism and increasing cultural
        responsiveness in, 183–87
*Social Work Training to Reduce Duration of
    Untreated Psychosis* study, 174–75
Society for Financial Education &
    Professional Development
    (SFEPD), 532–33
solidarity, fostering, 313–14
solitary confinement, 384–85
Solórzano, D. G., 388
soul wound, xxvii

Sparks, S., 465
Spinney, E., 419–20
spiritual health, effect of racism on, 201
SSP (School Success Project), 466–70
STARS (Suspension/Expulsion Tracking
    and Rating System), 467–68
Stephenson, R., 419
stereotypes, racial, 16
Stergiopoulos, V., 114–15
stigma, 172–73, 416
Straus, M., 460–61
Strengthening Families 10–14
    Program (SFP)
    innovative service-delivery
        models, 152–53
    overview, 148–49
    participatory processes in, 149–50
    tailoring to cultures, contexts, and
        conditions, 150–52
stress from racism, 203–4, 270–72, 308–9
structural interventions for Black family
    violence, 279
structural racism, 40–41
    anti-racism practice and theory
        narrative, 101–6
    closing health gap, 222–24
    denial of, confronting, 113–14
    ending, 117–19
    health disparities due to, 154–55
    impact on Black family
        violence, 272–77
    legal and policy infrastructure, 102–
        3, 117
    in mental healthcare, 175–76, 177
    practice approaches for
        reducing, 109–16
    in psychosis prevention, 183–87
    sustainability of racism in America, 99
    in youth psychosis-risk
        assessment, 178–83
Structured Interview for Psychosis Risk
    Syndromes (SIPS), 172
student loan debt, 492–93
subprime mortgage market, 542
substance abuse, possession, and
    trafficking, 431, 434, 439–40, 441–42
Sue, S., 316
surface structure fit efforts, 150–51

572 INDEX

Suspension/Expulsion Tracking and Rating System (STARS), 467–68
suspensions from school. *See* school suspensions and expulsions
suspiciousness, 181, 184–85
sustainability of racism in America, 99
SWPBIS (Schoolwide Positive Behavioral Interventions and Supports), 464, 465–66
syllabi development, 517
systemic racism, 14, 99–101, 102–3

Tālanoas, 221
Talking Circle, 220
targeted universalism, 136–37
task-centered practice, 112–13
taxes, 543
Teaching Equitable Asian American Community History Act (Illinois), 317
Temporary Assistance to Needy Families (TANF), 489
third system of structural racism, 102–3
third wave of environmental justice, 353
Thirteenth Amendment, 99–100
three-pronged theory of racism, 102–5
Three Strikes Laws, 433–34
TIC (trauma informed care), 214, 321
tornadoes, 345
Townes, E. M., 489
traditional values and practices, 218–19
traffic stops, 446–47
training perspective taking, 111–12
transitional justice, 223
trauma, racial, 12–13, 203–4, 308–9, 321, 431–32
trauma informed care (TIC), 214, 321
Trump, D. J., 76–77, 507–8
Truong, M., 208–9
truth and reconciliation process, 105–6, 117
Turner, M. A., 109

unbanked status, 534–35, 536
underbanked status, 534–35, 536
Unemployment Insurance (UI) system, 488
Unequal Treatment: Confronting Racial and Ethnic Disparities in Health Care report, Institute of Medicine, 207

universal income supplements, 493–94
Unleashing the Power of Prevention, 128, 129, 130–34
uranium mining, 343
urban heat islands (UHI), 344–45
U.S. Capitol storming, 104–5
U.S. Constitution, 99–101

VA (Department of Veterans Affairs), 374–76
Vagins, D. J., 20
Valdes, F., 388
Valinote, N., 513–14
values, role in reducing racial prejudice, 111
veterans, HUD-VASH program for, 374–76
Vietnam War, 313–14
violence. *See also* family violence in Black families
against Asian Americans, 304, 305, 306–7, 316–17
against Black families, history of, 262–67
individual racism, 104
by police, 184–85, 276, 293–94
upsurge of hate crimes, 76–77
volunteering by older adults, 243–45, 247–48
voting rights suppression laws, 99–100
Vulnerable Populations Strategic Initiative, 211

wage disparities, 268, 486–89
Walters, R. W., 507
war on drugs, 20
water insecurity, 340–42, 349–50
Waterstone, M., 23–24
wealth inequality
assets and, 489–91
Black/White wealth gap, 268–69, 482
financial capability and asset building and, 540–43
history of exclusionary policies, 479–86
labor and income disparities, 486–89
land loss, 491–92
policy to mitigate, 493–94
racial income and wealth gaps, 476–79

reparations, 494–95
social isolation/exclusion and, 392
social work practice and, 495
wage gap, 543
wealth stripping through fees and
fines, 492–93
welfare racism, 489
Wellman, D., 78–79
Whitbeck, L. B., 218–19
White Americans
deaths of despair among, 21
inequities among older adults, 238t
juvenile justice involvement, 413–14
racialized identity, 17–18
self-racial appraisal, 115
self-reflection needed to eradicate
racism, 83–85
White versus non-White concept, 7–8
White nationalism, 507–8
White privilege, 14, 84–85
white racial hegemony, 507
White supremacy
denial of racism, 508–10
effect of racism on health, 203–4
ending racism, 117
foundation of, 505–6
increase in, xxiii–xxiv
interprofessional education on, 210
overview, 503–5

policy practice addressing, 510–14
racism-centeredness in social welfare
policy course, 514–19
social policy as racial regulation, 507–8
Wildeman, C., 427
Wilson, C., 180
Wilson, W. J., 386
Winant, H., 14–16
Winchester, B., 345
Wise Feedback tool, 443–44
womanist pedagogy, 514–15
Woo, B., 309–10
workforce development, 112–13, 206t, 210

Yappalli: Choctaw Road to Health, 220
Yeide, M., 419
Yors, G., 109–12
Young, I. M., 509
Young, S. M., 309–10
Young, W. M. Jr., 524
youth, preventing behavioral health
problems in, 127–29. *See also* equity-
enhancing interventions; psychosis
prevention

Zamudio, M., 388
Zavaleta, D., 384
zero-tolerance legislation, 43–44, 460
zoomorphism, 118